Hellenic Studies 60

# EUSEBIUS OF CAESAREA

# Recent Titles in the Hellenic Studies Series

*http://chs.harvard.edu/chs/publications*

# EUSEBIUS OF CAESAREA

## TRADITION AND INNOVATIONS

*EDITED BY*
*AARON JOHNSON*
*JEREMY SCHOTT*

CENTER FOR HELLENIC STUDIES
Trustees for Harvard University
Washington, D.C.
Distributed by Harvard University Press
Cambridge, Massachusetts, and London, England
2013

*Eusebuis of Caesarea*
Edited by Aaron Johnson and Jeremy Schott
Copyright © 2013 Center for Hellenic Studies, Trustees for Harvard University
All Rights Reserved.
Published by Center for Hellenic Studies, Trustees for Harvard University, Washington, D.C.
Distributed by Harvard University Press, Cambridge, Massachusetts, and London, England
Production: Nancy Wolfe Kotary
Cover design: Joni Godlove
Printed by Edwards Brothers, Inc., Ann Arbor, MI

EDITORIAL TEAM

Senior Advisers: W. Robert Connor, Gloria Ferrari Pinney, Albert Henrichs, James O'Donnell, Bernd Seidensticker
Editorial Board: Gregory Nagy (Editor-in-Chief), Christopher Blackwell, Casey Dué (Executive Editor), Mary Ebbott (Executive Editor), Scott Johnson, Olga Levaniouk, Anne Mahoney, Leonard Muellner
Production Manager for Publications: Jill Curry Robbins
Web Producer: Mark Tomasko

LIBRARY OF CONGRESS CATALOGING-IN-PUBLICATION DATA

Eusebius of Caesarea : tradition and innovations / edited by Aaron Johnson and Jeremy Schott.
    pages. cm. -- (Hellenic studies ; 60)
ISBN 978-0-674-07329-6 (alk. paper)
1. Eusebius, of Caesarea, Bishop of Caesarea, approximately 260-approximately 340--Criticism and interpretation. 2. Christian literature, Early--History and criticism. I. Johnson, Aaron P. II. Schott, Jeremy M., 1977- III. Series: Hellenic studies ; 60.

BR65.E76E97 2013
270.1092--dc23

2013009760

# Contents

# Contents

# Acknowledgements

The editors wish to thank the members of the press, especially Scott F. Johnson and Jill Curry Robbins for enthusiasm, perceptiveness, and diligence. We are also most grateful to the contributors of this volume for providing intellectual energy, attentive insights, and new ideas both in the original presentation of the papers as well as in the print versions contained herein, as well as patience and good will throughout the editorial process. Their ongoing work evinces the powerful role that Eusebius must continue to play in the study of the ideas and literature of late antiquity. Of the volume editors, Johnson would like to express a special note of gratitude to Schott for much sound advice, firm judgment, and hours of investment in the editorial labors behind this volume. Schott, for his part, thanks Johnson for his leadership in organizing the conference sessions out of which this volume developed and in pursuing the publication of this volume, as well as for many years of convivial conversations and productive debates about Eusebius and his worlds.

*Additional note:* The editors decided to allow some flexibility among the different papers contained in this volume in rendering the titles of Eusebius' works (especially the *Praeparatio Evangelica* and the *Eclogae Propheticae*) according to the preference of the individual contributor, while maintaining uniformity in the abbreviations for these works. In addition, we opted to maintain the traditional BC/AD designations (rather than BCE/CE), though some contributors may have preferred otherwise; we did so in order to maintain uniformity, but also out of a recognition of the powerful conceptual (and political) framework that lies behind the chronological numeration, which BCE/CE otherwise occludes.

# Abbreviations

| | |
|---|---|
| C. Hier. | Eusebius, *Contra Hieroclem* (*Against Hierocles*) |
| C. Marc. | Eusebius, *Contra Marcellum* (*Against Marcellus*) |
| CCSL | *Corpus Christianorum Series Latina* |
| Chron. | Eusebius, *Chronicon* (*Chronicle*) |
| Chron. Can. | Eusebius, *Chronici Canones* (*Chronological Canons*) |
| CI | Eusebius, *Commentarius in Isaiam* (*Commentary on Isaiah*) |
| CPG | *Clavis Patrum Graecorum* |
| CPs | Eusebius, *Commentaria in Psalmos* (*Commentary on the Psalms*) |
| DE | Eusebius, *Demonstratio Evangelica* (*Gospel Demonstration/Demonstration of the Gospel*) |
| Eccl. Theol. | Eusebius, *De ecclesiastica theologia* (*Ecclesiastical Theology*) |
| Ecl. Proph. | Eusebius, *Eclogae Propheticae* (*Prophetic Extracts/Prophetic Eclogues*) |
| FGrH | *Die Fragmente der griechischen Historiker*, ed. F. Jacoby |
| GCS | *Die Griechischen Christlichen Schriftsteller* |
| Gen. El. Intr. | Eusebius, *Generalis elementaria introductio* (*General Elementary Introduction*) |
| HE | Eusebius, *Historia Ecclesiastica* (*Ecclesiastical History/Church History*) |
| LC | Eusebius, *De Laudibus Constantini* (*Tricennial Orations: In Praise of Constantine*) |
| LSJ | *Liddel and Scott Greek-English Lexicon*, rev. H. Stuart Jones |

| | |
|---|---|
| MP | Eusebius, *De martyribus Palaestinae* (*Martyrs of Palestine*) |
| MP(L) | Eusebius, *De martyribus Palaestinae* (*Martyrs of Palestine*), Syriac trans. |
| MP(S) | Eusebius, *De martyribus Palaestinae* (*Martyrs of Palestine*), Greek recension |
| NPNF | *Nicene- and Post-Nicene Fathers Series*, ed. Ph. Schaff and H. Wace |
| Onom. | Eusebius, *Onomasticon* (*Onomasticon*) |
| PE | Eusebius, *Praeparatio Evangelica* (*Gospel Preparation/Preparation for the Gospel*) |
| PG | *Patrologiae Cursus Completus, Series Graeca*, ed. J.-P. Migne |
| PL | *Patrologiae Cursus Completus, Series Latina*, ed. J.-P. Migne |
| SC | Eusebius, *De sepulchro Christi* (*Tricennial Orations: On Christ's Sepulcher*) |
| Theoph. | Eusebius, *De Theophania* (*Theophany*) |
| VC | Eusebius, *Vita Constantini* (*Life of Constantine*) |

All abbreviations of biblical books follow those of *The New Oxford Annotated Bible* (Oxford, 2001), xxv.

# 1

# Introduction

## Aaron P. Johnson

CURRENT STUDY of the cultures and literatures of late antiquity continues to find attractive the interpretive polarity of tradition and innovation.[1] The spectrum containing these two poles has fruitfully functioned to gauge the complex ways in which the history, literature, and thought of late antiquity can be identified as a coherent and distinctive age. This interpretive schema remains useful for identifying the ways in which particular late antique authors developed powerful conceptual frameworks in response to or in expectation of the great events, individuals, peoples, and forces of their changing world. Such changes could be represented as either of cataclysmic effect, altering the course of history, or as only the gentle drift of a world ossified by unbreakable and time- less laws of a cosmic nature. For a thinker like Eusebius of Caesarea, the literary modes of expression through which he formulated his own conceptual vision were at once carefully chosen and audaciously experimental. His wide-ranging corpus comprised works of historiographical, exegetical, and apologetic signifi- cance in one of the most stimulating and explosive periods of Christian literary history.

The present volume rests on the assumption that Eusebius is a thinker and writer worthy of great interest and deep investigation in his own right if we are properly to appreciate the literary and conceptual shifts marking the transition into late antiquity. The first decades of the fourth century were possessed not only of the Great Persecution, the conversion(s) of Constantine, the breakup of the brilliant administrative achievement of the Tetrarchy, and the imperial building of churches and hosting of ecclesiastical councils. These years also saw the production of new literary forms and the articulation of sophisticated and progressively precise philosophical and theological positions. Eusebius' prolific

---

[1]   See, for example: Goulet-Cazé 2000; Clover and Humphreys 1989; Kelly, Flower, and Williams 2010.

output lies at the heart of this literary profusion, as well as of the historical and theological transformations of the era. Yet, Eusebius has often been relegated to an inferior rank in the midst of the intellectual and literary currents of late antiquity, especially when compared with the literary style of Gregory Nazianzen, the political independence of Athanasius, or the theological precision of Gregory of Nyssa. As a stylist, he has been found wanting at least since the time of Photius;[2] as a thinker, he has been deemed a second-rate imitator of Origen; as an historian, he has been dubbed "the first thoroughly dishonest historian of antiquity."[3] The difficulty of his sometimes heavy periods and tangled syntax cannot be denied; his role as a purveyor of many of Origen's theological tendencies must not be understated (and will even be explored further in the present collection); and the pervasiveness of his particular historiographical agenda should not be ignored. We should, however, practice caution in these areas where later evaluations of Eusebius have often relied more on narrow literary tastes, an unhelpful elevation of the purported value of literary or intellectual originality, or historiographical assumptions foreign to late antiquity in general and Eusebius in particular.

A felicitous shift in scholarship on Eusebius in recent decades has made important advances in overcoming earlier shortsighted reactions to the man and his writings. Many of the latest studies have begun to approach his historical and biographical writings as literature.[4] Other studies have explored the social, theological, and cultural features of his exegesis.[5] His contributions to early apologetics have likewise received a number of important discussions.[6] Even his importance as a theologian has begun to be reassessed.[7] The essays contained in the present volume bear witness to the remaining vitality of these and other areas and approaches to Eusebius' writings and thought. At the same time they do not exhaust the possible ways in which Eusebius can be fruitfully appreciated. One element that deserves more adequate attention is the powerful ways in which his corpus evinces the creation of a new late antique aesthetic. Before turning, therefore, to a few introductory words on the main

---

[2]   Photius *Bibliothēkē* 13; see Clay 2012:42–45.
[3]   Burckhardt 1949:283; cf. 260 ("Constantine's historical memory has suffered the greatest misfortune conceivable . . . He has fallen into the hands of the most objectionable of all eulogists, who has utterly falsified his likeness. The man is Eusebius of Caesarea . . ."); 293 ("Eusebius . . . has been proven guilty of so many distortions, dissimulations, and inventions that he has forfeited all claim to figure as a decisive source"); 313 ("He presents an account of the [Arian] conflict which is unique in its kind for dishonesty and intentional meagerness").
[4]   See, for example: Cameron 1997; Morlet 2005; 2006; 2012; Morgan 2005; Verdoner 2011; De Vore forthcoming.
[5]   Hollerich 1999; Johnson 2006c.
[6]   Inowlocki 2006; Johnson 2006a; Schott 2008; Morlet 2009.
[7]   Lyman 1993; Spoerl 1997; DelCogliano 2006; 2008; Robertson 2007.

themes pursued in the essays of this collection, I would like to offer some brief remarks towards more properly recognizing his literary work as guided by and productive of what Jaś Elsner has aptly named the "cumulative aesthetic."

## Eusebius and the Late Antique Aesthetic

A significant part of the modern dismissal of Eusebius as a creative thinker lies in what has been taken as his inability to control his sources. Several of his most important productions contain numerous quotations of earlier authors. The *Ecclesiastical History* furnishes verbatim quotations from earlier authors to provide documentation of the veracity of Eusebius' historical claims or to serve as exempla of those authors' positions on particular issues. The pages of the *Preparation for the Gospel* are packed with often lengthy—and to the modern reader unwieldy—quotations from pagan and Jewish sources. Several chapters of his *General Elementary Introduction* as well as the *Proof of the Gospel* consist almost entirely of quotations from the Hebrew Scriptures with almost no comments of Eusebius' own. His initial response to what he claimed was the Sabellianizing theology of Marcellus based itself on quotations from his opponent's writing. The *Life of Constantine* provides lengthy imperial documentation that fills out (or, for many modern readers, interrupts) the biographical narrative.

Were he to have synthesized the contributions of Philo, Clement, and Plato (for example) and were he judiciously to have combined elements of each into his own thought and expressed the ideas more in his own voice, glossing over the abrupt breaks that we now experience in his verbatim quotations, he would probably receive a more favorable commendation among many readers today. It is the presence of polyphonic quotation, however, that highlights his position within the ongoing scholastic culture(s) of late antiquity. Schools of the late Roman Empire busied themselves with the careful reading and interpretation of the texts deemed relevant for study by the teacher. The teacher assumed the role of master reader, selecting and commenting on passages whose true meaning was not readily available to the amateur reader.[8] Some of Eusebius' treatises explicitly invoke such a scholastic context in which passages were to be read and appropriate interpretive techniques to be espoused for a student audience.[9] This scholastic context, however, only partly accounts for the bulky weight of his quotational works. Beyond the pedagogical processes of these works, his attempt to allow his sources to speak in their own voices, hostile though some of them were (for instance, Porphyry in his *Preparation* and *History*, or Marcellus

---

[8]   Mansfeld 1994; Snyder 2000.
[9]   See Gen. El. Intr. 6.1 (PG 22.1024D); PE 1.1.12; Johnson 2011.

in the *Against Marcellus*), marked a choice that was at once aesthetic, epistemological, moral, and theological.

Importantly, Eusebius' citational tendencies exhibit a literary manifestation of a more widespread phenomenon in architectural and artistic media of the cumulative aesthetic that arose precisely in this time. The reuse of older materials in new contexts was fostered in the early fourth century as never before. Such aesthetic tastes evinced a sense of the triumph of the new that was rooted in a transparent connectedness to past traditions (what would later be called "the new glory of the old," *nova vetustatis gloria*).[10] The cumulative aesthetic appeared in monumental art (such as the Arch of Constantine), in church buildings (such as the Lateran Basilica), and in entire cities (such as Constantinople, especially the Forum). The Arch of Constantine, erected in close proximity to the Colosseum at the east end of the Roman Forum soon after the newly-converted emperor's defeat of Maxentius in 312 (most likely 315), is probably the most well-known indication today of this new shift in taste.[11] Unlike the struggling ascent of aesthetically-homogeneous figures on the earlier Column of Marcus Aurelius, the Arch juxtaposed artistic pieces detached from their earlier contexts in the reigns of Trajan, Hadrian, and Aurelius, and placed them in a new triumphal whole with a carefully worded inscription (which may exhibit more an attempt to slow down the growing religious changes in the person and reign of Constantine on the part of the Senate than an ambiguous expression by the emperor of his new religious allegiances).[12] The panels of Trajan are made to collaborate in a new late antique visual program with the roundels of Hadrian, the artistic narratives of Aurelius, and friezes produced by Constantinian-age carvers. The heavy forms of Dacian soldiers (of Trajanic provenance), for instance, now collude with the lighter (Hadrianic) scenes of hunting; the formulaic sequences of a Constantinian *adventus* scene contrast with the individualism and spatial ease of a Hadrianic sacrifice scene. Though age has faded their original brilliance, the variegated marble (including Numidian yellow, white Proconnesian, and purple porphyry) contributed to a striking collage of images, styles, and colors. The Arch contained not only a sort of visual quotation of these earlier sources; Constantinian friezes narrated his campaigns in northern Italy and at the Milvian Bridge. More intrusively, the

---

[10] Theodoric, ap. Cassiodiorus, *Variae* 7.15; quoted by Brenk 1987:108.

[11] See esp. Elsner 2004; 2000, with bibliography. Controversy continues to surround the date of the construction of the Arch itself, as well as the messages it was intended to convey; see Panella and Pensabene 1997; 1999; Wilson Jones 2000.

[12] For a recent defense of the pagan senatorial origins of the inscription (which is, of course, ostensibly by the Senate and people of Rome), see Lenski 2008.

heads of the earlier pieces were recarved to resemble Constantine and another tetrarch (either his father or Licinius).

Like the compilation of images drawn from different ages and different conceptual worlds juxtaposed within a new unity on the Arch of Constantine, the works of Eusebius brought together the scattered, even disparate, voices of the classical, Hellenistic, and biblical literary traditions into a new, and therefore, a newly signifying, monument of words.[13] Both the Arch and Eusebius' corpus thus evince a critical moment in the cultural, literary, intellectual, and religious transformations of late antiquity. Both monuments exhibit a keen concern both to preserve and reframe more ancient works. They are, therefore, both deeply conservative in their traditionalism and strikingly innovative in their aesthetic sensibilities and conceptual expansion into a new age.

We may connect this aesthetic expression to the rise in the next generation of the erudite poetry of the cento poets, who stitched together lines (or half-lines) of Homer or Vergil in new (frequently Christian) poems.[14] As Ausonius' programmatic comments on the cento form declare, his own cento was at once "continuous, though made of disjointed tags; one, though of various scraps; playful, though of serious themes; mine, though the elements are another's."[15] Many of Eusebius' works extensively exhibit this same taste for the composite and cumulative. Unlike Eusebius in his lengthier quotations, however, the Latin poet played by stricter rules that limited the contiguous quoted material to, at most, one and a half lines, while the entirety comprised only a patchwork of quotations without any of the later centonist's own words. While Eusebius was no centonist, I would suggest that Puech goes too far when claiming that Eusebius "did not pretend to create a work of art,"[16] for there is nonetheless a related artfulness to his compositions. What strikes the modern reader as awkward and bulky citation can alternatively be appreciated for its gentle rhythms: "let us hear him as he writes in his own words"; "he writes word for word thus"; "these are the very syllables"; "and again, after other things, he adds." Suspicious of manipulation, wary of theological unorthodoxy, or desiring a different classical aesthetic, the modern reader of Eusebius may be too eager to resist this new cumulative aesthetic, which relished the bricolage of formerly disparate blocks of text placed within the frame of a new literary collage.

An example, taken at random from the *Praeparatio*, may suffice as an instance of this aesthetic affect. At 11.13.5, following quotations with commentary from

---

[13] For a related examination of the ways in which the visual arts contribute to a richer understanding of late antique literary art, see the important study of Roberts 1989, esp. 66–121.

[14] See Usher 1998; the cento form is directly compared at Elsner 2000:176.

[15] Ausonius, *Cento Nuptialis*, epistula ad Paulum; trans. modified from Evelyn White 1988:373.

[16] Puech 1930:3.219.

the *Timaeus* and *Epistle* 13, we read ten lines of quotation from Plato's *Laws*, followed by single lines of the Bible juxtaposed with single lines taken from the just-quoted text of Plato, or sometimes three separate biblical verses to one line of Plato. The progression begins with "compare" *a* to *b*, followed by "examine together" *c* to *d*, followed by merely *e* to *f* (in the dative), *g* to *h* (dative), and *i* to *j* (dative). Eusebius concludes: "These then are a few out of countless passages concerning *x*, but observe also the passages concerning *y*." These are presented in 11.14, which contains four lines of Eusebius' introductory words, approximately one line of the Bible (Moses, i.e. Genesis), four lines of Eusebius' remarks, one line from the Bible (David, i.e. the Psalms), five lines of Eusebius' remarks, one line from the Bible (David), one line of commentary, one line from the Bible (David), two lines of Eusebius (11.14.6), one line of the Bible (David), "then he adds," three lines of the Bible (Prov); "this is also from the same person," and one line of the Bible (Prov); "still further these things are said to be from the same person," and one line of the Bible (Wisdom), "then he adds," and two lines of the Bible (Wisdom) (11.14.9), "and next he clarifies such things," and nine lines of the Bible (Wisdom), "this [is what] Scripture says, but Philo presents the idea in this way . . ." Two lines of Philo open up 11.15, then "in the same author it also says this," followed by eight lines of Philo, "and again he adds," followed by eight lines of Philo, then eight lines of Eusebius' remarks.

These chapters from Book 11 exhibit well the ebb and flow of the commentator's guiding connective voice, gliding between the larger quotational units, which are themselves disproportional from each other in length as well as in style (thus evincing what Michael Roberts aptly named an "aesthetic of discontinuity").[17] This latter effect arises from a compositional choice that favored *variatio* over repetitive regularity. Such a cumulative progression is representative of the text as a whole. Yet the aggregation of variegated blocks of quotation could be omitted at key junctures in the overall structure of the *Preparation*. Most notably, sustained allusions to earlier master texts occur in the early portions of each of the two main segments of the work, namely Books One and Seven. A series of hitherto unnoticed allusions to the preface of Origen's *Contra Celsum* arise in the first book,[18] whereas Book Seven contains allusions to Philo of Alexandria's *On Abraham*.[19] Both instances avoid verbatim quotation or explicit naming of the source of the allusions. The agglomeration of allusive echoes nonetheless mingles with quotations of biblical passages to produce a similar, if more subtle, display of the cumulative aesthetic.

---

[17] Roberts 1989:61.
[18] Compare PE 1.5.3–8 with Origen, *contra Celsum* 1.9–11.
[19] See Johnson 2006b.

In a striking contrast to both the disproportional rhythms of Book Eleven and the two allusive passages of the first and seventh books, the final book of the entire work rises in a quotational crescendo that climaxes with twenty-nine chapters of direct quotation from Pseudo-Plutarch's doxographical lists with an almost complete lack of Eusebius' inserted remarks (PE 15.33–61). The overwhelming din of quotation from this doxography enumerates in quick succession the divided views of the enemy camp of Greek philosophers on a great number of subjects. Eusebius concludes the extended quotational *tour-de-force* with an apologetic summation of his own, an affirming quotation from Xenophon that evinced the similarity in response shared by both Socrates and Christians to the philosophical cacophony, and then his own commentary. With stirring effect, he mixes his final remarks with the staccato brevity of lines of verse from Timon of Phlius caustically lamenting the discord of the philosophers (PE 15.62).

The diversity, frequency, and rhythms of Eusebius' compositional accretions recognizably vary, therefore, among the different textual locations with their distinct purposes. Obvious variations in tone arise in the movement from an allusively strong passage to one that follows contrasting quotational units or an extended quotational string of dozens of pages. These variations further express the same aesthetic shift visible in monumental imperial art of the fourth century, which fostered a taste for irregularity in the aggregation of disparate visual units.

Even if we overlook the differences between centos and the text of Eusebius with respect to the length or disproportionality of quoted materials, Eusebius does not compose mere prose centos. Instead, he marks the "seams" between quoted material with formulaic phrases, provides an explanation, notes how the material fits within his overall argument, or inserts several paragraphs or pages of his own argument. Eusebius frequently magnifies the stitches holding the patchwork of compositional units together (to maintain the metaphor). Furthermore, direct classification of Eusebius' citational writings with the phenomenon of centonism would also require thorough knowledge on the part of his readers of the texts he was quoting; part of the appeal of centonism was the challenge of detecting the original contexts of quoted material. It seems unlikely that Eusebius' primary readers had such thorough knowledge. In fact, because the context for some of his heavily citational works was pedagogical, such knowledge seems to be precluded by the nature of the project (even if he himself admitted an openness of readership so that both the "advanced" and the beginners would derive benefit from his treatise).[20] Instead, centonism and citational pedagogy are very different yet twin expressions of a single,

---

[20]  Gen. El. Intr. 6.1 (PG 22.1024C).

broader cumulative tendency and its attendant aesthetic. In both cases, it was an aesthetic of erudition, though Eusebius exemplifies a process of both literary and stylistic bricolage, in which textual blocks from earlier authors of sometimes widely differing styles, linguistic registers, genres, and historical and intellectual milieus, which had hitherto not appeared to be related or assimilable, were made to form the gears of a new larger literary machine—which gears were sometimes intricately miniature like lines of Timon of Phlius, sometimes massive like the dozens of pages from Pseudo-Plutarch. Quoted within the same literary frame might be texts of Plato and the Hebrew Scriptures, or of Philo of Byblos and Diodorus Siculus, or of Porphyry and Eusebius' comments themselves, now forming innovative rotational movements in harmony with a larger conceptual, rhetorical, and textual whole.

Such literary practices go beyond the production of new late-antique tastes, however, since they prove to be the manifestation of a moral and theological choice as well.[21] Eusebius' literary collage could have comprised fuzzy pastel blotches of former thinkers' ideas if he had determined only to paraphrase their voices. This would have effectively muffled those distinctive voices under or behind his own clearer authorial voice.[22] His decision to quote many sources verbatim is thus a refusal to stifle those voices—even when they say more than he needed or wanted them to say, even when they spoke otherwise. We cannot and should not ignore Eusebius' active polemical edge; nearly every work is grounded in polemical concerns, whether of an offensive or defensive nature. We also cannot and should not ignore those few occasions where we have been able to catch Eusebius altering his source texts and thereby cheating at argumentation.[23] (However, we should also not exaggerate the extent to which he does so; given that he is quoting the writings from the enemy camp, he is remarkably sparing in the practice of altering texts.) Eusebius nonetheless chose to engage in polemical argument in a startlingly fair manner (given the much wider possibilities residing in the practice of paraphrase or innuendo) and placed rather restrictive limits upon himself by choosing to pursue literary controversy by means of quotation. Because his quotations could be selective, unrepresentative, or manipulated, we might be tempted to consider him a "thoroughly dishonest historian," apologist, theologian, and exegete. In doing so, however, we would fail to recognize the radical cost that he was willing to

---

[21] For the present I leave aside the way in which a cumulative aesthetic might interact with, or diverge from, a symbolic-allegorical aesthetic grounded in a Platonic ontology or a Christian Logos theology (both of which are pervasive, without necessarily being identical, in Eusebius' thought). On Eusebius' adaptation of a Platonic aesthetic, see most recently Schott 2011.

[22] An example of this is Plutarch's *de Iside*; cf. Johnson 2013: Chapter 6.

[23] Even where it is clear that Eusebius offers us an altered text, it is difficult to determine with any certainty that he is the producer of the alteration, rather than an earlier Christian author.

pay by allowing the multiplicity of other voices to be heard within the pages of his own corpus and often pulling in divergent or oblique directions from that of his own words. If this was a form of ventriloquism, it was a ventriloquism of limited freedom that even may have lost its independence altogether. Indeed, one often suspects that the voices of Eusebius' sources have ineluctably transformed his own expression when he is no longer quoting the views of others.

As with later imperial collections, where "meticulously ordered archives were the most dangerous documents of all" for the free play of imperial power, where the control of documents from the past or from the subjects of empire began to restrict the range of independence on the part of the possessor of those documents,[24] so also Eusebius' assemblage of other sources held a constraining force over his own authorial role. Eusebius' use of quotations from Marcellus in the two treatises against him is suggestive of this dynamic. As part of his assertion that Marcellus was renewing Sabellianism, Eusebius declared: "Marcellus calls one part of God the Father another part the Son, as if there was some kind of double and composite *ousia* in him" (Eccl. Theol. 1.5[63].1). Yet, a careful reading of the Marcellan quotations notices that nowhere is the language of part/whole adopted. Elsewhere, we are told that Marcellus held that the Word is like an indicative (*sēmantikon*) or imperative (*prostaktikon*) word (Eccl. Theol. 2.8[112].1). In spite of the quantity of quotation that follows Eusebius' allegation, the use of such grammatical language in describing the status of the Word is entirely absent. Likewise, with respect to Eusebius' avowal that Marcellus wrongly applied the distinction of *logos endiathetos* and *logos prophorikos*, his supporting quotations fail to use such terminology (Eccl. Theol. 2.11 [118–119].1–5). In the earlier anti-Marcellan treatise, Eusebius explained his opponent's line of argument: "As if realizing he has fallen into a depth of strangeness (*atopia*), he tries to recall himself, saying he doesn't know any of the things he said" (C. Marc. 2.4[53].15). The quoted material that follows only shows that Marcellus was unwilling to "dogmatize about what we have not learned precisely from the Scriptures" (C. Marc. 2.4.53.15–18), and thus shows the twist Eusebius has performed in his own representation.

While we may justly criticize the polemical smokescreen that Eusebius sought to produce in such instances, we must recognize that we are only able to check Eusebius' portrayal of Marcellus' thought from the verbatim material he himself preserves for us. In other words, Eusebius has provided us with the instruments of detecting the extent and nature of his representational manipulations. In spite of his claim that he quotes Marcellus "so no one may suppose I slander him" (C. Marc. 1.1[9].36), it is precisely from his quotations that we can

---

[24] Kelly 1994: quotation at 167–168; cf. 175–176.

now appreciate the force of his misrepresentations. As Brenk noted in a discussion of the artistic and architectural use of *spolia* from earlier sources, "It is far more difficult and inconvenient to work with spolia than with newly made, homogeneous building materials."[25] Though it would have made an easier task of dismantling a muted, paraphrased version of Marcellus' theology, Eusebius' quotational habit has tethered him to the still speaking, if fragmentary, voice of his rival.

We see, then, the importance of the cumulative aesthetic on levels beyond the merely artistic. Eusebius' corpus, comprised of texts building upon texts (whether of his polemical works emphasized here, or of others, such as the *Gospel Questions and Answers*, the commentaries, or the *Onomasticon*), stands as an exquisite manifestation of a cultural shift with incisive ramifications for an intellectual's argumentation, pedagogy, and aesthetic tastes. The brief remarks offered here merely hope to suggest some of the ways in which this phenomenon might have played itself out in particular texts. While the essays of the present volume do not (nor were they asked to) respond to the question of Eusebius' relationship to late antique aesthetic transformations, it has seemed appropriate to acknowledge the sorts of ongoing underlying attitudes and sensibilities that informed the range of works that are found in Eusebius' corpus.

## Traditions and Innovations in Eusebius' Writings: The Present Collection

The collection of essays contained in the present volume cannot match Eusebius' breadth. Indeed, even if taken together with another recent collection of studies on Eusebius (*Reconsidering Eusebius*, edited by Sabrina Inowlocki and Claudio Zamagni), to which this one owes its original impetus, there remains a good deal to be done in the exploration of Eusebius' importance as a writer and thinker. The present volume does, however, seek to address some of the gaps in the ongoing study of Eusebius' corpus and indicate promising directions for further investigation. It furthermore indicates the several salient modes of innovation and of preservation of traditional forms (whether in terms of genre, theological formulation, or exegetical movement).

Each contribution was invited to be presented at a series of sessions under the rubric of "Eusebius of Caesarea and the Making of Literary Culture in Late Antiquity" (which I organized and chaired at the annual meetings of the Society of Biblical Literature from 2009 to 2011). Following the rewarding and successful Brussels colloquium on Eusebius organized by Sabrina Inowlocki and Claudio

---

[25]   Brenk 1987:106.

Zamagni (the result of which was the just-mentioned volume *Reconsidering Eusebius*), it was determined at a later informal meeting of its participants that Eusebius' role as an author should be the object of the SBL sessions. Though I was given the responsibility of their organization, the papers presented at those sessions and published here (with some additional invited pieces) are collectively the offspring of the Brussels gathering. Aside from the contexts of the original invitation, the precise topics, approaches, and conclusions of the individual contributions were left solely to the interests and proclivities of their authors. In so doing, this collection captures the variety of productive ways in which Eusebius' works might be explored. As with Eusebius' corpus itself, the present volume exhibits the ways in which both traditional and innovative questions and methods remain significant in pushing Eusebian studies forward.

In significant ways, Eusebius did not perceive himself as doing anything innovative. His composition of the history of the Church from Origen to his own day made important representational connections that affirmed the continuity of Origen's school in that of Pamphilus, of which Eusebius had been a part during the years of persecution (see Penland). Eusebius saw himself as standing within the traditions of the Church; his theological position was designated as that fostered by "ecclesiastical men," that is, the men of the true Church. Again Origen played a formative role in Eusebius' articulation of a sound and orthodox theology (Ramelli) and of a proper reading of the Bible (Morlet). Even if his friends and associates might be deemed less than orthodox by later standards, he glossed over the doctrinal infelicities of thinkers like Asterius, but highlighted the innovating heretical ("Sabellianizing") formulations of his opponent Marcellus of Ancyra. Ecclesiastical tradition thus bound together a theological network from which subversive innovators could be rejected (Del Cogliano). Yet, at the same time that Eusebius articulated his theological concerns as merely the affirmation of traditional orthodoxy, the contemporary disputes prompted new emphases. In particular, his conflict with Marcellus served as a catalyst to develop further his doctrine of the Holy Spirit (his pneumatology) that had already been formulated in the *Preparation for the Gospel* (Drecoll). Even the earlier discussion in that work resisted the temptation to drift too deeply into the categories of his Platonist contemporaries—in spite of his asseverations that Platonists were indebted to biblical wisdom—and his distinctive pneumatological formulations rooted themselves in Christian, particularly Origenian, traditions.

Yet Eusebius himself was an innovator and even claimed as much in the prologues of his *Preparation for the Gospel* and his *Ecclesiastical History*. Though well read in the historiographic traditions of the Greek and Roman worlds, he explicitly had set himself the task of striking out on an untrodden path. The novelty of the *History*'s genre has been widely recognized, but the work has remained something of a literary anomaly. Even while invoking great historians of a previous generation (like Josephus), Eusebius advanced the conceptualization of history writing in new and productive ways (DeVore). The shifts and transformations that play out in the pages of the *History* provoked conceptual shifts about the role of the family and the place of Christianity within Roman society (Corke-Webster). The authority of tradition could even be invoked at the same time that it was being (re-)invented by Eusebius (Olson). If Olson's argument for the Eusebian origins of the so-called *Testimonium Flavianum* (the passage attributed to Josephus referring to Christ), it would affirm a further parallel with the Arch of Constantine developed above: just as Constantinian workers recarved the heads of earlier emperors as fourth-century ones, so Eusebius has intrusively infused his own work into that of his earlier predecessor. Innovation and tradition would thus certainly collide in an invention of Josephan tradition.

An especially powerful context for the directions Eusebius' corpus could take lies in the web of imperial discourses, speech-acts, and relations of benefaction fostered by Constantine. Moving beyond the trite assessments of Eusebius as a court theologian and sappy sycophant of the first Christian emperor (as much recent scholarship has attempted to do)[26] need not entail a complete dismissal of Eusebius' boundedness within imperial ways of writing and construing the subjects of his literary projects, as several essays in this volume indicate. Eusebius' well-known motif of Moses as a paradigm for Constantine, first in the *Ecclesiastical History*, then more fully in the *Life of Constantine*, is here suggestively placed in conversation with Constantine's own *Oration to the Saints* (Damgaard). Eusebius is recognized as carefully attending to Constantinian cues, while elaborating them in his own particular ways.[27] Nor would visual cues be lost on Eusebius: his *Life of Constantine* produced literary images of the emperor that played off of imperial portraits (Van Nuffelen). Significantly, the *Life of Constantine* is examined as literature rather than attempting to determine its historical accuracy or deficiency.[28]

Other Christian authors grappled with, at the same time that they were products of, broader imperial contexts. A member of the imperial courts of Diocletian and Constantine, Lactantius' corpus provides a precious counterpoint to Eusebius' writings that will continue to deserve sustained attention in the future.[29] Here, the Latin rhetor's *On the Anger of God* marks a path not taken (or only

---

[26] See Hollerich 1990; Johnson 2006a:174–196.

[27] For a related study of Eusebius' elaboration of Constantinian cues, see Del Cogliano 2011.

[28] See the perceptive paper of Cameron 1997.

[29] See Schott 2008; with older studies, see e.g. Laurin 1954.

partially taken) by Eusebius (Meinking). Lactantius' exposition of the character of God was distinctive from what we find formulated in Eusebius because he was formed not only by Roman philosophical tendencies but also stood firmly within the Latin rhetorical tradition. The two Christian intellectuals who exemplify so well the tetrarchic and Constantinian eras were formed by variant traditions. Further examination of Eusebius and Lactantius would also display similarity and difference in the multiple ways in which they were both bearers of traditions and inventive explorers in territory formed by the effects of imperialism. Indeed, textual and conceptual territory were drawn and redrawn by imperial discursive modes of writing and reasoning. Eusebius' commentary on Isaiah in particular may fruitfully be examined as the product of imperializing modes of textuality (Schott). Here Eusebius' commentary is shown to exhibit a series of "hypertextual" movements between the text of Isaiah, the imperial histories of key cities or regions, other texts defining those cities or regions (especially Eusebius' own *Onomasticon*), and the text of the commentary itself. Like the Arch of Constantine, in which the "Senate and People of Rome" and the emperor negotiated earlier imperial visual and ideological traditions, Eusebius' commentary bears the marks of a manifold negotiation between empires past and present, conceived within the shifting boundaries of biblical and imperial textual territories.

With less attention to the imperial dynamics at play in his exegetical treatments, the other studies of Eusebius' biblical scholarship contained in this volume reveal his negotiations between tradition and innovation through his exegetical determinations. On the one hand, this involved his experimentation with the appropriate genre within which to perform exegesis. However, the *Gospel Questions and Answers* does not easily fit in any readily circumscribed or stable genre, but marks an innovative move beyond other instances of question and answer literature (the *erōtapokriseis*, *zētēmata*, or *aporiai*) (Zamagni). Our appreciation of the nature of this text is unfortunately impeded by the loss of its original form (its fullest survival from antiquity is in an epitome). Future research of this text will be indebted to the catalogue of all the known fragments to date, with which Zamagni concludes his present contribution. The *Commentary on Psalms* and the more fragmentary *Commentary on Luke* are in similar need of critical assessment and editing. Their extant remains (especially the hundreds of pages of firmly identified material from the Psalms commentary) nonetheless allow for much exploration of Eusebius' work as a scholar and interpreter. His commentary dedicated to the Psalms is a central witness to processes of Christian "naturalization" in late antiquity, that is, the dual transformation wherein Christian reading practices came more fully to imitate those surrounding the texts of Homer, Plato, or Aristotle by contemporaries and then the countermovement in which the cultural imagination began to be formed by the biblical texts themselves (Hollerich). In a manner similar to the naturalizing performance of exegesis in the *Commentary on Psalms,* his work on the gospel of Luke exhibits an ongoing process of translating elements of the biblical text into a new fourth-century context (Johnson). Throughout Eusebius' exegetical endeavors, ancient traditional texts became reinvested with new value and seriousness as the culmination of the literary culture of the learned elite (a position formerly held by the canonical texts of the Greek heritage) and re-embedded within new frameworks of knowledge (imperial modes of textuality, innovative genres, cosmological and eschatological visions, and so on).

Collectively, the essays of this volume exhibit a sustained effort to appreciate Eusebius as an author and thinker who was at once a bearer of formative traditions and a creative shaping force in the contours and trajectories of those traditions. His historical works are here treated with due seriousness as literature. His theological formulations are recognized for their significance in the forming of theological communities and as contributions to the direction theological reflection would take in the fourth century. At the same time, his well-known role as an heir of Origen is analyzed here with the precision necessary for a proper appreciation of his engagement with the third-century master—it was neither a slavish nor an uncreative adoption of Origen's theological and exegetical legacy. Likewise, continuities abound amid new emphases, interpretive techniques, and imperializing visions in his commentaries and other exegetical works. The present collection is a promising harbinger of the future of Eusebian studies and its role in the broader and increasingly diversified study of late antique literary culture.

# Works Cited

Brenk, B. 1987. "Spolia from Constantine to Charlemagne: Aesthetics Versus Ideology." *Dumbarton Oaks Papers* 41:103–109.

Burckhardt, J. 1949. *The Age of Constantine the Great*. Trans. M. Hadas. Berkeley.

Cameron, A. 1997. "Eusebius' Vita Constantini and the Construction of Constantine." In *Portraits: Biographical Representation in the Greek and Latin Literature of the Roman Empire*, ed. S. Swain and M. Edwards, 145–174. Oxford.

Clay, A. 2012. *A Commentary on Eusebius of Caesarea, Ecclesiastical History, Book VIII*. PhD diss., University of Colorado, Boulder.

Clover, F., and R. Stephen Humphreys, eds. 1989. *Tradition and Innovation in Late Antiquity*. Madison, WI.

DelCogliano, M. 2006. "Eusebian Theologies of the Son as the Image of God before 341." *Journal of Early Christian Studies* 14:459–484.

————. 2008. "Basil of Caesarea on Proverbs 8:22 and the Sources of Pro-Nicene Theology." *Journal of Theological Studies* 59:183–190.

DeVore, D. Forthcoming. "Eusebius' Un-Josephan History: Two Portraits of Philo of Alexandria and the Sources of Ecclesiastical Historiography." *Studia Patristica*.

Elsner, J. 2000. "From the Culture of Spolia to the Cult of Relics: The Arch of Constantine and the Genesis of Late Antique Forms." *Proceedings of the British School at Rome* 68:149–184.

————. 2004. "Late Antique Art: The Problem of the Concept and the Cumulative Aesthetic." In *Approaching Late Antiquity*, ed. S. Swain and M. Edwards, 271–309. Oxford.

Evelyn White, H. G. 1988. *Ausonius*, 1, LCL 96. Cambridge, MA.

Goulet-Cazé, M.-O., ed. 2000. *Le commentaire entre tradition et innovation*. Paris.

Hollerich, M. 1990. "Religion and Politics in the Writings of Eusebius: Reassessing the First 'Court Theologian.'" *Church History* 59:309–325.

————. 1999. *Eusebius of Caesarea's Commentary on Isaiah: Christian Exegesis in the Age of Constantine*. Oxford.

Inowlocki, S. 2006. *Eusebius and the Jewish Authors: His Citation Technique in an Apologetic Context*. Leiden.

Johnson, A. P. 2006a. *Ethnicity and Argument in Eusebius' Praeparatio Evangelica*. Oxford.

————. 2006b. "Philonic Allusions in Eusebius, PE 7.7–8." *Classical Quarterly* 56:239–248.

————. 2006c. "The Blackness of Ethiopians: Classical Ethnography and Eusebius' Commentary on the Psalms." *Harvard Theological Review* 99:179–200.

———. 2011. "Eusebius the Educator: The Context of the General Elementary Introduction." In *Reconsidering Eusebius*, ed. C. Zamagni and S. Inowlocki, 99–118. Leiden.

———. 2013. *Religion and Identity in Porphyry of Tyre*. Cambridge.

Kelly, C. 1994. "Later Roman Bureacracy: Going Through the Files." In *Literacy and Power in the Ancient World*, ed. Alan Bowman and Greg Woolf, 161–176. Cambridge.

Kelly, C., R. Flower, and M. S. Williams, eds. 2010. *Unclassical Traditions*. Cambridge.

Laurin, J.-R. 1954. *Orientations maîtresses des apologistes chrétiens de 270 à 361*. Analecta Gregoriana 61. Rome.

Lenski, N. 2008. "Evoking the Pagan Past: Instinctu divinitatis and Constantine's Capture of Rome." *Journal of Late Antiquity* 1:204–257.

Lyman, R. 1993. *Christology and Cosmology: Models of Divine Activity in Origen, Eusebius and Athanasius*. Oxford.

Mansfeld, J. 1994. *Prolegomena: Questions to be Settled before the Study of an Author, or a Text*. Leiden.

Morgan, T. 2005. "Eusebius of Caesarea and Christian Historiography." *Athenaeum* 93:193–208.

Morlet, S. 2005. "Ecrire l'histoire selon Eusèbe de Césarée." *L'Information littéraire* 57:3–15.

———. 2006. "L'introduction de l'Histoire ecclésiastique d'Eusèbe de Césarée (HE I, II-IV): étude génétique, littéraire et rhétorique." *Revue des études augustiniennes et patristiques* 52:57–95.

———. 2009. *La Démonstration évangélique d'Eusèbe de Césarée. Étude sur l'apologétique chrétienne à l'époque de Constantin*. Paris.

———, ed. 2012. *Eusèbe de Césarée. Histoire ecclésiastique. Commentaire. Tome I. Études d'introduction*. Paris.

Panella, C. and P. Pensabene. 1997. "Riempego e progettazione architettonica nei monumenti tardo-antichi di Roma." *Atti della Pontificia academia romana di archeologia, Rendiconti*. 66:111–283.

———, eds. 1999. *Arco di Costantino. Tra archeologia e archeometria*. Rome.

Puech, A. 1930. *Histoire de la littérature grecque chrétienne*. 3 vols. Paris.

Roberts, M. 1989. *The Jeweled Style: Poetry and Poetics in Late Antiquity*. Ithaca.

Robertson, J. 2007. *Christ the Mediator: A Study of the Theologies of Eusebius of Caesarea, Marcellus of Ancyra, and Athanasius of Alexandria*. Oxford.

Schott, J. 2008. *Christianity, Empire and the Making of Religion in Late Antiquity*. Philadelphia.

———. 2011. "Eusebius' Panegyric on the Building of Churches (HE 10.4.2–72): Aesthetics and the Politics of Christian Architecture." In *Reconsidering Eusebius*, ed. S. Inowlocki and C. Zamagni, 177–198. Leiden.

Snyder, G. 2000. *Teachers and Texts in the Ancient World.* London.

Spoerl, K. 1997. "Anti-Arian Polemic in Eusebius of Caesarea's Ecclesiastical Theology." *Studia Patristica* 32:33–38.

Usher, M. D. 1989. *Homeric Stitchings: The Homeric Centos of the Empress Eudocia.* Lanham, MA.

Verdoner, M. 2011. *Narrated Reality: The Historia ecclesiastica of Eusebius of Caesarea.* Early Christianity in the Context of Antiquity. Vol. 9. Frankfurt am Main.

Wilson Jones, M. 2000. "Genesis and Mimesis: The Design of the Arch of Constantine in Rome." *Journal of the Society of Architectural Historians* 59:50–77.

# 2

# Genre and Eusebius' *Ecclesiastical History*
## Toward a Focused Debate[1]

### David J. DeVore

EUSEBIUS' *ECCLESIASTICAL HISTORY* is universally acknowledged as a watershed in historiographical presentation, the most innovative history since the fifth century BC: it quotes previous texts promiscuously, avoids placing orations into characters' mouths, incorporates literary history, and lacks causal relations between successive episodes. But it is *a priori* doubtful that the *Ecclesiastical History* either fell from the sky, distinctively formed and alien to classical tradition, or that its lines of participation in Greek historiographical genres are untraceable. The text explicitly participates in an 800-year, diverse tradition of Greek *historia*, competing with the Greek historiographical tradition.[2] The term *historia*, of course, could designate anything from a synchronic geographical survey to a novelistic narrative, labeling numerous subgenres and combinations of genres; nonetheless, Eusebius' title pointed to at least one of these groups of texts as precedent for its form, content, and/or rhetoric.[3]

[1] John DeVore, Hal Drake, Tom Hendrickson, Scott McGuiness, Alex Roberts, Megan Hale Williams, and the editors each read this paper at various stages and offered a multitude of helpful suggestions. I also thank John Dillery, Susanna Elm, and Rebecca Lyman for their generous help in shaping my thinking about the topics in this article, and the editors for the opportunity to publish it.
[2] See Perrone 1996:520–521, and Verdoner 2007:88–92; note also Calderone 1980:145–148. It is important to note that, unlike previous scholars of Eusebian historiography (e.g. Chesnut 1986, chapter 2), I exclude Latin histories and historiographies from discussion in this chapter. Although Eusebius probably knew some Latin—see HE 4.8.8, and note that almost all civic inscriptions in Caesarea Maritima before Constantine's reign were inscribed in Latin (Eck 2001:50–51, 55–61)—there is no evidence that he had any knowledge of literature written in Latin (see Carriker 2003:18, 18n53).
[3] As the greatest scholar of Greek historiography, Felix Jacoby, recognized in organizing his *Fragmente der griechischen Historiker* so as to include "virtually all Greek nonfictional prose" (in

Scholars have submitted a wide range of opinions as to what kind of history the *Ecclesiastical History* is. In 1892, Franz Overbeck argued that it presented the Christian past "als die Geschichte des Christenvolkes . . . gleich den anderen Völkern."[4] In his influential Pauly-Wissowa article published in 1907, Eduard Schwartz pronounced that the *historia* in *Ekklēsiastikē Historia* "bedeutet die Sammlung von überliefertem Material."[5] Timothy Barnes characterized the text in 1981 as combining both "a novel kind of national history" and "inevitably also a literary or philosophical history."[6] More recent assessments have described the *Ecclesiastical History* as "a 'media history,' a special genre on a new topic,"[7] or as "a transgeneric cross" between historiography and apologetics.[8]

This smattering of generic pronouncements brings into the open a mostly latent debate about the genre of Eusebius' new history.[9] As occurs with latent debates, scholars' views depend on categories that resonate in quite separate spheres of texts' operations. *Volksgeschichte* and "literary or philosophical history" classify a thematic subject; *Materialsammlung* names a method of research as manifested in mode of presentation; "media history" acts as an analogy that foregrounds the text's modes of influencing its target audience; and "apologetic historiography" emphasizes how the author intends the text to influence his readers.

Such a range of published views has the virtue of drawing numerous readings and insights from the text.[10] Yet scholars' disconnections about which traits determine a text's genre have occluded a focused debate on the kind of text that the *Ecclesiastical History* is. To take the categories employed in the generic pronouncements above: the same text can cover a people, take the form of a collection of sources, employ "medial" modes of influencing audiences, lack connections between units, and function to defend a social group—even though the scholars quoted above surely disagree with one another about many aspects of the *Ecclesiastical History*.[11] Discussion of Eusebian historiography has not yet forged a common set of questions or heuristic categories that can allow points

---

the words of Hägg 2001:192), though Jacoby did not include philosophy, medicine, or mathematical texts.

4   Overbeck 1892:42. The most sustained reading of the text as a national history is Beggs 1999.
5   Schwartz 1907:1395; note also Schwartz 1938:116 ("Materialsammlung").
6   Barnes 1981:128.
7   Mendels 1999:2–3.
8   Verdoner 2007:91–92.
9   Verdoner 2007 is already a step toward sharpening this debate.
10  Note also the generic (or quasi-generic) characterizations of Momigliano 1963:90–91; Gödecke 1987:24–26; Timpe 1989:196; Morgan 2005:196.
11  Another problem with these generic pronouncements is that, except for Schwartz's thesis that the *Ecclesiastical History* represented *Materialsammlung*, all of them marginalize narrative form.

of disagreement to emerge with clarity. Scholars, in short, are talking past each other.

Of course, the object of study itself resists easy classification: the *Ecclesiastical History's* universally acknowledged originality does not make easy work of generic identification.[12] We could sidestep the genre question altogether. In a commendable recent survey of Eusebius' historiographical influences, Sébastien Morlet judiciously avoided assigning a genre to the *Ecclesiastical History*.[13] Yet even in such a circumspect assessment, a tension surfaces: Morlet's conclusion conjoins an acknowledgment of Eusebian originality with the historian's concomitant influence from "[le] genre historiographique antique."[14] Eusebius' history was innovative, yet he drew his methods from a long and rich generic tradition. Historiography is considered a genre, yet the *Ecclesiastical History* is *sui generis*. Indeed, rather than discuss Eusebius' use of historiographical subgenres, Morlet points almost exclusively to specific Judean and Christian historical narratives (the Deuteronomistic history and Chronicles in the Hebrew Bible, Josephus' histories, the *Acts of the Apostles*) as Eusebian models, as well as some texts within "l'historiographique païenne."[15] Can we explain Eusebian historiography only in terms of specific paradigmatic texts, and not trace the *Ecclesiastical History's* participation in contemporary historiographical genres? Put another way: Eusebius had no way of knowing that others would write ecclesiastical history with his text as their model: *ekklēsiastikē historia* could have simply remained the title solely for his text, not the designation of a new genre. If Rufinus, Socrates, Sozomen, Theodoret, and the rest had not written, where would we locate the *Ecclesiastical History* within Greek historiography?

In this chapter I argue that the field of genre studies can help in articulating how the *Ecclesiastical History* participated in discourses circulating and proliferating at the time of its composition and aim to promote a more explicit discussion of the genre of the *Ecclesiastical History*. To do so I not only apply concepts through which such a debate may take place, but also stake out a position on the

---

[12] There are other obstacles to a tight debate. For example, the different disciplines whose scholars study Eusebius (theology and religious studies, Roman and late antique history, both political and cultural, and classical philology) do not facilitate unified discussion.

[13] Morlet 2005.

[14] Morlet 2005:14.

[15] Morlet 2005:11 (on the Hebrew Bible, merely citing Winckelmann 1991:65); 9, 11–12 (Josephus); 12–13 (Acts of the Apostles); 5–10 ("la tradition historiographique païenne"). However, note also Morlet 2005:8. The assumption that Eusebius was writing in the tradition of Greek *historia* is reflected in Morlet's choice of Eusebian models to survey: non- or para-historiographical models for the *Ecclesiastical History*, like apologetic oratory, martyrdom acts, and Irenaeus' *Examination and Refutation of Knowledge Falsely So-Called*, are omitted from his discussion. Yet surely there are more illuminating generic distinctions within Greek-language historical writing than the religio-ethnic identity of historical texts' individual author-narrators.

genre(s) of Eusebian historiography. As a theoretical foundation, I first summarize a theory of genre, that of the Australian literary theorist John Frow, to highlight what genre does in literary texts. Second, I apply five criteria for generic classification formulated by John Marincola, a leading scholar of ancient historiography, to the *Ecclesiastical History* in order to decipher some of the generic choices that Eusebius made. I conclude by outlining how Eusebius' choices in these five aspects of his text signaled his participation in carefully selected strands of the Greek historiographical tradition and shaped his construction of Christianity.

## Genre Theory and Generic Cues: A Framework for Approaching Eusebian Genre

All instances of human communication assume and convey meaning only as related to other instances of communication, as they fit into webs of similar kinds of communications. As Bakhtin famously argued, every kind of verbal communication, from a simple command from one individual to another all the way up to the modern novel, draws much of its meaning from its association with a recognizable class of speech.[16] To apprehend the genre of an enunciation, the speaker or recipient must determine certain formal, thematic, and rhetorical elements, as well as social situation and physical setting, that surround the enunciation.[17] The recipients of any enunciation can understand how the enunciation is meant to be received and can enter into dialogue with the speaker (or, as some might view it, with the enunciation) only by presuming the kind of enunciation that is expressed.

As Bakhtin recognized, societies collude to order their enunciations into particular generic groupings. These groupings contain latent networks of background information shared between speakers and audiences, which speakers can use to color and empower their enunciations, and upon which audiences must draw to interpret them. Drawing upon theoretical work in linguistics and cognitive science, John Frow has composed a perceptive synthesis of genre theory. Frow conceptualizes genre as a linguistic means of organizing information, one among the clusters of categories ("schemata") by which humans organize their knowledge of the world.

Cognitive science shows that our brains channel new knowledge into compartments containing the clusters of our previous knowledge. Information is thus processed as if through networks. In order to make new knowledge

---

[16] Bakhtin 1986:60–102. See also Frow 2006, chapters 2 and 4.
[17] For definitions and elaboration of these terms, see Frow 2006:7–9, 72–77.

meaningful within the structures of our already-constructed worldview, we cluster related bodies of knowledge together, storing information through "associative networks, 'knowledge nets,' the nodes of which are 'propositions, schemas, frames, scripts, production rules.'"[18] Thereafter, once new knowledge has been integrated into our cognitive networks:

> Knowledge nets allow . . . for the activation on an *ad hoc* basis of relevant knowledges, distributing resources between a foreground of active meanings and a background of encyclopaedic knowledge and beliefs. I take these knowledge nets to be in part generically organised . . .
>
> Frow 2006:85

If we conceptualize the cognitive processes of channeling, storing, and accessing knowledge as informational networks, then genres can be viewed as one of the network's nodes, functioning as one of Frow's "schemas, frames, scripts, production rules." "Genre cues act rather like context-sensitive drop-down menus in a computer program, directing me to the layers and sub-layers of information that respond to my purposes as a speaker or a reader or a viewer."[19] Thus, the recently fashionable concern with ancient practices of organizing knowledge must depend (at least in part) on an appreciation of the power of genre.[20] Furthermore, discussion of the *Ecclesiastical History's* genre (rather than historical veracity or use of sources, as so often) encourages sensitivity to its fundamental role in the organization of knowledge in the late Roman Empire.

Frow's articulation of genre as a frame for communicating information has several consequences relevant to understanding genre. First, genres will vary from reading community to reading community according to schemata available to and shared among each one. Any new literary work will show points of dialogue with kinds of speech salient in the author's culture. In seeking to map out generic connections, therefore, we cannot assume any universal genres, but must look for the communicative schemata available to communities of authors and audiences.[21]

---

[18] Frow 2006:85; quotation from Kintsch 1998:74 [*non vidi*].

[19] Frow 2006:84. Perhaps a more helpful metaphor would be that genre cues acts like hyperlinks, linking the brain to other information related to the phenomenon at hand and to apply that knowledge in understanding the new information. Genre, among other schemata, channels new information into certain categories of older knowledge.

[20] See, for example, the essays in König and Whitmarsh 2007.

[21] See Frow 2006:12–17, 124–139.

Second, unlike many prescriptive theories of genre, this theory of genre is fundamentally descriptive.[22] Genre becomes prescriptive only insofar as institutions within a society prescribe certain specific genres as normative. (To recognize such a practice is, of course, itself a descriptive act.)

Third, no literary genre is ever fully distinct from all other genres. As Bakhtin emphasized, speech genres in general, and individual texts in particular, absorb and incorporate many other genres into themselves. Similarly, if genres are the nodes of informational networks, then any network can create a node to channel information from any other network.[23]

Fourth, because speech genres result from individual societies' shared and organically ordered kinds of speech, genres—especially complex ones instantiated in written texts—wield the potential to change considerably over time.[24] It is true that genres must appear somewhat stable in order for societies to order knowledge around them. Genres would thus seem to be a mechanism for cultural stability. But as semiotic entities, genres are inherently incapable of maintaining stability.[25] Accordingly, the transposition or deconstruction of old configurations and generic signs remain available to any agent as strategies for reworking a culture's symbolic resources.[26] The historiographical tradition in which Eusebius participated had therefore undergone wide diversification, and thus offered many recognizable schemata through which he could impart his knowledge of the church.

Because genres are unstable and overlap with one another, the theory of genre employed here assumes that the schemata by which societies order their knowledge are in constant flux, a flux rooted in the reimagination and reconfiguration that each new text works upon the classes that it enters into. No text can "belong" to a genre, as if the genre is simply a class indistinct from all others. Whereas "belonging" indicates a fixed control that a classification exerts on a text, such control does not exist in practice, as texts are constantly

---

[22] *Pace* the influential Cairns 1972, e.g. p. 31. According to Cairns, ancient authors clung rigidly to their generic models.

[23] History resulted from a dialogue between epic narrative and geo-ethnographical literature, Athenian tragedy from mimesis meeting choral lyric. More complex genres naturally draw upon and refract simple ones. See Bakhtin 1981, chapter 2.

[24] A point made by Conte 1992:108–109; Marincola 1999:281–282, 299; Frow 2006:2, 124, 137–139. Cf. Bakhtin 1986:60, 64, 78–81.

[25] A point that has sunk into genre studies thanks to Fowler 1982. As William Sewell (2005:164–174, especially 165–167) points out, signs always carry their own networks of denotations and connotations, which vary among different groups within a society, at different times. For this reason, Sewell posits, the constellation of symbols that make up a society's culture can only possess a "thin coherence": that is, symbols are coherent enough to enable human agents to communicate, but are flexible enough for new configurations of symbols to transform a cultural system.

[26] On "transposition" of existing cultural structures, see Sewell 2005, chapter 4, especially 129–143.

reconfiguring each class's boundaries. A more fruitful conceptualization of the relationship between text and genre is that texts "perform" the latent schemata available in genres, so that a textual performance creates a relationship of dialogue or participation with generic schemata.[27] Since literary texts encompass and recontextualize different kinds of speech genres, each new literary performance will transpose various available genres with one another.[28] Each text can therefore be said to participate in the various schemata: each new performance, in textual, visual, or social form, will therefore re-form, extend, and test audiences' conceptions of their schemata, and thus change them.[29]

How should we identify the manifestation of Eusebius' performances within the historiographical (and the wider Greek literary) tradition? Drawing on the later work of Gérard Genette, Frow points to the concept of generic cues (alluded to above):

> The cues that alert us to what a text is doing are references to the text's generic frame, and work by either explicit or implicit invocation of the structures and frames that we characteristically associate with that frame . . . They are the ways in which texts seek to situate themselves rhetorically, to define and delimit their uptake by a reader—and, conversely, they are the way in which readers make sense of these markers, and indeed notice them and respond to them in the first place. Textual cues are thus metacommunications, aspects of the text that somehow stand out as being also, reflexively, *about* the text and how to use it.
>
> Frow 2006:114–115[30]

The determination of a text's genre is largely the detection of these generic cues, the formal, thematic, and rhetorical gestures that signify dialogue with salient groups of known texts. The next section will apply one method for revealing some of *Ecclesiastical History*'s generic cues.

---

[27] "Texts are acts or performances which work upon a set of generic materials. The relationship is one of elaboration rather than of derivation or determination" (Frow 2006:23–24).

[28] I draw the term "transpose" from Sewell 2005:140–143, who modifies its usage in the work of Pierre Bourdieu.

[29] First pointed out by Derrida 1980, especially pp. 55–66. See also the elaboration of Frow 2006:17–28.

[30] Frow goes on to offer some examples of generic cues: "They may stand out in very obvious ways, like the laugh track on a television sitcom or the moral appended to a fable; or they may be elements which seem to take on a particular weight in our reading, and to be indicative of what kind of thing this is." (Frow credits Genette 1987 [*non vidi*] at p. 105 as the foundation for his thinking about generic cues.)

## Interpreting the *Ecclesiastical History*'s Genres: Five Criteria

If "genre" refers to culturally contingent schemata for organizing communicated information, then we must locate the *Ecclesiastical History* within the genre(s) that were salient within Eusebius' literary culture. The Greek historiographical tradition in which the *Ecclesiastical History* participated was rich and wideranging, and in it there was constant tension between the paradigmatic texts inculcated as models and the incentives of literary competition that encouraged innovation.[31] We therefore need criteria for assessing genre that reveal a text's lines of connection with this historiographical tradition, viz. criteria that can expose its generic cues. Such criteria might serve as the common language needed to advance debate about the *Ecclesiastical History*'s genre.

Classicist John Marincola formulated just such a set of criteria a little over a decade ago, which seems not to have impacted the study of Eusebius as it could have. These criteria, Marincola writes, enable the scholar "to look at the totality of an historical work before forming conclusions about its nature and purpose."[32] They are neither independent from one another, nor do they constitute a closed system: their use is heuristic, as ciphers for identifying the schemata that distinguish historiographical subgenres. Marincola's criteria are:[33] (1) narrative or non-narrative, (2) focalization, (3) chronological limits, (4) chronological arrangement, and (5) subject matter. In what follows, I explain each criterion before applying it to the *Ecclesiastical History*.

What choices did Eusebius make in each of these areas of the *Ecclesiastical History*? The following exposition will reveal the outlines to Eusebius' generic cues, allowing me in the final section of this chapter to draw a hypothesis about which genre(s) within Greek historiography Eusebius put into performance in the *Ecclesiastical History*.

### Narrative or non-narrative?

Historians could "write an historical synchronic narrative or . . . a more diachronic descriptive method, or some combination of the two." Chronography, Marincola notes, may have different narrative patterns from *Zeitgeschichte*, but they are both equally narratival; and while "descriptions of the lands or customs of a people are usually diachronic and 'timeless,'" yet "these too can be

---

[31] For a discussion of how Greek educational practices under the Roman Empire created a virtual "canon" of historiographical texts, see Nicolai 1992, especially pp. 250–339. See also Gibson 2004. Theorizing genres as loci of competition in the Roman Empire is Conte 1992.

[32] Marincola 1999:302.

[33] Marincola 1999:302–309. For examples of their application, see Marincola 1999:309–320.

concerned with causation and explanation, as seen most easily in Herodotus." The Greek historiographical tradition offered several modes for narrating time and for explaining events, and the authorial decision of how to structure these (both for the text as a whole and for individual units) placed his text in a tradition immediately.[34]

For his part, Eusebius chose a narrative arrangement for the *Ecclesiastical History*, when he could have chosen to organize his history geographically—according to the events of each of the four apostolic sees, for instance—or thematically, like ethnographic *historiai*. Both modes of organization were common among Greek historians.[35] Eusebius' narratival structure thus signaled participation in the more specific traditions of Greek narrative history, such as war monographs (like Thucydides' *Peloponnesian War* or Josephus' *Judean War*), histories of a specific people or place (like local histories, Xenophon's *Hellenica*, Dionysius of Halicarnassus' *Roman Antiquities*, Josephus' *Judean Antiquities*, or Cassius Dio's and Herodian's *Roman Histories*), and "universal" (perhaps better termed "transnational") histories (like Polybius', Diodorus', and Appian's *Histories*).

On the other hand, Eusebius' ecclesiastical narrative is notable for its sequential discontinuity. The reader rarely gets the impression that one event or personal notice has any causal relationship with preceding or coming events. This disjunction between events lies behind the repeated scholarly comment that the *Ecclesiastical History* is a "static history."[36] It is necessary to note, however, that some subgenres of Greek historiography could shun causal connection between events. Certain kinds of local histories, including the "sacred histories" of temples, could avoid causal connectivity.[37] So too could Greek "lives" or biography, a genre with considerable overlap with history.[38] In short, Eusebius' choice to write a narrative, but a *discontinuous* narrative, of the church's past associated the *Ecclesiastical History* with certain strands of the Greek historical tradition.

---

[34] Marincola 1999:302–303.

[35] Strabo's *Geography*, for example, was a synchronic text that served as a companion to his diachronic pan-Mediterranean history (see 1.23). Other historians incorporated "timeless" ethnographies into their narrative histories: most famous are Herodotus' digressions, whereas Diodorus Siculus had begun his trans-Mediterranean history with geographically organized ethnographic surveys of the peoples that his narrative would discuss.

[36] For example, Barnes 1981:131–132; Twomey 1982:202–204; Timpe 1989:191–192; Winckelmann 1991:107; Carotenuto 2001:xix–xx; Morgan 2005:195–196; Morlet 2005:13; Willing 2008:487–488.

[37] For local histories, see the classic Jacoby 1949, pp. 86–99; and the more recent Clarke 2008, chapters 3, 4, and 6. For "sacred history," see e.g. Higbie 2003 and Dillery 2005.

[38] On the tense but kindred relations between biography and history, see Dihle 1986 (*passim*) and Dihle 1998:124–130. Note also Cooper 2004 on the complex relationship between Plutarch's *Lives* and narrative history.

Moreover, although the *Ecclesiastical History* is structured narratively, many of its individual units are non-narrative. I refer here specifically to the many non-narratival "profiles" that Eusebius inserts to describe individual Christians, Judeans, "heretics," and emperors.[39] In these profiles, the Eusebian narrator paints a generalized portrait of a character without regard for narrative sequence.[40] The character's location of activity and/or ethnicity, ecclesiastical office or professional identification, connections with teachers, students, and other important individuals, written works (including sacred texts used), travels, virtues or vices, and circumstances of death appear frequently in these profiles. The Eusebian narrator will sometimes compile this data in his own voice, and sometimes through quotation of other texts. Take, for example, Eusebius' profile of Julius Africanus:

> At that time Africanus also, the author of the books entitled *Kestoi*, was well known (ἐγνωρίζετο). A letter of his, written to Origen, is extant; he was at a loss as to whether the story of Susanna in the book of Daniel was a spurious forgery. Origen makes a very full reply to it. Of the same Africanus there have reached us as well five books of *Chronographies*, an endeavor toiled at with accuracy (ἐπ' ἀκριβὲς πεπονημένα σπουδάσματα). In these he says that he himself set out on a journey to Alexandria because of the great fame of Heraclas, who, as we have noted, was greatly distinguished for philosophical discourses and other Greek learning (διὰ πολλὴν τοῦ Ἡρακλᾶ φήμην, ὃν ἐπὶ λόγοις φιλοσόφοις καὶ τοῖς ἄλλοις Ἑλλήνων μαθήμασιν εὖ μάλα διαπρέψαντα), and who was entrusted with the bishopric of the church there. Another letter of the same Africanus is extant, to Aristides, *On the supposed discord between the Genealogies of Christ in Matthew and Luke*. In it he establishes very clearly the harmony of the evangelists (ἐν ᾗ σαφέστατα τὴν συμφωνίαν τῶν εὐαγγελιστῶν παρίστησιν) from an account that came down to him, which by anticipation I set forth in the proper place in the first book of the present work.

> HE 6.31, trans. Oulton, modified

Here the Eusebian narrator introduces Africanus through a temporal indication that synchronizes Africanus with contemporary Christian luminaries. The

---

[39] Aside from the so-called "Life of Origen," the profiles in the *Ecclesiastical History* have received little scholarly attention as formal units; the most extensive study of them is the neglected Alexandre 1998. See also Grant 1980:76–77; Carotenuto 2001:102–106; cf. Morlet 2005:8.

[40] Throughout this essay I use "the Eusebian narrator" or "the narrator" to denote the textual voice that narrates the *Ecclesiastical History*, and "Eusebius" to refer to the author of the *History*; narratological theory posits that we cannot identify the two as the same entity. See Bal 1997:19–31.

profile is ordered around a list of Africanus' written works, presenting some details about the arguments and debates he sets forth in these. Although mini-narratives—epistolary exchanges with Origen and (as can easily be inferred) with Aristides, a visit to the brilliant Heraclas—hover under the profile's surface, in itself the profile gives no indication of any specific chronological sequence of these events, nor does it indicate any causal relationships among them. Africanus' literary production garners praise (his *Chronographies* are ἐπ' ἀκριβὲς πεπονημένα, he proves the harmony of Matthew's and Luke's genealogies σαφέστατα—as the Eusebian narrator had indicated by quoting this letter at length in HE 1.7). On this list of literary works the narrator hangs data pertinent to two themes: interactions with important contemporaries and the character's researches into biblical history.

The *Ecclesiastical History*—particularly, but not exclusively, in books two through seven—deploys many such synchronic profiles of key individuals. It employs different structures for doing so, and sometimes (as in the cases of the apostle John, Irenaeus, Origen, and Dionysius of Alexandria) carries these profiles across several chapters.[41] While before Eusebius Greek narrative historians had paused their narratives to assess characters who participate in the narrated events,[42] it is difficult to find one who had so thoroughly interwoven characters' profiles with the course of passing time. The *Ecclesiastical History* thus opens up a seam in the binary between narrative and non-narrative history: macroscopically narrative, its constituent units are regularly non-narrative. Eusebius' use of the literary profile enables his history to straddle a border between two modes of historiographical organization.

## Focalization

Marincola defines this criterion, drawn from narratology, as "the focus or orientation or point of view from which one tells the story."[43] The possible focalizers defined by Marincola range on a spectrum according to their size, from individuals, to cities, to nations, to the entire known world. Marincola further notes that the focalization often corresponds to the arrangement of the history, and in particular to its dating system (see "Chronological arrangement" below).[44]

---

41   John 3:18.1–3; 3:20.9; 3:23; 3:24.7–14, 17; 3:31.2–3. Irenaeus 4.21; 4.25; 5.4; 5.5.8; 5.8; 5.20; 5.24.18; 5.26. Origen 6.2–6; 6.8; 6.14.10–6.19; 6.21.3–4; 6.23–25; 6.27; 6.30; 6.32; 6.33.2–4; 6.36–37; 6.39.5. Dionysius of Alexandria 6.35; 6.40; 6.45–46; 7.4–7.9; 7.11; 7.20–26; 7.28.3.

42   For example, Thucydides 2.65 on Pericles; 6.15 on Alcibiades; 7.86.5 on the Nicias; 8.68.1 on Antiphon.

43   Marincola 1999:303 (with diagram). For a more specific definition and discussion of its implications, see Bal 1997:142–161.

44   Marincola's criteria are interrelated on several points.

The *Ecclesiastical History* is nearly always told as through the eyes of the "orthodox" Christian church (as bounded by Eusebius). As Marie Verdoner has recently argued in a superb article on the *Ecclesiastical History*'s implied audience, the Eusebian narrator not only assumes knowledge of Christian holy texts, but also accepts their sacred status; the narrator omits discussion of Christian doctrine out of an assumption that the reader knows it; and the narrator is so unabashedly partisan—lacking defensiveness!—on behalf of the Christians as to presume a positive opinion of Christianity on the part of the reader.[45] The narrator rarely allows the text to reproduce the perspective of non-Christians, the only common contexts for extra-Christian perspective being quotations of Judean authors and imperial edicts and rescripts.[46]

The *Ecclesiastical History* thus maintains an intra-Christian perspective on the events and personalities that it recounts. But as Marincola's spectrum of focalizers indicates, a choice to limit a history's perspective to the collective viewpoint of a single (even if translocal) community was nothing new in Greek historiography: national histories like Josephus' *Judean Antiquities* and Cassius Dio's *Roman History* display the same focalization.[47] It cannot be coincidence that the Eusebian narrator labels the church as a "nation" (*ethnos*, 1.4.2, 10.4.19; cf. 5.pref.2, 9.1.5);[48] his focalization through Christian eyes follows the conventional focalizations of other national histories narrated from the point of view of a member of the portrayed group, as in the *Judean Antiquities*. The "orthodox" Christian focalization of the text places the *Ecclesiastical History* right into the center of Marincola's spectrum, mapping onto his category of perspective of a nation.

[45] Verdoner 2010: p. 368 (sacred texts); p. 367 (omission and tacit consensus with implied audience on dogma); pp. 369–370 (the narrator's presumption of ideological consensus with readers). Note also Morlet 2005:11.

[46] Quotations of Judean authors: Philo at 2.6.1–2 and 2.17 (on which see Inowlocki 2004); Josephus at 1.5.3–6, 1.8.4–15, 1.10.4–5, 1.11.4–9, 2.5.2–6, 2.6.3–4, 2.20.1–3, 2.23.20–21, 2.26, 3.6, 3.8. Imperial edicts and rescripts: 4.9, 4.13, 7.13, 8.17, 9.1.3–6, 9.7.3–15, 9.9A, 10.5–7. Other focalization through non-Christians: a famous quotation of Porphyry at 6.19.4–8, and a quotation of Hegesippus narrating the martyrdom of James the brother of Jesus uses multiple focalizations (2.23.14–17).

[47] Moreover, as T.J. Luce showed more than twenty years ago, ancient historians were expected to show partiality to their implied authors' native people, land, city, and family (Luce 1989, especially 20–21). To focalize a narrative from the perspective of one's own people permitted historians' prejudice to color the narrative.

[48] On the Christian self-conception as a "nation" or "ethnic" or "racial" group, see e.g. Lieu 2004 and Buell 2005; on Eusebius' own presentation of the place of Christians in the contemporary Greek world, see Johnson 2006:198–233.

## Chronological limits

Historians could choose to write starting at (or even before) their subject's origins, or could write only about more recent times, or could pick an intermediate period, or some time in between. The chronological boundaries reveal what Hayden White famously called the "emplotment" of a history: "... it cannot be denied that historians 'read' the events of their history in a certain way, and if, for example, an historian sees his subject as glorious, he might begin and end differently from one who saw the same events as comic and inglorious." In other words, "the choice of what time period to embrace carries with it consequences for the patterning of meaning produced by that work."[49] As Marincola notes, a longer, universal history can follow a tighter plot, but also feature "greater adornment," than a longer, national history.

Eusebius' chronological limits are fairly straightforward: he begins his continuous narrative from the reign of Herod and birth of Jesus at HE 1.5. True, after his preface (1.1) the narrator launches into some temporally transcendent theological prolegomena about the nature of Christ. But this does not stretch the narrative's chronological boundaries in any original way, for Herodotus and Thucydides (both of whose histories Eusebius knew)[50] had each written introductory "archaeologies" of protohistoric events that set the narratival tone for their respective war histories (Herodotus 1.1–4, Thucydides 1.2–19; and note also the internal "Sicilian Archaeology" at Thucydides 6.1–5). Eusebius' extended introduction has some of the same functions as these exemplary historiographical introductions.[51] On the other hand, the text's chronological boundaries are properly the reign of Herod and the author's own time.[52]

As Marincola suggests, the choice of chronological boundaries has consequences for the emplotment of the *Ecclesiastical History*. Eusebius' starting and ending points seem commonsensical for a narrative of the institution of the church, as Christianity was known to have arisen with the life of Jesus. Yet there

---

[49] Marincola 1999:304 (citing White 1988, chapter 1), 305.

[50] See Eusebius' *Theophany* 2.68–69; I owe this reference to Wallace-Hadrill 1960:184–185, who rightly notes Eusebius' knowledge of Thucydides. *Pace* Carriker 2003:151–152, who misses these references from the *Theophany*.

[51] Eusebius himself uses the term "archaeology" (which in historiography meant "account of prehistory") to summarize HE 1 at HE 2.pref.: ὡς ἐν προοιμίῳ διαστείλασθαι τῆς ἀρχαιολογίας τῶν τῆς ἡμετέρας διδασκαλίας. See Morlet 2006 on HE 1.2–4, though he does not compare the passage to the Herodotean and Thucydidean exemplars.

[52] His revisions of the HE notwithstanding. On the composition of the *Ecclesiastical History*, see Burgess 1997 (whose compositional theory of the HE has now forced Barnes to abandon his own earlier and widely accepted compositional theory: see Barnes 2009:6–7).

is a tension here, since Eusebius spent much of his "archaeology" arguing that Christianity was no revolutionary phenomenon. Several clever strategies enable the narrator to finesse the all-but-acknowledged novelty of Christianity (cf. 1.4.2). This "Christian Archaeology" (HE 2.pref.1) finds temporally deep roots for Christianity in claims that its founder had a transtemporal existence and a strong *Auswirkung* on the glorious Hebrews of the past (HE 1.2, elaborated more fully in Eusebius' *Praeparatio Evangelica* 7), in prophecies (HE 1.3), and in the claim that Christians were the real heirs of the ancient Hebrews (HE 1.4). After the narrative proper begins, the narrator creates legitimacy for Jesus as leader of the Hebrews: since Herod had appropriated the selection of Judean high priests, the Judean high priesthood no longer had a claim to act as God's earthly representative (HE 1.6).[53] The Eusebian narrator's insertion of an "archaeological" prolegomenon and a strained narrative of the end of the Judean high priesthood constitute external analepses[54] that create "preincarnate" origins for the Christian nation. Both techniques, drawing on previous historiographical traditions, allowed Eusebius to have it both ways, beginning at the foundations of Christianity, but projecting his nation's origins much further back in time.

## Chronological arrangement

Marincola points out how some Greek histories followed events annalistically, usually according to the sequence of holders of major offices. "One can also use kings or magistrates (κατ' ἄρχοντας καὶ βασιλέας) to give structure, especially where these rulers themselves are the instigators or subject of historical actions . . . Another method of arrangement is to write according to area or category (κατὰ γένος), treating the events by theater of action within a multi-year time

---

[53]  The only scholar I know of who has commented on this problem is Mendels 2001:204–205. To quote Mendels: "Eusebius deduced from the fact recorded by Josephus that Herod ceased to nominate High Priests from the legitimate Zadokite line, that Jesus's eternal High Priesthood was henceforward realized (1.6.9–11). Eusebius is mistaken here since the Hasmonean rulers were not legitimate high priests." To me it hardly seems plausible that such a well-informed biblical scholar as Eusebius had simply failed to do his homework about the high-priestly succession under the Hasmoneans (not to mention Antiochus IV's previous meddling with the institution!). More likely Eusebius presumed Jesus' and the apostles' legitimacy as successors to the divine authority of the high priesthood and therefore selected facts from his sources that he could manipulate into a narrative of Christians' legitimate accession to Judean institutions. See also Beggs 1999:106–113.

[54]  A narratological term. An analepsis designates "any evocation after the fact of an event that took place earlier than the point in the story where we are at any given moment" (Genette 1972:40); an "external analepsis" denotes an "analepsis whose entire extent remains external to the extent of the first narrative" (Genette 1972:49).

period."[55] Each arrangement associated a new history with certain paradigmatic texts. And these arrangements were not mutually exclusive: even annalistic historians like Thucydides took their readers on thematic or analeptic digressions.[56]

Eusebius famously organized the *Ecclesiastical History* not by years, but by corresponding terms in office of Roman emperors on the one hand, and on the other of contemporary Christian bishops of (in order of their foundation) Jerusalem, Antioch, Rome, and Alexandria. The reigns of emperors and the episcopates of leading bishops act as milestones between which the Eusebian narrator plants narratives or profiles of certain specified kinds of content.

Marincola associates chronological arrangement with historiographical focalization (see "Focalization" above), noting that "an annalistic arrangement clearly worked well for histories with a single focalization."[57] Despite his singular focalization, Eusebius rejected such an annalistic chronology. I would suggest five possible reasons for this. First, Eusebius had a historiographical precedent for structuring a history according to the term in office of the institutional head: the books of Kings and Chronicles in the Hebrew Bible, though in many respects the *Ecclesiastical History* diverges from these texts.[58] Second, unlike (say) Athenian archons, Spartan ephors, or Roman consuls, Christian bishops did not hold their office on annual, or otherwise fixed, terms, nor did churches traditionally count the number of years that bishops held their offices. It was therefore difficult for Eusebius to recover precise dates for his bishops' years in office in the first place, let alone synchronize them with the events that he narrated. Third, as most of the scanty narratival flowers that Eusebius picked from his meadow of sources (HE 1.1.3–4) lacked precise dates, an annular dating was impossible, though the Eusebian narrator supplies annual dates repeatedly.[59] To fudge the problem of his sources' chronological imprecision, Eusebius could date events to within a single emperor's reign—and sometimes his sources made even this impossible and it is transparent that his dating of an event represents a guess.[60] Fourth, Eusebius' relatively paltry number of narratives and profiles

---

[55] Marincola 1999:305–306; "κατὰ γένος" quotes Diodorus' description of how Ephorus organized his forty-book narrative history from the return of the Heracleidae to the present day (*FrGH* 70 F 11= Diodorus 5.1.4).

[56] See Rood 1998, chapter 5, and Dewald 2005, on the intricacies of Thucydides' temporal narration.

[57] Marincola 1999:306.

[58] Cf. Morlet 2005:11, following Winckelmann 1991:65, on Eusebius' debts to biblical historiography.

[59] For example, 2.24, 3.7.4, 3.13–15, 4.2.1–2, 4.5.5, 4.6.3, 4.10, 4.11.6, 5.pref.1, 5.9, 5.22, 6.2.2, 6.21.1–2, 6.26, 7.28.3.

[60] Whether due to inadequate information or because of his own agenda, Eusebius got the dates of some events horribly wrong. One famous example is the martyrdom of Pionius, which Eusebius

may have made an annual dating system less desirable in the first place. For example, Eusebius notes just two events during Hadrian's twenty-one-year reign (the Bar-Kochba revolt at HE 4.6, and Hadrian's rescript warning against seeking Christians out at 4.9). If the Eusebian narrator had dated each event to the year, the reader might easily have seen how few events Eusebius had to report. Fifth, dating according to emperors' and bishops' time in office made it easier to insert non-narratival profiles into the text: the narrator could simply say "at this time"[61] and begin his description of a key individual from the past, without having to date events involving that figure precisely.

While Eusebius' chronology is vaguer than that of most previous narrative histories of similar, "national," focalization, the arrangement nonetheless communicated an "orthodox" Christian perspective in part by foregrounding the institutional figureheads of the nation—just as the Atthidographers had foregrounded an Athenian perspective through their archon-dates, and Roman historians a Roman perspective by consular dating.[62]

## Subject matter

As noted above, since Herodotus *historia* could include almost any aspect of the life of a person or people: "there are, of course, political and military deeds, but there are also cultural events and activities; the religious life of a state and its people, the customs of a people . . . ; and even the lives and characters of a state's leaders, particularly important when a state is ruled by a single man or woman."[63] Thematic content that we now separate into ethnography, "antiquarianism," geography, biography (despite the declaration of Plutarch, *Alexander* 1),[64] political and war narratives, and even "paradoxography" (collections of marvels) all coexisted under the banner of *historia* in the ancient Mediterranean. Historians were always free to inject content from any of these thematic fields into their *historiai*.

More than just saying that he would narrate a history of a certain people, the Eusebian narrator famously (and, within the tradition of Greek historiography,

---

dates to the reign of Lucius Verus (4.15.47), but which internal evidence shows must be dated to Decius' principate. The classic study of the *Martyrdom of Pionius* is Robert 1994.

[61]   Cf. Julius Africanus' profile above, which begins with the words ἐν τούτῳ καί, "in this time also."

[62]   Simonetti 1997:54–55, compares Eusebius' bishop-dates with consular dates in Roman historiography.

[63]   Marincola 1999:307.

[64]   See the references in note 39 above.

idiosyncratically)[65] set forth the subjects of the *Ecclesiastical History* in the first, 167-word sentence of his history. In summary form, the topics are:[66]

1. The successions (διαδοχάς) of the holy apostles to the implied author's time.

2. Events transacted throughout ecclesiastical history.

3. Leaders and officials (ἡγήσαντό τε καὶ προέστησαν) in the most important church communities (παροικίαις).

4. Ambassadors (τὸν θεῖον ἐπρέσβευσαν λόγον) of the divine Logos, orally or in writing.

5. Innovators and introducers of knowledge falsely-called.

6. The Judeans' desserts for their plot against the Savior.

7. Attacks on the divine Logos (πεπολέμηται) by the nations (τὰ ἔθνη).

8. Martyrdoms in previous times and in the implied author's own time.

9. The rescue of the church by the Savior.

The Eusebian narrator clings closely to this list of topics for the duration of the text.[67] Some of these topics seem to correspond to the subject matter of

---

[65] The most comparable "list of topics" that I have been able to find in the prefaces of surviving pre-Eusebian Greek histories is in Dionysius' *Roman Antiquities* 1.8.2, which offers a brief array of themes (foreign and internal wars, forms of government, and customs and laws). See also Appian's *Roman History* pref.14–15, which sets down the subject of each book that he is about to narrate, whereas the Eusebian narrator offers a list of topics that are interwoven throughout the ten books of the text. Cf. also e.g. Diodorus 1.4.5–7; Josephus, *AJ* 1.5, 13–14 (but note the fuller projected list of topics for the *Judean Antiquities* at *Judean War* 1.17); and, in a parahistorical text, Philostratus, *Apollonius of Tyana* 1.4.3. Unlike the list of topics for the *Ecclesiastical History*, none of these topical lists is the first sentence of the history in which it appears. Morlet 2005:5n21 offers Polybius 1.2.8 as a comparandum, but this short notice merely announces that Polybius' *Histories* will tell how Rome gained power and how a reader could learn from history. Eusebius' first sentence makes no such explicit gesture about how the text's subject would edify his readers; indeed, the *Ecclesiastical History* presumes the importance of the church without argument (cf. Verdoner 2010).

[66] There are different ways of enumerating the topics in Eusebius' present: Overbeck 1892, p. 42 lists (and Overbeck 1898, p. 8 recapitulates) four topics, yet Overbeck 1898, p. 25 lists five; Grant 1980 is structured according to five topics read in HE 1.1.1–2; while six topics are noted in Schwartz 1907:1396–1401, Barnes 1981:129, Twomey 1982:21, and Willing 2008:487. For my list, I select the accusative noun phrases that are the grammatical objects of the object infinitive παραδοῦναι (1.1.2).

[67] While some (notably Grant 1980, chapter 11 and Barnes 1981:129) have argued that the canon of Christian sacred texts is a separate theme (Grant 1980:126 cites HE 3.3.3 on this point), I prefer to see this theme as merely a special case of "ambassadors of the divine Logos." Other

genres outside of, or at least marginal to, the domain of historiography: the reference to "knowledge falsely so-called" (ψευδωνύμου γνώσεως) echoes the title of Irenaeus' *Examination and Refutation of Knowledge Falsely-Called* (ψευδωνύμου γνώσεως, itself an echo of 1 Timothy 6:20) and thereby evokes the genre of Christian heresiological refutation;[68] while the last three topics allude to summaries of persecution in Christian apologetic speeches and to Christian martyr narratives.

The preface speaks, moreover, of major events transacted, and of portraits of ecclesiastical leaders and ambassadors—all subjects that one would expect in the history of a state. Of course, Eusebius uses some specifically Christian language to introduce these leaders of the church: *proistēmi* in participial form was a common generic term for Christian clergy.[69] The reader could thus expect to find specifically Christian officials transacting specifically Christian modes of "governance" in this narrative.[70]

In addition, it cannot be coincidental that the Eusebian narrator drops the verb *polemeō* to introduce his last three, martial topics. This corresponds to the generic cue sent in what I would call the *History*'s "second preface":

> Others who composed historical narratives would simply have handed down in writing victories in wars and trophies against enemies and the prizes of generals and the bravery of hoplites stained with blood and numerous murders for the sake of children and country and other advantage. Yet the narrative account by us of the community of God's followers will record *peaceful* wars contested for peace itself in the soul, wars among them for the sake of truth rather than country and for religious devotion rather than even the most loved ones, on permanent stelae, proclaiming the resolve and sought-after prizes of athletes for religious devotion, trophies against demons, victories against

---

passing Eusebian interests that do not fit into either of these themes include miracles (see HE 3.39.9, 5.3.3, 5.5, 5.7, 5.28.8–12, 6.6.6, 6.9.1–3, 6.11.2, 6.29, 6.44, 7.17, 9.9.3–4, *Martyrs of Palestine* (Greek, part of the first edition of the HE) 4.14–15, 9.12; on miracles in the *Ecclesiastical History*, see Sirinelli 1961:375–378, Grant 1980:151–153, and Gödecke 1987:60–70; *pace* Chesnut 1986, p. 47 and Morgan 2005, pp. 199 and 201), and buildings and monuments related to the church (e.g. HE 2.12.3, 2.13.3, 2.23.18, 3.9.2, 7.18–19, 7.32.29, 10.4; cf. also 5.pref.4, 10.2.2).

68 Of course heresiology was also a Jewish genre: see e.g. Boyarin 2004, chapters 5 and 6. The extent to which Eusebius may have engaged with Jewish heresiology in the *Ecclesiastical History* must remain an open question at this point. Ulrich 1999:14–27 has conjectured that Jewish-Christian dialogue was strong in Eusebius' Caesarea on the basis of Talmudic evidence and Origen's sermons. However, it is difficult to lend much historical credibility on third-century Caesarea even to the Yerushalmi, much less to the Bavli, and Origen delivered his sermons to a broader audience than that of Eusebius' literary compositions.

69 Lampe 1968 s.v. προΐστημι no. 6.

70 Note also that Eusebius refers to the church as a *politeuma* in his "second preface," HE 5.pref.3.

unseen adversaries, and crowns in all these contests, to the perpetual remembrance.[71]

HE 5.pref.2–4, my translation

Here the narrator contrasts himself with "other historians" who busied themselves with recording wars. A rhetorical tactic drawing on a then-prevalent dichotomy between the material and psychical realms underpins the critique of Greek *Kriegsgeschichte*: the narrator does not flinch at the subject of war, but elevates his characters' struggles to a higher plane. Eusebius must have made a strategic decision (pun intended) to place this second preface immediately before his lengthy reproduction of excerpts from the *Acts of the Martyrs of Lugdunum and Vienna*.[72] In this text, martyrs resist the pains and threats leveled against them by Satan (HE 5.1.5–6, 14, 16, 25–27, 35), remaining staunchly loyal to God through tortures and public humiliation.

While the martyrs of Lugdunum exemplify this new kind of Eusebian *Kriegsgeschichte*,[73] they (as well as the lengthy quotation of the *Martyrdom of Polycarp*, which had come shortly before at 4.15) are merely the most prominent martyrs in the *Ecclesiastical History*. Every book, from Book 2 through Book 8, records multiple martyrdom narratives.[74] The martyrdom narratives are spaced fairly evenly throughout the text, so that readers encounter frequent reminders that the church was under constant attack. As in the *Martyrs of Lugdunum and Vienna*, the reader is coaxed into seeing Satan's agency behind the attacks on the church. Accordingly, the Eusebian narrator twice quotes Dionysius of Alexandria's cries against the demons behind persecutions, and supports this identification of the church's enemy by locating demons behind Christians'

---

[71] ἄλλοι μὲν οὖν ἱστορικὰς ποιούμενοι διηγήσεις, πάντως ἂν παρέδωκαν τῇ γραφῇ πολέμων νίκας καὶ τρόπαια κατ᾽ ἐχθρῶν στρατηγῶν τε ἀριστείας καὶ ὁπλιτῶν ἀνδραγαθίας αἵματι καὶ μυρίοις φόνοις παίδων καὶ πατρίδος καὶ τῆς ἄλλης ἕνεκεν περιουσίας μιανθέντων· ὁ δέ γε τοῦ κατὰ θεὸν πολιτεύματος διηγηματικὸς ἡμῖν λόγος τοὺς ὑπὲρ αὐτῆς τῆς κατὰ ψυχὴν εἰρήνης εἰρηνικωτάτους πολέμους καὶ τοὺς ἐν τούτοις ὑπὲρ ἀληθείας μᾶλλον ἢ πατρίδος καὶ μᾶλλον ὑπὲρ εὐσεβείας ἢ τῶν φιλτάτων ἀνδρισαμένους αἰωνίαις ἀναγράψεται στήλαις, τῶν εὐσεβείας ἀθλητῶν τὰς ἐντάσεις καὶ τὰς πολυτλήτους ἀνδρείας τρόπαιά τε τὰ κατὰ δαιμόνων καὶ νίκας τὰς κατὰ τῶν ἀοράτων ἀντιπάλων καὶ τοὺς ἐπὶ πᾶσι τούτοις στεφάνους εἰς αἰώνιον μνήμην ἀνακηρύττων. (The resourceful translation of εἰρηνικωτάτους πολέμους must be credited to Williamson 1965:192.) Note that Eusebius refers to the Great Persecution as "the war against us" at HE 8.13.9 (a reference that I owe to Ferguson 2005:39).

[72] As both Perrone 1996:526 and Beggs 1999:257–258 astutely note.

[73] Cf. Mühlenberg 2002:200, who perhaps goes too far in asserting that "Euseb . . . benutzt [miterzähltes Leid], um die politische Militärgeschichte als historiographische Gattung zu diskreditieren."

[74] See 2.9, 2.23, 3.32, 3.36, 4.15, 4.17, 5.1, 5.21, 6.4–5, 6.39–42, 7.11–12, 7.14, and most of 8, not to mention the Greek *Martyrs of Palestine*, included after HE 8 in the first edition; cf. 3.18–20.

trials during persecutions in his own voice.[75] Both the narrator's own voice and his evocations of other Christian voices paint a Christianity in regular combat; and both the narrator's and other voices depict a diabolical enemy frequently attacking the Christian nation, until the very end of the text.[76]

Another crucial piece of Eusebian subject matter emerges in the preface, namely the text's emphasis on the intellectual achievements and achievers in the church's past. The clause noting ambassadors of the divine Logos "orally or in writing" prefigures the *Ecclesiastical History*'s emphasis on literary history, as noted earlier in relation to Eusebius' profile of Julius Africanus: one of the most frequent kinds of content in the profiles noted above are catalogues of literary texts written by Christian (and Judean, and sometimes "heretical") authors. In the same clause, it should not be overlooked that the verb πρεσβεύω, whose participial form is usually translatable as "ambassadors," could also signify "engagement," "study," or "interpretation" of a corpus of intellectual texts.[77] The intellectual reminiscences continue in the next clause with disparagement of "innovators of knowledge falsely so-called": this mention of teachers of false doctrines (met in Eusebius' profiles of and narratives involving "heretics") promised further intellectual-historical thematization.

Eusebius' very first clause suggested an additional intellectual-historical theme. It is true that since the second century Christian heresiologists had appealed to successions of bishops, who purportedly received the teaching of their predecessors in a chain of transmission back to Christ's apostles, to confirm their claim to the correct teachings of Christ. But in previous historiographical literature, *diadochē* had signified both successions of rulers and the successions of the leaders of philosophical sects.[78] Eusebius could hardly have been unaware that he was invoking historiographical traditions that stressed

---

[75] Dionysius: 6.41.2, 7.10.4; the narrator's voice: 5.21.2, 6.39.5, 8.1.6, 9.3, 9.10.2, 10.4.13–15. But cf. the caveat on the agency behind the *persecutors* (as opposed to the agency behind the *experience of the persecuted*) at Morgan 2005:203: "It is notable that with two exceptions Eusebius does not attribute Emperors' behaviour to divine influence, and he never attributes it to the devil."

[76] On the "spiritual"-militaristic aspects of the *Ecclesiastical History*, see above all Gödecke 1987, especially pp. 109–166, and Morgan 2005; on the place of daimonology in Eusebius' thought in general, see Sirinelli 1961, chapter 8.
Note also that Eusebius' "heretics" are depicted as Satan's or daimons' puppets (e.g. 2.13.1–3, 3.27) even more constantly than persecutors, on which see Willing 2008:436–452.

[77] I owe this insight to Inowlocki 2006:94 who notes that PE 11.1.2 clearly means "interpret" by πρεσβεύω. See LSJ s.v. πρεσβεύω I.2.b, whose examples for this usage include the prefatory remarks of Diogenes Laertius' *Lives and Opinions of the Famous Philosophers* (1.18) and Philostratus in the *Lives of the Sophists* (484), both of which use πρεσβεύω to denote intellectuals' engagement with the object of their studies.

[78] See Wehrli 1978 and Giannatasio Andria 1989 for the *reliquiae* of texts that chronicle the "successions of famous philosophers."

succession when he chose as the first five words of his *Ekklēsiastikē Historia*: τὰς τῶν ἱερῶν ἀποστόλων διαδοχάς.

## The *Ecclesiastical History*: Generic Participation and Generic Innovation

The previous section has yielded the generic cues embedded in the *Ecclesiastical History*; this section will outline the Greek genres to which those cues point.

That the *Ecclesiastical History*'s subject matter incorporates numerous elements from other prominent Christian literary genres poses no problem for, and even enhances, the text's self-situation as a history.[79] The Eusebian narrator quotes regularly from apologetic texts such as Justin's and Tertullian's *Apologies*, and, as Verdoner has recently shown, employs standard apologetic techniques both to defend Christianity and to settle certain scores on internal Christian debates.[80] Heresiological cues define the borders between Christians and their enemies that lurk within the church.[81] Citations of memoirs and textual commentaries yield anecdotes about historical individuals and allow the narrator to trace the sacralization of Christian holy books. Eusebius incorporates excerpts from each of these genres, prevalent in pre-Christian literature and all having an apologetic or polemical purpose, into his text. As a consequence, some modern scholars have labeled Eusebius' *History* as "apologetic history," a label that is accurate as far as it goes.[82] Greek historiography had always evoked, absorbed, entered dialogue with, and competed with other genres and remained no less historiographical.[83] But such pronouncements that

---

[79] As noted in Part I, all complex genres can absorb other genres: as a genre concerned with representing realities, history worked best when it absorbed the genres conventionally tasked with conveying these realities.

[80] Verdoner 2007.

[81] See the comprehensive treatment of Willing 2008.

[82] As Verdoner 2007 concludes after a sophisticated argument with close readings; for similar conclusions, see also Gödecke 1987:24–26, Burgess 1997:488–495, and Ulrich 2005. Interestingly, in her article, Verdoner seems to imply that Eusebius was innovative in "crossing" the two "genres" of apologetics and historiography in the *Ecclesiastical History*. ("Genre" is in scare quotes to acknowledge the ongoing debate about whether "apologetic" can legitimately be called a textual genre: see e.g. the nuanced Petersen 2009.) In constructing her argument, Verdoner makes no attempt to associate the *Ecclesiastical History* with previous "apologetic histories": in particular, she does not cite the stimulating Sterling 1991, who argued that a tradition of "apologetic historiography" underlay national histories from the early Hellenistic period up to Luke-Acts and the *Judean Antiquities* of Josephus.

[83] This can be seen in the very first words of the first Greek historiographical text, Hecataeus' *Genealogies* (Demetrius, *On Rhetoric* 12=Jacoby 1923, fr. 1a: "Hecataeus of Miletus tells the myths in the following way. I write these things as they seem true to me, for the tales of the Greeks are, as

Eusebius created a completely new genre must not obscure his participation in Greek historiographical genres.

Marincola's criteria for assessing an ancient history's genre have revealed that many of the formal and thematic cues that structure the *Ecclesiastical History* hearken to a genre narrating the temporally progressing course of events involving a particular nation, "national historiography." This associated Eusebius' *History* with other Greek histories that told the story of a particular nation, such as Dionysius of Halicarnassus' *Roman Antiquities*, Josephus' *Judean Antiquities*, and Cassius Dio's *Roman History*.[84] Like these texts, the *Ecclesiastical History* is structured as a narrative. Like the *Judean Antiquities*, it includes some discontinuities within that narratival structure, as it must juxtapose events from the same time that involve the same nation, but that are not causally related. Its chronological boundaries match those of these histories exactly: all relate events from the founding of the social group up to either the present, or some carefully chosen point in time.[85] The Eusebian chronological arrangement mirrors those of the national histories: where Dio dated events by consular year, Dionysius by Roman kings' and then consuls' years in office together with Olympian dates, and Josephus' *Judean Antiquities*, like the histories of the Hebrew Bible, by the reign of whatever monarch was head of the state ruling the Jews,[86] Eusebius ordered his events and personalities with emperors' reigns and bishops' episcopates. As in these histories, the *Ecclesiastical History's* narration is focalized through the perspective of its subject people, the Christian church, with only rare deviations. Much of the *History's* subject matter—events, leaders, and external conflicts—also parallels that of national historiography.

Picking up on this last theme, the war monograph receives special attention and dialogue from the Eusebian narrator. To insert content from the domain of *Kriegsgeschichte* into a national history was obviously nothing new, nor is

---

they appear to me, multiple and ridiculous." ('Εκαταῖος Μιλήσιος ὧδε μυθεῖται· τάδε γράφω, ὡς μοι δοκεῖ ἀληθέα εἶναι· οἱ γὰρ Ἑλλήνων λόγοι πολλοί τε καὶ γελοῖοι, ὡς ἐμοὶ φαίνονται, εἰσίν.)

[84] Of this trio, Eusebius had read Dionysius of Halicarnassus (see Carriker 2003:147) and Josephus' *Judean Antiquities*. The evidence for Eusebius' knowledge of Dio presented by Carriker 2003, pp. 153–154 is quite weak.

[85] Cassius Dio's *Roman History* went up to the narrator's present day; Josephus' *Judean Antiquities* went up to the beginning of the Judean War in AD 66, where Josephus' already-published *Judean War* took over the narrative; Dionysius' *Roman Antiquities* went up to the beginning of the First Punic War (1.8.2), at which point Polybius' already-published history began.

[86] Dio's dating system: Millar 1964:39–40; Dionysius': Schultze 1995. I have been unable to find a study of the *Judean Antiquities'* chronology; my own, admittedly cursory, study shows that Josephus dates by Judahite judges and kings (with events told according to reigns, not according to year within reigns, since Josephus' biblical sources rarely placed events in specific regnal years) until the fall of the Judahite monarchy to Babylon, and under the Hasmoneans; whenever there were no supreme, native Judahite kings, Josephus' chronological frame relied on a combination of Greek, Judean priestly, and Roman imperial terms in office.

Eusebius' participation in this historiographical genre any new revelation: over a century ago Franz Overbeck argued that the persecutions and martyrdoms, as well as the fate of the Judeans, correspond to the martial themes of national histories.[87] Focus on the woes of the Judeans, in Eusebius' presentation of the earliest foes of the Jesus movement, would provoke no surprise in readers of a national history. However, that the Eusebian narrator lines up martyrdom narratives to compete with earlier Greek *Kriegsgeschichte* was a bold and original literary stratagem. Whereas most national histories did not narrate a single, continuous war,[88] the *Ecclesiastical History* depicts one continuous conflict, the church's struggle with Satan and his demons, which persists from HE 2.13 until the end of the first edition of the *History*.[89] So martyrdoms, rather than traditional hand-to-hand combat, would be the struggle through which Christian warriors would defeat antagonists and win everlasting glory.

Finally, perhaps Eusebius' most original generic move was to insert topoi that foreground intellectual achievement into a national history of Christianity. It is difficult to find a pre-Eusebian Greek national historian who, for example, inscribed catalogues of authors' written texts into his history, or invested rhetorical capital into praising characters' intellectual achievements.[90] There was, however, a subgenre of *historia* that communicated such subject matter, which can be called intellectual historiography.

A number of scholars have suggested intellectual (or philosophical) historiography (or biography) as a model for Eusebian historiography.[91] Just one

---

[87] Overbeck 1892, especially pp. 42–43.

[88] Appian's *Civil Wars* comes closest among surviving Hellenophone histories before Eusebius, though it depicts a series of interrelated but separate wars rather than a single, continuous war.

[89] On the dating of the various editions of the *Ecclesiastical History*, I accept the consensus now emerging around the hypothesis of Burgess 1997, that the first edition of the text, containing what are now books 1–9 with a shortened version of the *Martyrs of Palestine* comprising most of book 8, was published around AD 313.

[90] However, on Greek local historians' notices of literary figures in their texts, see Clarke 2008:68–72, 77–81, 87–88, 224–227. Unfortunately, Greek local historiography survives almost exclusively in the works of later historians, so it is difficult to judge how the local historians arranged their intellectual history. Moreover, Eusebius probably decided to use intellectual historical topoi in a national history independently of any knowledge of these local historians—Carriker 2003 shows no evidence that Eusebius read any of the local historians cited by Clarke as including literary or intellectual history in their local histories.

[91] The only study of the *History*'s intellectual biographies is Alexandre 1998. Other scholars who have emphasized the *Ecclesiastical History*'s generic cues to intellectual biography are Momigliano 1962:140–141 and 1963:90–91; Carotenuto 2001:102–106; and Markschies 2007:230–235. Briefer gestures at the connection include Barnes 1981:128 (quoted at the beginning of this chapter); Schwartz 1938:117; Grant 1980:46–47; Twomey 1982:30–32; Perrone 2005:418; Morlet 2005:8. Arguing (without adducing any concrete evidence) against Eusebius' affinities with the genre are Timpe 1989:178–179 and Beggs 1999, especially pp. 36–39. (Incidentally, I expand the scope of Momigliano's "history of the philosophical schools" [Momigliano 1962:140] into "intellectual

scholarly treatment of the question longer than five pages has yet appeared; the generic cues that point toward intellectual historiography are numerous and unmistakable. First, as was hinted above, the first five words of the *Ecclesiastical History*—τὰς τῶν ἱερῶν ἀποστόλων διαδοχάς—evoke one particular Hellenistic historical subgenre of philosophical historiography, a series of texts entitled *Successions of Philosophers*.[92] Eusebius' use of concurrent successions of bishops to structure his history mirrored the successions of philosophers used by philosophical historians to confirm the continuity of the great philosophical schools.

Second, Eusebius' profiles invite comparison with intellectual biography: "lives" of intellectuals were often quite short and succinct, offering the most crucial details about a philosopher's life. One can compare the profile of Julius Africanus above to one of the shorter biographies of Diogenes Laertius (writing middle of the third century):

> Another of his [i.e. Cleanthes' of Assos, a famous Stoic philosopher] hearers after Zeno's death was Sphaerus the Bosporean, who, after displaying sufficient progress in arguments left for Alexandria to reside at the court of Ptolemy Philopator. Once when a conversation came up about the [Stoic] sage having opinions and Sphaerus said that he would not, the king wanted to test him. So he ordered waxen pomegranates to be presented to Sphaerus, and when Sphaerus was deceived, the king shouted out that Sphaerus had conceded to having a false apprehension. Sphaerus answered him readily: he had conceded not that the objects were pomegranates, but that it was plausible that they were pomegranates. Direct apprehension, he said, was a different thing from the plausible. When Mnesistratus accused him of denying that Ptolemy was king, he said that since Ptolemy was such a man as he was, he was a king. [A catalogue of 32 titles of philosophical and polemical books ensues.]

Diogenes Laertius, *Lives and Opinions of the Famous Philosophers*, 7.177–178

Diogenes Laertius begins with the homeland and teachers of Sphaerus of Bosporus. The connection to Zeno places Sphaerus in book 7 of the *Lives and Opinions of the Famous Philosophers*, in the "Stoic succession" (cf. Diogenes

---

historiography" because the genre was not applied solely to philosophers, as Philostratus' *Lives of the Sophists* attests.)

[92] See note 79 above. The *Successions* subgenre had not simply fallen into obscurity: within the century before Eusebius, Diogenes Laertius had incorporated this genre into his *Lives and Opinions of the Famous Philosophers*. (See especially Delattre 2006; note also Eunapius, *Lives of the Philosophers and Sophists* 454.)

Laertius 7.37). The Laertian narrator stresses the biographical subject's progress (προκοπήν), a key Stoic buzzword, similarly as Eusebius' narrator had complimented Julius Africanus with the scholarly virtue of *akribeia*. Diogenes not only connects Sphaerus to his Stoic teachers (analogously to Eusebius' association of bishops and teachers in *diadochai*), but also depicts him traveling to the court of another famous contemporary, king Ptolemy IV Philopator (r. 221–205 BC). Similarly, in HE 6.31, Eusebius' profile of Julius Africanus had connected its subject with Heraclas of Alexandria by noting Julius Africanus' journey to visit Heraclas. Diogenes' anecdote about Sphaerus trying to save face and philosophical doctrine before Ptolemy, and then against Mnesistratus' accusation, mirrors Eusebius' citation of Africanus' epistolary exchange with Origen, where (so the narrator implies) Origen corrects Africanus. A catalogue of Sphaerus' writings concludes the *Life*; as HE 6.31 exemplifies, Eusebius also catalogues the writings of profiled individuals frequently.[93]

Third, I would underscore Eusebius' use of the specific theme of literary history, in particular through the formal device of catalogues of written texts. As in Diogenes' *Life of Sphaerus*, cataloguing a subject's writings was a common strategy for intellectual historiographers. Sotion, the author of the prototypical *Successions of Philosophers* (ca. 200 BC), had included catalogues of texts written by the philosophers that he mentioned (frs. 6, 19, 24 Wehrli=Diogenes Laertius 2.85, 6.80, 8.7). Multiple catalogues of texts written by their subject authors had marked the philosophical lives of both Diogenes Laertius (*passim*) and Porphyry (*Life of Plotinus* 4–6, 24–26). Likewise, Eusebius' cataloguing of literary texts fixed a Christian stake in the field of literary achievement.

Fourth, the above-noted perception that Eusebius wrote a "static history" also mirrors the structural practices of intellectual historiography. The intellectual histories that survive from near Eusebius' time—along with Diogenes Laertius' *Lives and Opinions* and Porphyry's *Life of Plotinus*, we have Philostratus' *Lives of the Sophists*, Porphyry's *Life of Pythagoras*, which probably formed part of Porphyry's *Philosophical History*, and Iamblichus' *On the Pythagorean Life*—all marginalize or neglect the transformation of human groups and institutions, though Porphyry's two *Lives* supply a meta-narratival arc in relating the lives of their respective biographical subjects. It was perfectly typical for texts focused on the deeds and character of particular individuals—especially an individual not involved with political affairs—to paint a static image of their

---

93 Both Diogenes Laertius and Eusebius draw on a subgenre of "bio-bibliography" that went back at least to the famous *Tablets* of the Hellenistic Alexandrian scholar and poet Callimachus. For a discussion and the *reliquiae* of this text, see Asper 2004:49–50 (with frs. 493–499).

subject matter.[94] Instead of narrating periods of change in a society, intellectual historiographers described the beginning and end of an intellectual's life, and in between (or sometimes before and after these events) they would note friends, relatives, teachers, and other acquaintances, narrate anecdotes, present teachings and the habits of daily life, and quote texts written by or about their biographical subjects. Eusebius' profiles, written as mini- (or in some cases not-so-mini-) "lives," present virtually the same range of thematic content, using the same range of literary forms.[95]

## Conclusion

I hope to have shown that genre studies are a useful tool for understanding and interpreting the *Ecclesiastical History* and to have suggested a useful theoretical framework for debate on the genre of this tricky text. Rather than employing static and universalistic generic categories, we should view genres as dynamic and contingent, and more specifically, as culturally specific schemata for organizing and presenting information within humans' networks of knowledge. These schemata are constituted by certain formal, thematic, and rhetorical "cues," embedded in each text or other media that point to the pathways between cognitive nodes. By deploying such cues, texts both participate in these genres, and reconfigure them for the use of future readers and writers.

Eusebius incorporated several genres, both historiographical and extra-historiographical, both pre-Christian and Christian, into his text: cues toward heresiology, apology, and martyr drama amalgamate and overlap with national,

---

[94] The classic analysis of Leo 1901:15–16 and 316–318, made this point. Note also the comment of Wehrli 1973 (emphasis mine) on Hellenistic philosophical biography: "Ein gemeinsames Merkmal beinaher aller erhaltenen Biographien besteht darin, dass ihnen eine durchgehende Erzählung des Lebensablaufes fehlt, dass *sie vielmehr ein im wesentlichen statisches Bild der Persönlichkeit und ihrer Lebensweise (bios) zu vermitteln suchen.*" Conversely, the *Lives* of Diogenes Laertius that treat intellectuals involved in politics—e.g. the *Lives* of Solon, Plato, and Demetrius of Phaleron (Diogenes Laertius 1.45–66, 3, 5.75–85)—have the most pronounced narrative arcs.

[95] This analysis has supported Momigliano's opinion as expressed in a much-read 1963 article ("Pagan and Christian Historiography in the Fourth Century A.D."): "As he was dealing with a Church that represented a school of thought, there was much he could learn in the matter of presentation from the histories of philosophic schools which he knew well. These dealt with doctrinal controversies, questions of authenticity, successions of *scholarchs* . . . At the same time, Eusebius certainly had in mind Jewish-Hellenistic historiography, as exemplified for him and for us by Flavius Josephus. In Josephus he found the emphasis on the past, the apologetic tone, the doctrinal digression, the display (though not so lavish) of documents: above all there was the idea of a nation which is different from ordinary pagan nations." While I cannot concur with all of Momigliano's assertions in this remarkable (for anyone but Momigliano) burst of insight, his wide knowledge of historiography blazed a useful path for inquiry here that has gone shockingly underexplored.

war, and intellectual historiography. The *Ecclesiastical History* thus sets previous historiographical genres into dialogue—and sometimes pits them into contests—with genres anchored in contemporary Christian discourse.[96] The innovative blend of these genres not only constructed a novel subgenre named after this seminal *Ekklēsiastikē Historia* (though Eusebius could not have expected this): since generic schemata draw associations between different realms of knowledge, Eusebius' generic cues also became the ingredients for a new model of the Christian past. The product, if the generic associations presented here prove cogent, was a vision of a religious group whose past heroes constituted an ethnic nation, an intellectual sect, and an army against supernatural enemies.

---

[96] This conclusion nuances the thesis of Perrone 2005:420 that Eusebius' work reveals "the author's intention of distancing himself from the literary genres of paganism," repeated at Perrone 1996:526–527, and joined by Verdoner 2007:88–92.

# Works Cited

Alexandre, M. 1998. "L'approche des vies d'écrivains dans l'Histoire ecclésiastique de Eusèbe de Césarée." In *Actes de la table ronde Vies anciennes d'auteurs grecs: mythe et biographie*, ed. P. Brunet and M.-P. Noël. Tours.

Asper, M. 2004. *Kallimachos. Werke*. Darmstadt.

Bakhtin, M. 1981. *The Dialogic Imagination*, trans. C. Emerson and M. Holquist, ed. M. Holquist. Austin.

———. 1986. *Speech Genres & Other Late Essays*, trans. V. McGee, ed. C. Emerson and M. Holquist. Austin.

Bal, M. 1997. *Narratology: An Introduction to the Theory of Narrative*, second ed., trans. C. van Boheemen. Toronto.

Barnes, T. 1981. *Constantine and Eusebius*. Cambridge, MA.

———. 2009. "Eusebius of Caesarea." *Expository Times* 121.1.

Beggs, M. 1999. "From Kingdom to Nation: The Transformation of a Metaphor in Eusebius' *Historia Ecclesiastica*." Unpublished dissertation. Department of Theology, University of Notre Dame.

Boyarin, D. 2004. *Border Lines: The Partition of Judeo-Christianity*. Divinations: Rereading Late Ancient Religions. Philadelphia.

Buell, D. 2005. *Why this New Race: Ethnic Reasoning in Early Christianity*. New York.

Burgess, R. 1997. "The Dates and Editions of Eusebius' *Chronici Canones* and *Historia Ecclesiastica*." *Journal of Theological Studies* 48:471–504.

Cairns, F. 1972. *Generic Composition in Greek and Roman Poetry*. Edinburgh.

Calderone, S. 1980. "Questioni Eusebiane." In *La storiografia ecclesiastica nella tarda antichità*, ed. S. Calderone. Messina.

Carotenuto, E. 2001. *Tradizione e Innovazione nella Historia Ecclesiastica di Eusebio de Cesarea*. Bologna.

Carriker, A. 2003. *The Library of Eusebius of Caesarea*. Leiden.

Chesnut, G. 1986. *The First Christian Histories: Eusebius, Socrates, Sozomen, Theodoret, and Evagrius*, 2nd ed. Macon, GA.

Clarke, K. 2008. *Making Time for the Past: Local History and the Polis*. Oxford.

Conte, G. 1992. "Empirical and Theoretical Approaches to Literary Genre," trans. G. Most. In *The Interpretation of Roman Poetry*, ed. K. Galinsky. Frankfurt.

Cooper, C. 2004. "'The Appearance of History': Making some Sense of Plutarch." In *Daimonopylai: Essays in classics and the classical tradition presented to Edmund G. Berry*, ed. R. B. Egan and M. A. Joyal. Winnipeg.

Delattre, C. 2006. "L'ordre généologique, entre mythographie et doxographie." *Kernos* 19: mis en ligne le 24 mai 2011, consulté le 11 juin 2012. URL: http://kernos.revues.org/442; DOI:10.4000/kernos.442.

Derrida, J. 1980. "The Law of Genre," trans. A. Ronell. *Critical Inquiry* 7:55–81.

Dewald, C. 2005. *Thucydides' War Narrative: A Structural Study*. Berkeley.

Dihle, A. 1986. *Die Entstehung der historischen Biographie*. Heidelberg.

———. 1997. "Zur antiken Biographie." In *La Biographie Antique*, ed. W. Ehlers. Fondation Hardt 44. Geneva.

Dillery, J. 2005. "Greek Sacred History." *American Journal of Philology* 126:505–526.

Eck, W. 2001. "Ein Spiegel der Macht. Lateinische Inschriften römischer Zeit in Iudaea/Syria Palaestina." *Zeitschrift des deutschen PalästinaVereins* 117:47–63.

Ferguson, T. 2005. *The Past is Prologue: The Revolution of Nicene Historiography*. Leiden.

Fowler, A. 1982. *Kinds of Literature: An Introduction to the Theory of Genres and Modes*. Harvard.

Frow, J. 2006. *Genre*. London.

Giannatasio Andria, R. 1989. *I frammenti delle "Successioni dei filisofi."* Naples.

Gibson, C. 2004. "Learning Greek History in the Ancient Classroom: The Evidence of the Treatises on Progymnasmata." *Classical Philology* 99:103–129.

Gödecke, M. 1987. *Geschichte als Mythos. Eusebs "Kirchengeschichte."* Frankfurt.

Grant, R. 1980. *Eusebius as Church Historian*. Oxford.

Hägg, T. 2001. "Recent Work on Ancient Biography, I: Review Article." *Symbolae Osloenses* 76:191–200.

Higbie, C. 2003. *The Lindian Chronicle and the Greek Creation of their Past*. Oxford.

Inowlocki, S. 2004. "Eusebius of Caesarea's 'Interpretatio Christiana' of Philo's De vita contemplativa." *Harvard Theological Review* 97:305–328.

———. 2006. *Eusebius and the Jewish Authors: His Citation Technique in an Apologetic Context*. Leiden.

Jacobsen, A.-C. and J. Ulrich, eds. 2007. *Greek Apologists: Origen, Eusebius, Athanasius*. Frankfurt.

Jacoby, F. 1923. *Die Fragmente der griechischen Historiker, part 1*. Berlin.

———. 1949. *Atthis*. Oxford.

Johnson, A. 2006. *Ethnicity and Argument in Eusebius' Praeparatio Evangelica*. Oxford.

Jouanna, J. 2009. "Médecine et philosophie: sur la date de Sextus Empiricus et celle de Diogène Laërce à la lumière du Corpus Galénique." *Revue des études grecque* 122:359–390.

Kintsch, W. 1998. *Comprehension: A Paradigm for Cognition*. Cambridge.

Lampe, G. 1968. *A Patristic Greek Lexicon*. Oxford.

Leo, F. 1901. *Die griechische-römische Biographie nach ihrer literarischen Form*. Leipzig.

Lieu, J. 2004. *Christian Identity in the Jewish and Greco-Roman World*. Oxford.

Luce, T.J. 1989. "Ancient Views on the Causes of Bias in Historical Writing." *Classical Philology* 84:16–31.

Markschies, C. 2007. *Origenes und sein Erbe: Gesammelten Studien*. Berlin.

Marincola, J. 1999. "Genre, Convention, and Innovation in Greco-Roman Historiography." In *The Limits of Historiography: Genre and Narrative in Ancient Historical Texts*, ed. C. Kraus. Leiden.

Mendels, D. 1999. *The Media Revolution in Early Christianity: An Essay on Eusebius' Ecclesiastical History*. Grand Rapids.

——. 2001. "The Sources of the 'Ecclesiastical History' of Eusebius: The Case of Josephus." In *L'historiographie de l'Église des premiers siècles*, ed. B. Pouderon and Y.-M. Duval. Paris.

Millar, F. 1964. *A Study of Cassius Dio*. Oxford.

Momigliano, A. 1990. *The Classical Foundations of Modern Historiography*. Berkeley.

——. 1963. "Pagan and Christian Historiography in the Fourth Century AD." In *The Conflict Between Paganism and Christianity*, ed. A. Momigliano. Oxford.

Morgan, T. 2005. "Eusebius of Caesarea and Christian Historiography." *Athenaeum* 93:193–208.

Morlet, S. 2005. "Écrire l'Histoire selon Eusèbe de Césarée." *L'Information litteraire* 57:3–15.

——. 2006. "L'introduction de l'Histoire ecclésiastique d'Eusèbe de Césarée (HE I, ii-iv): étude génétique, littéraire et rhétorique." *Revue des études augustiniennes* 52:167–198.

Mühlenberg, E. 2002. "Die Geschichte in der Kirchengeschichte. Beobachtungen zu Eusebs Kirchengeschichte und ihren Folgen." In *Subjektiver Geist. Reflexion und Erfahrung im Glauben*, ed. K.-M. Kodalle and A. Steinmeier. Würzburg.

Nicolai, R. 1992. *La storiografia nell'educazione antica*. Pisa.

Overbeck, F. 1892. *Über die Anfänge der Kirchengeschichtsschreibung*. Basel.

——. 1898. *Die Bischofslisten und die apostolische Nachfolge in der Kirchengeschichte des Eusebius*. Basel.

Perrone, L. 1996. "Eusebius of Caesarea as a Christian Writer." In *Caesarea Maritima: A Retrospective After 2000 Years*, ed. A. Raban and K. Holum. Leiden.

——. 2005. "The Greek Apologists." In *Early Christian Greek and Latin Literature. A Literary History, vol. 1*, ed. C. Moreschini and E. Norelli, trans. M. O'Connell. Peabody, MA.

Petersen, A. 2009. "The Diversity of Apologetics: From Genre to a Mode of Thinking." In *Critique and Apologetics: Jews, Christians, and Pagans in Antiquity*, ed. A.-C. Jacobsen, J. Ulrich, and D. Brakke. Frankfurt.

Robert, L. 1994. *Le martyre de Pionios, prêtre de Smyrne*, ed. G.W. Bowersock and C. Jones, with contributions by J. Robert and A. Vaillant. Washington, DC.

Rood, T. 1998. *Thucydides: Narrative and Explanation*. Oxford.

Schultze, C. 1995. "Dionysius of Halicarnassus and Roman Chronology." *Proceedings of the Cambridge Philological Society* 41:192–214.

Schwartz, E. 1907. "Eusebios von Caesarea." *Pauly-Wissowas Realencyclopädie für Altertumswissenschaft* 6:1370–1439.

———. 1938. "Über Kirchengeschichte." In *Gesammelte Schriften, vol 1*. Berlin.

Sewell, W. 2005. *Logics of History. Historical Theory and Historical Transformation.* Chicago.

Simonetti, M. 1997. "Tra tradizione e innovazione: la storiografia cristiana." *Vetera Christianorum* 34:51–65.

Sirinelli, J. 1961. *Les vues historiques d'Eusèbe de Césarée durant la période prénicéenne.* Dakar.

Sterling, G. 1991. *Historiography and Self-Definition. Josephos, Luke-Acts, and Apologetic Historiography.* Leiden.

Timpe, D. 1989. "Was ist Kirchengeschichte? Zum Gattungscharakter der Historia Ecclesiastica des Eusebius." *Festschrift R. Werner zu seinem 65 Geburtstag*, ed. D. Werner. Konstanz.

Twomey, V. 1982. *Apostolikos Thronos. The Primacy of Rome as Reflected in the Church History of Eusebius and the Historico-apologetic Writings of Athanasius the Great.* Münster.

Ulrich, J. 1999. *Euseb von Caesarea und die Juden.* Berlin.

———. 2005. "Eusebius als Kirchengeschichtsschreiber." In Becker 2005: 277–287.

———. 2007. "Wie verteidigte Euseb das Christentum: Eine Übersicht über die apologetischen Schriften und die apologetische Methode Eusebs von Caesarea." In Jacobsen and Ulrich 2007:49–74.

Verdoner, M. 2007. "Transgeneric Crosses. Apologetics in the Church History of Eusebius." In Jacobsen and Ulrich 2007:75–92.

———. 2010. "Überlegungen zum Adressaten von Eusebs Historia Ecclesiastica." *Zeitschrift für Antike Christentum* 14:362–378.

Wehrli, F. 1973. "Gnome, Anekdote und Biographie." *Museum Helveticum* 30:193–208.

———. 1978. *Sotion.* Stuttgart.

Wallace-Hadrill, D. 1960. *Eusebius of Caesarea.* Oxford.

White, H. 1988. *The Content of the Form. Narrative Discourse and Historical Representation.* Baltimore.

Williamson, G. A., trans. 1965. *Eusebius. The History of the Church from Christ to Constantine.* Harmondsworth, UK.

Willing, M. 2008. *Eusebius von Cäsarea als Häresiograph.* Berlin.

Winckelmann, F. 1991. *Euseb von Kaisareia: der Vater der Kirchengeschichte.* Berlin.

# 3

# Mothers and Martyrdom

## Familial Piety and the Model of the Maccabees in Eusebius of Caesarea's *Ecclesiastical History*[1]

### JAMES CORKE-WEBSTER

STORIES CONCERNING FAMILY relationships in life-or-death situations possess both a peculiar magnetism and a surprising longevity. This is nowhere more true than the martyrdom of the Maccabean mother and her seven sons, which became a favorite literary motif of later Christian authors. This essay will explore Eusebius of Caesarea's use of this story in his *Ecclesiastical History*, written in the first quarter of the fourth century. It will compare his use with Origen of Alexandria's strikingly different treatment in his *Exhortation to Martyrdom*, written a century before in 235–236. Where Origen asserts the importance of renunciation for aspiring martyrs, Eusebius emphasizes instead the value of family unity. It is of particular literary interest that Eusebius counters Origen's use of this motif precisely when composing his own narrative about Origen's early life. Their varying use of Maccabean imagery is linked to the different circumstances in which Eusebius and Origen wrote, and the different attitudes they wanted to encourage in their readers. This case study should not only alert us to the depth of literary sophistication in Eusebius' narrative writing, but also contribute more broadly to our appreciation of the extraordinary significance of literature and rhetoric in forging attitudes and values in the Roman Empire. The *Ecclesiastical History*, like other imperial literature, must be understood as participating in this high-stakes landscape of literature and loyalty.

[1]  Versions of this paper were given at seminars in Manchester, Oxford, Cambridge, and Berkeley, to the participants of all of which I am grateful for corrections and suggestions. I am also grateful to the editors and the anonymous reader both for the invitation to contribute and for their helpful comments. Above all thanks are due to Kate Cooper, whose support has been, as ever, immeasurable.

# The Maccabean Family and Christian Storytelling

This article will assess Eusebius' use of one literary motif, that of the Maccabean mother and her children. The Maccabean story was a much-repeated Jewish tale. It tells how nine Jews refused to eat pork when commanded to do so by the Seleucid ruler Antiochus IV Epiphanes (175–164 BC), and were consequently tortured and killed. Eleazar, an elderly man, is hauled before the ruler, resists and is killed first. He is followed by seven anonymous brothers, who are tortured and die in descending age order in front of their mother (also anonymous) who encourages them in their suffering. Finally, the mother too is killed.

These stories find their most famous form in the intertestamental texts 2 Maccabees and 4 Maccabees. The original written form of these stories is unclear. The earliest extant written form is in 2 Maccabees 6:18–31 and 7, written probably between 124 BC and the first half of the first century AD. The account claims to be condensing the history of Jason of Cyrene, but there may have been other precedents too. This section of 2 Maccabees becomes the focus of 4 Maccabees, which will concern us more here. 4 Maccabees is a later text of even more uncertain date (there is no consensus, and hypotheses span from the mid-first century BC to beyond the mid-second century AD).[2] 4 Maccabees is a more philosophical discussion of the same core story. Its central concern is the primacy of reason over passion, and the author employs the Maccabean martyrs to illustrate the point.[3] The mother takes on real prominence here, as the text concludes with a lengthy encomium in praise of her.

The original intentions of the authors of these texts are less pertinent for my purposes than their later adoption by Christian authors. Linguistic and symbolic parallels have been identified in many Christian writings.[4] Language similar to that in 4 Maccabees, in particular concerning sacrificial death, is used in New Testament writings discussing Jesus' Passion. DeSilva also tentatively suggests that 4 Maccabees may have been a significant influence on the Judaizers with whom Paul contended.[5] The parallels between this text and the

---

[2]   The bibliography on the origins, dating, and sources of both 2 and 4 Maccabees is vast and need not overly concern us here, since our interest is almost entirely in their later reception. But for introductions and/or summary on these issues see: van Henten 1997; deSilva 1998 and 2006. For a particularly detailed summary of scholarship on the dating of 4 Maccabees, see Moore and Anderson 1998:251n4.

[3]   "I could prove to you from many and various examples that reason is dominant over the emotions, but I can demonstrate it best from the noble bravery of those who died for the sake of virtue, Eleazar and the seven brothers and their mother" (4 Maccabees 1:7–8). NRSV translation used throughout.

[4]   For a useful summary of work done prior to 1998, see deSilva 1998:143–155. The most important additions are Hilhorst 2000 and deSilva 2009.

[5]   DeSilva 1998.

Pastoral Epistles have also been noted, and deSilva discusses its influence on Hebrews as well.[6] Frend, van Henten and Perler have all discussed 4 Maccabees' influence on Ignatius' conception of his own martyrdom.[7] Similar parallels have frequently been drawn with both *The Martyrdom of Polycarp* and the *Letter of the churches in Lyons and Vienna to the church in Smyrna*.[8] The recurrent appearance of Maccabean motifs in these martyrological texts has thus been well documented. The use of Maccabean motifs by subsequent Christian thinkers however remains relatively underexplored.

There have been some attempts to discern the Maccabean motif's influence in later authors. R. B. Townshend in his 1913 study of 4 Maccabees briefly mentions treatments of the Maccabean martyrs in Gregory Nazianzen, John Chrysostom, Augustine, and Leo the Great.[9] At a similarly early date, W. Metcalfe published a brief note listing parallels observed between 4 Maccabees and Origen's *Exhortation to Martyrdom*.[10] D. Winslow published a very short survey of the use of the Maccabean motif in Cyprian, Origen, Augustine, and Gregory.[11] Origen's use of it, which will concern us here, is dealt with not only in Metcalfe and Winslow, but also briefly in studies of the *Exhortation* itself,[12] and in a recent lengthy article by deSilva.[13] Amid this meager literature, very little attention has been paid to these writers' conception of the Maccabean family or mother in particular, although deSilva's article has redressed the balance somewhat.[14] This article will, I hope, make some small further contribution.

As far as I am aware, Eusebius' use of Maccabean motifs has never been addressed.[15] This is in part because there persists within late antique scholarship an unflattering assessment of Eusebius' literary sophistication.[16] Recently

---

[6] See e.g. Staples 1966; see also D'Angelo 2003.

[7] Frend 1965; van Henten 1986; see also Perler 1949.

[8] It is intriguing that both are preserved in Eusebius' *Ecclesiastical History*, the latter exclusively so.

[9] Townshend 1913, see in particular 658–660.

[10] Metcalfe 1921.

[11] Winslow 1974. See also Ziadé 2007.

[12] E.g. Hartmann 1958:776–779.

[13] DeSilva 2009.

[14] J. W. van Henten is engaged in a longstanding project on the interaction of Jewish and early Christian martyrologies, which includes a survey of quotations and allusions to the Maccabean story in early Christian literature, but his final results are as yet unpublished. See e.g. van Henten 2012:118.

[15] Hilhorst mentions Eusebius' *Martyrs of Palestine* simply as one example of post-Diocletianic Christian texts, in which he sees a particular feature of 4 Maccabees (the characterization of persecutors as tyrants) repeated. See Hilhorst 2000:112.

[16] See for example the dismissal of Eusebius' style in Andrew Louth's introduction to Geoffrey Arthur Williamson's popular translation of the *Ecclesiastical History* (trans. Williamson 1965:xiii): "Such writing is enormously valuable to have, though tedious to read." This stems from Photius' dismissal of Eusebius in the ninth century: "his style is neither agreeable nor brilliant, but he was a man of great learning" (Photius *Bibliotheca* 13, trans. from Henry 1959:11).

however Eusebius' narrative abilities have begun to be appreciated. Doron Mendels's 1999 study *The Media Revolution of Early Christianity*, though its conclusions might be questioned, did much to highlight the care Eusebius takes in constructing narratives and his remarkable awareness of audience.[17] More recently in an under-appreciated article Erica Carotenuto has clearly demonstrated how Eusebius fabricated a story in *The Martyrs of Palestine* using material and motifs taken from elsewhere (including, significantly for this paper, Origen's *On First Principles* 4.3.6–8).[18] Joseph Verheyden's survey article on *The Martyrs of Palestine* does not go quite so far, but nevertheless highlights the text's rhetorical aspects.[19] Marie Verdoner's 2011 *Narrated Reality: The Historia ecclesiastica of Eusebius of Caesarea* has applied the principles of narratology to Eusebius' writing to afford it attention as text, rather than simply as a more or less reliable historical document.[20] A recent collection of essays on Eusebius can therefore claim in its introduction that, "The influence of post-modern studies has contributed to see Eusebius as an active participant in the construction of late antique history, theology and literature."[21] There is however significant scope for more extensive studies into the sophistication of Eusebius' compositions.

One area in which Eusebius' capacity for narrative composition has been appreciated is in his biographical material, in particular the stories he tells about Origen's childhood at the start of Book 6 of the *Ecclesiastical History*, which I will address in detail below. Doubts about the accuracy of these stories were raised as early as Eduard Schwartz, who thought Eusebius' picture of Origen was warped by apologetic concerns.[22] While many subsequent scholars were more trusting,[23] fresh skepticism from scholars of the caliber of Henry Chadwick has allowed consideration of this material as more than just an authentic record of Origen's childhood.[24] Recent scholars of ancient biography in particular see in these passages a prime example of sophisticated and politically motivated writing. Patricia Cox Miller's essay on Eusebius' "Life of Origen" represents a fresh approach, noting the parallels between Eusebius' enterprise and comparable ancient biographies. She concludes: "As Eusebius himself stated, the biographer was free to use exaggeration in developing his portrait so long as he

---

[17]   Mendels 1999.
[18]   Carotenuto 2002.
[19]   Verheyden 2010.
[20]   Verdoner 2011.
[21]   Inowlocki and Zamagni 2011:ix.
[22]   Schwartz 1909.
[23]   De Faye 1923–1928; Foakes-Jackson 1933; Cadiou 1935; Daniélou 1948.
[24]   Chadwick 1966. For subsequent cautious treatments, see in particular Nautin 1977; and in English, Trigg 1983.

maintained at least the semblance of historical truth."[25] Simon Swain too, in the initial contribution to a collection of essays on ancient biography, notes that "Eusebius' portrait of Origen . . . is not *about* Origen, but uses him to present to us the history and doctrine of the Church through the times he lived in and the events he experienced (as these are seen by Eusebius in his time)."[26] A number of extremely recent publications have continued this trend, arguing that the stories about Origen tell us as much about their author as their subject.[27] Joseph Verheyden labels his contribution to the latest edition of the *Origeniana* series "a modest contribution to the somewhat hesitant revival of a more positive appreciation of Eusebius' qualities as an author."[28]

These stories also have the potential to enlighten us as to the relationship between Origen and Eusebius, a figure of such prominence in third-century Christian thought that Eusebius could not fail to engage with his ideas in the process of developing his own. Eusebius was a prominent intellectual descendent of Origen, since his mentor Pamphilus was seemingly a student of Pierius, an early Origenist, and certainly collected Origen's works together. Origen relocated from Alexandria to Caesarea, and Eusebius (who eventually inherited the Caesarean episcopal see) had access to Origen's substantial library there.[29] Together with Pamphilus he had also co-authored a *Defense of Origen* during the Diocletianic Persecution (HE 6.33.4). Most scholars assume that Eusebius celebrated Origen in an uncomplicated fashion.[30] But while he does praise his ancestor, I suggest that this praise is qualified. Scholarship has revealed that the Origenist controversy of the late fourth and fifth centuries was presaged as early as the late third century by concerns over Origen's teaching.[31] For Eusebius, writing in the early fourth century, doubts about Origen's status would have been very real concerns. Therefore in the *Ecclesiastical History* I suggest we find Eusebius celebrating his great intellectual forebear, but in measured tones. In so doing he fulfills his filial piety but nevertheless signposts his awareness of his predecessors' extremist tendencies.

Eusebius' use of Maccabean imagery is one place we can see this attitude to Origen playing out. Eusebius utilizes Maccabean imagery in precisely these narratives about Origen's early life. And it is here that Eusebius' use of the motif

[25] Cox Miller 1983:18. See though the critique of Dillon 2006.
[26] Swain 1997:18.
[27] See e.g. Markschies 2004 (and other essays in that volume), Ferguson 2005 and Penland 2010.
[28] Verheyden 2011:725n31.
[29] See e.g. Carriker 2003; Grafton and Williams 2006.
[30] See e.g. Kannengiesser 1992; Grafton and Williams 2006.
[31] See e.g. the debate between Barnes 1981 and Vivian 1988. See also Ferguson 2005:22–29 on Eusebius' inheritance of disputes concerning Origen, although he too concludes that Eusebius simply defends Origen.

is so obviously different from Origen's in his *Exhortation*. Eusebius tells stories about Origen that seem to counter Origen's own writings.[32] We must therefore begin with Origen's own use of Maccabean motifs.

## Origen, Martyrdom, and the Maccabean Family

I suggest that Eusebius' use of Maccabean motifs in the early fourth century is a response to his own intellectual predecessor Origen's comparable use of them a century before. Origen makes extensive use of the Maccabean mother and her sons in his *Exhortation to Martyrdom*. This text was written in 235–236 as an encouragement for two of his associates in Caesarea, Protoctetus, a presbyter of that city, and Origen's own patron, Ambrose. The catalyst for writing was the accession of Maximin in 235 and, according to Eusebius, the ensuing persecution (HE 6.28.1). Encouraging the two to stand firm, the *Exhortation* discusses the requirements of successful martyrdom, and uses the Maccabean martyrs as a key case study between chapters 23 and 27.

There has been some debate over which written narratives of the Maccabean story Origen used. Winslow's treatment of Origen's discussion of the Maccabees refers throughout to 2 Maccabees alone, and the accuracy of Origen's quotations demonstrates that he certainly had a copy of that text.[33] But did he have more than one version? Origen indicates that his subject matter is "described in the books of Maccabees (δὲ ἐν τοῖς Μακκαβαϊκοῖς ἀναγραφέντες)" (*Exhortation* 23).[34] In addition, numerous similarities of language, phrasing and structure indicate that the *Exhortation* is also influenced, directly or indirectly, by 4 Maccabees. DeSilva notes that when Winslow attributes Origen's athletic imagery to 2 Maccabees but identifies as original his emphasis on the martyrs' freedom, he is missing that athletic imagery and freedom were already combined in 4 Maccabees.[35] Metcalfe had listed other such parallels as early as 1921, including the phraseology τὸ μητρικὸν . . . πῦρ and τὸ πρὸς θεὸν φίλτρον, found in Origen and 4 Maccabees but not in 2 Maccabees 6–7.[36] Perhaps most importantly, the language of piety in Origen's *Exhortation*, in particular the term εὐσεβεία, is found throughout 4 Maccabees, but not at all in 2 Maccabees 6–7.[37] Townshend calls this term "the keynote of his [the author of 4 Maccabees']

---

[32] Some recent work has demonstrated Eusebius' willingness to stray from or ignore Origen's intentions when discussing similar material elsewhere. See e.g. Johnson 2006.

[33] Winslow 1974; cf. also Hartmann 1958.

[34] For discussion of this point, see deSilva 2009:342–343.

[35] DeSilva 2009:340.

[36] Metcalfe 1921:269.

[37] Noted, for example, by Ziadé 2007:96n182.

whole book;"[38] it appears more times in 4 Maccabees than the entire rest of the Septuagint. Particularly striking is the phrase "athletes of piety (τῶν τῆς εὐσεβείας ἀθλητῶν)" (e.g. *Exhortation* 23). Structurally, too, Origen's use of the Maccabean family climaxes in a lengthy discussion of the mother in chapter 27. 4 Maccabees dedicates far more time to the mother than 2 Maccabees, and it too builds to a triumphant discussion of her.[39] It therefore seems likely that Origen had both 2 Maccabees and 4 Maccabees in mind when he wrote his *Exhortation*.

Origen's use of Maccabean motifs in the *Exhortation* is determined by that text's emphasis on renunciation. One of Origen's key points is the importance for the martyr of rejecting those things that concerned him most in life. In a list of conditions for Christian martyrdom, Origen includes the renunciation of all worldly ties, including those to friends and family. He says that "we have fulfilled the measure of the confession (ἐπληρώσαμεν τὸ μέτρον τῆς ὁμολογίας)" (*Exhortation* 11)[40] only when we are "not distracted or held even by affection for our children or for their mother or for one of those whom we regard as our dearest friends in this life (ὑπὸ τῆς περὶ τὰ τέκνα ἢ τὴν τούτων μητέρα ἢ τινα τῶν νομιζομένων εἶναι ἐντῷ βίῳ φιλτάτων φιλοστοργίας), so as to value their possession and to prize our earthly life." The successful martyr must "turn away from these ties (ταῦτα ἀπὸ στραφέντες) and become wholly dedicated to God and to living in his company and presence." This point is reiterated throughout the *Exhortation*,[41] and family is repeatedly the prime example of such ties. In chapter 15, true martyrs are described as those who can set aside "their normal attachment to the material world and for this life (τῷ φιλοσωματεῖν καὶ φιλοζωεῖν)" and thus "have cut free from very strong worldly ties because of their profound love for God (τοὺς τοσούτους κοσμικοὺς δεσμοὺς διακόψαντες καὶ διαρρήξαντες)." The family unit is for Origen a hindrance to martyrdom that must be overcome.

It is to illustrate precisely this point about renunciation that Origen employs Maccabean imagery.[42] He states that he has included the Maccabees'

---

38   Townshend 1913:663.
39   Having summarized all the evidence available, deSilva concludes: "While the value of any one of these pieces of evidence could be disputed, the accumulation of data strongly suggests that Origen read both 2 and 4 Maccabees, and that he incorporated a substantial amount of vocabulary, imagery, and thought from the latter both in his retelling of the story of 2 Maccabees 6–7 in particular and in his exhortation to Ambrose and Protoctetus in general."
40   All translations of the *Exhortation* are taken from Oulton and Chadwick 1954 (suitably modified); Greek from Baehrens 1925; online at http://stephanus.tlg.uci.edu/.
41   See e.g. *Exhortation* 14–16, 50.
42   See deSilva 2009:350, where he notes that by picking up this point about the family's potential for distraction: "Origen thus uses a topic highlighted by the author of 4 Maccabees in regard to the general ethical achievement of the Torah-observant, and the Maccabean martyrs in particular, to speak of an essential obstacle to be overcome by Christian martyrs . . ."

example because: "I believe that this story which I have quoted from Scripture in abbreviated form is most valuable to our purpose (χρησιμώτατα πρὸς τὸ προκείμενον)" (*Exhortation* 27). This value is precisely that it demonstrates the principle of renunciation: "It enables us to see how piety and love for God (εὐσέβεια καὶ τὸ πρὸς θεὸν φίλτρον), in face of the most painful agonies and the severest torments, is far more powerful than any other bond of affection (παντὸς φίλτρου καθ' ὑπερβολὴν πλεῖον δυνάμενον)." Such bonds of affection, by which he means familial love, are subsequently described as "human weakness (ἀνθρωπίνη ἀσθένεια)"; a weakness which for the martyr is "exiled and altogether driven out of our soul and is rendered entirely impotent (ὑπερόριος ἀφ' ὅλης τῆς ψυχῆς ἐλαυνομένη καὶ οὐδὲ κατὰ ποσὸν ἐνεργεῖν δυναμένη)." The repeated language of renunciation here is pronounced, and Origen concludes his discussion of the Maccabees on this note.[43]

In fact, Origen makes renunciation more pronounced than it was originally in 4 Maccabees. The term φίλτρ—identified as early as Metcalfe as a parallel between 4 Maccabees and Origen's *Exhortation* (and infrequent in Origen's other works)[44]—is actually used slightly differently in both. In Origen, it is used with the clear intention to prioritize love for God over love for the family. In 4 Maccabees, though, on the three occasions it is used it refers simply to love between family members (13:19, 13:27, 15:3). Origen has therefore inherited this phrase from 4 Maccabees, but with it makes a very particular point about the priority of the martyr's relationship with God over that with his family, which was not the term's purpose in its original context. Origen molds 4 Maccabees to his own purpose, to stress the necessity of renouncing family ties.

Origen's purpose is particularly apparent in his climactic eulogy to the Maccabean mother in *Exhortation* 27, where he declares:

> At that moment one could have seen how the mother of these heroes, for her hope in God, bravely bore the torments and deaths of her sons. For the dew of piety and the cool breath of holiness did not allow to be kindled within her maternal instinct which in most mothers faced with such severe pains would have been a burning fire . . .[45]

---

[43] Winslow in his brief treatment of the *Exhortation* agrees for example that "His [Origen's] conclusions are simple: love for God and human weakness cannot dwell together, while true piety and devotion are the equal of any adversary." See Winslow 1974:78.

[44] Metcalfe 1921:269.

[45] Ἦν δὲ τότε τὴν μητέρα τῶν τοσούτων ἰδεῖν „εὐψύχως" φέρουσαν „διὰ τὰς ἐπὶ τὸν θεὸν ἐλπίδας" τοὺς πόνους καὶ τοὺς θανάτους τῶν υἱῶν· δρόσοι γὰρ εὐσεβείας καὶ πνεῦμα ὁσιότητος οὐκ εἶων ἀνάπτεσθαι ἐν τοῖς σπλάγχνοις αὐτῆς τὸ μητρικὸν καὶ ἐν πολλαῖς ἀναφλεγόμενον ὡς ἐπὶ βαρυτάτοις κακοῖς πῦρ . . .

Firstly, we must note Origen's distinctive phraseology here, which will become important when we turn to Eusebius later. The unnamed mother is the object of divine inspiration rather than an active agent. It is "the dew of piety (δρόσοι . . . εὐσεβείας)" and "the cool breath of holiness (πνεῦμα ὁσιότητος)" which "did not allow to be kindled (οὐκ εἴων ἀνάπτεσθαι)" her maternal instinct. This phrasing gives prominence to divine action. I will return to this when looking at Eusebius' similar language below. Secondly, and more immediately important, the father of the Maccabees is completely absent here. Origen ignores him. Thirdly, as noted by a number of authors, this description of the Maccabean mother is closely modeled on 4 Maccabees.[46] We read in 4 Maccabees 16:3–4 that:

> The lions surrounding Daniel were not so savage, nor was the raging fiery furnace of Mishael so intensely hot, as was her innate parental love, inflamed as she saw her seven sons tortured in such varied ways. But the mother quenched so many and such great emotions by devout reason . . .[47]

Again, Origen has foregrounded the theme of renunciation. DeSilva notes but dismisses a difference between 4 Maccabees and Origen's *Exhortation* here: "There is a significant difference in that Origen claims that piety prevented the maternal fire from being kindled in the mother, while the author of 4 Maccabees speaks of the mother feeling the pain of this fire fully, but nevertheless 'quenching it by means of pious reasoning.' This difference, however, pales before the commonalities . . ."[48] This merits more attention, however, since Origen's changes indicate his priorities in the Maccabean story. Where in 4 Maccabees reason triumphs over the fire of parental love, in Origen that same love is not even permitted to begin burning. Elsewhere in 4 Maccabees the author actually emphasizes the strength of the mother's love for her children (e.g. 4 Maccabees 15:9–10). The mother's enthusiasm for her sons' martyrdoms is not a rejection of her love for them, but a further demonstration of that love and concern for their future. Hence, in 4 Maccabees 15:3, we read: "She loved piety more, the piety that preserves them for eternal life according to God's promise (τὴν εὐσέβειαν μᾶλλον ἠγάπησεν τὴν σῴζουσαν εἰς αἰωνίαν ζωὴν κατὰ θεόν)." Her encouragement of their dying is part and parcel of her continued

---

[46] See e.g. Ziadé 2007:99; deSilva 2009:348–349.

[47] καὶ οὐχ οὕτως οἱ περὶ Δανιηλ λέοντες ἦσαν ἄγριοι οὐδὲ ἡ Μισαηλ ἐκφλεγομένη κάμινος λαβροτάτῳ πυρί ὡς ἡ τῆς φιλοτεκνίας περιέκαιεν ἐκείνην φύσις ὁρῶσαν αὐτῆς οὕτως ποικίλως βασανιζομένους τοὺς ἑπτὰ υἱούς ἀλλὰ τῷ λογισμῷ τῆς εὐσεβείας κατέσβεσεν τὰ τοσαῦτα καὶ τηλικαῦτα πάθη ἡ μήτηρ . . .

[48] DeSilva 2009:349.

affection, since eternal life will be superior to temporary deliverance.[49] For Origen, though, family affection must be completely renounced.

Origen's innovative use of 4 Maccabees is still clearer when we consider the interactions of the Maccabean brothers. 4 Maccabees repeatedly emphasizes their solidarity. The first (9:23), third (10:1–3), fourth (10:15), sixth (11:13–16), and seventh (12:16) brothers all either exhort the others to follow their lead or state that they were educated with and share the values of their siblings. The first brother's words in particular bear repeating: "'Imitate me, brothers (μιμήσασθέ με ἀδελφοί),' he said. 'Do not leave your post in my struggle or renounce our courageous family ties (τὴν τῆς εὐψυχίας ἀδελφότητα).'" The brothers are repeatedly said to be linked by shared upbringing and education, and to be dying with and for each other. This mutual encouragement has disappeared in Origen's retelling. The solidarity of the family in martyrdom was, I suggest, counterproductive for Origen's purposes. But it was not for Eusebius, as we will see below.

That Origen makes no mention of the Maccabean mother's own demise also illustrates his priorities. In his telling, the mother's role is simply to encourage her children's deaths and separation from herself. In both 2 and 4 Maccabees, though, her own death is a prominent feature. In 2 Maccabees 7:41 the mother's death is simply recorded; in the longer discussion of 4 Maccabees 17 her voluntary death upon a pyre is discussed at greater length. The subsequent discussion again emphasizes the solidarity of this family fatality (4 Maccabees 17:1–24). Origen omits this.

Similarly, the differing discussions of the martyrs' future post-mortem by the author of 4 Maccabees and Origen reveal their disparate interests. 4 Maccabees confirms the reunion of the Maccabean family, declaring: "the sons of Abraham with their victorious mother are gathered together (συναγελάζονται) into the chorus of the fathers" (4 Maccabees 18:23).[50] Origen's promise of reward on the other hand gives little regard to the specific nuclear family: "Notice at the same time the gravity of the scripture which promises multiplication, even to a hundred times, (πολυπλασιασμὸν καὶ ἑκατονταπλασιασμὸν) of brothers, children, parents, land, and homes (ἀδελφῶν καὶ τέκνων καὶ γονέων καὶ ἀγρῶν καὶ οἰκιῶν)" (*Exhortation* 16). Contrary to 4 Maccabees, Origen has no interest in the future of this devastated nuclear family.

Origen's renunciation-directed use of 4 Maccabees is evidenced at the linguistic level too. The term *eusebeia* deserves particular attention. Mary Rose D'Angelo has argued that where *eusebeia* usually has connotations of religious

---

[49] This is in fact noted in deSilva 2006:260: "The actions of the mother thus embody not the neglect of love for offspring, nor its negation, but its perfection and fullest fruition."

[50] See also 4 Maccabees 17:5. DeSilva comments on this in e.g. 2006:266.

duty and devotion to the divine, in 4 Maccabees it also indicates familial duty and affection. She suggests that, in 4 Maccabees, "it [the martyrs' piety] is expressed in their family relationship, their loyalty and love for each other and for their mother and hers for them. In choosing piety toward God over their temporary safety, both mother and sons achieve the highest level of familial piety."[51] This, she suggests, aligns *eusebeia* with the Roman value of *pietas*. Though D'Angelo does not cite him directly, Richard Saller's work on the Roman family is highly pertinent.[52] Where traditional pictures of the Roman father, for example, had focused on his disciplinary, authoritarian function, Saller argued that the ideal Roman father was better characterized by mutual affection and reciprocal regard for his family. Saller states: "*pietas* was not associated, first and foremost, with filial submission and obedience ... it was a reciprocal obligation owed by all family members, including the father, to all others."[53] In its presentation of the whole family's "love and loyalty for each other," 4 Maccabees is highly reminiscent of Saller's family ideal.

Saller argues that this familial piety was characteristic of the Roman family throughout its history, but it is also true that it takes on greater rhetorical force in the imperial period. *Pietas* was the key virtue in Augustus' public program of moral reform. It was prominent on Augustan virtue lists and became key to his own self-presentation as *pater patriae*. Beth Severy, for example, has explored how Augustus' reforms and self-stylizing encouraged a familial model of government. She suggests that there developed "a new way of conceiving of Augustus' role in the state—as the father of a Roman family."[54] These cultural and moral reforms were in fact key to the maintenance of the Empire, which was held together by a shared "familial" bond to the emperor and a shared cultural and ethical program stemming from him. This was particularly true in the provinces, and provincial literature should therefore be read with this in mind.[55] D'Angelo therefore suggests that 4 Maccabees' distinctive use of *eusebeia* is a deliberate appropriation of imperial ideology. The picture of the Maccabean family here is designed to appeal to Roman imperial conceptions of morality. I will return below to the significance of this link between familial piety and imperial ideology.

The solidarity of the Maccabean family's martyrdom is lost—deliberately, I suggest—in Origen's retelling. As a result, his use of the language of piety changes accordingly, making no reference to family values. Origen uses *eusebeia*

---

51  D'Angelo 2003:150.
52  See e.g. Saller and Shaw 1984; Saller 1984; 1986; 1988; 1999b.
53  Saller 1988:395.
54  Severy 2003:61; see also 158–186.
55  See famously Price 1983.

and its various declinable forms thirteen times in the *Exhortation*, none of which has a positive connotation of family duty. Often, in keeping with his desire that the martyr be focused entirely on the divine, it refers explicitly to love and duty towards God alone.[56] Typical, for example, is chapter 47 where we read: "But why did our Maker implant in us a longing for pious communion with him (πόθον τῆς πρὸς αὐτὸν εὐσεβείας καὶ κοινωνίας)?"[57] *Eusebeia*, in the context of martyrdom for Origen, implies none of the concern for family characteristic of 4 Maccabees. As we shall see, this is very different from Eusebius' use of the same term.

Origen's central theme in the *Exhortation* is renunciation, illustrated primarily in the insistence upon severance of family ties. He uses the story of the Maccabees to this end, against the intentions of the author of 4 Maccabees. Eusebius' use of the Maccabean motif can be read as reacting against this use of Origen's. It is precisely the theme of renunciation with which Eusebius, I suggest, is uncomfortable.

## Eusebius, Martyrdom, and the Maccabean Family

Having inherited Origen's library in Caesarea, when he wrote the *Ecclesiastical History* Eusebius had access both to Origen's own texts and many of his sources. Eusebius knew Origen's *Exhortation* (HE 6.28.1),[58] but tells us nothing of its contents, which is surprising given his interest in both Origen and martyrdom. I ascribe this neglect to Eusebius' discomfort with that text, and specifically with Origen's stress on the necessity of renouncing family. Eusebius also knew 4 Maccabees, and his mistaken attribution of it to Josephus and brief discussion of its contents indicate more than a passing familiarity.[59] Most interestingly, Eusebius uses imagery from 4 Maccabees,[60] but differently from Origen, thereby encouraging his audience to think differently too.

The first story I wish to consider in which we glimpse the literary specters of the Maccabean martyrs is in book 8 of the *Ecclesiastical History*. There Eusebius

---

[56] D'Angelo 2003:140 notes that this is the standard use of *eusebeia* in contemporary Greek texts.

[57] Origen's other uses of the term are found in chapters 5 (x3), 23 (x3), 27 (x3), 25, 29, 42, and 47. This data was based on an online search of the TLG.

[58] For Eusebius' collection of Origen's works (though without explicit discussion of the *Exhortation*), see Carriker 2003:235–243; also 308.

[59] In HE 3.10.6–7, while listing Josephus' work, he states that "he has composed another, and no unworthy, work, *On the Supremacy of Reason*, entitled by some *Maccabaicum*, because it contains the conflicts of those Hebrews who contended valiantly for piety towards the Deity, to be found in the books of the *Maccabaica*, as they are in like manner called."

[60] Carriker 2003:162 notes that in HE 6.25.2 in a list of canonical Hebrew Scriptures inherited from Origen: "The last work in the list is τὰ Μακκαβαικά, probably *1 Maccabees*, though it is evident that Eusebius also knew the other Maccabean books, 2 Maccabees, 3 Maccabees, and 4 Maccabees."

tells of a mother and two daughters arrested under Diocletian at Antioch. The mother, identified only as "A certain holy person,—in soul admirable for virtue, in body a woman (τις ἱερὰ καὶ θαυμασία τὴν τῆς ψυχῆς ἀρετήν, τὸ δὲ σῶμα γυνή),"[61] fearing "the threat of fornication (πορνείας ἀπειλήν)," "exhorted both herself and her girls that they ought not to submit to listen to even the least whisper of such a thing (μηδὲ ἄκροις ὠσὶν ὑπομεῖναι δεῖν ἀκοῦσαι ἑαυτῇ τε καὶ ταῖς κόραις παρακελευσαμένη)" (HE 8.12.3). She therefore suggests that they martyr themselves together with her. Her two daughters "agreed to her opinion (ὁμοῦ τῇ γνώμῃ συνθέμεναι)" (HE 8.12.4), and having arranged their clothing modestly, all three drown themselves. Various elements here evoke Maccabean motifs.

Firstly, a mother persuading her children to martyr themselves is clearly evocative of the Maccabean legacy. Both mother and daughters here are unnamed, as famously were the Maccabean family.[62] The mother in Eusebius' story is also described as "illustrious beyond all in Antioch for wealth and family and reputation (τὰ ἄλλα τῶν ἐπ᾽ Ἀντιοχείας πλούτῳ καὶ γένει καὶ εὐδοξίᾳ παρὰ πᾶσι βεβοημένη)" and her daughters as "in the freshness and bloom of life (τῇ τοῦ σώματος ὥρᾳ καὶ ἀκμῇ)." Even setting aside that Antioch had strong Maccabean links,[63] these descriptions are comparable with those in 4 Maccabees 8:3; here the boys are "handsome, modest, noble, and accomplished in every way (καλοί τε καὶ αἰδήμονες καὶ γενναῖοι καὶ ἐν παντὶ χαρίεντες)." Furthermore, as the mother and daughters in Eusebius' story fear bodily abuse from their guards, the Maccabean mother too "threw herself into the flames so that no one might touch her body (ἵνα μὴ ψαύσειέν τις τοῦ σώματος αὐτῆς ἑαυτὴν ἔρριψε κατὰ τῆς πυρᾶς)" (4 Maccabees 17:1). These cumulative echoes must have put Eusebius' readers in mind of the Maccabean story.

The key concern of Eusebius' anecdote is family solidarity. In stark contrast with Origen, Maccabean imagery is used to emphasize that the integrity of the family unit is preserved even in death. The girls die having listened to the advice of their mother, who dies together with them. The mother is said explicitly to

[61] All translations of the *Ecclesiastical History* taken from Lawlor and Oulton 1927 (suitably modified); Greek from Bardy 1952; 1955; 1958; online at http://stephanus.tlg.uci.edu/.

[62] Tessa Rajak attributes this anonymity to a desire in Jewish martyrology to "curb the cult of individuals," and through the example of the martyrs encourage a focus on Israel as a whole; see e.g. Rajak 1997:57–58. The mother acquired the name "Maria" or "Miriam" in some later Rabbinic literature, and "Hannah" in Spanish versions of the mediaeval writer Josippon. The sons do not acquire names until Erasmus provides them in the sixteenth century; see also Townshend 1913:660–662. I note too, though, that traditionally in Greek prose, and in the Attic Orators especially, proper Greek women were unnamed. See Schaps 1977.

[63] For a summary of scholarship on this idea, see e.g. deSilva 1998:19.

have "brought up in the principles of piety (θεσμοῖς εὐσεβείας ἀναθρεψαμένη)" (HE 8.12.3) her two daughters. *Eusebeia* here seems to refer both to divine and familial piety, conforming to that definition which D'Angelo marks as characteristic of 4 Maccabees, but which Origen had rejected. The girls are martyred on the basis of their piety, but their piety also means that the family unit is not renounced, and they all die together. Eusebius' use of Maccabean imagery thus differs from that of Origen.

Eusebius also employs Maccabean imagery in the biographical stories about Origen in book 6 of the *Ecclesiastical History*.[64] His distinctive use of this imagery here and its variance from Origen's use is striking. The childhood stories about Origen concern his relationship with his parents and a thwarted martyrdom attempt. Eusebius tells us how Origen's father Leonidas was martyred in the "persecution against the churches (διωγμὸν κατὰ τῶν ἐκκλησιῶν)" (HE 6.1.1) under Severus in 203. Origen was eager to join him, but was prevented from so doing by his mother who, having failed to persuade him, hid his clothes and thus rendered him housebound. This is followed by a wonderfully vivid picture of Origen's prior loving instruction by his father. With his father dead the story then sketches the start of Origen's ascent in pedagogical, literary, and clerical circles. Though these stories are much studied (see above), the significance of Maccabean imagery here has been missed.

As in book 8, mothers, sons, and martyrdom together would itself have been evocative of Maccabean traditions. But again, Origen's mother, in stark contrast to his father Leonidas, remains unnamed, like the Maccabean mother. Even more striking is Eusebius' passing remark that after the death of his father Origen "was left destitute with his mother and six smaller brothers (μητρὶ καὶ βραχυτέροις ἀδελφοῖς τὸν ἀριθμὸν ἕξ), when he was not quite seventeen" (HE 6.2.12). A single mother and seven sons in the context of martyrdom is a clear allusion to the Maccabean story. Moreover, it is linguistically clear that Eusebius is referring specifically to 4 Maccabees. In the very first sentence of book 6, for example, Eusebius uses the phrase "athletes of piety (τῶν ὑπὲρ εὐσεβείας ἀθλητῶν)" (HE 6.1.1), characteristic of 4 Maccabees. Structurally too Eusebius' story echoes 4 Maccabees, as I will discuss below. All this flags for the alert reader this intended inter-text.

However, Eusebius is not simply evoking 4 Maccabees. More interestingly, I suggest he calls to mind here too a second inter-text, namely Origen's own previous use of 4 Maccabees in his *Exhortation*. This is most apparent in their

---

[64] Eusebius' interest in Origen's early life is noteworthy in itself. Gregory Thaumaturgus in his comparable *Oration and Panegyric Addressed to Origen* states specifically that he will not discuss Origen's youth or education: "And it is not his birth or bodily training that I am to praise"; trans. from Coxe, Roberts, and Donaldson 1971.

treatments of the mother figures. As with Origen's discussion of the mother of the Maccabees, Eusebius paints Origen's mother as the subject of divine agency. When Origen desires martyrdom, Eusebius states that it was prevented because "the divine and heavenly Providence, acting for the general good through his mother, stood in the way of his zeal (τῆς θείας καὶ οὐρανίου προνοίας εἰς τὴν πλείστων ὠφέλειαν διὰ τῆς αὐτοῦ μητρὸς ἐμποδὼν αὐτῷ τῆς προθυμίας ἐνστάσης)" (HE 6.2.4). Eusebius' story about Origen and his mother not only appeals to Maccabean imagery, but alludes to Origen's own story about the Maccabean mother.

As in both the original Maccabean story and Origen's retelling, in Eusebius' story the mother figure remains the heroine. But now it is for acting in an exactly opposite manner to the Maccabean mother. Whereas the latter encourages her children's martyrdoms, Origen's mother prevents his death and is unambiguously praised by Eusebius for doing so. Where in Origen's *Exhortation* divine agency enabled the Maccabean mother to overcome her "maternal instinct (τὸ μητρικὸν)," here Origen's own "mother's feelings (τῆς . . . μητρικῆς διαθέσεως)" are supported by divine agency in preventing the boy's martyrdom. Eusebius in fact seems closer to the original intentions of 4 Maccabees. In 4 Maccabees 13:19, for example, we read: "You are not ignorant of the affection of family ties (τὰ τῆς ἀδελφότητος φίλτρα), which the divine and all-wise Providence (ἡ θεία καὶ πάνσοφος πρόνοια) has bequeathed through the fathers to their descendants and which was implanted in the mother's womb." In both 4 Maccabees and the *Ecclesiastical History*, divine Providence (τῆς θείας . . . προνοίας and ἡ θεία πάνσοφος πρόνοια, respectively) supports maternal affection and strengthens family ties. This is in direct contrast to Origen's insistence on the renunciation of family ties. We can clearly observe Eusebius picking up different elements of 4 Maccabees from Origen.

Indeed, while his mother's actions are providential, Origen's own desire for martyrdom is conceived by Eusebius as impetuous and even rash. In emphatic language, we are told that "Origen's soul was possessed with such a passion for martyrdom (ἔρως τοσοῦτος μαρτυρίου), while he was still quite a boy, that he was all eagerness to come to close quarters with danger (ὁμόσε τοῖς κινδύνοις χωρεῖν προπηδᾶν), and to leap forward and rush into the conflict (ὁρμᾶν ἐπὶ τὸν ἀγῶνα προθύμως ἔχειν)" (HE 6.2.3). The term *erōs* is rare in the *Ecclesiastical History*, and is not the term normally used there when Eusebius talks about the passion of martyrs.[65] In fact, Origen's enthusiasm for martyrdom is conceived

---

65  Ἔρως and its declinable forms appear only three other times in the *Ecclesiastical History*: once as a proper name (HE 4.20.1), and twice as passion for philosophy, of which one refers again to Origen and his teaching of pupils (HE 6.30.1), and one to the early disciples leading up to Clement (HE 3.37.2).

by Eusebius similarly to his ill-advised subsequent self-castration. His abortive martyrdom is "the first proof of Origen's boyish readiness of mind (τοῦτο πρῶτον τῆς Ὠριγένους παιδικῆς ἀγχινοίας . . . τεκμήριον)" (HE 6.2.6), and his castration "a thing which gave abundant proof of an immature and youthful mind (πράγμάτι . . . φρενὸς μὲν ἀτελοῦς καὶ νεανικῆς . . . μέγιστον δεῖγμα περιέχον)" (HE 6.8.1). That his mother can prevent him only with a gesture as ridiculous as hiding his clothes lends the episode an unexpected farcical element and hints that Origen's intentions are themselves faintly laughable. Eusebius therefore seems to implicitly criticize Origen's desire to renounce his family and be martyred, and praises his mother as a rational heroine when she prevents him.[66]

Eusebius' sparing use of the term *eusebeia* here also deserves comment. This language, distinctive of 4 Maccabees, is also a common Eusebian term found in its various cognate forms exactly one hundred times in the *Ecclesiastical History*. We have already encountered the phrase "athletes of piety (εὐσεβείας ἀθλητῶν)" in Eusebius' introduction to the story. Leonidas, Origen's father, is one of these athletes. But then, tellingly, Eusebius refrains from using *euseb*- language for the remainder of the story, returning to it only in a later discussion of Origen's own pupils' martyrdoms (HE 6.4.3). Eusebius seems to avoid thus describing Origen, whose desire to abandon his family does not conform to the familial loyalty that 4 Maccabees and Eusebius both understand as integral to the term. In other words, Eusebius steps back from Origen's contrary use of the term and reimbues it with the familial implications it originally had in 4 Maccabees.

In a fascinating passage, Eusebius seems to acknowledge Origen's own opinions on martyrdom and the role of the family, while distancing himself from them. Eusebius recounts that, clothes hidden and unable to venture outside, "since there was nothing else he could do (ὡς οὐδὲν ἄλλο πράττειν αὐτῷ παρῆν)" (HE 6.2.6), Origen wrote to his father "a letter on martyrdom most strongly urging him on (προτρεπτικωτάτην περὶ μαρτυρίου ἐπιστολήν)." In this he advises him "'Take care not to change your mind on our account (ἔπεχε μὴ δι' ἡμᾶς ἄλλο τι φρονήσῃς).'" This cannot fail to recall Origen's actual *Exhortation* (ΕΙΣ ΜΑΡΤΥΡΙΟΝ ΠΡΟΤΡΕΠΤΙΚΟΣ), which contains precisely this advice on family renunciation. Eusebius states: "This may be recorded as the first evidence of Origen's youthful wisdom (τῆς Ὠριγένους παιδικῆς ἀγχινοίας) and of his genuine love for piety (τὴν θεοσέβειαν γνησιωτάτης διαθέσεως)". Eusebius' construction of this passage is very interesting. Firstly, Origen's advice is born of the fact that: "his rising zeal beyond his age (τῆς προθυμίας ὑπὲρ τὴν ἡλικίαν ἐπιτεινομένης) would not suffer him to be quiet." We have already been told

---

[66] Swain 1997:10, for example, briefly mentions the entertainment value of the second sophistic novels.

that Origen's youthful zeal was somewhat intemperate. Eusebius' unambiguous support of Origen's mother in opposing her son's zeal, and his unwise castration attempt, are fresh in the reader's mind. Secondly, "piety" here is not *eusebeia* but the variant *theosebeia*, indicating a piety specifically towards God. That is characteristic, as we have seen, of Origen's attitude to martyrdom in his own writings. Eusebius here qualifies his praise of Origen by his careful use (or here avoidance) of Maccabean imagery and language.

In telling this unparalleled story, Eusebius uses Maccabean imagery in a context where neither mother nor son are martyred, and where the mother is even praised for actively preventing martyrdom. The effect, I suggest, is to question Origen's principle of renunciation. Thanks to the actions of the mother in Eusebius' story, the family unit is not broken. In smothering her impetuous son's desire to leave his family and die, Origen's mother acts exactly as Eusebius himself does symbolically here, in constructing a picture of Origen using a Maccabean motif that "smothers" how Origen himself had used it. There is no overt criticism of Origen here, nor does Eusebius inaccurately record his opinions. But the whole passage is constructed so the reader knows that Eusebius questions Origen's views on the topic, and to cause the reader to doubt them too.

Eusebius' motivations are revealed by the second part to this childhood anecdote. The real climax of the story is a surprisingly lengthy description of Origen's relationship with his father Leonidas. The first point of note is that Leonidas' relationship with his son is remarkably affectionate. In a touching tableau, Eusebius paints a portrait of a dutiful father, describing how Leonidas "would stand over the sleeping boy and uncover his breast, as if a divine spirit were enshrined therein, and kissing it with reverence (φιλῆσαί τε σεβασμίως) count himself happy in his goodly offspring (τῆς εὐτεκνίας μακάριον ἑαυτὸν ἡγήσασθαι)" (HE 6.2.11). This portrait of a loving father is reminiscent of Richard Saller's picture, described above, of the ideal relationship between Roman father and son, characterized by love and reciprocity rather than discipline. Eusebius constructs this passage carefully to deliberately create this impression.

The second point of note is that this affection is directly linked to Leonidas' education of his son. Eusebius tells us that Origen "had been trained in the divine Scriptures from the time that he was still a boy (ταῖς θείαις γραφαῖς ἐξ ἔτι παιδὸς ἐνησκημένος)" (HE 6.2.7) because "his father, in addition to the customary curriculum, took pains that these also should be for him no secondary matter (τοῦ πατρὸς αὐτῷ πρὸς τῇ τῶν ἐγκυκλίων παιδείᾳ καὶ τούτων οὐ κατὰ πάρεργον τὴν φροντίδα πεποιημένου)." Invariably, we are told, before Origen's normal lessons his father "kept urging him to train himself in the sacred studies (ἐνῆγεν τοῖς ἱεροῖς ἐν ἀσκεῖσθαι παιδεύμασιν)" (HE 6.2.8) and kept "exacting from him each day learning by heart and repetition (ἐκμαθήσεις καὶ ἀπαγγελίας ἡμέρας ἑκάστης αὐτὸν εἰσπραττόμενος)." When Origen asked questions inappropriate to his age, his father would "ostensibly rebuke him to his face (τῷ μὲν δοκεῖν εἰς πρόσωπον ἐπέπληττεν αὐτῷ)" (HE 6.2.10) but "secretly in himself he rejoiced greatly (ἰδίως δὲ παρ' ἑαυτῷ τὰ μεγάλα γεγηθώς), and gave profound thanks to God, the Author of all good things, that He had deemed him worthy to be the father of such a boy (αὐτὸν τοιοῦδε πατέρα γενέσθαι παιδὸς ἠξίωσεν)." Leonidas' parental authority and affection are tied to the successful education of his son.

Eusebius, in his emphasis on upbringing and education, is again borrowing motifs from 4 Maccabees. Leonidas combines the figures of Eleazar, the martyr who dies before the brothers, and their actual father. In 4 Maccabees 9:6, the boys refer to Eleazar, who has just been martyred, as "our aged instructor (ὁ παιδευτὴς ἡμῶν γέρων)." More tellingly, in placing this diversion on Origen's education by his father after the latter's death and the former's attempted death (i.e. out of chronological sequence), he follows the exact model of 4 Maccabees, which concludes with a speech of the mother relating her seven sons' instruction by their father.[67] She describes at length how: "While he was still with you, he taught you the law and the prophets (ἐδίδασκεν ὑμᾶς ἔτι ὢν σὺν ὑμῖν τὸν νόμον καὶ τοὺς προφήτας)" (4 Maccabees 18:10), and lists the Scriptural content of his teaching.[68] Eusebius' story echoes this education-focused conclusion from 4 Maccabees (note that Scripture was also the focus of Leonidas' teaching to Origen) but places greater emphasis upon it.

In fact, 4 Maccabees has a strong focus throughout on the impact of shared upbringing and education on the family's behavior in this crisis. We read in 4 Maccabees 13:24, for example: "Since they had been educated by the same law and trained in the same virtues (νόμῳ γὰρ τῷ αὐτῷ παιδευθέντες καὶ τὰς αὐτὰς ἐξασκήσαντες ἀρετὰς) and brought up in right living (τῷ δικαίῳ συντραφέντες βίῳ), they loved one another all the more." Family solidarity, crucial in 4 Maccabees, derives from shared education. When Origen used 4 Maccabees, he ignored the father, and the family history, both of which were for him simply hurdles to be overcome. Eusebius, however, highlights these elements of 4 Maccabees. Where Origen focuses on the renunciation of the family, Eusebius highlights its lasting value, not least as a locus for education.

---

[67] On the sudden appearance of the father and his role as educator, see in particular D'Angelo 2003:156.

[68] The authenticity of 4 Maccabees 18 has provoked debate precisely because it breaks the chronological sequence (also because of the patriarchal and moderating limits placed on the mother). For a summary of the literature surrounding this speech, see Moore and Anderson 1998:270. Current consensus supports the passage's authenticity, though this need not concern us here. As D'Angelo 2003:152n51 says, even if it is not original, "the speech deserves attention as a very important reading of the work of the whole . . ."

# Christian History, Martyrdom, and the Role of the Family

Their respective use of Maccabean imagery has indicated the different motivations of Origen and Eusebius. Origen employed it to hammer home his belief that renouncing earthly ties, including and especially those of the family, underlies the pious Christian's successful martyrdom. Eusebius reinterprets that same imagery and language to the opposite end, suggesting that the Christian martyr need not renounce family, and that family solidarity is more important than the headlong pursuit of martyrdom. Where Origen foregrounds the mother's ability to endure her sons' agony, Eusebius highlights their family education. These differing attitudes can be linked to the different contexts of writing. As Simon Swain says: "In this period the biographical focus on individuals does not aim simply to recount the facts of their lives: it is concerned with the setting of these portraits in social, political, and religious contexts."[69] Winslow too acknowledges this for the four patristic figures whose use of the Maccabean motif he surveys. He notes that while Origen and Cyprian lived in "a period of persecution" and thus "their writings will reflect the immediacy of this situation," Augustine and Gregory Nazianzen wrote after Constantine so "their writings will reflect a calmer and less occasional approach to the subject."[70] We must understand Origen and Eusebius' usage by looking again at the historical contexts of their writing.

Eusebius and Origen can both usefully be read within the literary movement sometimes commonly called the "second sophistic."[71] Much modern scholarship has encouraged a reading of literary Greek culture of the imperial period as the identity negotiations of provincial Greek elites struggling with their newfound subordination in the Roman Empire. Texts produced in this context are seen as providing identity models, values, and vocabulary with which provincial readers could explore their imperial existence. As Tim Whitmarsh summarizes: "The extant literature of the period was the fundamental vehicle of self-definition for the urban elites of the eastern Empire."[72] Many such texts, produced by local elites, co-opted cultural media to cultivate Roman values in provincial communities. Such literature was thus a means by which the Roman Empire anchored

---

[69] Swain 1997:1.

[70] Winslow 1974:79. Winslow says little though about these authors' attitudes to the family in the context of martyrdom.

[71] Whether Eusebius can be read as a sophistic author has been much debated, with the central question being his disputed authorship of the *Against Hierocles,* which if he did write it, would establish his knowledge of the second sophistic. Barnes 2001 and 2009 continue to assert that Eusebius of Caesarea was not the author, citing Hägg 1992. However, Jones 2006 and Borzi 2003 have established Eusebian authorship.

[72] Whitmarsh 2001a:273. See also Whitmarsh 2001b.

itself in the minds of its inhabitants. Origen and Eusebius were geographically and socially both members of that local Greek elite, and their writings can be productively read in this light.

Within second sophistic literature, treatments of the family are particularly important. The family was both the key unit of Roman society and a common literary metaphor representing the "state" itself. Eve Marie Lassen notes that: ". . . since the family formed an important social unit and held a prominent place in Roman tradition, metaphors of the family had the capacity to form very powerful, and to the Romans meaningful, images."[73] In the Greek second sophistic novels, for example, the eventual reunion of the protagonists with their families has been read as a symbolic affirmation of that family's worth and thus, for Greek provincial readers, of the worth of the Roman administration.[74] D'Angelo reads 4 Maccabees along these same lines. She suggests that this text, written from a provincial Jewish perspective, affirms and presents as imitable the values of the Roman hegemony. 4 Maccabees paints the nine Jewish martyrs as exemplifying a mode of piety (*eusebeia*) aligned with post-Augustan Roman imperial values. As such, the text adopts and recommends the virtue central to the Roman ideal, and so aligns itself with that Roman reality. D'Angelo states that: "The display of familial orthodoxy, particularly as incumbent on women, offers a guarantee of the moral and religious excellence of the [provincial Jewish] community, and a basis of apologetic appeal to emperors, governors and all in authority."[75] 4 Maccabees is a concrete example of the second sophistic principle in action. It both represents and constructs provincial Greek culture.

Pre-Constantinian Christian texts, particularly those concerning martyrdom, have also been read in this way, but as providing alternative, non-accommodating identity models for their readers. Martyrdom was a key symbol of resistance. In valorizing martyrs as imitable figures, these Christian texts reject the potential for happy coexistence under the Roman hegemony.[76] Here too family motifs are crucial. Family renunciation is a key feature, for example, in the early third century *Passion of Saints Perpetua and Felicitas*, where Perpetua's threefold rejection of her father and wider family is a prime focus of her diary account. Her rejection of her father has been read as a deliberate precursor to her confrontation with Hilarianus, the Roman governor in Carthage.[77] Rejections of family and of Empire are linked. Such renunciations in martyr narratives are

---

[73] Lassen 1997:110.
[74] Cooper 1996:21–44.
[75] D'Angelo 2003:141; see also 145–147.
[76] See e.g. Tilley 1991; Perkins 1995 and 2009. See also Shaw 1996; Cooper 1998.
[77] See in particular Cooper 2011a.

an identity model for other would-be martyrs to aspire to.[78] They are also a symbolic rejection of the current earthly reality and the Roman hegemony that dominates it. Family renunciation is a refusal of social reproduction, and death is presented as a preferable goal to education, marriage, and family life. Such literature was profoundly subversive. As Kate Cooper puts it: "Left unchecked, rival cognitions could destabilize a social system."[79] Christian imperial literature too then can be read within this complex sophistic culture.

Origen and Eusebius can both be understood better if we bear this in mind. Origen wrote his *Exhortation* during this period when Christian communities often conceived themselves in opposition to Roman hegemony, and valorized martyrs as symbols of their resistance.[80] The work's title indicates its design to encourage individuals in martyrdom and, like the second and third century martyr *acta* mentioned above, can be read as providing identity models of resistance.[81] The theme of renunciation so central to the *Exhortation* is part of this mentality of resistance to and separation from the current world order. In this text Origen rejects social reproduction in favor of pursuit of heavenly reward. His stress on family renunciation and his use of 4 Maccabees is partly due to the period when this text was written, when many Christian texts encouraged a resistance mentality towards Rome.

Eusebius, though, wrote in the early fourth century, when the Christian church was moving into increasing alignment with the principles and mechanisms of the imperial institution. Though the exact dates when Eusebius composed book 6 and book 8 of the *Ecclesiastical History* are uncertain, the current consensus on questions of dating places both between 311 and 315 at the end of Diocletian's "Great Persecution."[82] Furthermore, until that trouble commenced in 303, Eusebius had lived through forty years of peace. Where Origen is writing to encourage potential martyrs, Eusebius is writing to memo-

---

[78]  For a survey and discussion of anti-family sentiments in martyr narratives, see Bradley 2003; with supplements and corrections in Bremmer 2006.

[79]  Cooper 2007:8. "Rival cognitions" are defined here as "interpretations of hierarchy favoring the subject position of the subordinate."

[80]  For a selection of views on Origen's attitude to martyrdom see e.g. Trigg 1983; Crouzel 1989; Bright 1988; Heisey 2000; Weidmann 2004; Rizzi 2009. The most comprehensive linguistic assessment is Smith 2008.

[81]  One might question how great the threat to Christianity posed by Maximin actually was; see e.g. Trigg 1983:163. Regardless of the reality however, Origen writes rhetorically as if there were an immediate threat, and the tone of the work clearly envisages would-be-martyr readers. See also deSilva 2009:337–338.

[82]  For the debate over dating and editions of the *Ecclesiastical History*, see Burgess 1997, whose suggestions are currently widely accepted. The literature here is extensive; key contributions include: Lawlor and Oulton 1927:1–11; Barnes 1980; 1981:148–150, 154–158; 1984; 2009 (accepting Burgess' suggestions); Louth 1990.

rialize past martyrs, but with neither the need nor the will to encourage similar behavior in his own time since such resistance had become unnecessary. That particular valence of martyrdom was simply less applicable.[83] The "sophistic" Eusebian martyr narratives we have considered are not spaces for espousing resistance or renunciation. Instead they have become vehicles for a firm affirmation of the importance of the Christian family unit. As above however, family is symbolic of more. I suggest that Eusebius is also endeavoring to realign the loyalties of his provincial Christian readers towards the Roman administration.[84]

Eusebius is attempting to realign his readers' sympathies to match the church's new situation via literary means. It is important to appreciate the real-life importance of such rhetoric. Kate Cooper has suggested that the public/private divide imposed by modern scholars on late antiquity masks a reality where much of what we consider "public" actually came within the purview of the "sphere of private influence." This is crucial to understanding exactly how rhetoric and imagery worked in the Roman Empire. Since Fergus Millar's famous 1977 work *The Emperor in the Roman World*, scholars have largely agreed that concrete Roman administration in the provinces was thin on the ground. The Empire's continuation relied on the construction and persistence of ideologies that favored its hegemony. As a result of this, literary constructs impacted society. This is nowhere more true than with representations of the family. For example, while the ideology of the ideal Roman father that Richard Saller has traced was rooted in the household, it actually had a concrete effect on public life and the running of the Empire, since Roman men were judged worthy of public office on the basis of their perceived behavior within the household. What Cooper evocatively calls "the threatening vitality of private power" was the key means by which the Empire was governed.[85] The inherited ideal of *pietas* was the key means by which Roman families, with their "core activities of production and reproduction," were practically regulated day by day.[86] Celebration of this ideal in provincial literature had concrete effects.

Eusebius' literary "sophism" must therefore be read with an eye to the potential "real-life" effects of his writing. Eusebius was attempting to renegotiate the relationship between the church and the Roman administration, and to realign his Christian readership's attitude towards the latter. The significance of the Roman *domus* to the Empire's self-understanding and operation

---

[83] I have addressed elsewhere other ways in which Eusebius re-appropriates the martyr *topos*; see e.g. Corke-Webster 2012.

[84] Though Mendels 1999 argues that Eusebius is writing for a sympathetic pagan audience, the evidence of the *Ecclesiastical History* itself indicates clearly that Eusebius is writing for an "internal" Christian audience (e.g. HE 8.2.3; 7.18.1). See further Verdoner 2010.

[85] Cooper 2007:22–23; see also Cooper 2011.

[86] Cooper 2007:26; though Cooper notes too the legal safeguards regulating the *domus*.

means that renegotiating Christian attitudes to the family unit was central to that process. In narratives of martyrdom, Eusebius demonstrates the abiding importance of the family unit, since he asserts that family is not to be discarded even in the moment when divine loyalty is most pressing. It is no coincidence that Eusebius' picture of Leonidas (tenderly kissing his son's forehead, and gently disciplining while diligently educating his son) fits Richard Saller's ideal of the sympathetic Roman *pater*. The antagonistic Roman *pater* of texts like *The Martyrdom of Perpetua*, of whom many Christians were deeply suspicious, is replaced by a sympathetic and affectionate Christian father demonstrating those attributes that characterize the good Roman *pater*. The stress on the father's educative role only demonstrates further that Eusebius is concerned to enable the process of social reproduction.[87] In Eusebius' complex narratives, his audience encounters Christian heroes imagined in traditional Roman terms. This encourages a new sympathy with the imperial institution in whose circles the Christian church was starting to move.

In fact, Eusebius goes so far as to suggest that Christians can be the best representatives of true Roman values.[88] Elsewhere in the *Ecclesiastical History*, Eusebius portrays renunciation of one's family as a characteristically "un-Christian" action, characteristic of both Jewish and pagan behavior in times of crisis. Eusebius' quotation of Josephus' account of Jewish misfortunes during the Jewish War focuses on poor family relationships.[89] We read how in the accompanying famine "wives would snatch the food out of the very mouths of their husbands, children from their fathers, and—most lamentable of all (τὸ οἰκτρότατον)—mothers from their babes (μητέρες νηπίων)" (HE 3.6.5). More dramatically still we read that: "there was no pity for grey hairs or for babes (οὐδέ τις ἦν οἶκτος πολιᾶς ἢ νηπίων), they lifted up the little children as they clutched their scraps of food, and dashed them to the ground" (HE 3.6.7–8). Relatives were not buried, partly from physical weakness, partly from fear (HE 3.6.14). In addition, "neither weeping nor wailing accompanied these calamities; but famine stifled the affections (ὁ λιμὸς ἤλεγχε τὰ πάθη)" (HE 3.6.15). The horrific climax comes in the lengthy tale of the Jewish mother also "distinguished for birth and wealth (διὰ γένος καὶ πλοῦτον ἐπίσημος)" (HE 3.6.21) like

---

[87] Like 4 Maccabees, Eusebius does not unduly upset gender hierarchies here. There the mother's final speech submits her to her husband. Here Origen's mother fails to persuade her son by normal means; Leonidas as father and tutor remains the dominant authority figure. Origen's parents also conform to the traditional Roman family's division of labor, with mother concerned for *cura* and father for *tutela*. In book 8, the two daughters' mother's concern for sexual honor was also a key attribute of the Roman *mater familias*; see e.g. Saller 1999a:193–196.

[88] See also Corke-Webster 2012. D'Angelo 2003:157 suggests that 4 Maccabees too demonstrates "a familial piety that fulfills and surpasses Roman standards."

[89] For more on Eusebius' use of Josephus see e.g. Mendels 2001; Inowlocki 2006.

the Maccabean mother and the mother of the two daughters in book 8. But this Jewish mother does not echo their piety. Instead, she "took Wrath and Necessity as her fellow-counselors, and made an onslaught upon Nature (ἐπὶ τὴν φύσιν ἐχώρει)" (HE 3.6.23), and roasted and ate her own child. When Jewish rioters discover her, demand to share her food, and then balk when they discover its origin, she mocks them for their piety (εὐσεβεῖς) (HE 3.6.26). This sick joke rests upon the familial connotations of εὐσεβεία. This outrage to piety provides "the final piece of the disasters of the Jews (ὁ μόνος ἐλλείπων ταῖς Ἰουδαίων συμφοραῖς)" (HE 3.6.24). This criticism of Jewish behavior presents a disregard for family ties as characteristic.

Eusebius' selective quotations from a letter of Dionysius of Alexandria describing a plague in Alexandria apply the same stereotype to "pagans." Their behavior is also condemned precisely because they reject the ties of family and community that the Christians revere. Christians "in their exceeding love and affection for the brotherhood (δι' ὑπερβάλλουσαν ἀγάπην καὶ φιλαδελφίαν) were unsparing of themselves and clave to one another (ἀλλήλων ἐχόμενοι), visiting the sick without a thought as to the danger" (HE 7.22.7). Many Christian leaders died this way, a mode of death which Eusebius says came from "much piety and strong faith (διὰ πολλὴν εὐσέβειαν καὶ πίστιν ἰσχυρὰν)" (HE 7.22.8). We find εὐσέβεια here again, clearly referring to care and duty towards those around one, rather than simply towards the divine. Against this, "the conduct of the heathen was the exact opposite (τὰ δέ γε ἔθνη πᾶν τοὐναντίον)." Dionysius states how "Even those who were in the first stages of the disease they thrust away, and fled from their dearest (ἀπέφευγοντοὺς φιλτάτους)." They would even cast them in the roads half dead, and treat the unburied corpses as vile refuse (HE 7.22.10). It is precisely a concern for the ties of family and friendship that distinguishes Christian over against non-Christian behavior.

Eusebius is thus not simply seeking in his presentation of the family to align his Christian audience with the Roman administration. He is also presenting the Christians as true exemplars of classic Roman familial piety. Eusebius wrote at a transitional period in the history of both the church and the imperial institution. As these slowly came into alignment, Eusebius is visibly exploring the possibilities presented. In his narratives about martyrdom and family, as well as turning away from the ideologies of resistance and renunciation which had characterized earlier treatments, he also seems to suggest that the future of the Roman Empire is with the church, since it is in the church that classic imperial virtues are now best represented.

## Eusebius, the Family, and Christian Authority

This article has illustrated a number of points. First, in his creative use of Maccabean motifs, and in particular his use of those motifs in a manner different *from* Origen in a story *about* Origen, the subtlety of Eusebius' narrative craft should be apparent. Though this is increasingly realized, Eusebius' writings still deserve closer and more systematic readings of this kind. Second, his use of the Maccabean motif compared with Origen's indicates distinct motivations in writing about martyrdom.[90] Eusebius' attention is directed here more towards family solidarity than martyrdom. This is not simply because martyrdom and the resistance to dominant culture it had often stood for were a progressively less pressing concern as Eusebius wrote. More than that, Eusebius' embrace of the current world order and the institutions of Empire lent fresh motivation in writing about the family. His attempt to encourage his Christian audience to warm to the value system and process of social reproduction that drove the Roman Empire stands in a long tradition of literature concerned to direct and mold its readers' sympathies. It is precisely Christianity's novel position in the early fourth century that motivates Eusebius' complex writing.

We have also glimpsed here one example of Eusebius' more comprehensive realignment of Christian authority models. Eusebius' concern for the family's continuing validity is strongly tied to its educative potential. The aspect of Origen's childhood he foregrounds, and the aspect of 4 Maccabees he echoes most strongly, is the would-be martyrs' prior education by their parents. The brief anecdote from Book 8 also focuses on the daughters' education and obedience. I suggest that these examples illustrate a more general tendency in Eusebius—the value ascribed to intellectual and pastoral qualities. Consistently in the *Ecclesiastical History* and beyond, Eusebius associates legitimate Christian authority with the well-educated and in particular those who use their skills for the welfare of the Christian community, especially in their writings.[91]

---

[90] It is interesting that both Origen and Eusebius found a suitable source of imagery for very different purposes in 4 Maccabees. A comment of D'Angelo 2003:157 is evocative here: "One of the reasons that 4 Maccabees is so difficult to date is that it might equally well rally the Jews against imperial force during the crisis of 41 or 117–118, or help them appeal to a more complaisant gentile world in less turbulent periods." 4 Maccabees seems a particularly multivalent text.

[91] I note that the upshot of Origen's abortive martyrdom attempt is his first pastoral epistle, written to his father. The rest of book 6 focuses above all on Origen's intellectual, literary, epistolary, and pastoral abilities.

Origen's father Leonidas' value for Eusebius is not his martyrdom, mentioned only briefly, but his education of his son.[92] Similarly it is precisely "for the general good (εἰς τὴν πλείστων ὠφέλειαν)" that Providence and his mother prevent Origen's martyrdom. To what can this refer except the vast intellectual and pastoral contribution to the Christian community with which almost all of Eusebius' subsequent discussion of Origen is concerned? Eusebius' manipulation of Maccabean motifs contributes to the positive portrayal of the family at least in part because it was a locus of education. Eusebius' narrative complexity therefore does not simply assert the value of the Christian family. It is also part of a more far-reaching attempt to co-opt his readers' views on the very nature of Christian authority.

---

[92]  I am not suggesting that Eusebius did not ascribe any value to martyrdom; numerous examples make it clear that he did, including that of the mother and her two daughters discussed here. But it is noteworthy that the gender of those martyrs might well have diminished their intellectual and literary value to the church in Eusebius' mind. I hope to discuss this issue in more detail elsewhere.

# Works Cited

Baehrens, W. A. 1925. *Origenes Werke.* Vol. 8. Die Griechischen Christlichen Schriftsteller 33. Leipzig.

Bardy, G. 1952, 1955, 1958. *Eusèbe de Césarée. Histoire ecclésiastique.* 3 vols. *Sources chrétiennes* 31, 41, 55. Paris.

Barnes, T. D. 1980. "The Editions of Eusebius' *Ecclesiastical History.*" *Greek, Roman and Byzantine Studies* 21:191–201.

———. 1981. *Constantine and Eusebius.* Cambridge, MA/London.

———. 1984. "Some Inconsistencies in Eusebius." *Journal of Theological Studies* n.s. 35:470–475.

———. 2001. "Monotheists All?" *Phoenix* 55.1/2:142–162.

———. 2009. "Eusebius of Caesarea." *Expository Times* 121.1:1–14.

Borzì, S. 2003. "Sull' autenticità del 'Contra Hieroclem' di Eusebio di Cesarea." *Augustinianum* 43.2:397–416.

Bradley, K. 2003. "Sacrificing the Family: Christian Martyrs and their Kin." *Ancient Narrative* 3:150–181.

Bremmer, J. N. 2006. "The Social and Religious Capital of the Early Christians." *Hephaistos* 24:269–278.

Bright, P. 1988. "Origenian Understanding of Martyrdom and its Biblical Framework." In *Origen of Alexandria: His World and His Legacy*, ed. C. Kannengiesser and W. L. Petersen, 180–199. Notre Dame.

Burgess, R. 1997. "The Dates and Editions of Eusebius' *Chronici Canones* and *Historia Ecclesiastica.*" *Journal of Theological Studies* 48:471–504.

Cadiou, R. 1935. *La Jeunesse d'Origène.* Paris.

Carotenuto, E. 2002. "Five Egyptians Coming from Jerusalem: Some Remarks on Eusebius, "De martyribus palestinae" 11.6-13." *Classical Quarterly* 52:500–506.

Carriker, A. J. 2003. *The Library of Eusebius of Caesarea.* Leiden.

Chadwick, H. 1966. *Early Christian Thought and the Classical Tradition.* Oxford.

Cooper, K. 1996. *The Virgin and the Bride: Idealized Womanhood in Late Antiquity.* Cambridge, MA.

———. 1998. "The Voice of the Victim: Gender, Representation and Early Christian Martyrdom." *The Bulletin of the John Rylands Library of Manchester*, 80:147–157.

———. 2007. "Closely Watched Households: Visibility, Exposure and Private Power in the Roman *Domus.*" *Past & Present* 197:3–33.

———. 2011a. "A Father, a Daughter, and a Procurator: Authority and Resistance in the Prison Memoir of Perpetua of Carthage." *Gender and History* 23:685–702.

————. 2011b. "Christianity, Private Power and the Law from Decius to Constantine: The Minimalist View." *Journal of Early Christian Studies* 19:327–343.

Corke-Webster, J. 2012. "Author and Authority: Literary Representations of Moral Authority in Eusebius of Caesarea's *The Martyrs of Palestine*." In *Martyrdom in Late Antiquity (300-400 AD): History and Discourse, Tradition and Religious Identity*, ed. P. Gemeinhardt and J. Leemans. Arbeiten zur Kirchengeschichte 116. Berlin/New York.

Cox Miller, P. 1983. *Biography in Late Antiquity: A Quest for the Holy Man*. Berkeley.

Coxe, A. C., A. Roberts, J. Donaldson, eds. 1971. *The Ante-Nicene Fathers: Translations of the Writings of the Fathers Down to A.D.325. Vol.6, Gregory Thaumaturgus, Dionysius the Great, Julius Africanus, Anatolius and Minor Writers, Methodius, Arnobius*. Grand Rapids, MI.

Crouzel, H. 1989. *Origen*. Edinburgh.

D'Angelo, M. R. 2003. "Εὐσέβεια: Roman Imperial Family Values and the Sexual Politics of 4 Maccabees and the Pastorals." *Biblical Interpretation* 11:139–165.

Daniélou, J. 1948. *Origène*. Paris.

De Faye, E. 1923–1928. *Origène, sa vie, son oeuvre, sa pensee*. 3 vols. Paris.

DeSilva, D. A. 1998. *4 Maccabees*. Guides to Apocrypha and Pseudepigrapha. Sheffield.

————. 2006a. *4 Maccabees: Introduction and Commentary*. Septuagint Commentary Series. Leiden.

————. 2006b. "The Perfection of 'Love for Offspring': Greek Representations of Maternal Affection and the Achievement of the Heroine of 4 Maccabees." *New Testament Studies* 52:251–268.

————. 2009. "An Example of How to Die Nobly For Religion: The Influence of 4 Maccabees on Origen's *Exhortation ad Martyrium*." *Journal of Early Christian Studies* 17:337–356.

Dillon, J. 2006. "Holy and Not So Holy: On the Interpretation of Late Antique Biography." In *The Limits of Ancient Biography*, ed. B. McGinn and J. Mossmann, 155–167. Swansea.

Ferguson, T. C. 2005. *The Past is Prologue: The Revolution of Nicene Historiography*. Vigiliae Christianae Supplements 75. Leiden.

Foakes-Jackson, F. J. 1933. *Eusebius Pamphili, A Study of the Man and his Writings*. Cambridge.

Frend, W. 1965. *Martyrdom and Persecution in the Early Church. A Study of Conflict from the Maccabees to Donatus*. Oxford.

Grafton A., and M. Williams. 2006. *Christianity and the Transformation of the Book: Origen, Eusebius and the Library of Caesarea*. Cambridge, MA/London.

Hägg, T. 2002. "Hierocles the Lover of Truth and Eusebius the Sophist." *Symbolae Osloenses* 67: 138–150.

Hartmann, P. 1958. "Origène et la théologie du martyre d'après le Protreptikos de 235." *Ephemeridae Theologicae Lovanienses* 34:776–779.

Heisey, N. R. 2000.*Origen the Egyptian: A Literary and Historical Consideration of the Egyptian Background in Origen's Writings on Martyrdom*. PhD diss., Temple University.

Henry, R. 1959. *Photius. Bibliothèque*. Paris.

Hilhorst, T. 2000. "Fourth Maccabees in Christian Martyr Texts." In *Ultima Aetas: Time, Tense and Transience in the Ancient World*, ed. C. Kroon and D. den Hengst, 107–121. Amsterdam.

Inowlocki, S. 2006. *Eusebius and the Jewish Authors: His Citation Technique in an Apologetic Context*. Leiden.

Inowlocki, S. and Claudio Zamagni, eds. 2011. *Reconsidering Eusebius: Collected Papers on Literary, Historical and Theological Issues*. Vigiliae Christianae Supplements 107. Leiden.

Johnson, A. P. 2006. "The Blackness of Ethiopians: Classical Ethnography and Eusebius's *Commentary on the Psalms*." *Harvard Theological Review* 99:165–186.

Jones, C.P. 2006. *The Life of Apollonius of Tyana*, Vol. 3. Cambridge.

Kannengiesser, C. 1992. "Eusebius of Caesarea, Origenist." In *Eusebius, Christianity and Judaism*, ed. Harold Attridge and Gohei Hata, 435–466. Leiden.

Lassen, E. M. 1997. "The Roman Family: Ideal and Metaphor." In *Constructing Early Christian Families: Family as Social Reality and Metaphor*, ed. H. Moxnes, 103–120. London/New York.

Lawlor, H. and J. Oulton, trans. 1927. *Eusebius: The Ecclesiastical History and the Martyrs of Palestine*, Vol. 2. New York/Toronto.

Louth, A. 1990. "The Date of Eusebius' *Historia Ecclesiastica*." *Journal of Theological Studies* n.s. 41:111–123.

Markschies, C. 2004. "Eusebius als Schriftsteller: Beobachtungen zum sechsten Buch der Kirchengeschichte." In *La biografia di origene fra storia e agiografia. Atti del VI Convegno di Studi del Gruppo Italiano di Ricerca su Origene e la Tradizione Alessandrina*. Biblioteca di Adamantius, 1, ed. A. Monaci Castagno, 33–50. Villa Verucchio.

Mendels, D. 1999. *The Media Revolution of Early Christianity: An Essay on Eusebius's Ecclesiastical History*. Grand Rapids, MI.

———. 2001. "The Sources of the 'Ecclesiastical History' of Eusebius: The Case of Josephus." In *L'historiographie de l'Église des premiers siècles*, ed. B. Pouderon and Y.-M. Duval, 195–205. Paris.

Metcalfe, W. 1921. "Origen's Exhortation to Martyrdom and 4 Maccabees." *Journal of Theological Studies* 22:268–269.

Moore, S. D., and J. C. Anderson. 1998. "Taking it Like a Man: Masculinity in 4 Maccabees." *Journal of Biblical Literature* 117:249–273.

Oulton, J., and H. Chadwick, eds. 1954. *Alexandrian Christianity.* Vol. 2. London.

Penland, E. C. 2010. *Martyrs as philosophers: The school of Pamphilus and ascetic tradition in Eusebius's "Martyrs of Palestine."* PhD diss. Yale University.

Perkins, J. 1995. *The Suffering Self: Pain and Narrative Representation in the Early Christian Era.* London/New York.

———. 2009. *Roman Imperial Identities in the Early Christian Era.* London/New York.

Perler, O. 1949. "Das vierte Makkabäerbuch, Ignatius von Antiochien und die ältesten Martyrerberichte." *Real lexicon für Antike und Christentum* 35:47–72.

Price, S. 1983. *Rituals and Power: The Roman Imperial Cult in Asia Minor.* Cambridge.

Rajak, T. 1997. "Dying for the Law: The Martyr's Portrait in Jewish-Greek Literature." In *Portraits: Biographical Representation in the Greek and Latin Literature of the Roman Empire,* ed. M. Edwards and S. Swain, 39–67. Oxford.

Rizzi, M. 2009. "Origen's Conceptions on Martyrdom: Theology and Social Practices." In *Origeniana Nona. Origen and the Religious Practice of His Time,* ed. G. Heidl and R. Somos, 469–476. Leuven.

Saller, R. 1984. "*Familia, Domus,* and the Roman Conception of the Family." *Phoenix* 38:336–355.

———. 1986. "*Patria potestas* and the Stereotype of the Roman Family." *Continuity and Change* 1:7–22.

———. 1988. "*Pietas,* Obligation, and Authority in the Roman Family." In *Alte Geschichte und Wissenschaftsgeschichte: Festschrift für Karl Christ zum 65. Geburstag,* ed. P. Kneissl and V. Losemann, 392–410. Darmstadt.

———. 1999a. "Pater Familias, Mater Familias, and the Gendered Semantics of the Roman Household." *Classical Philology* 94:182–197.

———. 1999b. "Roman Kinship: Structure and Sentiment." In *The Roman Family in Italy: Status, Sentiment, Space,* ed. B. Rawson and P. Weaver, 7–34. Oxford.

Saller, R. and B. Shaw. 1984. "Tombstones and Roman Family Relations in the Principate: Civilians, Soldiers and Slaves." *Journal of Roman Studies* 74:124–156.

Schaps, D. 1977. "The Woman Least Mentioned: Etiquette and Women's Names," *Classical Quarterly* 27:323–330.

Schwartz, E. 1909. *Eusebius: Die Kirchengeschichte.* GCS 9. 3 vols. Berlin.

Severy, B. 2003. *Augustus and the Family at the Birth of the Roman Empire.* London/ New York.

Shaw, B. 1996. "Body/Power/Identity: Passions of the Martyrs." *Journal of Early Christian Studies* 4:269–312.

Smith, J. 2008. *Testify: Origen, Martyria, and the Christian Life.* PhD diss. Florida State University.

Staples, P. 1966. "The Unused Lever? A Study of the Possible Literary Influence of the Greek Maccabean Literature in the New Testament." *Modern Churchman* 9:218–224.

Swain, S. 1997. "Biography and Biographic in the Literature of the Roman Empire." In *Portraits: Biographical Representation in the Greek and Latin Literature of the Roman Empire*, ed. M. Edwards and S. Swain, 1–17. Oxford.

Tilley, M. 1991. "The Ascetic Body and the (Un)making of the World of the Martyr." *Journal of the American Academy of Religion* 59:467–479.

Townshend, R. B. 1913. "The Fourth Book of Maccabees." In *The Apocrypha and Pseudepigrapha of the Old Testament*, ed. R. H. Charles, 2.653–685. Oxford.

Trigg, J. W. 1983. *Origen: The Bible and Philosophy in the Third-century Church.* Atlanta.

Van Henten, J. W. 1986. "Datierung und Herkunft des Vierten Makkabäerbuches." In *Tradition and Re-interpretation in Jewish and Early Christian Literature*, ed. J. W. van Henten and H. J. de Jonge, et al., 136–149. Leiden.

———. 1997. *The Maccabean Martyrs as Saviours of the Jewish People: A Study of 2 and 4 Maccabees.* Leiden.

———. 2012. "The *Passio Perpetua* and Jewish Martyrdom: The Motif of Motherly Love." In *Perpetua's Passions: Multidisciplinary Approaches to the Passio Perpetua et Felicitas*, ed. J. N. Bremmer and M. Formisano, 118–133. Oxford.

Verdoner, M. 2010. "Überlegungen zum Adressaten von Eusebs *Historia ecclesiastica.*" *Zeitschrift für antikes Christentum* 14:62–78.

———. 2011. *Narrated Reality: The Historia ecclesiastica of Eusebius of Caesarea.* Early Christianity in the Context of Antiquity 9. Frankfurt am Main.

Verheyden, J. 2010. "Pain and Glory: Some Introductory Comments on the Rhetorical Qualities and Potential of the Martyrs of Palestine by Eusebius of Caesarea." In *Martyrdom and Persecution in Late Ancient Christianity: Festschrift Boudewijn Dehandschutter*, ed. Johan Leemans. Bibliotheca Ephemeridum Theologicarum Lovaniensium, 241. 353–391. Leuven.

———. 2011. "Origen in the Making: Reading Between (and Behind) the Lines of Eusebius' Life of Origen" (HE 6)." In *Origeniana Decima: Origen as Writer*, ed. S. Kaczmarek and H. Pietras, 713–725. Leuven.

Vivian, T. 1988. *St. Peter of Alexandria: Bishop and Martyr.* Studies in Antiquity and Christianity. Philadelphia.

Weidmann, F. 2004. "Martyrdom." In *The Westminster Handbook to Origen*, ed. J. A. McGuckin, 147–149. Louisville.

Whitmarsh, T. 2001a. "'Greece is the World': Exile and Identity in the Second Sophistic." In *Being Greek Under Rome: Cultural Identity, the Second Sophistic and the Development of Empire*, ed. S. Goldhill, 269–305. Cambridge.

———. 2001b. *Greek Literature and the Roman Empire: The Politics of Imitation.* Oxford.

Williamson, G. A., trans. 1965. *The History of the Church: From Christ to Constantine.* London.

Winslow, D. 1974. "The Maccabean Martyrs: Early Christian Attitudes." *Judaism* 23:78–86.

Ziadé, R. 2007. *Les martyrs Maccabées: De l'histoire juive au culte chrétien.* Leiden.

# 4

# The History of the Caesarean Present:
# Eusebius and Narratives of Origen

ELIZABETH C. PENLAND

WHEN EUSEBIUS PRESENTS the life of Origen in Book 6 of the *Ecclesiastical History*, he interrupts the narrative framework to present an extended biographical sub-narrative focused on Origen with interspersed details from other sources and from Origen's writings.[1] Unlike the other books, where biographical details are subjugated to chronology, Book 6 is framed by the biographical events of the life of Origen: his early life, his teaching activity, his move to Caesarea, his death. Although the biographical framing of the book fits into the chronographical structure of the *Ecclesiastical History*, it is stylistically a singular appearance in the work. No other life of a figure changes the formulaic presentation of Eusebius' *History*. The life of Origen seems to be part of a biographical tendency that Eusebius' writings evince when touching upon figures with some meaning to his own teaching circle, and Origen did have direct meaning for Eusebius' own context and day.

Eusebius of Caesarea's closely related historical works, the *Ecclesiastical History* and the *Martyrs of Palestine*, were both composed in the early fourth century and show interdependent composition—the chronicle format of the *Martyrs* in years of persecution, for example, has been shown to have strongly influenced the eventual form of the *History*—and they were frequently

---

[1] Although assessments of Eusebius's merits as a historian vary, the importance of the *Ecclesiastical History* to scholarship on the life of Origen—and indeed Christianity at Alexandria—remains constant. For the biographical material on Origen in the context of the *History*, see Grant 1971; Nautin 1977: Chapters 1 and 2; Barnes 1981: Section Two, "Eusebius"; the papers collected in *La biografia di Origene fra storia e agiografia*, 2004, especially Junod, *"L'apologie pour Origène* de Pamphile et Eusèbe et les développments sur Origène dans le livre VI de l'*Histoire écclesiastique"* and Mazzucco, "Il modello martirial nella 'Vita di Origene' di Eusebio." Discussions of the material on Origen in Book 6 appear also in modern surveys of Origen's life and works, e.g. Daniélou 1948; Greer 1979; Crouzel 1989; Trigg 1998; and Heine 2010.

transmitted together in Greek.[2] There is also material overlap between the *Martyrs of Palestine* and the *Ecclesiastical History*, specifically, in the later books, on the persecution and the material on the martyred church officials. When read together, the works provide valuable insight into the circle around Eusebius and his master, Pamphilus, and their Christian philosophical school at Caesarea.

The search for Origen defines the character and practices of the late-third- and early-fourth-century school at Caesarea. According to the *Ecclesiastical History*, Eusebius' master Pamphilus comes to Caesarea from Berytus to collect the works of Origen, which become the foundation of his own library and biblical copying efforts. There had been a disruption of Origen's teaching activity, such that it was necessary for Pamphilus to recollect the texts and also to search for texts written in Origen's own hand. As witnessed in the *Ecclesiastical History*, Pamphilus—and by extension, his student and biographer, Eusebius—is a restorer of the tradition of Origen at Caesarea, even though the closest physical teaching connection is through Pierius, the "younger Origen," at Alexandria, according to Photius *Library* 117. In collecting texts and writing both a biography and an *Apology for Origen*, Pamphilus and Eusebius participate actively in the definition and preservation of Origen's tradition of scholarship and teaching at Caesarea. The scholastic connection between Origen's theological work and the later circle around Pamphilus at Caesarea is frequently overlooked, although the continuity of biblical editions and textual scholarship is well known.[3] Textual preservation, annotation, and criticism of the sort pursued by the circle around Pamphilus at Caesarea are highly literate school activities which were also accompanied by theological training in the tradition of Origen, if not in direct succession from him.

In the *Ecclesiastical History*, Eusebius devotes Book 6 to a discussion of historical events framed by the life of Origen. This is a radical and significant departure from the structure of the other books. As Helene Hohmeyer has pointed out, extended biographical asides could form sections of earlier histories, a technique notable in Herodotus.[4] The biography of Origen and its emergence from the general historical overview underlines the importance of Origen as a figure to Eusebius' examination of general history and also to the history of

---

[2] On the *Chronographical Tables* and their relationship to the structure of the *Martyrs* and the *Ecclesiastical History*, see Burgess 1997 and Burgess with Witakowski 1999, as well as Louth 1990. For the contextualization of the *Chronographical Tables* within the history of the genre, see Mosshammer 1979; Adler 1992.

[3] For recent discussions, see Grafton and Williams 2006; Heine 2010.

[4] Hohmeyer 1962. [Editors' note: See DeVore's contribution on pp. 41–44 of this volume, "Genre and Eusebius' Ecclesiastical History: Toward a Focused Debate."]

Eusebius' interpretative projects. His role as biographer is inseparable from his role as reader, interpreter, and preserver of the works of Origen.[5]

In Eusebius' depictions, there are numerous parallels between the representation of Origen's teaching work at Alexandria and Caesarea and the teaching work of Pamphilus. Both teachers are learned in secular and sacred texts, enough to win converts from philosophical schools. They are both integrated into a church hierarchy and both are presbyters at Caesarea. They also both come to Caesarea from famous cities of learning: Origen is a native of Alexandria and Pamphilus of Berytus, which was famous for its legal academies. Both teachers have dedicated their lives to study, and both seem to use the house as a place of instruction. In Origen's case, the status of his experienced pupils as living in the same house with him is not clear. In Pamphilus' case, his pupils live with him, and even the slaves of his house are his pupils. In contrast to Origen, Pamphilus has no female students listed in the surviving material from Eusebius, although Jerome tells us in *On Illustrious Men* 75 that Pamphilus instructed women and in *Against Rufinus* 1.9 that he gave bibles to women. Both teachers are active during major persecutions. They both have students who are martyred and, as Eusebius tells it, they both eventually become martyrs themselves.[6] Both practice divinely inspired philosophical asceticism, and both are learned in pagan Greek and Christian sources.

This likeness of the activities of the two teachers combined with the physical transmission of Origen's teaching to Caesarea and the subtext of Pamphilus' training at the Alexandrian school suggests a mimetic relationship between the two figures in Eusebius. As exemplary lives transmit the values of the material taught, Pamphilus' life and teaching activity is shown in consonance with both the teachings and the lived practice of Origen. Although he had not been a direct student of Origen, he is made an "as-if" student, in every way, for the sake of the narrative of the *Ecclesiastical History* and the coherence of teaching between Alexandria and Caesarea. In turn, the example of Pamphilus is transmitted to his own students, including Eusebius.

Eusebius connects Pamphilus to Origen in his narrative through parallelism, direct homage, and juxtaposition when the evidence does not suffice. Eusebius' depiction of the Alexandrian school reflects a desire to establish a lineage of

---

5    Jaap Mansfeld adduces Cicero's *On Invention* 2.117 in a discussion of the importance of biography to the sectarian study of philosophical doctrine. As he writes: "The study of the life, activities and sayings of a philosopher was regarded as an indispensable preliminary to that of his writings" (Mansfeld 1999:20).

6    Origen's martyrdom during the Decian persecution is not at all certain; see Crouzel 1989:33–36. Eusebius, HE 7.1 reports that Origen lived until the time of Gallus and Volusian. Photius credits Pamphilus' *Apology for Origen* with the report of his martyrdom at Caesarea under Decius, *Library* 119.

teaching at Caesarea.[7] Although he is not the direct heir of the Alexandrians—for one thing, the school continued at Alexandria after Origen's departure for Caesarea—Eusebius portrays himself as a member of a Caesarean offshoot of the Alexandrian tradition. This involves some fancy narrative footwork. He ties Origen to Caesarea through historical accounts and his teacher Pamphilus to Origen through repetitive language, and, ultimately, books. Through his strategic deployment of information interposed with significant silences, Eusebius suggests that the school of Pamphilus and the school of Origen are united in common tradition, a tradition that ties Eusebius' teaching lineage to the antiquity and everything else he claims for the Alexandrian school tradition. The physical link between the two traditions is Origen. Eusebius portrays the gradual shift of Origen's teaching authority to Caesarea. The fact that he casts this move in terms of teaching is significant for his project of establishing teaching lineage. In *Ecclesiastical History* 6, Eusebius shows how Origen brings Alexandrian Christian philosophical erudition to Caesarea. This process begins with a visit by Origen to Caesarea during a period of civil unrest in Alexandria. In describing Origen's activities at Caesarea at this time, Eusebius writes that he came to the city to pursue his studies: ἐν Καισαρείᾳ δὲ τὰς διατριβὰς ἐποιεῖτο (HE 6.19).

After Heraclas succeeds Origen and Origen moves to Caesarea, Origen is in demand as a teacher. According to Eusebius, Firmilianus, the Bishop of Caesarea in Cappadocia, would summon Origen to visit "for the benefit of the churches" and also travel himself to Origen to "spend time (*sundiatribein*) with him for the sake of his own improvement in divine subjects" (HE 6.27). In Eusebius' account and in the witnesses he marshals, Origen instructs bishops and others in small groups or individually and also preaches sermons and scriptural exegeses to larger audiences in the churches. The smaller group is composed of the pupils of his *diatribê* and the larger group comprises the congregations he speaks in.

Although Eusebius is explicit in his descriptions of the distinction and the authority with which Origen taught, he is remarkably quiet on the explicit relationship of his own teacher, Pamphilus, to Origen and his teaching. When Eusebius lists the students of Origen in *Ecclesiastical History* 6.30, he does not mention Pamphilus or one of Pamphilus' teachers among them. The lack of concrete information about the teaching relationship, and the chronological gap, shows that Pamphilus was not an immediate student of Origen. However, Eusebius never comes out and says this. He does nothing to exclude the possibility of direct succession and includes many things to associate Pamphilus with the tradition of Origen.

---

[7]  For a historical overview of the Alexandrian school, see Vacherot 1851; Bardy 1937; Jakab 2001. Van den Hoek 1997 provides a nice overview of modern work on the school and ancient terminology. On Jewish and Christian schools at Caesarea, see Lieberman 1944; Lapin 1996.

Eusebius does not mention the intervening teachers between Pamphilus and Origen in the *Ecclesiastical History* or the *Martyrs of Palestine*, although he was probably taught by Pierius of Alexandria (on the evidence of Photius). As far as can be ascertained from Eusebius' work, the only intellectual forefather of Pamphilus' lineage is Origen. The absence of Pamphilus' "other lineage" seems analogous to the absence Buell identifies of Clement's teachers in the *Stromateis* and its function in the lineage and legitimation discourse in that text: "Regardless of his motive, Clement's decision to mask his teachers' names removes Clement's claim to apostolic inheritance beyond scrutiny—one cannot question Clement's pedigree since he does not fully elaborate his own lineage."[8] The succession between Pamphilus and Origen can be inferred from the fact that they were both at Caesarea and they were both the most learned and respected teachers of their day. Eusebius provides just enough information to allow the reader to connect them, to fill in the gap between their lives and their teaching activities.

In addition to his evocative silences, Eusebius uses a rhetorical strategy to connect the teaching lineages of Origen and Pamphilus: he associates them both with the technical vocabulary of the *diatribê* and the material and intellectual objects of Origen's books and letters. In the *Ecclesiastical History* and the *Martyrs of Palestine*, the term *diatribê* is strongly associated with Origen and with the catechetical school. Uses of *diatribê* cognates (*sun/diatribein*) and of the plural, *diatribai*, appear in the discussion of Origen's teaching activity in Book 6. The term *diatribê* refers to philosophical/theological teaching activity. In the *Ecclesiastical History*, there is one usage of the term *diatribê* to refer to non-Christian philosophical teaching: Eusebius' description of the Antiochene churchman and teacher, Malchion, who played a central role in the deposing of Bishop Paul of Samosata. Malchion is described as both a presbyter and the head of a *diatribê* for Greek studies at Antioch. Except for this instance, *diatribê* in the *Ecclesiastical History* refers to Christian teaching activity, and the only two cities to have a Christian *diatribê* in the *Ecclesiastical History* and *Martyrs of Palestine* are Alexandria and Caesarea. The term first appears in the introduction of the catechetical "school" in *Ecclesiastical History* 5.10, in which it is called a *diatribê* for the faithful. The term next appears in the course of Origen's young adulthood, when he teaches in a *diatribê* because there is no one in charge of catechetical instruction at Alexandria (HE 6.3). The διατριβὴ τοῦ κατηχεῖν is what Origen leads when Bishop Demetrius puts him in charge of teaching catechumens at Alexandria. After a large chronological and narrative gap, the term reappears in the context of succession, when Heraclas succeeds Demetrius as Bishop of

---

8    Buell 1999:85.

Alexandria and Dionysius succeeds Heraclas as the head of the catechetical school (HE 6.4).

In *Ecclesiastical History* 7.14, Bishop Theoktistos of Caesarea is listed as belonging to Origen's teaching (τῆς δ' Ὠριγένους διατριβῆς). In mentioning Theoktistos, Eusebius creates a continuity between the *diatribê* of Origen and his own time. Theoktistos is an important witness for Origen's school before Eusebius: although Theoktistos represents an actual student of Origen's who was still alive in Eusebius' time and a contemporary of Pamphilus, Eusebius does not mention anything about his intellectual activities, separate from the establishment of Origen's teaching authority at Caesarea. It is almost as though Theoktistos is a masked counterpart to the emphasized Pamphilus; Eusebius uses Theoktistos to establish Origen in Caesarea and then drops him off of the intellectual map. Eusebius describes Pamphilus' erudition and zeal for divine topics directly after Theoktistos, but Theoktistos is distinguished among his contemporaries only for the "zealous" exercise of his office (HE 7.32).

In the *Ecclesiastical History*, Pamphilus is the only person other than Origen to have a *diatribê* at Caesarea, and the *diatribê* at Caesarea is the only counterpart to the Alexandrian school in the works of Eusebius. Eusebius writes that the lost biographical work about Pamphilus contained details about the *diatribê* that Pamphilus established (συνεστήσατο) at Caesarea (HE 7.32.25). Here it is explicit that Pamphilus is the founder of a school, so the teaching lineage of Origen at Caesarea is not continuous, or at least, not continuous with Eusebius' own teaching lineage. Still, the use of *diatribê* belies the fact that Pamphilus did not succeed Origen. Rhetorically, Pamphilus' teaching endeavors are continuous with Origen's. Pamphilus is Origen's "as-if" intellectual heir at Caesarea, the only one to share the mastery of a *diatribê*.

The transmission of Origen's teachings to Pamphilus is effected through the physical intermediaries of books. The library substitutes for the school until Pamphilus can restore the legacy of Origen. It functions in the place of a person to connect Origen and Pamphilus without actual personal contact.[9] Eusebius has to perform rhetorical work to construct and enhance this lineage. The appeal to lineage is always an imaginary map, a narrative explanation, the creation of connections between points to form a line. Lineage is the struggle to relate elements to one another and to present the illusion that they have always been integrally related. The idea of the "restoration," that is, the creation of Origen's inheritance, is present not only in the repetition of the *diatribê* but also in the intermediary organ of the library. In Eusebius' account, Pamphilus makes a

---

9   For the internalization of the divine library in Origen and the embodiment of Scripture, see Cox Miller 2009:29–30.

great effort to gather the works of Origen. Eusebius mentions his effort on the topic of Origen's writing activity at Caesarea, shortly after the mention of the international fame of his school and the students who came to it. Eusebius tells that his work about the life of Pamphilus collected a full catalogue of the works of Origen and other Christian writers (HE 6.32). What he gathers are library lists (πίνακες) that act as a testimony to his "zeal for divine subjects (τὰ θεῖα)" (HE 6.32.3). This use of τὰ θεῖα resembles Bishop Firmilianus of Cappadocia's visits to Origen to better himself in τὰ θεῖα (HE 6.27). The lists themselves are book lineages, linking together individual works to reveal more than the individual titles. The catalog reveals the character of Pamphilus and his gathering of τὰ θεῖα relating to Origen. Moreover, Eusebius states that these lists confirmed the status of Pamphilus as the best representative of Origen: "from these [lists], anyone who wishes can gather the most complete knowledge of the works of Origen that have reached us (τὰ εἰς ἡμᾶς ἐλθόντα)" (HE 6.32). In this statement, through identification with the works of Origen, Pamphilus becomes the living repository of the most complete knowledge of Origen. The lists are the proof, the chronicle of this status, and the books are the physical tokens of exchange of knowledge. Pamphilus is an authoritative teacher who inherits Origen's teaching mantle at Caesarea and is also in possession of the fullest knowledge of Origen's knowledge, which passes in turn to Eusebius.

When Eusebius writes the stories of the martyrs who died in the persecutions of Diocletian and Galerius in the *Martyrs of Palestine*, he presents a collection of texts focused on individual figures and their suffering and deaths. Many of these figures are singled out as exemplary in life before their exemplary deaths, but a few accounts stand out by length. The two longest accounts in the collection are of the martyrs with whom Eusebius had the closest association, his teacher Pamphilus and Apphianus. Apphianus was a pupil of Pamphilus who had come from Asia Minor and who was martyred before his eighteenth birthday.

The connection of the Caesarean school of Pamphilus to Origen also appears within the text of the *Martyrs of Palestine* in the form of allusions to the *Thanksgiving Address* of Gregory Thaumaturgus in the descriptions of school members. The oration eulogizes the school of Origen, praising its course of instruction and the discipline it fosters. Eusebius parallels significant features in his eulogizing of the martyrs of his school. He does this through internal and external parallels, internal allusions to the text and external analogy to the biographical details of Gregory Thaumaturgus. Using the *Thanksgiving Address* as a model of Origen's school, Eusebius connects it in the *Martyrs* to his own school at Caesarea.

Gregory belonged to Origen's teaching circle at Caesarea. From what we know of his background, he was a pagan convert to Christianity from Pontus.[10] He came to Caesarea ca. AD 233 and began to study Christian teachings and scripture with Origen. After several years of instruction with Origen, Gregory left Caesarea and returned to his home of Neocaesarea. His *Thanksgiving Address* (λόγος χαριστήριος) was delivered at the end of his time with Origen as he was taking his leave of his teacher and his fellow students. It presents a glimpse into the student's perspective on his teacher, the school, and the teaching methods, as well as containing biographical testimony of Gregory's own path to Origen and to Christianity.

When treating the members of the school of Pamphilus, Eusebius presents several parallels to the material found in the *Thanksgiving Address* of Gregory and also to his own account of Gregory's time at Caesarea in *Ecclesiastical History* 6.30. One of the most obvious places of scholastic parallelism is found in the narrative of Apphianus in the *Martyrs*. Apphianus' journey to join the school of Pamphilus at Caesarea in the *Martyrs* has significant overlap with Gregory's journey to Caesarea to join the school of Origen in the *Address*. Both trajectories begin in the ancestral home, with parents who are not Christians and with ancestral customs of error.

Gregory begins the story of his journey with an account of where he came from before his time in the school of Origen. This account does not begin with a pedigree and heritage, but with a disavowal of his pagan upbringing and former beliefs: "From birth our parents gave us our first upbringing including the erroneous customs of our native land" (*Address* 5 (§48), trans. Slusser). In beginning the *Address*, Gregory separates himself from his parental home and from the practices he learned there. He views his early experience from the post-conversion perspective of his time in the house of Origen.

Eusebius portrays the life of the martyr Apphianus before his time in the school of Pamphilus in a similar light. Apphianus grew up in a pagan household and left because he had converted to Christianity in Berytus and was no longer able to abide by the customs in his parental home. Eusebius shows Apphianus leaving because of ancestral customs (MP(L) 13). Apphianus had converted to a form of ascetic Christianity during his study in Berytus. Upon returning home, much like Gregory, Apphianus (through the eyes of Eusebius) sees his parents' practices as foreign to his own.[11]

---

10 Much of the early biographical data about Gregory's life before and during his time in Caesarea comes from the *Address* and Eusebius, HE 6.30.

11 The shorter recension of the *Martyrs* has a fuller account of Apphianus's conversion to Christian philosophy and the conflicts with his parents' way of life, which occur because they did not live according to Christian practices. It says that Gregory's father offered him the benefits of being

Both Gregory and Apphianus engage on a long journey to their teacher in Caesarea, aided by divine providence. In Gregory's case, he is called to accompany his sister on an official trip to Palestine. He thinks he will be able stop in Berytus, but he is pressed forward and comes to Caesarea. For one who wanted to study in the famous legal schools of Berytus, Caesarea may have at first seemed an empty backwater. However, in recalling the events, Gregory speaks of the "marvelous providence (ἡ θαυμαστὴ οἰκονομία)" that kept him from stopping in Berytus and led him to Origen: "But I do not know how my discourse got stuck at this point since I wish to narrate methodically the remarkable dispensation by which I came to this man" (*Address* 5 (§55), trans. Slusser). This marvelous providence takes many forms in Gregory's account of the journey. He describes the soldier who escorted his family as an angelic figure, guiding them to Caesarea to meet Origen. In fact, Gregory depicts his entire life as a journey to meet Origen. He suggests that, although the beginning of his life was under pagan education, he had been predestined to come to Origen's school.

Apphianus' journey in the *Martyrs* is no less providential, particularly its practical details. When Apphianus realizes he cannot remain at home with his erring parents, according to Eusebius, the young man leaves with no preparation for the journey, not even provisions for one day (MP(L) 14). According to Eusebius, the power of God leads Apphianus to Caesarea, "the city in which the crown of martyrdom was prepared for him" (MP(L) 14).

One of the strongest parallels between Gregory and the *Martyrs of Palestine* is the biographical parallel between Apphianus and Aedesius. According to Eusebius' biographical account, Gregory had his brother with him as he joined this new web of philosophical kinship ties. Much like the fraternal situation among the martyrs of Eusebius' school, where Apphianus and Aedesius both study with Pamphilus, Gregory appears in *Ecclesiastical History* 6.30 at the school of Origen with his own brother, Athenodorus. Both fraternal relationships are mysterious. In the *Martyrs of Palestine*, the Aedesius narrative is a rhetorical doubling of Apphianus'—Eusebius even stresses how much like his brother Aedesius is, so the brother is included by analogy and with some deeds of his own, but the details are a bit hazy and vary significantly between versions of the *Martyrs*. It is also unclear when and how Aedesius comes to join Apphianius and whether he is an older or a younger brother, although, much like a contemporary census, Eusebius does tell us that they are brothers on both their mother's and their father's sides (MP(L)18).

---

the first son (τὰ πρωτεῖα τῆς πατρίδος), but that he rejected common life with his family (τὴν ἅμα τῷ πατρὶ καὶ τοῖς τῷ γένει προσήκουσιν συνουσίαν). The reason for this rejection, in the expanded narrative, is that their manner of life was contrary to the rules of his newly adopted Christian life (κατὰ τοὺς τῆς θεοσεβείας θεσμούς), MP(S) 4.

Aedesius is portrayed going to Alexandria and challenging the governor there to defend virgins and using both Roman law and Christian dialectic. Aedesius also studies with Pamphilus: "Aedesius, too, spent many years in the *diatribê* of Pamphilus" (MP(L)18). The use of "too" suggests that one brother is better known than the other, but the narrative of the brother is used to strengthen the narrative of the better-known figure. In the case of Gregory, we know about his brother Athenodorus only from Eusebius' account in the *Ecclesiastical History*. His very presence in the biography of Gregory is unclear and Eusebius is the primary witness for Gregory having a natal brother in the school of Origen. So, in the *Martyrs*, Apphianus and his brother Aedesius act as a sort of contemporary Caesarean version of Gregory and his brother Athenodorus.

As Arnaldo Momigliano asserts: "[T]o be a credible biographer of a holy man one had to claim close personal knowledge. There was need of intimacy with a holy man. The biographer mediated the intimacy between saint and reader by asserting intimacy between saint and biographer."[12] Similarly, in the conclusion to her study of the lives of Origen and Plotinus, Patricia Cox describes the images of the biographical subject as a "reflection of the author's deep sense of himself" and the biographical lens as a prism in which the hero reflects the many faces of the biographer.[13] Many who read the biography of Origen focus on the figure of Origen and his life and neglect the questions of what Eusebius was writing about his own time and his own context in Caesarea by composing a long biography and singular opus focused on this figure, a figure strongly connected to the contemporary philosophical, text-critical, and historical endeavors of his own school. In presenting the life of Origen in the midst of the *Ecclesiastical History*, Eusebius is writing Origen into the Caesarean present, presenting his almost ancestral connection to the famous theologian who was active at Caesarea over sixty years prior to Eusebius' writing activity.

Admittedly, many questions will remain open to interpretation. It is beyond the interpreter's grasp to reconstruct fully the Caesarean present of Eusebius, nor can the evidence of Eusebius be easily triangulated with other texts in historical perspective to create a fact-checked and definitive biography of Origen. The fact remains that Eusebius' works preserve the most biographical information about Origen. Jerome included material in his short chapter in *On Illustrious Men*, but this was mostly taken from his stay at Caesarea. Photius' material in the *Library* is brief and much, much later. There is a possible silver lining in Gregory Thaumaturgus' *Thanksgiving Address*, and the companion *Letter to Gregory*, which reflect school activity and the relationship of the student to

---

[12]  Momigliano 1987:77.
[13]  Cox 1983:135–136.

the founder and the school during Origen's time at Caesarea, a source which appears in redacted form in Eusebius, both explicitly in the biography of Origen and also compositionally in the narratives Eusebius writes about the martyrs of Palestine, particularly those associated with Pamphilus at Caesarea.

So the search for Origen ends where it starts, in the compositional present of Eusebius and the origin narratives of the school at Caesarea. The written biography of Origen can be read profitably within the writing project of the *Ecclesiastical History* and its many forms of appealing to the memory and the authority of Origen. The parallel material from the *Martyrs* supports a reading of Eusebius as a figure living in a school context with explicit interest in establishing, maintaining, cultivating, and, in part, creating the legacy of Origen at Caesarea.

# Works Cited

Adler, William. 1992. "Eusebius' Chronicle and Its Legacy." In *Eusebius, Christianity, and Judaism*, ed. Harold W. Attridge and Gohei Hata, 467–491. Leiden.

Bardy, Gustav. 1937. "Aux origines de l'ecole d'Alexandrie." *Revue des Sciences Religieuses* 27:65–90.

Barnes, Timothy D. 1981. *Constantine and Eusebius*. Cambridge, MA.

Buell, Denise Kimber. 1999. *Making Christians: Clement of Alexandria and the Rhetoric of Legitimacy*. Princeton.

Burgess, Richard W. 1997. "The Dates and Editions of Eusebius' *Chronici Canones* and *Historia Ecclesiastica*." *Journal of Theological Studies* 48:471–504.

Burgess, Richard W., with Witold Witakowski. 1999. *Studies in Eusebian and Post-Eusebian Chronography*. Stuttgart.

Cox, Patricia. 1983. *Biography in Late Antiquity: A Quest for the Holy Man*. Berkeley.

Cox Miller, Patricia. 2009. *The Corporeal Imagination: Signifying the Holy in Late Ancient Christianity*. Philadelphia.

Crouzel, Henri. 1989. *Origen*. Trans. A. S. Worall. Edinburgh.

Daniélou, Jean. 1948. *Origène*. Paris.

Grant, Robert M. 1971. "Early Alexandrian Christianity." *Church History* 40:133–144.

Greer, Rowan A. 1979. *Origen*. Mahwah.

Heine, Ronald E. 2010. *Origen: Scholarship in Service of the Church*. Oxford.

Hoek, Annewies van den. 1997. "The 'Catechetical School' of Early Christian Alexandria and Its Philonic Heritage." *Harvard Theological Review* 90:59–97.

Jakab, Attila. 2001. *Ecclesia alexandrina : Evolution sociale et institutionnelle du christianisme alexandrin, IIe et IIIe siècles*. Bern.

Lapin, Hayim. 1996. "Jewish and Christian Academies in Roman Palestine." In *Caesarea Maritima: A Retrospective after Two Millennia*, ed. Kenneth G. Holum and Avner Raban, 496–512. Leiden.

Lieberman, Saul. 1939–1944. "The Martyrs of Caesarea." *Annuaire de l'institut de philologie et d'histoire orientale et slaves* 7:395–446.

Louth, Andrew. 1990. "The Date of Eusebius' *Historia Ecclesiastica*." *Journal of Theological Studies* 41:111–123.

Mansfeld, Jaap. 1999. "Sources." In *The Cambridge History of Hellenistic Philosophy*, ed. Algra Keimpe, et al., 3–30. Cambridge.

Momigliano, Arnaldo D. 1987. *On Pagans, Jews, and Christians*. Hanover, NH.

Monaci, Adele Castagno, ed. 2004. *La biografia di Origene fra storia e agiografia: Atti del VI Convegno di studi del Gruppo italiano di ricerca su Origene e la tradizione alessandrina*. Rimini.

Mosshammer, Alden. 1979. *The Chronicle of Eusebius and Greek Chronographic Tradition*. Lewisburg, PA.

Nautin, Pierre. 1977. *Origène: Sa vie et son oeuvre*. Paris.

Slusser, Michael. 1998. *St. Gregory Thaumaturgus: Life and Works*. Washington, DC.

Trigg, Joseph W. 1998. *Origen*. London.

Vacherot, Étienne. 1851. *Histoire Critique de l'École d'Alexandrie*. 3 vols. Paris.

# 5

# A Eusebian Reading
# of the *Testimonium Flavianum*

## Ken Olson

IN HIS LAUDATORY *LIFE OF CONSTANTINE*, written shortly after the emper-
or's death in 337, Eusebius of Caesarea gives an account of a battle Constantine
fought against his colleague and rival, Licinius, the emperor of the eastern
part of the empire. Eusebius presents a speech that he claims Licinius made to
his troops just before he was defeated in battle by Constantine. Eusebius has
Licinius say:

> The present occasion shall prove which of us is mistaken in his judg-
> ment, and shall decide between our gods and those whom our adver-
> saries profess to honor. For either it will declare the victory to be
> ours, and so most justly evince that our gods are the true saviours and
> helpers; or else, if this God of Constantine's, who comes from we know
> not whence, shall prove superior to our deities (who are many, and in
> point of numbers, at least, have the advantage), let no one henceforth
> doubt which god he ought to worship, but attach himself at once to the
> superior power, and ascribe to him the honors of the victory. Suppose,
> then, this strange God, whom we now regard with ridicule, should
> really prove victorious; then indeed we must acknowledge and give
> him honor, and so bid a long farewell to those for whom we light our
> tapers in vain. But if our own gods triumph (as they undoubtedly will),
> then, as soon as we have secured the present victory, let us prosecute
> the war without delay against these despisers of the gods.

*Eusebius Life of Constantine* 2.5.3–4[1]

---

[1]    Eusebius 1890:992, E. C. Richardson's translation.

Eusebius then assures his readers: "Such was his speech to those present. The author of the present work was given this information shortly afterwards by those who personally heard his words" (Eusebius *Life* 2.5.5).[2]

Modern scholars have long been skeptical about Licinius' speech as recorded by Eusebius. Some defended Eusebius by claiming that he merely reports in good faith what his sources told him.[3] In recent scholarship, however, there seems to be a tendency among commentators to ascribe the composition of Licinius' speech to Eusebius himself. In their 1999 translation and commentary on the *Life of Constantine*, Averil Cameron and Stuart Hall comment:

> Eusebius claims (2.5.5) to have heard about Licinius' speech (2.5.2–4) shortly afterwards from those actually present, though he had not mentioned it at the relevant place in *Ecclesiastical History* 10.9; more probably it is his own invention. He uses the speech to heighten the religious character of the conflict, and makes Licinius himself concede that his defeat will prove Christianity true.[4]

If Cameron and Hall are correct, Eusebius apparently provided his own allegedly outside witness to the truth of Christianity. Might there be other cases where Eusebius has employed this technique of *prosōpopoeia*, "face-making" (or "character-crafting"), to further his own argument in the voice of another?[5]

This brings us to the topic of this chapter.[6] In current scholarship, the brief passage about Jesus found in the manuscripts of Josephus' *Antiquities*, called the

---

[2]  Translation Cameron and Hall 1999:97.

[3]  Richardson in Eusebius 1890:992n7.

[4]  Cameron and Hall 1999:232. (I have altered the format of the references given in the quotation.) Similarly, in his commentary in the recent Brepols edition of the *Life of Constantine*, Horst Schneider finds Licinius' speech to be the work of Eusebius in both its form and content (Bleckmann and Schneider 2007:43n240).

[5]  Eusebius also employs *prosōpopoeia* in *Demonstration* 1.6.64–67, writing in the voice of Jesus or the personified gospel teaching, and also 3.4.48–3.5.59, in which he satirizes the idea that Jesus' disciples were charlatans by writing a speech in the voice of the supposed charlatans. In both of these cases, he writes in the first person, but makes no effort to represent the speech-in-character as anything but his own composition.

[6]  The argument presented here, that Eusebius is the true author of the *Testimonium*, is a substantial reformulation of the thesis I articulated earlier in Olson 1999:305–322. In particular, I no longer think it necessary to suppose that Eusebius may have intentionally adopted Josephan phrases in particular cases in his "second edition" (i.e. the version of the *Testimonium* found in the *Ecclesiastical History*) in order to sound more like Josephus. Eusebius' language does not appear to go beyond what might be expected in an author employing *prosōpopoeia* or the variations in wording found in any author. I have also brought out the relationship between the contents of the *Testimonium* and the larger argument Eusebius is making in the *Demonstration of the Gospel* more clearly. In his recent review article on the *Testimonium Flavianum*, Louis H. Feldman has also argued for the identification of Eusebius as the author of the received text (2012:13–30). The thesis of Eusebian authorship of the *Testimonium* has been criticized by James

Testimonium Flavianum (Antiquities 18.63–64) is often considered to be an independent source for material about the historical Jesus. This places it alongside the Gospels of Mark and John and the hypothetical Q document as one of several sources to which the criterion of multiple attestation may be applied.[7] This criterion, widely considered to be one of the strongest of the criteria of authenticity used in historical Jesus research, posits that any data found in more than one independent source is more likely to be historical. Parts of the Testimonium are commonly used in historical Jesus scholarship as supporting evidence for reconstructing various aspects of Jesus' career, especially those having to do with his miracle-working, his teaching, and his trial and execution.

The passage has been controversial for some time. There is some evidence that the Testimonium was rejected by Jews in the Middle Ages, but as this evidence comes second-hand through Christian sources, we do not have an especially good idea as to why they did so.[8] In the sixteenth century, some Christian scholars began to reject the text on the grounds that it seemed to be a Christian confession of faith greatly at odds with what the non-Christian Jew Josephus says elsewhere in his works. Some earlier interpreters tried to reconcile this discrepancy by suggesting that Josephus in fact confessed the truth about Jesus yet continued to be a Jew and not a Christian.[9]

Few scholars would resort to such an explanation today. More commonly, scholars who wish to retain the Testimonium as an authentic Josephan text have adopted one or both of two methods. The first is to interpret the text in ways that seem less Christian or even hostile toward Jesus. By this method of interpretation, Josephus may have written the text, but it does not mean what Christians before the Enlightenment took it to mean. Josephus may have intended at least some parts of the text, especially those that others have taken as Christological confessions, to be read ironically.[10] The second is to alter the text, usually by omission of the most overtly Christian material, and possibly altering or adding material so that the passage becomes more negative toward Jesus and Christianity.[11]

---

Carleton Paget (2003:539–624) and at greater length by Alice Whealey (2007:73–116). While I will give a more detailed response to their criticisms in my forthcoming dissertation, in this chapter I have set out some of the major reasons for my disagreement with their positions.

[7] Meier 1991:91, 92, 98; 1994:621–622.

[8] See the discussions in Sanford 1935:136–139; Schreckenberg 1972:117–118; Whealey 2003:58–61.

[9] See Whealey 2003:86–89.

[10] This is the general position of the recent treatments of Whealey 2003, 2007; and Bardet 2002, though both allow that a few words may have been altered in transmission and Bardet expresses caution toward arguments based on tone.

[11] Meier 1991:56–68, discussed further below, falls largely within this approach, though he also argues for the possibility of deliberately ambiguous meanings in the parts of the text he considers authentic.

Probably the dominant opinion on the *Testimonium Flavianum* in recent historical Jesus scholarship follows the second method and supposes that the received text is not what Josephus wrote, but that we can recover what Josephus wrote by conjecturally emending the passage. By removing the three most overtly Christian statements from the text, we are left with a "core" text that is Josephan in language and non-Christian in content. This is the approach taken by John Meier in his widely cited and influential treatment of the issue in the first volume of *A Marginal Jew: Rethinking the Historical Jesus*.[12]

This approach is seriously flawed. The text does not divide easily into Christian and non-Christian sections on the basis of either language or content.[13] Both the language and the content have close parallels in the work of Eusebius of Caesarea, who is the first author to show any knowledge of the text. Eusebius quotes the *Testimonium* in three of his extant works: the *Demonstration of the Gospel* 3.5.106, the *Ecclesiastical History* 1.11.8, and the *Theophany* 5.44. The most likely hypothesis is that Eusebius either composed the entire text or rewrote it so thoroughly that it is now impossible to recover a Josephan original.

In the course of defending his proposition that this summary description of Jesus is not conceivable in the mouth of an ancient Christian, Meier asks: "What would be the point of a Christian interpolation that would make Josephus the Jew affirm such an imperfect estimation of the God-man? What would a Christian scribe intend to gain by such an assertion?"[14] This is an excellent question and one that deserves an answer. The question itself reveals a key assumption made by Meier and other scholars who have examined the issue. They assume that the interpolation (or interpolations) in the text of *Antiquities* 18 was composed by the scribes engaged in copying the manuscripts of Josephus and first appeared in its present context between *Antiquities* 18.62 and 18.65. This is possible, but there is a more likely alternative. The passage fits much better into the larger literary context it occupies in Eusebius' work. Eusebius uses the passage as part of an extended argument that he makes in the *Demonstration* and later reproduces in the *Theophany*.[15] In this context, the *Testimonium* sounds very

---

[12]  Meier 1991:56–88.

[13]  In his comparison of the vocabulary and usage of the *Testimonium* with that of the New Testament and of Josephus, Meier notes that in the parts of the passage he considers to be Christian interpolations: "In a few cases, the usage is more Josephan that that of the N[ew] T[estament] . . . Hence, in the case of the three interpolations, the major argument against their authenticity is from content" (Meier 1991:83n42). I am skeptical of Meier's initial assumption that the language of the New Testament can serve as a representative sample for the language used by early Christians. While Christian writers were undoubtedly influenced by the language of the New Testament, they were by no means limited to it.

[14]  Meier 1991:64.

[15]  On the role of the *Ecclesiastical History* in the transmission of the *Testimonium*, see note 50 below.

different from the way it sounds when Meier and other scholars read it as the work of Josephus. The theory of Josephan authorship controls their interpretation of the text. I will therefore offer a different reading of the text that highlights what the text might mean in the context of Eusebius' work.

Eusebius wrote the *Demonstration* for a Christian audience, both to instruct them in the truth of the Christian faith and to counter pagan and Jewish criticisms of Christianity. Among the pagan critics to whom Eusebius was responding was Porphyry of Tyre, but they included Eusebius' contemporary Hierocles and the earlier critic Celsus as well.[16] Eusebius' rhetorical technique is to present the criticisms made by pagan critics of Christianity anonymously. He explicitly cites Porphyry several times, but always to establish a point in favor of Christianity. This makes it difficult to know exactly which critic made the criticism to which Eusebius is responding, except where that criticism can be documented from an outside source.

In the *Demonstration*, Eusebius is responding to the argument that Christianity is an unreasonable belief. The Christians not only deserted the Hellenic traditions of their ancestors but, having adopted the scriptures of the Jews, deserted Judaism as well, and erroneously interpret the Jewish scriptures and the Messianic prophecies contained therein as referring not to the Jews but to themselves. Eusebius uses the *Demonstration* to defend the intellectual respectability of Christianity. The main argument of the work is that Jesus and Christianity are indeed the subject of the Hebrew scriptures and the fulfillment of the prophecies in them.

In Book III of the *Demonstration*, the book in which the *Testimonium* is found, Eusebius is carrying on an extended defense of the incarnation and answering the charges of critics of Christianity. One of these is Porphyry's argument against the divinity of Jesus. Departing from other pagan critics like Celsus who had disparaged Jesus, Porphyry said that Jesus was one of the wise men of the Hebrews, but that the Christians had mistakenly taken him to be divine.[17] Porphyry attributes his information to oracles of the gods Apollo and Hecate. Eusebius quotes a truncated form of one oracle in the final chapter of Book III, but we can establish a fuller text of these oracles from citations in Augustine's *City of God* 19.23 and Lactantius' *Divine Institutes* 4.11.[18]

---

[16]   See the discussion in Morlet 2009:272–283.

[17]   See Robert Wilken (1979:120–123; 2003:152–155). Michael Bland Simmons argues that Porphyry's ostensible praise of Jesus is actually disparaging (1995:222–229). For a mediating position, see Jeremy Schott (2005:310–312; 2008:74–76).

[18]   Eusebius and Augustine explicitly name Porphyry as their source for these oracles. Andrew Smith provides a synopsis of the parallels between them in Porphyrius 1993:395–398. While Lactantius quotes (and subsequently discusses) an oracle of Apollo which refers to Jesus as wise in *Divine Institutes* 4.11, it is disputed whether he knew Porphyry's work directly. I accept the

What Eusebius is seeking to show in Book III is that Jesus has not only a human nature, but a divine one as well. He goes about this by arguing that Jesus' coming as Christ was foretold in prophecy, that he was not a deceiver but a teacher of true doctrines, that he performed superhuman feats, and that he did not perform these feats by sorcery. At the end of Book III, Eusebius concludes that a man who was not a sorcerer but a man of good character (as Porphyry himself allowed he was), yet could perform wonders beyond human ability, must necessarily have been superhuman in his nature.[19] As an ostensibly outside witness to the fact that the man Jesus was not merely human in his nature but evidenced the things foretold of the Christ in prophecy, the *Testimonium* represents an encapsulation of Eusebius' argument. It therefore has its most plausible *Sitz-im-Leben* in the pagan-Christian controversies of the fourth century. This was the period in which the question of whether Jesus was merely a wise man or something more was being debated. The first half of the *Testimonium* seems to address precisely this issue. While the manuscripts and the external witnesses do contain significant variants, for simplicity I will give a translation of the text based on Niese's critical edition of Josephus' *Antiquities*, with the sections Meier takes to be interpolated in italics:

> About this time arose Jesus, a wise man, *if indeed one ought to call him a man*, for he was a maker of miraculous works, a teacher of human beings who receive the truth with pleasure, and he won over both many Jews and also many from the Gentiles. *This one was the Christ.*[20]

Meier argues that "This one was the Christ" is an interpolation, both because it is clearly a Christian profession of faith and because it "seems out of place in its present position and disturbs the flow of thought. If it were present at all, one would expect it to occur immediately after either 'Jesus' or 'wise man' where further identification would make sense."[21]

But Meier's reading does not do justice to the text as it stands. Meier is quite correct in arguing that the statement "this one was the Christ" is an overt Christian confession, but his assertion that it is out of sequence in its current position fails to recognize the internal logic of the passage. The *Testimonium*

---

common identification of the unnamed philosopher who wrote three volumes against the name and faith of Christians in *Divine Institutes* 5.3–11 as Porphyry. The best case for the identification is made by Digeser 2000:91–114.

[19] For a discussion of Jesus' miracles in Eusebius' apologetics, see Kofsky 2002:165–214, especially 170–173.

[20] Γίνεται δὲ κατὰ τοῦτον τὸν χρόνον Ἰησοῦς σοφὸς ἀνήρ, εἴγε ἄνδρα αὐτὸν λέγειν χρή· ἦν γὰρ παραδόξων ἔργων ποιητής, διδάσκαλος ἀνθρώπων τῶν ἡδονῇ τἀληθῆ δεχομένων, καὶ πολλοὺς μὲν Ἰουδαίους, πολλοὺς δὲ καὶ τοῦ Ἑλληνικοῦ ἐπηγάγετο· ὁ χριστὸς οὗτος ἦν (18.63).

[21] Meier 1991:60.

initially labels Jesus a wise man, but then immediately puts in question whether the word "man" is adequate to describe him, and offers three reasons for doing so: first, "because he was a maker of miraculous works"; second, because he was "a teacher of human beings who receive the truth with pleasure"; third, because "he won over many Jews and also many from the Gentiles." Immediately following these three facts about Jesus, the *Testimonium* declares: "This one was the Christ."[22] It would seem reasonable to suppose that the identity of Jesus as the Christ (a suitable label for Jesus), and not merely a wise man (a true but inadequate classification for Jesus), is established based on the three reasons that have been given in the text.

The term "maker of miraculous works" παραδόξων ἔργων ποιητής, contrary to what one frequently finds in the literature on the *Testimonium*, is far more characteristic of Eusebius than of Josephus. Josephus never elsewhere uses the word ποιητής in the sense of "maker" or "doer" rather than "poet." Nor does he ever elsewhere combine a form of ποιέω with παράδοξος in the sense of wonder-working. The combination of παράδοξος and ποιέω to mean "wonder-working" is extremely common in Eusebius and occurs more than a hundred times. With the disputed exception of the *Testimonium* itself, the word ποιητής modified by παραδόξων ἔργων does not show up *anywhere* in the *Thesaurus Linguae Graecae* database of extant Greek literature before Eusebius, who uses this combination of words ten times outside the *Testimonium*,[23] usually of Jesus, but also of God. He says, for example, that God became "a maker of miraculous works" for the emperor Constantine in *Life of Constantine* 1.18.2. Two features of the way the term is used in the *Testimonium* are noteworthy. First, Eusebius uses the fact that Jesus was a "maker of miraculous works" in the *Demonstration* to show that Jesus was beyond human in his nature. In *Demonstration* 3.3.20, Eusebius says that he has been discussing Christ as though he had only a common human nature and will now move on to discussing his diviner side. The next section begins with his first use of the term παραδόξων ἔργων ποιητής as a label for Jesus (3.4.21).[24] Eusebius appears to be using the term to suggest that Jesus was more than an ordinary man, just as the *Testimonium* uses it to justify questioning whether it is proper to call Jesus a man. Second, Eusebius frequently claims that it was fore-told in prophecy that the Christ would be a miracle-worker, and once even that he would be a παραδόξων ἔργων ποιητής (*Ecclesiastical History* 1.2.23), and this would seem to be implied by the *Testimonium* as well.

---

[22] The use of the imperfect verb is paralleled in *Ecclesiastical History* 1.4.12 in which Eusebius is identifying a figure he has been discussing with the Christ.

[23] *Ecclesiastical History* 1.2.23; *Demonstration of the Gospel* 3.4.21, 3.5.59, 3.5.103, 3.7.4; *Commentary on Isaiah* 2.57.62; *Life of Constantine* 1.18.2; *Commentary on Psalms* PG 23 cols. 541, 984, 1033.

[24] English translation in Ferrar 1920:1.126–127.

The description of Jesus as "a teacher of human beings receiving the truth with pleasure" has caused some difficulties for the theory of authenticity because it seems to be calling Jesus' teachings the truth. Some scholars have advocated conjecturally emending the word from τἀληθῆ to τ' ἀλλ' ἤθη, "other customs" to avoid the difficulty.[25] Others have argued that the word ἡδονή ("pleasure") has a distinctly negative connotation in New Testament usage (and thus presumably other early Christian usage as well), but Josephus employs the word in both positive and negative senses.[26]

Meier finds it difficult to be precise about what this text might mean for Josephus:

> The Greek phrase τῶν ἡδονῇ τἀληθῆ δεχομένων could imply simple-minded enthusiasm, even self-delusion. Yet, while possible, that is not necessarily the sense. We may have here one example of what Josephus is doing throughout the *Testimonium*: carefully writing an ambiguous text that different audiences could take in different ways.

Meier 1991:76n19

Meier thus posits that Josephus deliberately crafted an ambiguous text so that we cannot be sure what he means by it.

We can find a much better explanation of what the text actually says if we investigate the possibility that Eusebius wrote it. In two different works (*In Praise of Constantine* 17.11, *Martyrs of Palestine* 6.6), Eusebius praises Christians who undergo martyrdom with ἡδονή ("pleasure"), and in his comments on Psalm 67.4 (PG 23 col. 684D) he speaks of delighting in divine pleasure in the presence of God.[27] Eusebius, like Josephus and other writers, recognizes both good and bad forms of pleasure.

Like the phrase "maker of miraculous works," the phrase διδάσκαλος ἀνθρώπων ("teacher of human beings") is also more characteristic of Eusebius than of Josephus. Neville Birdsall, who tentatively rejected the authenticity of the *Testimonium* based on an examination of its language, observed that the word διδάσκαλος followed by the recipients, rather than the contents, of the

---

[25] Dubarle 1977:52–53 prefers τ' ἀλλ' ἤθη to the alternative conjecture τὰ ἀήθη, and is tentatively followed by Whealey 2003:33.

[26] Meier 1991:80–81n41.

[27] ἡδονῇ τε θείᾳ ἐντρυφᾷν; Whealey 2007:85 argues that Eusebius uses the dative form ἡδονῇ in a negative or unfavorable sense, but fails to note this counterexample in her discussion. The problem with Whealey's argument goes beyond merely missing a particular counterexample (she could always introduce further distinctions to exclude any counterexample); the more serious issue is that her initial assumption that grammatical case lends words positive or negative senses in Eusebius' writings is insecure.

teaching in the genitive is extremely rare in Josephus. It is found only at *Jewish War* 7.444,[28] where Josephus places both the recipients and the content of the teaching in the genitive.[29] Eusebius on the other hand calls Jesus a "teacher of human beings" elsewhere in the *Demonstration* and he even claims it was foretold in prophecy that the Christ would be a "teacher of human beings" (*Demonstration* 3.6.27, 9.11.3; note also the variants in 3.7.6 and 5.Proem.24). In another case, Eusebius identifies Jesus as the savior of human beings and the teacher of barbarians and Greeks alike and places the recipients of the teaching in the genitive (*Demonstration* 5.Proem.25). In all of these cases the content of Jesus' teaching is εὐσέβεια, religion or piety, and in two of them specifically the "true religion," a term which he defined in the introduction to his *Preparation for the Gospel* as worship of the one God who is creator of all (*Preparation* 1.1). That is likely to be the meaning here, because Eusebius does sometimes use the neuter plural τὰ ἀληθῆ to denote the monotheistic religious beliefs of the ancient Hebrews which Jesus re-instituted by teaching them to his disciples, as in *Demonstration* 4.13, where Eusebius says:

> He taught them *truths* (τὰ ἀληθῆ) not shared by others, but laid down as laws by Him or by the Father in far distant periods of time for the ancient and pre-Mosaic Hebrew men of God.
>
> *Demonstration* 4.13.169[30]

Taken together, all of this suggests that when the text describes the recipients of Jesus' teachings as "human beings receiving the truths with pleasure," it is neither polemical nor intentionally ambiguous. It means that Jesus taught the truths *about the One God* to those who were willing to receive them.

The statement that "he won over both many Jews and also many from the Gentiles," has been one of the main points brought in support of the position that the text is partially authentic. A number of scholars contend that a Christian would not have said that Jesus won over many Jews and Gentiles because the gospels portray Jesus' mission as being only to the Jews and that the mission to the Gentiles did not begin until after his death.[31] But here we have

---

[28] διδάσκαλος ἦν τῶν σικαρίων τῆς ψευδολογίας.

[29] Birdsall 1984–1985:619.

[30] Ferrar 1920:1.189.

[31] Whealey 2007:86–87 takes this position, but her evidence shows that Jesus did not send his apostles on a mission to the Gentiles until after his resurrection. This does nothing to negate the evidence from Eusebius' works stating that Jesus himself attracted Gentiles during his ministry.

to acknowledge that what the gospels say to modern readers is not necessarily what they said to ancient interpreters.[32]

Eusebius introduces the *Testimonium* in the course of his defense of the witness of the disciples as given in the gospels. Following his citation of the *Testimonium* and brief mentions of Acts and the Jewish bishops of Jerusalem, he says:

> Thus the whole slander against his disciples is destroyed, when *by their evidence*, and also apart from their evidence, it has to be confessed that *many myriads of Jews and Gentiles* were brought under His yoke by Jesus the Christ of God through the miracles that he performed.
>
> *Demonstration* 3.5.109 (emphasis mine)[33]

Eusebius not only accepts the *Testimonium*'s claim that Jesus won over many Gentiles, but exaggerates the number—"many myriads"—and claims that this is the testimony of the evangelists as well. Nor is this the only context in which Eusebius claims that Jesus attracted Gentiles during his ministry. In *Demonstration* IV, 10, Eusebius lists among other deeds of Jesus during his incarnation: "He set all that came to Him free from age-long superstition and the fears of polytheistic error" (4.10.14).[34] He is presumably not referring to Jews. In *Demonstration* 8.2, Eusebius claims that "by teaching and miracles He revealed the powers of His Godhead to all equally whether Greeks or Jews" (8.2.109).[35] In the *Ecclesiastical History*, Eusebius introduces the story of the conversion of King Abgar and the city of Edessa by saying: "The divinity of our Lord and Saviour Jesus Christ

---

[32] A century ago, Walter Bauer noted the tendency of some later Christian writers to increase Jesus' contacts with Gentiles during his ministry beyond what a strict reading of the gospels might suggest. He includes the *Testimonium*, which he took to be a Christian interpolation, among his examples (1909:344–345).

[33] ὡς καὶ ἐκ τούτων λελύσθαι πᾶσαν τὴν κατὰ τῶν μαθητῶν αὐτοῦ διαβολήν, ὅτε καὶ πρὸς αὐτῶν καὶ δίχα τῆς αὐτῶν μαρτυρίας μυρία ὁμολογεῖται πλήθη Ἰουδαίων τε καὶ Ἑλλήνων αὐτὸς Ἰησοῦς ὁ Χριστὸς τοῦ θεοῦ, δι' ὧν ἐπετέλει παραδόξων ἔργων, ὑφ' ἑαυτὸν πεποιημένος. Translation from Ferrar 1920:1.144 (adapted). Both Whealey (2003:27; 2007:85–88) and Paget (2001:562) argue that the *Testimonium*'s statement that Jesus won over both Jews and Gentiles was problematic for Eusebius because it contradicts the gospels, but neither discusses this passage in which Eusebius attributes precisely this view to the evangelists, though Whealey does quote the passage earlier (2003:26). Whealey's failure to note the significance of *Demonstration* 3.5.109 leads her to misinterpret the text that precedes it. She takes Eusebius' statements about the Acts of the Apostles and the bishops of Jerusalem as an attempt to support the *Testimonium*'s claim that Jesus attracted multitudes of Jews and finds it significant that he produces no biblical or other evidence to support the *Testimonium*'s claim that Jesus also won over many Gentiles (2007:86–87). But this is a misreading of Eusebius' argument. He is not trying to demonstrate the reliability of the *Testimonium*; he is using the *Testimonium*, Acts, and the bishops of Jerusalem as evidence supporting the reliability of the evangelists.

[34] Ferrar 1920:1.183.

[35] Ferrar 1920:2.135.

became famous among all men because of his wonder-working power, and led to him myriads even of those who in foreign lands were far remote from Judea, in the hope of healing from diseases and from all kinds of suffering" (1.13.1).[36] In Book VII, he also tells of a statue of Jesus in Caesarea Philippi erected to honor Jesus' healing of the woman with a flow of blood. Eusebius comments: "And it is not at at all surprising that those Gentiles, who long ago received benefits from our Savior, should have made these things" (7.18.4). Whatever we may suppose as to whether Jesus attracted Gentiles during his ministry, we should allow that Eusebius thought he did. Further, Eusebius devotes the entirety of Book II of the *Demonstration* to answering the charge that the Christ was promised to the Jews. Eusebius argues, to the contrary, that the hope of the Christ was promised equally to the Jews and Gentiles and that the Christian church contains both Gentiles and the remnant of the Jews.

The fact that Jesus taught the true religion not only among Jews, but among Gentiles as well, is what allows the conclusion that follows in the *Testimonium*: "This one was the Christ". In the second chapter of Book III of the *Demonstration*, three chapters before he introduces the *Testimonium*, Eusebius presents a lengthy argument that Jesus is the prophet like Moses whose coming was fore-told in Deuteronomy 18. Both Moses and Jesus had worked miracles. Both Moses

---

[36]  Translation from K. Lake 1926:1.85. Whealey objects to the use of Eusebius' introduction to the story of King Abgar and the conversion of Edessa quoted here as an example of Jesus attracting a multitude of Gentiles during his ministry on two grounds. First, while Eusebius allows that Abgar petitioned Jesus, Jesus did not immediately grant Abgar's request, but after his resurrection the disciple Thomas sent Thaddeus to Edessa, so the mission to Gentiles still began only after Jesus' death. Second, the Syriac-speaking Edessenes are barbarians and not the "Greeks" (τοῦ Ἑλληνικοῦ) of the *Testimonium*, because, according to Whealey, Eusebius constantly differentiates between Greeks and barbarians throughout his works (Whealey 2007:87). Neither objection is sustainable. First, in the Abgar story Eusebius says that Abgar was one among the myriads that were led to (ἐπήγετο) Jesus in search of healing, which is enough to establish that Eusebius thought many Gentiles were led to Jesus during his ministry. That Abgar's actual healing and the disciples' mission to the Gentiles came about only later is irrelevant to the case. One cannot dismiss a relevant parallel on the basis of an irrelevant distinction. Second, while Eusebius does often differentiate between Greeks and barbarians on the basis of language in his works, in the *Demonstration* he also distinguishes between Greeks and Jews on the basis of religion. In this context, "Greek" has the more general sense of pagan or polytheist. See especially *Demonstration* 1.2.2: "Hellenism you might summarily describe as the worship of many gods according to the ancestral religions of all nations" and the discussion that follows it. Further, all of our ancient Latin and Syriac translators of the *Testimonium* understood τοῦ Ἑλληνικοῦ in the sense of "Gentiles" or "idolaters," rather than "Greeks." Nor is there warrant for Whealey's implicit assumption that the myriads from outside Judea mentioned in *Ecclesiastical History* 1.13.1 were composed solely of Aramaic-speakers, nor for believing that Eusebius might have accepted the idea of Jesus attracting Aramaic-speaking Gentiles but not Greek-speaking Gentiles, nor for the assumption that Eusebius and other early Christians considered only those characters specifically identified as Gentiles in the gospels to be such (the story of the woman with the flow of blood, cited above, contradicts this assumption).

and Jesus had taught the truth about the One God. But while Moses had taught this truth only among Jews, Jesus was the first to have taught the true religion of the One God not only among Jews, but to human beings of all nations. It is the fulfillment of prophecies about the Christ that allows the *Testimonium* to conclude at this point in the text that, in fact, this one was the Christ.

The proposed reading for the first half of the *Testimonium*, therefore, is that it puts in question whether it is adequate to call Jesus a man and concludes that he was not only a man, but the Christ. The justification for this conclusion is that he was a maker of miraculous works, taught human beings the truth *about the one God*, and brought over not only Jews but Gentiles as well—that is, all people regardless of nationality or prior religious affiliation. These are things which Eusebius claims elsewhere were foretold about the Christ in prophecy.[37]

The second part of the *Testimonium*, with the section Meier and many other scholars take to be interpolated in italics, reads:

> Although, on the accusation of the first men among us, Pilate condemned him to the cross, those who adhered at first did not cease, *for he appeared to them on the third day, living again, as the divine prophets had spoken these and myriads of other wonders about him.* And still to this day the tribe of Christians, named after him, has not failed.[38]

I have followed Meier here in translating the initial genitive absolute as a concessive clause.[39] On Meier's reading, the second half of the *Testimonium* suggests that the author of the text is surprised that Jesus' following continued after Jesus' death. Meier says:

> The implication seems to be one of surprise: granted Jesus' shameful end (with no new life mentioned in the core text), one is amazed to

---

[37] See especially the first chapter of the *Preparation for the Gospel* on Eusebius' conception of the role of Christ as the mediator of true religion to all human beings without distinction; see also John Robertson, *Christ as Mediator: A Study of the Theologies of Eusebius of Caesarea, Marcellus of Ancyra, and Athanasius of Alexandria* (Oxford University Press, 2007) 37–96, and particularly 60–70, on Christ's role and the mediator of God to human beings.

[38] καὶ αὐτὸν ἐνδείξει τῶν πρώτων ἀνδρῶν παρ' ἡμῖν σταυρῷ ἐπιτετιμηκότος Πιλάτου οὐκ ἐπαύσαντο οἱ τὸ πρῶτον ἀγαπήσαντες· ἐφάνη γὰρ αὐτοῖς τρίτην ἔχων ἡμέραν πάλιν ζῶν τῶν θείων προφητῶν ταῦτά τε καὶ ἄλλα μυρία περὶ αὐτοῦ θαυμάσια εἰρηκότων. εἰς ἔτι τε νῦν τῶν Χριστιανῶν ἀπὸ τοῦδε ὠνομασμένον οὐκ ἐπέλιπε τὸ φῦλον (18.64).

[39] Meier 1991:78n35. Meier finds the fact that the *Testimonium* does not deal with the question of why Jesus was condemned to death to be an argument for Josephus' authorship (1991:65). As will be argued further below, I find, to the contrary, that the fact that the *Testimonium* introduces the denunciation and crucifixion of Jesus in order to describe the conditions under which his adherents did not abandon his teaching to be an argument in favor of Eusebius' authorship.

note, says Josephus, that this group of post-mortem lovers is still at it and has not disappeared even in our own day.[40]

Meier is again quite correct in understanding that the text communicates that the continuance of Christianity after Jesus' death is surprising. But if we read the text as it stands and include the claim that Jesus appeared to the disciples alive again, we have an explanation for this surprising event. Moreover, this is a key argument that Eusebius makes for the reliability of the disciples' report of the resurrection earlier in the same chapter of the *Demonstration* in which he produces the *Testimonium*. Eusebius, like the *Testimonium*, finds the behavior of the disciples surprising. He says: "surely they had all seen the end of their teacher, and the death to which He came. Why then after seeing His miserable end did they stand their ground?" (3.5.39); and again: "I ask you how these pupils of a base and shifty master, who had seen His end, discussed with one another how they should invent a story about Him which would hang together?" (3.5.113).[41] Eusebius' argument in this part of the chapter is that the disciples' continued adherence to Jesus' teachings and the subsequent success of their mission is inexplicable apart from the reality of the resurrection appearances, which demonstrated the truth of what Jesus taught. Later in the *Demonstration*, Eusebius enumerates the reasons for the resurrection itself and ranks as number five Christ's need to give his disciples ocular proof of life after death so that they would have the courage to preach his message to all nations (*Demonstration* 4.12). In his later work *In Praise of Constantine*, Eusebius ranks this reason for the resurrection first (*Tricennial Orations: On Christ's Sepulcher* 15.7).

In addition, some of the language used in this section of the *Testimonium* is paralleled in Eusebius' work, but not in Josephus. These include: καὶ ἄλλα μυρία ("and myriads of other things"), which occurs eight times elsewhere in Eusebius' work;[42] τῶν Χριστιανῶν . . . τὸ φῦλον ("tribe of Christians"), which occurs twice elsewhere;[43] and εἰς ἔτι τε νῦν ("to this very day"), which occurs

---

[40] Meier 1991:66.

[41] Ferrar 1920:1.128; 130. As with many of his arguments in the *Demonstration*, Eusebius is expanding on an idea found in Origen (*Against Celsus* 2.56).

[42] *Demonstration of the Gospel* 1.Proem.3, 1.7.4, 5.16.3; *Ecclesiastical Theology* 1.20.18; *Commentary on Isaiah* 1.62.81, 1.98.56, 1.98.58; *Commentary on Psalms* PG 23 col. 1080B. Meier, of course, does not consider these words to come from Josephus, but from a Christian interpolator (1991:61, 83n42).

[43] *Ecclesiastical History* 3.33.2, 3.33.3. Whealey 2007:97–100 argues against the use of "tribe of Christians" as an indication of Eusebian authorship on the grounds that Eusebius uses the term in the *Ecclesiastical History* under the influence of a source. I think the point that Eusebius uses the term independent of Josephus stands regardless. Whealey's supplementary point that Eusebius uses φῦλον to describe groups to which he is hostile is insecure (e.g. Eusebius is not polemicizing against stars when he refers to their "tribes and families" in *Preparation* 7.15.12).

six times elsewhere.[44] Some scholars have suggested that the author of the *Testimonium*, in saying that the tribe of Christians has not died out until now, expects or even desires that it will come to an end, but this inference is unnecessary.[45] In *Ecclesiastical History* 1.3.19, Eusebius argues that Jesus alone, "out of all those who have ever yet been until now (εἰς ἔτι καὶ νῦν), is called Christ among all men,"[46] and he by no means expects or desires that this will change. Perhaps a closer parallel to the *Testimonium* is in Eusebius' *Commentary on Psalms*: "the Pharisees and Sadducees have *disappeared* (ἐξέλιπον) so much that no mention is made of them *even till now* (εἰς ἔτι νῦν), nor is their name preserved among the Jews" (PG 23 col. 684C).[47] Both the failure of the Sadducees and Pharisees in the *Commentary* and the success of the Christians in the *Testimonium* exhibit one of the principle themes of Eusebius' historiography: whatever does not come from God will fail, but what comes from God cannot be stopped.[48] The fact that Christianity has not failed, but continues to this day despite all that has been thrown against it, is proof of its truth.

I do not expect to be able to overturn the majority opinion of modern scholarship in the course of a short chapter. There are several other pieces of evidence that different scholars have cited as reasons for accepting at least the partial authenticity of the text, such as the passage mentioning James the brother of Jesus in *Antiquities* 20.200, Origen's claims in *Against Celsus* 1.47 and *Commentary on Matthew* 10.17 that Josephus did not believe Jesus to be the Christ, Agapius' tenth century Arabic version of the text, and the very presence of the text in the manuscript tradition of Josephus.[49]

---

[44] *Preparation for the Gospel* 1.3.10, *Demonstration of the Gospel* 4.16.3; 9.3.7; *Ecclesiastical History* 2.1.7, *Commentaria in Psalmos* PG 23 col. 1305, *Generalis elementaria introductio* 168.15. The phrase εἰς ἔτι νῦν (with an occasional καί or τε inserted) occurs over a hundred times in Eusebius. The use of this phrase as evidence of Eusebius' authorship is challenged by Whealey 2007:100–105, who presents a text-critical argument against ἔτι having stood in the *Antiquities*. Even if one accepted her case for the original reading of the *Antiquities* (and I am dubious), εἰς . . . τε νῦν is still found in the given cases in Eusebius and not in Josephus.

[45] Meier 1991:66. Schwartz 2002:167 contends that the use of the negative formulation that the movement "has not ceased to exist" rather than positively saying that it continued to grow contradicts the positive tone of the rest of the *Testimonium* and is thus an argument for Josephan authenticity. The argument is insecure. The *Testimonium* contains two negated verbs: οὐκ ἐπαύσαντο and οὐκ ἐπέλιπε. The first has a near parallel in οὐκ ἐπαύοντο διδάσκοντες καὶ εὐαγγελιζόμενοι in Acts 5:42, which may well have influenced it. In his commentary on Acts, C.K. Barrett notes: "οὐκ ἐπαύοντο is stronger than the imperfects of διδάσκειν and εὐαγγελίζεσθαι would have been" (Barrett 1994:301). Thus, the negated verbs in the *Testimonium* may readily be understood as litotes or negative iteration, rhetorical devices used to strengthen the statements made with them.

[46] Translation Lake 1926:37.

[47] I am indebted to Aaron Johnson for the reference.

[48] This theme in Christian historiography goes back at least to Gamaliel's speech in Acts 5:38–39.

[49] I will be addressing those issues in a fuller treatment of Eusebius and the *Testimonium Flavianum* (forthcoming).

What I have tried to show here is that many of the usual reasons given to support the authenticity of the text are weak or reversible, and this is particularly true of arguments about Josephan language and non-Christian content. Further, arguments about negative tone and ironic or ambiguous readings are almost entirely subjective. Our ability to perceive them depends on who we think wrote the text in the first place. The frequently employed argument that the language is "Josephan," and therefore must either come from Josephus himself or be a masterful forgery, runs into difficulties especially in places where we find parallels in Eusebius but not in Josephus. Such language, of course, could still conceivably have been used by Josephus. It is impossible to prove absolutely that it was not. But it is difficult to see how it can be used as a positive argument for authenticity. And if we adopt the hypothesis that Eusebius is so deeply influenced by the *Testimonium* that he has imitated not only its language but its apparent Christology as well in several of his works, this seems not only improbable but comes near to removing the hypothesis of authenticity from any possibility of falsification. The confidence that many scholars place in the *Testimonium* or its reconstructed core text is misplaced.

The discussion offered here, if correct, contributes to our understanding of Eusebius as an author, polemicist, and preserver of Hellenistic Jewish texts. He has frequently been recognized for his extensive use of quotations. I have argued here that, at least in this one highly charged case, Eusebius not only used quotations, he also produced one *and* his production was carried over into the manuscripts of Josephus' *Antiquities*.[50] The suggestion that Eusebius has sometimes been guilty of misattribution is in itself hardly novel. Sabrina Inowlocki has recently drawn attention to the passage Eusebius attributes to Philo in *Demonstration* 8.2.402d–403. Rather than directly quoting the passage in which Philo discusses the incident in which Pilate brought golden shields with inscriptions into Jerusalem from *Embassy to Gaius* 299, Eusebius attributes to Philo a passage combining language drawn from Josephus' account from *Antiquities* 18.55–59 with his own redaction which has Pilate bringing images into the temple itself.[51] In that instance, of course, the Eusebian passage was not carried over into the manuscripts of Philo.

---

[50] I have been arguing in this chapter that Eusebius composed the *Testimonium* following the line of argument he uses in the *Demonstration* and later in the *Theophany*. The form of the text found in the manuscripts of Josephus' *Antiquities*, however, more closely resembles that found in the *Ecclesiastical History*, from which the scribes who copied the text of Josephus probably took it (unless Eusebius himself oversaw the insertion). A discussion of the dating of the composition of Book III of the *Demonstration*, the editorial history of Book I of the *Ecclesiastical History*, and the date and contents of the lost *Against Porphyry* will have to await fuller treatment elsewhere.

[51] Inowlocki 2006:214–220, arguing against the view that the passage in the *Demonstration* quotes some unknown lost work of Philo.

Is it plausible to think that in other cases Eusebius may have influenced the transmission of the texts he used as sources? There are, in fact, a few cases where Eusebius' influence on the manuscript tradition of Josephus is hardly disputable. Alice Whealey has pointed out that the sixth-century Latin translators of the *Antiquities* did not provide original translations of the *Testimonium Flavianum* or the passage about John the Baptist in Book XVIII, but used the existing translations of those passages from Rufinus' Latin version of Eusebius' *Ecclesiastical History*.[52] In the Greek manuscript tradition of Josephus, there is a note at the end of the table of contents attached to Book I of the *Antiquities*: "The book covers a period of 3008 years according to Josephus, of 1872 according to the Hebrews, of 3,459 according to Eusebius."[53]

Beyond these specific cases, there is the more general question, which David Runia has addressed, of the role that Caesarea played in the transmission of Hellenistic Jewish texts. Runia argues, for example, that our manuscripts of the works of Philo are all descended from a single Caesarean exemplar. However, he sets aside the works of Josephus as outside the scope of his study:

> It is not likely that the Caesarea library was alone responsible for the survival of these works, which soon after their publication gained a lasting popularity among Christians, and to a lesser extent, pagan readers.

Runia 1996:477–478

Runia's description of the Josephan corpus as a whole, however, does not apply to the *Antiquities*, and particularly not to Books XI–XX. As Whealey has argued, the earliest Christian writers to discuss Josephus were concerned mostly with *Against Apion* and the *Jewish War*. Origen and Eusebius are the first Christian authors to show unmistakable familiarity with the *Antiquities*,[54] and Porphyry is the only pagan author who does. The full extent of Eusebius' influence on both Christian interpretation of Josephus and on the transmission of Josephus' text remains an open question. In the particular case of the *Testimonium*, however, it seems very likely that Eusebius' work influenced the transmission of the Greek manuscripts of Book XVIII of the *Antiquities*.

---

[52] Whealey 2002:34–35.

[53] Translation Thackeray 1930:643.

[54] Whealey 2003:1–29, especially 11–12, though allowing for the possible exception of a fragment of Irenaeus. Admittedly, Whealey's case may be overstated. In particular, the theory recently revived by Steve Mason (2001:251–295) and Richard Pervo (2009:12) that the author of Luke-Acts may have known the *Antiquities* is a possibility. Nevertheless, the *Antiquities* was hardly a well known text before Eusebius.

# Works Cited

## Primary Sources

Eusebius. *Church History, Life of Constantine the Great, and Oration in Praise of Constantine. A Revised Translation, with Prolegomena and Notes.* 1890, repr. 2004. Ernest Cushing Richardson, trans. Nicene and Post-Nicene Fathers, Second Series, v.1, ed. Philip Schaff and Henry Wace. Peabody, MA.

Eusebius. *Ecclesiastical History: Books I–V.* 1926. K. Lake, ed. Cambridge, MA.

Eusebius. *Life of Constantine.* 1999. A. Cameron and S.G. Hall, eds. Oxford.

Eusebius von Caesarea. *De Vita Constantini. Über das Leben Konstantins.* 2007. B Bleckman and H. Schneider. Fontes Christiani. Turnhout.

Josephus. *Jewish Antiquities: Books 1–IV.* 1930. H. Thackeray, ed. Cambridge, MA.

Porphyrius. *Fragmenta.* 1993. A. Smith, ed. Stuttgart.

## Secondary Sources

Bardet, S. 2002. *Le Testimonium Flavianum: Examen historique considérations historiographiques.* Paris.

Barett, C. K. 1994. *Acts: Volume I: I–XIV.* Edinburgh.

Bauer, W. 1909. *Das Leben Jesu im Zeitalter der neutestamentlichen Apokryphen.* Tübingen.

Birdsall, N. 1984–1985. "The Continuing Enigma of Josephus's Testimony about Jesus." *Bulletin of the John Rylands Library of Manchester* 67:609–622.

Digeser, E. 2000. *The Making of a Christian Empire: Lactantius and Rome.* Ithaca.

Dubarle, A. M. 1977. "Le Témoignage de Josèphe sur Jésus d'après des publications récentes." *Revue biblique* 84:28–58.

Feldman, L. H. 2012. "On the Authenticity of the Testimonium Flavianum Attributed to Josephus." In *New Perspectives on Jewish-Christian Relations,* ed. E. Carlebach and J. Schachter, 13–30. Leiden.

Inowlocki, S. 2006. *Eusebius and the Jewish Authors: His Citation Technique in an Apologetic Context.* Leiden.

Kofsky, A. 2002. *Eusebius of Caesarea Against Paganism.* Boston and Leiden.

Mason, S. 2003. *Josephus and the New Testament.* Peabody, MA.

Meier, J. 1991. *A Marginal Jew. Volume 1: Rethinking the Historical Jesus.* New York.

———. 1994. *A Marginal Jew. Volume 2: Mentor, Message, and Miracles.* New York.

Morlet, S. 2009. *La Démonstration Évangélique d'Eusèbe de Césarée: Étude sur l'apologétique chrétienne à l'époque de Constantin.* Paris.

Olson, K. 1999. "Eusebius and the Testimonium Flavianum." *Catholic Biblical Quarterly* 61:305–322.

Paget, J. C. 2001. "Some Observations on Josephus and Christianity." *Journal of Theological Studies* 52:539–624.

Pervo, R. 2009. *Acts: A Commentary*. Minneapolis.

Runia, D. 1996. "Caesarea Maritima and the Survival of Hellenistic Jewish Literature." In *Caesarea Maritima: A Retrospective after Two Millenia*, ed. A. Raban and K. Holum, 476–495. Leiden.

Sanford, E. 1935. "Propaganda and Censorship in the Transmission of Josephus." *Transactions and Proceedings of the American Philological Association* 66:127–145.

Schott, J. 2005. "Porphyry on Christians and Others: 'Barbarian Wisdom', Identity Politics, and Anti-Christian Polemics on the Eve of the Great Persecution." *Journal of Early Christian Studies* 13.3:277–314.

———. 2008. *Christianity, Empire and the Making of Religion in Late Antiquity*. Philadelphia.

Schreckenberg, H. 1972. *Die Flavius-Josephus-Tradition in Antike und Mittelalter*. Leiden.

Schwartz, D. 2002. "Should Josephus Have Ignored the Christians?" In *Ethos und Identität: Einheit und Vielfalt des Judentums in hellenistisch-römischer Zeit*, ed. M. Konradt and U. Steinert, 165–178. Paderborn/München/Wien/Zürich.

Simmons, M. 1995. *Arnobius of Sicca*. Oxford.

Whealey, A. 2003. *Josephus on Jesus: The Testimonium Flavianum Controversy from Late Antiquity to Modern Times*. New York.

———. 2007. "Josephus, Eusebius of Caesarea, and the *Testimonium Flavianum*." In *Josephus und das Neue Testament*, ed. C. Böttrich and Jenz Herzer, 73–116. Tübingen.

Wilken, R. 1978. "Pagan Criticism of Christianity: Greek Religion and Christian Faith." In *Early Christian Literature and the Classical Intellectual Tradition*, ed. W. Schoedel and R. Wilken, 117–134. Paris.

———. 2003. *The Christians as the Romans Saw Them*. New Haven and London.

# 6

# Propaganda Against Propaganda

## Revisiting Eusebius' Use of the Figure of Moses in the *Life of Constantine*

### FINN DAMGAARD

## Introduction

IN THE LAST TWO DECADES there has been an increasing interest in the literary aspects of the *Life of Constantine* (VC) and a number of recent studies have touched on Eusebius' use of the figure of Moses in this work.[1] In the introduction and commentary to their translation, Averil Cameron and Stuart G. Hall show a keen interest in the parallels between Constantine and Moses and even call these parallels "the most obvious device used by Eusebius in the *Life of Constantine* to bring home his ideological message."[2] In a similar way, Claudia Rapp has called these parallels a *Leitmotif* in the work.[3] Several recent studies

---

[1]  The present article reproduces parts of a chapter in my forthcoming book, Damgaard 2013.

[2]  Cameron and Hall 1999:35.

[3]  Rapp 2005:130. Of the four books that constitute the *Life of Constantine*, the comparison between Constantine and Moses is most pronounced in the first book and the beginning of the second book. In the latter half of the second book, the nature of the work changes radically. Whereas hitherto the work has comprised a narrative with next to no documentary evidence, more than half of the remaining work contains documents with only a minimum of narrative to link them. Since these documents are now usually accepted as mostly or entirely genuine (cf. Jones and Skeat 1954:196–200, Cameron and Hall 1999:16–21), we may assume that Eusebius did not shape the latter half of the work to the same degree as the first half. This may explain why the explicit comparison between Constantine and Moses fades out at this point of the narrative. Whether this be due to Eusebius' primary commitment to bring documentary evidence or because of the unfinished character of the *Life of Constantine* (Pasquali's thesis that Eusebius died before finishing the *Life of Constantine* and that the unfinished work was published by an unknown editor has long been adopted by most scholars, cf. Pasquali 1910) or simply because he ran out of steam, we cannot say. It may also be that Eusebius simply left it for his readers to decide. Since the readers have been presented with the comparison between Constantine and Moses in

have also sought to explain why Eusebius chose precisely the model of Moses for his term of comparison. According to Cameron and Hall, the comparison between Constantine and Moses "was perfectly suited to the work's apologetic purpose."[4] By portraying Constantine as the successor of Moses, Eusebius provided a precise and detailed demonstration of how God's plan for Christian government on earth was realized.[5] Michael J. Hollerich also stresses the apologetic purpose of Eusebius' use of Moses. According to Hollerich, however, Eusebius was not only drawn to Moses as a biblical exemplum for Constantine in order to stress his divinely inspired mission and his example of a godly life, he also invoked the figure of Moses in order "to sanction behavior that appeared to contradict traditional Christian views on the taking of life."[6] Taking a somewhat different approach, Sabrina Inowlocki has suggested that: "Eusebius' portrayal of Moses also testifies to the ambiguity of the legislator in Christianity."[7] According to Inowlocki, Eusebius skilfully exploits the ambivalence of Moses in order to achieve apologetic purposes. Thus Eusebius compared Constantine with Moses in order to identify him as a *figure de l'entre deux*. According to Inowlocki, Moses himself is portrayed as a *figure de l'entre deux* in Eusebius' thought as being both a Hebrew and the founder of Judaism. Referring to Eusebius' apologetic works, the *Praeparatio Evangelica* and the *Demonstratio Evangelica*, Inowlocki demonstrates that Moses appears as an ambivalent character whose different facets are exploited according to the context. On the one hand, the figure of Moses is continuously glorified in the pagan-Christian debate described in the *Praeparatio Evangelica*. On the other hand, the description of Moses is far less enthusiastic in the Jewish-Christian debate described in the *Demonstratio Evangelica*. According

---

the first half of the work, they are in a sense made susceptible to such reasoning and may find themselves continuing keying Constantine to Moses as the (sporadic) narrative proceeds. Thus, for instance, just as Moses became occupied with internal threats immediately after the exodus event (Exodus 15:24), so in Eusebius' own narrative, Constantine had to deal with the rumblings of the later internal Christian dissension, the Easter dispute and the Arian controversy. Also the account of Constantine's death seems to be wholly consistent with the narratives of the death of Moses. Both Moses and Constantine are depicted as enjoying good health prior to their death and as being of advanced age (VC 4.53, Deuteronomy 34:7) and both deliver a kind of farewell speech before dying, since they know that their death is approaching (VC 4.55.2–3, Deuteronomy 1:1–33:29); they are, of course, mourned (VC 4.65–67, Deuteronomy 34:8) and, more importantly both narratives conclude unanimously by claiming that its protagonist was without a peer (VC 4.75, Deuteronomy 34:10–12).

4   Cameron and Hall 1999:37.
5   Cameron 1997:161.
6   Hollerich 1989b:81; see also Hollerich 1989a:425.
7   Inowlocki 2007:244. Inowlocki relies on the work of Gilbert Dagron, who has argued that Eusebius was reluctant to present the emperor as a "universal bishop" by signalling the title as metaphorical by a "like" and emptying the words of its institutional sense (VC 1.44.1), cf. Dagron 1996:133–134.

to Inowlocki, Eusebius thus implicitly identifies Constantine as a *figure de l'entre deux* by choosing Moses as an *exemplum* for Constantine.

What is common to these suggestions is that they all take for granted that the comparison with Moses was invented by Eusebius himself. In this article, I shall suggest another approach, namely that it was actually Constantine (or his near advisers) who originally fabricated the comparison with Moses as part of his propaganda. As we shall see, Eusebius' use of the comparison probably reuses much material from Constantine's Moses propaganda, but he also seems to have reshaped some parts of it in order to promote his own interests. Moreover, I shall argue that Philo's portrait of Moses as a model ruler in his *Life of Moses* was an important source for Eusebius' idealized portrait of Constantine and his revision of Constantine's Moses propaganda.

## Moses in Constantine's own Political Propaganda

Interestingly, it is in the speech that Eusebius attaches to the *Life of Constantine* that we come upon Constantine's own use of Moses. In order to support his paraphrase of Constantine's speeches (VC 4.29.2–5), Eusebius promises to append to the *Life of Constantine* an example of one of the emperor's own speeches which he refers to as "To the Assembly of the Saints" (VC 4.32).[8] The authenticity of the speech was long in doubt, but is now generally considered to be authentic by the majority of scholars.[9] The speech seems to address a Christian audience—most likely bishops—but the date as well as the venue and occasion for the speech are still in question. I shall come back to this issue later.

As Mark Edwards has argued in the introduction to his new translation, the speech should probably be read as a "manifesto of ambition."[10] The speech does not have Christianity per se as its focus; rather Christianity seems a means of persuading the Christian audience of the emperor's right to rule. Constantine's appeal to Moses at approximately the middle of the speech is a particularly illustrative example of this. In his attack on the fallen ideologies of Christianity's enemies, Constantine suddenly hints at his own experience when he claims that he himself has been "an eyewitness of the miserable fortune of the cities [Memphis and Babylon]"[11] (*Oration to the Saints* 16). By claiming himself to be an eyewitness, Constantine succeeds in drawing a parallel between himself and Moses, since it was Moses who desolated Memphis when he:

---

8  I shall follow Mark Edwards 2003 and refer to the speech as the *Oration to the Saints*.
9  Dörries 1954:129–161, Barnes 2001:26–36, Edwards 2003:xviii–xxii.
10  Edwards 2003:xxii.
11  Translations of Constantine's *Oration to the Saints* are from Edwards 2003.

> [. . .] in accordance with the decree of God shattered the arrogance of Pharaoh, the greatest potentate of the time, and destroyed his army, victor as it was over many of the greatest nations and fenced round with arms—not by shooting arrows or launching javelins, but just *by holy prayer and meek adoration.*
>
> *Oration to the Saints* 16, my emphasis

Though Constantine does not explicitly cast himself as a new Moses, he seems to imply this when, later in the oration, he claims that everything has also turned out "according to *my prayers*—acts of courage, victories, trophies over my enemies" (*Oration to the Saints* 22, my emphasis) and finally concludes:

> Now in my view a ministry is most lovely and excellent when someone, before the attempt, ensures that what is done will be secure. And all human beings know that the most holy devotion of these hands is owed to God with pure faith of the strictest kind, and that all that has been accomplished with advantage *is achieved by joining the hands in prayers and litanies,* with as much private and public assistance as everyone might pray for on his own behalf and that of those dearest to him. They indeed have witnessed the battles and observed the war in which God's providence awarded victory to the people, and have seen *God co-operating with our prayers.* For righteous prayer is an invincible thing, and no-one who pays holy adoration is disappointed of his aim.
>
> *Oration to the Saints* 26, my emphasis

Constantine could of course hardly claim to have won by conquest without having "shot arrows or launched javelins," but he might have hoped that his audience would catch the parallel to Moses when he piously claims that his palm of victory was similarly based on prayers and God's co-operation. Also the fact that Constantine does not dwell on priestly or visionary aspects of the Moses figure, but rather turns the figure into a *military* and *political* leader suggests that Constantine constructed Moses as his own model:[12]

> What could one say about Moses to match his worth? Leading a disorderly people into good order, having set their souls in order by

---

[12] Note that this is in contrast to Raymond Van Dam who has recently claimed that: "Unlike Eusebius, Constantine had not promoted Moses as a biblical paradigm for his imperial rule" (Van Dam 2011:81).

persuasion and awe, he procured freedom for them in place of captivity, and he made their faces bright instead of blear.

*Oration to the Saints* 17

As Michael Williams has recently suggested, "It is difficult to read this as anything other than a kind of idealised portrait of the first Christian emperor—that is, as a portrait of Constantine himself."[13] Williams' suggestion is, I believe, right on target. There are, however, some rather important political motives for Constantine's use of Moses that Williams does not examine, probably because he regards the speech as a conventional defense of Christianity.[14] For if Constantine should be seen as a new Moses, how should Christian subjects then catch the spirit of their own part? An audience acquainted with Paul's use of the Israelites as negative examples in 1 Corinthians 10 (where the wayward followers of Moses were destroyed in the wilderness)[15] would probably not be slow to hear Constantine's reference to the Moses narratives as a dire warning to themselves concerning internal discord. Thus, Constantine continues his panegyric of his predecessor by describing how the Israelites "became superhumanly boastful" though Moses was their sovereign. If Constantine had only referred to Moses in order to legitimize his own rule, he would probably not have touched on the Israelites' acts of disobedience in the wilderness. Like Paul, Constantine seems, by contrast, to exploit the Moses narratives in order to control his Christian audience. Thus, when he reminds his audience that "no people would ever or could ever have been more blessed than that one [the Israelites], had they not voluntarily cut off their souls from the Holy Spirit" (*Oration to the Saints* 17), he makes a convenient agreement between the Holy Spirit and Moses, since it was of course Moses who had set their souls in order in the first place. By appending the *Oration to the Saints* to his *Life of Constantine*, Eusebius provides us with a fascinating glimpse of Constantine skilfully making use of the example of Moses in order to advance his own political agenda, namely to control the bishops.

## Playing Constantine's Game

The first time Eusebius himself invokes the Moses narratives in relation to Constantine is in the well-known passage in the ninth book of the *Ecclesiastical History* (HE) probably composed in 314 or 315.[16] In this passage, Eusebius compares

---

[13]  Williams 2008:29.

[14]  Williams 2008:28.

[15]  1 Co 10:5; cf. Heb 3:16–19.

[16]  According to Schwartz, book 9 and the beginning of book 10 (including the Constantinian documents) were composed in 315 (Schwartz 1909:lviii); Louth and Barnes argue for 313 or 314 (Louth 1990:123; Barnes 1980:201).

Constantine's victory over Maxentius at the Milvian Bridge in 312 with the defeat of Pharaoh at the Red Sea (HE 9.9.2–8). Though the passage seems to be Eusebius' own invention, he could actually have been inspired by Constantine's *Oration to the Saints* if we accept an early date of delivery. According to Girardet, the speech was delivered by Constantine in Trier or Rome at Easter 314.[17] With Girardet and Edwards, I take the field "prepared for battle" mentioned in chapter 22 to be the battlefield of the Milvian Bridge, and Constantine's reference to the tyrant of the most dear city "who was suddenly overtaken in a fitting manner worthy of his atrocities" (*Oration to the Saints* 22) as referring to Maxentius.[18] Though Constantine does not himself compare the battle at the Milvian Bridge explicitly with the battle at the Red Sea, he refers to the defeat of Pharaoh earlier in the speech and even in a context that, as we have seen, might be viewed as an implicit comparison of Constantine with Moses. As Girardet has argued, the speech was probably also sent out as a circular letter to all bishops in Constantine's part of the empire and therefore also translated into Greek at the same occasion in order to address congregations in places such as South Italy and Sicily.[19] If the speech had received such a wide distribution, Eusebius could have learned about it as he composed the ninth book of the *Ecclesiastical History*.[20] Eusebius' comparison of Constantine's victory at the Milvian Bridge with the battle at the Red Sea might thus develop a potential in Constantine's own speech.[21] However, while Constantine would probably approve Eusebius' comparison in the *Ecclesiastical History* (and perhaps even regret that he had not developed it himself), I shall argue that not all Eusebius' parallels between Constantine and Moses in the *Life of Constantine* would play Constantine's game. On the contrary, some of Eusebius' parallels might be read as an attempt to turn Constantine's own Moses propaganda upside down.

---

[17] Girardet 2007:78. Edwards has also argued for an early date of delivery (Edwards 2003:xxix). See also Kurfess 1950:164–165.

[18] Giradet 2007:76–77; Edwards 2003:xxviii–xxix.

[19] Girardet 2007:79.

[20] The speech was not the only document that Eusebius had obtained a copy of quickly. As normally pointed out, the six Constantinian documents that he quotes in book 10 of the *Ecclesiastical History* may also have had a rapid transmission. If book 9 was composed at the same time as the beginning of book 10, such as Schwartz argued, Eusebius may have received the speech together with the other Constantinian documents. Concerning the provenance of Eusebius' copies of the six Constantinian documents and their translation, see Carotenuto 2002:56–71.

[21] Just as Constantine does in the speech (*Oration to the Saints* 22), Eusebius also calls Maxentius a tyrant, and in so doing Eusebius recasts Maxentius as a new pharaoh (compare *Ecclesiastical History* 9.9.4 and 9.9.8). Concerning Eusebius' use of the Greek word *tyrannos* as reflecting Constantinian propaganda, see Barnes 2011:55 and Grünewald 1990:68–69.

## Revisiting the Use of Moses in the Life of Constantine

Eusebius' portrait of Constantine in the *Life of Constantine* has often been seen as only an encomiastic portrait of the deceased emperor, and several of his comparisons with Moses in the *Life of Constantine* are certainly flattering. The comparison known from the *Ecclesiastical History* between Constantine's victory over Maxentius and the defeat of Pharaoh is for instance turned into an even more complimentary comparison, since Eusebius now compares Constantine explicitly to Moses (VC 1.39.1). Also Eusebius' portrait of Constantine's child-hood told in close connection to Moses' upbringing (VC 1.12.1-2) seems to be written by a servile panegyrist. Thus, Eusebius claims that Moses' youth resembles the youth of Constantine, since Constantine, like Moses, "sat at the tyrant's hearth, yet though still young he did not share the same morality as the godless"[22] (VC 1.12.2). Very little is known about Constantine's involvement at Diocletian's court and his role in the great persecution. The fact, however, that Constantine was present at Diocletian's court during the persecution may have given rise to Christian criticism. Thus, Constantine seems to make an effort to dissociate himself from the persecutors when, in a letter against polythe-istic worship which Eusebius included in the *Life of Constantine*, he stresses that he was just a boy (VC 2.51.1) when the persecution began—even though he may have been about thirty.[23] In his comparison of Constantine's presence at Diocletian's court to Moses' stay at the court of Pharaoh, Eusebius also seems to acquit Constantine of blame. Like the Constantinian letter, in his own narrative Eusebius stresses that Constantine was still young when he sat at the tyrants' hearth like Moses, whom Eusebius claims was still in his infancy (VC 1.12.1).[24] And just as the book of Exodus implicitly describes Moses as being in opposition to Pharaoh's policy, since Moses observed the Hebrews' toil and struck down one of the Egyptians who was beating one of the Hebrews,[25] so Constantine, says Eusebius, conducted himself in the same way as Moses (VC 1.19.1). Just as Moses withdrew from Pharaoh's presence because Pharaoh sought to kill him

---

[22] Unless otherwise noted translations of the *Life of Constantine* are from Cameron and Hall 1999.

[23] Barnes 1982:39-42. T. G. Elliott suggests that Constantine was already a Christian during the persecution and lied about his age in order to avoid answering embarrassing questions about the way in which he, as a Christian, had escaped from the court of Diocletian (Elliott 1987:425-427). See now Barnes 2011:46-60.

[24] Eusebius gives Constantine's correct age at his death, namely 64 (VC 4.53, see also 1.5). This age is, however, in direct opposition to the age given here in the VC 1.12.1-2 and in 1.19.1 (and the age Constantine himself gives in the VC 2.51.1), where he makes Constantine younger than he actually was. The emphasis on youth at the accession and advanced age at the death are both panegyrical *topoi*.

[25] Exodus 2:11-12 LXX.

as a result of his murder of the Egyptian,[26] so Constantine "sought his safety in flight, in this also preserving his likeness to the great prophet Moses" (VC 1.20.2). Constantine's "flight" was due in part to the circumstance that those in power devised secret plots against him based on envy and fear,[27] since "the young man was fine, sturdy and tall, full of good sense" (VC 1.20.1).[28]

Eusebius does not, however, follow the lead of Constantine in all of his Moses parallels. Thus, for instance, his portrait of Constantine differs from Constantine's self-portrait in the *Oration to the Saints*. In his description of Constantine's miraculous vision before the battle with Maxentius, Eusebius claims that Constantine decided to venerate his father's God (VC 1.27.3) though Constantine claims that he had *not* been raised a Christian (*Oration to the Saints* 11).[29] Eusebius probably changed this, because he wanted to enhance the parallel between Constantine's vision and Moses' vision in Exodus 3:6 where God identifies himself to Moses as "the God of your father."[30] But there may also be another and more important reason for the change, namely Eusebius' wish to turn Constantine into a convenient model for his own sons. As most scholars agree, the *Life of Constantine* should probably be read as a "mirror for princes." Perhaps Eusebius, who had recently hymned Constantine (as he himself notes in the very first lines of the work, cf. VC 1.1.1), might even have planned to take

---

[26] Exodus 2:15.

[27] It seems not improbable that Galerius, the junior Augustus to Constantius after May 1, 305, would have wanted to prevent Constantius' son from leaving Nicomedia and joining his father (cf. Cameron and Hall 1999:198). See also Lactantius' story of Constantine's wild escape, *On the Deaths of the Persecutors* 24.5–6. Since Constantine (together with Maxentius) had surprisingly been passed over in May 305 when Severus and Maximinus were named Caesars, he may have been seen as a potential threat to the new settlement. Eusebius, however, obscures any sign of ambition on Constantine's part and claims that it was God who revealed the danger to him and that God intended that Constantine should succeed his father (VC 1.20.2)

[28] In his description of Constantine's character, Eusebius claims that he himself had known Constantine as one with "an imperial quality of mind" (VC 1.19.1) when he travelled through Palestine in the company of Diocletian (apparently in 301–302). Moreover, Eusebius portrays Constantine as: "In handsome physique and bodily height no other could bear comparison with him; in physical strength he so exceeded his contemporaries as even to put them in fear; he took pride in moral qualities rather than physical superiority, ennobling his soul first and foremost with self-control, and thereafter distinguishing himself by the excellence of his rhetorical education, his instinctive shrewdness and his God-given wisdom" (1.19.2). Eusebius' portrait is one of the ideal emperor where inner virtue is reflected in the outward appearance.

[29] In the *Latin Panegyrics*, Constantius is also presented as a pagan, see *Latin Panegyrics* 6(7).3.3–4 (from the year 307) and *Latin Panegyrics* 9(12).25 (from the year 313). On Constantius' religion, see also Cameron 2006:22–23.

[30] The change is somewhat inconsistent, since Constantine is said to be unacquainted with the cross in VC 1.32. As H. A. Drake has argued, Eusebius' concern here seems to be to make Constantine dependent on "those expert in his words" (VC 1.32.1), namely the bishops or clergy (Drake 2000:391).

the liberty to present copies of his *Life of Constantine* to the new Augusti.[31] In presenting to Constantine's sons a portrait of their father as a Christian emperor, Eusebius was in the privileged position that such a portrait was without precedent. Thus he was in a sense free to claim a particular action as characteristic of a Christian emperor and thereby bring his influence to bear on what did and did not fall within the sphere of Christianity.[32] When Eusebius implicitly claims that Constantine had been raised as a Christian and that he turned to his "father's God" at a crucial point in his career, Eusebius has probably the three brothers Augusti in mind. Thus, in Eusebius' version, the scene is laid for Constantine's sons imitating their father (like Constantine, cf. VC 1.12.3) in order for them to adhere to the God of *their* father.

Actually, however, Eusebius' use of the figure of Moses seems somewhat misplaced in this context, since Christians hitherto had used the figure of Moses to argue against succession through descent. In his homilies on Numbers (22.4.1–2), Origen, for instance, praises Moses because he did not pray to God in order to have his own kin appointed leaders of the people. The interpretation seems to derive from Philo's *Life of Moses*, which Eusebius had probably used as an inspiration for some of his comparisons between Constantine and Moses. Thus in the famous passage of the *Life of Moses* where God requites Moses the kingship of the Hebrews, Philo keenly stresses that Moses subdued his natural affection for his own sons and avoided promoting them as his heirs (*Life of Moses* 1.150). Eusebius could hardly have failed to notice the telling difference between Constantine's and Moses' attitude to dynasties. While Philo seems to reproduce and imitate a Roman aristocratic and senatorial opposition to dynasties probably in polemical contrast to the degeneracy of the Julio-Claudian dynasty, Eusebius, by contrast, flatteringly describes Constantine's sons as "new lamps" (VC 1.1.3) and "as virtuous and God-beloved sons" (VC 2.19.3) who succeeded

---

[31] If he had such a plan, he died before carrying it into effect. Eusebius praises Constantine's sons mainly in the introduction and conclusion to the work, see VC 1.1.3, 2.19.3, and 4.68–72. See also 4.51–52 for an account of their preparation for succession. The *Life of Constantine* seems to have been generally unknown in the fourth century and does not appear in Jerome's list of Eusebius' works (cf. Winkelmann 1964:91–119). As Cameron notes, the glories and the details of Constantine's life and acts were soon past history, since there was no particular need for verification and no particular interest in this type of work under Constantius II (Cameron 1983:87).

[32] As several scholars have pointed out, Eusebius may have worked energetically in the *Life of Constantine* to establish the rightness of his own cause and to claim imperial support for it (cf. Barnes 1981:269–270, Cameron 1997:166–168). Thus, according to Barnes and Cameron, Eusebius' account of the Arian controversy and the Council of Nicaea (VC 2.61–3.24) was designed to conceal any hint of Eusebius' own recent condemnation and his subsequent change of heart. Cameron and Barnes also call attention to the fact that Eusebius omits any reference to the change in Constantine's stance later in the reign when the exiles of Nicaea were recalled and the baptism of Constantine by Eusebius of Nicomedia whom he had earlier exiled took place (4.41–42, 61).

Constantine by law of nature (VC 1.9.2). Despite these panegyrical titles, the *Life of Constantine* reflects a latent sense of unease concerning the continuation of the Roman Empire under the direction of the new Augusti. Thus, for instance, Eusebius took pains to stress that the Augusti had really been instructed in "godly piety" by Constantine himself:

> Sometimes he [Constantine] encouraged them [his sons] while they were with him with personal admonitions to copy him and taught them to make themselves imitators of his godly piety. Sometimes when communicating with them in their absence about imperial matters he would express his exhortations in writing, the greatest and most important of these being that they should prize the knowledge of God the King of all and devotion to him above all wealth and even above Empire. By now he had also given them authority to take action for the public good by themselves, and he urged them that one of their prime concerns should be the Church of God, instructing them to be frankly Christian.
>
> VC 4.52.1–2

The agreement between this passage and the introduction to the *Life of Constantine* is rather significant. At the beginning of the work, Eusebius provided the reader with the basic threads of the work, namely the contrast between Constantine and his rivals and the likeness between the life of Constantine and the lives of the God-beloved men as recorded in Scripture—in particular, the life of Moses. Here Constantine is claimed to be a present "example to all mankind of the life of godliness" (VC 1.3.4) and "a lesson in the pattern of godliness to the human race" (VC 1.4.1). By claiming agreement between how Constantine had presented himself to his sons and the way Eusebius now presents him to "all mankind," Eusebius probably hoped to oblige the Augusti to comply with his picture of their father. For if they would choose another line of action than suggested in Eusebius' portrait of Constantine, they would find themselves in conflict with the way they had purportedly been instructed by their own father. From the biblical narratives, Eusebius would know that succession through descent was a difficult undertaking. However, by reusing Constantine's comparison with Moses, Eusebius was able to stress that good kingship was not based on descent, but on godliness. Ironically, Eusebius pays Constantine back in his own coin, so to speak. For just as Constantine used Moses to control the bishops, so Eusebius uses the same figure to promote his own view of how Constantine's sons should rule.

## Constructing a Christian Dynasty

As H. A. Drake reminds us in his *Constantine and the Bishops*, praise is a means of control, and panegyrics could be an effective "means of indicating the actions that would delegitimize an emperor."[33] Far from being innocent analogies, Eusebius' comparison of Constantine and Moses represents a wish to influence the Constantinian dynasty by controlling and defining the imperial role and by presenting an imperial model that the Christian bishops could support. According to Eusebius, a Christian emperor would, for instance, "shut himself at fixed times each day in secret places within his royal palace chambers, and would converse with his God alone with the alone (*monos monôi*, VC 4.22.1)"[34] and in so doing, he would imitate Moses whom the Lord used to speak with "face to face (*enôpios enôpiôi*), as if someone should speak to his own friend."[35] Though Neoplatonists such as Numenius and Plotinus had also used the expression *monos monôi* in relation to their metaphysics and mystical philosophy,[36] I find it more likely that Eusebius may have alluded to Exodus 33:11, given the fact that Philo also rephrases the same biblical passage in this way (*Life of Moses* 1.294; 2.163).[37]

Also Eusebius' emphasis on the close affinity between piety and philanthropy in government seems to construct an imperial portrait characteristic of a Christian emperor. As is well known, Eusebius puts great emphasis on piety in the *Life of Constantine*. According to Eusebius, Constantine's physical bearing

---

[33] Drake 2000:68.

[34] Translation slightly modified.

[35] Exodus 33:11 LXX. (Translations of LXX-Exodus are by Perkins 2007.) Interestingly, Johnson has argued that Eusebius uses the phrase *enôpios enôpiôi* in the *Eclogae Propheticae* (*General Elementary Introduction*) to lessen the spiritual level of Moses (Johnson 2006:118).

[36] Numenius uses the phrase in a fragment that is actually preserved by Eusebius himself in his *Praeparatio Evangelica* 11.22.1: "Thus, far from the visible world, must he commune with the Good, being alone with the alone (*monôi monon*), far from man, or living being, or any body, small or great, in an inexpressible, indefinable, immediately divine solitude. There, in radiant beauty, dwells the Good, brooding over existence in a manner which though solitary and dominating, is both peaceful, gracious and friendly" (English translation: Guthrie 1987). Plotinus uses the phrase in his *Enneads* I 6.7: "So we must ascend again to the good, which every soul desires. Anyone who has seen it knows what I mean when I say that it is beautiful. It is desired as good, and the desire for it is directed to good, and the attainment of it is for those who go up to the higher world and are converted and strip off what we put on in our descent; [. . .] until, passing in the ascent all that is alien to the God, one sees with one's self alone That alone, simple, single and pure, from which all depends (*heôs an tis parelthôn en têi anabasei pan hoson allotrion tou theou autôi monôi auto monon idêi eilikrines, haploun, katharon, aph' hou panta exêrtêtai*) and to which all look and are and live and think: for it is cause of life and mind and being" (English translation: Armstrong 1966, my emphasis).

[37] Later Gregory of Nazianzus did also rephrase Exodus 33:11 LXX in this way in his *On Virtues* (*Carmina* 1.2.10.501–502).

was indicative of his piety: "his fear and reverence for God [. . .] was shown by his eyes, which were cast down, the blush on his face, his gait, and the rest of his appearance" (VC 3.10.4). His piety led him to write statutes forbidding private sacrifice and favoring the building of churches (VC 2.45.1–2) and to repeal a law that had forbidden childless couples to inherit property (VC 4.26.2). He piously acknowledged God as the author of victory at his *adventus* into Rome (VC 1.39.3, see also 1.41.1–2, 46; 2.19.2; 3.72; 4.19); and at the end of the work, Eusebius claims that no other Roman emperor could be compared with him in exceeding godly piety (VC 4.75). In close connection with Constantine's piety, Eusebius also stresses his philanthropy. According to Eusebius, Constantine:

> [. . .] traveled every virtuous road and took pride in fruits of piety (*eusebeias*) of every kind. By the magnanimity of his helpful actions he enslaved those who knew him, and ruled by humane (*philanthrôpias*) laws, making his government agreeable and much prayed for by the governed.

VC 1.9.1

Similarly, Eusebius later claims that Constantine's decrees were not only full of philanthropy: they were also a token of his piety towards God (VC 2.20.1). In sum, philanthropy is said to have been Constantine's most conspicuous quality (VC 4.54.1).

Though both virtues are, of course, stock virtues in encomiastic literature of antiquity, the insistence on the close affinity between them cannot be found in other ancient writers such as, for instance, Plutarch, who is otherwise well known for his extensive reference to philanthropy.[38] In his insistence on the centrality of these virtues in government, Eusebius probably again constructs Constantine as a new Moses. Indeed, Philo had also singled out Moses as the one who has embodied both virtues to the highest degree.[39] According to Philo, piety and philanthropy are the queens of virtue (*On the Virtues* 95) and Philo stresses time and again how essential they are to the Mosaic legislation (*On the Virtues* 51–174).[40] Thus, in the *Life of Moses*, he claims that Moses was the most pious of men ever born (*Life of Moses* 2.192; see also 1.198; 2.66); and, as for philanthropy,

---

[38] I have only found one reference in which Plutarch mentions philanthropy and piety in close connection, namely in his *On the Fortune of Alexander*. In enumerating Alexander's virtues, Plutarch mentions among other things philanthropy and piety, but does not link them in any substantial way (Plutarch *Moralia* 342F). On philanthropy in the writings of Plutarch, see Hirzel 1912:23–32, Ruiter 2004:824–839, Hubert 1961:164–175.

[39] See also Veldhuizen 1985:215–224.

[40] For Philo's use of piety and philanthropy, see for instance Sterling 2006:103–123, Winston 1984:372–416.

Philo asserts that Moses was the best of all lawgivers in all countries (*Life of Moses* 2.12) because he acquired all the legislative virtues, among which philanthropy is the one mentioned first (*Life of Moses* 2.9). In the inquiry devoted to philanthropy in *On the Virtues* (51–174), which Philo regarded as a supplement to the *Life of Moses* (*On the Virtues* 52), he also stresses the connection between philanthropy and piety. Thus Moses:

> [. . .] perhaps loved her [philanthropy] more than anyone else has done, since he knew that she was a high road leading to piety, [and he accordingly] used to incite and train all his subjects to fellowship, setting before them the monument of his own life like an original design to be their beautiful model.
>
> *On the Virtues* 51[41]

Eusebius and Philo also both employ *topoi* typical of philanthropy, for instance the sparing of the lives of prisoners of war (*Life of Constantine* 2.10.1, 13.1–2, *Life of Moses* 1.249).[42] In addition, like Philo, Eusebius adds to the classical definition of philanthropy the idea of the king's kindness toward widows and orphans.[43] Eusebius' repeated references to Constantine's gifts to the poor, widows, and orphans thus resemble Philo's emphasis on the benefit of Moses' philanthropic legislation for the needy and unfortunate. For both authors, such generosity is equated with piety and philanthropy (*On the Virtues* 90–95, *Life of Constantine* 1.43.1–3; 2.20.1).[44]

---

[41] Translations of *On the Virtues* are from Colson 1939 (here slightly modified).

[42] The typical *topoi* of philanthropy are treated in the third-century treatise on epideictic rhetoric attributed to Menander of Laodicea. The treatise recommends dealing with the virtue of philanthropy in relation to the victories of the emperor suggesting the author of a *basilikos logos* to write that, "Justice is a portion of his philanthropy: for when victorious, the emperor did not repay the aggressors in kind, but divided his actions in just proportion between punishment and humanity; having done what he thought enough to chastise, and having stopped at this point out of humane feeling, he conceded that the relics of the race should be saved, partly in order that the remnant might remain as a memorial of what had befallen them, but partly also to demonstrate his philanthropy" (Menander Rhetor 374.27–375.4; English translation: Russell and Wilson 1981).

[43] Goodenough 1938:94–95.

[44] Gerald S. Vigna, who originally suggested that Eusebius depends on Philo in singling out piety and philanthropy as the main virtues in the *Life of Constantine*, argues that Constantine's almsgiving should be situated within his kingly function rather than his duties as a Christian, since he couches it in traditional royal language by referring to him as a philanthropist and a benefactor and by using sun imagery (VC 1.43.1–3). It therefore seems likely that this motif should be seen in the light of Philo's elucidation of Moses' philanthropic legislation as much as in comparison with the Christian theology of almsgiving (Vigna 1980:125–126). Philo and Eusebius also use the same imagery of Moses and Constantine, speaking of them as people who cared for the orphaned in their father's stead (*On the Virtues* 91, VC 1.43.2). See also *Praeparatio Evangelica* 8.14

In his use of Philo's figure of Moses as a model for his own portrait of Constantine, Eusebius shows himself to be more like an independent biographer than a servile eulogist. By using Philo's *Life of Moses* as an inspiration for his idealized portrait of Constantine as a *Christian* emperor, Eusebius revises Constantine's Moses propaganda in order to influence those with influence at court—not least Constantine's sons themselves.

## Conclusion

As we have seen, Constantine himself already appeals to Moses and the Exodus narratives in his *Oration to the Saints*. Eusebius was accordingly not the first to compare Constantine and Moses; on the contrary, the comparison probably came into being in Constantine's own propaganda machine. Eusebius, however, not only reproduces the propaganda, he also adapts the comparison to his own agenda. Thus, whereas Constantine used the comparison to issue a subtle warning to his audience of bishops concerning their divisive behavior, Eusebius, by contrast, focuses on the similarities between Constantine and Moses in order to control and define the character of the Constantinian dynasty.

In addition to the figure of Moses, the *Life of Constantine* also offers other comparisons with heroes of myth and history as is typical of the genre of the *basilikos logos*. Thus, Eusebius contrasts Constantine with Cyrus and Alexander the Great (VC 1.7–9)[45] and later with the rivals from whom he had delivered the empire (VC 3.1–3).[46] Apart from the tetrarchs who as Constantine's rivals could hardly be ignored, Eusebius did not compare Constantine with Roman emperors before him such as Trajan, Hadrian, and Marcus Aurelius, who all featured in Late Antique panegyric.[47] In this way, Eusebius divorced Constantine "almost entirely from the society which seemed to have produced him."[48] By consigning the history of imperial Rome to oblivion, Eusebius claims that a new

---

where Eusebius quotes from Philo's lost treatise on Providence to the effect that the title father was the most fitting for a king.

[45] The comparison with Cyrus and Alexander the Great conforms entirely to conventional practice. They are both mentioned in the treatise on epideictic rhetoric attributed to Menander as appropriate subjects for comparison in the section devoted to the *basilikos logos*; see Menander *Rhetor* 371.3–10; 377.2–10. As such, the choice of Cyrus and Alexander as exemplars appears somewhat vapid. Perhaps they have been selected in order to exclude the history of imperial Rome, as Williams has suggested (Williams 2008:50).

[46] Friedrich Focke notices in his excellent essays on *synkrisis* that comparison has almost become a mania in encomia. Thus, in the comparison between the tyrants and Constantine in the VC 3.1–3, Eusebius uses the pattern *hoi men—ho de* as many as fifteen times (Focke 1923:338).

[47] Williams 2008:51. Eusebius does, however, mention Nero briefly in VC 1.10.2 and he makes a general and brief comparison with "all the Roman emperors" in VC 4.75 (see below).

[48] Williams 2008:50.

beginning has taken place. Constantine and his dynasty were more on a par with Moses than with their Roman predecessors. Symptomatically, even when Eusebius ends the *Life of Constantine* with a brief comparison with "all the Roman emperors," he actually once again compares Constantine with Moses:

> He [Constantine] alone of all the Roman emperors has honoured God the All-sovereign with exceeding godly piety [. . .] and surely he alone has deserved in life itself and after death such things as none could say has ever been achieved by any other among either Greeks or barbarians, or even among the ancient Romans, for his like has never been recorded from the beginning of time until our day.
>
> VC 4.75

Compared with the Greeks, the barbarians and even the ancient Romans, Constantine was, so Eusebius flatteringly asserts, without peer; and yet, the message of the *Life of Constantine* is that Constantine was only second to none, because he actually followed in the footsteps of a figure equal to himself, namely Moses.[49]

---

[49] Cf. Deuteronomy 34:10–12.

# Works Cited

Armstrong, A. H. 1966. *Plotinus, with an English translation.* (Loeb). Cambridge, MA.

Barnes, T. D. 1980. "The Editions of Eusebius' Ecclesiastical History." *Greek, Roman and Byzantine Studies* 21:191–201.

———. 1981. *Constantine and Eusebius.* Cambridge.

———. 1982. *The New Empire of Diocletian and Constantine.* Cambridge.

———. 2001. "Constantine's Speech to the Assembly of the Saints: Place and Date of Delivery." *Journal of Theological Studies* 52:26–36.

———. 2011. *Constantine. Dynasty, Religion and Power in the Later Roman Empire.* Malden.

Cameron, A. 1983. "Eusebius of Caesarea and the Rethinking of History." In *Tria Corda: Scritti in onore di Arnaldo Momigliano,* ed. E. Gabba, 71–88. Como.

———. 1997. "Eusebius' Vita Constantini and the Construction of Constantine." In *Portraits. Biographical Representation in the Greek and Latin Literature of the Roman Empire,* ed. M. Edwards and S. Swain, 145–174. Oxford.

———. 2006. "Constantius and Constantine: An Exercise in Publicity." In *Constantine the Great. York's Roman Emperor,* ed. E. Hartley et al. 18–30. York.

Cameron, A. and S. G. Hall, eds. 1999. *Eusebius: Life of Constantine.* Oxford.

Carotenuto, E. 2002. "Six Constantinian Documents (Eus. H.E. 10, 5–7)." *Vigiliae Christianae* 56:56–71.

Colson, F. H. 1939. *Philo, vol. 8.* (Loeb). Cambridge, MA.

Dagron, G. 1996. *Emperor and Priest: The Imperial Office in Byzantium.* Trans. J. Birrell. 2003. Cambridge.

Damgaard, F. Forthcoming. *Recasting Moses: The Memory of Moses in Biographical and Autobiographical Narratives in Ancient Judaism and 4th-Century Christianity.* Frankfurt am Main.

Dörries, H. 1954. *Das Selbstzeugnis Kaiser Konstantins.* Göttingen.

Drake, H. A. 2000. *Constantine and the Bishops: The Politics of Intolerance.* Baltimore.

Edwards, M. 2003. *Constantine and Christendom. The Oration to the Saints, The Greek and Latin Accounts of the Discovery of the Cross, The Edict of Constantine to Pope Silvester.* Liverpool.

Elliott, T. G. 1987. "Constantine's Conversion: Do We Really Need It?" *Phoenix* 41:420–438.

Focke, F. 1923. "Synkrisis." *Hermes* 5:327–368.

Girardet, K. M. 2007. "Konstantin und das Christentum: Die Jahre der Entscheidung 310 bis 314." In *Konstantin der Grosse—Geschichte—Archäologie—Rezeption, Kolloquiumsband,* ed. A. Demandt and J. Engemann, 69–81. Trier.

Goodenough, E. R. 1938. *The Politics of Philo Judaeus: Practice and Theory.* New Haven.

Grünewald, T. 1990. *Constantinus Maximus Augustus. Herrschaftspropaganda in der zeitgenössischen Überlieferung.* Stuttgart.

Guthrie, K. 1987. *The Neoplatonic Writings of Numenius.* Lawrence, KS.

Hirzel, R. 1912. *Plutarch.* Leipzig.

Hollerich, M. J. 1989a. "Myth and History in Eusebius's De Vita Constantini: Vit. Const. 1.12 in Its Contemporary Setting." *The Harvard Theological Review* 82:421–445.

———. 1989b. "The Comparison of Moses and Constantine in Eusebius of Caesarea's Life of Constantine." *Studia Patristica 19:* 80–85.

Hubert, M. Jr. 1961. "The Concept of Philanthropia in Plutarch's Lives." *The American Journal of Philology* 82:164–175.

Inowlocki, S. 2007. "Eusebius's appropriation of Moses in an Apologetic Context." In *Moses in Biblical and Extra-Biblical Traditions.* Beihefte zur Zeitschrift für die alttestamentliche Wissenschaft 372, ed. A. Graupner and M. Wolter, 241–255. Berlin.

Johnson A. P. 2005. *Ethnicity and Argument in Eusebius' Praeparatio Evangelica.* Oxford.

Jones, A. H. M., and T. C. Skeat. 1954. "Notes on the Genuineness of the Constantinian Documents in Eusebius' Life of Constantine." *Journal of Ecclesiastical History* 5:196–200.

Kurfess, A. 1950. "Zu Kaiser Konstantins Rede an die Versammlung der Heiligen." *Theologische Quartalschrift* 130:145–165.

Louth, A. 1990. "The Date of Eusebius' 'Historia Ecclesiastica'." *Journal of Theological Studies* 41:111–123.

Pasquali, G. 1910. "Die Composition der Vita Constantini des Eusebius." *Hermes* 45:369–386.

Perkins, L. 2007. "Exodus, translated." In *A New English Translation of the Septuagint,* ed. A. Pietersma and B. G. Wright, 52–81. Oxford.

Rapp C. 2005. *Holy Bishops in Late Antiquity: The Nature of Christian Leadership in an Age of Transition.* Berkeley.

Ruiter, S. T. D. 2004. "On the Meaning and Usage of the Word 'Philanthropia'." Trans. and ed. M. Sulek. In *Philanthropy in America. A Comprehensive Historical Encyclopedia. vol. 3,* ed. D. F. Burlingame, 824–839. Santa Barbara.

Russell, D. A., and N. G. Wilson, eds. 1981. *Menander Rhetor.* Oxford.

Schwartz, E. 1909. "Einleitungen, Übersichten und Register." In *Eusebius Werke. vol. 2:3,* xvii–ccxlviii. Leipzig.

Sterling, G. E. 2006. "'The Queen of the Virtues': Piety in Philo of Alexandria." *The Studia Philonica Annual* 18:103–123.

Van Dam, R. 2011. *Remembering Constantine at the Milvian Bridge.* Cambridge.

Veldhuizen, M. V. 1985. "Moses: A Model of Hellenistic Philanthropia." *Reformed Review* 38:215–224.

Vigna, G. S. 1980. *The Influence of Epideictic Rhetoric on Eusebius of Caesarea's Political Theology.* Unpublished dissertation. Northwestern University. Evanston.

Williams, M. S. 2008. *Authorised Lives in Early Christian Biography.* Cambridge Classical Studies. Cambridge.

Winkelmann, F. 1964. "Die Beurteilung des Eusebius von Cäsarea und seiner Vita Constantini im griechischen Osten: Ein Beitrag zur Untersuchung der griechischen hagiographischen Vitae Constantini." In *Byzantinische Beiträge*, ed. J. Irmscher, 91–119. Berlin.

Winston, D. 1984. "Philo's Ethical Theory." *Aufstieg und Niedergang der Römischen Welt* II.21.1:372–416.

7

# The *Life of Constantine*
## The Image of an Image

Peter Van Nuffelen

IN HER 1991 CLASSIC, *Christianity and the Rhetoric of Empire*, Averil Cameron commented that Eusebius' *Life of Constantine* (also referred to as the VC) is "a work over-criticized on historical grounds and understudied as a literary text."[1] This statement still holds true. To cite but one example, Cameron's own brief but stimulating discussion of the importance of signs and images in the *Life* has not been followed up, not even by herself in the 1999 translation and commentary that she co-authored with S.G. Hall.[2] The complaint has been echoed since,[3] but apart from persistent attempts to pin down the genre of what is usually called a "hybrid" text[4] and to define the role played by Moses as a point of comparison for Constantine,[5] little work has been done to remedy this deficiency. The purpose of this chapter is to take a first step into that direction by returning to the issue of the omnipresence of images in the *Life*. As noticed by Cameron, images are ubiquitous in the *Life of Constantine* and take many forms, ranging from divine visions shown to Constantine, over *ecphraseis* of statues, paintings, and coins, to earthly signs of the divine. Many of them can be seen as drawn from the stock imagery of late antique panegyric, or can be related to Christian, indeed ancient, beliefs about the role played by divine signs in human action. Tracing the use of images back to specific sources and traditions does not, however, suffice as an explanation for their striking presence in the *Life of*

---

[1]   Cameron 1991:53.

[2]   Cameron 1991:61–64. A few more comments can be found in Cameron 1997:162.

[3]   Dräger 2007:380 ("der üblichen, Einzelstellen auf 'historische Steinbrüche' reduzierenden partikularistischen Betrachtungsweise eines letzlich 'poetischen' Textes.").

[4]   This debate, which picks up the older one about the authenticity of the *Life of Constantine* (Winkelmann 1962), was spurred anew by Barnes 1989 and 1994. See Cameron and Hall 1999:27–34; Cameron 2000; Tartaglia 2003; Bleckmann and Schneider 2007:27–38; Dräger 2007:384–385.

[5]   Hollerich 1989; Wilson 1998; Rapp 1998; Cameron and Hall 1999:35–39; Williams 2008:25–57.

*Constantine*, nor may such an approach do justice to the implicit, yet complex and dense, reflection on the nature of images that is developed by Eusebius.

My aim is in the first place to show how Eusebius uses a variety of images to generate meaning in his text and authority for himself as an author. This literary analysis cannot but lead to questions of a more metaphysical nature, namely to what extent Eusebius was willing to allow that images could provide access to the truth. I hope, thus, to illuminate his general attitude towards images, whilst at the same time contributing to a better understanding of the literary choices made by Eusebius in composing the *Life of Constantine*. To state it with the title of another of Averil Cameron's contributions, I hope to show how form and meaning hang together.[6] My main focus will be on the preface to the *Life* (1.1–11), where Eusebius' diverse attitude towards images is elaborated, and where the themes are adumbrated that are then pursued in the remainder of the biography.

Before I turn to the preface, I need to address briefly one last issue. One could argue that I lump together many different items and issues under the general denominator of "images." Whereas *ecphraseis* clearly belong to literary theory, they are not obviously related to visions of the divine, which are rather the subject of the history of religion. My response to this argument is double. First, all these different items share that they stand in a relationship of similitude to an object: this is evident for *ecphraseis*, but visions of the divine are only truthful visions on the condition that they bear some resemblance with the powers or representatives of God. Such a relational definition of an image is not a modern one; it was, for example, put forward by Augustine.[7] I therefore use "image" in such a relational sense: X is an image of Y if X imitates, reflects, depicts, etc., Y. Second, as we shall see, for Eusebius all the various forms of images are part of one reflection on their nature and usefulness. Focusing on just one of them would thus not allow us to grasp the full breadth of his thought.

## "Logos stands agape"

The *Life of Constantine* opens with a strong antithesis between speech and sight. The first sentence describes how until recently Constantine was celebrated by panegyrics, including by Eusebius himself. "But now our speech (*logos*) stands paralyzed." Then, wishing to say something: "it is at a loss where to turn, stunned by the sheer amazement at a wondrous sight (*tōi thaumati tēs xenizousēs*

---

[6]  Cameron 2000.
[7]  Augustine, *De diversis quaestionibus* LXXXIII 74.

*opseōs katapeplēgmenos*)" (VC 1.1.2).[8] That wonder is the ubiquity of Constantine: he himself is now in heaven, but through his sons he still rules the earth here below. The act of viewing is emphasized throughout the rest of the first chapter and the second one,[9] which declares that: "our speech is completely disconcerted (*ho logos hyperekplēttetai*)" by seeing Constantine still present after his death. Eusebius then depicts human speech and thought (the Greek term *logos* covers both meanings) as ascending to heaven and seeing Constantine in all his heavenly glory, united with God. The sight again transcends the capacity of human speech: "thought in its mortality (*hoia thnētos logos*) stands agape, uttering not a word, but convicted by itself of its impotence" (VC 1.2.3).[10] Human *logos* can thus perceive the wondrous sight of Constantine in heaven, but not express it: indeed, only the divine *logos* is explicitly said to be capable of that (VC 1.2.3).

That the *Life of Constantine*, a written text, not to say a verbose one, opens on a confession of the impotence of speech in the face of a wondrous sight is a carefully constructed paradox. Eusebius' confessed inability to express the greatness of Constantine in his heavenly glory is obviously also a theologically underpinned illustration of the panegyrical *topos* of modesty,[11] but, in the light of the recurring presence of the visual in the *Life of Constantine*, it points to more than that. The first two chapters of the preface throw up a major issue, namely the incapacity of mankind to translate sights, especially of the divine, appropriately into words. This seems, at first consideration, to stand in contrast with the apparent omnipresence of visual images in the *Life of Constantine*, thus again underlining the paradoxical nature of the preface.

A paradox is only an apparent contradiction. In order to show that the preface does not profess a total rejection of the power of visual images, we must take a closer look at the various roles images play in the preface and confront these with those used later in the *Life*. In fact, three different but interrelated kinds of images can be detected in the work, and to a greater or lesser degree, also in the preface. As any good preface, that of the *Life* can thus be said to introduce the themes of the work.

## A Cascade of Images

The first use of an image is covert but no less important. As we have seen, the *Life* opens with an evocation of Constantine's "absent presence" after his death.

---

[8]   Translations are my own except when indicated as drawn from Cameron and Hall 1999. For some corrections to that translation, see Dräger 2007 and Van Nuffelen 2008.

[9]   VC 1.1.2: *opseōs, emblepseien, theōrei*; 1.1.3: *sunorai*; 1.2.1: *horōmenon, theōmenos*.

[10]   Trans. Cameron and Hall 2008:68.

[11]   Cameron and Hall 1999.

The rhetoric of the opening paragraphs, with their emphasis on the wondrous sight of Constantine's continued heavenly and earthly existence, obscures the fact that the sons of Constantine are, at best, images of their father: Constantine is "paradoxically present with us, even after the end of his life" (*paradoxotata*, VC 1.2.1). As Constantine's absent presences, his sons are his image.[12] As has been underlined by B. Bleckmann, Eusebius' political goal in keeping Constantine alive—albeit it merely rhetorically—may have been to remind the new emperors to pursue the path of their father.[13] Changes of imperial rule could, indeed, lead to a change of policy and so soon after Constantine's conversion there was no guarantee that the reversal of fortunes that Christianity had experienced could not be turned back. Yet the conceptualization of the relationship between the father and his sons as that of an archetype and its images also has a purpose within the makeup of the *Life*. Indeed, if one looks closely, image relationships are ubiquitous in the preface.

The opposition between human speech and sight of the divine in VC 1.2 is further developed in 1.3 into a contrast between the eternal rewards of God and the frail and limited images mankind creates in painting or sculpture to commemorate individuals. This contrast, to which we shall return, justifies the superiority of Constantine as an image for all of us: because of his piety, he has become a model for all of us. As Eusebius states it, Constantine gave "a clear example to all mankind of the pious life (*enarges...paradeigma*)" (VC 1.3.4). If the first paragraph suggests a factual relationship of archetype and image between Constantine and his sons, now a normative relationship is suggested between the emperor and us: we should imitate Constantine so as to become his images. An additional justification is given further on in the preface: Constantine was made by God into "the image of his own monarchical rule (*tēn eikona dous*)" (VC 1.5.1).[14]

The density of such image-relationships in the first five chapters suggests that it is legitimate to connect them all, thus generating a series of images that cascades down from God: Constantine is an image of divine rule, his sons are images of Constantine, and we should try to become images of Constantine. Through Constantine, we are thus connected to God. Unavoidably, in such a presentation, the question arises as to the status of the text that presents us with this series of images. Unsurprisingly in the light of the preceding analysis, Eusebius presents the *Life of Constantine* also as an image at the very end of the preface: "Even if saying something appropriate about the blessedness of this man is virtually impossible and staying silent safe and without danger, I

---

[12]  For the Platonic idea of an image as an absent presence, see Ricoeur 2000.

[13]  Bleckmann and Schneider 2007:36.

[14]  For *eikōn* I prefer "image" to "model," as Cameron and Hall 1999:69 have it. See also VC 3.5.2, 4.74.

must set up an image in words (*tēn dia logōn eikona*) in commemoration of the Godbeloved man, in imitation of human painting, so as to acquit myself of the charge of sluggishness and laziness" (VC 1.10.1). The *Life* is thus an image in words of Constantine, and the last chain in a series of images that connects God, through Constantine and his biography by Eusebius, to us.

In this cascade, Eusebius has deftly combined two strands of earlier thought. First, it was common, at least since Post-Hellenistic political philosophy, to depict rulers as part of a cascade of images from the highest God down. The idea recurs, to cite but a few examples, in Dio and Plutarch,[15] and hence passed on into Neoplatonic thought.[16] The imitation of the divine as a characteristic of the ruler is a recurring element in other 'political' works of Eusebius, in particular the oration in praise of Constantine.[17] In the *Life of Constantine*, this is combined with a traditional idea from the biographical tradition, namely that the text sets up an image of virtue that the reader should imitate and even interiorize.[18] By combining both elements, Eusebius succeeds in raising the status of the *Life of Constantine*. The work is not just a biography of any virtuous individual, but it partakes in this cascade that comes down from heaven. As much as Constantine is helping to spread God's work on earth, the *Life of Constantine* helps in making it known and, by setting Constantine up as an example to imitate, it furthers God's rule on earth. A discussion of the second type of reflection on images that the preface introduces will help us to understand further implications of this combination of political and literary strands in the *Life*.

## The Power of Images

The presence of a cascade of images and the suggestion that we should imitate the image that is presented to us may seem to conflict with the confession of speech's inability to create true images in the first chapters of the preface and thus to exacerbate the paradox with which we started this essay. It may, however, repay to take a closer look at what Eusebius is saying there. As we have seen, human *logos* can see Constantine in heaven, but not translate that vision into words: only the divine *logos* can do so (VC 1.2.3). This statement rests on two assumptions that are rendered explicit elsewhere in the preface.

---

[15] Dio Chrysostom, *Oration* 1.44–46 and 3.50; Plutarch, *To an uneducated ruler* 3–5. These and other texts are discussed in Van Nuffelen 2011 with further references.

[16] O'Meara 2003:40–49.

[17] See Maraval 2001.

[18] Plutarch, *Life of Alexander* 1.2–3, *Life of Pericles* 1. Johnson 2004:255 plausibly suggests Plutarch as the direct model for Eusebius. Morlet 2006 points to parallels with Philo of Alexandria.

First, images created by humans are always imperfect and cannot be substitutes for reality. If this is true as a general proposition, this deficiency becomes most evident in the case discussed in the preface, namely the sight of the divine, which is perfect and transcends human *logos*—that is, speech and understanding. By stating that only the divine *logos* is capable of grasping and expressing divine sights, Eusebius points to a fundamental dividing line. The images humans can make (be they in words or in visual arts) are properly human: they are imperfect and perishable, and thus at best approximations. The point is driven home in chapter 3, where Eusebius contrasts human memorials to the everlasting memorial that is the soul: "For the nature of the mortals, finding a consolation for a mortal and perishable end, supposed to glorify the memories of the ancestors with immortal honors through the dedication of images (*eikonōn anathēmasi*)," such as encaustic painting, statues, and inscriptions. "But all of this was mortal and destroyed by the passage of time, inasmuch that they were appearances of perishable bodies and not from an impression of the eternal soul" (VC 1.3.2). The Platonic tone of that last expression (*athanatou psychēs apotypounta ideas*) cannot be ignored,[19] enhancing the emphasis on the true reality that constitutes the divine level of being. Eusebius echoes here a common concern that indeed can be traced back to Plato, namely that an image always represents a loss in reality: it never can be identical to what it depicts. As the preface suggests, this problem is most acutely felt in cases where one tries to translate the divine into an image, be it in art or in words. More radically, the ephemeral quality of every human image must also include the *Life of Constantine* itself: conceived "in imitation of mortal painting" (VC 1.10.1), it logically will undergo the same fate as painting and perish with the course of time. What reads at first sight as the habitual *topos* of modesty, namely that Eusebius is unable to say anything worthy of his subject (VC 1.10.1),[20] is thus philosophically underpinned by the fundamental distance that separates image and archetype.

Yet the awareness of the deficiency of images in relation to their archetype does not lead to a wholesale rejection of images, as the omnipresence of images in the preface and the rest of the *Life* shows. Indeed, the depiction of the ascent of human *logos* to heaven also illustrates the power of sight in contrast with that of speech. Human *logos* can perceive Constantine in heaven, but cannot express that vision. Sight therefore is more potent than speech. The power of the visual was recognized in rhetorical theory and most explicitly conceptualized in the mode of *enargeia*. For its most explicit theorist, Quintilian, *enargeia* is an enhancement of an essential feature of narrative, perspicuity (*perspicuitas*):

---

[19] Plato, *Theaetetus* 191D, *Timaeus* 39E.
[20] This topos is repeated often in the VC: 3.10.4, 3.15.2, 3.20.3, 3.30.1–2, 3.40, 3.64.3, 4.35.1–3.

"Instead of being merely transparent [as the latter], [the former] somehow shows itself off."[21] As such, it increases the quality of the narrative, for "it is a great virtue to express our subject clearly and in such a way that it seems to be actually seen."[22] The task of the orator is therefore to conjure up in the minds of his audience a truthful image of what has happened. "The result will be *enargeia*, what Cicero calls *inlustratio* and *evidentia*, a quality which makes us seem not so much to be talking about something as exhibiting it."[23] True *enargeia* is speech that transcends the limitations of speech and creates the illusion that one is an eyewitness. In making absent things present, it thus creates truthful images. As it was expressed elegantly by Ruth Webb: "L'enargeia verbale est, bien sûr, une forme de mimêsis, mais qui—à la différence des arts du théâtre et de la peinture, auxquels elle est souvent comparée—fonctionne en imitant la perception même. Plutôt que faire voir une illusion, elle crée l'illusion de voir."[24] Rhetorically trained, Eusebius was obviously aware of the qualities of *enargeia*. It can even be argued that he explicitly alludes to it in the preface. In 1.3.4, Constantine is said to have given "a clear example to all mankind of the pious life (*enarges . . . paradeigma*)" (VC 1.3.4). The term *enarges* is immediately echoed in the next sentence when Eusebius states that God himself has guaranteed that Constantine is a paradigm for all "with clear support (*enargesi psēphois*)" (VC 1.4.1).[25] The term *enarges* (visible) refers in the first instance to the visibility and clarity of Constantine as an example, but it is hard not to attribute a wider meaning to it and see it as an allusion to the rhetorical mode that creates almost real images in the minds of the readers: Constantine is as good an image as one can get of the pious life. Indeed, it is striking that Eusebius repeatedly takes as a model for his own writing the art forms that chapter 1.3 seems to depreciate.[26] This again shows the recognition of the power of the visual and underscores that their depreciation in the first chapter of the preface was based on the contrast with divine images. Human images cannot render the divine perfectly, but that does not mean that images cannot be extremely powerful in the human realm.

---

[21] Quintilian, *Institutes of Oratory* 8.3.61: *illud patet, hoc se quodam modo ostendit.* Trans. Bailey.

[22] Quintilian, *Institutes of Oratory* 8.3.62: *magna virtus res de quibus loquimur clare atque ut cerni videantur enuntiare.*

[23] Quintilian, *Institutes of Oratory* 6.2.32: *insequetur enargeia, quae a Cicerone inlustratio et evidentia nominatur, quae tam non dicere videtur quam ostendere.* Webb 2009 shows that *ecphraseis* are just one form of *enargeia.*

[24] Webb 1997:248. See also Webb 2009:105. "Enargeia is therefore more than a figure of speech, or a purely linguistic phenomenon. It is a quality of language that derives from something beyond words: the capacity to visualize a scene. And its effect also goes beyond words in that it sparks a corresponding image, with corresponding emotional associations, in the mind of the listener."

[25] See also VC 3.5.2, 3.15, where Constantine appears as an image of God.

[26] See VC 1.10, 3.16, 4.7.2.

Quintilian sees *enargeia* as a powerful tool in persuading audience and judge during a legal speech, as it puts the situation before their eyes and thus provides proof for the guilt or innocence of the orator's client. The highly visual descriptions of paintings, coins, and churches that we encounter in the *Life*[27] can hence be read as more than literary embellishments. In fact, they aim at displaying to the reader the proofs of Constantine's Christian convictions and his actions in support of the Church. Although these images are only traces of Constantine's Christianity, their detailed description suggests that they are true signs of the emperor's beliefs. Again, this is implicitly self-referential: by stating that the *Life of Constantine* provides an image of the emperor as a painting would do, the work is set up as something to look at, an imitation of reality, and, one could say, a collection of all the proofs of Constantine's Christianity one needs to see.

## Idols

The paradox with which this chapter has opened can now be explained. The concomitant awareness of both the deficiency and the power of images can be understood as different perspectives on the cascade of images. When looking downwards, the greater the distance is from the original, the less accurate the image must become. In particular, there is a qualitative threshold when images of the divine are concerned: as images are by their very nature the work of humans, they remain imperfect and may thus not do justice to the divine. At the bottom of the cascade, in our human world, images are, however, extremely powerful: making things visible is the highest achievement of an orator because sight is more powerful than just hearing. The power of the visual becomes evident in the famous vision before the battle of the Milvian Bridge: Constantine is shown a sign, and said to copy it, but the exegesis of it follows much later, and is, in essence, a secondary act to the belief in the vision.[28] Constantine even declares that he would not "worship any other God than the one he had seen" (VC 1.32.1).

The recurring references to images of Constantine, as well as the repeated *ecphraseis* of some of them in the *Life*[29] therefore point in a double direction. On the one hand, they are part of the cascade of images that makes Constantine omnipresent: just as his sons are absent presences of Constantine, so are his statues, coins and paintings. They remind us of Constantine. At the same time, such images confirm the omnipotence of God: Constantine being an image

---

27  *Life of Constantine* 1.30–1, 3.2–3, 3.35–40, 4.7.2, 4.15, 4.69, 4.72–73.
    See also 3.7.2 on the council of Nicea as "a replica of the apostolic assembly" (Trans. Cameron and Hall 1999:124).
28  VC 1.28–32. See also a later vision in 2.12.
29  See the references in note 26.

of God, they show the power of God, be it at a distance, in shaping the world according to his plans. On the other hand, these images do not simply display but also provide proof: proof that Constantine indeed converted to Christianity and that this has had a fundamental influence on the empire. They may be mere human fabrications, but that does not disqualify their power within a human discourse and for human perception.

The end of the *Life* therefore consciously concludes on a reminder of the numerous portraits of Constantine and his sons that were set up all over the empire, and in particular the consecration coins, depicting Constantine's ascent to heaven (4.72–73). It recapitulates the major themes of the preface: the continued presence in absence of Constantine and the fact that the omnipresence of such signs indicates Constantine's unique and enduring—and God-willed—success. So much is spelled out explicitly by Eusebius: God has "shown these things (*tauth'*) to us and our very eyes in the case of Constantine, who, alone among all his predecessors, clearly exhibited himself as a Christian" (4.74). Indeed, says Eusebius, the catastrophic death of persecuting emperors is sufficient and clear proof (*enargē elenchon*) of this. As we have seen, the term *enargēs* was also used in the preface to qualify Constantine as an example for all of us and its use here may be meant to recall in the reader's mind the suggestion there that the *Life* is a clear proof of Constantine's Christianity and his divinely supported success. Indeed, the initial *tauta* ("these things") refer primarily to the preceding section that refers to the portraits and the coins. But, capable of extension to everything said in the *Life*, it is also an apt conclusion to the work, which is as much an inventory of the signs that demonstrate Constantine's Christian success as a sign of this itself.

The contrast between Constantine and his idol-worshipping predecessors points to a third, and final, aspect of Eusebius' attitude towards images. Any Judeo-Christian discussion of images is valued, in that only images that entertain a relationship with a true object are acceptable. If ordinary human images are deficient because an image is never identical to its archetype, idols are simply false as they depict non-existent beings. Throughout the *Life*, Eusebius defines paganism as idol worship and underlines, as he does in the final chapters we have just discussed, their ineffectiveness.[30] Christian signs, such as the labarum, are powerful because they are true: they point to the real God who supports those who march behind it.[31] Eusebius can be taken to suggest that the church provides the criteria for determining which images are true and which are not. As we have seen, Constantine's vision of the cross leads to his conversion and

---

[30] VC 2.16, 3.26, 3.48, 54, 58, 4.15, 4.72. Similarly, pagan predictions of the future are dismissed as false in 2.4.3.
[31] VC 1.29, cf. 2.6–9, 2.16.

the acceptance of the God who has disclosed himself to the emperor, but the vision is also crucially confirmed and explained by priests, who set out the true teachings of the Church to the emperor.[32] In Eusebius' presentation, Constantine understands the crucial distinction between true and false images and Eusebius has him forbid the display of his portraits in pagan temples, "so that he would not be polluted, even in an image, by the error of what is forbidden" (VC 4.16). Constantine's picture of himself trampling a dragon, explained by Eusebius as an allegory based on Isaiah 27.1, is, in turn, a "true representation in painting" (*alēthōs entitheis mimēmata tēi skiagraphia*, VC 3.3.3).

The opposition between idols and true images coincides in the *Life of Constantine* with that between light and dark. The importance of the latter contrast has been noted before and needs no detailed elaboration here.[33] It suffices to note that from the preface onwards, where the sons of Constantine are described as "new lamps" (VC 1.1.3), the rule of Constantine is associated with bright light that illuminates an earth that for a long time had been in the clutches of darkness, namely idolatrous tyrannical rule.[34] In the light of this symbolism, it was a convenient coincidence—if not rhetorical invention—that Constantine died at noon.[35]

## The Holy Sepulchre

For Eusebius, the world is full of images that have a powerful impact on mankind. Some of these are connected to the truth, that is, via a cascade of images to God. As images are man-made, they always represent that truth imperfectly, but at least they have a connection with the truth, in contrast with idols that are false and dangerous: representing nonexistent beings, they exploit the power of an image to delude its viewers. As I have shown, the various strands of Eusebius' understanding of images recur repeatedly in the *Life*. In this final section, I wish to focus on one crucial passage in which they appear all interwoven: the discovery of the Holy Sepulchre.

Eusebius' account of how the grave of Christ was found is based on the opposition between true and false images. In graphic language, he describes how the impious had sought to give over the sign of Christ's immortality "to darkness and forgetfulness" (VC 3.26.1). Just as light shone over the grave when the angel turned the stone aside to liberate Jesus, so Constantine's cleansing of the place does away with the darkness that had reigned over it. The pagans

---

[32] VC 1.32.
[33] Tantillo 2003a: 48–54 and 2003b. A similar idea can be found in the *Praise of Constantine* 3.4.
[34] VC 1.5, 2.16, 2.19, 1.8.4, 1.41.1, 3.10.3, 3.26.4, 4.22.2, 4.41.1, 4.58.
[35] VC 4.64.

consciously erected a sanctuary of Aphrodite on the spot, but their dark designs were overcome by the divine light of Christ: Constantine ordered his people to do away with the idols, as well as all the earth that had been soiled by pagan sacrifice. The disposal of the idol led to the discovery of the grave, "the sign of the resurrection of the Savior." In that way, "the most holy cave became a resembling image of the return to life of the Savior (*homoian . . . eikona*)" (VC 3.28). The substitution of idols by a true sign of Christ is highly significative, symbolizing the transition of the empire as a whole to Christianity. It is also the substitution of a false by a true image: the pleonastic expression "resembling image" emphasizes that in the holy Sepulchre we are faced with an image that connects us with the truth of God. That image now presents itself as a "clear" proof (*enargē*, VC 3.28) to those that visit the place, "testifying by facts louder than any voice to the resurrection of the Savior."[36] The cave, as an image, is thus a strong proof for the truth of what is written in the Bible. The role of the cave as a true sign of Christ and of the truth of Christianity is enhanced by the fact that the discovery is presented, one can argue, as an epiphany. Eusebius twice emphasizes that Constantine's desire to make the site of Christ's burial known to all (*prophanē*, VC 3.25) happened under divine inspiration.[37] Indeed, it was not even Constantine's intention to find the cave. The finding of the Holy Sepulchre is thus at once a highly symbolic and an eminently tangible fact: in its materiality and because it is the image of the resurrection, the cave is proof of the truth of Christianity.[38] This interweaving of the material and the spiritual is predicated on the importance Eusebius ascribed to true images, that is, those that entertain a relationship with the truth.

## Conclusion

Averil Cameron has remarked that the use of images and signs in the *Life of Constantine* demands further study, as their omnipresence seemed paradoxical.[39] Indeed, Eusebius rejected the production of images of Christ in his letter to Constantia, a document that unsurprisingly resurfaced during the iconoclast controversy. Given its late first attestation and the apparent contrast in attitude with Eusebius' extensive use of images elsewhere in his writings, its authenticity has been questioned.[40] Nevertheless, it is now generally accepted

---

[36] Cameron and Hall 1999:133.

[37] VC 3.25, 3.26.6.

[38] It used to be believed that Eusebius distanced himself from the material world and only attributed importance to the spiritual. Such positions are reviewed by Cameron and Hall 1999:275 and conclusively refuted by them.

[39] Cameron 1991:64. The paradox is also noted by Johnson 2004:260–261.

[40] Murray 1977; Schäferdiek 1980; Sode and Speck 2004.

that the letter is a genuine piece by Eusebius.[41] Extensive discussion of this issue cannot be attempted here. Rather, I wish to argue that, even if the letter were authentic, the position it takes on images is not very different from the one I have detected in the *Life of Constantine*. In fact, the circumspect reflection on images we have recovered from the *Life of Constantine* squares rather well with the position found in the letter to Constantia. Indeed, it would be misleading to state that the letter rejects all kinds of images and that the *Life* embraces all of them. Even in the *Life of Constantine*, the use of images is limited on theological grounds in two ways. On the one hand, images are assigned to the human realm. As a consequence, they are imperfect and incapable of fully and truly reflecting the divine.[42] At best, they are imperfect approximations of higher truths.[43] This position is well illustrated by the idea we encountered in the preface that the human *logos* can ascend to heaven and view divine splendor but not express it. On the other hand, images are for Eusebius not fictions and only admissible on condition that they stand in a relation of truth to their model: if that condition is not fulfilled, as is the case with idols, false images are generated. This position is paralleled in Eusebius' *Praeparatio Evangelica* where he attacks Porphyry's *On images*, for stating that Zeus stands for the mind of the world.[44] The critique picks up the same two elements. It is impossible to depict accurately the divine mind of the world in a statue of Zeus, as it transcends our human capacity of under-standing: "what likeness can a human body have to the mind of God?" Pagan statues hence have to be fictions and thus idols.[45] The letter to Constantia makes a similar point, but now in relation to images of Christ. Eusebius asks Constantia what kind of image she had in mind: "the true and unchangeable image which bears by nature the likeness of Christ, or rather the one which he took on for us when he clothed himself with the form of a servant?"[46] Eusebius rejects both: the first one is impossible since one cannot depict the divine with human craft; the second one is undesirable because of the elevated nature of the incarnated Christ: "that what is mortal has been swallowed by life." Hence, it is impossible to produce an accurate image even of the human form of Christ. Moreover, even the incarnated Christ is God, and thus falls under the prohibition of images of

---

[41]   Gero 1981; Thümmel 1984; Stockhausen 2000; Gwynn 2007:227n5 and 6. Barnes 2010 argues that the letter is genuine but retouched after Eusebius' death.

[42]   VC 1.43, 47, 49, 58.4.

[43]   In a letter, Constantine states that one cannot speak worthily about divine mysteries (*Life of Constantine* 4.35.1).

[44]   PE 3.10.14–19

[45]   See Stockhausen 2000: 94–96; Williams 2007.

[46]   Eusebius, Letter to Constantia Frg. 7 (Stockhausen 2000:100). Trans. Schönborn 1994:59, slightly modified.

God expressed in the Ten Commandments (Deut 5.8).[47] Christ's incarnation is obviously a crux in Eusebius' thought about images, as it is the point where the human and the divine meet. Ultimately, however, it is Eusebius' emphasis on the divinity of Christ that rules out the possibility of representing him in a true fashion. Indeed, making a painting of Christ would reduce him to his human form and is hence highly undesirable.

If, then, human images are problematic when relating to the divine, they are very powerful within the human realm. This potential is fully and consciously exploited by Eusebius. The *Life of Constantine* does not aim at merely describing the actions of Constantine in relation to the church,[48] but at displaying them. The repeated *ecphraseis* of images in paintings, statues, and coins, themselves images of Constantine, bear testimony to this fact. Eusebius' own vivid style, as well as the numerous documents quoted, allow the reader to form a vision of the emperor's support for Christianity. The embrace of the visual and tangible is more than a choice for a literary style and a rhetorical mode. By inserting the *Life of Constantine* in the cascade of images that comes down from God, Eusebius can, at least implicitly, claim great authority for his own work. It is not just a biography of an emperor; it is the privileged access the reader has to the actions of an emperor who modeled his rule on that of God. Moreover, if Constantine is a model for all Christians, the *Life* is their access to that model. It is, Eusebius suggests, a good access: his detailed descriptions of the proofs of Constantine's support for Christianity put these before the eyes of the reader. The recurrence of images of Constantine within the *Life* can thus be interpreted as showing that the *Life* itself is, so to speak, a super-image of Constantine and really stands in a relation of truth to the emperor.

It has recently been argued that later antiquity is marked by a fundamental shift in the act of viewing: images came to be seen as a gateway to a superior reality and their contemplation could hence transform the viewer.[49] James Francis has suggested that it is typical for Late Antiquity that individuals could become "living icons" and thus function as images of a higher reality.[50] Eusebius can indeed be seen as part of that trend, in particular in the way in which he sets Constantine up as a living image of God's rule. Nevertheless, this emphasis on Constantine as a "living icon" is complicated in the *Life of Constantine* in two respects. First, there is the pervading consciousness that human images always fall short of the divine. It is indeed significant that, for Eusebius, Constantine is

---

[47] Eusebius, Letter to Constantia Frg. 8–12 (Stockhausen 2000:108–109)

[48] In contrast with the classical biographical tradition, Eusebius states that his subject are Constantine's actions (*praxeis*), and not his character (VC 1.11.1).

[49] Elsner 1998 and 2007.

[50] Francis 2003.

not a direct image of God, but of "his own monarchical rule" (VC 1.5.1). Secondly, the *Life of Constantine* is written after the death of the emperor. The image that is Constantine is hence only accessible through the traces that he has left: the *Life* collects images of an image. The omnipresence of images in the *Life of Constantine* can thus be understood as Eusebius' attempt to gather these traces and make them visible again for his readers, whilst at the same time making the point that only true images can convey some truths about their object. It is that true likeness of Constantine that the reader finds in the *Vita Constantini*.

# Works Cited

Barnes, T.D. 1989. "Panegyric, History and Hagiography in Eusebius' *Life of Constantine.*" In *The Making of Orthodoxy. Essays in Honour of Henry Chadwick*, ed. R. Williams, 94–123. Cambridge.

———. 1994. "The Two Drafts of Eusebius' Vita Constantini." In *From Eusebius to Augustine*. Aldershot.

———. 2010. "Notes on the Letter of Eusebius to Constantia (CPG 3503)." *Studia Patristica* 46:313–317.

Bleckmann, B. and H. Schneider. 2007. *Eusebius von Caesarea. De Vita Constantini. Über das leben Konstantins.* Fontes christiani 83. Turnhout.

Cameron, A. 1991. *Christianity and the Rhetoric of Empire.* Berkeley.

———. 1997. "Eusebius' Vita Constantini and the Construction of Constantine." In *Portraits. Biographical Representation in the Greek and Latin Literature of the Roman Empire*, ed. M.J. Edwards and S. Swain, 145–174. Oxford.

———. 2000. "Form and Meaning. The Vita Constantini and the Vita Antonii." In *Greek Biography and Panegyric in Late Antiquity*, ed. P. Rousseau and T. Hägg, 72–88. Berkeley and Los Angeles.

Cameron, A. and S.G. Hall. 1999. *Eusebius. Life of Constantine.* Clarendon Ancient History Series. Oxford.

Dräger, P. 2007. *Eusebius. De vita Constantini. Über das Leben des glückseligen Kaisers Konstantin.* Oberhaid.

Elsner, J. 1998. *Imperial Rome and Christian Triumph: The Art of the Roman Empire AD 100-450.* Oxford History of Art. Oxford.

———. 2007. *Roman Eyes: Visuality and Subjectivity in Art and Text.* Princeton.

Francis, J. 2003. "Living Icons: Tracing a Motif in Verbal and Visual Representation from the Second to Fourth Centuries C.E." In *American Journal of Philology* 124:575–600.

Gero, S. 1981. "The true image of Christ: Eusebius' letter to Constantia reconsidered." In *Journal of Theological Studies* 32:460–470.

Gwynn, D. M. 2007. "From Iconoclasm to Arianism: the Construction of Christian Tradition in the Iconoclast Controversy." *Greek, Roman, and Byzantine Studies* 47:225–251.

Hollerich, M.J. 1989. "The Comparison of Moses and Constantine in Eusebius of Caesarea's Life of Constantine." *Studia Patristica* 10:80–85.

Johnson, A. 2004. "Ancestors as Icons: The Lives of Hebrew Saints in Eusebius' Praeparatio Evangelica." *Greek, Roman, and Byzantine Studies* 44:245–64.

Maraval, P. 2001. *Eusèbe de Césarée. La théologie politique de l'Empire chrétien. Louanges de Constantin (Triakontaétérikos).* Paris.

Morlet, S. 2006. "L'Ecriture, image des vertus: la transformation d'un thème philonien dans l'apologétique d'Eusèbe de Césarée." *Studia Patristica* 42:187–192.

Murray, S.C. 1977. "Art and the Early Church." *Journal of Theological Studies* 28:303–345.

O'Meara, D. 2003. *Platonopolis: Platonic Political Philosophy in Late Antiquity.* Oxford.

Rapp, C. 1998. "Imperial Ideology in the Making: Eusebius of Caesarea on Constantine as 'Bishop.'" *Journal of Theological Studies* 49:685–695.

Ricoeur, P. 2000. *L'histoire, la mémoire, l'oubli.* Paris.

Schäferdiek, K. 1980. "Zu Verfasserschaft und Situation der epistula ad Constantiam de imagine Christi." *Zeitschrift für Kirchengeschichte* 91:177–186.

Schönborn, H. von. 1994. *God's Human Face. The Christ-Icon.* San Francisco. (English translation of 1984. *Die Christus-Ikone. Theologische Hinführung.* Schaffhausen).

Sode, C. and P. Speck. 2004. "Ikonoklasmus vor der Zeit? Der Brief des Eusebius von Kaisareia an Kaiserin Konstantia." *Jahrbuch der Österreichischen Byzantinistik* 54:113–134.

Stockhausen, A. von. 2000. "Einige Anmerkungen zur Epistula ad Constantiam des Euseb von Caesarea." *Die ikonoklastische Synode von Hiereia 754,* ed. T. Krannich, C. Schubert, C. Sode, 92–112. Tübingen.

Tantillo, I. 2003a. "Attributi solari della figura imperiale in Eusebio di Cesarea." *Mediterraneo Antico* 6:41–59.

———. 2003b. "L'impero della luce: riflessioni su Costantino e il sole." *Mémoires et études de l'école française de Rome: Antiquité* 115:985–1048.

Tartaglia, L. 2003. "La forma letteraria della Vita Constantini di Eusebio di Cesarea." *Forme letterarie nella produzione latina di IV–V secolo,* ed. F.E. Consolino, 7–17. Rome.

Thümmel, H.G. 1984. "Eusebius' Brief an Kaiserin Konstantia." *Klio* 66:210–222.

Van Nuffelen, P. 2008. *Review of Bleckmann and Schneider 2007, Bryn Mawr Classical Review* (2008.02.14).

———. 2011. *Rethinking the Gods. Philosophical Readings of Religion in the Post-Hellenistic Period.* Cambridge.

Webb, R. 1997. "Mémoire et imagination: les limites de l' 'enargeia' dans la théorie rhétorique grecque." *Dire l'évidence. Philosophie et rhétorique antiques,* ed. C. Lévy and L. Pernot, 225–248. Paris and Montréal.

———. 2009. *Ekphrasis, imagination and persuasion in ancient rhetorical theory and practice.* Aldershot.

Williams, M.S. 2008. *Authorised Lives in Early Christian Biography. Between Eusebius and Augustine.* Cambridge.

Williams, R.L. 2007. "Eusebius on Porphyry's 'Polytheistic Error.'" *Reading Religions in the Ancient World*. Novum Testamentum Supplements 125, ed. D. E. Aune and R. D. Young, 273–288. Leiden.

Wilson, A. 1998. "Biographical Models. The Constantinian Period and Beyond." In *Constantine: History, Historiography and Legend*, ed. S. Lieu et al., 107–135. London.

Winkelmann, F. 1962. "Zur Geschichte des Authentizitätsproblem der Vita Constantini." *Klio* 42:187–243.

# 8

# Eusebius' *Commentary on the Psalms*
# and Its Place in the Origins
# of Christian Biblical Scholarship

## Michael J. Hollerich

Eusebius' *Commentary on the Psalms* (hereafter CPs) is probably the longest book he ever wrote. It came late in his career, at a time when the Church was basking in the emperor's favor and when the party of those with misgivings about the Council of Nicaea felt that politico-dogmatic momentum had swung in their favor, with the rehabilitation of Arius and the ascendancy of Eusebius of Nicomedia at court. It is one of only two line-by-line biblical commentaries that he appears to have written. It is the first Christian commentary on the entire Psalter. And it shows Eusebius both in the full possession of the skills he had acquired during his tutelage under Pamphilus and refined in his many books, and also exploiting the resources in the library at Caesarea, the richness of which recent scholarship has given us fresh appreciation.[1]

All of this being so, one may ask why the CPs has drawn relatively little scholarly attention. Reasons are not hard to find. A major problem is the condition of the text. Like so much of the patristic exegetical legacy, the CPs has survived exclusively in the tangle of anthologies known as the catenae. The authentication problems are well known. Existing manuscripts may represent multiple stages of revision and editing, during which selections may be shortened, paraphrased, or combined with selections from other authors, and the authorship confused (just such a confusion has given us Eusebius' commentary on Psalm 37, preserved in the works of Basil of Caesarea[2]) or simply dropped altogether. The labors of several generations of scholars, mainly French, have shed much light on the landscape. We now have a new survey of the state of

---

[1]  Grafton and Williams 2006; Carriker 2003.
[2]  PG 30.81–104; cf. CPG 3467 (1).

research on the catenae available in English, thanks to the publication (in 2006) of the last volume of the *Patrology* completed by Angelo Di Berardino and his team of scholars. That volume contains a fifty-page survey of research on the Greek exegetical catenae. We are doubly fortunate that the lead scholar on that chapter was the late Carmelo Curti (d. 2003), who contributed a discussion of the basic literary problems posed by the catenae and a special section on the catenae based on the Psalter. Curti devoted a good portion of his life's work to Eusebius' Psalms commentary. His goal, announced years ago but never completed, was a new edition. Failing that, we at least have his republished papers and his survey of the manuscript remains in the *Patrology* volume.[3]

The edition of the Psalms commentary in PG 23 (and a small portion of PG 24) is basically the work of Montfaucon. Modern research has shown that the section of PG 23 commenting on Ps 51 through Ps 95:3 is certainly Eusebius'.[4] That material comprises almost 800 columns, about sixty percent of the volume. Substantial portions of the commentary on the first 50 psalms are also Eusebius'.[5] Also available in a sound edition are extracts in the Palestinian Catena on Ps 118 edited by Marguerite Harl.[6] Its value is heightened by the editor's thesis that the Palestinian Catena in its earliest form originated in the library at Caesarea, a conclusion partly based on Origen's dominance among the selections, followed by Eusebius himself—she notes the numerous citations of non-LXX versions in the Eusebian extracts and suggests that that was an important part of their appeal to the original redactors of the catena.[7]

A second discouragement to research may be the suspicion that Eusebius merely borrowed from Origen. No one would deny Origen's influence. Eusebius apparently knew two Psalms commentaries by Origen, neither of which covered the whole Psalter. The first one was written perhaps as early as 214–218[8] while Origen was still in Alexandria and dealt only with the first twenty-five psalms (HE 6.24.2). The second and much longer one was written in Caesarea late in Origen's life (Nautin has dated it to 246–248). It probably stopped at Ps 72, with

---

3    Curti 1989a; idem 2006. A team of German scholars at the academic initiative "Die alexandrinische und antiochenische Bibelexegese in der Spätantike" (under the aegis of the Berlin-Brandenburgische Akademie der Wissenschaften) has begun a ten-year project to produce a critical edition of the commentary. See the project's website: http://www.bbaw.de/forschung/bibelexegese/projekte.

4    Curti 1989c:3–17. MS. Coislin 44 is based on a direct tradition from Eusebius' actual commentary. Curti notes that it is by no means free from errors.

5    See the detailed review of the extracts on the first fifty psalms in Rondeau and Kirchmeyer 1967:col. 1689.

6    Harl 1972.

7    Harl 1972:90, 153.

8    The dating of Cadiou 1936, cited in Harl 1972:154n1.

an appended treatment of Ps 118, though the precise terminus is uncertain.[9] The confirmed remains of Eusebius' commentary extend to Ps 95:3, and the length and substance of its comments on individual psalms differ not at all before and after Ps 72. Eusebius did not need to depend on Origen for his exegesis, as the parallel case of his *Commentary on Isaiah* shows: he certainly used Origen's Isaiah commentary for as much of Isaiah as Origen had commented on (up to Isa 30:6), but his own commentary covered the whole of the book of Isaiah. In one notable instance in the Psalms commentary (see below on the question of the significance of the numbers of the psalms), Eusebius unequivocally separates himself from his master's opinion.[10]

There is also the fact that patristic exegetical works tend to be low yield for the kinds of interest that have typically driven research in the past. In the case of our bishop-scholar, there are, as we know, texts that have for a very long time drawn the attention of scholars from a host of disciplines. If we were to rank them, the historical works would take first place, followed closely by the Constantinian literature; then the apologetic writings; the polemical theological tracts; and, last of all, the biblical commentaries. Yet numerous publications over the last decade indicate the landscape is changing, and elaborate productions like Charles Kannengiesser's new handbook on patristic exegesis show that scholars—and publishers—have recognized the patristic exegetical legacy as a whole as worthy of and in need of (re?) consideration.[11]

My preference for reading patristic biblical interpretation is to treat it as an outstanding instance of Christianity's naturalization within the high literary culture of late antiquity, a process in which Eusebius and the library at Caesarea indisputably played central roles, as Megan Williams' and Anthony Grafton's splendid book has shown. By "naturalization" I mean the two-fold process of performing the sort of exegetical care with respect to a corpus of texts that was already being done on Homer, Plato, and Aristotle by the educated elite of the Roman Empire and the widespread shaping of the cultural imagination by the biblical texts. Elsewhere, I have sketched the basic contours of Eusebius'

---

[9]  On the complex questions surrounding the fragmentary evidence for Origen's engagement with the Psalter, see Nautin 1977:249–250, 258–259, and 261–292. Nautin identifies two true commentaries, the ones just mentioned, plus a collection of short explanations or *sêmeiôseis*, a word which Jerome translated as *excerpta* (Nautin 1977:259n73), consisting of various passages culled from throughout the Psalter; Nautin argues that Jerome's own *Excerpta in Psalterium* is heavily dependent on Origen's (cf. Nautin 1977:249–250 on the length of the Caesarean commentary).

[10]  The *Philocalia* (1.29) preserves a fragment of Origen's commentary on Ps 50, but what is said there bears no resemblance to Eusebius' treatment of that psalm—assuming that we can accept that the passage is really Eusebius'. Considering the emphasis it gives to *to theosebes politeuma* as an *eikôn* of the heavenly City of God (PG 23.441), I see no reason to doubt that it belongs to Eusebius.

[11]  Kannengiesser 2004.

work as a biblical scholar, in an article surveying current research on his many-sided engagement with the Bible. It looks especially at the literary, textual, and historical aspects of Eusebius' biblical scholarship and was based in part upon consideration of the sections of his Psalms commentary that can with reasonable certainty be identified as his.[12] My contribution to the present volume will consist of a general characterization of the commentary as I have become acquainted with it, under the assumption that it has not been a frequently visited text.[13] It is hoped that this introduction to the CPs will prompt greater appreciation of this important work and of its significance for the "making of late antique literary culture."

## The Date of the Commentary

The CPs is a late work of Eusebius', as proven by the mention in his commentary on Ps 87:11 of the *mnêma* (tomb) and *martyrion* of the Savior in Jerusalem, where, he says, miracles were being performed among the faithful.[14] This is a reference to the buildings constructed by Constantine over the alleged site of Christ's burial, sometime between 326 and 333. That is also the time when he was composing the *Commentary on Isaiah*, which can be dated to the years immediately after the Council of Nicaea.[15] The two works have a great deal in common, though the CPs, unlike the Isaiah commentary, shows Eusebius occasionally reverting to the subordinationist theological vocabulary that marks all of his books prior to 325.[16] Rather than indicating a pre-Nicene date, this could

---

[12] To appear in vol. 1 of Carleton Paget and Schaper forthcoming.

[13] A recent exception is Johnson 2006.

[14] CPs on Ps 87:11 (PG 23.1064a), already noted by Montfaucon, the original editor (PG 23.20b–21b), as a *terminus post quem*. On the Constantinian buildings, cf. Eusebius *Life of Constantine* 3.25–40, and the commentary of Cameron and Hall 1999:274–291. Montfaucon's late dating is followed by Harnack 1904:II 122–123; Wallace-Hadrill 1960:52, 57; Moreau 1966:col. 1064; and Curti 1989c:196n7. Rondeau 1982:66–69 presents arguments for a slightly earlier date and for the hypothesis that there were two editions of the commentary. Barnes 1981:391n38 also admits the possibility of an earlier edition before 324 that was later updated. Curti 1989a:196n7 comments that even if there was an earlier edition, the present version is the only one that has survived, and the datum of the comment on Ps 87:11 trumps efforts to lower the date on the basis of such things as an alleged change in Christological vocabulary.

[15] Hollerich 1999:19–26.

[16] Commenting on Ps 67:23–25, Eusebius several times calls the Logos "a secondary Lord" (cf. PG 23.705d and 709b, with reference to Ps 109:1) but never, that I can see, a secondary *God*, a usage that does show up in the pre-Nicene works, such as DE 5.Proem.23, which speaks of "the secondary Lord and God after the supreme Father." Neither usage, secondary God or secondary Lord, occurs in the Isaiah commentary, which was written in the immediate wake of the Council of Nicaea.

suggest that Eusebius was at work on the Psalms commentary when the political fortunes of Arius's supporters were turning in their favor.

## Purpose and Occasion for Writing

Eusebius only chose two biblical books on which to write line-by-line commentaries (though the fragments on Luke may represent a third).[17] Those two books were the primary Christian sources for prophetic exegesis of the Old Testament, and he returned to them repeatedly throughout his career. That tells us how profoundly he cared about the historical fulfillment of prophecy (*hê tôn pragmatôn ekbasis*), a concern that grew first of all out of traditional Christian competition with Judaism for interpretive hegemony over the Jewish scriptures. The ugly anti-Judaism of the Constantinian documents in Eusebius' *Life of Constantine*, which he wrote (and left incomplete) in the immediate aftermath of the emperor's death,[18] shows that the emperor's conversion may have only whetted Christian ambitions in the struggle with Judaism. But Eusebius' predilection for historically oriented proofs is a dominant feature of all his writings. It may have originated in the Palestinian setting in which he lived his whole life, and it certainly suited his scholarly training and temperament.

It also reflected his long preoccupation with Porphyry. One element of Porphyry's attack on the Christian scriptures seems to have consisted of denying that the psalms qualified as authentic prophecy. Porphyry apparently conceded that Hebrew prophecy could in principle be genuine, so long as the gift of prophecy was not thought of as the exclusive property of the Jews. In his *Demonstration of the Gospel*, Eusebius quotes an unnamed pagan, who is usually understood to be Porphyry, as saying: ". . . for the God of the universe . . . is God not only of the Jews but of all the rest of the human race as well. He does not care for some more than others, but his providence watches over all equally" (DE 5.Proem.3–5, ed. Heikel; my trans.). Elsewhere in the *Demonstration*, Eusebius defends the Psalter against unnamed critics:

> As it has been proposed by some that the Book of Psalms merely consists of hymns to God and sacred songs, and that we shall look in vain in it

---

[17] See Johnson 2011, for the argument that the fragments on Luke derive from an otherwise lost commentary on that gospel, rather than from the tenth book of the *General Elementary Introduction* (as argued by Wallace-Hadrill).

[18] Cf. Barnes 1981:265–271 and Cameron and Hall 1999:9–12 on the incomplete status of our text of the VC.

for predictions and prophecies of the future, let us realize distinctly that it contains many prophecies, far too many to be quoted now . . .[19]

This statement comes from Eusebius' preface to his exposition of Ps 40, one of the psalms of Asaph, who is credited with divine inspiration according to 1 Chronicles 16:4. To Asaph scripture also attributed Ps 73, which Eusebius construed as prophesying the destruction of both the first and the second temples (DE 10.1.6–10), and Ps 78, which he thought predicted the temple desecration and the persecution of Antiochus Epiphanes (DE 10.1.10–12). In the same way, Eusebius proceeds to read Ps 40 as a highly specific prophecy of Judas' betrayal of Jesus (DE 10.1.13–40). The whole Psalter becomes an interconnected skein of biblical prophecy fulfilled historically in both the Old and the New Testaments—and thus cements Christian claims to both.[20]

## Content and Character

The general character of the Psalms commentary resembles that of the Isaiah commentary: its laborious textual exposition based on the resources of the *Hexapla*; its theology, though with a more candid subordinationism; its anti-Judaic apologetic theses, the rejection of Israel and the calling of the Gentiles; and its constant attention to prophetic fulfillment, both in the history of Israel and the history of the Church, which to Eusebius is really the same history. Of the type of spiritual exegesis that Origen pioneered and that came to dominate patristic commentary on the Psalter, there is proportionately less. Spiritual exegesis was not, however, necessary in Eusebius' mind to justify his steady attention to the Church, "the godly polity" (*to theosebes politeuma*), which he regarded as the literal fulfillment (*kata lexin*) of biblical prophecy, just as he did in the Isaiah commentary. Finally, the CPs devotes a great deal of space to distinctively literary questions involving the authorship, the genre, and the

---

[19]  DE 10.1.3 (trans. Ferrar). Cf. also DE 6.18.11 (= frag. 19, Berchman), where Eusebius identifies unnamed skeptics as claiming that Zech 14:1–10 was fulfilled in the days of Antiochus, not in the coming of Christ and the destruction of the sacrificial cult of the Temple. For the identification of Porphyry as the critic, see Barnes 1981:363n96. For criticisms of attempts to see Porphyry as the anonymous critic, see Morlet 2009. Even if Morlet's caution is well placed, it remains clear from other fragments of Porphyry's *Against the Christians* that he was opposed to Christian attempts to interpret the Jewish Scriptures as prophetic of Christ or Christian events.

[20]  And beyond the New Testament into the Christian era: Hollerich 1989 proposes Porphyry as one of those who regarded the Exodus story as a "myth." Eusebius saw Constantine's victory at the Milvian Bridge as a typological fulfillment of the defeat of Pharaoh and his troops—providing perhaps the first of what would become many political extrapolations from the book of Exodus.

ordering of the psalms; perhaps Eusebius worried that these were areas that were particularly vulnerable to intelligent pagan criticism.

Of the Psalter as the medium of the prayer of the Church, we need only say the obvious: Eusebius, in common with most other Christians, thought that many passages were spoken by the Psalmist *in persona Christi*.[21] Ps 58:16–18, for example, represents words that the Prophetic Spirit led the prophetic author of the psalm to speak *ek prosôpou tou Sôtêros*, just as was true of Ps 21:23 (PG 23.549d). Words spoken by Christ to the Father are thus also the Spirit's way of teaching Christ's followers to pray, so that Ps 58:16, "I will sing your mercy at the dawn," anticipates the universal Church's morning worship every Sunday (PG 23.552a–b). To assist readers in identifying the various speakers and authors of the individual psalms, Eusebius created a tabular reference tool in the format that we are familiar with from his universal history, known as the *Chronological Canons*, and from his *Evangelical Canons*, a table of gospel pericopes for comparative study of the four gospels. Little evidence of it survives, although a version of the work may have recently been identified in a medieval manuscript preserved at Oxford.[22]

Of the theological content of the commentary, I will mention only the occasional Christological expositions that speak of the divine and the human in the Incarnation as such distinct entities as to appear Antiochene, if the anachronistic category may be permitted, e.g. the comment on Ps 88:6, in which Eusebius speaks rather casually of "the Son of God who dwells in him [= the Son of David]" (PG 23.1084c). Compare the similar language with which Eusebius comments on Ps 87:5: "For just as Zion, being the city of God, is the locality of the man who will be born in her, so too is the man himself a locality and receptacle (*dokheion*) of the divine Word who is begotten in him, as in a holy place and temple, or rather, as in a statue (*agalma*) and receptacle of his divinity that dwells in him" (PG 23.1049a).

Of the apologetic topoi, the calling of the Gentiles is fitted in wherever Eusebius thinks he can find a sufficiently universalizing or "open" passage in a

---

[21] For a fine recent survey of patristic exegesis of the Psalter, with special emphasis on its spiritual internalization as Christian prayer, see Daley 2003. Rondeau 1985:169–195 offers a detailed analysis of Eusebius' *méthode prosopologique* in identifying the various speakers or referents in the Psalms.

[22] See Grafton and Williams 2006:198–199, who cite both Rondeau 1982:71–72 ("a supplementary trace of the scholarly endeavors of Eusebius on the Psalter") and Mercati 1948:95–104, which latter work I have not been able to consult. We do have a short list by Eusebius of the subject matter of each of the 150 Psalms, entitled *Hupotheseis* ("Themes"; reprinted in PG 23.68–72). On the newly identified version of the Psalms canon tables, see the paper of Martin Wallraff presented at the Oxford International Patristics Conference in 2011: http://oxfordpatristics. blogspot.com/2011/07/martin-wallraff-canon-tables-of-psalms.html. His paper deserves publication, which I expect to happen in the near future.

given psalm. Of anti-Judaism there is all too much, though not in a measure that distinguishes the CPs from any of Eusebius' earlier works. The staple elements are all there: their rejection of Christ led to their destruction, and their "fleshly" interpretation of the Scriptures had led them into error and ignorance. More than once he refers to the Roman expulsion of Jews from Jerusalem after the revolt of 132–135 (at PG 23.541c, on Ps 58:7; also PG 23.753c, on Ps 68).

Just as in the Isaiah commentary, the Church understood as the godly polity is a significant subject in the CPs.[23] The Roman state is not, however: in one of his rare political references, Eusebius celebrated the end of "polyarchy," i.e. national and ethnic divisions and warfare, which he believed was prophesied in Ps 71:7 (PG 23.801d–804a[24]). Polyarchy, along with other lamentable forms of government like tyranny, democracy, and oligarchy, has been overcome by monarchy (*monarkhia*). That is a staple element in Eusebius' political theology. In the *Demonstration of the Gospel*, he had already interpreted Ps 71:7 in terms of monarchy's elimination of polyarchy (DE 8.4). But in the Psalms' commentary on Ps 71, it is the *Church* more than the empire that heals humanity's divisions: the Church, established in every city and land, ". . . is called the city of God because of the legal and evangelical *politeia* which she embodies" (PG 23.816d). This "legal and evangelical *politeia*" is not a reference to the Church's juridical establishment in the empire but to its incorporation of a dual way of life, one that is fitting both to the Law and to the Gospel. The Church thus recapitulates biblical Israel's two grades of piety, one for the masses and one for a spiritual elite.[25]

In the passages that refer to the godly polity, a common theme is the various orders (*tagmata*) that constitute it. The community is hierarchical, being governed by the successors of the apostles, among whom Peter was the *koruphaios* (PG 23.449c). But bishops per se aren't all that prominent. The true elite are the spiritual virtuosos, the ascetics. And when the Church's "archons and hegemons" are referred to, it is more in terms of spiritual advancement than of ordination to clerical office.[26] The first *tagma*, he says in one place, are the monks (he actually calls them *monakhoi*, adopting the word from Symmachus's version of Ps 67:7a). Eusebius cites four different versions, beginning with the LXX, which reads: *ho theos katoikizei monotropous en oikôi* ("God makes the single-minded

---

23  Hollerich 1999:165–203.

24  A passage that contains a quotation from Homer *Odyssey* i 23–24, on the location of the Ethiopians at the ends of the earth (PG 23.805b); see Johnson 2006:179.

25  See Eusebius' exposition of this apologetic motif in DE 1.8 and Hollerich 2002:172–184.

26  CPs on 64:14 (PG 23.644d). Eusebius' esteem for celibacy is well documented; see the previous note and also Eusebius' defense in his *Life of Constantine* of Constantine's repeal of the Augustan legislation that penalized childless marriages (VC 4.26.2–4; cf. the discussion in Cameron and Hall 1999:322–324).

to dwell in a house"). Symmachus has *didôsin oikizein monakhois oikian*; Aquila, *kathizei monogeneis oikonde*; and "the fifth edition," *katoikizei monozônous en oikôi*. The passage is worth quoting:

> And this is his [God's] first virtuous action, and indeed the greatest of the favors which have been given to the human race. For the first *tagma* of those who have progressed in Christ is that of the *monakhoi*. They are rare; therefore according to Aquila they were named *monogeneis* for having been likened to the only-begotten Son of God. According to the Seventy they are *monotropoi*, but not *polutropoi* [!—a critical swipe at the wily Odysseus?], nor in any other way fluctuating in their way of life but keeping only to one, and so have come to a pitch of virtue. The fifth edition calls them *monozônous*, 'those who journey alone,' since they were solitaries and as it were girded up for travel by themselves. Such were the first disciples of the Savior, to whom it was said, 'Do not take gold or silver for your belts, or a bag for the journey, or sandals, or a staff (Mt 10:9–10)'.[27]

Among other passages on the godly polity, I point in passing to one on Ps 52, dealing with the existence of two *tagmata* already in Israel (PG 23.449c), and another on Ps 86:3, "Glorious things have been said of you, O City of God," which Eusebius says refers to *to theosebes politeuma*, the Church spread throughout the world and the *eikôn* of "the great *politeuma* of the heavenly Zion" (PG 23.1045a). This of course is the great psalm text that gave Augustine the title for *On the City of God*. Eusebius is equally fond of it; note how he cites Ps 86:3 when commenting on Ps 71:16–17 (PG 23.816d) and on Ps 59:11 (PG 23.572b–c)—where he follows immediately with a reference to Mt 16:18!

The most distinctive features of Eusebius' exegetical production are his use of philological methods and material and his interest in literary questions and topics. Timothy Barnes' assessment still seems right: "Eusebius was by instinct and training a scholar; he became an apologist only because circumstances demanded that he do so, and his style of argument in apology and polemic continually betrays the biblical exegete."[28]

Citations from Origen's *Hexapla* are ubiquitous in the Psalms commentary, as they also were in the Isaiah commentary. A rough estimate of their respective frequencies shows that Aquila and Symmachus are quoted most often,

---

[27] PG 23.689c.

[28] Barnes 1981:164. That was also Carmelo Curti's judgment, expressed in an excellent survey of Eusebius' exegesis: "L'approccio filologico al testo è peculiare di tutta la produzione di Eusebio, dalle opere giovanili a quelle della maturità e della vechiaia, ma in poche è condotto con tanta acribià come nei Commentarii in Psalmos" (Curti 1989b:205).

frequently as a pair. An unnamed third version, which Eusebius calls simply the "fifth edition" (*pemptê ekdosis,* or *Quinta* as modern scholars have labeled it), appears half as many times as the first two. Theodotion, whom in the Isaiah commentary Eusebius routinely lumped with Aquila and Symmachus as *hoi loipoi,* in the Psalms commentary has retreated to fourth place, showing up less than a third as often as Aquila and Symmachus.[29] Once Eusebius cites "yet another version"[30] besides Aquila, Symmachus, and Quinta. That is presumably the unnamed "sixth edition" which in the *Church History* Eusebius credits Origen with discovering (along with still another, *seventh* version) and adding to the Psalms portion of the *Hexapla* (HE 6.16.2–3). In addition to the Greek versions, Eusebius frequently appeals to *to Hebraïkon,* "the Hebrew."

Two questions to ask about his use of the *Hexapla:*

1. What is the interpretive status of the Greek versions in relation to the LXX?

2. And what use, if any, was Eusebius making of the Hebrew?

I will deal with the second question first. His synopsis must have had a Hebrew column in Hebrew script, not merely a Hebrew text in Greek transliteration, because he frequently alludes to the "Hebrew writing" (*graphê,* PG 23.809c), the "Hebrew reading" (*lexis*), or "Hebrew letters" (*stoicheia*). Most often his gestures towards the Hebrew serve to verify that instances of *sôtêrion* in the LXX are based on some form of the Hebrew name for Jesus (although he is also interested in the Hebrew names for God as well).[31] He notes that the Hebrew original of Ps 52:2 (= Ps 53:2 MT) is verbally identical with the Hebrew of Ps 13:1 (= Ps 14:1b–c MT) because "the same words *and the same letters* are contained in both" (PG 23.456b). That tells us he is doing a painstaking check, letter by letter, of the Hebrew column of the *Hexapla.* Did Origen's commentary tell him this or did he discover it himself? Even if it is not his own discovery, the care to specify the Hebrew reading—in a passage in which Eusebius did not have an apologetic investment—is suggestive. We can attribute it partly, I propose,

---

[29] Theodotion's diminished significance compared to *Quinta* becomes more intriguing when seen in connection with Mercati's discovery that the Milan *Hexapla* palimpsest, which has five columns of Greek translations of the psalms (fragments of Psalms 17 through 88), contains a transliterated Hebrew column, Aquila, Symmachus, the LXX, and *Quinta*—not Theodotion—in the fifth and final column on the right. See Fernández Marcos 2000:212–213.

[30] CPs on Ps 61:5 (PG 23.592c).

[31] Including one instance when he knows that the LXX rendering of *Iêsouach* (to use the Greek transliteration) as *tou sôtêrion sou* reflects the addition of the pronominal suffix, and that the abstract noun *sôtêria* would be "the commoner form among the Hebrews," thus signaling (to him, anyway) that something or someone special is indicated by the more unusual *sôtêrion* (PG 23.440d, on Ps 50:14/Ps 51:14 MT).

to scholarly precision.[32] But it also reflected the motive behind the very existence of the *Hexapla*: to gain access to the Hebrew original as a necessary instrument for correcting the Church's own scriptures. That at least is what Origen gives as the purpose of the *Hexapla* in a celebrated passage in his *Commentary on Matthew*.[33] The project was controversial, which perhaps explains the rather different and somewhat defensive motive he expounds in his *Letter to Africanus*, where he says that his retention of the Hebrew text, even when it contained material missing from the Church's bible, was necessary for the sake of discussions with the Jews—it did not mean the devaluing of the Church's scriptures.[34]

Eusebius' practice regarding the authority of the Septuagint is not totally consistent with his theory, so far as we can reconstruct that theory. He certainly accepted the privileged status of the LXX, though in one programmatic passage in *The Demonstration of the Gospel*, he describes its status as a matter of custom:

> We must recognize that the sacred oracles include in the Hebrew much that is obscure both in the literal sense (*pros lexin*) of the words and in their deeper interpretation (*pros dianoian*), and are capable of various translations into Greek because of their difficulty. The Seventy Hebrews in concert have translated them together, and I shall pay the greatest attention to them, because it is the custom of the Christian Church to use their work (*têi tou Christou ekklêsiai toutois kekhrêsthai philon*). But wherever necessary, I shall call in the help of the editions of the later translators, which the Jews are accustomed to use today, so that my proof may have stronger support from all sources.[35]

In more than one place, he explains (or explains away) the obscurity of the LXX prophecies about Jesus as the result of an exercise in discretion (*oikonomia*) on the part of the Seventy. An example of this is his commentary on Ps

---

[32] He is not beyond a certain pedantic pride, which at one point trips him up. Commenting on the puzzling repetition of "Saba" in both Aquila's and Symmachus' translations of Ps 71:10 (=72:10 MT) as "the kings of Saba and Saba," Eusebius notes that the Hebrew has two different words that to a Greek ear are not easily distinguished because both begin with sibilants, *sheba'* and *seba'*. Unfortunately, he gets the letters wrong, saying that the first word begins with a *shin* (in Greek *sen*) and the second with a *tsade* (in Greek *sadê*). But the second word actually begins with a *samekh* (23.808b). See the discussion in Johnson 2006:181–182.

[33] Origen *Commentary on Matthew* 15.14, as cited and discussed in Fernández Marcos 2000:208–210.

[34] Cf. Origen's *Letter to Africanus* 5. See the comments of Nicholas de Lange in his edition of the letter (de Lange 1983:496, 500, and 535).

[35] DE 5.Proem.35–36, trans. Ferrar (slightly revised). Like Origen, he accepted the authenticity of the *Letter to Aristeas*, but also like Origen, he avoided the later elaboration of the legend of the mysteriously identical translations. Irenaeus, on the other hand, had accepted it, in a passage that Eusebius quoted in the *Church History* (HE 5.8.10–15). See now Wasserstein and Wasserstein 2006:109–112.

86:5–7, for which the LXX differs notably from the other Greek versions (and Eusebius usually presumed that that meant the LXX differed from the Hebrew as well). Recalling the Septuagint's origins in Ptolemaic Egypt, he argued that the Seventy had intentionally made their text "dark and enigmatic" because they knew their work would be preserved under foreign rulers (he mentions the foreign rulers because the LXX of Ps 86:6 introduced an anomalous reference to *arkhontes*). Predictions about Christ could not be too overt lest they threaten the powers that be, who were not yet ready to receive them. But when the time came, the verse that spoke of the Most High's registering of the peoples would then be seen fulfilled in the census that attended the birth of Jesus.[36]

In practice, Eusebius treats the *Hexapla* as if the whole synopsis were authoritative scripture. The LXX is the base text, but the versions are drawn upon for all manner of purposes: linguistic obscurity in the LXX, apologetic and dogmatic needs, or simply the desire to preserve and record the sheer diversity of witnesses. Scientific his practice is not, but at least it recognizes the difficulty of interpreting an inspired text if so much labor must be devoted just to the text itself. To further complicate the status of the *Hexapla*, the translators of the other Greek versions were believed to have been Jewish or Jewish-Christians, which in Christian eyes meant their work was compromised.[37] So Eusebius (and of course Origen) should be honored for his willingness to use whatever instruments were at hand to interpret divine scripture. It has recently been suggested that his synthetic approach was "a turning point in the de-canonization of the Greek Torah."[38] That seems overstated (certainly the LXX's place remained secure in the Greek East). But he does appear to be groping towards the position that Jerome would embrace unambiguously several decades later.

Perhaps an even deeper concern was at work in Eusebius' forays, however limited, into the Hebrew text. Pierre Nautin once suggested that Origen entertained the belief, acquired from his Jewish teacher (so Nautin), that the very letters of the Hebrew alphabet were revealed by God.[39] Did Eusebius entertain a similar conception, or at least feel compelled to pay it respect? It appears

---

[36] CPs 86:6 (PG 23.1049b–c). Cf. also PE 8.1. The Armenian translation of Eusebius' *Chronicle* preserves a more scurrilous explanation for deviations between the LXX and the Hebrew text possessed by the Jews of Eusebius' time: see Schoene 1967:I 84.22–35, 94.5–28, 96.3–5.

[37] See Fernández Marcos 2000:111–113 (traditions about Aquila), 123–126 (Symmachus), and 142–143 (Theodotion). The Christian devaluing of the versions because of their Jewish associations has recently been emphasized by Rajak 2009:310–311.

[38] Veltri 2006:56.

[39] Nautin 1977:268, citing a passage from Origen's first commentary on the Psalms, on Ps 1, as preserved in the *Philocalia* 3 (Harl 1983:260.1–13; see her commentary, 262–268, esp. 264n2), and Origen's comments on the parallel between the twenty-two books in the Hebrew scriptures and the twenty-two letters in their alphabet (cf. Eusebius HE 6.25.1–2).

that he did. Elsewhere, in his apologetic work *The Preparation for the Gospel*, he presented a philological argument for the historical priority of the Hebrew alphabet over the Greek alphabet, based on the fact that the names of the individual letters were intelligible as distinct words in Hebrew and that the words could even be clustered as intelligible phrases (PE 10.5). Hebrew, he said, has an exceptional "correctness" (*orthotêta*) in its names for things, befitting the language of a people whose very name is taken from "Heber" (cf. Gn 14:13), the etymology of which means "to pass over," from the things of this world to things divine (PE 11.6.36–40).[40]

Besides his attention to the actual text, a second literary preoccupation in the CPs is the status of the Psalter as a composite work. Eusebius devotes much time to explaining the ordering of the psalms and to establishing connections among them, based on verbal parallels, similar titles, and common authors or ascriptions (not all Christians were happy with the notion that David wasn't the author of the whole Psalter).[41] He acknowledges the traditional division of the Psalter into five parts[42] but introduces divisions of his own as well, such as his identification of Pss 51–70 as a unit defined by their location in the life of David while Saul was still alive, whereas Ps 50, the great psalm of repentance, was composed by David after his adultery with Bathsheba. The chronological reversal is explained away with the moralizing interpretation that David did not want those who prayed the psalms to see what was better give way to what was worse.[43] In contextualizing Ps 56, Eusebius notes that the title might refer either to the cave story in 1Sa 22:1–2 or the one in 1Sa 24:2–8. He solves his dilemma by appealing to the similar title in Ps 141 and splitting the narrative difference: Ps 56 refers to the cave of Odollam, and Ps 141 to the second cave story, set in Engaddi (PG 23.504).

In other places Eusebius is more candid about the redaction of the psalms. To be sure, he believes that the process as a whole was inspired. Recognizing that the psalms originated in the prayers of Israel, he says ". . . the things that were uttered were rightly no longer regarded as ordinary prayers but as prophetic words, and the ones who had received the *charisma* of the discernment of spirits inserted them into the divine books" (PG 23.580c). But he knows that many hands must have been involved in that discernment and perhaps

---

[40]  My thanks to Aaron Johnson for pointing out this interesting passage; see Johnson 2006:134–135. Eusebius is partially dependent here on Origen's discussion in *Contra Celsum* 1.24–25.

[41]  See Curti's detailed account of Eusebius' elaborate web of cross-comparisons in Curti 1989b:206–210.

[42]  PG 23.65a–68a (Pss 1–40, 41–72, 73–88, 89–105, 106–150). At Ps 40:14 (PG 23.365d), he draws attention to the first of the four doxologies that divide the Psalter.

[43]  PG 23.445d–448a, the conclusion to his preface to Ps 51, in which he presents a detailed review of the jumbled chronology of the psalms attributed to David in the first two portions of the Psalter.

more than a little contingency. In two separate passages, he proposes scenarios for explaining how the Psalter may have assumed its present shape.[44] The basic hypothesis is that the psalms were composed by numerous authors over a long period of time, and then assembled gradually by an editor or editors as the individual psalms came to their attention. Eusebius says he isn't sure whether that person was actually Ezra, as "the children of the Hebrews" allege. In this way, e.g. of the twelve psalms eventually attributed to "the sons of Kore," eight were found and numbered 41 through 48; then later, two more (83 and 84), after which one of David's was placed (85); and then the last two of the sons of Kore (86–87).[45] Eusebius compares the process to what he thinks may also have happened to the books of Jeremiah and of Ezekiel. There too, he says, the order of events and of prophecies is sometimes reversed, with prophecies from later times being found in earlier parts of the books. In both cases, the "probable" (*eikos*) explanation is that the unhistorical sequencing of the books is due to the fact that those who preserved the prophecies added them to the book as they incidentally came to their attention, following disruptions like the Babylonian Exile. The same explanation applies to the Psalter—unless, he adds, someone wishes to propose a deeper meaning (*bathuteros nous*) that has escaped him (PG 23.1041d). He flatly denies that the psalm numbers themselves could carry inherent significance, as if ". . . the fiftieth in number contains the understanding of the forgiveness of sins because of the fifty year period referred to in the Law, the period which the children of the Hebrews call a 'jubilee' . . ."[46] As Eusebius well knew, the author of that symbolic interpretation was none other than Origen.[47]

With that blunt testimony to his scholarly independence, we take our leave of Eusebius and his commentary. Its importance lies mainly in its summation of the exegetical prowess achieved by Christian scholarship at Caesarea, in the century-old trajectory going back to Origen's residence. Eusebius of Vercelli, banished to Palestine in 355, discovered the commentary at Caesarea and made a Latin translation, which unfortunately has not survived. But the massive scale of the original made it unlikely that it would survive intact for too many generations. It was fated to leave its mark mainly in the ample selections in

---

[44] Curti has already drawn attention to these two passages, one on Ps 62 and the other on Ps 86 (Curti 1989b:208). My translation of the commentary on Ps 62:2–3 (PG 23.601a–604b) will appear in the Eusebius chapter in the forthcoming *New Cambridge History of the Bible*.

[45] See PG 23.1040b–1041d (on Ps 86).

[46] Not everyone was comfortable with this contingent explanation. Hilary of Poitiers, Theodoret, and Cassiodorus are among those who thought that the arrangement and the numbering were the inspiration of the Spirit and were therefore essential to the psalms' interpretation (Daley 2003:199).

[47] Origen *Selecta in psalmos* (PG 12.1073d–1076b). In fairness it should be noted that Origen recognized the possibility of a historical explanation as well.

the catenae, beginning with the Palestinian Catena, which appears to have been assembled in the library at Caesarea. We can expect much new light to be shed on the commentary by the German team that has now begun work on a critical edition.[48] It is gratifying to know it will receive the careful attention it deserves, and that Carmelo Curti's efforts will find an appropriate completion. As we have seen, the CPs shows the heights to which Eusebius rose in his exegetical industry and the ways in which such industry could be formative of ecclesiological notions, anti-Judaism, and late antique literary culture generally.

[48]   See note 3 above.

# Works Cited

Attridge, H.A. and Fassler, M.E., eds. 2003. *Psalms in Community: Jewish and Christian Textual, Liturgical, and Artistic Traditions.* Atlanta.

Barnes, T.D. 1981. *Constantine and Eusebius.* Cambridge, MA.

Berardino, A. di, ed. 2006. *Patrology: The Eastern Fathers from the Council of Chalcedon (451) to John of Damascus (d. 750).* Trans. Adrian Walford. Cambridge.

Berlin-Brandenburg Academy of the Sciences. 2012. "Alexandrian and Antiochene Biblical Exegesis in Late Antiquity." Berlin-Brandenburgische Akademie der Wissenschaften. Accessed May 15, 2012. http://www.bbaw. de/forschung/bibelexegese/projekte.

Blowers, P.M. et al., eds. 2002. *In Dominico Eloquio, In Lordly Eloquence: Essays on Patristic Exegesis in Honor of Robert Wilken.* Grand Rapids, MI.

Cadiou, R. 1936. *La jeunesse d'Origène.* Paris.

Cameron, A., and Hall, S. G., eds. 1999. *Eusebius: Life of Constantine.* Oxford.

Carleton Paget, J. and J. Schaper, eds. Forthcoming. *The New Cambridge History of the Bible.* Cambridge.

Carriker, A. J. 2003. *The Library of Eusebius of Caesarea.* Supplements to Vigiliae Christianae 67. Leiden.

Curti, C. 1989a. *Eusebiana I: commentarii in Psalmos.* Saggi e testi classici, cristiani e medievali 1. Catania, Sicily.

———. 1989b. "L'esegesi di Eusebio di Cesare: caraterri i sviluppo." In Curti 1989a:195–213.

———. 1989c. "Per una nuova edizione dei 'Commentarii in Psalmos' di Eusebio di Cesarea (MS. Coislin 44)." In Curti 1989a:3–17.

——— 2006. "Greek Catenae on the Psalms." In Berardino 2006:618–626.

Daley, B. E. 2003. "Finding the Right Key: The Aims and Strategies of Early Christian Interpretation of the Psalms." In Attridge and Fassler 2003:113–123.

Fernández Marcos, N. 2000. *The Septuagint in Context: Introduction to the Greek Versions of the Bible.* Leiden.

Grafton, A. and Williams, M. 2006. *Christianity and the Transformation of the Book: Origen, Eusebius, and the Library of Caesarea.* Cambridge, MA.

Harl, M., ed. 1972. *La chaîne palestinienne sur le Psaume 118.* Sources chrétiennes 189. Paris.

———., ed. 1983. *Sur les Écritures: Philocalie 1-20/Origène.* Sources chrétiennes 302. Paris.

Harnack, A. 1904. *Die Chronologie der altchristlichen Literatur bis Eusebius.* 2 vols. Leipzig.

Hollerich, M. J. 1989. "Myth and History in Eusebius' De vita Constantini: Vita Const. 1.12 in its Contemporary Setting." *Harvard Theological Review* 82:421–445.

———. 1999. *Eusebius of Caesarea's Commentary on Isaiah: Christian Exegesis in the Age of Constantine.* Oxford Early Christian Studies. Oxford.

———. 2002. "Hebrews, Jews, and Christians: Eusebius of Caesarea on the Biblical Basis of the Two States of the Christian Life." In Blowers 2002:172–184.

Johnson, A. 2006. "The Blackness of Ethiopians: Classical Ethnography and Eusebius' Commentary on the Psalms." *Harvard Theological Review* 99:165–186.

Kannengiesser, C., ed. 2004. *Handbook of Patristic Exegesis: The Bible in Ancient Christianity.* Leiden.

Lange, N. de, ed. 1983. *Sur les Écritures: La lettre à Africanus sur l'histoire de Suzanne.* Sources chrétiennes 302. Paris.

Mercati, G. 1948. *Osservazioni a proemi del Salterio di Origene, Ippolito, Eusebio, Cirillo Alessandrino e altri, con frammenti inediti.* Studi e Testi 142. Vatican City.

Moreau, J. 1966. "Eusebius von Caesarea." *Reallexikon für Antike und Christentum* 6:col. 1064.

Nautin, P. 1977. *Origène: sa vie et son oeuvre.* Christianisme antique 1. Paris.

Rajak, T. 2009. *Translation and Survival: The Greek Bible of the Ancient Jewish Diaspora.* Oxford.

Rondeau, M.-J. and Kirchmeyer, J. 1967. "Eusèbe de Césarée." In *Dictionnaire de Spiritualité* 4, 2:1688–1691.

Rondeau, M.-J. 1982, 1985. *Les commentaires patristiques du Psautier (IIIe–Ve siècles)* I, II. Orientalia Christiana Analecta 219–220. Rome.

Schoene, A., ed. 1967. *Eusebii Chronicon.* 2 vols. Zurich.

Veltri, G. 2006. *Libraries, Translations, and 'Canonic' Texts: The Septuagint, Aquila, and Ben Sira in the Jewish and Christian Traditions.* Leiden.

Wallace-Hadrill, D. S. 1960. *Eusebius of Caesarea.* London.

Wallraff, M. 2011. "The Canon Tables of the Psalms. An Unknown Work of Eusebius of Caesarea." Oxford Patristics: The Conference Blog, July 13, 2011. http://oxfordpatristics.blogspot.com/2011/07/martin-wallraff-canon-tables-of-psalms.html.

Wasserstein, A., and Wasserstein, D. 2006. *The Legend of the Septuagint: From Classical Antiquity to Today.* Cambridge.

# 9

# Textuality and Territorialization
## Eusebius' Exegeses of Isaiah and Empire

JEREMY M. SCHOTT

THAT WE SHOULD STUDY Eusebius' works within the context of late-ancient Roman imperialism appears self-evident. Eusebius lived and wrote in one of Rome's provincial capitals. He lived under and had direct contact with Roman imperial power—he witnessed the persecution of Christians in Caesarea under the governors Flavianus, Urbanus, and Firmilianus, but also met, delivered panegyrics for, and corresponded with Constantine. Consequently, Eusebius figures prominently in all histories of late-ancient political theology and political philosophy. In the 310s and 320s, works like his *Ecclesiastical History* and *Gospel Demonstration* developed a salvation history that linked Roman imperial expansion and Christian mission. In the 330s, the *Life of Constantine* and the Tricennial Orations pressed these connections further and more explicitly by offering a political theology amalgamated from Hellenistic philosophies of monarchy, Roman imperial ideology, and Christian theologies. Studies of "Eusebius and Politics" or "The Politics of Eusebius" traditionally focus on the explicit political messages recorded in his works. Certain questions dominate: What is Eusebius' theology of empire? Where do the emperor and the empire fit in salvation history? What is his theology of Christian monarchy?[1]

This essay asks that we consider what it might mean to study Eusebius' works as imperial *texts*. In emphasizing textuality rather than *oeuvre*, I am adopting an approach to "politics" that begins from an examination of form, structure, and process, rather than message and meaning. This approach is one of the key insights of post-colonial theory. Drawing upon the distinction

---

[1] The bibliography is vast, but some key works that focus on or include important discussions of Eusebius and the politics of empire include: Peterson 1935; Sirinelli 1961; Dvornik 1966; Farina 1966; Hollerich 1990: 309–325; Drake 2000.

between work and text elaborated by Roland Barthes and other Tel Quel theorists, this approach understands the "work" as the relatively bounded object printed between the covers of a book (or inscribed in a scroll or codex). A text, on the other hand, is a network of signification, a field produced in and through the work of production.[2] Works (or books) make arguments, have theses, and offer, for example, "theologies of empire." Textualities are produced within, and productive of, existential possibilities. To say that Eusebian texts are imperial is to say that they participate in a textuality of empire, a semiotic field produced within, and productive of, territory, conquest, and colonization.

This essay lays particular stress on imperial textuality as spatiality. Empire, after all, brings into being/is brought into being as particular kinds of places: metropolis, province, border, frontier, and so forth. My essay's emphasis on space, territory, and aesthetics is, moreover, suggested by Eusebius' *oeuvre* itself. For all of his bookishness, Eusebius was also profoundly interested in the visual and spatial world around him. He travelled fairly widely in the eastern Mediterranean, from Egypt to Constantinople.[3] He was responsible for the earliest extant detailed descriptions of early Christian architecture and played a key role in mapping a Christian "Holy Land" onto the geography of fourth-century Roman Palestine.[4] And as Peter Van Nuffelen's contribution to this volume shows, theorizations of image and vision were important in Eusebius' thought. Eusebian texts demand (and exploit) an aesthetics of movement and viewing. This essay explores several of Eusebius' texts cartographically, aiming to trace the spaces they mediate and types of movement they effect.

## Theorizing Imperial Space and Textuality

Space is never merely "there," a neutral, three-dimensional vacuum within which we live and history unfolds. Rather, as Henri Lefebvre influentially contended, space is a production.[5] Like other products, space (and our experience and analysis of it) tends to become divorced from the labors that produce it.[6] But space, like other products, is shaped by, and bears the traces of, the specific

---

2 Barthes 1977; Kristeva 1980a:36–63; Kristeva 1980b:64–91.
3 Eusebius spent time in Egypt during the 310's, and recounts martyrdoms of Christians he witnessed in the Thebaid (HE 8.9.4); he had also spent time in Tyre (HE 8.7.1–8.1) and Antioch (HE 7.32.2). Eusebius visited Constantinople in 336, where he delivered an oration in honor of Constantine's Tricennalia.
4 Wilken 1992 and Jacobs 2004 are two excellent studies (with different methodological approaches) within the vast bibliography on this subject. On Eusebius' architectural description see Smith 1989:226–247 and Schott 2011:177–198.
5 Lefebvre 1991.
6 Lefebvre 1991:113.

modes of production that generated it. In Lefebvre's words, "[s]pace is social morphology."[7] The activity of production simultaneously produces space(s) that make the relations of production possible.[8] In a passage worth quoting at length, Lefebvre likens the work of the historian of space to interpreting a manuscript:

> ... one might say that practical activity writes upon nature, albeit in a scrawling hand, and that this writing implies a particular representation of space. Places are marked, noted, named. Between them, within the 'holes in the net,' are blank or marginal spaces ... Paths are more important than the traffic they bear, because they are what endures in the form of the reticular patterns left by animals, both wild and domestic, and by people ... Always distinct and clearly indicated, such traces embody the 'values' assigned to particular routes: danger, safety, waiting, promise. This graphic aspect ... has more in common with a spider's web than with a drawing or plan. Could it be called a text, or a message? Possibly, but the analogy would serve no particularly useful purpose, and it would make more sense to speak of texture rather than of texts in this connection.
>
> Lefebvre 1991:117–118

Here, Lefebvre's contrast between "text" and "texture" is homologous to the post-structuralist distinction between "work" and "text." Space, in other words, is not a "book" legible through linear "reading," but like the post-structuralist text, is a complex web of interrelations. To press the scribal analogy: space, in its depth and texture, is much like a hand-made, hand-penned manuscript that bears the marks of its creation and has experienced the vicissitudes of transmission (blemishes in the skin/parchment, the marks of cutting and assembly, errors, erasures, additions, and so forth). A historical account of a written or artistic work that takes account of space, then, would aim to understand the relations of power and political interests at work in these textured webs (or textualities).

But if space is textual, if it is semiotic, it may also be submitted to rhetorical analysis. As we might pose aesthetic questions about what it feels like to read or write a written work, we can consider the aesthetics of working over spatial texts. Hence Michel de Certeau describes the negotiation of space as an enunciative practice homologous to other rhetorical practices and having its own grammar and figures of speech.[9] In pointing to the broad homologies

---

[7]   Lefebvre 1991:94.
[8]   Lefebvre 1991:115.
[9]   De Certeau 1984:91–110.

between verbal acts and spatial acts, de Certeau's insights help to elucidate the complex relationships between texts and social space. As writing appropriates the parameters of language and the page, enacting new relationships among semiotic and scribal positions, movement (walking, sitting, standing, pausing, entering, exiting, and so forth) appropriates and improvises upon the possibilities of social space. Like Lefebvre, moreover, de Certeau recognizes that spatial enunciation is also a production: "... if it is true that the spatial order organizes an ensemble of possibilities ... and interdictions ..., then the walker actualizes some of these possibilities. *In that way, he makes them exist as well as emerge.*"[10]

If we take these insights seriously, to say that Eusebius' works are "imperial" demands that we examine the spatial modalities that produced them and that they, in turn produce(d). Empire can be described in terms of spatial enunciation (in de Certeau's sense) and as a particular kind of space or spatiality (in Lefebvre's sense). Imperial spatial enunciation, for its part, involves a particular set of figures of speech, for example: invasion (movement into a space territorialized as both foreign and conquerable), destruction (the clearing of conquered space), provincialization (the redistribution or reterritorialization of space[s] within [and as] imperial territory), and colonization (movement from space territorialized as [another's] homeland to space re-territorialized as colony or province). There is a "feel," a poetics to an imperial text/texture.

The space of empire is a production brought into being by and in turn productive of specific relations of production. The Roman province (its boundaries as well as its bureaucratic structure) served to administer the exploitation of resources within the empire. The roads and seaways that crossed the Mediterranean developed and were maintained to facilitate flows of labor and material. The literary productions of the Roman Empire, then, are likewise spatial productions. Apuleius' *Metamorphoses* and the *Acts of the Apostles*, to take two examples, are imperial productions in that the narrative vectors of these texts—Odysseys that unfold along the highways and shipping routes of the Mediterranean—"embody the 'values'"[11] of the spatialities that made possible the economics of empire. The space of empire, in turn, made possible the transnational literary culture(s) of which these works were a part. The scribal labor force, concentrated in major metropolises, produced volumes that then circulated through networks of friendship and patronage, via the same roads and seaways as other products.[12]

---

[10] De Certeau 1984:98 (emphasis added).

[11] Lefebvre 1991:118; though without the theoretical implications explored here, compare Millar 1981:63–75.

[12] For an excellent discussion of early Christian "publication" and "circulation" in the context of ancient book production, see Gamble 1995:82–143.

Caesarea, an intermodal trade hub and provincial capital, is a case in point. The historical narrative we might write of the processes that created its famed Christian library, for example, embodies the social relations of production (themselves embodied in roads, harbors, and so forth) that bound Caesarea to the towns and villages of Palestine and other urban centers, such as Tyre, Laodicea, Alexandria, and Antioch. Such a narrative would include the "transnational" travels of Origen, Origen's inter-city and inter-province patronage relationship with Ambrose, Pamphilus' efforts to acquire manuscripts of Origen's works from other locales, the migration of Anatolius (the Aristotelian philosopher, mathematician, and later, bishop of Laodicea) from Alexandria to Caesarea after the defeat of Zenobia's Palmyrene kingdom,[13] and, of course, Eusebius' drawing together of sources for his literary projects, his sending of dedication copies of texts to friends and patrons such as Paulinus of Tyre[14] and Theodotus of Laodicea,[15] and the dossier of missives so integral to the *Life of Constantine*— all of which could be plotted as vectors within and constitutive of the space of imperial power and economy.

What follows focuses on selected passages from Eusebius' *Commentary on Isaiah* as a test case for exploring the aesthetics and poetics of imperial textuality in early Christian literature. As a genre, exegetical works are not fertile territory for explicit discussions of monarchy and empire. Michael Hollerich has shown, however, that the relative dearth of explicit engagement with Constantine and the Christian Empire in texts like the *Commentary on Isaiah* offers a necessary corrective to stock portraits of Eusebius as a "court theologian."[16] Instead, Hollerich presents a more politically nuanced Eusebius; a theologian and exegete concerned primarily with the theology and ecclesiology of the Christian polity than the details of Constantinian politics.

But Eusebius' *Commentary on Isaiah* is also an excellent example of an aesthetic of imperial territorialization. Eusebius' exegesis of the first verses of Isaiah lists, in effect, the figures of spatial speech just mentioned above. Isaiah's vision, he writes, was "just as if someone could see the approach of wars and the sacking and enslavements of besieged lands represented in color on a great tablet (*pinax*)" (*Commentary on Isaiah* [CI hereafter] 3.20–23).[17] Here, the reference to "tablets (*pinakes*)" invokes a territorialized and territorializing writing. Isaiah previews history on figurative tablets like those upon which classical city-states would record their histories. Such tablets offered, in the concise but powerful

---

13 HE 7.32.6–21.
14 HE 10.1.2; HE 10.4; Onom., praefatio.
15 PE 1.1.1.
16 Hollerich 1990:309–325.
17 Greek text in Ziegler 1975, my translation throughout.

form of chronological lists, a linear narrative (or, in the case of Eusebius' own *Chronicle* and *Chronological Canons*, a linear narrative comprised of the parallel chronologies of several peoples) marked by the ebb and flow of wars, conquest, victory, and defeat. Written in colored inks, these figurative tablets also suggest particular scribal technologies. Colored inks aided the presentation of large sets of information—like that presented in tables and chronographies. The colored inks also hint at Eusebius' own scribal practices. He adverts to using colored inks as a visual aid in his *Gospel Canons*, while later versions of the *Chronicle* also employed the device.[18] Eusebius' likening of Isaiah's vision to the reading of a particular kind of book produced with particular scribal technologies locates Isaiah as a narrative of territory, its acquisition, its loss, and recovery—that is, as an imperial textuality.

The book of Isaiah as we have it, and as Eusebius had it, is itself, of course, patterned on the strophe and antistrophe of the loss and recovery of the Land of Israel. We can conceptualize the relations among the text of empire, the text of Isaiah, and the text of Eusebius' exegesis, I suggest, as "hypertextual." Here I adapt this term as defined by literary theorist Gerard Genette.[19] For him, "hypertextuality" defines any situation in which two or more texts are inter-connected, in ways *other than* that of explicit commentary; for him the intertex-tual relationship among Homer's *Odyssey*, Vergil's *Aeneid*, and Joyce's *Ulysses* is "hypertextual." Genette also distinguishes "hypertextual" relations from direct commentary (a relation he terms "metatextuality"[20]). Hypertextuality is char-acterized by relationships of dependence and transformation.[21] Genette's use

---

[18] Eusebius mentions the use of different colored inks in the letter that accompanies his *Canon Tables* (*Epistula ad Carpianum*), text in Nestle and Aland 1969:32*–37*; on Eusebius' use of colored inks and their subsequent use by Jerome and others, see Grafton and Williams 2006:199–201, 344n54.

[19] Genette 1997. Others have also recognized a hypertextual quality in Eusebius work; Grafton and Williams, for example, drawing on and adding to James J. O'Donnell's observations: "the . . . Canon Tables were extraordinarily original and effective information retrieval devices: the world's first hot links. They enabled readers not simply to rely on memory or to use rearranged texts of the Bible, but to turn the four Gospels into a single web of cross-commentary—to move from text to text as easily as one could move from kingdom to kingdom in the *Canon*" (Grafton and Williams 2006:199; 344n53 cites http://ccat.sas.upenn.edu/jod/jod.html, but this link does not currently function). These observations do capture the innovation of Eusebius' method and point to important points of contact between modern and ancient media technologies; in drawing on Genette's work, however, I aim to trace the specific kinds of (spatial) movements and (political) forces (the aesthetics) at work in this hypertextual web.

[20] ". . . *metatextuality*, is the relationship most often labeled "commentary." It unites a given text to another, of which it speaks without necessarily citing it" (Genette 1997:4). Eusebius' *Commentary on Isaiah* does bear such a relationship to the text of Isaiah, and the analysis of that relationship is the basis of most studies of early Christian commentary.

[21] ". . . such as text B not speaking of text A at all but being unable to exist, as such, without A, from which it originates through a process I shall provisionally call *transformation*, and which

of terms like "transformation" and "transposing" signals the kinetic quality that operates in hypertextual relationships.[22] Taking Genette's example of the hypertextual relationship between the *Odyssey* and *Ulysses*, for instance, a reader of the latter must constantly transpose Homeric plot, characters, idioms, and the present text of *Ulysses*. Of course, these analogical movements are not always linear; Bloom is not *the same as* Odysseus, but a reading of Bloom refers, that is, carries back or returns (Latin: *refero*) the reader to Odysseus and the *Odyssey*.[23] Genette develops and applies this terminology only to written texts, but the concept is easily extended to "textuality" in its broadest sense—any semiotic network, including spatial textures. Joyce's *Ulysses* again provides an apt example. Not only does Bloom refer to Odysseus, but as the narrative traces his wanderings it also effects a doubled spatial movement within the cityscape of Edwardian Dublin and, referentially, back to and within the epic spatiality of the Homeric text. Contemporary Bloomsday pilgrimages, of course, enact these movements on the streets of contemporary Dublin, territorializing the post-modern city as epic space. The contemporary experience of navigating Internet hyperlinks also offers a good example of the kinetic aspects of hypertextuality. Web pages do not read in a linear, unidirectional way; rather, the structure of the "web" refers us constantly to new (web)sites, and so on. The "web," however, is not a limitless space offering unbounded possibilities for movement. It is a structured space, a "net," that makes possible specific forms of movement within and among particular types of spaces. Indeed, as Lefebvre would remind us, the feeling of free movement that the web effects is the territorializing effect of a particular economic modality (e.g. the "free, global market"). Similarly, then, we might conceptualize imperial textuality as the "net" or "web" of metaphors, references, figures of (spatial and rhetorical) speech, and so forth, that structure the (politically and economically interested) space of Eusebius' *Commentary*, the text of Isaiah, the spatial text of the late-ancient Levant, and referentiality among them.

---

it consequently evokes more or less perceptibly without necessarily speaking of it or citing it" (Genette 1997:5).

[22] For "transposing," see Genette 1997:5–6.

[23] De Certeau plays on words to make a similar point about the movements effected by written texts: "In modern Athens, the vehicles of mass transportation are called *metaphorai* . . . Stories could also take this noble name: every day, they traverse and organize places; they select and link them together; they make sentences and itineraries out of them. They are spatial trajectories"; where de Certeau emphasizes the way in which (verbal) narratives "regulate changes in space" and "organize walks"—that is, how written or spoken texts produce enunciations of space (de Certeau 1984:115–116), I have adapted Genette's concept of "hypertextuality" because it better blurs the distinction between verbal and geographic/architectural space. Hypertextuality connotes the interconnectedness of written and geographic texts as different planes within a spatial continuum.

# Eusebius' *Commentary on Isaiah* and Imperial Textuality

## The vision against Tyre

I have chosen to focus on Eusebius' exegesis of Isaiah chapters 15 and 16 (the vision against Moab) and chapter 23 (the vision against Tyre) because they pertain to territory with which we might assume Eusebius had at least some personal familiarity. He identifies Moab with the Roman province of Arabia, portions of which had been incorporated into the province of Palestine by Diocletian.[24] Some of this territory, then, would have been within Eusebius' purview as metropolitan of Palestine. He had also traveled through portions of this region when he visited martyrs at the mines at Phaeno during the Great Persecution.[25] He had visited Tyre on several occasions and was closely allied with the city's bishop, Paulinus.[26]

First, Tyre. Eusebius opens with remarks characteristic of his exegesis of the ten visions against the nations:

> If the prophecies concerning foreigners pertained only to matters undertaken of old and to deeds completed a long time ago, it would be superfluous to be curious about things which have nothing to do with us, but in addition to saying what will happen to the nations mentioned in each prophecy, the text addresses piety. Indeed, it is amazing how it prophesies something specific about each nation individually, yet in these same verses conveys things pertaining to the godly doctrine at the same time.

CI 149.5–11

Here, Eusebius' hermeneutic seems rather simple—a tempered Origenist exegesis that looks for deeper meanings, the *dianoia*, behind the *lexis*, or letter, of the text. The body of the text consists of prophecies against the nations, while

---

[24] Barnes 1982.

[25] Eusebius was in Phaeno on or around May 4, 311, when the martyr Silvanus of Gaza (who was presiding as bishop of a church set up by Christians working as forced labor at the copper mines there) was executed; it was also at this time that Eusebius reports hearing John the Egyptian recite scripture from memory (Eusebius, MP 13.1–10, Greek text in Schwartz, et al. 1999).

[26] Eusebius was invited to deliver his oration for the dedication of the rebuilt and remodeled basilica at Tyre ca. AD 315 (HE 10.4); he had visited Tyre on previous occasions, however: he was in Tyre at least once during the Great Persecution, sometime between 311–313 (HE 8.7.1–8.1). Eusebius also reports having "come to know" the learned presbyter Dorotheus in Tyre or Antioch in the 280's or 290's (HE 7.32.2–4); any overland travel to Antioch would have taken Eusebius along the coastal Roman road that passed through Tyre.

the *dianoia* of the text concerns the *parousia* and the coming kingdom of God. Yet, Eusebius' explanation of his exegetical principles leaves unspoken or unexamined the precise mode in which *lexis* and *dianoia* are related. That relation is effected through a hermeneutic of territorialization.

The exegesis depends on Eusebius' implicit claim to read the spatial text of Tyre correctly. Isaiah 23:1 ("Wail, ships of Carthage, because she has been destroyed and they no longer come from the land of Kitieon") prompts Eusebius to explain the historical geography of Tyre and its colonies. This is a history territorialized imperially:

> Now at this time, during which the city of the Tyrians remained such a desolate place, it was likely that those who were nautical and dedicated in all respects to oceangoing commerce no longer plied their accustomed trade. Thus he has said: *Wail, ships of Carthage, because she has been destroyed and they no longer come.* Why else has the prophecy mentioned Carthage in these verses, but for the fact that there was an ancient kindred relationship between the Tyrians and Carthaginians, when the Tyrians took control of those inhabiting Africa, and became the first founders of Carthage. Therefore, with Tyre destroyed, there no longer were those who transported goods from Tyre to Carthage nor those accustomed to sail from Carthage to Tyre. Thus he says: *Wail, ships of Carthage, because she has been destroyed, and they no longer come from the land of Kitieon,* or from the *land of Chetteim* according to the rest of the translators. But Cyprus is said to be indicated here and Kition to be a city there, by way of which seafarers from Tyre sailed. And the reason why the usual commerce of Tyre ceased he declares next, saying: *they have been taken captive*—clearly this means Tyre.

> CI 150.9–23

The invasion of Tyre by the Assyrians, he infers, would have disrupted economic movement within the Phoenician empire. The deeper meaning, the *dianoia*, of the prophecy is determined by reflection on the deterritorialization and reterritorialization of Tyrian space. When Tyre asks: "Who planned this for Tyre" the answer must be that the Assyrian invasion teaches the lesson of Proverbs 3:34: "God is opposed to the boastful, but gives favor to the humble" (CI 151.14–15). Imperial figures of speech thus provide a hermeneutical key to exegesis: the boastfulness and humbleness of Proverbs map, respectively, the imperial hubris and subsequent conquest of Tyre as an imperial power.

Eusebius' interpretation of the final verses of the vision against Tyre is also illustrative of the *Commentary* as an imperial textuality. He reads the final verses of the vision—"And her commerce and her wages shall be consecrated to the Lord, and it shall not be collected for them, but all her commerce will be for those who reside in the presence of the Lord to eat, and drink, and be satiated"—as prophesying the establishment of the Christian church in Tyre and donations to its clergy. Here, Eusebius' exegesis depends on a text-critical argument based on his reading of the *Hexapla*. Eusebius states that the LXX reads *pasa hē emporia autēs* ("all her commerce"). He notes, however, that Symmachus and the Hebrew lack the adjective "all." Symmachus reads *hē emporia autēs* ("her commerce"), while the Hebrew has *saherat* ("her commerce"). Eusebius then opines a corrected version: "some of her commerce" (*ta apo tēs emporias autēs*). The Hebrew lacks a definite article before "commerce" and "wages," and so it seems did the *Hexapla*, for Eusebius' proposed emendation assumes that the lack of the definite article in the Hebrew indicates an indefinite with a partitive sense: that is, "some of the commerce." This must be the case, Eusebius explains:

> For not *all* her commerce nor *all* her profits, but a *portion* of the commerce and a *portion* of the wages will be consecrated to the Lord. This is indeed fulfilled in our very own day, for when God's Church was established in the city of the Tyrians much of her profits, gained from business, are consecrated to the Lord, when donated to his Church.
>
> CI 152.30–34, emphasis added

This exegesis is based, ostensibly, on (inaccurate) knowledge of Hebrew. The Hebrew, though it lacks a definite article, does have a pronominal suffix, making the word definite, so Eusebius' reading is philologically incorrect. Rather, the changed economic distributions within imperial space lead Eusebius to opine about the Hebrew. His suggested reading of the verse looks, on its surface, to account for the economy of article usage in the Hebrew, but it is driven by the present system of wealth distribution in Tyre. Tyre's place as a merchant city bookends Eusebius' exegesis of the vision against Tyre. The movement of the exegesis follows the flow of Tyrian commerce through a sequence of imperial spatialities; the city is territorialized as a metropolis of the Phoenician empire, reterritorialized as conquered land under the Assyrians, and reterritorialized as Christian metropolis.

> Therefore what other refuge will you find, or where will you procure hope of salvation? Thus it is reasonable that your colonists—I mean the Carthaginians—sing dirges for you who were at that time their *fortress of Tyre*, and that all the things prophesied against Tyre would be fulfilled in a few years, during such time as the city of Jerusalem, purified by

God, remained desolate. For God determined that Tyre would be seized by the coming desolation for a time equal to the lifespan *of one man*—I mean *seventy years*—or the *reign of one king* who rules for many years.

During these *seventy years* all those people who in times past correctly perceived that you were like a woman who has lost her proper virtue will sing an ode and a lyric about your desolation. And you yourself spent the period of your desolation *roaming* and moving from place to place and prostituting yourself to the rest of the Gentiles, inasmuch as, indeed, you had been *forgotten* by God. But if, when you no longer *take up* your own *lyre* like a harlot, you are able to use your own instrument skillfully, *strum much and sing much* in the form of prayers and supplications to God. For thus a *remembrance* of you will be before God, if you use the parts of your body and your well-orchestrated senses themselves skillfully like a lyre, living a life of self-control and singing pleasingly to God—for thus *there will be a remembrance of you*, since God's memory of you deemed you worthy. For immediately after the aforementioned time has been completed, he will make his own *visitation*[27] and *she will be reestablished* again *as she was at the beginning*, so that there will once again be *commerce* in you and those from everywhere will stream eagerly to you and ship their goods to you.

CI 151.30–152.19

The *dianoia* refers to the present Christian reterritorialization of Tyre, and, hypertextually, situates the present space of Tyre, colonized by the Church, in terms of Isaiah's reterritorialization of Tyre as tributary of the God of Israel (via his clergy).

Who happening upon these words would not marvel that a prediction made so long ago, which says that idolaters and those especially crazed by polytheistic error, who were always enemies of and hostile towards the Jews, will have changed so much that they will know the God who is honored among the Jews and bring him gifts! Indeed, it shows that these things have come to perfect completion in actuality through the grace of our Savior Jesus Christ.

CI 153.24–29

---

[27]  The word *episkopē* ("visitation" or "watching over") would also, of course, suggest "bishop" (*episkopos*) and "the espiscopal office" (*episkopē*) to Eusebius.

# Prophecies against Moab

Eusebius argues for an explicitly historical exegesis (*kata tēn historian*) of the prophecies against Moab in Isaiah chapters 15 and 16, contending that "a figurative interpretation of these passages is forced" (CI 108.4; 19). The prophecy against Moab was given because the Moabites "thought their own gods great and laughed at and mocked the God of Israel" (CI 107.26–28). This he infers from references to regional cult at 15:1–2: "Debon will perish. Where your altar is, there you will go up to weep," and 16:12: "Moab has become weary at the altars, and she will enter the works of her hands to pray but will not be able to deliver him." Eusebius argues that these verses were fulfilled in historical fact "at the time of the invasion of the Assyrians and Babylonians and at the time of those who controlled the territory of Arabia after them" (CI 108.3–5). As he does frequently in the *Commentary* and elsewhere, Eusebius claims that the prophecy refers to the defeat of this nation's tutelary demon.[28] Thus Isaiah 16:4 ("The ruler who trampled upon the land has perished") refers to "the wicked demon who presides over the nation, or 'ruling' the nation, like the one ruling the kingdom of the Persians, the one ruling the kingdom of the Greeks, and the one ruling the Babylonians" (CI 108.33–36).

The passages about Moab also prompt Eusebius to locate these biblical sites within past and contemporary landscapes. He notes that the prophecy mentions a series of Moabite cities and that "these places and villages are still known today in the territory around what is now called Areopolis" (CI 108.14–16). In the *Onomasticon*, an earlier work, he identifies several of these villages. Debon, for instance, is described as a stop along the Israelites' Exodus journey and in Eusebius' day as the site of "another immense village" near the Arnon; Eusebius also recounts that this village passed from Moabite to Amorite control before it was conquered by the Israelites.[29] Essebon "is now called Esbus, the famous polis in Arabia. It lies in the mountains opposite Jericho about twenty miles from the Jordan,"[30] while Elealeh is explained as the site where "a very large village is still preserved, not more than a mile from Heshbon."[31] Indeed, the formula "Isaiah mentioned it in the vision against Moab" that appears at

---

[28] See discussion in Hollerich, *Commentary on Isaiah* 90.

[29] Onom. 372: ἐπὶ τῆς ἐρήμου σταθμὸς τῶν υἱῶν Ἰσραήλ. ἔστι δὲ καὶ ἄλλη εἰς ἔτι νῦν κώμη παμμεγέθης παρὰ τὸν Ἀρνωνᾶν, ἣν τὸ παλαιὸν οὖσαν τῶν υἱῶν Μωὰβ καὶ μετὰ ταῦτα Σηῶν τοῦ Ἀμορραίου οἱ υἱοὶ Ἰσραὴλ ἀπέλαβον, καὶ γέγονε φυλῆς Γάδ. μέμνηται δὲ αὐτῆς Ἡσαΐας ἐν ὁράσει τῇ "κατὰ τῆς Μωαβίτιδος," καὶ Ἰερεμίας (Greek text and English translation: Notley and Safrai 2005).

[30] Onom. 408: καλεῖται δὲ νῦν Ἐσβοῦς, ἐπίσημος πόλις τῆς Ἀραβίας, ἐν ὄρεσι τοῖς ἀντικρὺ τῆς Ἰεριχοῦς κειμένη.

[31] Onom. 410: καὶ σῴζεται εἰς ἔτι νῦν κώμη μεγίστη, οὐ πλεῖον σημείου ἑνὸς ἀπέχουσα τῆς Ἐσβοῦς.

least 14 times in the *Onomasticon* establishes hypertextual links among references to these sites in the contemporary landscape, the historical books of the Hebrew Bible, and Isaiah.[32]

According to Eusebius, the prophecy against Moab may in fact signify several historical invasions of this *chōra*, that is, "space" or "territory." These include the invasions of the Assyrians and Babylonians, but also the "Arabs" that Isaiah 15:7 and 9 says God will send against Moab. "Arabs," Eusebius explains, can refer either to the "adjacent Arabs" or "the Saracens who lie beyond them" (CI 108.6–7). By "adjacent Arabs," Eusebius likely means the Nabataean kingdom, which controlled the area until its annexation in AD 106 as part of the new province of Arabia.[33] "Saracens," on the other hand, probably refers to what was for Eusebius the more recent past. In AD 291, a panegyric to Diocletian's co-Augustus Maximian mentions a recent victory over "Saracens" who border Syria.[34] In the *Onomasticon*, Eusebius locates the biblical Midian (e.g. Gen 25:2) "beyond Arabia to the south in the desert of the Saracens, east of the Red Sea," and Pharan (e.g. Gen 14:6) as "a city beyond Arabia near the desert of the Saracens."[35] The panegyric and Eusebius' comments in the *Commentary* and *Onomasticon* mark the earliest references to Roman conflict with *Sarakenoi*, and suggest that Diocletian, known from other sources to have been in Syria in AD 290, had repulsed some type of incursion or series of incursions along the frontier of the provinces of Arabia and Syria.[36] Diocletian's innovative border defenses were concentrated in this region and several elements of the emperor's new defensive installations are mentioned by Eusebius.[37] In the *Onomasticon*, for example, the Arnon of Isaiah 16:2 is identified with a river/wadi to the east of the Dead Sea. He writes that the Arnon marked the border between the Moabites and Amorites in the days of Joshua, and served as the site of a series of contemporary border posts along the *Strata Diocletiana*, the system of Roman roads that ran from the Red Sea to Damascus and Palmyra and was the backbone of Diocletian's frontier defenses in the East.[38]

> [Arnon] is located between "Moab and the Amorites." It is *a boundary of Moab*, which is Areopolis in Arabia. Until the present day the place

---

[32] Onom. 173, 175, 176, 360, 372, 388, 408, 410, 647, 525, 725, 745, 795, 815, 822.

[33] On the establishment of the province of Arabia, see Bowersock 1983:76–89, Millar 1993:414–428, and Sartre 2005:133–135.

[34] *Panegyrici Latini* III.5,4; 7,1. See also discussion in Millar 1993:177, 399.

[35] Onom. 650; 914, translation slightly modified for clarity.

[36] Millar 1993:177; Williams 1985:63.

[37] For Eusebius' references to garrisons (*phrouria stratiōtōn*) stationed on the *limes* see for example Onom. 193 (Bela), 676 (Mephaath), 953 (Carmel), 227 (Beer-sheba).

[38] For maps showing the Arnon and the portion of the *Strata Diocletiana* crossing it to the east of the Dead Sea, see Millar 1993:572 and the map included in Notley and Safrai 2005:endpapers.

is still shown of a very dangerous canyon trail that is named Arnon extending to the north of Areopolis. On it also garrisons of soldiers watch on every side because of the fear of the place.

*Onom. 18*

Here again, the underlying exegetical poetic is that of imperial territorialization. The "Moab" of Isaiah marks a space (*chōra*) that for Eusebius bears the traces of a number of spatial writings and rewritings. Eusebius produces the meaning of these verses by establishing a hypertextual link between the space of the prophetic text and the present demographic situation of Roman Arabia: the prophecy ends with a prediction of Moab's dishonor and depopulation, "as is easily observed by those who travel to the place" (CI 112.30–33). "Moab," identified by Eusebius with the *chōra* of fourth-century Areopolis, is a polysemic spatial text that is spread (again, spatially) across several textual planes: the prophetic text of Isaiah, the historical geography of Moab, and the present territory of Roman Arabia marked by imperial defenses and marking the limits of Roman power.

Eusebius goes on to interpret Isaiah 16:5: "Then a throne shall be restored with mercy, and he shall sit on it with truth in the tent of David, judging and seeking decisions and striving after justice." For Eusebius, this passage indicates a radically new enunciation of "Moabite" territory being inscribed in the present:

Who would not be astounded at the fulfillment of this verse, when he sees with his own eyes the churches of God and the "throne" of Christ in them that have been established in Areopolis itself and the territory around it, and in the rest of the cities of Arabia, when those demons who in former times worked terrible things among them no longer have even their names remembered.

CI 110.6–9

The verse from Isaiah is explicitly concerned with land and territory, but establishing a hypertextual link between Isaiah and Roman Arabia was not the only exegetical avenue open to Eusebius. Commenting on the same verse, Jerome notes a range of explanations: some interpreters read the verses as a prophecy of Hezekiah's reign after the return from exile, while others saw an eschatological prophecy of Christ's eternal kingdom after the defeat of the anti-Christ.[39] Given that Jerome claims to draw on both Eusebius' and Origen's commentaries on

---

[39] Jerome, *Commentariorum in Esaiam* 16.5, Latin text in Adriaen 1968.

Isaiah, Jerome's comments could suggest that these other interpretations stood in Origen's work. Since at other points in his *Commentary*, Eusebius clearly refers to alternative exegeses that likely derive from Origen, Eusebius may deliberately ignore these less-territorialized exegeses here. For Eusebius, the verse points to a material, historical alteration of Moabite/Arabian space: the altars of the demons have been scraped from the land and churches with bishops' thrones now dot the landscape. That this different enunciation of space is a conquest and colonization was not lost on Jerome as he drew upon Eusebius' exegesis. His vocabulary makes the hypertextual references between the prophetic past and ecclesiastical and Roman imperial presents even more explicit: "in the whole land of Moab the *imperium* of Christ is evidenced by the signs of the churches that have been built."[40]

Eusebius' hypertextual reading of Isaiah 15 and 16 *kata historian* may appeal to history, but it is not a diachronic or unidirectional mode of reading. Eusebius' figurative readings of the text's *dianoia* are marked by the same hypertextual connections between geographic and textual space as his historical exegeses. A good example is Eusebius' treatment of a portion of the prophecies against Ethiopia in Isaiah 18:2–3: "Now the rivers of the earth will all become an inhabited territory," though one might also render the phrase used here, *chōra katoikoumenē*, as "colonized territory." Eusebius reads the two previous verses of chapter 18, which describe ships and messengers sent "beyond the rivers of Ethiopia," as a figurative reference to universal Christian mission.[41] Eusebius explains that the "rivers" and "territory" of 18:3, however, do not correspond to any identifiable literal/historical rivers or territory:

> But through these verses it seems to me that *rivers* enigmatically signify the multitude of the peoples that have come to know God, and *territory* [to enigmatically signify] the churches. For as above he compared *the multitude of the unbelieving nations to the wave of the sea and to troubled waters* (Isa 17:12–13a), so too he now likens the peoples of Christ to *rivers* that are sweet and flow tranquilly, indicating the Church by their *territory*. Of old, then, these *rivers* were uninhabited and foreign to God (cf. 1 Clem. 7:7), and their *territory* was devoid of piety, but now, he says, through your (pl.) preaching, those designated *rivers* and their *territory will become inhabited.*

CI 120:34–121:6

---

40  Jerome, *Commentariorum in Esaiam* 16.5.
41  For a detailed study of Eusebius' treatment of "Ethiopians" as contrasted with Origen see Johnson 2006:165–186.

Here, the spatial logic of the imperial text points to what is for the book of Isaiah a future and for Eusebius' commentary a present colonization of people and peoples, souls and nations, by the "preaching (*kerygma*)" of the apostles (CI 121.5). This reterritorialization is not figurative:

> But how *the rivers* and their aforementioned *territory* will be able calmly to be inhabited he necessarily teaches, saying: *Therefore in this way the Lord says to me, 'There will be security in my city'* (Isa 18:4). And the afore-mentioned *territory* is *my city*, the Lord's. Thus, *there will be security in it*, as it were with me guarding it and in every way securing it, so that naturally it will be said about it: *Glorious things have been spoken about you, the City of God* (Ps 87:3 LXX) and: *The rushings of the river gladden the City of God* (Ps 45.5a). Thus scripture is wont to call the community (*politeia*) that is according to God, in which, it adds, saying *there will be security* and *there will be light in the same city*, not the common kind, but of a sort such that compared it to the brightest *noon-time* ray of the sun (e.g. Isa 18:4) . . . Now the *light* is the very Word of God that illumi-nates his church everywhere, [while] *cloud full of water* is the Holy Spirit that casts the shadow of the highest theology of the Only-begotten Son of God to those not making room for it, so that, having coalesced, the greatness and purity of the theology concerning Christ would be brought to perfection through the diffusion of the Holy Spirit, just like that of a cloud.

> CI 121: 11–28

As we have seen in the examples of Tyre and Moab, churches, and here in the prophecies about Ethiopia, the preaching of the "theology of Christ," are indeed material enunciations upon real (material) people and peoples and interpolated between the real (material) lines of Roman inscriptions of imperial power.

## Conclusions and Speculations

In this chapter, I have asked that we take seriously, even literally, that texts are spaces—that they subsist in the kinetics of intertextual relationships and are productive of ways of being in spatial relation. To be in the text of Eusebius' *Commentary* is to *be in* an imperial space. The text is *textual*, rather than a paper nowhere, because it is a space produced in, or a *chōra* occupied through, hyper-textual relationships with other productions of space. Its parameters, its borders, its spatial possibilities are all shaped by the forces that draw and redraw the space of the Levant. Imperial spatiality is the text—the metaphors, the figures of speech, the semiotic web—that suffuses the text of Eusebius' commentary, the text of Isaiah, and the spatial text of late-ancient Palestine, Arabia, and Ethiopia.

It can be tempting to read geography and landscape as stable and univocal in contrast to texts as rhetorical, tendentious, or even manipulative. Like late-ancient pilgrims, historians can feel a thrill at visiting or recovering the "real" places mentioned in biblical or other texts. But, as I have hoped to show in this chapter, the relationship between ancient political landscapes and Eusebius' works is not a simple matter of texts and contexts, but a complex problem in semiotics and spatial theory. Landscapes are formed through political processes of conquest, settlement, displacement, administration, and so forth. In fact, landscapes and cityscapes *are* landscapes and cityscapes, rather than empty nowheres, only because they are seen, walked, sailed, and inhabited by politically situated residents and sojourners. The space of the written text, like the geographic space or *chōra*, is never blank. Eusebius cannot merely write the Levant anew on the blank page of a codex. This is a space already territorialized by the text of Isaiah, redrawn in the Septuagint translation and those of Symmachus, Aquila, and Theodotion, repositioned in the *Hexapla* from which Eusebius reads Isaiah, and redistributed further in Origen's lost *Commentary on Isaiah*, which Eusebius had on hand as he wrote his own. The poetics of this hypertextual web is constituted by decidedly spatial figures: halts, invasions, attacks, sieges, sackings, colonizations. The strophe and antistrophe from the prophetic past to the late-Roman present acts as the shuttle weaving the warp and woof of the text. This strophic movement is itself a territorialization or colonization: the spatial text of the seventh and sixth centuries BC are biblicized and the spatial texts of the late-Roman present Christianized.

If it is productive to think about space and territory as texts, collapsing the homology in the other direction—again, attending seriously to the spatiality of textuality—may offer new perspectives on works not explicitly concerned with space and geography. Eusebian texts were produced as and in particular spaces—the page, the codex, the library, or rather, the page-scape, the codex-scape, the library-scape. Eusebius was a pivotal and innovative figure in the development of new technologies of the book. We might well ask if there might be any historical connection between the changing landscape of Eusebius' Levant and the changing landscape of the late-ancient book.

Eusebius' *Commentary on Isaiah* and *Onomasticon* are the pieces of his *oeuvre* that yield most readily to hypertextual and territorial analyses. But we can appreciate other, less explicitly geographical of his works in new ways by reading them in terms of the enunciation of imperial spatiality and territorialization. Eusebius' quotational habits, for instance, involve the marking off or seizure of other literary territories and resettling them in the territory of his own works. The *Gospel Canons*, moreover, another of Eusebius' innovative biblical study aids, seems to operate similarly to the *Onomasticon*. By providing a cross-referencing system for parallel material in the gospels, the *Canons* encourages at least two modes of territorialization. First, it subdivides each gospel text into regions. Second, it asks readers to colonize the text of Mark with the text of Matthew, populate Luke with John, and so forth.

To conclude with a final speculation, let us imagine again the spaces and movements produced by the *Onomasticon*. The *Onomasticon* is readable neither as a travel manual nor as historical geography. Rather, it consists of toponymic lemmata, or nodes. One either enters a node after alighting on an obscure place-name while reading scripture, or alternatively, one visits the node in order to reconnoiter the location of a geographic place in scriptural space. To use the *Onomasticon*, then, is to enact various movements across several textual planes. Consequently, when we examine the production of imperial spatialities in Eusebius' late-ancient works we are not looking at an ossified, ancient "representation" of a since-disappeared ancient geography. To study space-as-production is an historical enterprise with "presentist" implications. Indeed, the continued popularity of biblical atlases and similar study aids, not to mention the centrality of the *Onomasticon* itself for scholarly reconstructions of Holy Land geography,[42] should make us consider to what extent these Eusebian spatialities and territorializations remain very much alive, productive, in the contemporary academy and beyond.

---

[42] One might also note the tendency to render or market editions and translations of the *Onomasticon* as, after the application of critical analysis and the insights of biblical archaeology, a relatively transparent "map" or "plan" of ancient Palestine. Thus Brill's three-column "triglot" edition (Greek edition, English translation, Jerome's Latin, in that order) is in fact a four-column edition, as the running notes along the bottom of each page aim to correct or corroborate Eusebius' remarks (e.g. the note for Onom. 372 [Dibon]: "The present-day village of Dibban," and Onom. 410 [Elealeh]: "This is al-Al, four kilometers to the north of Heshbon. The distance cited by the author [i.e. Eusebius] is inaccurate (Notley and Safrai 2005:75, 82). The title of another recent resource, *Palestine in the Fourth Century A.D.: The* Onomasticon *by Eusebius of Caesarea* (Taylor and Freeman-Grenville 2003) adverts to the volume's intended use as an accessible resource for studying the historical geography of late-ancient Palestine; in asking the reader to refer the *Onomasticon* to the present territorial enunciations of Israel/Palestine (and vice versa), the book extends the very hypertextual web of reference it aims to "read past" at the same time that it obscures the *textuality* of the *Onomasticon* ("our principal aim is to provide an accessible translation, with a helpful index, for use by anyone interested in *the sites of this remarkable area of the world*, as recorded in the fourth century" (8, emphasis added). Notably, both volumes conclude with maps that effectively immobilize hypertextual movements of the text into a reconstructed aerial "snapshot." My criticism is not that such volumes are not useful or important works of scholarship, merely that they attend to but one aspect of the spatiality of the *Onomasticon* as a textuality/texture.

# Works Cited

Adriaen, M. 1968. *Commentariorum in Esaiam Libri I-XI*. S. Hieronymi Presbyteri Opera. Pars I. Opera Exegetica. CCSL 73. Turnhout.

Barnes, Timothy. 1981. *Constantine and Eusebius*. Cambridge, MA.

———. 1982. *The New Empire of Diocletian and Constantine*. Cambridge, MA.

Barthes, Roland. 1977. "From Work to Text." In *Image, Music, Text*, trans. Stephen Heath. New York.

Bowersock, Glen. 1983. *Roman Arabia*. Cambridge, MA.

de Certeau, Michel. 1984. *The Practice of Everyday Life*, trans. S. Rendall. Berkeley.

Drake, Harold. 2000. *Constantine and the Bishops: The Politics of Intolerance*. Baltimore.

Dvornik, Francis. 1966. *Early Christian and Byzantine Political Philosophy*. 2 vols. Dumbarton Oaks Studies 9. Washington, DC.

Farina, Raffaella. 1966. *L'impero e l'imperatore cristiano in Eusebio di Cesarea: la prima teologia politica del cristianismo*. Zurich.

Gamble, Harry. 1995. *Books and Readers in the Early Church: A History of Early Christian Texts*. New Haven.

Genette, Gerard. 1997. *Palimpsests: Literature in the Second Degree*, trans. C. Newman and C. Doubinsky. Lincoln, NE.

Grafton, Anthony and Megan Williams. 2006. *Christianity and the Transformation of the Book: Origen, Eusebius, and the Library of Caesarea*. Cambridge, MA.

Hollerich, Michael. 1990. "Religion and Politics in the Writings of Eusebius of Caesarea: Reassessing the First Court Theologian." *Church History* 59:309–325.

Inowlocki, Sabrina and Claudio Zamagni, eds. 2011. *Reconsidering Eusebius: Collected Papers in Literary, Historical, and Theological Issues*. Supplements to Vigiliae Christianae 107. Leiden.

Jacobs, Andrew. 2004. *Remains of the Jews: The Holy Land and Christian Empire in Late Antiquity*. Stanford.

Johnson, Aaron. 2006. "The Blackness of Ethiopians: Classical Ethnography and Eusebius's Commentary on the Psalms." *Harvard Theological Review* 99:165–186.

Kristeva, Julia. 1980. "The Bounded Text." In *Desire in Language: A Semiotic Approach to Literature and Art*, ed. Leon Roudiez, trans. A. Jardin, T. Gora, and L. Roudiez, 36–63. New York.

———. 1980. "Word, Dialogue, Novel." In *Desire in Language*, 64–91.

Lefebvre, Henri. 1991. *The Production of Space*. Trans. Donald Nicholson-Smith. Oxford.

Millar, Fergus. 1981. "The World of the Golden Ass." *Journal of Roman Studies* 71:63–75.

————. 1993. *The Roman Near East: 31 BC–AD 337*. Cambridge, MA.

Nestle, Eberhard and Kurt Aland, eds. 1969. *Novum Testamentum Graeca*. London.

Notley, Steven and Ze'ev Safrai. 2005. *Eusebius. Onomasticon: The Place Names of Divine Scripture*. Boston and Leiden.

Peterson, Eric. 1935. *Der Monotheismus als politisches Problem: Ein Beitrage zur Geschichte der politischen Theologie im Imperium Romanum*. Leipzig.

Sartre, Maurice. 2005. *The Middle East Under Rome*. Trans. C. Porter, E. Rawlings, and J. Routier-Pucci. Cambridge, MA. (Abridged translation of Maurice Sartre. 2001. *D'Alexandre à Zénobie*. Paris.).

Schott, Jeremy M. 2011. "Eusebius' Panegyric On the Building of Churches (HE 10.4.2–72): Aesthetics and the Politics of Christian Architecture." In Inowlocki and Zamagni 2011:177–198.

Schwartz, E., T. Mommsen, and F. Winkelmann, eds. 1999. *Eusebius. Werke Band 2, Teils 1–3. Die Kirchengeschichte*. Die Griechischen christlichen Schriftsteller der ersten Jahrhunderte N.F. 6. Berlin.

Sirinelli, Jean. 1961. *Les vues historiques d'Eusèbe de Césarée durant la period prénicéenne*. Dakar.

Smith, Christine. 1989. "Christian Rhetoric in Eusebius' Panegyric at Tyre." *Vigiliae Christianae* 43:226–247.

Taylor, Joan, ed. 2003. *Palestine in the Fourth Century AD: The Onomasticon by Eusebius of Caesarea*. Trans. G.S.P. Freeman-Grenville. Jerusalem.

Wilken, Robert. 1992. *The Land Called Holy: Palestine in Christian History and Thought*. New Haven.

Williams, Stephen. 1985. *Diocletian and the Roman Recovery*. New York.

Ziegler, Joseph. 1975. *Eusebius. Werke, Vol. 9. Der Jesajakommentar*. Die griechischen christlichen Schriftsteller. Berlin.

# 10

# The Ends of Transfiguration

## Eusebius' *Commentary on Luke* (PG 24.549)

### AARON P. JOHNSON

IN AN ILLUMINATING TREATMENT of the rise of Platonic commentaries, David Sedley has argued that at the origins of such a parasitic genre as the commentary lies the need to explain a text whose meaning is no longer clear, primarily because of temporal distance, to its readers.[1] Commentaries on Plato's dialogues were necessitated by the linguistic shift from the classical Attic of Plato to the *koine* of Platonists in the late Hellenistic period. Hence, the occurrence of what may seem to modern readers as the simple and uninteresting paraphrase of lines of the source text in the commentaries. Plato's expression in Greek required translation into a more comprehensible idiom. Pierre Hadot had already suggested another reason for the rise of the Platonic commentary, which was at once political and personal, or even spiritual. Following the rupture of continuity in the philosophical schools caused by the Roman conquest under Sulla (88 BC), a fissure was opened up between the intellectual heritage formed by the line of Plato's successors at Athens in the previous generations and the now scattered groups of Platonists (especially at Rome itself).[2] Commentaries filled the gap and provided a sort of intellectual and spiritual parentage for the orphaned Platonic diaspora. Commentaries were an attempt to maintain continuity and stability in the transmission of Plato's philosophy across disruptions of time and geographical space.

Both of these approaches to the rise of the Platonic commentary bear an important point for appreciating any particular commentary or commentary tradition. The relation of a text and its commentary involves the transference of meaning across a space or gap between the source and the target, whether this

---

[1] Sedley 1997:112–116.
[2] Hadot 1987.

be of a temporal, conceptual, linguistic, or even spiritual nature. Commentary is the practice of transposing units of meaning from one ("native") frame of reference and system of conceptual interconnections to another ("foreign") one. Hence, commentary is the practice of translation—a term which, unlike "interpretation," evokes this image of carrying across a space, of transport between textual territories.[3] The translation (whether this was presented in the form of paraphrase or segments of a philological or philosophical commentary) created a second conceptual place that was at once rooted in, and yet different from, the source text. As Eusebius would note in the *Praeparatio Evangelica*, those who gave a translation and explanation of the biblical texts for those who needed it were named *deuterōtai*, those who carved out a second (*deuteros*) space across from and connected to the biblical textual frame.[4] Eusebius' description of these experts highlights an important element of any translation in its placement of these translators in relation to other readers. Besides the transfer of truths "overshadowed in enigmatic riddles" out into the light, the *deuterōtai* stood at a higher level above the "first teachings" to those who were intent on hearing the biblical words. Translation instantiated relations of authority between the master of the second, deeper level of meaning and the student-reader, who would otherwise be left with the mere surface of the letter and so remain "infants in their souls," and not yet "matured in their disposition."[5]

A related image brings us to the passage of Eusebius that will concern us below: commentary may fruitfully be characterized as an act of "transfiguration"—of figuring meaning differently across conceptual and textual boundaries. In figural terms, I suppose it could be represented variously depending on how optimistic or pessimistic we might be about such an enterprise. Is the work of commentary (as translation) merely like the removal and transporting of a framed picture from one room to another, from one gallery to another? Or is it, rather, the removal of the myriad fragments of a mosaic and their subsequent re-assemblage within a different space? In the first instance, the arrangement of many elements remains intact from one space to another; but, in the second, any purportedly original scheme of ordering is replaced. Such different modes of translation, exposition, paraphrase, commentary, and selection depend upon the contexts, needs, and training of the transmitter of meaning. For my present purposes, I only want to make explicit the ways in which we might construe the task of the commentator in late antiquity and raise the metaphoric possibilities

---

[3]  See Sturge 2007:8, 10, 19–21; Bhabha 1994:325.
[4]  PE 11.5.3; cf. Hollerich 1999:143–153.
[5]  PE 12.1.4, where Eusebius is explicitly drawing a parallel between the *deuterōtai* of the Hebrews and Christian teachers. For Eusebius' pedagogical concerns, see Johnson 2011a:99–118.

of translation and transfiguration when reading the commentaries of Eusebius in particular.

Sometime after 311 (probably much later), Eusebius composed a remarkable—yet remarkably under-studied—commentary on the gospel of Luke.[6] In its treatment of the Transfiguration of Christ (Lk 9:28–36) we can appreciate the ways in which certain elements of the biblical text could be transposed into a different frame of reference in the fourth century so as to produce a vision of the world and its peoples that was resonant of, and yet quite different from, the vision of the biblical account. In what follows, I would first like to offer some very brief comments on the background to the *Commentary on Luke*; then I would like to consider two frameworks into which Eusebius translated or transfigured Luke's Transfiguration account.

## Background

The precise form, nature, and scope of Eusebius' original *Commentary on Luke* elude us. The surviving thirty-eight columns of Greek text published in Migne's series (PG 24.529–606) are dwarfed by the extensive remains of his important commentaries on Isaiah and on the Psalms. Extracted from the pages of the eleventh-century Nicetas of Heraclea's Luke catenae, the *Commentary on Luke* has received almost no modern scholarly attention: it remains in need of a critical edition, translation (into any modern language), and analysis in terms of the history of biblical interpretation, especially the commentary genre, as well as with respect to Eusebius' theological positions. The most notable exception to this modern neglect has been Wallace-Hadrill's exposition of the *Commentary* in support of his thesis that the fragments had not been taken from a full-length commentary at all, but originated rather in the tenth book of the *General Elementary Introduction*.[7] Yet, close analysis of both sets of texts shows Wallace-Hadrill's thesis to be quite unlikely.

The content, proportions, emphases, and style of the fragments on Luke and the four extant books of the *General Elementary Introduction* are sufficiently different as to be, in my mind, irreconcilable within the limits of the same original work.[8] The fragments from Nicetas would scarcely fit within the average

---

[6] The only clear internal indication of date is the reference to Maximinus Daia's destruction of a statue set representing Christ and the woman with the hemorrhage in Caesarea Paneas; see *Commentaria in Lucam* 541D–544A; cf. HE 7.18. The references to persecution and the eschatological elements need not indicate an early persecution-era date; see Johnson 2011b. For other considerations of date, see Schwartz 1909:1387; Wallace-Hadrill 1960:51; followed by Moreau 1966:1064.

[7] Wallace-Hadrill 1974.

[8] See Johnson 2011b.

length of the books of the *Introduction*. There is little hint of how any of the material contained in the Luke fragments would cohere with the themes and purpose of the *Introduction*. Even the inclusion of material from the other evangelists, especially Matthew, is directed toward the goal of explicating the passages from Luke. Persecution seems to be a thing of the past (whereas it was a pressing threat in the *Introduction*). Furthermore, in the closing comments of the surviving *Introduction*, Eusebius promises that he would turn to dispelling the errors of the heretics in his next book (the tenth); if the fragments on Luke come from that missing book, then we would have to conclude that he entirely failed to keep his promise.[9] Thus, all the indications point to the existence of a full commentary—or possibly a series of homilies—on the Gospel of Luke, from which our fragments in Nicetas' catenae derive. The treatment of the Transfiguration to which we now turn was part of a continuous linear treatment of Luke quite similar to the extant commentaries on Isaiah and the Psalms.

## Text and Translation

"Παραλαβὼν τὸν Πέτρον καὶ Ἰωάννην καὶ Ἰάκωβον." [5] Καὶ ἐν μὲν τῇ μεταμορφώσει τρεῖς μόνοι τὴν δυνάμει ὀφθεῖσαν αὐτοῖς βασιλείαν τῶν οὐρανῶν θεάσασθαι ἠξιώθησαν· ἐν δὲ τῇ συντελείᾳ τοῦ αἰῶνος, ἐπειδὰν μετὰ τῆς δόξης τῆς πατρικῆς ὁ Κύριος ἀφίκηται, οὐκέτι Μωϋσῆς μόνον καὶ Ἠλίας δορυφορήσουσιν [10] αὐτόν, οὐδὲ τρεῖς μόνοι τῶν μαθητῶν αὐτῷ συνέσονται, ἀλλὰ πάντες προφῆται καὶ πατριάρχαι καὶ δίκαιοι· καὶ οὐκ εἰς ὄρος ὑψηλόν, ἀλλ' εἰς τὸν οὐρανὸν ἀνάξει τοὺς ἀξίους τῆς αὐτοῦ θεότητος. Τότε δὲ λάμψει ἡ θεότης αὐτοῦ οὐχ ὡς ὁ ἥλιος, [15] ἀλλ' ὑπὲρ πᾶν ἐπινοούμενον ἔν τε αἰσθητοῖς καὶ ἐν νοητοῖς

---

[9]   Since the publication of my recent argument that the fragments on Luke are not derived from the tenth book of the *Introduction*, it has occurred to me that one might argue that a decision to focus on Luke could have responded to the Marcionite privileging of that gospel, as well as Marcion's distinctive version of that gospel (see Tertullian, *adversus Marcionem* 4.22; the modern scholarship is scarcely in agreement on the precise relationship between any original version of Luke and Marcion's version, see most recently Tyson 2006, but also, e.g. Von Harnack 1990; Knox 1942; for a corrective account of the earlier phase of the German scholarship, see Roth 2008). I have found, however, no instances of Eusebius' concern with the rendering of Luke's text against Marcionite rivals (e.g. in the Transfiguration passage discussed here, Eusebius does not seem to notice Marcionite variants; see Harnack 1990:37; Knox 1942:86). If one nonetheless adopts this line of reasoning in order to continue to see the fragments on Luke as parts of the lost book of the *Introduction*, one would need to account for the complete absence of any anti-Marcionite expression in the fragments. One looks in vain for an anti-heretical subtext to the *Commentary on Luke*. Instead, it favors asceticism in a way that an anti-encratite work would have avoided, and it lacks concern to show Christ as the fulfillment of the Law or the Old Testament prophets as would be fitting if it were aimed at heretical disparagements of the Hebrew Scriptures (as is frequently found in the *Introduction*).

γεννητὸν φῶς· ἐπείπερ ἐστὶν αὐτὸς τὸ φῶς τὸ φωτίζον πάντα ἄνθρωπον
ἐρχόμενον εἰς τὸν κόσμον· ὅτε καὶ δείξει αὐτοῦ τὸ πρόσωπον· οὐ γὰρ
ὡς πάλαι τῷ Μωϋσεῖ ποτε ἔλεγεν, ὅτι Τὰ ὀπίσω μου ὄψει, τὸ [20] δὲ
πρόσωπόν μου οὐκ ὀφθήσεταί σοι, οὕτω καὶ τότε ποιήσει· ἀλλ' οὕτως
ἑαυτὸν παρέξει τοῖς ἁγίοις, ὡς δύνασθαι πάντας λέγειν· Ἡμεῖς δὲ,
ἀνακεκαλυμμένῳ προσώπῳ τὴν δόξαν Κυρίου κατοπτριζόμενοι, τὴν
αὐτὴν εἰκόνα μεταμορφούμεθα ἀπὸ [25] δόξης εἰς δόξαν. Καὶ τότε οὐ
νεφέλη βοήσει, οὐδὲ διὰ νεφέλης ὁ Πατὴρ μαρτυρήσει τῷ Υἱῷ, ἀλλ'
αὐτὸς δι' ἑαυτοῦ δίχα παντὸς ἐπισκιάσματος, καὶ δίχα παντὸς ἑρμηνέως,
αὐτῷ τῷ ἔργῳ τὸν μονογενῆ αὐτοῦ Υἱὸν ἐπὶ πάντων τῶν ἁγίων αὐτοῦ
δοξάσει, σύνθρονον [30] αὐτὸν ἑαυτῷ καὶ συμβασιλέα ἀποδείξας, καὶ
ὑπεράνω πάσης ἀρχῆς καταστήσας αὐτόν· οὔτε οὐκέτι ὥσπερ τότε οἱ
τρεῖς μαθηταὶ μόνοι ἐπὶ τοῦ ὄρους ἀκούσαντες τῆς φωνῆς ἐπὶ πρόσωπον
ἔπεσον, καὶ ἐφοβήθησαν, ἀλλὰ καὶ πᾶν γόνυ κάμψει ἐπουρανίων
[35] καὶ ἐπιγείων καὶ καταχθονίων. "Φωνὴ ἐγένετο ἐκ τῆς νεφέλης
λέγουσα," κ. τ. λ. Φωνὴ πατρικὴ διὰ νεφέλης, οὕτως γὰρ φαίνεται ὁ
Θεός, ἐμαρτύρει Χριστῷ τὴν υἱότητα· ἔδει γὰρ μὴ παρὰ Πέτρου μόνου
γνωσθῆναι, ὅτι αὐτὸς εἴη ὁ Χριστὸς [40] ὁ Υἱὸς τοῦ Θεοῦ τοῦ ζῶντος·
μηδ' αὐτὸν μόνον τῷ Πέτρῳ μεμαρτυρηκέναι ὡς παρὰ τοῦ Πατρὸς
τοῦ ἐν τοῖς οὐρανοῖς τὴν περὶ αὐτοῦ γνῶσιν εἰληφὼς εἴη· ἀλλὰ καὶ
αὐτὴν τὴν πατρικὴν φωνὴν ἐπισφραγίσασθαι τὴν ἀλήθειαν τοῦ λόγου,
μαρτυροῦσαν αὐτὸν [45] εἶναι Υἱὸν τοῦ Θεοῦ, δεῖν τε ἀκούειν αὐτοῦ
παρακελευομένην.

"Taking Peter, John and James . . ." (Lk 9:28) [5] In the Transfiguration
(*metamorphosis*),[10] only three disciples were deemed worthy of seeing the
kingdom of heaven when it appeared to them with power; but in the consum-
mation of the age, when the Lord returns with the Father's glory, no longer will
Moses and Elijah alone attend [10] Him, nor will only three disciples be with Him,
but [it will be] all prophets, patriarchs and just people; and He will lead those
worthy of His divinity up to heaven, not to a lofty mountain. At that time His
divinity will shine not like the sun [15], but beyond every conceivable begotten
light, both in perceptible and in intelligible realms; since He Himself is 'the light
illumining all humanity coming into the world' (Jn 1:9); at which time He also
will show His face (*prosōpon*); for at that time, he will not do as he did long ago
when he said to Moses, 'You shall see my back, [20] my face shall not be seen
by you' (Ex 33:23); on the contrary, He will show Himself to the saints in such

---

[10] It should be noted that Luke, unlike the other evangelists, avoids *metamorph-* and its cognates;
it has been suggested that he does so to avoid evocation of pagan parallels (Fitzmeyer
1981:798–799).

a way that they will be able to say, 'We, with unveiled face (*prosōpon*) reflecting the glory of the Lord are transfigured (*metamorphoumetha*) into the same image from [25] glory to glory' (2 Cor 3:18). At that time, a cloud will not speak, nor will the Father bear witness to the Son in a cloud, but He Himself, through Himself, apart from any darkness and apart from any translator (*hermēneus*) will glorify His only-begotten Son before all His saints in very deed [not merely in word], proving that He is a co-ruler [30] and fellow sovereign and establishing Him beyond all power. No longer [will it be] like it was at that time when only three disciples fell on their face when they heard the voice on the mountain and were afraid; but 'every knee will bow, of heavenly [35], earthly and netherworld [beings]' (Phil 2:10). "A voice came from the cloud saying . . . ," etc. (Lk 9:35) It was the Father's voice in the cloud, for God appears in this way, when He used to confirm Christ's status as a Son; for it was necessary not only for Peter to make Him known, because He was 'the Christ [40] the Son of the living God' (Mt 16:16); nor that He alone testified to Peter that He had received knowledge about Himself from the 'Father who is in heaven' (Mt 6:9); but on the contrary, the very voice of the Father sealed the truth of the account, testifying that He [45] was the Son of God, and exhorting them that they must listen to Him.

## Eschatology and Transfiguration

What is striking about this passage is Eusebius' unequivocal claim to see in the episode of the Transfiguration a window of a future transformation. Earlier readings of the passage in Luke had found the narrative to be an attempt to confirm and authorize Jesus' status as God's Son (through the voice from heaven) as well as His fulfillment of the Law and prophets (through the figures of Moses and Elijah).[11] Indeed, Eusebius would likewise assert that the divine voice "sealed" the truth of Christ's status as God's Son (549CD).[12] Just such an interpretation of the Transfiguration would find a place in the considerations seeking to problematize the making of icons of Christ in Eusebius' *Letter to the Empress Constantia*. There, he claimed that the Transfiguration gave a glimpse of the divine nature, which was otherwise unrepresentable (hence, Christ's prohibition of the building of shrines to memorialize it).[13]

---

[11] See Origen, *Commentarius Matthaeum* 12.38, 43; *contra Celsum* 6.68. A valuable collection and translation of patristic sources on the Transfiguration (including the two passages from Origen referenced here) is provided in McGuckin 1986:145–316.

[12] Cf. Clement *Stromateis* 6.16.140.

[13] For recent discussion of the letter's authenticity (though allowing for the addition of later material), see Barnes 2010.

The commentary had, however, begun its discussion of the passage with a series of contrasts between the Transfiguration as reported in Luke (with echoes of Matthew's account)[14] and the final, glorious end toward which the episode was merely a prefigured image: in the past only three disciples were deemed worthy of seeing the kingdom of heaven in its power, "but at the end of the age, when the Lord returns with the Father's glory, no longer will Moses and Elijah alone attend Him, nor will only three disciples be with Him, but [it will be] all prophets, patriarchs and just people" (549A). In the Transfiguration, Jesus and the three disciples had gone up a lofty mountain;[15] but at the end, He would lead his followers up to heaven (549A). In the Transfiguration, His face had only shone like the sun;[16] but at the end, He would shine "beyond every conceivable begotten light, both in perceptible and in intelligible realms" (549B).[17]

Such an eschatological emphasis in his interpretation of the passage resonates with a general tendency throughout the *Commentary on Luke*.[18] Numerous fragments discuss the Antichrist (584A), the "son of destruction" (585B; 596C), the rapture (584D–585A; 585CD), the subsequent great apostasy (584A, C; 585BC; 588CD), the upheavals of cosmic phenomena (597B–D; 600C-601B), the second coming of Christ (548B, D; 549A-C), and the final judgment of the Jews, about whom Christ will say, according to Eusebius, "Bring them here, and slaughter them before me" (593C).[19] In his comments on the Transfiguration, the eschatological themes comprise the raising of the faithful (549A), the glorification of the only-begotten Son as a co-ruler (*sunthronon . . . kai sumbasilea*, 549BC), and the submission of all cosmic phenomena to Christ (549C).

It has often been remarked that Eusebius' anti-millenarianism and openness to the prospects of a Christian Roman Empire under a Christian emperor produced in him only a very weak eschatological sensibility. Because of the eschatological elements enumerated here, however, the *Commentary on Luke* has been assigned an earlier date under persecuting emperors when a desire for a final, awesome reparation of wrongs committed would have been more natural.[20] Yet, Maximinus Daia is referred to without any special hostility on the part of

---

[14]  On the inclusion of Matthean material in the *Commentaria in Lucam*, see Johnson 2011b:150–156.

[15]  For similar emphasis on the small number of disciples granted the vision of the Transfiguration, see Origen, *contra Celsum* 2.64–65. Otherwise, this point seems to be unique to Eusebius.

[16]  Christ's face shining like the sun only occurs in Matthew's version.

[17]  Cf. Origen, *Commentarius in Matthaeum* 12.37; *Homilia in Genesim* 1.7.

[18]  See Johnson 2011b:149.

[19]  Quoting from Lk 19:27. That the "fellow-citizens" of Christ who receive such punishment are to be identified with the Jews is made explicit at 592D.

[20]  See Wallace-Hadrill 1960:51; Schwartz 1909:1387.

Eusebius (541D–544A),[21] and, if he was concretely concerned with persecuting emperors, he missed every opportunity to connect them with the Antichrist or the "son of destruction" when he discussed these figures (if they are not, in fact, one and the same). Instead, after noting that the "vultures" of a biblical passage symbolize those who persecute the saints, he quickly moves on to assert that they also designate any kings who had besieged Jerusalem (such as Nebuchadnezzar in Ezeckiel, 588B).[22] A sense of Christian triumphalism, as may be found in almost all of Eusebius' works, is also present in the commentary (553BC; 569AB; 572C; 593B; 597C).[23] Furthermore, Thielman has already argued cogently for an acknowledgment of eschatological elements even in Eusebius' later writings.[24]

The eschatological expressions in the passage on the Transfiguration are thus of little help in any attempt to delineate a theological or political development in Eusebius' thought over time. Instead, they provide us with an important instance of the interpretive mechanisms that could be utilized in order to evince an eschatological image even without explicitly eschatological material in the biblical text at hand. In most of the other fragments of the *Commentary on Luke*, where the end of the age receives elaboration, the biblical text had presented him with details requiring a relatively small interpretive step (e.g. a landlord returns to deal with wicked servants). His eschatological comments on the Transfiguration, on the other hand, depend upon two interpretive means to arrive at their ends. First, details surrounding the description of Christ (some not taken from Luke's account at all) are made to stand as partial types of a future glorification: his being flanked by attendants, his brilliant face,[25] his standing atop a mountain, and the voice from heaven. Based on these features, Eusebius sees the Transfiguration as a clearly typological prefiguration of the final glory.

Secondly, his interpretation of the passage invokes biblical cross-referencing.[26] Christ's shining face recalled John's declaration that he was

---

[21] The PG editor, Angelo Mai, notes that Asterius, cod. B, f. 85 inserts Maximian rather than Maximinus here and reports that the emperor destroyed the statue set (of Christ and the women with the flow of blood); but Eusebius HE 7.18 refers to the statue set as still standing in his day (later authors, e.g. Philostorgius 7.3 and Sozomen 5.21, would claim that pagans under Julian were responsible for its destruction).

[22] On Eusebius' interpretation of other biblical birds, see Johnson 2007.

[23] *Pace* Tabbernee 1997, triumphalist expressions (e.g., the claim that Christianity is spreading throughout the entire earth) cannot be used as indicators of the relative date of any of Eusebius' works; triumphalism is a consistent feature of nearly all of his works, even those that can be securely dated to the period of persecution, e.g. the Gen. El. Intr.

[24] See Thielman 1987; Barnes 1981:172–173; see also the important contribution of Ilaria Ramelli in this volume.

[25] Only at Mt 17:2.

[26] For general remarks on the importance of cross-referencing in Eusebius' commentaries, see Johnson forthcoming.

"the light illumining all humanity coming into the world" (Jn 1:9, at 549B). The metamorphosis of Christ himself recalled the metamorphosis of his followers, who "with unveiled faces reflect the glory of the Lord and are metamorphosed into his same image" (2 Cor 3:18, at 549B), which Eusebius then identified with the final ascent of believers. Or again, the disciples' act of falling on the ground[27] recalled Paul's assertion that "every knee will bow, of heavenly, earthly and netherworld [beings]" (Phil 2:10, at 549C).[28] Such inter-biblical evocations provided a richer texture to his interpretation, provided it with a greater legitimization and authority, and made his eschatological interpretive move seem much more natural and even obvious.

The translation of Lucan meaning into Eusebius' fourth-century context thus involved the assemblage of words and images from different, even disparate, locations in the biblical corpus into a newly constructed unity. Verses from John or the epistles of Paul were carefully excised from their original literary, moral, and theological contexts and made to contribute to a new, distinctively eschatological vision. The Transfiguration narrative in Luke was put to creative ends through Eusebius' transfiguring performance.

One of the biblical cross-references in his commentary on the Transfiguration prompts us to turn to a second fundamental feature of this text. Christ's shining face, made manifest to his disciples, recalled a similar, yet less revelatory, encounter in the Old Testament. "For in that time, he will not do as he did long ago when he said to Moses, 'You shall see my back, my face shall not be seen by you'" (Ex 33:23, at 549B). This passing juxtaposition of the New Testament theophany with that of Moses may have been prompted by Irenaeus' earlier connection of the two episodes.[29] But, Eusebius himself had already shown great concern over the proper interpretation of the Exodus theophany, and his comments on the Transfiguration find their proper contextualization within his larger framework for interpreting Old Testament theophanies, which we find expressed most frequently in his *General Elementary Introduction* (a work which, as already noted, has been improperly identified with the *Commentary on Luke*).

All that survives of the *General Elementary Introduction* are Books Six through Nine, and even these are in damaged and lacunose form.[30] They were published by Migne under the title *Prophetic Eclogues*, since that was Eusebius' own subtitle

---

[27] Only at Mt 17:6.

[28] Interestingly, Eusebius appears to avoid an allusion to the vision of God enthroned in Revelation; on Eusebius' general treatment of the book of Revelation, see the balanced treatment (aside from an inappropriate appeal to a "realized eschatology") of Mazzucco 1979.

[29] Irenaeus, *adversus Haereses* 4.20.9.

[30] On its textual problems, see variously, Nolte 1861; Selwyn 1872; Smith 1916–1917; Mercati 1948; Dorival 2004. For a general account of the work, see Barnes 1981:167–174; Des Places 1982:133–134, 158–188; Kofsky 2000:50–57; Johnson 2006b and 2011a.

for that section of his *Introduction*. These four books are united in their aim of locating and discussing passages of the Hebrew Scriptures that contained manifestations of the Logos, who was second in divinity only to the "God over all." In Book Six of the *Introduction*, Eusebius makes some illuminating distinctions in God's revelations to Abraham, on the one hand, and to Moses, on the other.[31] Whereas He had appeared to Abraham openly at Mamre in a "face to face" encounter, the appearances to Moses were always at a second remove: in a fire, a cloud, or even when the divine presence was fullest to Moses, it was only God's back. In spite of the fact that the Scriptures declared that God spoke with Moses "as with a friend," Eusebius emphasized that the biblical text only granted Moses an encounter that was "visage to visage" (using *enōpios*), not "face to face" (using *prosōpon*) as with Abraham. The "visage to visage" theophany was obscured by the cloud. "He used to speak, therefore, in a cloud, and certainly he did not appear to him like he did to Abraham, Isaac, or Jacob. For it is recorded that he appeared to them openly (*gumnōs*) and clearly without any [physical] form (*eidous*), but to Moses in a so-called form (*eidous*) and the cloud" (Gen. El. Intr. 6 [= Ecl. Proph. 1].12, 1061B).

The clouded vision of the Mosaic theophany was a result of years of spiritual and moral decline under Egyptian servitude. The lofty radiance of a more direct access to the divine, which was allotted to the Hebrew forefathers, was beyond the visionary abilities of the children of the Hebrews. As Eusebius declared in another treatise, the label of Jews was only attached to the ancient Hebrews' descendants during and after their sojourn in Egypt, the land of idolatry.[32] While Moses was able to recall them to the monotheism of their forebears, they were capable of only a moderate form of piety and wisdom. The Law's deepest truths were concealed in riddles of which the Jews were scarcely aware.[33] God's backside theophany was all that Moses, though a "Hebrew of Hebrews,"[34] was granted. Along with the Jews who had largely forgotten the ways of their holy forefathers, Moses saw the divine only through the murkiness of a cloud. He was something of a lone Hebrew who had seen more of God than the Jewish nation but less than his ancestors.

It was precisely this sort of delimited theophanic spirituality that Eusebius was now invoking in his interpretation of the Transfiguration in the *Commentary on Luke*. In Luke's text, "the appearance of His face (*prosōpon*) was changed" (Lk 9:29),

---

[31] I have already signaled the importance of this discussion at Johnson 2006a:117–119.

[32] PE 7.6.2; 7.8.20–21, 37; 10.14.2; 11.6.39. For Egypt as a land of idolatry, see e.g. Eusebius CPs 67.2–4 (PG 23.680B); DE 5.4.3; for classical representations of Egypt, see Smelik and Hemelrijk 1984; Vasunia 2001.

[33] PE 7.8.39. For general discussion, see variously Johnson 2006a:94–125; Ulrich 1999:57–131; Kofsky 1996.

[34] PE 7.7.1; cf. Paul at Phil 3:5.

while in Matthew's account, alluded to by Eusebius, Christ's face (*prosōpon*) shone like the sun (Mt 17:2). This was clearly a "face to face" encounter between Christ and the disciples, which was unlike Moses' theophanies. Instead, it would appear to be on the level of the Patriarchs or even higher. The disciples receiving such a privileged access to the divine face could thus be identified as renewing the pure spirituality of the ancient Hebrews before such rarified closeness to the divine was sullied by the national decline from the Hebrew to the Jewish way of life.[35] Indeed, the *Commentary* itself had earlier clarified the distinction between Hebrews and Jews: the world comprised two orders (*tagmata*),[36] that of the Israelitic race and that of the foreign nations (*allophula ethnē*), represented by the tax collectors in Luke (540BC). Significantly, Eusebius overturns the biblical ordering, "first to the Jews, then to the nations,"[37] with the bold claim that God had first called the nations and only secondly the Jews, or "the circumcision" (540C):[38]

> For before there was Israel there were the nations, and it was to the nations first that the oracles of God and theophanies were given, when the Israelitic name was not yet even present among men. For Enoch, being uncircumcised, was a gentile (*ethnikos*) . . . and Noah . . . was deemed worthy of receiving oracles from God, though he, too, was uncircumcised; and Melchizedek was more ancient than the people of the circumcision . . . and Abraham, Isaac and Jacob were deemed worthy of oracles from God . . . And Job was an Idumean . . .

> *Commentary on Luke*, 540CD[39]

The nation of the Jews, on the other hand, feigned obedience to God, but were deemed unworthy of higher forms of revelation and ultimately rejected his fullest theophany (541AB).

The devaluing and delimiting attitude towards the Mosaic encounter with God that we find in the comments on the Transfiguration thus resonates with a consistent attitude of the *Commentary on Luke* as well as a general feature of Eusebian thought. Again, Eusebius has transfigured the Lucan narrative so as to confirm his ethnic representations and theology of theophany. The Jews were neither named nor targeted in the gospel text. The Transfiguration's relevance for conceptions of spiritual clarity or depth was left ambiguous at best.

---

[35] For Christ and the disciples as renewers of the Hebrew piety, see Ulrich 1999:113–116; Gallagher 1989; Johnson 2006a:227–232.

[36] For similar terminology, see PE 8.10.18–19.

[37] See e.g. Rom 1:16; 2:9.

[38] Cf. *ad Stephanum* 7.7.

[39] For a similar appeal to these holy men, see PE 7.8; Gen. El. Intr. 6 (= Ecl. Proph. 1).7 (PG 22.1041C); Johnson 2004.

Indeed, whatever Paul may have meant by his claim that "we are the true Israel" (Romans 9:3–8), it is doubtful that he possessed the same conceptual apparatus that guided Eusebius' historiographical assumptions about Hebrews, Jews, and Christians.

Yet, we ought not categorize this passage as merely another instance of the same anti-Jewish moves scattered throughout his corpus. For that would be to ignore the ways in which Eusebius' eschatological tendencies in this passage serve to defuse, at least partly, the distinction between Hebrew/Christian spirituality and Jewish/Mosaic spirituality. Consistent with his interpretation of the Transfiguration as a prefiguring of future glory, Eusebius located this Transfiguration within the same sphere of spirituality as Moses' glimpse of the divine back in Exodus. The cloud on the mountain carried the same valence for Eusebius as the cloud that visited the wandering Jews under Moses; it was a sign of epistemological uncertainty and of partial or confused knowledge of the divine.

This ambivalence in the present passage stands in sharper focus if we recall Origen's interpretation of the cloud. In his *Commentary on Matthew*, Origen concluded that Peter was denied the construction of a tabernacle since the cloud was a better, more divine, tabernacle than any that could be built by human hands. Like a tabernacle, whose function was to shelter those within it, the cloud was a divine pattern of the resurrection. "The bright cloud overshadows the just who are at once protected, illuminated and enlightened by it." Origen goes even further: "Perhaps the bright cloud that overshadows the just and prophesies of the things of God is the Holy Spirit who works within it and says 'This is my beloved Son in whom I am well-pleased.'"[40] In a final expansive move, Origen continues, "The bright cloud of the Father, Son and Holy Spirit overshadows the genuine disciples of Jesus. Or else the cloud perhaps overshadows the Gospel and the Law and the Prophets and then becomes bright to the man who can see its light in the Gospel, Law and Prophets."[41]

The antithesis between Origen's and Eusebius' interpretation is sharp. Origen's was no murky cloud that brought confusion and haze; its brightness illuminated rather than concealed. The transcendent glory of the Trinity swirled around the human witnesses in a cloud that protected and revealed, as the whole sweep of revelation from Law and Prophets up to the Gospel was made present in the grandeur of the Father, Son, and Holy Spirit. Such revelatory

---

[40] Origen, *Commentarius in Matthaeum* 12.42 (trans. McGuckin).

[41] Origen, *Commentarius in Matthaeum* 12.42 (trans. McGuckin); I have omitted a section where the text is corrupt. Origen's mention of the Law and prophets here is consistent with his interpretation of Moses as embodying the Law and Elijah as embodying the prophets; see *Commentarius in Matthaeum* 12.38, 43; *contra Celsum* 6.68.

brilliance and nearness to the divine was, for Eusebius, delayed until the end of time. Eusebius' cloud was a veil of obscurity that tantalized the theophanic desires of disciples and readers alike. It would only be at a future time that the Son would "show himself to his saints in such a way that they would be able to say, 'We, with unveiled face (*prosōpon*) reflecting the glory of the Lord . . .' (2 Cor 3:18)" (549B). Eusebius notes that the revelation of the Son's divinity through God's voice in the Transfiguration had come through the darkness of a cloud, a point reminiscent of the cloud of God in the Exodus narrative that Eusebius, in his *Introduction*, had emphasized for its obscuring qualities.

The logic that here denied full theophanic disclosure to those who none-theless caught a glimpse of future glory is likewise the same that prohibited the manufacture of a visual icon of Christ in the *Letter to Constantia*. There, Eusebius had reminded the empress that the divine nature could not be represented in the world of sensible images. It had flashed forth with brilliance on the mountain of Transfiguration, but the intelligible could not be captured in the sensible. The disciples of the New Testament and the Christians of Eusebius' present had not fully transcended, then, the ambiguities and shadows of Jewish theophanic knowledge. Like the Jews, they must await a coming time in which, "no longer will a cloud speak, nor will the Father bear witness to the Son in a cloud, but he himself, through himself, apart from any darkness and apart from any translator (*hermēneus*) will glorify his only-begotten Son before all his saints in very deed [not merely in word]" (549B).

This final assertion of Eusebius returns us to the presence of a space between the source text and its commentary with which we began. For Eusebius, only the end of the age could bring about the end of translation—his role as a transmitter of meaning from the biblical framework to his own contemporary framework was ensured. The Transfiguration required a commentator, since the divine voice continued to speak out from behind clouds and within darkness. In such a world of shadows and ambiguous spiritualities, much might be lost (as well as gained) in translation, or at least be transfigured. But in Eusebius' dim and shrouded world, even with its glints of the Word's presence, translation was a spiritual and theological necessity; and so, the translator's authoritative status remained secure.

The commentary's exposition of the Transfiguration cautions us with respect to several dominant assertions about Eusebius. While he certainly promoted notions of Christian supercessionism and triumphalism over the Jews, his emphasis on the cloud's obscuring effects confined even Christ's disciples to the realm of ambiguity. The achievement of the clear-sighted vision of the divine, such as that of Abraham and other Hebrew holy men, was deferred. Also, in spite of the frequent declarations of Eusebius' dependence on Origen, the preceding discussion has discovered an independent and less optimistic interpretive approach to the biblical text. Furthermore, the eschatology of the passage (and of the remainder of the *Commentary on Luke*) is firm and widespread (contrary to the modern emphasis on his anti-millenarianism, which flattens his multifaceted approach to eschatological elements of Scripture); and it remains consistently future-oriented (in contrast to declarations of a "realized escha-tology" in Eusebius' thought). It is hoped the present remarks, brief though they are, might offer some hint of the rich material that repays the modern reader's careful investigation. The fragments on Luke carried on the incessant work of transfiguring meaning within and between the biblical and late-antique worlds in erudite, creative, and wide-ranging ways.[42] Together with Eusebius' *Introduction* and other commentaries they participated within and creatively developed the broader commentary culture of late-antique philosophical and theological schools.[43]

---

[42] For the impact of the biblical vision(s) in shaping Eusebius' thought and works, see Williams 2008.

[43] See Philippe Hoffman's illuminating discussion (2009), as well as the relevant chapters of Hadot 1995. See also Hollerich's perceptive remarks on Eusebius' commentaries as part of naturalizing processes in late antiquity (in the present volume).

# Works Cited

Barnes, T. D. 1981. *Constantine and Eusebius*. Cambridge, MA.

———. 2010. "Notes on the Letter of Eusebius to Constantia (CPG 3503)." *Studia Patristica* 46:313–317.

Bhabha, H. 1994. "How Newness Enters the World: Postmodern Space, Postcolonial Times and the Trials of Cultural Translation." In *The Location of Culture*, 303–337. New York.

Des Places, E. 1982. *Eusèbe de Césarée commentateur*. Paris.

Dorival, G. 2004. "Remarques sur les *Eklogai Prophétiques* d'Eusèbe de Césarée." In *Philomathestatos. Studies in Greek and Byzantine Texts Presented to Jacques Noret for his Sixty-Fifth Birthday*, ed. B. Janssens, B. Roosen, and P. Van Deun, 203–224. Leuven.

Gallagher, E. 1989. "Piety and Polity: Eusebius' Defense of the Gospel." In *Religious Writings and Religious Systems*, ed. J. Neusner, E. S. Frerichs, and A. J. Levine, 2.139–55. Atlanta.

Hadot, P. 1987. "Théologie, exégèse, revelation, écriture dans la philosophie grecque." In *Les Règles de l'interprétation*, ed. Michel Tardieu, 13–34. Paris.

———. 1995. *Philosophy as a Way of Life*. Trans. M. Chase. Oxford.

Hoffman, P. 2009. "What Was Commentary in Late Antiquity? The Example of the Neoplatonic Commentators." In *Companion to Ancient Philosophy*, ed. Mary Louise Gill and Pierre Pellegrin, 597–622. Oxford.

Hollerich, M. 1999. *Eusebius of Caesarea's Commentary on Isaiah*. Oxford.

Johnson, A. P. 2004. "Ancestors as Icons: The Lives of Hebrew Saints in Eusebius' *Praeparatio Evangelica*." *Greek, Roman and Byzantine Studies* 44:245–264.

———. 2006a. *Ethnicity and Argument in Eusebius' Praeparatio Evangelica*. Oxford.

———. 2006b. "Eusebius' *Praeparatio Evangelica* as Literary Experiment." In *Greek Literature in Late Antiquity: Dynamism, Didacticism, Classicism*, ed. S. Johnson, 67–89. Aldershot.

———. 2007. "Eusebius and Memnon's Ethiopians." *Classical Philology* 102:307–310.

———. 2011a. "Eusebius the Educator: The Context of the *General Elementary Introduction*." In *Reconsidering Eusebius*, ed. C. Zamagni and S. Inowlocki, 99–118. Leiden.

———. 2011b. "The Tenth Book of Eusebius' *General Elementary Introduction*: A Critique of the Wallace-Hadrill Thesis." *Journal of Theological Studies* 62:144–160.

———. Forthcoming. *Eusebius*. Introducing Classics series. London.

Knox, J. 1942. *Marcion and the New Testament*. Chicago.

Kofsky, A. 1996. "Eusebius of Caesarea and the Christian-Jewish Polemic." In *Contra Iudaeos. Ancient and Medieval Polemics between Christians and Jews*, ed. O. Limor and G. Stroumsa, 59–83. Tübingen.

———. 2000. *Eusebius of Caesarea Against Paganism*. Leiden.

Mazzucco, C. 1979. "Eusèbe de Césarée et l'*Apocalypse* de Jean." *Studia Patristica* 17:317–324.

McGuckin, J. 1986. *The Transfiguration of Christ in Scripture and Tradition*. Lewiston.

Mercati, G. 1948. "La grande lacuna delle Ecloghe profetiche di Eusebio di Cesarea." In *Mémorial L. Petit*, 1–3. Bucharest.

Moreau, J. 1966. "Eusebius von Caesarea." *Reallexikon für Antike und Christentum* 6:1052–1088.

Nolte, T. 1861. "Zu den *Eclogis propheticis* des Eusebius von Cäsarea." *Theologische Quartalschrift* 43:95–109.

Roth, D. 2008. "Marcion's Gospel and Luke: The History of Research in Current Debate." *Journal of Biblical Literature.* 127:513–527.

Schwartz, E. 1909. "Eusebios von Caesarea." *Realencyclopädie der Classischen Altertumswissenschaft* 11:1370–1439.

Sedley, D. 1997. "Plato's *Auctoritas* and the Rebirth of the Commentary Tradition." In *Philosophia Togata II: Plato and Aristotle at Rome*, ed. Jonathan Barnes and Miriam Griffin, 110–129. Oxford.

Selwyn, W. 1872. "Emendations of Certain Passages of Eusebii *Eclogae Propheticae*." *Journal of Philology* 4:275–280.

Smelik, K. A. D., and E. A. Hemelrijk. 1984. "Who Knows Not What Monsters Demented Egypt Worships?" *Aufstieg und Niedergang der Romischen Welt* 2.17.4:1852–2000.

Smith, H. 1916–1917. "Notes on Origen and Eusebius." *Journal of Theological Studies* 18:77–78.

Sturge, K. 2007. *Representing Others: Translation, Ethnography and the Museum*. Manchester.

Tabernee, William. 1997. "Eusebius' 'Theology of Persecution:' As Seen in the Various Editions of his Church History." *Journal of Early Christian Studies* 5:319–334.

Thielman, F. S. 1987. "Another Look at the Eschatology of Eusebius." *Vigiliae Christianae* 41:226–237.

Tyson, J. B. 2006. *Marcion and Luke-Acts*. Columbia, SC.

Ulrich, J. 1999. *Euseb von Caesarea und die Juden. Studien zur Rolle der Juden in der Theologie des Eusebius von Caesarea*. Berlin and New York.

Vasunia, P. 2001. *The Gift of the Nile: Hellenizing Egypt from Aeschylus to Alexander*. Berkeley.

Von Harnack, A. 1990. *Marcion: The Gospel of the Alien God.* Trans. J. E. Steely and L. D. Bierma. Durham, NC.

Wallace-Hadrill, D. S. 1960. *Eusebius of Caesarea.* London.

———. 1974. "Eusebius of Caesarea's *Commentary on Luke*: Its Origin and Early History." *Harvard Theological Review* 67:55–63.

Williams, M. S. 2008. *Authorised Lives in Early Christian Biography: Between Eusebius and Augustine.* Cambridge.

*Author's note:* The important article of A. Whealey (in VC 67 [2013]: 169–183) appeared only at the last stages of editing the present volume, and hence the argument made there against attributing the fragments of the Comm.Luc. to Eusebius of Caesarea (Eusebius of Emesa being a more likely source) could not be answered in the present treatment. Whealey's argument against the Caesarean's authorship is not entirely compelling, but certainly prompts the need for further inquiry.

# 11

# Origen as an Exegetical Source in Eusebius' *Prophetic Extracts*

Sébastien Morlet

T HE STUDY OF THE RELATIONSHIP between Eusebius and Origen as exegetes is still conditioned by Carmelo Curti's article "L'esegesi di Eusebio di Cesarea: caratteri e sviluppo."[1] This article contains, in my view, three major hypotheses:

1. Throughout his life, Eusebius was attached to the principle that Scripture contains two meanings, the letter and the spirit. In the *Prophetic Extracts* (hereafter Ecl. Proph.), Eusebius would concentrate on the search for the "allegorical" meaning; the *Demonstratio Evangelica* (hereafter DE) would witness a certain balance between the two senses; in the *Commentary on the Psalms* (hereafter CPs), finally, Eusebius would have favored the literal meaning.

2. These differences would attest to an *evolution* of Eusebius' exegetical practice.

3. The search for the "allegorical" sense in Eusebius would be indebted to Origen; on the contrary, the "literalism" of the CPs would foreshadow the so-called "Antiochene school."

---

[1] See Curti 1985. The influence of this article is notable in Kannengiesser 2004, though the author seems to have totally misunderstood Curti's description of the Ecl. Proph. as witnessing a taste for allegorical interpretation (p. 677: "In the Eclogae he stresses the literal meanings of the prophecies"). The first global study on Eusebius' exegesis is C. Sant's study (Sant 1964). After C. Curti, M. J. Hollerich provided the first monograph on Eusebius' *Commentary on Isaiah* (Hollerich 1999). A few studies dealt with Eusebius' possible use of Origen in the *Demonstratio Evangelica*, the *Commentary on Isaiah,* or the *Commentary on the Psalms* (see, in chronological order: Curti 1980; Carpino 1986; Guinot 1987; Tuccari 1987; Hollerich 1992 and 1992b; Dorival 1996; Pennachio 2002; Morlet 2009:585–622; Bandt 2011 and forthcoming). Such a study should take into account the recent discovery of homilies on the codex *Monacensis gr.* 314 by Marina Molin Pradel. According to Lorenzo Perrone, these homilies must be attributed to Origen.

In an earlier analysis of the first two hypotheses,[2] I tried to show that Curti's description seems correct, generally speaking, but that his hypothesis of an evolution of Eusebius is difficult to sustain, since it appears, rather, that Eusebius could have commented differently on the same text because he had specific *interests* in doing so. This is not to say that Eusebius was a "cynical" interpreter. But his interpretation may slightly change according to his rhetorical strategy (i.e. more or less polemical) or the literary genre of the work (i.e. commentary, apology, theological speculation, etc.). Hence, it is often not necessary to hypothesize an intimate *evolution* of Eusebius's exegesis.

What is particularly striking in Curti's article is that the scholar discusses the relationship between Eusebius and Origen only in terms of general *hermeneutics*, according to the principle "allegory is Origenian" (which is, moreover, extremely reductive); he never tries to evaluate the debt of Eusebius to Origen's *commentaries* and, significantly, he never quotes any text by Origen in the core of his demonstration. This gives his inquiry a very abstract turn. Our aim is to proceed along more philological grounds. We already began this inquiry in the case of the DE. We would like to ask here how far we can identify the Origenian background of the Ecl. Proph. Such an inquiry, as one knows, is far from simple, since huge parts of Origen's commentaries are no longer extant, at least in direct tradition. But this study will show that the research is not impossible.

In a previous publication, I argued that the prologue of the Ecl. Proph.'s book 4 is based on several passages from *Against Celsus* (see Appendix 2).[3] It remains to be seen if Eusebius is also indebted to Origen's *commentaries* in this work.

## Eusebius' Method in the Ecl. Proph.

The exact date of the Ecl. Proph. is unknown.[4] It was composed between 304 and 313, and probably around 311/312 if one accepts Burgess' dating of the *Chronicle*.[5]

---

[2] See Morlet 2007 and 2009:585–622.

[3] Morlet 2009:333–339. A. P. Johnson, without knowing my argument, also noticed the use of *Against Celsus*, 1.36 in this passage (Johnson 2011).

[4] We are still dependent on T. Gaisford's edition (Gaisford 1842). I am preparing a new critical edition for the Sources chrétiennes. Very few studies have dealt with that work since Gaisford's edition. Except A. P. Johnson's recent article (Johnson 2011), most of them are not "studies," properly speaking, but aim at correcting Gaisford's text or filling in the lacunas of the works (in books 1 and 2): Nolte 1861; Selwyn 1872; Smith, 1916–1917; Mercati 1948; Dorival 2004. Note the French translation, with a few comments, by M. Jaubert Philippe (Jaubert Philippe 2001).

[5] Burgess 1997: the first edition of the *Chronicle* would date to 311. Burgess thinks however that at the time Eusebius was working on the Ecl. Proph., he had probably not finished the *Chronicle*, which is a way of interpreting the vague mention of the *Chronological canons* at the beginning of the Ecl. Proph. E. Schwartz thought he could date the work before 310 because of a supposed allusion to Pamphilus, who died in 310, in Ecl. Proph. 4.31; but his analysis seems incorrect (Morlet 2009:81n109).

It formed books 6 to 9 of the *General Elementary Introduction* (Gen. El. Intr.), from which we only have fragments from the first books. There is no reason to think that this work was not, as the title indicates, a real "introduction," viz. an exposition of the Christian faith addressed to beginners.[6] The plan was probably the following: first, exposition of the fundamental principles of Christian doctrine, with a discussion about Christ (books 1–5); second, prophetical proofs about Christ (books 6–9); third, refutation of heresies (book 10).[7]

The Ecl. Proph. are a collection of proof-texts (*testimonia*) about Christ and associated ecclesiological themes (the calling of the nations, the rejection of the Jews), with a commentary by Eusebius. The work contains several passages in which Eusebius explains his own method.[8] At the beginning of the Ecl. Proph., he specifies the kind of interpretation he will make:

Ἔσται δὲ καὶ διὰ βραχέων μετρία τις ἡμῶν ἐξήγησις, ὅτε μὲν ἀπόδειξιν περιέξουσα τοῦ κατὰ μόνον τὸν ἡμέτερον Σωτῆρα πεπληρῶσθαι τὰς ἱερὰς τοῦ Θεοῦ προρρήσεις, ὅτε δὲ τὴν ἡμετέραν γνώμην ἣν ἐχόμεν περὶ τῶν ἐκτεθησομένων σημαίνουσα.

"And our interpretation will be short and moderate. On the one hand, it will contain a proof that the sacred predictions of God have been

---

[6] It remains to be seen if such an introduction could have been a real "manual" used at Caesarea in a course (see Schwartz 1907:1386; Barnes 1981:169), or a "literary" introduction, such as the *Preparation* appears to be.

[7] The few fragments we possess from the first part of the Gen. El. Intr. indicate a discussion about ethical themes (good and evil, free will). Fragment 2, from book 1, alludes to the Logos. Eusebius says at the beginning of the Ecl. Proph. that he has spoken about the doctrine and life of Christ before (so, in the previous book or books). It is thus difficult to know if the ethical themes were treated for themselves, or rather within a demonstration about Christ, which is very possible. This discussion was founded on "the testimonies about our Lord and Savior" (= probably the Gospels); "true demonstrations and syllogisms" (= logical argumentation); also, "at the end," short quotations from the OT, because, as Eusebius indicates, it was not time for him to give a long exposition of the prophecies for readers who were still not convinced that the Scriptures are divinely inspired. The previous development about the prophecies contained, however, a proof of that point, so that the reader is supposed, now (ἤδη), to believe that the Scriptures are divinely inspired. The Ecl. Proph. will thus complete (ἀποπληροῦντα) what "is lacking to them" (τὸ λεῖπον ἐκείναις), viz. the Scriptures or, more probably, the "expositions" (τὰς συστάσεις) mentioned before. At the end of book 4 of the Ecl. Proph. (viz. book 9 of the Gen. El. Intr.), Eusebius announces a discussion on the heresies. This tends to undermine D. S. Wallace Hadrill's contention that Eusebius' fragments on Luke (see PG 24.529–606) originally come from book 10 (Wallace-Hadrill 1974:55–63) of the Gen. El. Intr. A. P. Johnson recently refuted Wallace Hadrill's hypothesis and suggested that these fragments may come from a commentary on Luke (Johnson 2011).

[8] This makes the Ecl. Proph. a very valuable (and underestimated) testimony about ancient exegetical practices.

accomplished only at the time of our Savior. On the other hand, it will show the opinion we have concerning the passages we will quote."

This text defines the σκοπός[9] of the commentary in a twofold way: not only will Eusebius comment on a selection of passages, but he will also content himself with a selective commentary. The latter will be based on the demonstration that Jesus has fulfilled the prophecies. But Eusebius states that he will also give his *own opinion* concerning the texts. At first sight, this way of defining the commentary is rather puzzling, since one does not clearly see why Eusebius' opinion could not be the same thing as the conviction that Christ has fulfilled the prophecies. Besides, this conviction is expressed in *every* commentary. For this reason, it seems impossible to understand the text as if Eusebius was saying that he will "sometimes" (ὅτε μέν) demonstrate the accomplishment of the predictions, and "sometimes" (τότε δέ) give his own opinion. One should probably rather understand ὅτε μέν . . . τότε δέ as meaning "on the one hand, on the other hand." Thus, the text could mean that Eusebius intends primarily to show that Jesus accomplished the prophecies, and also (probably secondarily) to provide *other* comments, which do not necessarily correspond directly to the first and fundamental issue of his commentary.

In the commentary itself, Eusebius follows this principle. He comments on the *testimonia* only by referring them to Christ or associated themes.[10] In that respect, the commentary is only a development of the ὑποθέσεις that are given at the beginning of the books (except at the beginning of book 1, which is lost, and of book 4, which apparently lacks such a *pinax* in the preserved manuscripts). It is short (διὰ βραχέων),[11] gives only indications "in passing" (ἐν παρέργῳ καὶ παραδρομῇ),[12] and Eusebius compares it to an ἐπιτομή.[13]

# "Concluding Formulas" in the Ecl. Proph.
## as Indications to Readers

Eusebius, however, often feels the need to give some indications to the reader who would like to go further and would be in need of a complete commentary. Eusebius gives these indications at the very end of his comments.[14] Their

---

[9]   The word is used in 1.8; 2.7.
[10]   There are some exceptions: in 1.8, Eusebius admits that he has gone beyond his σκοπός, because a clear understanding of the passage needed such a development.
[11]   1.19.
[12]   2.9.
[13]   3.46.
[14]   See Appendix 2. We have already discussed analogous passages contained in the DE (Morlet 2009:117–134).

recurrence is striking. The "formulaic" character of the phrases used by the exegete is also notable. Eusebius addresses himself to the "lover of learning" (the φιλομαθής).[15] He often explains that his σκοπός prevents him from going beyond a selective commentary and that a deep investigation of the texts must be left for another time (καιρός[16]) and would require some leisure (σχολή[17]). Sometimes, the concluding remarks allude to a section of the text that Eusebius does not want to comment upon because it would be too long and too far from his aim, or because it would lead him to too difficult an explanation, and such an explanation must be rejected from a work that is addressed to the beginners. At other times, the indication does not allude to a portion of the text that is not commented upon, but to a level of understanding that Eusebius, for the same reason, prefers to leave unaddressed.

Sometimes, Eusebius concludes commentaries by noting that he cannot go further, but does not include any indication to the reader who would like to know more. At other times, Eusebius explains the kind of exegesis which the text would need: he may indicate that it needs a spiritual interpretation, or give a more specific indication, for instance, that the text is to be understood with reference to Christ alone, or that the reader would only have to adapt to the whole text Eusebius' comments about another passage or passages (see Appendix 1).

A few times, Eusebius even refers his reader to other commentaries. He sometimes makes it clear that if he does not need to give a complete commentary, it is *because* such commentaries exist.[18] The problem is: what are these other commentaries?

Most often, the reference is anonymous: about the Psalms, Eusebius refers to τοῖς εἰς αὐτὸν ὑπομνηματισαμένοις (2.1), τὰ ὑφ' ἑτέρων εἰς τὸν Ψαλμὸν ὑπομνηματισθέντα (2.7), or to a πληρεστάτη διήγησις (2.2); about Isaiah, he alludes to τὰ εἰς τοὺς τόπους ὑπομνήματα (4.7). But it is not difficult to identify these commentaries. About the same Isaiah, Eusebius refers one time to τὰ εἰς τοὺς τόπους τοῦ θαυμασίου ἀνδρὸς ἐξηγητικά, "the exegetical remarks of the marvelous man about these passages" (4.7). About the Song of Songs, Eusebius writes that the book has already found a "very complete clarification" (πληρεστάτη σαφηνεία) "in the commentaries of the very industrious exegete of the divine Scriptures" (ἐν οἷς ὁ φιλοπονώτατος τῶν θείων γραφῶν ἐξηγητὴς ὑπεμνημάτισατο).[19] These two texts can hardly refer to a man other than Origen.

---

[15]  1.6.8; 4.7.20.
[16]  4.11.18.
[17]  3.14; 4.17.
[18]  See 2.2; 3.6.
[19]  3.6.

They tend to prove that each time Eusebius refers to another commentary (that is to say about the Psalms, Isaiah, and the Song), he refers primarily, and highly probably, only, to Origen's commentaries.[20] Besides, the possibilities are not many.[21]

But one could and perhaps should go further. These few references to Origen's works already indicate that Eusebius has in mind his predecessor's commentaries when he composed the Ecl. Proph. and that these commentaries were for him (at least at that time) the best commentaries one ever wrote or would write (as he presents the *Against Celsus*, at the beginning of the *Against Hierocles*, as the prototype of every possible refutation).[22] Thus, it is reasonable

---

[20] The question remains: why does Eusebius not *name* Origen (the same phenomenon occurs in Ecl. Proph. 4 Prologue: Eusebius depends on Origen, but speaks about his "predecessors," οἱ πρὸ ἡμῶν)? He may have done so in the first books of the Gen. El. Intr. or in the "lacuna" of the Ecl. Proph.'s book 2. If he had not done so, one could wonder if his silence has to do with the fact that Origen's ideas (and commentaries) were suspected at that time, as the *Apology for Origen* witnesses. Is it a literary device or even a kind of "code" for the happy few? Do we have to think that Eusebius did not *need* to name Origen for his audience (which would suggest that the work was intended primarily for a circle of friends, that of Pamphilus); and/or, that this audience revered Origen so much that it would have seemed too irreverent to *name* the master? Significantly, perhaps, Eusebius does not refrain from naming Origen at the beginning of his *Against Hierocles* (see note 22), but he probably addresses here an external audience, which did not necessarily know who he was.

[21] The other exegete who is known to have written a commentary on the Psalms before Eusebius is Hippolytus (see Jerome, *De uiris illustribus* 61, and the so-called "statue of Hippolytus" [see Prinzivalli 1983]). If such a commentary existed, the question remains to be seen if the few fragments on the Psalms preserved belong to this work (see CPG 1882). Apart from the fragments, we possess a "homily" edited by P. Nautin (Nautin 1953). The question of whether the bishop of Caesarea knew and used these commentaries must remain open. The question is not posed by A. J. Carriker (Carriker 2003:209–215). On the one hand, there is no clear evidence that Eusebius knew any of them. In the catalogue of Hippolytus's works, he does not mention them, though he names a few of Hippolytus' books (HE 6.22: *About the Hexaemeron; About what follows the Hexaemeron; On the Song of songs; On parts of Ezechiel*). On the other hand, Eusebius states that apart from the list he gives, there were other works of Hippolytus that were not in his possession, but were "preserved among many people" (HE 6.22): thus, he also heard of other works by Hippolytus, and one cannot exclude that he had a knowledge of at least parts of his commentaries on the Psalms (which he may have copied, for instance, from another library than his own one). In Ecl. Proph. 2.7, he refers to the commentaries written by "others" (ἑτέρων): the plural sometimes hides a single source, but if Eusebius has not only Origen in mind, he may also refer here to Hippolytus. The fact that both Origen and Hippolytus seem to be the only ones to have interpreted Ps 1 as a prophecy about Christ before Eusebius (see *infra*) makes it possible to believe that, though Origen appears to be his main source when he comments on the Psalm, he may also have Hippolytus in mind. One must admit, however, that Origen is, generally speaking, a more "natural" source for Eusebius: if he used Hippolytus (which is not clear), the bishop of Caesarea must have used him only as a very marginal source.

[22] About Hierocles' arguments: ἃ τύχοι μὲν ἂν καὶ αὐτὰ τῆς προσηκούσης κατὰ καιρὸν ἀπελέγξεως, δυνάμει δ᾽ ἤδη καὶ πρὸ τῆς ἰδίας κατ᾽ αὐτῶν γραφῆς ἀνατέτραπται καὶ προαπελήλεγκται ἐν ὅλοις ὀκτὼ συγγράμμασι τοῖς Ὠριγένει γραφεῖσι πρὸς τὸν ἀλαζονικώτερον τοῦ Φιλαλήθους ἐπιγεγραμμένον Κέλσου Ἀληθῆ λόγον, ᾧ τὰς εὐθύνας ἀπαραλείπτως, ἐν ὅσοις εἰρήκαμεν,

to think that the concluding formulas in the Ecl. Proph. are *often*, if not *always*, an allusion to Origen's commentaries.

The type of exegesis that Eusebius excludes from his *Extracts* tends to sustain this hypothesis. This exegesis is excluded because it is too long,[23] too precise,[24] or too respectful of every word (ἑκάστη λέξις) in the text;[25] it is too deep,[26] too difficult for a beginner; it deals with the deepest meaning of the text (called by Eusebius ἡ δι' ἀλληγορίας ὑπονοία,[27] νοῦς,[28] διάνοια,[29] or θεωρία[30]), which would need to be understood *spiritually* (πνευματικῶς),[31] with the help of "tropology alone" (μονὴ τροπολογία),[32] or "the laws of allegory" (νόμοι ἀλληγορίας).[33] It would be the commentary of someone who could search (ἐξετάζειν)[34] and scrutinize (ἐρευνᾶν).[35] These phrases not only suggest Origen's exegesis, which was known in antiquity to be at the same time precise, respectful of every letter in the text, and based on the research of the deepest meaning, but they are part of Origen's own exegetical vocabulary.[36]

Now, if we must be convinced that Eusebius has Origen in mind when he speaks about what he *could* do, but *does* not, does that mean that his commentary is *not* indebted to Origen, or, on the contrary, that it *is*? The only way to know is to compare, every time it is possible, Origen's preserved exegesis with Eusebius'. It would be impossible to discuss every commentary in the Ecl. Proph. We will concentrate on book 2, which deals with the Psalms, and will take only three examples. Origen's exegetical works on the Psalms included a long commentary (the *Tomoi* on the Psalms); homilies; and at least two collections of scholia (or

---

ὁ δεδηλωμένος παραγαγὼν συλλήβδην ὅσα εἰς τὴν αὐτὴν ὑπόθεσιν παντί τῳ εἴρηταί τε καὶ εἰρήσεται, προλαβὼν διελύσατο, ἐφ' ἃ τοὺς ἐπ' ἀκριβὲς τὰ καθ' ἡμᾶς διαγνῶναι ἔχοντας φιλαλήθως ἀναπέμψαντες. The way Eusebius refers here to Origen's *Against Celsus* recalls our "concluding formulas" (except that he names Origen: see note 20). This would be a confirmation that Eusebius, in the Ecl. Proph., does refer to Origen.

23   1.19; 3.27: πολλὴ ἐξέτασις.
24   1.1; 3.14.
25   1.6; 3.14; 4.4; 4.20; 23.
26   2.9; 3.6; 33: βαθυτέρας θεωρίας; 4.11.
27   1.8.
28   2.14 (νοήσειας).
29   4.24.
30   1.3; 3.33.
31   2.14. See also 4.24.
32   4.10. Compare to 4.24: κατὰ μόνην διάνοιαν.
33   1.6.
34   3.27; 4.23.
35   1.12; 4.27.
36   Origen quotes seven times the passage of John 5:39, ἐρευνᾶτε τὰς γραφάς (*Against Celsus* 3.33; 5.16; *Commentary on John* 5.6.1; 6.20.109; *On Principles* 4.3.5; *Philocalia* 1.21; 5.5). About the necessity of ἐξετάζειν, see for instance *Commentary on John* 6.14.84; 41.215; *Commentary on Matthew* 13.4; 15.6; 16.2; *Homilies on Jeremiah* 10.1; *On prayer* 5.2.

"excerpts").[37] Of this material, almost nothing remains. From the *Tomoi* and the excerpts, we only have a few fragments given in the catenae. Origen, though, often mentions the Psalms in his other works. His exegesis may correspond partly to what he wrote in his commentaries on the Psalms, but may sometimes also be different. Jerome's *Commentarioli in Psalmos*, however, are a good (but selective) witness to the *Tomoi*, since Jerome writes in his preface that he will give some brief indications about the Psalms derived from Origen's *Tomoi* and homilies, or based on his own opinion.[38] The following analysis will show the difficulty, but also the interest of comparing Eusebius' Ecl. Proph. to what remains of Origen's exegesis on the Psalms.[39]

## Eusebius' Exegesis of the Psalms in the Ecl. Proph.

### Psalm 1, 1-2[40] (= Ecl. Proph. 2.1)

1    Blessed is the man who did not walk in the counsel of the wicked,
        Nor stand in the path of sinners,
        Nor sit in the seat of scoffers!
2    But his will is in the law of the Lord,
        And in his law he will meditate day and night.[41]

Eusebius' commentary aims at showing that the text can in no way refer to a simple man, but only to Christ, since the virtue of the man mentioned in the Psalm "surpasses every human nature."[42]

---

[37]  The "Enchiridion" mentioned in Jerome's *Commentarioli in Psalmos* is sometimes seen as a third collection of excerpts (see for the problem Rondeau 1982:46–47). E. Prinzivalli notices that it is usual to identify this *Enchiridion* with the *Excerpta in totum Psalterium* (Prinzivalli 2000:422). It is sometimes believed that at least one of the two collections of "excerpts" was a collection of extracts from Origen's other commentaries, viz. *Tomoi*, *Homilies*, and *Scholia* (if one accepts the idea that the other collection of "excerpts" was actually a selective commentary by Origen himself, and not a collection of extracts constituted by later exegetes): see Rondeau 1982:48–49, who notes V. Peri's hypothesis that the *Tractatus in Psalmos* attributed to Jerome are a Latin translation of passages from Origen's homilies and are identical with the *Excerpta in totum Psalterium*. Many scholars have remained sceptical towards this hypothesis. M.-J. Rondeau admits however that the *Excerpta in totum Psalterium* would have been extracts from Origen's homilies.

[38]  *Commentarioli in Psalmos*, Prologus, 18–21 Morin.

[39]  This research is indebted to the *Biblia patristica*, now on the Internet under the name "Biblindex." From the many texts attributed to Origen in the catenae, some are now placed among the *spuria*, others, in the *dubia*. In the following analysis, I concentrate exclusively on the texts whose authenticity is not questioned.

[40]  The Psalms are quoted according to the Septuagint numbering.

[41]  The translations of the Septuagint text are inspired by the New American Standard Bible.

[42]  Gaisford 1842:68.21–22.

This passage is often referred to in the first three centuries, though always as an allusion to the faithful or the just man (not to Christ).[43] The only two exceptions before Eusebius are Hippolytus and Origen. The former left a very short commentary applying the text to Christ.[44] The other commented many times upon the two verses. Most often, Origen reads it as an allusion to the faithful,[45] and sometimes more precisely to those who are eager to find the deepest meaning of the Scriptures (they "meditate on the law day and night").[46] There are, however, at least two fragments of Origen's *Tomoi* on the Psalms, preserved in the catenae, which apply the text to Christ. The first fragment is attributed to Origen in three manuscripts.[47] Because Origen seems more often to apply the text to the faithful, E. Goffinet is a bit skeptical towards this fragment. He judges that it does not reflect Origen's "usual doctrine" (*sic*) but that it "might" have been contained in his commentary on the Psalms as an illustration of a "current theory" (that is to say, an interpretation that Origen did not completely admit). The problem is that we also have another fragment from the same commentary, which contained two close parallels with Eusebius' commentary in the Ecl. Proph.[48] This fragment explains that Christ alone must be indicated in the Psalm, because of his exceptional virtue, and argues, exactly like Eusebius in the Ecl. Proph., that this interpretation is confirmed by reference to the Hebrew text, which contains an article before the word ἀνήρ, which demonstrates, to the commentator's view, that the text does not refer to "a" man, but to "the" only man who could accomplish the prophecy.[49]

---

43   *Epistle of Barnabas* 10.10; Justin *Apology* 1.1–6; Irenaeus *Demonstration of the Apostolic Preaching* 2; *Against Heresies* 5.8.3; Tertullian *Against Marcion* 2.19.1–3; 4.42.8; *On Modesty* 6.4; *On Spectacles* 3.3; 5; 8; *To his Wife* 1.4.4; Clement of Alexandria *The Pedagogue* 1.90.1; 92.1; *Stromateis* 2.67.1; 3–4; 68.1; 5.31.1; 7.109.2; Cyprian *On the Unity of the Church* 10; *To Quirinus* 3.120; *Teaching of the Apostles* (anonymous work of the third century) 26; Lactantius *Divine Institutes* 4.16.6; Methodius of Olympus *Banquet* 5.4; *On foods* 14.2; *On the leech* 1.5.

44   See *Homily on the Psalms* 20 (Nautin 1953:183).

45   *Against Celsus* 3.60; *Commentary on the Song of Songs* 3 (p. 181.21 Baehrens); *Commentary on Matthew* 10.15; *Commentary on Romans* 9.2; *Fragments on Ezechiel* C 543.34; *Fragments on Lamentations* 260.24; *Fragments on the Psalms* PG 12.1085 B; *Fragments on Romans* 31 Ramsbotham; *Homilies on Leviticus* 6.1; 6; 7.6; 9.5; 11.1; 12.4; *Homilies on the Psalms* 3.10 (PG 12 1346 A 5); *On Prayer* 29.9.

46   *Commentary on the Song of Songs* Prologue (p. 77.17 Baehrens); *Homilies on Leviticus* 7.6; *Homilies on Luke* 39.218.3.

47   See fr. 1 Goffinet (Goffinet 1963): cod. *Vindobonensis Theol. Gr.* 8; cod. *Coislianus* 80; cod. *Vatopedinus* 240.

48   See fr. 3 Goffinet. Another problem is that there is no evidence that this theory was "current" at that time, at least concerning verses 1 and 2 of the Psalm.

49   See both texts: Τὸ δ' ἐπιδεδεγμένον τῆς ἐκδοχῆς παρίστησιν ἡ κατὰ τὸ Ἑβραϊκὸν ἐντεῦξις ἐπιτετηρημένως οὕτως ἔχουσα, μακάριος ὁ ἀνήρ, μετὰ τῆς ἄρθρου προσθήκης (Eusebius, Gaisford 1842:68.28–69.1); τοῦτο δ' ἔοικεν ἡ Ἑβραϊκὴ φωνὴ παριστᾶν, καθ' ἣν μακάριος ὁ ἀνὴρ μετὰ τῆς ἄρθρου προσθήκης εἴρηται (fr. 3 Goffinet).

In one manuscript (*Vindobonensis Theologicus Graecus* 59), the fragment is attributed to Origen; in another manuscript (*Oxoniensis Bodleianus Baroccianus* 235), it is attributed both to Eusebius and to Origen, the manuscript suggesting that the text is derived from Eusebius using Origen (Εὐσεβ. Καισαρ. ὁμοίως ωρ.). Goffinet thinks that the text is a Eusebian commentary exactly reflecting Origen's, which is possible.[50]

In any case, these different testimonies attest that:

> Origen, in his *Tomoi*, also applied the Psalm to Christ;

> Eusebius used this interpretation in his own *Commentary on the Psalms*, probably rewriting (at least partly) Origen's exegesis;

> the Ecl. Proph. already reflect Origen's interpretation in the *Tomoi*; moreoever, since the passage about the article in the Hebrew text is found again in the catenae and is attributed both to Origen and to Eusebius, there is a strong probability that at least this passage is already, in the Ecl. Proph., a rewriting of Origen's *Tomoi*. It is thus also probable that the rest of the commentary is strongly inspired by Origen's commentary. This intuition is confirmed by Jerome's *Commentarioli in Psalmos*. Jerome first applies the text to the just man who meditates upon the Law of God, but since the Jews, as he says, apply the Psalm to Josias, he explains that it would better (*melius*) be applied to Christ.[51]

We can thus demonstrate that in his *Tomoi*, Origen suggested at least two interpretations (and referred to a third, "Jewish" one, if Jerome follows him in this as well): first, that the Psalm refers to the just man; second, that it would refer to Josias, according to the Jews; third, but that it better applies to Christ. Thus, Origen was not reluctant towards the Christological interpretation of the text, as Goffinet tended to think.[52] The testimony of the Ecl. Proph. could already have permitted Goffinet to revise his opinion, since at the end of the commentary, Eusebius, as we noted, tells the reader that he will find every detail of the christological meaning of the text in commentaries which, as we have shown, are Origen's *Tomoi*.

---

[50] "Le caténiste a eu en mains le texte d'Eusèbe et celui d'Origène. Il a donné sa préférence à celui d'Eusèbe (...). La seule interprétation possible de ὁμοίως est que le caténiste n'a pas voulu faire de répétition et qu'il a éliminé ce qui se trouvait déjà dans le texte d'Eusèbe" (p. 157).

[51] *Commentarioli in Psalmos*, in Ps 1:26–43 Morin.

[52] See also the text edited in the PG 12.1085B–1088D, which applies verse 3 to Christ. Note in the fragment the word προσοχή (1088 B 5) also used by Eusebius (see Gaisford 1842:68.5).

The conclusion is that Eusebius' commentary in the Ecl. Proph. is directly inspired by Origen's *Tomoi*.[53] The bishop of Caesarea selected, from the three possible exegeses mentioned by Origen, the one that best suited his purpose.

## Psalm 2, 1-2 (= Ecl. Proph. 2.2)

1     Why have the nations been in an uproar
      And the peoples devised a vain thing?
2     The kings of the earth have taken their stand
      And the rulers have taken counsel together
      Against the Lord and against His Anointed.

Eusebius' commentary is that the text not only (οὐ μόνοι) refers to those who plotted against Christ during his lifetime (e.g. Herod and Pilate), but also (ἀλλὰ καί) to all the kings and even to all those who ever plotted against him in any time. Besides, the "kings" and the "rulers" would not only refer to the human and visible sort, but also, and far better (πολὺ μᾶλλον) to the "intelligible and invisible rulers of this age" (τοὺς νοητοὺς καὶ ἀοράτους ἄρχοντας τοῦ αἰῶνος τούτου). The "nations" and the "peoples" could also be the Jews.

First quoted in the NT as a prophecy of Herod and Pilate (Acts 4:25–26), this passage is often mentioned by the first Christian exegetes.[54] They often reference the quotation of the text in Acts 4, but there is no elaborate interpretation of the passage before Tertullian.[55] The latter does not see in the text simply an allusion to Herod and Pilate, but also to all the persecutions against the Christians. In the *De resurrectione*,[56] he specifically applies "nations" to Pilate, "peoples" to the Jews, "kings" to Herod, and "rulers" to Annas and Caiaphas. This partly recalls Eusebius' interpretation. But analysis shows that the latter is far closer to Origen.

The Greek tradition transmits several commentaries by Origen. They show the close dependence of Eusebius on his spiritual master. Most often, Origen

---

[53] In the *Commentary on Romans* PG 14.1255 A1, Origen does not go so far as to say that the text is a prophecy of Christ alone, but underlines the difficulty of being perfectly faithful to God. In his *Homilies on Numbers* 26.2, he admits that the Psalm must only refer to an elite. This recalls Eusebius' commentary.

[54] See for instance Irenaeus *Demonstration of the Apostolic Preaching* 74; *Against Heresies* 3.12.5; Melito *On the Passover* 62; Tertullian *Against Praxeas* 28.10; *Against Marcion* 1.21.1; 3.22.3; 5.3.8; 4.9; 14.8; *On Resurrection* 20.4; Cyprian *To Quirinus* 1.13; 3.119; Hippolytus *On Genesis* p. 56.13 Achelis; *Homily on the Psalms* 20 (Nautin 1853:183).

[55] Irenaeus seems to apply the text only to Herod and Pilate (*Demonstration of the Apostolic Preaching* 74; *Against Heresies* 3.12.5).

[56] *On Resurrection* 20.4.

applies "kings" and "rulers" to the demons,[57] which tends to suggest that he had at least a preference for this spiritual interpretation of the text. The phrases he uses strongly recall Eusebius (ἀντικείμεναι ἐνεργείαι,[58] ἀόρατοι δυνάμεις,[59] ἄρχοντες τοῦ αἰῶνος τούτου[60]). A Latin translator speaks of the "invisible kings and rulers of this world" (*inuisibiles reges et principes saeculi huius*).[61] Once again, however, Origen's exegesis seems to have been changing. In his *Homilies on Ezechiel*, he states that the text can in no way refer to physical rulers.[62] But in the Latin version of the *Commentary on Matthew*, Origen (if it really is Origen) says that it can refer to all those who plot against Jesus.[63]

Now if we turn to Jerome's *Commentarioli*, the dependence of Eusebius on Origen's *Tomoi* becomes particularly clear. Jerome states that the Psalm not only (*non solum*) refers to Herod, but also (*sed etiam*) to the demons (*quorum regna ei in puncto temporis diabolus ostendit*).[64] The idea and the style clearly recall Eusebius. Thus, the double testimony of Jerome and Origen himself tends to demonstrate that Eusebius' commentary in the Ecl. Proph. is closely inspired by Origen's *Tomoi*. Let us add that Jerome's commentary, like Eusebius', begins with an allusion to Acts 4:27, where the Psalm is quoted by Peter. This element also must stem from Origen's commentary.

A fragment from Origen's *Tomoi* confirms this view: it applies the text to Herod and Pilate, all the kings and nations who ever plotted against Jesus, and finally to the demons and the Jews, who would be the "peoples" mentioned in the text.[65] This is exactly the movement of Eusebius' commentary in the Ecl. Proph. Moreover, the text also alludes to Acts 4. The consequence is, at least in this respect, that Eusebius' more complete commentary on verse 2 is a more faithful witness of Origen's commentary in the *Tomoi* than Jerome's. Another conclusion of this analysis is that there is no need to assume any other source than Origen behind Eusebius' commentary. The only discrepancy between Eusebius' and Origen's (preserved) commentaries is that Eusebius sees an allusion to the Jews not only in the "peoples" but also in the "nations." He is apparently the first one to do so. This interpretation seems paradoxical since the word ἔθνη in Greek

---

57   *Commentary on Matthew* 12.1; 13.9; *Fragments on Lamentations* 107; *Fragments on the Psalms* (SC 189, 226, 4); *Homilies on Genesis* 9.3; *Homilies on Numbers* 26.7; *Homilies on Ezechiel* 13.1; *On First Principles* 3.3.2.

58   *Commentary on Matthew* 12.1.

59   *Commentary on Matthew* 13.9.

60   *Fragments on the Psalms* (SC 189, 226, 4); *On First Principles* 3.3.2.

61   *Commentary on Matthew* A 125.

62   *Homilies on Ezechiel* 13.1.

63   *Commentary on Matthew* A 115.

64   *Commentarioli in Psalmos*, in Ps 2:4–6 Morin.

65   PG 12.1109 A 9ff.

would have been more naturally interpreted as an allusion to the "pagans," not the "Jews." There is a good reason to think that Eusebius is the "inventor" of this exegesis. In a work such as the Ecl. Proph., he preferred to apply the negative passage about the "nations" to the Jews for an obvious polemical purpose (the nations being always presented in the work in a positive way).

## Psalm 18, 4-7 (= Ecl. Proph. 2.10)

4　　There is no speech, nor words;
　　　　Their voice is not heard.
5　　Their sound has gone out through all the earth,
　　　　And their utterances to the end of the world
　　　　In the sun He has placed his tent.
6　　Like a bridegroom coming out of his chamber,
　　　　It rejoiced as a giant to run his course.
7　　Its exit is from one end of the heaven,
　　　　And its circuit to the other end of it.

According to Eusebius, the beginning of the text could only refer to the apostles. The "sun" could be the "divinity" in which Christ took his "sojourn" (μονή, κατασκήνωσις) or the body he took from the Virgin. Verse 6 would refer to Christ as the Church's "bridegroom," victorious over his enemies. The end of the passage would be a prophecy of Christ's Ascension.

Until Eusebius, the most frequently quoted verse is verse 5, already mentioned in the NT (Rom 10:18). Christians before Eusebius see it as a prophecy of the preaching of the Gospel.[66] The "giant" (verse 6) is identified with Christ.[67] The "bridegroom" is always interpreted as Christ engaged to the Church (Tertullian),[68] the flesh (Novatian),[69] or the Church (Cyprian).[70] Usually, verse 7 is considered as an allusion to the Ascension.[71] The most problematical passage seems to have been "in the sun He has placed his tent." Hermogenes is probably the first to interpret the passage as an allusion to the "body" (the

---

[66]　Justin *Dialogue with Trypho* 42.1; Irenaeus *Demonstration of the Apostolic Preaching* 21; 86; Tertullian *Against the Jews* 7.3; *On Flight from Persecution* 6.5; *Against Marcion* 3.22.1; 4.43.9; 5.19.2; Hippolytus *Benedictions of Isaac* 2 (*Patrologia Orientalis* 27 p. 176.7); Methodius of Olympus *On the leech* 7.1; 9.7.

[67]　Justin *Apology* 1.54.9; *Dialogue with Trypho* 69.3.

[68]　*Against Marcion* 4.11.7.

[69]　*On Trinity* 13.4.

[70]　*To Quirinus* 2.18.

[71]　Irenaeus *Demonstration of the Apostolic Preaching* 85; *Against Heresies* 4.33.13; Novatian *On Trinity* 13.4. Hippolytus seems to be the first one to apply the verse to the second coming of Christ (*On Antichrist* 64).

tent) that Christ placed in a region called "the belt of the sun" at the time of his Ascension.[72] Clement of Alexandria says that certain people interpret the "tent" as the body of Christ, others, as being the Church.[73] He himself applies the passage to the second coming of Christ and prefers to see the "tent" as the Church;[74] the "sun" would be either the brightness which will illuminate the just ones, either the physical sun where they will be placed at that time,[75] or God himself (because of the false paronomasia Ἐl/ἥλιος),[76] but in that case, it seems that Clement prefers to see the "tent" as an allusion to the angels.[77]

Origen's commentary in the *Tomoi* is not directly known, apart from Origen's comment about the "sun" (thanks to Pamphilus' *Apology of Origen*[78]) and Jerome's *Commentarioli* (which do not comment on the other verses). Jerome only writes that "By 'sun,' we understand mystically 'Christ'" (*Per solem mystice de Christo intellegitur*).[79] In the fragment preserved in the *Apology*, Origen refutes the Hermogenian exegesis, which consists in seeing the "tent" as the body that Christ will bring to the "belt of the sun." Instead, he thinks that the tent is the Church, which Christ has placed in the sun of justice. This interpretation recalls Clement, but Origen refers to the first coming of Christ, and identifies the "sun" with the "sun of justice," which was, however, probably identified in another passage of the *Tomoi* with Christ himself.[80] Here, the only common point between Eusebius and Origen is that both, it seems, applied the passage to Christ. Eusebius' exegesis stems, perhaps, from Clement's own *Prophetic Extracts*. Even if it is not Clement's own exegesis, the latter may be the source for Eusebius' identification of the "tent" as the body of Christ and of the "sun" as his divinity (or God, in Clement). It is all the more tempting to think that Eusebius' *Prophetic Extracts* depend here on Clement's work of the same title. But it remains of course possible that this exegesis, though it may be inspired by Clement, was also mentioned in Origen's *Tomoi* as another way of understanding the text—this would be quite consistent with his habits as a commentator, even if Origen may have preferred the interpretation preserved in Pamphilus' (and

---

[72]   See R. Gounelle 1994.

[73]   Ecl. Proph. 56–57.

[74]   Ecl. Proph. 56–57.

[75]   Ecl. Proph. 56–57.

[76]   Ecl. Proph. 56–57.

[77]   See Gounelle 1994:211.

[78]   *Apology of Origen*, 147–148.

[79]   *Commentarioli in Psalmos*, in Ps 18:8 Morin.

[80]   Jerome identifies the "sun" with the Christ (see *supra*) and Didymus, who probably uses Origen's commentary, clearly identifies the "sun of justice" with Christ (*Expositio in Psalmos* 155 Mülhenberg). Besides, Mal 3:20, from which Origen draws the phrase "sun of justice," was often read in antiquity as a prophecy of Christ. Thus, one can imagine that after saying that Christ has placed his Church in the "sun of justice," Origen identified the latter with Christ himself.

Eusebius') *Apology for Origen*. As a variant of this hypothesis, we could imagine that the identification "tent" = "body" stems from Origen's preserved passage in the *Apology of Origen*, and that Origen had said in another passage that the "sun" could also be understood, as Clement did, as the "divinity."

Concerning the beginning of verse 2, the loss of any trace of Origen's *Tomoi* does not prevent us from detecting a possible dependence of Eusebius on Origen, since the latter frequently commented on the passage, like Eusebius (but also like his own predecessors), as a prophecy of the preaching of the apostles.[81]

Finally, Origen's exegesis of verse 6 is known from two texts that apply the passage to Christ.[82] In a fragment about the Song of Songs, Origen (if he is really the author of the fragment) alludes to the verse by telling that Christ is the bridegroom of the angels and the archangels.[83] But this does not mean that in the *Tomoi*, Origen's exegesis could not have been the same as Eusebius' (first attested, as it seems, in Tertullian). Besides, the theme "Christ as the bridegroom of the Church" is coherent with Origen's interpretation of the Song of Songs. It is difficult to imagine that this interpretation was not mentioned in the *Tomoi* on the Psalms.

The conclusion here is more problematical than in the previous two cases. First, Eusebius agrees with Origen only on verse 2, but here his exegesis is also traditional. Second, there is an apparent contradiction between Eusebius' and Origen's interpretations of the end of verse 5. And, third, there is no clear connection between their interpretations of verse 6, though the theme of Eusebius' commentary recalls Origen (but also Tertullian). We should not, however, automatically conclude that this commentary is not derived from Origen. On the contrary, there is no reason to think that Eusebius elaborated this commentary differently from the others. We *must* think that he used, as a primary material, a commentary by Origen. But this time, two possibilities appear:

> On the basis of the available evidence, Eusebius seems to have followed Origen's commentary, except in the case of the "tent" placed in the "sun." His commentary *appears* here to be original. He may have drawn it from Clement, because he could not find in Origen a clear christological interpretation of the text.

> Another hypothesis would be that every element of Eusebius' commentary stems from Origen's *Tomoi*. But this hypothesis is less economical

---

[81] *Against Celsus* 1.62; 3.2; *Commentary on John* 4 (99.1); 13.115; *Commentary on Matthew* A 46; *Commentary on Romans* PG 14 848 B 15; 853 A 11; 1171 C 14–1172 A 3 (the text commented on here corresponds exactly to Eusebius' initial lemma); *Homilies on Genesis* 13.3; *Homilies on Joshua* 3.3; *Homilies on Jeremiah* 10.2; *Homilies on Luke* 6 (Rauer:38.24).

[82] *Fragments on the Song of Songs* A 277 D 8; *Homilies on Leviticus* 12.2.

[83] *Fragments on the Song of Songs* A 277 D 8.

than the first, because it is not based on facts, but on an assumption. It is not impossible, but it has no philological foundation.

# Conclusions

This analysis tends to confirm that Origen's *Tomoi* were Eusebius' main source in Ecl. Proph. 2.[84] The same *must* be true in the other books. Origen was his main source, but that did not prevent him from using other authors (such as Clement) and giving original comments.[85] Moreover, some of the texts mentioned above tend to confirm the comparison between the prologue of Book IV and Origen's *Against Celsus*: Eusebius may follow his master so close that when he does, he sometimes *reproduces literally* (with little or no modifications) what Origen writes.[86] The consequence is that the Ecl. Proph. are a *major* witness of Origen's lost exegesis.[87] This is not surprising. At that time, Eusebius had learned, in the circle of Pamphilus, to read and admire the Alexandrian. Before the death of Pamphilus in 310, he had spent a long time copying Origen's *opera omnia* along with his friend. We can guess that the "teaching" of Pamphilus, alluded to in the *History of the Church* and the *Martyrs of Palestine*, was based of course on the Bible, but probably as much on Origen's works.[88] The friends of Pamphilus would have spent a long time reading and meditating on the thought of their spiritual

---

[84] See Morlet 2009:453 for the assumption that Eusebius used Origen's *Commentary on Genesis* in book 1 of the Ecl. Proph.

[85] The fact that Eusebius used Origen's commentaries as his primary material is not contradictory to the fact that he could also express more personal comments, but it remains very difficult to determine precisely the part of his originality. One should probably be careful about interpreting Eusebius' own remarks about his "personal" ideas (see for instance, the allusion to his γνώμη in the already mentioned prologue, Gaisford 1842:3.26) as reliable testimonies about his originality. In the *Demonstratio Evangelica* (10.5.2–3), he says *he* found a portion of Jeremiah that is not contained in the Septuagint; but the same "biographical" testimony occurs first in Origen (*Homilies on Jeremiah* 16.10), and it is obvious that Eusebius simply reproduces what his master says (see Morlet 2009:612–614). In a few instances, Eusebius feels the need to justify the quotation of a text within a collection of *testimonia* about Christ (3.15; 3.27). But such passages tend to show Eusebius' originality in the *testimonia* tradition; they do not prove that he is not dependent on Origen. Moreover, we have shown that Eusebius' originality in the *testimonia* tradition often stems from the fact that he is the first to quote as a christological proof-text a biblical passage which Origen was apparently the first to apply to Christ (Morlet 2009:358–404).

[86] There is, apparently, a great variability in the way Eusebius can use Origen: sometimes, he simply copies the text he has under the eyes; sometimes, he rewrites his source more freely.

[87] That is not to say of course that one may uncritically use the Ecl. Proph. to reconstruct Origen's lost exegesis. We only mean that the work certainly contains an important trace of Origen's commentaries. Only the careful use of the work, along with a comparison of other supposed testimonies of Origen's commentaries, may sometimes lead to what Origen could have written.

[88] About the nature of Pamphilus' teaching, see the *Martyrs of Palestine* (long recension) 4.6 and Morlet 2010; Le Boulluec 2012.

master. We can imagine that Eusebius knew whole passages of Origen by heart.[89] But that should not lead us to think that in a work like the Ecl. Proph., he draws upon Origen from memory. The fact that he may *rewrite* Origen's commentaries proves that he had a text under the eyes. On the other hand, this text cannot be constituted of Origen's whole commentaries. We should not imagine Eusebius sat at a desk writing the Ecl. Proph. with Origen's *opera omnia* (in the form of rolls, possibly)[90] on the table (a rather awkward way to compose a work, I may add). As writers in antiquity were accustomed to do,[91] he used one or several anthologies of extracts derived from Origen's works.[92] These anthologies cannot be confused with the one he made with Pamphilus when both friends composed the *Apology for Origen*. The latter anthology contained passages supposed to show the orthodoxy of Origen's thought. We may assume that before Eusebius worked at the Ecl. Proph., he had composed at least two other anthologies: an anthology from the *Against Celsus*, from which he took at least the passages on the prophets he used in book 4, and an anthology derived from Origen's commentaries, where he selected only the *christological* comments. But since readers in antiquity were often reluctant to *read* without also taking notes (in the form of extracts), we are also quite sure that Eusebius had made specific anthologies when he read each one of Origen's works. We cannot know whether these "primary" anthologies where already selections of exclusively christo-logical passages, or also contained other kinds of extracts which could not be used directly for the purpose of a demonstration about Christ. In any case, the Ecl. Proph. are not only extracts from the Bible; they also *are* or at least *reflect*

---

[89] Learning by heart was a current practice in Late Antiquity: Palladius tells that Ammonius, a monk from Nitria, had learned by heart passages from Pierius, the master of Pamphilus, himself the master of Eusebius (*Lausiac History* 12; 14). Amelius, Plotinus' disciple, had learned by heart passages from Numenius (see Porphyry, *Life of Plotinus* 3.44).

[90] It seems that the process of transferring the rolls contained in the library of Caesarea onto codices did not begin before the successors of Eusebius, Acacius, and Euzoius (see Jerome, *De uiris illustribus*, 113; Letter 34, 1). See Carriker 2003:23–24 (who discusses the question whether the allusion to a transfer from "papyri" to "parchments," according to Jerome, is to be understood as a transfer from "rolls" to "codices") and Cassin/Debié/Perrin 2012:205.

[91] See, for instance, the famous testimony of Pliny the Younger *Letters* 3.5.17; Suetonius *Diuus Augustus* 89.4; Aulus Gellius *Attic Nights* Praefatio. We have organized at the University of Paris/Sorbonne, with Olivier Munnich, a project about ancient extracting practices called "Lire en extraits: une contribution à l'histoire de la lecture et de la littérature, de l'Antiquité au Moyen Âge" / "Reading in extracts: a contribution to the history of reading and literature, from Antiquity to the Middle Ages" (2010–2012).

[92] Such a hypothesis is all the more probable that Eusebius himself appears to have been a notable user of the *Extracts* as a literary genre (the *Praeparatio Evangelica* contains a collection of pagan texts; the *Demonstratio Evangelica*, a collection of prophecies; the *History of the Church* itself is presented by Eusebius as a literary library: see HE 1.1.4). The composition of personal antholo-gies is coherent with his activities as a scholar (see Grafton and Williams 2006:205; Morlet 2011:31).

extracts from Origen's commentaries. Such a conclusion should lead us to reexamine the hypothesis that at least some of Origen's "extracts" on the Psalms known to Jerome were actually anthologies constituted from his works, perhaps by Pamphilus and Eusebius.[93]

It is quite sure that the Origenian anthologies Eusebius used for the Ecl. Proph. were used again in the DE, as we can be quite sure that the anthologies of Josephus and Philo Eusebius certainly used in the DE and the HE,[94] were already available to him when he wrote the Ecl. Proph. This would tend to prove that a good part of the matrix of the HE and the DE was constituted before Eusebius wrote the Ecl. Proph.

If this analysis is correct, it sheds new light on a work that has long been considered as a minor work or as an "early work" of Eusebius (which is paradoxical: if Eusebius was born around 260/265 as we think, he would have been around forty years old when he composed it). The Ecl. Proph. were not only a collection of proof-texts. They were also a kind of *epitome* of Origen's exegesis addressed to the beginners. The "concluding formulas" show that it could even be used, in Eusebius' view, as an *introduction* to Origen's commentaries.

---

[93] See note 37. As far as we know, the idea that both friends could be the "authors" of at least one of Origen's collections of "excerpts" stems from R. Cadiou (Cadiou 1936 and 1936b). In the same way, we recall that É. Junod suggested some years ago that the *Philocalia* may have originated in the circle of Pamphilus and Eusebius (Junod 1988:360).

[94] For the very reasonable assumption that Eusebius composed a Josephan anthology, see Inowlocki 2006:212.

# Appendix 1: "Concluding formulas" in the Ecl. Proph.

| Ecl. Proph. | | Passage |
|---|---|---|
| I 2 | μυστικῆς δὲ καὶ ἀπορρήτου θεωρίας ἐχόμενα τὰ κατὰ τὸν τόπον οὐ νῦν ἀναπτύσσειν καιρός. | Gen 11, 5–7 |
| I 3 | πολλῆς δὲ καὶ βαθυτάτης δεομένων θεωρίας τῶν κατὰ τὸν τόπον, ἱκανὰ καὶ ταῦτα πρὸς τὴν παροῦσαν ὑπόθεσιν. | Gen 12, 1–19, 19 |
| I 6 | ἅπερ εἰ οὕτως ἔχοι ὁ φιλομαθὴς ἑκάστην λέξιν νόμοις ἀλληγορίας ἐξετάσας εἴσεται. | Gen 27, 29 |
| I 8 | τὰ δ' ἑξῆς ἀπὸ τοῦ, δεσμεύων πρὸς ἄμπελον τὸν πῶλον αὐτοῦ, τῆς δι' ἀλληγορίας ὑπονοίας ἀρτημένα τοῖς φιλομαθέσι ζητεῖν καταλείψομεν, πλεονάσαντες καὶ ἐν τοῖς εἰρημένοις, οὐ κατὰ τὸν προτεθέντα μὲν σκοπόν, ὅμως δ' ἐξ ἀνάγκης ὑπὲρ σαφοῦς διηγήσεως τῶν κατὰ τὸν τόπον. | Gen 49, 1; 8–10 |
| I 12 | πῶς τε εἴρηται τό, σκεπάσω τῇ χειρί μου ἐπὶ σέ, καλύμματος καὶ σκέπης ἐπιτιθεμένου τῷ νόμῳ, ὡς διὰ τοῦτο τὸ κάλυμμα τὰ μὲν ὀπίσω δύνασθαι ὁρᾶν, οὐκέτι δὲ τὰ προηγούμενα καὶ διαφέροντα· ἰδίᾳ κατὰ καιρόν, ᾧ μέλει τῆς τούτων ἐρεύνης, ἐπιστήσας εἴσεται. | Ex 33, 9–34, 9 |
| I 19 | πλείονος δὲ σαφηνείας δεομένων τῶν τόπων, τούτοις ὡς οἷόν τε ἦν διὰ βραχέων εἰρημένοις ἀρκεσθησόμεθα. | 1 Kings 2, 27; 35–36 |
| I 23 | καὶ ταῦτα, ὅμοια ὄντα τοῖς ἐκ τῆς δευτέρας τῶν Βασιλειῶν προεκτεθείσης, σημειωσάμενοι, διὰ τὸ μὴ πολλὴν εἶναι τὴν τούτων πρὸς ἐκεῖνα παραλλαγὴν ἀρκεσθησόμεθα τοῖς εἰς ἐκεῖνα εἰρημένοις. | 1 Chr 17, 11–14 |
| II 1 | ὅτῳ δὲ φίλον διαγνῶναι τὸ ἀκριβὲς τῆς ἐπὶ τὴν Σωτῆρα τῶν ἐν τῷ ψαλμῷ λεγομένων ἀναφορᾶς, τοῖς εἰς αὐτὸν ὑπομνηματισαμένοις ἐντυχὼν εἴσεται. | Ps 1, 1–3 |
| II 2 | ὅλα δὲ τὰ κατὰ τὸν ψαλμὸν διηγεῖσθαι οὐ τοῦ παρόντος τυγχάνει καιροῦ, μάλιστα ὅτε πληρεστάτης ἤδη τετύχηκεν διηγήσεως. | Ps 2, 1–2; 4–5; 6–8 |

| Ecl. Proph. | | Passage |
|---|---|---|
| II 7 | τοῦ δὴ Πέτρου τοίνυν ἀποδεδωκότος εἰς τὸν Σωτῆρα τὴν τῆς προφητείας ἑρμηνείαν, παρέσται τῷ μὴ πάρεργον τὴν τούτων ἔρευναν ποιουμένῳ, ἤτοι ἐπ᾽ αὐτῷ πᾶσαν τὴν ἐν τῷ Ψαλμῷ λέξιν ἀκολούθως ἐφαρμόζειν οἷς καὶ ὁ Πέτρος ἐξείληφεν, ἢ τοῖς ὑφ᾽ ἑτέρων εἰς τὸν Ψαλμὸν ὑπομνηματισθεῖσιν ἐντυχεῖν· ἡμῖν γὰρ ὁ σκοπὸς οὐδέν τι πλεῖον τῶν εἰρημένων λέγειν εἰς τοὺς τόπους ἐπιτρέπει. | Ps 15, 8–11 |
| II 9 | οἶμαι δὲ καὶ τὰ περὶ τῆς θεότητος καὶ τῆς εἰς ἀνθρώπους καταβάσεως αὐτοῦ ἐν τοῖς πρώτοις δηλοῦσθαι τοῦ Ψαλμοῦ· ἅπερ οὐ τῆς ἐν παρέργῳ καὶ παραδρομῇ δέοιτ᾽ ἂν ἐξηγήσεως ἀπορρητότερον εἰρημένα, οἷά ἐστιν ἀπὸ τοῦ, καὶ ἔκλινεν οὐρανοὺς καὶ κατέβη, καὶ γνόφος ὑπὸ τοὺς πόδας αὐτοῦ· καὶ ἐπέβη ἐπὶ Χερουβὶν καὶ ἐπετάσθη, ἐπετάσθη ἐπὶ πτερύγων ἀνέμων· καὶ ὅσα τούτοις παραπλησίως ἐπὶ τὸν τοῦ Θεοῦ Λόγον ἀναφέρεται. | Ps 17, 10–11; 44–46 |
| II 10 | εὐχερῶς δ᾽ ἄν τις ἑαυτῷ τούτοις ἀναλόγως ἐξεργάσεται τὰ κατὰ τὸν τόπον. | Ps 18, 4–7 |
| II 11 | καὶ ὅλα δὲ τὰ κατὰ τὸν τόπον ἐφαρμοσθείη ἂν αὐτῷ τῆς προσηκούσης τυχόντα ἐξηγήσεως. | Ps 19, 6–7 |
| II 12 | καὶ τὰ λοιπὰ δὲ τὰ ἐν τῷ ψαλμῷ ὡς περὶ τῆς τοῦ βασιλέως δόξης λεγόμενα, οὐ μικρὰ ὄντα, ἁρμόττοι ἂν τῷ Χριστῷ μᾶλλον ἢ τῷ Δαυὶδ τῆς ἀξίας τυχόντα σαφηνείας. | Ps 20, 2; 5 |
| II 13 | καὶ ὅλα δὲ τὰ ἐν τῷ ψαλμῷ ἐφαρμόσαι ἂν τῷ Χριστῷ, τὰ κατὰ τὴν ἐνανθρώπησιν αὐτοῦ, καθ᾽ ἣν ἐπεβουλεύθη, περιέχοντα. | Ps 141, 8; 3–4; 7 |
| II 14 | καὶ τὰ λοιπὰ δὲ τοῦ ψαλμοῦ πνευματικῶς ἐκλαμβάνων νοήσεις. | Ps 143, 3–5 |

| Ecl. Proph. | | Passage |
|---|---|---|
| III 6 | καὶ ὅσα ἄλλα ἐναποκέκρυπται τῇ βίβλῳ ἀπορρητότερα μαθήματα, ἃ καὶ πληρεστάτης ἤδη σαφηνείας ἔτυχεν, ἐν οἷς ὁ φιλοπονώτατος τῶν θείων γραφῶν ἐξηγητὴς ὑπεμνηματίσατο. | Song of Songs (whole book) |
| III 14 | καὶ διὰ τούτων σαφῶς τὰ τῆς εἰς ἀνθρώπους ἐπιδημίας τοῦ Χριστοῦ προφητεύεται· ἐπὶ σχολῆς δ᾽ ἂν ἑκάστη λέξις ἀκριβεστέρας τύχοι σαφηνείας. | Am 4, 12–13 |
| III 23 | πολλῆς δὲ τῶν κατὰ τὸν τόπον δεομένων ἐξηγήσεως ἱκανὰ καὶ ταῦτα ὡς πρὸς τὴν παροῦσαν ὑπόθεσιν. | Zech 3, 1; 4–5; 8; 6, 9–10; 11–14 |
| III 27 | καταλείψαντες αὐτὸν οἱ μαθηταὶ διεσκορπίσθησαν· τούτου δὴ χάριν καὶ ἡμεῖς ἐσημειωσάμεθα τὸ ῥητόν, ὃ καὶ πολλῆς δεόμενον ἐξετάσεως εἰς ἐπιτήδειον ἀναθησόμεθα καιρόν. | Zech 13, 7 |
| III 33 | εἰ δὲ καὶ βαθυτέρας ἔχοιτο θεωρίας τὰ κατὰ τὸν τόπον, οὐδὲν πρὸς ἐκεῖνο λυπεῖ καὶ τὰ εἰρημένα. | Jer 11, 18–19 |
| III 46 | ἀλλὰ ταῦτα μὲν ἐπιτεμόμενοι τὴν διήγησιν παρατεθείμεθα. | |
| IV 4 | τὰ δὲ κατὰ τὴν λέξιν ἕκαστα ὁποῖον ἔχει νοῦν, τοῖς εἰς τοὺς τόπους τοῦ θαυμασίου ἀνδρὸς ἐξηγητικοῖς ἐντυχὼν ὁ φιλομαθὴς εἴσεται. | Isa 7, 10–16 |
| IV 7 | δι᾽ ὅπερ ἀναπέμψαντες τοὺς φιλομαθεῖς ἐπὶ τὰ εἰς τοὺς τόπους ὑπομνήματα, ἡμεῖς τὸ προτεθὲν διαπερανούμεθα. | Isa 9, 5–7 |
| IV 10 | τὰ δ᾽ ἑξῆς τῆς προφητείας ἅπαντα διὰ μόνης ἀποδοθήσεται τροπολογίας. | Isa 19, 1 |
| IV 11 | καὶ ὅλα δὲ τὰ ἑξῆς τῆς προφητείας βαθυτέρας ἤρτηται διανοίας, ἣν οὐχ ὁ παρὼν ἀναπτύσσειν καιρός. | Isa 19, 19–21 |

| Ecl. Proph. | | Passage |
|---|---|---|
| IV 17 | ἐν τῇ πάλαι δὲ ἐρήμῳ, τῇ ἐξ ἐθνῶν ἐκκλησίᾳ, ἡ τοιαύτη γενομένη φωνὴ ἑτοιμάζειν παρακελεύεται τὴν ὁδὸν Κυρίου, καὶ τὰ ἑξῆς· ἅπερ ἐπὶ σχολῆς ᾧ μέλει τῆς τούτων γνώσεως ἐρευνήσας εἴσεται. | Isa 40, 3–5 |
| IV 18 | τὰ μέντοι γε λοιπὰ οὐκ ἔτι νῦν καιρὸς ἀπαιτεῖ διηγεῖσθαι· ὅθεν ἐφ' ἑτέραν τραπησόμεθα περικοπήν. | Isa 40, 9–11 |
| IV 20 | πρόκειται δὲ τῷ φιλομαθεῖ ἑκάστην ἐξετάζειν τῆς προφητείας λέξιν, καὶ ἀναλόγως τοῖς ὑφ' ἡμῶν εἰρημένοις ἐπὶ τὸν Χριστὸν τοῦ Θεοῦ τὰ ὑποπίπτοντα μεταφέρειν. | Isa 42, 1–7 |
| IV 23 | ἑκάστην μέντοι γε λέξιν τῆς περικοπῆς ἐξετάζειν οὐ τῆς παρούσης ἐστὶν πραγματείας. | Isa 48, 12–16 |
| IV 24 | ἅπερ ἐπιπλεῖον βασανίζειν πνευματικώτερα ὄντα, καὶ κατὰ μόνην διάνοιαν ἀποδιδόμενα, οὐ τῆς παρούσης πραγματείας τυγχάνει. | Isa 49, 1–11 |
| IV 26 | ὁποῖον ἔχει νοῦν ὁ φιλομαθὴς ἐρευνήσας εἴσεται. | Isa 52, 5–7 |
| IV 27 | ἐπιμελέστερον οὗτος ἐρευνήσας τὰ ἐν αὐτοῖς εἴσεται. | Isa 52, 10–54, 1 |

## Appendix 2: Eusebius' Use of Origen's *Against Celsus* in Ecl. Proph. IV Prol.

| Eusebius' Ecl. Proph. IV Prol.* | Origen *Against Celsus* (main source of the passage) | Other parallels in Origen |
|---|---|---|
| Τὰς ἀπὸ τῶν Ἡσαΐου Προφητικὰς Ἐκλογὰς μόνας ἡμῖν λειπούσας ἀπανθίσασθαι πειρώμενοι, πρὸς τοὺς ἀπίστως περὶ τὰς προφητείας διακειμένους ὀλίγα προδιαληψόμεθα εἰς παράστασιν τῆς τῶν προφητῶν ἀληθείας, καὶ δὴ πρῶτον καλῶς καὶ τοῖς πρὸ ἡμῶν τετηρημένον παραθήσομαι λογισμόν. Εὖ γοῦν εἴρηκέναι μοι δοκοῦσιν, ὡς ἄρα τοῖς ὑπὸ τὸν Μωσέως νόμον αὐτὸς ὁ νόμος διαμαρτύρεται, ὅτι δὴ τὰ ἔθνη ὧν μεταξὺ πολιτεύσονται κληδόνων καὶ μαντειῶν ἀκούσονται· σοὶ δέ, φησιν, οὐχ οὕτως ἔδωκε Κύριος ὁ Θεός σου· καὶ ἔτι γε εἴργων αὐτοὺς ὁ θεῖος λόγος ἔκ τε οἰωνιστικῆς καὶ πάσης τῆς διὰ δαιμόνων περιέργου μαντείας ἐπιφέρει, | Τὸ δ' ἀναγκαῖον οὕτω παραστήσομεν. Τὰ ἔθνη, ὡς γέγραπται καὶ ἐν αὐτῷ τῷ τῶν Ἰουδαίων νόμῳ, κληδόνων καὶ μαντειῶν ἀκούσονται· τῷ δὲ λαῷ ἐκείνῳ εἴρηται· Σοὶ δὲ οὐχ οὕτως ἔδωκε κύριος ὁ θεός σου. Καὶ ἐπιφέρεται τούτῳ τὸ Προφήτην ἐκ τῶν ἀδελφῶν σου ἀναστήσει σοι κύριος ὁ θεός σου. | |

* Gaisford's text has been corrected when necessary (especially concerning Greek accents).

| Eusebius' Ecl. Proph. IV Prol. | Origen Against Celsus (main source of the passage) | Other parallels in Origen |
|---|---|---|
| λέγων, προφήτην ἐκ τῶν ἀδελφῶν σου ἀναστήσει σοι Κύριος ὁ Θεός σου. Ἆρ᾽ οὖν τούτων αὐτοῖς ἀναγεγραμμένων, μὴ ἔργῳ δὲ γενομένων, μηδὲ παρόντων αὐτοῖς προφητῶν ἀνδρῶν, δύνατον ἦν αὐτοὺς πιστεύειν τῷ νόμῳ, καὶ τῷ ταῦτα ἐπαγγειλαμένῳ λόγῳ οὕτω προφανῶς καὶ ἐναργῶς ψευδομένῳ, ἢ δῆλον ὅτι ὑπ᾽ αὐτῆς τῆς περὶ τὴν πρόγνωσιν τῶν ἐσομένων λιχνείας ἀγόμενοι κατεφρόνησαν <μὲν> τῶν ἰδίων, ὡς οὐδὲν ἀληθὲς ἐχόντων οὐδὲ θεῖον, διὰ τὸ μὴ εἶναι παρ᾽ αὐτοῖς προφήτας, αὐτόμολοι δὲ ἐπὶ τὰ τῶν ἐθνῶν μαντεῖά τε καὶ χρηστήρια μετῄεσαν <ἄν>; Ἀλλὰ γὰρ φαίνονται οὐ μόνον Μωσέα, ἀλλὰ καὶ πλείους μετ᾽ αὐτὸν ὡς Θεοῦ προφήτας προσειέμενοι, οὐκ ἄλλως δῆλον ὅτι ἢ τῷ πείραν τῆς ἐν αὐτοῖς θειότητος εἰληφέναι· οὔτε γὰρ | Εἴπερ οὖν τῶν ἐθνῶν χρωμένων μαντείαις εἴτε διὰ κληδόνων εἴτε δι᾽ οἰωνῶν εἴτε δι᾽ ὀρνίθων εἴτε δι᾽ ἐγγαστριμύθων εἴτε καὶ διὰ τῶν τὴν θυτικὴν ἐπαγγελλομένων εἴτε καὶ διὰ Χαλδαίων γενεθλιαλογούντων, ἅπερ πάντα Ἰουδαίοις ἀπείρητο, Ἰουδαῖοι εἰ μηδεμίαν εἶχον παραμυθίαν γνώσεως τῶν μελλόντων, ὑπ᾽ αὐτῆς ἂν τῆς ἀνθρωπίνης περὶ τὴν γνῶσιν λιχνείας τῶν ἐσομένων ἀγόμενοι κατεφρόνησαν μὲν ἂν τῶν ἰδίων ὡς οὐδὲν ἐχόντων θεῖον ἐν ἑαυτοῖς καὶ οὐκ ἂν μετὰ Μωϋσέα προφήτην προσήκαντο οὐδ᾽ ἀνέγραψαν αὐτῶν τοὺς λόγους, αὐτόμολοι δὲ ἐπὶ τὰ τῶν ἐθνῶν μαντεία καὶ χρηστήρια μετέστρεψαν ἢ ἐπεχείρησαν ἂν ἱδρῦσαί τι τοιοῦτον καὶ παρ᾽ ἑαυτοῖς, Ὥστ᾽ οὐδὲν ἄτοπον ἐστι καὶ περὶ τῶν τυχόντων τοὺς παρ᾽ αὐτοῖς | |

| Eusebius' Ecl. Proph. IV Prol. | Origen *Against Celsus* (main source of the passage) | Other parallels in Origen |
|---|---|---|
| αὐτοῖς οὐ μόνον περὶ τῶν μακροῖς ὕστερον χρόνοις μελλόντων ἔσεσθαι προὐθέσπιζον, ἀλλὰ καὶ περί τινων προχείρων καὶ βιωτικῶν προὔλεγον· οἷον περὶ ὄνων ἀπολωλυιῶν, καὶ περὶ νοσοῦντων ἐπισφαλῶς εἰ βιώσονται ἢ μή, καὶ περὶ μελλούσης ἔσεσθαι τῷ λαῷ εὐθηνίας, καὶ περὶ ἄλλων μυρίων, ἃ ταῖς κατ' αὐτοὺς ἱστορίαις ἐμφέρεται· ἅπερ εἰ μὴ τοῦτον γεγόνει τὸν τρόπον, ἀποκρινέσθω τις, τίνι δὴ ποτε οὖν λόγῳ προφήτας ἡγοῦντό τε καὶ ἀπεκάλουν, ἢ διὰ τί γραφῆς τοὺς λόγους αὐτῶν ἠξίουν· Τίς δ' ἡ αἰτία, δι' ἣν καὶ τοῖς μετέπειτα παισὶν ἑαυτῶν, ὡς ἂν δὴ θείας, αὐτῶν τὰς γραφὰς παρεδίδοσαν; μηδὲν γάρ τι θεῖον μηδὲ παράδοξον ἐν τοῖς ἀνδράσιν ἑορακότας εἰκῇ καὶ μάτην οἴεσθαι περὶ αὐτῶν τοιαῦτα διειληφέναι πάντων ἐστὶν ἀπιθανώτατον. Εἰ δ' ἀναδράμοι τις ἐπὶ τοὺς τότε χρόνους τῇ διανοίᾳ, τί ἄρα ἐπινοήσειεν, ὁρῶν ἄνδρας ἀγροίκους καὶ τὸ σχῆμα λιτούς, | προφήτας εἰς παραμυθίαν τῶν τὰ τοιαῦτα ποθούντων προειρηκέναι, ὥστε καὶ περὶ ὄνων ἀπολωλυιῶν προφητεύειν τὸν Σαμουὴλ καὶ περὶ νόσου παιδὸς βασιλικοῦ τὸν ἐν τῇ τρίτῃ τῶν Βασιλειῶν ἀναγεγραμμένον. (I.36)<br><br>Ἆρα γὰρ ὡς ἔτυχε ταῦτ' ἔλεγον οἱ προφῆται σὺν οὐδεμιᾷ πιθανότητι, τῇ κινούσῃ αὐτοὺς ἐπὶ τὸ μὴ μόνον εἰπεῖν ἀλλὰ καὶ ἀναγραφῆς ἀξιῶσαι τὰ λεγόμενα; Ἆρά γε τὸ τοσοῦτο τῶν Ἰουδαίων ἔθνος, πάλαι χώραν ἰδίαν εἰληφὸς οἰκεῖν, σὺν οὐδεμιᾷ πιθανότητι τινας μὲν ὡς προφήτας ἀνηγόρευον ἑτέρους δὲ ὡς ψευδοπροφήτας ἀπεδοκίμαζον; Καὶ οὐδὲν ἦν παρ' αὐτοῖς τὸ προκαλούμενον συναριθμεῖν ταῖς ἱεραῖς εἶναι πεπιστευμέναις Μωϋσέως βίβλοις τοὺς λόγους τῶν ἑξῆς νενομισμένων εἶναι προφητῶν; (III.2) | |

| Eusebius' Ecl. Proph. IV Prol. | Origen Against Celsus (main source of the passage) | Other parallels in Origen |
|---|---|---|
| αἰπολούς τινὰς καὶ ποιμένας, εἰς μέσον παντός τοῦ ἔθνους παριόντας, καὶ ὡς ἐκ προσώπου τοῦ θεοῦ τινα λέγοντας, καὶ τάδε λέγει Κύριος ἀναβοωμένους, ἐπί τε βασιλέων καὶ παντὸς τοῦ λαοῦ μετὰ παραστήματος <u>ἀκαταπλήκτου</u> δημηγοροῦντας, καὶ σοφίαν ὑπὲρ ἄνθρωπον ἐνδεικνυμένους, τὴν καὶ εἰς ἔτι νῦν ἐν ταῖς <u>προφητείαις</u> αὐτῶν φερομένην, μυρία τε ἄλλα <u>δι' αἰνιγμάτων καὶ παραβολῶν</u> ἀπόρρητα φιλοσοφοῦντας, ἠθικήν τε καὶ δογματικὴν τῇ Ἑβραίων φωνῇ διδασκαλίαν τῷ λαῷ παραδιδόντας, καὶ πρὸς ἐπὶ τούτοις τὸν βίον τοῖς λόγοις αὐτῶν κατάλληλον ἐνδεικνυμένους, καὶ τοῖς πᾶσιν ἀκολακεύτως ὁμιλοῦντας, εἰς πρόσωπόν τε τοὺς ἀσεβεῖς διελέγχοντας, ὡς καὶ <u>ἐπιβουλεύεσθαι πρὸς αὐτῶν μέχρι θανάτου</u>, ῥωμαλέῳ καὶ γενναικῷ παραστήματι τῷ ἀληθεῖ | ... διὰ τὸ τοῦ βίου δυσμίμητον καὶ σφόδρα εὔτονον καὶ ἐλευθέριον καὶ πάντη πρὸς θάνατον καὶ κινδύνους <u>ἀκατάπληκτον</u> (...) Δι' ἀλήθειαν γοῦν καὶ τὸ ἐλευθερίως ἐλέγχειν τοὺς ἁμαρτάνοντας ... (VII.7)<br>Τῶν δ' ἐν Ἰουδαίοις προφητῶν οἱ μὲν πρὸ τῆς προφητείας καὶ τῆς θείας κατακωχῆς ἦσαν σοφοί, οἱ δ' ἀπ' αὐτῆς τῆς προφητείας φωτισθέντες τὸν νοῦν τοιοῦτοι γεγόνασιν ... (VII.7)<br>Οὗτοι δὴ καὶ ἄλλοι μύριοι προφητεύσαντες τῷ θεῷ καὶ τὰ περὶ Ἰησοῦ τοῦ Χριστοῦ προεῖπον. (VII.7)<br>Ταῦτα δι' αἰνιγμάτων καὶ ἀλληγοριῶν καὶ τῶν καλουμένων σκοτεινῶν λόγων καὶ τῶν ὀνομαζομένων παραβολῶν ἢ παροιμιῶν ἀπεφήναντο. (VII.10)<br>Ἐλιθάσθησαν, ἐπρίσθησαν, ἐπει-ράσθησαν, ἐν φόνῳ μαχαίρας <u>ἀπέθανον.</u> (VII.7) | Οὐ μόνον προφητείας Ἱερεμίας ἀνέγραψεν, ἀλλὰ καὶ ἴδια πάθη, ταῖς μὲν διδάσκων βασιλείας οὐρανῶν μυστήρια, τοῖς δὲ διδάσκων ὑπομονῆς παραδείγματα, τῶν ψευδοπροφητῶν τοιοῦτον οὐδὲν διὰ τὴν κολακείαν πασχόντων. (FrJr 63)<br><br>Ἐλιθάσθησαν, ἐπρίσθησαν, ἐπει-ράσθησαν ... (CmMt X.18) |

| Eusebius' Ecl. Proph. IV Prol. | Origen Against Celsus (main source of the passage) | Other parallels in Origen |
|---|---|---|
| λόγῳ παριστάμενος; Ταῦτά τις εἰς νοῦν εὐγνωμόνως θέμενος, πῶς οὐκ ἂν ὁμολογήσειεν κατὰ θείαν ὡς ἀληθῶς <u>ἐπίπνοιαν</u> ταῦτα πάντα περὶ αὐτοὺς γεγονέναι; Διὸ καὶ τότε θαυμάζεσθαι αὐτοὺς εἰκός ἦν παρὰ τοῖς ἔμφροσιν, καὶ τοὺς λόγους αὐτῶν ἀναγράπτους παρὰ τοῖς ἱερογραμματεῦσι φυλάττεσθαι, εἰς ἔτι τε νῦν παρ' ὅλῳ τῷ ἔθνει προφήτας γεγονέναι τοῦ Θεοῦ πιστεύεσθαι· ὁ καὶ ἐναργέστατα μάλιστα παρίστησιν ἡ ἡμετέρα περὶ τοῦ Χριστοῦ διάληψις, καθ' ἣν ἀποδείκνυμεν πᾶσαν τὴν κατ' αὐτὸν οἰκονομίαν γεγενημένην, τά τε περὶ τῆς διδασκαλίας αὐτοῦ, καὶ τῆς ἐξ ἁπάντων ἐθνῶν γενομένης δι' αὐτοῦ κλήσεως ἀκριβῶς προεγνῶσθαί τε καὶ πρὸ μυρίων ὅσων ἐτῶν τοῖς θεσπεσίοις ἐκείνοις ἀνδράσι προειρῆσθαι· ὧν τὰς ἱερὰς βίβλους Ἰουδαῖοι μᾶλλον ἂν ἡμῶν εἶεν ἀξιοπιστότεροι μετὰ πάσης σεβασμίου τιμῆς περιέποντές τε καὶ προφέροντες, | Ἐπεὶ δ'ἅπαξ εἰς τὸν περὶ τῶν προφητῶν ἤλθομεν λόγον, Ἰουδαίοις μέν, τοῖς πιστεύουσι <u>θείῳ πνεύματι</u> αὐτοὺς λελαληκέναι, οὐ μόνον οὐκ ἔσται ἄχρήσιμα τὰ ἐπιοθησόμενα καὶ τοῖς <u>εὐγνωμονοῦσι</u> δὲ τῶν Ἑλλήνων. (I.36) | |

# Notes to Appendix 2[95]

Eusebius' text is inspired by several passages from *Against Celsus*, and probably by other parallels in Origen's works. Such parallels may also indicate that he *also* depends on a lost work by Origen, maybe the prologue of the lost commentary on Isaiah. This would account for the presence of this discussion at the beginning of a book devoted to Isaiah.

Since Eusebius speaks about his "predecessors" at the beginning of the passage, we cannot exclude that he also depends on other writers (we have already noticed possible echoes of Clement of Alexandria: see Morlet 2009:338–339).

The comparison shows the way Eusebius can rewrite Origen: sometimes, he is very close to his source (cf. *Against Celsus* 1.36 here); sometimes, he rewrites Origen more freely (see here *Against Celsus* 7.7 and 10).

The comparison also shows that Gaisford's text, which makes no sense, has to be corrected (the mistake is in the codex *Vindobonensis Theol. Gr.* 29, fol. 43v). According to this edition, one reads that the Jews *despised* (κατεφρόνησαν) the prophets and *passed* (μετῄεσαν) to the pagan ones. That is exactly the contrary to what Eusebius means: if God would not have allowed the Jewish prophets to speak about daily problems, the Jews *would have despised* (κατεφρόνησαν <μὲν ἄν>) them and *would have passed* (μετῄεσαν <ἄν>) to the pagan prophets. Origen's text confirms that we ought to assume the fall of the word ἄν in both cases, probably due to the similarity of the word with the ending of both verbs. The copyist thought Eusebius was dealing with the anger of the Jews against the prophets, to which Eusebius indeed alludes, but only in the second part of the text.

---

[95] For a more thorough commentary, see Morlet 2009:333–339.

# Works Cited

Baehrens, W.A. 1925. *Origenis Libri X in Canticum canticorum*. Leipzig.

Bandt, C. 2011. "Reverberations of Origen's Exegesis of the Psalms in the Work of Eusebius and Didymus." *Origeniana Decima. Origen as Writer*, ed. S. Kaczmarek and H. Pietras, 891–905. Leuven/Paris/Walpole, MA.

Bandt, C. Forthcoming. "Some Remarks on the Tone of Eusebius' Commentary on Psalms." *Studia Patristica*.

Barnes, T.D. 1981. *Constantine and Eusebius*. Cambridge, MA.

Brière, M., Mariès, L., and Mercier, C. 1954. *Hippolyte de Rome. Sur les bénédictions d'Isaac, de Jacob et de Moïse*, Patrologia Orientalis 27, 2–115. Paris.

Burgess, R.W. 1997. "The Dates and Editions of Eusebius' Chronici Canones and Historia Ecclesiastica." *Journal of Theological Studies* 48:471–504.

Cadiou, R. 1936. *Commentaires inédits des Psaumes. Études sur les textes d'Origène contenus dans le manuscrit Vindobonensis 8*. Paris.

———. 1936b. "La bibliothèque de Césarée et la formation des chaînes." *Revue des sciences religieuses* 16:474–483

Carriker, A. J. 2003. *The Library of Eusebius of Caesarea*. Leiden/Boston.

Carpino, F. 1986. "Origene, Eusebio e Ilario sul Salmo 118." *Annali di storia dell'esegesi* 3:57–64.

Cassin, M., Debié, M., and Perrin, M.-Y. 2012. "La question des éditions de l'Histoire ecclésiastique et le livre X." *Eusèbe de Césarée, Histoire ecclésiastique, commentaire. T. I.: études d'introduction*, ed. S. Morlet and L. Perrone, 185–206. Paris.

Curti, C. 1980. "L'interpretazione di Ps 67, 14 in Eusebio di Cesarea. La sua fortuna presso gli esegeti greci e latini del Salterio." *Paradoxos Politeia. Studi patristici in onore di Giuseppe Lazzati,* ed. R. Cantalamessa and L. F. Pizzolato, 195–207. Milano.

Curti, C. 1985. "L'esegesi di Eusebio di Cesarea: caratteri e sviluppo." *Le trasformazioni della cultura nella Tarda Antichità.* Atti del Convegno tenuto a Catania, Università degli Studi, 27 Sett.–2 Ott. 1982, I: 459–478. Roma.

Dorival, G. 1996. "Un astre se lèvera de Jacob. L'interprétation ancienne de Nombre 24, 17." *Annali di storia dell'esegesi* 13:295–353.

———. 2004. "Remarques sur les 'Eklogai prophétiques' d'Eusèbe de Césarée." *Philomathestatos: Studies in Greek and Byzantine Texts Presented to Jacques Noret for His Sixty-Fifth Birthday/Études de patristique grecque et textes byzantins offerts à Jacques Noret à l'occasion de ses soixante-cinq ans*, ed. B. Janssens, B. Roosen and P. Van Deun, 203–224. Leuven.

Gaisford, T. 1842. *Eusebii Pamphili episcopi Caesariensis Eclogae propheticae*. Oxford.

Goffinet, E. 1963. "Recherches sur quelques fragments du commentaire d'Origène sur le premier psaume." *Le Muséon* 76:145–163.

Gounelle, R. 1994. "*Il a placé sa tente dans le soleil* (Ps 18(19), 5c(6a)) chez les écrivains ecclésiastiques des cinq premiers siècles." *Le Psautier chez les Pères.* Cahiers de Biblia Patristica 4:197–220. Strasbourg.

Grafton, A. and M. Williams. 2006. *Christianity and the Transformation of the Book. Origen, Eusebius, and the Library of Caesarea.* Cambridge, MA.

Guinot, J.-N. 1987. "L'héritage origénien des commentateurs grecs du prophète Isaïe." *Origeniana quarta*, ed. L. Lies, 379–389. Innsbruck.

Hollerich, M.J. 1992. "Eusebius as a Polemical Interpreter of Scripture." *Eusebius, Christianity, and Judaism*, ed. H. W. Attridge and G. Hata, 585–615. Leiden.

———. 1992b. "Origen's Exegetical Heritage in the Early Fourth Century: The Evidence of Eusebius." *Origeniana quinta*, ed. R.J. Daly, 542–547. Leuven.

———. 1999. *Eusebius of Caesarea's Commentary on Isaiah: Christian Exegesis in the Age of Constantine.* Oxford.

Inowlocki, S. 2006. *Eusebius and the Jewish Authors: His Citation Technique in an Apologetic Context.* Leiden.

Jaubert Philippe, M. 2001. *Les Extraits prophétiques au sujet du Christ d'Eusèbe de Césarée. Introduction, traduction, annotations.* PhD diss., Université du Provence.

Johnson, A. P. 2011. "The Tenth Book of Eusebius' General Elementary Introduction: A Critique of the Wallace-Hadrill Thesis." *Journal of Theological Studies* 62:144–160.

———. 2011. "Eusebius the Educator. The Context of the General Elementary Introduction." In *Reconsidering Eusebius. Collected Papers on Literary, Historical, and Theological Issues*, ed. S. Inowlocki and C. Zamagni, 99–118. Leiden.

Junod, É. 1988. "Basile de Césarée et Grégoire de Nazianze sont-ils les compilateurs de la Philocalie d'Origène? Réexamen de la *Lettre* 115 de Grégoire." *Mémorial Jean Gribomont (1920-1986).* Roma.

Kannengiesser, C. 2004. "The Achievement of Eusebius of Caesarea." *Handbook of Patristic Exegesis* II:675–683. Leiden.

Le Boulluec, A. 2012. "Pamphilos de Césarée." In *Dictionnaire des philosophes antiques*, Vol. 5.1, ed. R. Goulet, 111–115. Paris.

Mercati, G. 1948. "La grande lacuna delle Ecloghe profetiche di Eusebio di Cesarea." *Mémorial L. Petit. Mélanges d'histoire et d'archéologie byzantine*, Archives de l'Orient Chrétien 1.1-3. Bucharest.

Morin, G. 1959. *S. Hieronymi presbyteri commentarioli in Psalmos.* Turnhout.

Morlet, S. 2007. "Le commentaire d'Eusèbe de Césarée sur Is 8, 4 dans la *Démonstration évangélique* (VII, 1, 95–113): ses sources et son originalité." *Adamantius* 13:52–63.

———. 2009. *La Démonstration évangélique d'Eusèbe de Césarée. Étude sur l'apologétique chrétienne à l'époque de Constantin*. Paris.

———. 2011. "Eusèbe de Césarée: biographie, chronologie, profil intellectuel." *Eusèbe de Césarée, Histoire ecclésiastique, commentaire. T. I : études d'introduction*, ed. S. Morlet and L. Perrone, 1–31. Paris.

Nautin, P. 1953. *Le dossier d'Hippolyte et de Méliton*. Paris.

Pennachio, M. C. 2002. *Propheta insaniens: l'esegesi patristica di Osea tra profezia e storia*. Roma.

Prinzivalli, E. 1983. "Hippolyte (Statue d')." *Dictionnaire encyclopédique du christianisme ancien* II:1163–1166. Paris.

———. 2000. "Salmi." *Origene. Dizionario*, ed. A. Monaco-Castagno, 422–424. Rome.

Rondeau, M.-J. 1982. *Les commentaires patristiques du Psautier (IIIᵉ-Vᵉ siècles), I*. Rome.

Sant, C. 1964. *The Old Testament Interpretation of Eusebius of Caesarea*. PhD Diss. Pontificium Institutum Biblicum. Rome. (First part published under the title *The Old Testament Interpretation of Eusebius of Caesarea. The Manifold Sense of Holy Scripture*. Valletta. 1967).

Schwartz, E. 1907. "Eusebios von Caesarea." *Realencyclopädie der classischen Altertumswissenschaft* VI:1370–1439.

Selwyn, W. 1872. "Emendations of Certain Passages of *Eusebii Eclogae Propheticae*." *Journal of Philology* 4:275–280.

Smith, H. 1916–1917. "Notes on Origen and Eusebius." *The Journal of Theological Studies* 18:77–78.

Tuccari, L. 1987. "Eusebio e Basilio sul Salmo 59." *Annali di storia dell'esegesi* 4:143–149.

Von Nolte, T. 1861. "Zu den Eclogis Propheticis des Eusebius von Cäsarea." *Theologische Quartalschrift* 43:95–109.

Wallace-Hadrill, D.S. 1974. "Eusebius of Cesarea's Commentary on Luke. Its Origin and Early History." *Harvard Theological Review* 67:55–63.

# 12

# New Perspectives on Eusebius' *Questions and Answers on the Gospels*

## The Manuscripts[1]

### Claudio Zamagni

EUSEBIUS WROTE A LARGE NUMBER of works; each of them would probably have been enough to make him one of the major Christian authors of
his time. Among his less famous works stand the *Questions and Answers on the
Gospels*,[2] an innovation in Christian literature—a sort of compendium of exegesis
concerning different controversial passages of the Gospels.

This work consisted exclusively of a series of questions and answers, and
was divided into two parts. The first was devoted to difficulties concerning
Jesus' genealogies according to Matthew and Luke and other related topics. This
first part had probably fifteen questions,[3] was composed of two books, and was
dedicated to a certain Stephanos, who is presented as having asked the questions which Eusebius answers. The second part, probably in a single book, is also
dedicated to another unknown figure, named Marinos, who is also supposed to
have asked a set of questions. The questions in the second part totaled more than
four and concern the resurrection of Jesus and the events that follow it, such as
the manifestations of angels at Jesus' grave and the appearances of the resur-
rected Jesus in Jerusalem or elsewhere. The two parts circulated in antiquity

[1] I am grateful to Pierluigi Piovanelli (Ottawa), who suggested some improvements to me, and to
Christophe Guignard (Lausanne), who read a first draft of this paper and kindly directed me to
two manuscripts of the Meteors. I am also very pleased to thank Diane Barraud (Lausanne), who
checked the first version of my list of manuscripts, more than ten years ago. Part of this essay
has been prepared thanks to a grant of the Swiss National Science Foundation.
[2] CPG 3470. On the exact title of this work, cf. Zamagni 2008:11.
[3] Actually, we have sixteen questions to Stephanus, but the questions 3 and 4 were originally joined
together, as the manuscripts and the content of the text show. On this point, cf. Spitta 1877:13–
14; Reichardt 1909:23–24; Bardy 1932:210–236; Perrone 1990:417–435; Guignard 2011:48–49.

separately,[4] which indicates that they were possibly composed at different times, although the unity of the work is assured by the preface dedicated to Marinos. Concerning the date of composition, we can assume that at least the first part of the book to Stephanos was composed in the same period as the *Demonstration of the Gospel* (before 320), as both the *Questions* and the *Demonstration* contain explicit cross references.[5]

One can easily get an idea of the content of Eusebius' text by considering four of the questions of Marinos that Eusebius answered (translation by David J. D. Miller, slightly modified):[6]

> How is it that the Savior's resurrection evidently took place, in Matthew, "late on the Sabbath" (Mt 28:1), but in Mark, "early in the morning on the first day of the week" (Mk 16:2)?

> How is it that the Magdalene, who according to Matthew had witnessed the resurrection "late on the Sabbath" (Mt 28:1) is, according to John, the very person who stands at the tomb in tears "on the first day of the week" (Jn 20:1, 11)?

> How is it that the same Magdalene who has, according to Matthew, touched the Savior's feet with the other Mary, "late on the Sabbath" (Mt 28:1), is told "do not touch me" (Jn 20:17) early in the morning on the first day of the week, according to John?

> How is it that in Matthew Mary of Magdala, with the other Mary, has seen one angel outside the tomb, sitting on the stone of the tomb (Mt 28:1-2), and how, according to John, does Mary of Magdala see two angels, sitting inside the tomb (Jn 20:11-12); but according to Luke it was two men that appeared to the women (Lk 24:1-4), and according to Mark it was a young man that was seen by them—Mary of Magdala, James' Mary, and Salome—sitting to the right of the tomb (Mk 16:1-5)?

---

[4] Many ancient witnesses refer to the second part of the work only, using the title of "Questions to Marinos," while the Syriac versions apparently only know the part of the work dedicated to Stephanos, as does Nicetas of Herakleia, who has only the first half of the questions dedicated to Marinos (which possibly corresponds to the first of the two books to Stephanos); cf. Zamagni 2008:12–13.

[5] We can exclude, with John Lightfoot, that such cross references came from a revised edition of these two works by Eusebius himself (Lighfoot 1880:338); on the dating debate, cf. also Zamagni 2008:42–46.

[6] Pearse 2010:3; this volume reprints the Sources Chrétiennes' text and biblical apparatus of the *ekloge* wrongly ascribing the copyright to the Cerf publishing company, while it is still mine.

As one can clearly see, it is quite possible to locate these kinds of questions on the Gospels within the context of anti-Christian polemic, because their content mirrors the criticisms made by the philosopher Porphyry against Christian Scriptures not many years before Eusebius wrote his questions.[7] It has even been argued by Pierre de Labriolle and others that the questions proposed by Eusebius were asked in a polemical context.[8] This is certainly not true, for many reasons. For example, many of the questions had already been discussed among Christians for centuries, and the two people supposed to have asked the questions, Stephanos and Marinos, are clearly Christians, as we learn from the epilogue to the first part and from the preface of the second part. Furthermore, Eusebius sometimes proposes open answers, or answers that contradict each other, and certainly such a habit does not seem appropriate in a controversial context. The questions of Eusebius are certainly not an apologetic text in themselves, although much of their content could have been of some utility in responding to anti-Christian polemics.[9]

The genre of the book was new among Christian texts, but was not new in itself. Since the beginnings of the Hellenistic period, and in the first centuries of our era, books written as a collection of questions-and-answers were relatively common. But, although the scheme of question-and-answer literature is plain, we lack a clear comprehension of this genre in antiquity. This is partly because we do not have many relevant examples of this genre earlier than the *Questions and Answers on the Gospels* by Eusebius. But it is also because the definition of this genre is somewhat unclear in most of the secondary literature. Gustave Bardy, for example, considers even texts that clearly belong to other well-defined literary genres, like epistles or commentaries, as pertaining to this genre as long as these texts use a question-and-answer scheme in at least one of their sections.[10] In such cases, I prefer to consider the question-and-answer scheme simply as a rhetorical tool. That is why we need to differentiate between a *literary genre* and a *literary pattern* (or *literary format, procedure*).[11] In other words, for practical reasons, and on a purely formal basis, we can find and recognize the pattern of a question (and its answer) in any kind of text, but only the works composed exclusively of a collection of questions-and-answers should be considered as pertaining to the literary genre of questions-and-answers.

---

[7]   And, of course, Eusebius did know well the book of Porphyry against Christians, as he is credited with having written a now-lost refutation of Porphyry's criticism in twenty-five books.

[8]   Labriolle 1948:292–293, 487–508; among many followers, Courcelle 1959:133–169; against this hypothesis see especially Perrone 1994:161–185

[9]   For a wider perspective on this debate, concerning Eusebius as well as the whole literature of questions and answers in Christian antiquity, cf. Zamagni 2011a:357–370.

[10]   Bardy 1932:210–236, 341–369, 515–537; Bardy 1933:14–30, 211–229, 328, 352.

[11]   I have developed this distinction in Zamagni 2004:7–24 and Zamagni forthcoming.

The book of Eusebius is one of the first true specimens of this genre that we possess. It is also one of the more studied; yet, we still lack a complete comprehension of its cultural setting, of its transmission and influence, and—most of all, of course—we lack a global explanation for its context. After Eusebius, this genre had an immediate impact in Christian literature of the fourth and fifth centuries, and the work of Eusebius had an important impact among the Christian writers of that period.[12] We find that many of the questions asked by Eusebius, as well as the content of his answers, can be found within many other Christian texts, both Greek and Latin. We find the content of his questions in very different works, such as the letters of Jerome, the homilies of Ambrose of Milan, works of John Chrysostom, and collections in Syriac, Coptic, Arabic and Ethiopic.[13]

In the centuries that follow, the questions-and-answer genre becomes a way for Christians to express their attempts to define themselves and their relationships with others—heretics or pagans—in a process of religious and philosophical interaction that lasted for centuries. This is why we have many question-and-answer books coming from ancient and medieval Christian authors.[14] This is not, however, the case for the classical and Hellenistic question-and-answer texts that inspired our Christian examples.[15]

I would argue that one of the reasons for the success of Eusebius' *Questions* lies in the way they have been written, much more than in the collection's innovative form. In his questions, Eusebius tries to consider all the sources available to him in his rich library. He works as if he were trying to prepare for each question a complete *status quaestionis* that considered all possible questions and solutions involved, as long as they had been discussed by earlier authors. His major point of reference is obviously Origen, although he is far from being Eusebius' only influence. Only in the second place does he try to sum up all his findings, eventually also proposing *his* new explanation to the given question. This method is not so distant from the way in which Eusebius writes his better known and more complex works, like the *Ecclesiastical History* or the *Preparation of the Gospel*, in which he always tries to be as complete as possible, tends to use the greatest number of sources available to him in the library of Caesarea, tries to compare different versions of each single episode, or in our case all the exegeses made on the passage at hand.[16]

---

[12] See especially Perrone 1991:485–505 and idem 1990:417–421.
[13] Concerning the fortune of Eusebius' questions, cf. the commentary I have provided in my dissertation, Zamagni 2003.
[14] Cf. Papadoyannakis 2006:91–105, and Papadoyannakis, forthcoming.
[15] Cf. Jacob 2004:25–54.
[16] Cf. my commentary in Zamagni 2003, as well as the example study of the background of the first question to Stephanos in Zamagni 2011b:151–176.

Eusebius probably worked by making card-files based upon his lectures, eventually also using copyists and secretaries to prepare his final draft, based on these card-files. In any case, he usually does not take a precise position on a question, except when he is sure of his evidence or is willing to demonstrate something that is for him a theological truth.[17] He probably knew that there is no "objective" historian, nor an "objective" exegete, at least in the sense that history and exegesis are "interpretations" of raw data and, because of this, they are always susceptible to corrections and adjustments and open to new explanations. In this sense, Eusebius is very different from Origen and much more a "literalist," not only because his interests were not mainly devoted to allegory, but because they were especially devoted to documents and to their interpretation. Eusebius seems generally to prefer literal exegesis, but his version of literal exegesis is enhanced by his broad cultural interests and by his great erudition.[18] Although they contain very few explicit quotations, Eusebius' *Questions* are still written in a complex dialogue with the exegetical tradition of the past centuries on the same topics. The *Questions* only *seem* a very simple and not at all erudite text. And, in this sense, the library of Caesarea certainly represents the condition that has made the *Questions* possible, which is of course also true for most of his other works.[19]

The *Questions* of Eusebius are unfortunately lost in their original form, but there are two main Greek textual traditions that retain parts of Eusebius' lost work. There is a shortened Greek form, containing twenty questions-and-answers, the *ekloge* (selection, choice), as it is titled. This shortened form exists in a single manuscript (*Vaticanus Palatinus Graecus* 220), which was edited by Angelo Mai in 1825.[20] Then we have many Greek fragments in the *Catena* on Luke by Nicetas of Herakleia (eleventh century).[21] These two traditions partly cover the same sections of the text, but each one also has its own sections. This demonstrates that both come directly from the original lost text, and that both are equally important to its reconstruction. The texts from the *Catena* on Luke by Nicetas were published in 1847 by Angelo Mai, and their edition is based on a single manuscript (*Vaticanus Graecus* 1611).[22]

Besides these two main Greek traditions, there are also other Greek fragments. The majority of those available were also published by Angelo Mai in

---

[17] Secondary literature is rich here; as an example, see the remarks on Eusebius' reconstruction of Christian origins according to Papias and Hegesippus in Norelli 2001:1–22.

[18] See the remarks in Hollerich 1999:67–80 and Perrone 1996:515–530.

[19] Cavallo 1988:65–78; Carriker 2003; Grafton and Williams 2006.

[20] Mai 1825:1–82; Mai 1847:218–267 (reprinted in PG 22.879A–957A); Zamagni 2008:80–230 (republished by Pearse 2010:6–128). On the whole textual tradition, cf. Zamagni 2008:13–21.

[21] CPG C135.

[22] Mai 1847:268–277, 283–298 (PG 22.957B–972D, 984A–1005D; Pearse 2010:134–154, 180–212).

1825 and 1847. In his first edition of 1825, Mai published what is essentially the shortened text of the *ekloge*, followed by some minor fragments in Greek, both of which come primarily from exegetical *catenae* or from unpublished manuscripts that he could read directly in the Vatican Library where he worked, for a total of nineteen Greek fragments and a single fragment in a Latin translation.[23] This first edition has an introduction that also collects indirect evidence on the Eusebian questions (*testimonia*).[24] In his second edition, Mai offers again the *ekloge*, together with a larger section of fragments, including some very long sections of the text, that derive mainly from the *Catena* on Luke by Nicetas of Herakleia. In his first edition, the *ekloge* represented more than 80 percent of the published text; in his second only some 50 percent of the text is occupied by the *ekloge*. This is due to the fact that a great number of fragments had arisen from the *Catena* by Nicetas, wherein Mai identifies a total of twenty-three new fragments (his numbering is questionable, but it remains a widespread reference).[25] Some of these fragments are of the utmost importance, as many of them preserve parts of the original text that are not reproduced in the *ekloge* or elsewhere. Mai also added seven other new Greek fragments that derive from minor textual traditions.[26]

Nevertheless, in his second edition Mai omitted nine fragments he had published in his first edition: two fragments from the questions to Stephanos (including the fragment in Latin translation),[27] five from the questions to Marinos,[28] and two other fragments that were reproduced in a footnote to his first edition.[29] Mai also left out a quotation of Eusebius' text reproduced in the *Questions* of Anastasius of Sinai (seventh century),[30] but adds other quotations that come from the same Anastasius and other authors,[31] as well as a very large

---

[23] Mai 1825:89–101; Mai actually counts only twelve Greek fragments, but this is just because he joins all fragments coming from a same source. The Latin fragment comes from a translation by Balthasar Cordier based on a Greek *catena* on Luke (Corderius 1628:95).

[24] Mai 1825:x–xvii.

[25] According to Charles Kannengiesser, Eusebius' fragment *On Easter* that comes from the *catena* of Nicetas may belong to the *Questions* (CPG 3479; PG 24.693A–705D); cf. Kannengiesser 2004:676. Although not mentioned in the commentary by Averil Cameron and Stuart Hall (1999:326–327), it is nevertheless more than likely that this extract comes from the treatise on Easter that Eusebius sent to Constantine and referenced in VC 4.35, as the first editor Angelo Mai already indicated (Mai 1847:208).

[26] Mai 1825:83–101, 374; Mai 1847:268–278, 298–303 (all republished in Pearse 2010:154–167, 214–232).

[27] Mai 1825:88–89. The first fragment is now reprinted in Pearse 2010:164–166.

[28] Mai 1825:90, 94–100. Two of these fragments have been now reprinted in Pearse 2010:228–232.

[29] Mai 1825:78–79. (These fragments have not been republished by Pearse.)

[30] Mai 1825:85–87, republished by Pearse 2010:160–164.

[31] Mai 1825:100–101, 374; Mai 1847:298, 300–303, and cf. also 298n3, which refers to the fragment at p. 90 of the first edition; Pearse 2010:220–228.

section of Latin fragments that are nothing more than *testimonia* from Ambrose of Milan (*Sermons on Luke*) and from Jerome (*Commentary on Matthew*).[32]

All the fragments that Mai omits in his second edition are discarded because the new ones he identifies and publishes cover the same parts of Eusebius' original text, but in a more complete form. This shows that the intention of Mai in publishing his second edition was not to provide all the evidence available, but to offer instead only the fragments that were most likely to complete the text of the *ekloge*, avoiding any duplication as far as possible.[33] Excluding Nicetas, the total number of Greek fragments Mai edited in his two editions is twenty-seven fragments. Other Greek fragments, however, have been found in other sources published after Mai's editions, especially the eight fragments from the *catenae* on the Gospels edited by John Cramer,[34] another transmitted in a letter of Isidore of Pelusium (or, perhaps better, together with it),[35] and another partially published from a Venice manuscript by Christophe Guignard.[36] Besides Nicetas, the total number of known published fragments is thus at least thirty-seven. As in the case of Nicetas' fragments, we still lack a critical edition for these fragments, and many other Greek fragments probably remain in unpublished manuscripts. Certainly, from what we can determine, these Greek fragments seem less important for the reconstruction of the original lost text than the textual remains in Nicetas' *catena* or in the *ekloge*, but a complete study of their text is required in order to provide an edition of the *Questions* prepared according to modern standards.

---

[32] Mai 1825:101–106; Mai 1847:304–309. While Migne already chose not to republish these Latin *testimonia* (PG 22), David Miller and Roger Pearse reprint them among Eusebius' fragments (Pearse 2010:258–300).

[33] Cf. Zamagni 2008:13–16. The second edition of Mai is reprinted by Migne in PG 22, which omits the fragments only printed in the first edition (now partly republished in Pearse 2010:notes 26, 27, 28).

[34] Cf. Zamagni 2003:65, 69, 70, 134, 154, 165; Cramer 1840:7–8, 10, 12, 15, 251; Cramer 1844:399–402, 404–406. All these fragments are reprinted in Pearse 2010:166–174, 232–249, which also locates for the first time a fragment in Cramer 1840:13.

[35] Isidore of Pelusium, *Epistles* 2.212 (PG 78.652B–653C). Until otherwise proven, this text is to me a *testimonium* (Zamagni 2003:196), although Pearse 2010:248–253 considers it as a new fragment (Fr. Mar. Supp. 17 according to his numbering). Similar statements can be found also among Mai's fragments and it is not my intention to discuss their pertinence in this *status quaestionis*: to me it is obvious that a new study of the published fragments and of the whole corpus of new manuscripts containing fragments is necessary to make sense of this textual tradition. In this regard, I have to mention that some manuscripts containing fragments of the *Questions to Marinos* also contain this letter of Isidore—for example: Athos, Laura, G119; Paris, Bibliothèque Nationale 201; B.N. 206; B.N. 700; B.N. 701; B.N. 702; B.N. 704.

[36] This fragment from the Biblioteca Marciana in Venice is used in the critical apparatus of Guignard 2011:296–304. I had independently recorded this manuscript in my list, but I am pleased to learn from Guignard's dissertation that it certainly comes from Eusebius' *Questions* (cf. note 55 below).

In his second edition, Mai also reported the existence of a Syriac version, providing an edition of two "questions" in Syriac.[37] The Syriac textual tradition has since been studied and published by Gerhard Beyer between 1925 and 1927.[38] The results of his study show that, rather than a plain version of Eusebius' text, there were two different Syriac translations. The best known version is a resumed translation, partially edited by Mai (ms. *Vaticanus Syriacus* 103); it is an appendix to the *catena* on the Gospels by Severus of Antioch, to be dated between the end of the seventh and the beginnings of the eighth century. Among the indirect *testimonia*, George of Beelthan (eighth century) witnesses a second, more ancient and literal Syriac translation, to be dated to the fifth century (ms. *Vaticanus Syriacus* 154).[39]

Other indirect and less important textual traditions have been found in Coptic (Bohairic), Arabic, and Ethiopic translations that derive from a Greek *catena* or, perhaps, from a monophysite dogmatic florilegium; this text, to be dated from the sixth or seventh century, was once considered written in Egypt, but it is more likely to have come from the Palestinian (perhaps Antiochian) region.[40] The Coptic translation was published in 1886 by Paul de Lagarde (born Paul Boetticher) using a Robert Curzon manuscript now at the British Library (*Orientalis* 8812).[41] This Coptic tradition seems to contain three fragments that come from the *Questions* of Eusebius.[42]

---

[37] Mai 1847:279–282 (republished in PG 22.976B–981D).

[38] Beyer 1925:30–70, 1927 (Dritte Serie, 1):80–97, 284–292; 1927 (Dritte Serie, 2):57–69.

[39] On this topic, see also Zamagni 2008:16–18; Guignard 2011:118–131. Only the main Syriac textual tradition (*Vaticanus Syriacus* 103) has been republished in Pearse 2010:306–344, with a useful vocalized text by Adam McCollum. If I understand correctly, Pearse and McCollum also identify two new Syriac *testimonia* (cf. Pearse 2010:304, 344–348).

[40] CPG C117, C118, C127, C138, C148 (the Ethiopic and Arabic forms are not recorded in the *Clavis*, except for the Arabic on Matthew). Concerning this text, usually referred to as a *catena*, cf. Dorival 1984:166–167 and Dorival 1986:28–29. See also Caubet Iturbe 1970:xxxix–xl; Graf 1944:481–482, and Achelis 1897:167–168. Regardless of the origins of the exegetical extracts, the text actually has the shape of a *catena* on selected passages of the four gospels, and its Coptic version even provide an old textual form of their text (Lagarde 1887a and Lagarde 1887b:373–374).

[41] Lagarde 1886; According Lagarde (1886:iii), and to other sources depending on him, this manuscript had the number 102 in the Curzon library at Parham, but this could be a mistake for 106, as indicated by Layton (1987:xlviii, 393).

[42] Roger Pearse and Carol Downer have reprinted all the passages of this work attributed to any "Eusebius" mentioned, without taking any stand (Pearse 2010:352–383), though in my estimation only fragments 1, 4, and 6 (Pearse's numbering) can be considered as certainly deriving from Eusebius' *Questions*; these correspond to the texts in Lagarde 1886:2, 80, 119. Concerning the numbering, it is worth mentioning that the total number of passages which have an attribution to Eusebius is twenty-three (Lagarde 1886:vi), but Pearse and Downer merge many extracts together and include among their fragments two texts that have no attribution: their fragments 5 and 12 are composed of three different passages in each, the fragment 14 of four, and the fragment 15 of two, while their fragments 11 and 17 have no attribution (Pearse 2010:360–362, 368–374, 376–382).

The Arabic version seems to be translated from Coptic, but from a slightly different textual tradition of the text; for example, among the extracts concerning Matthew's Gospel, the Arabic has five extracts of Eusebius, two of which are not in the Coptic, while the Curzon manuscript has just four extracts, one of which is not in the Arabic. There is a partial critical edition of this Arabic version, covering the texts on Matthew's Gospel, published in 1969 by Francisco Caubet Iturbe using nine manuscripts divided into three families.[43] In the introduction to the translation, Caubet Iturbe correctly indicates that two of the five passages attributed to Eusebius of Caesarea came from his *Questions*.[44] In the unpublished part of this Arabic version, there should be at least another fragment of Eusebius' work.[45]

The Ethiopic version is translated from Arabic, but no recent study of it has been undertaken since its identification by Hermann Zotenberg in the Catalogue of the French National Library of 1877.[46] Of course, there are also dozens, if not hundreds, of indirect *testimonia* of Eusebius' *Questions* in many other authors, many of them already indicated by Mai.[47]

As a first step toward a complete critical edition, I have started a new search of Greek manuscripts. My research has not been limited to the catalogs of Greek manuscripts, but also extended to the Latin manuscripts and those in other ancient languages containing indices of authors, works, and biblical passages. Consulting the catalogs of Greek manuscripts was simplified by the use of the latest available edition of the classic guide of Marcel Richard,[48] whose references have been almost completely verified in the collection of the Greek section of the *Institut de Recherche et Histoire des Textes* in Paris, where I also searched the *Pinakes* database of the Greek Index Project, originally created by the Pontifical

---

[43] Caubet Iturbe 1969. This edition is based on the Vaticanus Arabicus 452, the most important and ancient manuscript, and the apparatus gives mainly variants of the other manuscripts (cf. x, xlvii–l, liii–liv and lvii–lix). Caubet Iturbe knows all fourteen Arabic manuscripts I list hereafter, but excludes five of them from his edition because they do not represent the same textual tradition he is editing (containing the extracts on Matthew), or, in the case of the manuscript of Bagdad, because he couldn't have access to it (cf. xlvi–xlvii).

[44] According to Caubet Iturbe 1969, only passages n. 1 (= Coptic 1) and 5 (= Coptic 6) really come from Eusebius' *Questions* (1944:xxi–xxii). For texts and translations of these passages, cf. Caubet Iturbe 1969:8, 251; Caubet Iturbe 1944:9, 268. Again, Pearse republishes all five passages in his edition (Pearse 2010:386–392).

[45] On Luke 1:39–40, cf. Lagarde 1886:119–120; Pearse 2010:362–363 (fragment 6 according to his numbering).

[46] Zotenberg 1877:73 (the catalogue is published anonymously); cf. Achelis 1897:165.

[47] Cf. Mai 1825:notes 24 and 32, as well as my commentary (Zamagni 2003:73–75, 90, 99, 108–110, etc.) and Guignard 2011:86–161.

[48] Richard and Olivier 1995.

Institute of Medieval Studies at Toronto and now freely available online.[49] For manuscripts in other languages (as well as for catalogs missing at the I.R.H.T.), I have used the collections of catalogs available at the Library of Lausanne, at the Library of Geneva, as well as the catalogs available at the Vatican Apostolic Library in Rome. This research was carried out mainly between 1998 and 2000 (although it is still in progress), and was primarily intended to search for other manuscripts of the *ekloge*, or for a complete copy of Eusebius' *Questions*, which was reported to be in Sicily in a letter by Latino Latini written 1563 and quoted by Mai.[50] Unfortunately, I have found no trace of a complete manuscript of the *Questions*, nor of another copy of the *ekloge*, but I nevertheless found many manuscripts containing parts or fragments of Eusebius' *Questions*.[51]

As for the *catena* of Nicetas on Luke, this research has identified a total of thirty-seven manuscripts, only some of which have been studied so far. The edition that Angelo Mai published in 1847 remains the only available edition and was made using a single manuscript (*Vaticanus Graecus* 1611). In 1902 Joseph Sickenberger studied a total of eighteen manuscripts of this catena and demonstrated that this is one of the best manuscripts available,[52] at least among the manuscripts he studied. This would not, however, exempt us from a study of all the known manuscripts, especially since, even according to Sickenberger's study, the manuscript used by Mai does not represent the only textual tradition of the *catena*.[53]

Concerning the other Greek fragmentary traditions that are not in Nicetas' *catena*, the results are even more challenging.[54] I have prepared a comprehensive list of Greek manuscripts containing (or probably containing) one or more fragments of Eusebius' *Questions*. The list identifies sixty-one Greek manuscripts that are likely to contain parts of this text (only a further study of these manu-

---

49  <http://pinakes.irht.cnrs.fr>. I have also occasionally used the Schoenberg Database of Manuscripts, <http://dla.library.upenn.edu/cocoon/dla/schoenberg>, and the online catalogues of the Bibliothèque Nationale de France, <http://archivesetmanuscrits.bnf.fr>.

50  Mai 1825:xii; Mai 1847:217 (reprinted in PG 22.877–878). This letter is now republished in complete form in Pearse 2010:398–402.

51  Excepting the catalogues of Greek manuscripts listed in Richard (cf. note 48), I checked a total of 1174 catalogues. My search terms included Eusebius as an author, as well as fragments attributed to him, Nicetas as an author, Julius Africanus as an author, and any anonymous text concerning arguments or biblical passages discussed in Eusebius' *Questions*, as well as the characters he mentioned (Stephanos and Marinos). These search criteria were however reduced in the case of catalogues lacking sufficiently comprehensive indexes.

52  Together with *Parisinus Coislinianus* 201 and Athos, *Iviron* 371; on this manuscript, cf. also Krikonis 1973.

53  Sickenberger 1902, and cf. Sickenberger 1898:55–84. See also the recent study of Nicetas' textual tradition by Guignard 2011:69–76.

54  On the fragments of the *Questions*, cf. also Burgon 1871:43–44 (note), 47–48 (note x); Schwartz 1907:1387–1388; Preuschen 1893:578–579; Pearse 2010:ix, refers to forty or more Greek manuscripts, using information I provided him by email on March, 1, 2008.

scripts will permit us to refine such a number). The number of manuscripts thus identified suggests that this fragmentary Greek tradition may contain something more than the thirty-seven fragments that have been hitherto printed,[55] although many manuscripts often contain the same questions. In any case, no direct study has ever been undertaken on these manuscripts.

During the making of this inventory, I have prepared a list of manuscripts containing unidentified fragments of Eusebius. There are a total of 146 manuscripts (mostly Latin) that should contain fragments taken from the works of Eusebius, but that the printed catalogues do not define more precisely. It is rather usual that catalogues, especially the oldest, merely state the authors of the texts in describing collections of miscellaneous works, sometimes with a very brief note on the fragment's content, without trying to identify its original source, nor giving an exact number of folios. Of course, it is likely that these fragments derive from other and better known works of Eusebius; in many cases, especially in the case of Latin texts, I also suspect that these extracts may come from another homonymous author.

Concerning traditions in other ancient languages, we already know of a total of five manuscripts containing different traditions of Eusebius' questions in Syriac, published partly by Mai in 1847 and partly by Beyer between 1925 and 1927.[56] The research for new Syriac witnesses has brought me to a total of ten manuscripts possibly containing remains of Eusebius' *Questions*. Although I have checked all catalogs of manuscripts in other ancient languages (mainly at the Vatican Library), I spotted only a Coptic manuscript hitherto unknown, but no new Arabic or Ethiopic manuscript of the so-called monophysite dogmatic florilegium published by De Lagarde and Caubet Iturbe.[57]

This inventory is intended as a provisional list of manuscripts, and certainly much in the list remains to be checked and verified. In preparing this catalog, I tried to be as complete as possible concerning the reported manuscripts, listing each manuscript, the description of its content vis à vis Eusebius, and, originally, the bibliographical references to the catalogs (or to other sources) examined.[58] This explains, though certainly does not excuse, the lack of some technical data

---

[55] The study of the *Venetus Marcianus Graecus* 61 by Guignard (2011:79–82, 189–193) has demonstrated in practice this statement, because the manuscript has been proved to be a new fragment coming from Eusebius' *Questions*.

[56] Beyer 1925–1927. Beyer actually edits the *Vaticanus Syriacus* 103, the *Vaticanus Syriacus* 154, and the *Florentinus Orientalis* 47.

[57] See notes 41 and 43 above.

[58] I have skipped here the description of the manuscripts' content because it needs a careful checking on the manuscripts themselves and skipped also the bibliographic references because of a lack of space.

on the manuscripts, as well as many inconsistencies in the way of indicating the manuscripts themselves.[59]

To get a complete critical edition of this Eusebian text, we must study all these manuscripts and all the different textual traditions they embody. This is of course a very challenging task, and obviously not a task for a single scholar. We should in any case carefully study the *catena* on Luke by Nicetas, which contains very interesting passages that have no corresponding passages in the *ekloge*, especially for the questions to Marinos. And the yet-unpublished Greek fragments? May they also contain some new sections of this lost work of Eusebius? To answer this simple question, much work still has to be done.

## I. Manuscript of the *ekloge*

1. Città del Vaticano, Biblioteca Apostolica Vaticana, Pal. Gr. 220 (parch.; X), fol. 61–96.

## II. Manuscripts of the *catena* on Luke by Nicetas of Herakleia

1. Athos, Vatopedi, 457.
2. Athos, Vatopedi, 529 (XIV), fol. 30r–122v.
3. Athos, Vatopedi, 530 (XII), 1–585v.
4. Athos, Dionysiou, 377 (n. 3911; paper; XVII).
5. Athos, Iviron, 371 (n. 4491; fol. 1–409: parch.; XIII; fol. 410–626: paper; a. 1576), 1–626.
6. Athos, Iviron, 1439 (XIII), fol. 1–8.
7. Bruxelles, Bibliothèque Royale Albert I, I.8232–33 (n. 3337; XVII), fol. 271–272.
8. Città del Vaticano, Biblioteca Apostolica Vaticana, Gr. 759 (paper; XIV), fol. IV.264.
9. Città del Vaticano, Biblioteca Apostolica Vaticana, Gr. 1611 (parch.; a. 1116–1117), fol. I.320.
10. Città del Vaticano, Biblioteca Apostolica Vaticana, Gr. 1642 (parch.; XI/XII), fol. I.296.
11. Città del Vaticano, Biblioteca Apostolica Vaticana, Gr. 1933 (paper; XVII), fol. XII.626.
12. Città del Vaticano, Biblioteca Apostolica Vaticana, Pal. Gr. 20.
13. Città del Vaticano, Biblioteca Apostolica Vaticana, Ottob. 100 (XV/XVI), fol. 2–105.
14. Firenze, Biblioteca Mediceo Laurenziana, Conventi Soppressi 176 (XII/XIII).
15. Istambul, Taphou 466 (XII/XII).
16. London, Lambeth Palace Library, 763 (XVIII), fol. 63–79v.
17. Milano, Biblioteca Ambrosiana, O 245 sup. (n. 608; XVI), fol. 19r–v.
18. München, Bayerische Staatsbibliothek, Gr. 33 (a. 1553), fol. 1–397v.
19. München, Bayerische Staatsbibliothek, Gr. 146 (XI), fol. 249–254.
20. München, Bayerische Staatsbibliothek, Gr. 318 (XIII), fol. 1–69.
21. München, Bayerische Staatsbibliothek, 473 (XIII).
22. Napoli, Biblioteca Nazionale, Gr. 3* (Vind. Suppl. Gr. 6; XI) fol. 196–314.
23. Oxford, St. John's College, 44 (XVI), fol. 201–266v.
24. Paris, Bibliothèque Nationale, Gr. 193 (paper; XVI).
25. Paris, Bibliothèque Nationale, Gr. 208 (paper; XIV).

---

[59] More than occasionally, these lacks are due to incomplete catalogues, or to the fact that folios containing Eusebius' passages are not explicitly mentioned.

26. Paris, Bibliothèque Nationale, Coislin 201 (paper; XIV/XV), fol. 1–605.
27. Paris, Bibliothèque Nationale, Suppl. Gr. 71 (paper; a. 1659), fol. 1–43.
28. Patmos, Moni Agiou Ioannou tou theologou, 203 (XIII).
29. Roma, Biblioteca Angelica, Gr. 100 (XII).
30. Roma, Biblioteca Casanatense, 715.
31. Sankt Peterburg, Rossiyskaya Natsionalnaya Bibliotyeka [National Library of Russia], Duh. Akad. 370, fol. 41–42.
32. Schleusingen, Henneberg. Gymn., 3 (XVII).
33. Venezia, Biblioteca Nazionale Marciana, Gr. 26.
34. Venezia, Biblioteca Nazionale Marciana, Gr. 331 (XIII/XIV).
35. Venezia, Biblioteca Nazionale Marciana, Gr. 494 (coll. 331; paper, XIII), fol. 3–58.
36. Venezia, Biblioteca Nazionale Marciana, Gr. 495 (coll. 1048; paper; XIV/XV), fol. 373–435.
37. Wien, Österreichische Nationalbibliothek, Theol. Gr. 71 (parch.; XIII).

## III. Greek Manuscripts Containing Parts of Eusebius' *Questions*

1. Athinai, Ethnike bibliotheke tes Hellados, 2164 (parch.; a. 1088), fol. 96; fol. 98.
2. Athinai, Katholikon Orthodoxon Patriarcheion [Jerusalem], 22, fol. 159.
3. Athinai, Katholikon Orthodoxon Patriarcheion [Jerusalem], Saba 31 (XI), fol. 88–100.
4. Athos, Lavra, Γ119 (n. 359; X), fol. 108r–v; fol. 110–111.
5. Alexandria, Bibliotheke tou Patriacheiou, 71 (n. 219; paper; XII), fol. 175r–184v.
6. Cambridge, University Library, Oo. VI. 91. (n. 3163; paper/parch.; XV/XVI/XVIII), fasc. 19, n. 17.
7. Cambridge, Trinity College, B. 7. i vac. (n. 178; X), fol. 140–145; fol. 148–149.
8. Città del Vaticano, Biblioteca Apostolica Vaticana, Gr. 358 (parch.; XI), fol. 110r; fol. 110v–111v.
9. Città del Vaticano, Biblioteca Apostolica Vaticana, Gr. 384 (paper; a. 1553), fol. 127–129; fol. 131–133.
10. Città del Vaticano, Biblioteca Apostolica Vaticana, Gr. 840 (paper; XIV), fol. 173v–174r.
11. Città del Vaticano, Biblioteca Apostolica Vaticana, Gr. 1532 (paper; XI), fol. 140v–142r; fol. 143v–145r.
12. Città del Vaticano, Biblioteca Apostolica Vaticana, Gr. 1692 (parch.; X), fol. 85r–v; fol. 86r–87r.
13. Città del Vaticano, Biblioteca Apostolica Vaticana, Gr. 1767 (paper; XVI), fol. 103r–105v.
14. Città del Vaticano, Biblioteca Apostolica Vaticana, Gr. 1915 (parch.; X/XI), fol. 37v–38v.
15. Città del Vaticano, Biblioteca Apostolica Vaticana, Gr. 2658 (X/XI), fol. 238r–278v.
16. Città del Vaticano, Biblioteca Apostolica Vaticana, Barb. Gr. 562 (X/XI), fol. 120v–125v.
17. Città del Vaticano, Biblioteca Apostolica Vaticana, Pii II Gr. 9 (paper; XV), fol. 141.
18. Città del Vaticano, Biblioteca Apostolica Vaticana, Reg. Gr. 46 (Montfaucon 938; paper; XV/XVI), fol. 82–83.
19. Città del Vaticano, Biblioteca Apostolica Vaticana, Ross. Gr. 7 (XIII), fol. 2v–4r.
20. Città del Vaticano, Biblioteca Apostolica Vaticana, Ross. Gr. 211 (XIII), fol. 2v–3v.
21. El Escorial, Madrid, Biblioteca de S. Lorenzo, K. II. 10. [deperditus] (parch.), fol. 116v–117v; fol. 119–120.

22. El Escorial, Madrid, Biblioteca de S. Lorenzo, K. III. 12. [deperditus] (n. 534; paper; a. 1580 circa), fol. 122r–123v; fol. 125v–128r.
23. Firenze, Biblioteca Medicea Laurenziana, Plut. VI. cod. 5 (parch.; XII), fol. 68–75; fol. 76–77.
24. Firenze, Biblioteca Medicea Laurenziana, Plut. VI. cod. 33 (parch.; XI).
25. Firenze, Biblioteca Medicea Laurenziana, S. Marco 687 (X/XIV), fol. 83v–86v.
26. Leiden, Bibliotheek der Rijkuniversiteit, Voss. Misc. 22 (paper; XVII), fol. 59–61.
27. London, British Library, Harley 5643 (XVI/XVII), fol. 11r–v.
28. Meteora, Moni Metamorphoseos, 28 (bomb., XIV), fol. 97–99; fol. 126v–127.
29. Milano, Biblioteca Ambrosiana, A 62 inf. (n. 797; parch.; XI), fol. 26r–27v.
30. Milano, Biblioteca Ambrosiana, H 257 inf. (n. 1041; parch.; XIII), fol. 156r–158v.
31. München, Bayerische Staatsbibliothek, Gr. 146 (XI), fol. 249–254.
32. Oxford, Bodleian Library, Barocc. 197 (XIV), fol. 212v–227.
33. Oxford, Bodleian Library, Laud. Gr. 33 (XI), fol. 79–80; fol. 80.
34. Oxford, Bodleian Library, Misc. 182 (T.1.4; X/XI), fol. 80; fol. 169–172.
35. Paris, Bibliothèque Nationale, Gr. 186 (parch.; XI).
36. Paris, Bibliothèque Nationale, Gr. 199 (parch.; XII), fol. 176v.
37. Paris, Bibliothèque Nationale, Gr. 200 (parch.; XI/XII), fol. 130v.
38. Paris, Bibliothèque Nationale, Gr. 201 (parch.; XI/XII), fol. 112r–v.
39. Paris, Bibliothèque Nationale, Gr. 206 (parch.; a. 13071308), fol. 1r–v; fol. 3v–5v.
40. Paris, Bibliothèque Nationale, Gr. 255 (paper; XV).
41. Paris, Bibliothèque Nationale, Gr. 572 (paper; XV/XVI), fol. 239r–240.
42. Paris, Bibliothèque Nationale, Gr. 700 (parch.; X), fol. 43v–46r.
43. Paris, Bibliothèque Nationale, Gr. 701 (parch.; IX/X), fol. 137v–143.
44. Paris, Bibliothèque Nationale, Gr. 702 (parch.; X), fol. 122–126.
45. Paris, Bibliothèque Nationale, Gr. 704 (parch.; X/XII), fol. 53v–57.
46. Paris, Bibliothèque Nationale, Coislin 195 (parch.; X), fol. 165–168.
47. Patmos, Moni Agiou Ioannou tou theologou, 59 (IX–X), fol. 105r–106r; fol.107v–108r; fol. 235r–236r.
48. Patmos, Moni Agiou Ioannou tou theologou, 60 (XI), fol. 375v–377r; fol. 379r–381r.
49. Roma, Biblioteca Angelica, B. 1. 7. (n. 67; parch.; X/XI), fol. 59r–60r; fol. 61v–63r.
50. Roma, Biblioteca Vallicelliana, C 34 (n. 36; paper/parch.; XII/XVI), fol. 402r–404r; fol. 407v–411r.
51. Roma, Biblioteca Vallicelliana, F 25 (n. 89; paper; XIV), fol. 37–38.
52. Sankt Peterburg, Rossiyskaya Natsionalnaya Bibliotyeka [National Library of Russia], Gr. 216 (parch.; a. 862/863), fol. 346r.
53. Venezia, Biblioteca Nazionale Marciana, Gr. I, 34 (coll. 1070; parch.; XII), fol. 111v–112v; fol. 114r–115v.
54. Venezia, Biblioteca Nazionale Marciana, Gr. II, 144 (coll. 1362; parch.; X), fol. 3r–4r (marg.).
55. Venezia, Biblioteca Nazionale Marciana, Gr. 61 (parch.; X; fol. 1–2: XI), fol. 1–2.
56. Venezia, Biblioteca Nazionale Marciana, Gr. 494 (paper, XIII), fol. 111–112; fol. 143–144.
57. Venezia, Biblioteca Nazionale Marciana, Gr. 495 (coll. 1048; paper; XIV/XV), fol. 143bis–144.
58. Wien, Österreichische Nationalbibliothek, Theol. Gr. 153 (paper; XIII), fol. 260r.
59. Wien, Österreichische Nationalbibliothek, Theol. Gr. 199 (paper; XVI), fol. 1–45.

60. Unknown, Paris, Collège de Clermont, 75 (Schoenberg n. 188178; paper; XV).
61. Unknown, Den Haag, Gerard and Johan Meerman Collection, Ms. 76 (Schoenberg n. 45161; parch.; XII).

## IV. Syriac Manuscripts Containing Parts of Eusebius' *Questions*

1. Berlin, Alte Bibliothek [Königliche], Syr. 81 (n. 311; XVI/XVII [fol. 1–15.157–259: XIX]); fol. 84.
2. Firenze, Biblioteca Medicea Laurenziana, Pal. Or. 47, fol. 1v–2v [published by Beyer, but to be considered a *testimonium*].
3. London, British Library, Syr. 853, fol. 176–182; fol. 232.
4. London, British Library, Add. 12144 (a. 1801) [copy of Vatican Library, Syr. 103].
5. Città del Vaticano, Biblioteca Apostolica Vaticana, Syr. 103 (parch.; IX/X), fol. 302r–307v; fol. 368v.
6. Città del Vaticano, Biblioteca Apostolica Vaticana, Syr. 154 (parch./bomb.; VIII/IX), fol. 3–9; fol. 21–22; fol. 209.
7. Città del Vaticano, Biblioteca Apostolica Vaticana, Syr. 155, fol. 26r and 35v at least.
8. Città del Vaticano, Biblioteca Apostolica Vaticana, Syr. 156, fol. 11–13; fol. 32r; fol. 159v; fol. 315r.
9. Città del Vaticano, Biblioteca Apostolica Vaticana, Syr. 284 [or 283] (paper).
10. Città del Vaticano, Biblioteca Apostolica Vaticana, Syr. 541 (paper; a. 1555), fol. 153r–225r [a *catena* on Luke containing Eusebius' texts, text to be checked].

## V. Coptic Manuscripts of the So-called Monophysite Dogmatic Florilegium

1. London, British Library, Or. 8812 (n. 249; Parham 106; parch.; a. 888/889).
2. London, British Library, Add. 14740 (n. 740; parch.).

## VI. Arabic Manuscripts of the So-called Monophysite Dogmatic Florilegium

1. Al-Qahira, Coptic Museum, 1157–Graf 166 (XIV/XV).
2. Al-Qahira, Coptic Patriachate, 41–Graf 195 (paper; a. 1735).
3. Al-Qahira, Coptic Patriachate, 567–Graf 411 (paper; XIV).
4. Città del Vaticano, Biblioteca Apostolica Vaticana, Ar. 410 (paper; XIII/XIV).
5. Città del Vaticano, Biblioteca Apostolica Vaticana, Ar. 411 (paper; XIV).
6. Città del Vaticano, Biblioteca Apostolica Vaticana, Ar. 452 (paper; a. 1214).
7. Città del Vaticano, Biblioteca Apostolica Vaticana, (Karšhuni) Syr. 531 (a. 1486).
8. Città del Vaticano, Biblioteca Apostolica Vaticana, (Karšuni) Syr. 541 (paper, a. 1555).
9. Bagdad, Chaldean Patriarchate, Library of Mossul Chaldean Patriarchate, 131 (Diyarbakır, 131; a. 1498).
10. Göttingen, Niedersächsische Staats und Universitätsbibliothek Göttingen, Ar. 103 (paper; XIII/XIV, restored a. 1811).
11. Oxford, Bodleian Library, Hunt. 262 (n. 26; paper; XVI, before a. 1575).

12. Paris, Bibliothèque Nationale, Ar. 55 (paper; a. 1619).
13. Paris, Bibliothèque Nationale, Ar. 93 (paper; XIV).
14. Strasbourg, Bibliothèque Nationale et Universitaire, Or. 4315 (paper; XVI).

## VII. Ethiopic Manuscripts of the So-called Monophysite Dogmatic Florilegium

1. London, British Library, Aeth. 11 (add. 16220; parch.; XVII).
2. Paris, Bibliothèque Nationale, Aeth. 65 (parch.; XVII).

## VIII. Greek and Latin Manuscripts Containing Other Eusebius' Extracts or Unidentified Questions on the Gospels

1. Arras, Abbaye Saint-Vaast, 158 (XII).
2. Athinai, Ethnike bibliotheke tes Hellados, 408.
3. Athinai, Katholikon Orthodoxon Patriarcheion [Jerusalem], Saba, 232 (parch.; XI).
4. Athinai, Katholikon Orthodoxon Patriarcheion [Jerusalem], Panagiou Taphou, 257 (paper; XVII), fol. 9–21.
5. Athos, Dionysiou, 71 (n. 3605; parch.; X).
6. Athos, Koutloumousiou, 178 (n. 3251; paper; XIII), fol. 11–13.
7. Athos, Lavra, A37 (n. 37; X), fol. 1–9 et 9–20.
8. Athos, Xenophontos, 53 (n. 755; paper; XVII), sect. 3.
9. Bamberg, Staatsbibliothek [Königliche], Q. VI. 58. (n. 110; paper; XV), fol. 221v.
10. Bamberg, Staatsbibliothek [Königliche], Domkapitel, 141 [B. III. 36] (n. 86; parch.; XI–XII).
11. Basel, Universitätsbibliothek, A XI 71 (paper; XV), fol. 161.
12. Bern, Bibliotheca Bongarsiana, AA 90 fasc. 4 (parch.; XI–XII), fol. 1–3.
13. Besançon, Bibliothèque, 186 (parch.; IX), miscellanea patristica, fol. 32–70.
14. Bologna, Biblioteca Universitaria, 3637 (paper; XIV), fol. 81–83.
15. Brescia, Biblioteca Civica Queriniana, F II 1 (parch.; IX).
16. Brescia, Biblioteca Civica Queriniana, C V 10 (paper; XVII–XVIII).
17. Cambridge, Corpus Christi College, 404, fol. 7–9.
18. Cambridge, Trinity College, O. 8. 22 5939–53 (n. 1397), fol. 15–16; fol. 77–81.
19. Cambridge, Public Library, 151 (n. 2331).
20. Città del Vaticano, Biblioteca Apostolica Vaticana, Lat. 3832, fol. 29.46.
21. Città del Vaticano, Biblioteca Apostolica Vaticana, Gr. 875 (paper; XIII), fol. 300–301.
22. Città del Vaticano, Biblioteca Apostolica Vaticana, Gr. 1618 (paper, XVI), on Mt 1:1–21.
23. Città del Vaticano, Biblioteca Apostolica Vaticana, Gr. 1637 (parch.; XVI), fol. 103r–105v.
24. Città del Vaticano, Biblioteca Apostolica Vaticana, Gr. 1890 (paper; XV/XVI), fol. 123r–128v.
25. Città del Vaticano, Biblioteca Apostolica Vaticana, Ott. Gr. 100 (paper; XV/XVI).
26. Città del Vaticano, Biblioteca Apostolica Vaticana, Ott. Gr. 134 (paper; XVII).
27. Città del Vaticano, Biblioteca Apostolica Vaticana, Ott. Gr. 408 (paper; XVI).

28. Città del Vaticano, Biblioteca Apostolica Vaticana, Pal. Gr. 20 (bomb.; XIII).
29. Città del Vaticano, Biblioteca Apostolica Vaticana, Pal. Gr. 129 (paper; XV/XVI).
30. Città del Vaticano, Biblioteca Apostolica Vaticana, Reg. Gr. 46 (Montfaucon 938; paper; XV/XVI), fol. 59–60; fol. 66.
31. Città del Vaticano, Biblioteca Apostolica Vaticana, Reg. Gr. 57 (paper; XV–XVI), fol. 456.
32. Dublin, Trinity College Library, 148 (XV), fol. 15–45v.
33. Dublin, Trinity College Library, 422, fol. 39.
34. Dublin, Trinity College Library, 2100, fol. 152v.
35. El Escorial, Madrid, Biblioteca de S. Lorenzo, Cod. Gr. E. (4 codici).
36. El Escorial, Madrid, Biblioteca de S. Lorenzo, Γ 14. 118.
37. El Escorial, Madrid, Biblioteca de S. Lorenzo, Γ II. 4.
38. El Escorial, Madrid, Biblioteca de S. Lorenzo, Γ II. 7.
39. El Escorial, Madrid, Biblioteca de S. Lorenzo, X. IV. 11. (n. 406; paper; XIV), fol. 8v–36v.
40. El Escorial, Madrid, Biblioteca de S. Lorenzo, Λ. IV. 20. [deperditus] (n. 601; parch.), fol. 15r–v.
41. El Escorial, Madrid, Biblioteca de S. Lorenzo, K. II. 13.
42. Firenze, Biblioteca Moreniana, 13 (paper; XVIII), fol. 272–276.
43. Firenze, Biblioteca Medicea Laurenziana, Plut. IV. cod. 26 (paper; XVI).
44. Firenze, Biblioteca Medicea Laurenziana, Plut. VI. cod. 4 (parch.; XIV).
45. Firenze, Biblioteca Medicea Laurenziana, Plut. VII. cod. 15 (parch.; XI), fol. 150; fol. 154; fol. 189; fol. 192.
46. Firenze, Biblioteca Medicea Laurenziana, Plut. IX. cod. 26 (parch.; XIV), fol. 84.
47. Firenze, Biblioteca Riccardiana, Ricc. 907 (N III 16; paper; XV a.).
48. Graz, Universitätsbibliothek, 996 (paper; a. 1579).
49. Hamburg, Staats- und Universitätsbibliothek, Theol. 1518c.
50. Istambul, Maurogordateios Bibliotheke, 264.
51. Klosternburg, Bibliotheca Augustiniana, 205 (paper, XV), fol. 188–247.
52. Lyon, Bibliothèque Municipale, 598 (parch.; XII), cf. fol. 112–114.
53. London, British Library, Harley 3089.
54. London, British Library, Harley 3651.
55. Madrid, Biblioteca Nacional, 4749 (n. 198; paper; a. 1555), fol. 43–46; fol. 183v–185v.
56. Marseille, Bibliothèque, 198 (paper; XVII).
57. Meteora, Moni Barlaam, 137 (paper; XVI), fol. 76–87.
58. Meteora, Moni Barlaam, 195 (paper; XVII), fol. 50–105.
59. Meteora, Moni Metamorphoseos, 243 (paper; XIV).
60. Meteora, Moni Agiou Stephanou, 110 (paper; XIX), fol. 124r; fol. 126v.
61. Meteora, Moni Agiou Stephanou, 130 (paper; XIX), fol. 5.
62. Milano, Biblioteca Ambrosiana, A 84 sup. (n. 273; parch.; XIII), fol. 86.
63. Milano, Biblioteca Ambrosiana, C 30 inf. (n. 850; parch.; XII).
64. Milano, Biblioteca Ambrosiana, E 16 sup. (n. 273; parch.; XIII), fol. 57.
65. Milano, Biblioteca Ambrosiana, E 20 sup. (n. 276; parch.; XIII), fol. 74.
66. Milano, Biblioteca Ambrosiana, E 64 sup. (n. 290; paper; XV), fol. 218.
67. Milano, Biblioteca Ambrosiana, F 140 sup. (n. 375; parch.; XIII).
68. Milano, Biblioteca Ambrosiana, G 76 inf. (XVI).
69. Milano, Biblioteca Ambrosiana, M 57 sup. (n. 520; parch.), fol. 139.
70. Milano, Biblioteca Ambrosiana, M 83 sup. (n. 529; parch.; XIII).

71. Milano, Biblioteca Ambrosiana, Q 50 sup. (n. 678; paper; XIV), fol. 160–231.
72. Milano, Biblioteca Ambrosiana, Q 74 sup. (n. 681).
73. Milano, Biblioteca Ambrosiana, S 23 sup. (n. 732; parch.; XII), fol. 163; fol. 165–168.
74. Milano, Biblioteca Ambrosiana, Z 75 sup. (n. 752; paper; XVI).
75. Mons, Bibliothèque Publique, 47/217, fol. 26r–32v; fol. 32v–38r.
76. Moscau, Gosudarstvyenniy Istorichyeskiy Muzyey [State Historical Museum], Gr. 29–119/CXX.
77. Moscau, Rossiyskaya Gosudarstvyennaya Bibliotyeka [Russians State Library], 82 (n. 137; IX), fol. 170r–175r.
78. München, Bayerische Staatsbibliothek, Gr. 381 (XIII), fol. 1–69.
79. München, Bayerische Staatsbibliothek, 26690 (n. 2213; XV).
80. Nürnberg, Pfarriche St. Sebald Bibl., 141 [B. III. 36] (n. 86).
81. Oxford, Bodleian Library, Ashmol. 393, fol. 80.
82. Oxford, Bodleian Library, Barrocc. 76 (n. 76) fol. 177–215.
83. Oxford, Bodleian Library, Digbeian. 196 (n. 1797), fol. 18.
84. Oxford, Corpus Christi College Library, 232 (n. 1699).
85. Oxford, Christ Church College Library, 45 (XIII/XV), fol. 241–245.
86. Oxford, Jesus College Library, 25.
87. Oxford, Jesus College Library, 65, fol. 138–140.
88. Mons, Bibliothèque Publique, 47/217, fol. 26–32; fol. 32–38.
89. Paris, Bibliothèque Mazarine, 968 (paper; a. 1462), fol. 87–89; fol. 94–134.
90. Paris, Bibliothèque Mazarine, 1631 (paper; XVII).
91. Paris, Bibliothèque Sainte Geneviève, 212 (paper; a. 1743–1745).
92. Paris, Bibliothèque Sainte Geneviève, 1416 (parch.; XIII), fol. 135r–142r.
93. Paris, Bibliothèque Nationale, Gr. 221 (parch.; XII).
94. Paris, Bibliothèque Nationale, Gr. 633 (parch.; a. 1186).
95. Paris, Bibliothèque Nationale, Gr. 854 (bomb.; XIII), fol. 17.
96. Paris, Bibliothèque Nationale, Gr. 922 (parch.; XI), fol. 236–240.
97. Paris, Bibliothèque Nationale, Gr. 1555A (bomb.; XVI), fol. 179–186.
98. Paris, Bibliothèque Nationale, Gr. 2511 (paper; XV), fol. 46–55.
99. Paris, Bibliothèque Nationale, Gr. 2665 (paper/bomb.; XIV/XV), fol. 209–210.
100. Paris, Bibliothèque Nationale, Supplément grec 771 (XV).
101. Paris, Bibliothèque Nationale, Coislin 20 (parch.; X), fol. 165–168.
102. Paris, Bibliothèque Nationale, Coislin 23 (parch.; XI).
103. Paris, Bibliothèque Nationale, Coislin 112 (paper; a. 1329).
104. Paris, Bibliothèque Nationale, Coislin 115 (parch.; XII).
105. Paris, Bibliothèque Nationale, Coislin 120 (parch.; X), fol. 31–204.
106. Paris, Bibliothèque Nationale, Coislin 122 (paper; XIV).
107. Paris, Bibliothèque Nationale, Coislin 296 (parch.; XII), fol. 120–162.
108. Paris, Bibliothèque Nationale, Coislin 371 (parch.; X), fol. 51–55; fol. 91–92; fol. 94.
109. Paris, Bibliothèque Nationale, Lat. 1568 (parch.; IX–XV), fol. 40–67 [IX].
110. Paris, Bibliothèque Nationale, Lat. 1860 (parch.; XIII), fol. 153v–217r.
111. Paris, Bibliothèque Nationale, Lat. 3396 (XVI).

112. Paris, Bibliothèque Nationale, Lat. 3497 (parch.; XIV); fol. 37.
113. Paris, Bibliothèque Nationale, Lat. 3508 (paper; XV).
114. Paris, Bibliothèque Nationale, Lat. 3508A (paper; XV).
115. Paris, Bibliothèque Nationale, Lat. 10685 (XII).
116. Patmos, Moni Agiou Ioannou tou theologou, 56.
117. Patmos, Moni Agiou Ioannou tou theologou, 203, fol. 120–191.
118. Praha, Státní Knihovna [National Library], XIII D 24 (n. 2316), fol. 333–335.
119. Praha, Státní Knihovna [National Library], XXV B 7 (parch.; X/XI), fol. 9v–10r; fol. 115v; fol. 183r; fol. 298r; fol. 191r–v; fol. 307r.
120. Reims, Bibliothèque, Saints Pères 284 (parch.; XI).
121. Roma, Biblioteca Angelica, A. 4. 1. (n. 57; paper; XV), fol. 192.
122. Roma, Biblioteca Vallicelliana, E 40 (n. 72; parch.; XI).
123. Roma, Biblioteca Vallicelliana, Gr. 137 (n. 213).
124. Salisbury, Library of the Cathedral Church, 61, fol. 35.
125. San Daniele del Friuli, Biblioteca Guarneriana, 87, fol. 77v–78v.
126. Sinai, Aghia Katerina, 529 (XVII), fol. 8v–10v.
127. Skiathos, Moni Evangelistria, 11 (XIV), fol. 2–25.
128. Toulouse, Bibliothèque, 624 (n. 82), fol. 2; fol. 37.
129. Uppsala, Universitätsbibliothek, C 937 (n. 339), fol. 18–21.
130. Venezia, Museo Civico Correr, Fondo Morosini-Grimani, 94 (XVII), fol. 229.
131. Venezia, Biblioteca Nazionale Marciana, Gr. II, 77 (paper; XVI), fol. 97.107.
132. Venezia, Biblioteca Nazionale Marciana, Gr. II, 90 (paper; XVI), fol. 212–231.
133. Venezia, Biblioteca Nazionale Marciana, Gr. III, 4 (paper; XVI).
134. Venezia, Biblioteca Nazionale Marciana, Gr. 27 (coll. 341; parch.; X–XI), fol. 93.
135. Venezia, Biblioteca Nazionale Marciana, Gr. 28 (coll. 364; parch.; XI), fol. 4–136; fol. 137–281.
136. Venezia, Biblioteca Nazionale Marciana, Gr. 138 (parch.; X).
137. Venezia, Biblioteca Nazionale Marciana, Gr. 139 (parch.; XI/XII), fol. 50–51.
138. Venezia, Biblioteca Nazionale Marciana, Gr. 410.
139. Venezia, Biblioteca del monastero di S. Michele, 120.
140. Wien, Österreichische Nationalbibliothek, Phil. Gr. 248 (paper; XIV/XV), fol. 132r–191r.
141. Würzburg, Universitätsbibliothek, Ehemaligen Dombibliothek, M. p. th. f. 61 (parch.; VIII/IX).
142. Unknown, *apud* P. Labbe, *Nova bibliotheca manuscriptorum librorum*, Parisiis 1653, 184, 'De triduo sepulturae Domini.'
143. Unknown, Sens, Library of M. [Gratien-Théodore] Tarbé, 22 (parch.).
144. Unknown, Toulouse, Bibliothèque de l'archévêque Charles de Montchal, 220.
145. Unknown, [York,] Library of Thomas Gale, 115 (Schoenberg n. 163425; n. 5949; [E. Bernard,] *Catalogi librorum manuscriptorum Anglie et Hiberniae in unum collecti*, II,1, Oxoniae 1697, 188), 'Eusebi sermo de sepultura Christi triduana.'
146. Unknown, Aedes Jacobaei, 591 (*ibid.*, 244S; Schoenberg n. 165132; n. 8313).

# Works Cited

Achelis, H. 1897. *Hippolytstudien*, Texte und Untersuchungen 16.4. Leipzig.

Bardy, G. 1932–1933. "La littérature patristique des 'Quaestiones et responsiones' sur l'Écriture sainte." *Revue biblique* 41:210–236, 341–369, 515–537; 42:14–30, 211–229, 328–352.

Beyer, G. 1925–1927. "Die evangelischen Fragen und Lösungen des Eusebius in jakobitischer Überlieferung und deren nestorianische Parallelen. Syrische Texte, herausgegeben, übersetzt und untersucht." *Oriens Christianus*, Neue Serie, 12–24 (1925), 30–70; Dritte Serie, 1 (1927), 80–97; 284–292; Dritte Serie, 2 (1927), 57–69.

Burgon, J. W. 1871. *The Last Twelve Verses of the Gospel According to S. Mark, Vindicated Against Recent Critical Objectors and Established.* Oxford/London.

Cameron, A. and S. G. Hall. 1999. *Eusebius, Life of Constantine. Introduction, translation and commentary*, Clarendon Ancient History Series. Oxford.

Carriker, A. J. 2003. *The Library of Eusebius of Caesarea*, Supplements to Vigiliae Christianae 67. Leiden and Boston.

Caubet Iturbe, F. J. 1969. *La cadena árabe del evangelio de san Mateo, I. Testo.* Studi e testi, 254. Vatican City.

———. 1970. *La cadena árabe del evangelio de san Mateo, II. Versión.* Studi e testi, 255. Vatican City.

Cavallo, G. 1988. "Scuola, scriptorium, biblioteca a Cesarea." In *Le biblioteche nel mondo antico e medievale*, Biblioteca Universale Laterza 250, G. Cavallo, ed., 65–78. Bari.

Courcelle, P. 1959. "Critiques exégétiques et arguments antichrétiens rapportés par Ambrosiaster." *Vigiliae Christianae* 13:133–169.

Cramer, J. A. 1840. *Catenae in evangelia s. Matthaei et s. Marci, ad fidem codd. mss.*, Catenae Graecorum patrum in Novum Testamentum 1. Oxford.

———. 1844. *Catenae in evangelia s. Lucae et s. Joannis, ad fidem codd. mss.*, Catenae Graecorum patrum in Novum Testamentum 2. Oxford.

Corderius, B. 1628. *Catena sexaginta quinque Graecorum patrum in S. Lucam . . ., luce ac Latinitate donate.* Antwerp.

Dorival, G. 1984. "Apercu sur l'histoire des chaînes exégétiques grecques sur le Psautier (Vᵉ-XIVᵉ siècles)." In *Studia patristica*, vol. XV, Texte und Untersuchungen 128, E.A. Livingstone, ed., 146–169. Berlin.

———. 1986. *Les chaînes exégétiques grecques sur les Psaumes, contributions à l'étude d'une forme littéraire*, t. 1., Spicilegium sacrum lovaniense, Études et documents 43. Leuven.

Graf, G. 1944. *Geschichte der christlichen arabischen Literatur, I. Die Übersetzungen*, Studi e testi 118. Vatican City.

Grafton, A and M. Williams. 2006. *Christianity and the Transformation of the Book. Origen, Eusebius and the Library of Caesarea.* Cambridge, MA/London.

Guignard, C. 2011. *La lettre de Julius Africanus à Aristide sur la généalogie du Christ. Analyse de la tradition textuelle, édition, traduction et étude critique,* Texte und Untersuchungen 167. Berlin/Boston.

Hollerich, M. J. 1999. *Eusebius of Caesarea's* Commentary on Isaiah. *Christian Exegesis in the Age of Constantine,* Oxford Early Christian Studies. Oxford.

Jacob, C. 2004. "Questions sur les questions: archéologie d'une pratique intellectuelle et d'une forme discursive." In *Erotapokriseis. Early Christian Question-and-Answer Literature in Context. Proceedings of the Utrecht Colloquium, 13–14 October 2003,* Contributions to Biblical Exegesis and Theology 37, ed. Volgers, A., and C. Zamagni, 25–54. Leuven/Paris/Dudley, MA.

Kannengiesser, C. 2004. *Handbook of Patristic Exegesis, II.* The Bible in Ancient Christianity 1/2. Leiden/Boston 2004.

Krikonis, Ch. Th. 1973. *Συναγωγὴ πατέρων εἰς τὸ κατὰ Λουκᾶν εὐαγγελίον ὑπὸ Νικήτα Ἡρακλείας.* Thessaloniki.

Labriolle, P. de. 1948. *La réaction païenne. Étude sur la polémique antichrétienne du Ier au VIe siècle.* Paris.

Lagarde, P. de. 1886. *Catenae in Evangelia Aegyptiacae quae supersunt.* Göttingen.

———. 1887a. "Selbstanzeige meiner letzten Schriften." *Göttingische gelehrte Anzeigen* 15 Juni.

———. 1887b. *Mittheilungen, II. Band,* Göttingen.

Layton, B. 1987. *Catalogue of Coptic literary manuscripts in the British Library acquired since the year 1906.* London.

Lightfoot, J.B. 1880. "Eusebius of Caesarea, also known as Eusebius Pamphili." In *A Dictionary of Christian Biography, Literature, Sects and Doctrines,* ed. Smith, W. and H. Wace, 308–348. London/New York.

Mai, A. 1825. *Scriptorum veterum nova collectio, e Vaticanis codicibus edita, tomus I [pars prior],* Rome. Reprinted in 1931 and republished in PG 22.

———. 1847. *Novae patrum bibliothecae tomus IV.* Rome. Republished in PG 22.

Norelli, E. 2001. "La mémoire des origines chrétiennes: Papias et Hégésippe chez Eusèbe." In *L'historiographie de l'église des premiers siècles,* Théologie historique 114, ed. Pouderon, B. and Y.-M. Duval, 1–22. Paris.

Papadoyannakis, Y. 2006. "Instruction by Question and Answer: The Case of Late Antique and Byzantine Erotapokriseis." In *Greek Literature in Late Antiquity. Dynamism, Didacticism, Classicism,* S. F Johnson, ed., 91–105. Burlington.

———. Forthcoming. "'Encyclopedism' in the Byzantine Question-and-Answer Literature: The Case of Pseudo-Kasairios." In *Encyclopaedic Trends in Byzantium?,* ed. van Deun, P. and C. Macé. Leuven.

Pearse, R. 2010. *Eusebius of Caesarea, Gospel Problems and Solutions. Quaestiones ad Stephanum et Marinum (CPG 3470)*, Ancient Texts in Translation 1, ed. D.J.D. Miller (Greek, Latin), A.C. McCollum (Syriac, Arabic), C. Downer (Coptic), and others. Ipswich.

Perrone, L. 1990. "Le Quaestiones evangelicae di Eusebio di Cesarea. Alle origini di un genere letterario." *Annali di storia dell'esegesi* 7:417–435.

———. 1991. "Sulla preistoria delle 'quaestiones' nella letteratura patristica. Presupposti e sviluppi del genere letterario fino al IV sec." *Annali di storia dell'esegesi* 8:485–505.

———. 1994. "Echi della polemica pagana sulla Bibbia negli scritti esegetici fra IV e V secolo: Le Quaestiones Veteris et Novi Testamenti dell'Ambrosiaster." *Annali di storia dell'esegesi* 11:161–185.

———. 1996. "Eusebius of Caesarea as a Christian Writer." In *Caesarea Maritima. A Retrospective after Two Millennia*, ed. Raban, A. and K.G. Holum, 515–530. Leiden/New York/Köln.

Preuschen, E. 1893. "Eusebius, Bischof von Cäsarea (c. 265–340), Schriften." In Harnack, A. von, *Geschichte der altchristlichen Literatur bis Eusebius, I. Die Überlieferung und der Bestand, bearb. unter Mitwirkung von E. Preuschen*, 551–586. Leipzig.

Reichardt, W. 1909. *Die Briefe des Sextus Julius Africanus an Aristides und Origenes.* Texte und Untersuchungen 34.3. Leipzig.

Richard, M. and J.-M. Olivier. 1995. *Répertoire des bibliothèques et des catalogues de manuscrits grecs.* Turnhout.

Schwartz, E. 1907. "Eusebios von Caesarea." In *Paulys Realenzyklopädie*, VI/1. Stuttgart.

Sickenberger, J. 1898. "Aus römischen Handschriften über die Lukaskatene des Niketas." *Römische Quartalschrift für christliche Altertumskunde und für Kirchengeschichte* 12:55–84.

———. 1902. *Die Lukaskatene des Niketas von Herakleia, untersucht.* Texte und Untersuchungen 22.4. Leipzig.

Spitta, F. 1877. *Der Brief des Julius Africanus an Aristides, kritisch untersucht und herg-estellt.* Halle.

Zamagni, C. 2003. *Les "Questions et réponses sur les évangiles" d'Eusèbe de Césarée. Étude et Édition du résumé grec.* PhD Dissertation, Université de Lausanne – EHPE. Paris.

———. 2004. "Une introduction méthodologique à la littérature patristique des questions et réponses: le cas d'Eusèbe de Césarée." In *Erotapokriseis. Early Christian Question-and-Answer Literature in Context. Proceedings of the Utrecht Colloquium, 13-14 October 2003*, Contributions to Biblical Exegesis and Theology 37, ed. Volgers A., and C. Zamagni, 7–24. Leuven/Paris/ Dudley, MA.

———. 2008. *Eusèbe de Césarée: Questions évangéliques. Introduction, texte critique, traduction et notes.* Sources chrétiennes 523. Paris.

———. 2011a. "Porphyre est-il la cible principale des 'questions' chrétiennes du IVe et Ve siècles?" In *Le traité de Porphyre contre les chrétiens. Un siècle de recherches, nouvelles questions. Actes du colloque international organisé les 8 et 9 septembre 2009 à l'Université de Paris IV-Sorbonne,* Études Augustiniennes, Série Antiquité 190, S. Morlet, ed., 357–370. Paris.

———. 2011b. "Eusebius' Exegesis Between Alexandria and Antioch: Being a Scholar in Caesarea—A Test Case from Questions to Stephanos I." In *Reconsidering Eusebius Collected Papers on Literary, Historical, and Theological Issues,* Supplements to Vigiliae Christianae 107, ed. Inowlocki, S. and C. Zamagni, 151–176. Leiden/Boston.

———. Forthcoming. "Is the Question-and-Answer Literature from IVth and Vth Century an Homogeneous Group?" In *Actes du colloque « La littérature de questions et réponses dans l'Antiquité : de l'enseignement à l'exégèse »,* Université d'Ottawa, 25–26/9/2009, Instrumenta patristica et mediaevalia 64, M.-P. Bussières, ed., 241–268. Turnhout.

Zotenberg, H. 1877. *Manuscrits orientaux: Catalogue des manuscrits éthiopiens (gheez et amharique) de la Bibliothèque nationale.* Paris.

# 13

# Eusebius of Caesarea on Asterius of Cappadocia in the Anti-Marcellan Writings

## A Case Study of Mutual Defense within the Eusebian Alliance

### Mark DelCogliano

THE THEOLOGICAL CONTRIBUTIONS of Eusebius of Caesarea have long been overshadowed by his achievements as a historian, apologist, and biblical scholar. But in recent scholarship on the fourth-century Trinitarian controversies, he has been identified as one of the leading lights in the articulation of the theology of the "Eusebian alliance." One of the features of an ecclesiastical alliance is mutual defense. This essay explores this activity within the Eusebian alliance, particularly by examining to what extent Eusebius defended the views of another leading member of the Eusebian alliance, Asterius of Cappadocia, in his anti-Marcellan works (*Contra Marcellum* and *De ecclesiastica theologia*).[1] Asterius was one of the principle targets of Marcellus, and so the question investigated here is whether Eusebius' anti-Marcellan works can in some sense be construed as writings *pro Asterio*. By determining the contours of the theological relationship between Asterius and Eusebius, not only do we see evidence for development within the theological tradition of the Eusebian alliance, but also we come away with a new appreciation for the crucial role played by Eusebius himself in the transmission of an influential theological culture.

## The Eusebian Alliance

In a series of articles I have explored conceptualizing ecclesio-political and theological divisions in the fourth century in terms of "alliances" instead of "church

---

[1]   Edition: Klostermann and Hansen 1991 (hereafter Kl/H).

parties" as traditionally understood.[2] It is notoriously difficult to account for the cohesiveness of discrete "church parties" since any traditional typology of parties that relies principally upon simplistic or monolithic doctrinal criteria breaks down when one examines the theologies of individuals placed within a single category. In recent scholarship, the notion of an "alliance" or "ecclesial alliance" has been used instead of "church party" to name groups or networks that arise because of some common value or are formed for the promotion of a specific agenda in the ecclesiastical sphere.[3] These values or agendas may or may not be theological. Such groups are characterized by features such as the performance of ecclesiastical communion, sufficient doctrinal agreement with respect to both principles and terminologies, the struggle with common enemies, mutual defense (and perhaps critique), the exercise of public ecclesio-political support, loyalty to revered figures, local ecclesiastical traditions, and personal friendship. No single feature, value, or agenda is necessary to consti-tute an ecclesial alliance, and individuals or individual churches may be part of a larger ecclesial alliance for different reasons.

Calling the alliance to which Eusebius and Asterius belonged "Eusebian" is admittedly problematic since this label was first coined by Athanasius in the heat of his anti-"Arian" polemics to discredit his opponents, as recently discussed by David M. Gwynn.[4] Gwynn ably deconstructs Athanasius' description of his oppo-nents as a collective heretical party, whom the Alexandrian bishop branded the "Eusebians," because he saw Eusebius of Nicomedia as the fountainhead of the ecclesio-political movement, and accused them of "Arianism" because Eusebius and his allies defended Arius. Gwynn concludes that the "Eusebians"—as depicted by Athanasius—were neither a "party" nor "Arian," and that Athanasius' depic-tion of the fourth-century church as polarized between his own "orthodoxy" and the "Arianism" of the "Eusebians" is a polemical construct. Gwynn does not deny that those whom Athanasius called "Eusebians" shared political and theological concerns, but proves that Athanasius' polemical construction of the group distorts the reality.

I use "Eusebian" in contrast to the Athanasian usage deconstructed by Gwynn and in line with other recent usage to name the *ad hoc* alliance of eastern bishops and theologians initially formed around the figures of Eusebius of Nicomedia and Eusebius of Caesarea that lasted from ca. 320 to ca. 355.[5] The alliance emerged when several eastern bishops rallied around Arius in common cause against what they deemed to be Alexander of Alexandria's doctrinal

---

2  See my research on the theological and ecclesio-political cohesiveness of the Eusebians: DelCogliano 2006; 2008; 2011b.
3  See Ayres 2004:13; DelCogliano 2006:480–483.
4  Gwynn 2007.
5  For a definition of the category, see Ayres 2004:52, and Lienhard 1999:34–35.

innovations and his mistreatment of Arius. But they did not agree with Arius' theology in every detail, and there were theological differences among them. In the ensuing years, the Eusebian alliance was animated by a common set of values and a shared agenda in the ecclesiastical sphere, but displayed considerable diversity in theology.[6] The chief architects of Eusebian theology are recognized to have been Asterius of Cappadocia[7] and Eusebius of Caesarea.[8] The theology of the Eusebian alliance came to be decisively shaped by its emerging debate with Marcellus of Ancyra.[9] The Eusebians positioned themselves as advocates of a middle way between the extremes of Arius' theology and the purported neo-Sabellianism of Marcellus of Ancyra. From the early 340s through the late 350s, the Eusebians orchestrated various councils that sought to achieve theological consensus by eliminating what they considered extreme views, those of Arius, Athanasius, Marcellus, and Photinus. Tensions inherent to Eusebian theology caused the alliance to splinter in the late 350s, giving rise to new alliances, the Homoiousians, the Homoians, and the Heteroousians.

## A Eusebian Tradition of Mutual Defense: The Two Eusebii and Asterius

The members of the Eusebian alliance engaged in mutual defense from the beginning. Indeed, the alliance emerged when several eastern bishops rose to the defense of Arius when he sought refuge with them after being expelled from Alexandria. There is, however, no evidence for personal interaction between Eusebius and Asterius. Yet, as they moved in the same ecclesiastical circles, it is hard to imagine that they did not know each other. But this is unimportant for our purposes since this study focuses on their literary relationship, even if it is somewhat complicated to delineate. In the early 320s, Eusebius of Nicomedia wrote to Paulinus of Tyre urging him to write to Alexander of Alexandria to protest his excommunication of Arius.[10] Paulinus did so.[11] These letters are

---

[6]  E.g. DelCogliano 2006.

[7]  For accounts of Asterius' theology, see: Kopecek 1979:28–34 and 55–57; Hanson 1988:32–38; Kinzig 1990:125–132; Vinzent 1993:38–71; Lienhard 1999:92–101; Ayres 2004:53–54; Gwynn 2007:205–211; and Anatolios 2011:53–59.

[8]  For accounts of Eusebius' theology, see Ayres 2004:58–60; Hanson 1988:46–59; Lienhard 1999:104–135; Strutwolf 1999; and Anatolios 2011:59–69.

[9]  On Marcellus' theology, see Ayres 2004:62–69; Hanson 1988:217–235; Lienhard 1999:49–68; Vinzent 1997; and Anatolios 2011:86–92. On Marcellus' career, see Parvis 2006.

[10]  The whole letter is extant; see Urk. 8 (Urk. = Opitz 1934–1935, cited by document number). Opitz dates the letter to 320–321; ca. 323 is the proposal of Williams 2001:58. For analyses of this letter, see Stead 1973; Luibhéid 1976; Lienhard 1999:78–82; and DelCogliano 2010:111–119. Stead argues that the letter was condemned at the Council of Nicaea.

[11]  Only fragments of the letter are extant; see Urk. 9. For an analysis of this letter, see Lienhard 1999:84–87.

instances of how members of the Eusebian alliance struggled with a common enemy. The theological language used by Eusebius in his widely circulated letter became in the years following the Council of Nicaea so outdated that it was a cause of embarrassment among his Eusebian associates.[12] Presumably sharing this embarrassment, Asterius wrote in defense of it.[13] I shall refer to this writing as the *Apologia*.[14] It is an excellent example of mutual defense among the Eusebian alliance, and it will be examined below. Opinions vary on its exact date.[15] It was probably written around the time Eusebius of Nicomedia returned from exile (he was deposed and exiled at the Council of Nicaea in 325), either just before or just after, that is, around 327 or 328.[16]

Whenever the *Apologia* was written, Marcellus of Ancyra soon attacked Asterius because of it.[17] It is likely that after writing it Asterius traveled around the East, visiting churches, publically reading his books, and winning the support of influential churchmen.[18] This self-promotion undoubtedly attracted the attention of Marcellus. But in writing against Asterius, Marcellus sought to refute not only Asterius, but also Eusebius of Caesarea, Eusebius of Nicomedia, Paulinus of Tyre, and Narcissus of Neronias—in other words, he sought to discredit the theology of the Eusebian alliance as a whole, even if Asterius was his main target.[19] It is difficult to date the anti-Asterian writing of Marcellus

---

[12] Lienhard 1999:92.

[13] Kopecek 1979:55, suggests that Asterius was also protesting the letter's condemnation at Nicaea (see note 10 above).

[14] On the *Apologia*, see Bardy 1936:336–338; Kopecek 1979:55–57; Lienhard 1999:95–98. The only other extant work of Asterius is his *Syntagmation*, fragments of which are preserved by Athanasius.

[15] The various opinions are discussed by Bardy 1936:323–324; Vinzent 1993:34; and Parvis 2006:100–101 and 111–116.

[16] Lienhard 1999:92.

[17] On this writing, see Lienhard 1999:47–68.

[18] Eusebius, C. Marc. 1.4.48 (GCS 14:28,3–4 Kl/H); Socrates, *Historia ecclesiastica* 1.36.3.

[19] See Eusebius, C. Marc. 1.4.1–3 (17,30–18,12 Kl/H): "I will first present the passages in which he [Marcellus] tries to contradict the things that were written correctly and in accordance with ecclesiastical teaching, attacking their authors and engaging in a battle that all but demanded everything he had. For now he directs the refutation against Asterius, now against Eusebius the Great [Eusebius of Nicomedia]. And then he turns to the man of God, the so truly thrice-blessed Paulinus, a man who was honored with the sovereignty of the Antiochene Church, but who served as bishop of the Tyrians and shined so brightly in the episcopacy there that the Antiochene Church shared in its goodness as their own. But even this man, who lived blessedly and died blessedly, who not long ago fell asleep and is now disturbed by nothing, this astonishing author mocks. And passing on from this man he makes war on Origen, who passed from this life very long ago. Then he marches against Narcissus and persecutes the other Eusebius [Eusebius of Caesarea], and at the same time rejects all the church fathers, satisfied with none whatsoever except only himself." Origen of course is not associated with the Eusebian alliance. In this anti-Asterian writing Marcellus polemically depicts the Eusebians as nothing more than slavish adherents of Origen.

with precision.[20] It seems most likely that it began to be circulated at some point in the early 330s.[21]

Marcellus's polemical writing prompted the Eusebians to adopt a strong anti-Marcellan position that would characterize the alliance for the remainder of its existence.[22] His anti-Asterian writing was first condemned at the Eusebian-controlled Council of Tyre in 335. And then Marcellus was deposed and exiled at a synod in Constantinople in 336, specifically for his theological opinions, on the basis of a dossier of Marcellan texts collected by Eusebius of Caesarea.[23] Asterius may have been in attendance at the Council of Tyre, or at least may have been present when the synod traveled to Jerusalem to dedicate the Church of the Holy Sepulcher.[24] If so, this would have been a prime opportunity for Asterius and Eusebius to meet, if they had not earlier. In 337–338 Eusebius of Caesarea published two anti-Marcellan works, one based on his earlier dossier and another with more elaborate argumentation to demonstrate the heresy of Marcellus, namely, *Contra Marcellum* and *De ecclesiastica theologia*.

Thus, we see here a tradition of mutual defense among the Eusebians spanning about fifteen years. Eusebius of Caesarea defended Asterius, who had earlier defended Eusebius of Nicomedia. While the letter of the Nicomedian bishop has been preserved in its entirety, unfortunately neither Asterius' *Apologia* nor Marcellus' anti-Asterian writing is intact. The only extant fragments of Asterius' *Apologia* are preserved in the anti-Asterian work of Marcellus, and the only extant fragments of Marcellus' anti-Asterian writing are preserved in the two anti-Marcellan writings of Eusebius. Thus, the extant fragments of Asterius' *Apologia* are indirectly preserved in the quotations of Marcellus preserved in Eusebius of Caesarea.[25]

---

[20] The title of the work is not preserved and scholars have referred to it by many names, most commonly *Contra Asterium.*

[21] Parvis 2006:118–123, lays out the evidence and the various scholarly opinions for dating the work. I find the case for a composition before rather than after the Council of Jerusalem in 335 more compelling. Parvis argues for an early date of 329–330, which is not outside the realm of possibility, but also contributes to her "heroic" narrative of Marcellus, in that it makes the Eusebians "unable to depose Marcellus on the basis of it for a further six years" (2006:123).

[22] Lienhard 1999:104–209.

[23] Parvis 2006:123–132.

[24] Socrates, *Historia ecclesiastica* 1.36.5. See Bardy 1936:325–326; and Kinzig 1990:18.

[25] Two editions of the fragments of Asterius have been published, each with their limitations. See Bardy 1936:341–353; and Vinzent 1993:82–141. In this study I have for the most part elected not to refer to the fragments according to the enumeration of these editions to avoid complicating the references.

While Eusebius is recognized to have accurately quoted the very words of others,[26] there is no way to evaluate Marcellus' habits of citation.[27] In line with ancient citation practices in polemical contexts, we cannot always be certain that what he presents as Asterius' words were in fact written by Asterius or if they report his thought with bias.[28] There is no evidence in the anti-Marcellan works that Eusebius attempted to confirm the accuracy of Marcellus' citations of Asterius by comparing them with the *Apologia*.[29] Perhaps Eusebius did not have the *Apologia* available to him, though this seems unlikely given Asterius' promotion of the text and Eusebius' book-collecting proclivities. It is more likely that Eusebius did not undertake such a comparison as a matter of methodological principle, in that his chief concern was to refute Marcellus, not to defend Asterius. Of course, even if this was his principle goal, it does not mean that he did not also engage in a defense of Asterius. In fact, in the first book of *Contra Marcellum*, Eusebius not only defends Asterius but also the other members of the Eusebian alliance whom Marcellus had attacked: Eusebius of Nicomedia, Paulinus, Narcissus, and himself. However, as we shall see, just as Marcellus targeted Asterius far more than the others, so too Eusebius expends far more energy on defending Asterius than the others.

## Asterius' *Apologia* for Eusebius of Nicomedia

Before investigating Eusebius' defense of Asterius, it will be helpful to examine the *Apologia* for comparative purposes. Unfortunately the fragmentary state of the *Apologia* makes the project of reconstructing Asterius' defense of Eusebius difficult. Simply put, no extant fragment of the *Apologia* contains Asterius' explicit defense of specific doctrines of Eusebius. But other fragments reveal some of the tactics used by Asterius to defend Eusebius. Furthermore, Asterius agrees with some of the teachings of Eusebius, but modifies, rejects, and improves upon others. These doctrinal relationships between the two theologians provide further evidence for Asterius' defense of Eusebius in the *Apologia*.

Some fragments preserved by Marcellus indicate that Asterius attempted to stem criticism of Eusebius' letter by articulating a framework in which the letter should be interpreted. First, Asterius formulated the "main point of the letter" as "ascribing the generation of the Son to the will of the Father and denying that

---

[26] Inowlocki 2006.

[27] Bardy 1936:340 asserts that Marcellus cited his sources more precisely than Athanasius, but does not give reasons for this judgment.

[28] On ancient citation practices, see Inowlocki 2006:35–47; Most 1997:vii; and Kidd 1997:226.

[29] Bardy 1936:341 commenting on Marcellus' habit of citing only a few words of Asterius out of context: "Il est assez curieux qu'Eusèbe n'ait pas cherché, sur ce point, à compléter ou à préciser sa documentation."

this birth involves change on the part of God. This is the very thing," continues Asterius, "that the wisest of the fathers declared in their own treatises, guarding against the impiety of heretics, who falsely alleged that God's childbearing was in some way corporeal and involved change by teaching the issuings (*probolas*)."[30] While ascribing the generation of the Son to the Father's will was controversial, denying that the divine birth involved suffering and change on the part of God was not. This statement thus defends Eusebius by connecting his main ideas (or at least his second idea) with long-standing anti-heretical traditions.[31] Another intention of this statement was presumably to draw attention away from other more problematic and controversial aspects of the letter, as well as to enable Asterius to interpret its unclear or poorly expressed portions in the light of these main points. Second, he claimed that Eusebius did not intend to offer authoritative, "official" teaching in his episcopal capacity; rather, it was a private letter to Paulinus.[32] Thus, Asterius is suggesting that the theology of the letter was provisional and subject to revision. Indeed, there are good grounds for this perspective, since at the conclusion of his letter Eusebius asked Paulinus to revise it (ἐξερασάμενος), that is, work out its contents in greater detail and bring it to completion, before writing to Alexander.[33] Third, Asterius spoke of "the depth of the thought of Eusebius that lies hidden in his brief words."[34] Presumably, in his *Apologia*, Asterius attempted to extract and enunciate the deep thoughts of Eusebius in a way that corresponded to current theological sensibilities. Hence the revision of Eusebius' theology is rhetorically constructed as an expansion of obfuscating terseness. And so, these texts demonstrate that Asterius undertook an explicit defense of Eusebius. This is corroborated by certain comments of Marcellus, who speaks of Asterius as "recommending (συνιστάμενος) the evil writings of Eusebius,"[35] and "intending to advocate (συνηγορῆσαι βουλόμενος) for Eusebius."[36]

In enunciating "the depth of the thought of Eusebius," Asterius engaged in a good deal of updating and revision. A comparison of the doctrines of Eusebius and Asterius reveals the latter's agreements and disagreements with the former. Eusebius almost completely avoids "Father-Son" language, preferring to speak of "the unbegotten" and "the one generated by him."[37] He seems to have been

---

[30]  C. Marc. 1.4.9–10 (19,11–20 Kl/H).

[31]  Lienhard 1999:98n148 claims that the "wisest fathers" to whom Asterius refers are Paulinus and the two Eusebii, but it seems rather that Asterius intends more remote figures like Origen. On this point, see also DelCogliano 2011a:49n19.

[32]  C. Marc. 1.4.17–18 (20,32–21,6 Kl/H).

[33]  See Urk. 8.8 (17,8–9 Opitz).

[34]  C. Marc. 1.4.11 (19,26–27 Kl/H).

[35]  C. Marc. 1.4.9 (19,11–12 Kl/H).

[36]  C. Marc. 1.4.11 (19,23–24 Kl/H); 1.4.17 (20,32–33 Kl/H).

[37]  Urk. 8.3 (16,2–3 Opitz).

reluctant to use such language because of his understanding of "begetting." He rejected the idea that the Father begets the Son "from his substance" (ἐκ τῆς οὐσίας αὐτοῦ) as materialistic and as resulting in an "identity of nature" (ταυτότητα τῆς φύσεως) between two unbegotten beings (and thus destructive of monotheism).[38] As a result, for Eusebius "begetting" signified something quite different than the production of an ontologically identical offspring. Eusebius grounds this viewpoint in scripture, noting that it describes as "begotten" (γεννητόν) by the Father not only the Son, but also many other creatures who are unlike God in nature. Hence "begotten" is not a unique designation for the Son but refers to all beings generated "from the will" of God.

In contrast, for Asterius, "Father-Son" language is primary.[39] He repeatedly speaks of the Father begetting the Son and even affirms that the Father begot the Son "from himself" (ἐξ αὐτοῦ).[40] Joseph Lienhard claims that "from him" is tantamount to "from his substance," and so concludes that Asterius is more or less rejecting Eusebius' teaching on this point.[41] While no extant fragment of Asterius preserved by Marcellus contains explicit comments on the phrase "from his substance," either for or against it, I submit that by using the phrase "from him" Asterius is purposely backing away from the controversial "from his substance" in favor of a less controversial, yet more ambiguous, scriptural expression. The idea that the Son was begotten from the Father, that is, from his substance, was central to Alexander of Alexandria's theology (and a line to this effect was included in the Nicene Creed), but was suspicious to the Eusebians for the reasons articulated by Eusebius of Nicomedia.[42] Other Eusebians before Asterius such as George of Laodicea had attempted to find common ground between the disputing parties on this very point by using scriptural language that was similarly less controversial but more ambiguous.[43] Hence Asterius backs away from the more precise and radical language of Eusebius in order to defend him against his detractors and make his theology more acceptable. Finally, nowhere in the extant fragments preserved by Marcellus does Asterius deal with the issue of whether "begotten" is unique to the Son. He does, however, describe the main point of Eusebius' letter as "ascribing the generation of the

---

[38]  Urk. 8.6–7 (16,15–17,5 Kl/H).

[39]  E.g. C. Marc. 1.4.4–7 (18,12–32 Kl/H).

[40]  C. Marc. 1.4.12 (19,31–20,1 Kl/H); 1.4.30 (24,12 Kl/H); 1.4.33 (25,4 Kl/H).

[41]  Lienhard 1999:97.

[42]  For more details, see DelCogliano 2010:115–119.

[43]  Urk. 13 (19 Opitz): "Why do you find fault with Alexander the Pope when he says that the Son is from the Father? For you should not fear to say that the Son is from God. For if the Apostle wrote: 'All things are from God' [1 Cor 11:12], and it is clear that all things are made from nothing, and the Son too is a created thing and one of things that have been made, then it can be said that the Son is from God just as all things are said to be from God." See also DelCogliano 2011b:671–672.

Son to the will of the Father," but this topic does not appear in any other of the Marcellan fragments. Thus, it remains unclear if Asterius endorsed this idea in the *Apologia*.[44]

In other areas, Eusebius and Asterius more or less agree, with differences of emphasis. Eusebius taught that the Father and Son were completely different in nature (φύσις) and substance (οὐσία), the one unbegotten, the other begotten. Yet the Son has perfect likeness (τελείαν ὁμοιότητα) to the Father in other ways such as in disposition (διάθεσις) and power (δύναμις).[45] Like Eusebius, Asterius speaks of the Father and Son as having two distinct natures and otherwise stresses their ontological distinctiveness.[46] But no text of his preserved by Marcellus speaks of the Father and Son as two substances. For Asterius too the Son is like the Father, particularly in terms of substance, will, power, and glory, so much so that the one is indistinguishable from the other and they agree in everything.[47] While Eusebius emphasized the difference between the substances of the Father and Son, Asterius stressed the likeness of their substances. Nonetheless, both Eusebius and Asterius subscribe to the idea that the Father and Son are different at the level of nature and substance, but very similar at other levels. One departure between the two in this regard is that Asterius speaks of the Father and Son as different *hypostases* and persons (πρόσωπα), terms which never appear in Eusebius' letter. In the same vein, the Son's status as image of God has no place in the theology of Eusebius, whereas it is a major component of Asterius', supporting his doctrine of the Father and Son's simultaneous difference and likeness.[48]

In sum, Asterius clearly defends Eusebius and agrees with much of his theology. Yet at the same time, Asterius does not shy away from distancing himself from some of Eusebius' more controversial and archaic formulations, affirming them in more ambiguous terms, or simply passing over them in silence, in order to focus on the main points of the Nicomedian's teaching. Note that Asterius' disagreement with Eusebius is never explicitly expressed. His critiques are always implicit as he interprets the bishop's theology in the light of his own, putting his own stamp upon it and placing the emphases elsewhere. And so, Asterius' *Apologia* is an example of Eusebian mutual defense in which the defense is coupled with revisionist critiques.

---

[44] In the fragments of the *Syntagmation* preserved by Athanasius, however, Asterius does seem to subscribe to the idea; see *Orationes contra Arianos* 3.60.

[45] Urk. 8.3.

[46] C. Marc. 1.4.11 (19,24 Kl/H).

[47] C. Marc. 1.4.33–34 (24,35–25,17 Kl/H); C. Marc. 1.4.55 (29,7–12 Kl/H); C. Marc. 2.2.15–19 (37,29–38 Kl/H); C. Marc. 2.2.20–22 (38,25–39,10 Kl/H); Eccl. Theol. 2.4.2 (102,27–30 Kl/H).

[48] On this, see below p. 277.

## Eusebius' Defense and Critique of the Other Eusebians

In order to further contextualize Eusebius of Caesarea's defense of Asterius, it will also be helpful to examine his defense of the other Eusebians attacked by Marcellus. In fact, only in the first book of *Contra Marcellum* does Eusebius present fragments of Marcellus that criticized the theologies of Paulinus, Eusebius of Nicomedia, Narcissus, and himself.[49] While on two occasions he defends his own views against Marcellus' misinterpretation,[50] he never defends specific opinions of Paulinus and Narcissus.[51] In fact, when one examines the views of Paulinus and Narcissus censured by Marcellus, it becomes clear that Eusebius does not endorse any of them. Marcellus accuses Paulinus of teaching that "Christ is a second God and became a more human God," that "Christ is a creature," that "there are many Gods," and that "there are newer Gods."[52] As for Narcissus, Marcellus records that he taught that there were "three substances" and that "there is a first and second God."[53] None of the views imputed to Paulinus or Narcissus is defended by Eusebius, who rejected any polytheistic language of "two gods"[54] and explicitly denied that the Son was a creature.[55] In addition, Eusebius denies that there are two substances, preferring to call the Father and Son two *hypostases*.[56]

Nonetheless, despite Eusebius' implicit rejection of the theological language of Paulinus and Narcissus, the first book of the *Contra Marcellum* concludes with a general defense of the ecclesiastical writers impugned by Marcellus:

> Having set forth such awful teachings and ones even far worse than these, not only against the bishops, but also against the sound and ecclesiastical faith, it will be clear that Marcellus stands guilty of great

[49]   On these texts, see Lienhard 1999:70–89.

[50]   C. Marc. 1.4.51–52 and 1.4.63–66.

[51]   Marcellus does not accuse Eusebius of Nicomedia of specific teachings; he only refers to him in the context of responding to Asterius' comments on his letter to Paulinus. But he does repeatedly say that Eusebius wrote badly (κακῶς); see C. Marc. 1.4.9 (19,11–12 Kl/H); 1.4.11 (19,23 Kl/H); 1.4.17 (20,32–33 Kl/H). On this expression, see Lienhard 1999:82.

[52]   C. Marc. 1.4.49 (28,8–12; 28,14; 28,20 Kl/H) = Urk. 9.2–4.

[53]   C. Marc. 1.4.39 (26,10 Kl/H); 1.4.53 (28,33–34 Kl/H).

[54]   Marcellus also accused Eusebius himself of this; see C. Marc. 1.4.46 (27,24–25 Kl/H) and 1.4.46 (27,28 Kl/H). Marcellus tended to see no difference between a theology of two divine realities, *hypostases*, powers, or even substances and a theology of two gods. On Eusebius' belief in the unity of God, see Eccl. Theol. 2.23.1 (133,11–17 Kl/H) and below p. 280. He does, however, refer to the Son as a "second God" throughout *Praeparatio Evangelica*. But this usage seems to arise only in cases where he is seeking to find references to the Son in non-Christian literature, where the phrase originally occurs.

[55]   Eccl. Theol. 1.9.

[56]   On the denial of two substances, see Eccl. Theol. 2.23.1 (133,9–17 Kl/H). On *hypostases*, see below pp. 279–280.

heresy. You will learn that the truth is of no concern to this man if you read the letters of the bishops, in which you will find him mutilating the overall sense of their statements and hiding all the connections between them, seizing upon short phrases and wickedly using them to come up with slanderous accusations.[57]

It is clear that Eusebius is defending his fellow Eusebians from what he thinks are unfair attacks by Marcellus, even though he has declined to defend their specific formulations. And so, this example of mutual defense among the Eusebians is a kind of critique rhetorically presented as defense.[58]

## Eusebius' Defense and Critique of Asterius

The case is different for Asterius, to whom Eusebius gives far more attention than he does to Eusebius of Nicomedia, Paulinus, and Narcissus. And he really defends Asterius, with very little criticism, if any, even implicit. Note that in the passage quoted above, Asterius, who was not a bishop, is apparently omitted from Eusebius' defense, perhaps on purpose, but more likely the Caesarean bishop meant to include him and spoke imprecisely. But in fact several scholars have claimed that Eusebius did not defend Asterius in the anti-Marcellan writings. Eduard Schwartz suggests this was because Eusebius wanted to distance himself from the too "Arian" Asterius.[59] Both Gustave Bardy and Joseph Lienhard rightly doubt Schwartz's explanation, but still affirm that Eusebius never attempted to defend Asterius.[60] Both are struck by the praise that Eusebius lavished upon Paulinus of Tyre and the absence of anything comparable for Asterius.[61] Yet Eusebius' esteem for Paulinus should not be taken as disparagement of Asterius. Eusebius had known Paulinus since at least 315, a good twenty years before writing his anti-Marcellan works, when Eusebius delivered an oration for the dedication of the basilica at Tyre, in which he also acclaimed Paulinus.[62] Furthermore, Paulinus had died around 326,[63] so Eusebius is also

---

[57]  C. Marc. 1.4.63 (30,25–32 Kl/H).

[58]  Thus, the judgment of Wallace-Hadrill 1960:37 seems correct. He describes the anti-Marcellan works of Eusebius as "repeating considerable portions of the work of Marcellus without providing much defense of Paulinus, Narcissus, Eusebius of Nicomedia, Origen and the others whom Marcellus had attacked." But if he meant to include Asterius in this judgment, as he seems to have done, below I argue the opposite.

[59]  Schwartz 1911:367–368.

[60]  Bardy 1936:341; Lienhard 1999:100.

[61]  See Eusebius, C. Marc. 1.4.1–3 (cited above at note 19). See also C. Marc. 1.4.48 where Eusebius again calls Paulinus "the man of God" (28,5–6 Kl/H).

[62]  *Historia ecclesiastica* 10.4. See also Schott 2011:189–96.

[63]  Lienhard 1999:83–84.

probably honoring the memory of his dead friend. If the "omission" of praise of Asterius needs to be explained, it could be due to the fact that Asterius was still alive. Also still alive were Eusebius of Nicomedia and Narcissus of Neronias, whom Eusebius of Caesarea similarly did not extol.[64] Thus the praise accorded to Paulinus does not preclude Eusebius defending Asterius. In contrast to these scholars, Markus Vinzent claims that Eusebius both defended and critiqued Asterius.[65] However, Vinzent offers no specific evidence to substantiate Eusebius' defense of Asterius and only points to Eusebius' rejection of Asterius' opinion on the question of the creatureliness of Christ. But as I will argue below, there is no evidence in the fragments of the *Apologia* that Asterius held that the Son was a creature. Accordingly, Eusebius did not "reject" this opinion of Asterius.

In what follows I proceed more or less sequentially through the anti-Marcellan works of Eusebius examining his engagement with Asterius. No fragment of Asterius is omitted from investigation in what is intended to be an exhaustive analysis. Two distinct kinds of defense emerge, both of which we have already encountered in Asterius' *Apologia*: first, an *explicit* defense where Eusebius specifically rejects Marcellus' view of Asterius and voices his support for Asterius; and second, an *implicit* defense where Eusebius does not specifically mention the views of Asterius reported by Marcellus, but in the course of his discussion reveals his tacit agreement with Asterius. In this latter case, usually Eusebius agrees with the doctrinal principles and terminology of Asterius, but sometimes explains these with a somewhat different theology, either expanding upon Asterius' views or taking them in another direction. Never in the anti-Marcellan writings does Eusebius explicitly reject Asterius or his theology.

In one of the first fragments preserved by Eusebius, Marcellus accuses Asterius of altering the main verb of Psalm 109:3 to support his opinion that it refers to the Word's pre-cosmic birth from the Father, not the birth of the incarnate Word as he himself thought.[66] Marcellus' reading is ἐξεγέννησα, but Asterius used ἐγέννησα. On this issue Eusebius sides with Asterius, noting that it is Marcellus who has misquoted the verse. Thus, concludes Eusebius, there is no basis for Marcellus' accusation of Asterius in this case.[67] Furthermore, like

---

[64] Eusebius of Caesarea, however, does refer to his namesake of Nicomedia as "Eusebius the Great" (C. Marc. 1.4.1 (17,33–18,1 Kl/H); 1.4.9 (19,8–9 Kl/H)).

[65] Vinzent 1993:23 and 26.

[66] C. Marc. 1.2.20–22 (12,8–21 Kl/H). See C. Marc. 1.4.55 (24,31–34 Kl/H) for Marcellus' interpretation of this verse.

[67] Textual criticism has vindicated Marcellus. The majority of manuscripts read ἐξεγέννησα instead of ἐγέννησα. Lienhard 1999:98 mistakenly ascribes the Marcellan reading to Asterius and vice versa.

Asterius, Eusebius applies Psalm 109:3 to the pre-cosmic birth of the Son, not the incarnation.[68]

In a similar vein, Marcellus sought to undermine Asterius' teaching that one can say that the Son was begotten from the Father in eternity by claiming that his words, "before the ages the Word was begotten," contradicted Proverbs 8:23, "before the age he established me."[69] Eusebius does not explicitly contest Marcellus' accusation of misquotation. It is, however, unclear whether Asterius intended his words to be a scriptural citation; they are more likely a shorthand phrase for Proverbs 8:23–25.[70] Elsewhere in the anti-Marcellan writings Eusebius affirms that the Son was begotten from the Father before all ages[71] and appeals to Proverbs 8:25 (interpreted in the context of Proverbs 8:22–24) to make the same point.[72] Thus, he supports Asterius' interpretation of the Proverb passages as referring to the Son's pre-cosmic birth from the Father over Marcellus' view that they spoke of the incarnation.

In another fragment, Marcellus quotes a few lines from what seems to be a rather innocuous statement of faith found in Asterius' *Apologia*.[73] Most of it Marcellus accepts without reservation. But he finds one line problematic because it advances what he considers a newly concocted heresy that conceives of the Father and Son in all too human terms: "it is necessary to think that the Father is truly a father, and the Son truly a son, and likewise the Holy Spirit."[74] In his comment on this fragment, Eusebius notes that the new idea that Marcellus attributes to Asterius has actually been part of the church's faith since even before Origen.[75] So, according to Eusebius, the charge of heretical innovation that Marcellus leveled against Asterius has no basis.

One of the fragments of Asterius preserved by Marcellus reads: "For another is the Father, who begot from himself the only-begotten Word and the firstborn of all creation."[76] Marcellus censures Asterius for connecting "only-begotten"

---

68  C. Marc. 2.3.30 (50,5–6 Kl/H). See also DE 5.1.19, as well as PE 7.12 and DE 4.15; 4.16; 5.3. The local "Caesarean" creed that Eusebius quotes in his letter to his church after the Council of Nicaea contains the line: "begotten from the Father before all ages" (Urk. 22.4 (43,11–12 Opitz)).

69  C. Marc. 1.4.27–29 (23,25–21 Kl/H); see also C. Marc. 2.2.7–8 (36,2–8 Kl/H).

70  "Before the age he established me in the beginning; before he made the earth and before he made the depths, before he brought forth the springs of the waters, before the mountains were set in place, before all the hills, he begets me." Eusebius of Nicomedia had cited an abbreviated version of Prov 8:22–25, which excludes "in the beginning ... set in place" (see Urk. 8.4). Perhaps Asterius' words were inspired by Eusebius'.

71  Eccl. Theol. 1.2.1 (63,20–21 Kl/H).

72  Eccl. Theol. 1.11.6 (70,22–25 Kl/H); 3.3.27–42 (150,18–153,7 Kl/H).

73  C. Marc. 1.4.4–6 (18,14–29 Kl/H).

74  C. Marc. 1.4.6 (18,28–29 Kl/H).

75  C. Marc. 1.4.7–9 (18,30–19,10 Kl/H).

76  C. Marc. 1.4.12 (19,31–20,2 Kl/H).

and "firstborn" since each means something quite different. "For it is clear," writes Marcellus, "that the only-begotten, if he really is only-begotten, can no longer be firstborn, and if the firstborn is firstborn, he cannot be only-begotten."[77] In reply, Eusebius writes: "Now in these remarks, [Marcellus] finds fault with Asterius in vain. For it is not him but the holy scripture that speaks of the Son of God at one time as the only-begotten Son and at another time as the firstborn of all creation."[78] Here Eusebius refers to John 1:18 and Colossians 1:15. So Asterius is not guilty of confused and heretical thinking as Marcellus claims, but merely citing scripture.

Marcellus faults Asterius for claiming that his theology was both "from the divine scriptures"[79] and "the very thing that the wisest of the fathers declared in their own treatises."[80] The latter is the problem for Marcellus since the opinions and dogmas declared by the fathers, he believes, were arrived at through their own deliberation. For Marcellus, "the word 'dogma' implies human will and judgment."[81] Hence Marcellus suggests that a theology based on both scripture and ecclesiastical tradition, as Asterius claimed about his own, is necessarily corrupted by mere human opinions. Thus, he advocates a *sola scriptura* position *avant la lettre*. Eusebius admits that Marcellus' denigration of dogma has apostolic approbation (see Ephesians 2:15), but rejects the notion that tradition plays no role in theology. In this connection he cites Deuteronomy 32:7 and Proverbs 22:28 as proof-texts about the necessity of following the fathers.[82] And so, Eusebius defends Asterius' appeal to the tradition of the fathers for his theology.

On numerous occasions, Marcellus attacks Asterius' doctrine of the image of God. Perhaps Asterius' most famous statement on this subject is his identification of the only-begotten Word (Jn 1:18) and the firstborn of all creation (Col 1:15) as the indistinguishable (ἀπαράλλακτος) image of the Father's substance, will, power, and glory.[83] Elsewhere Asterius calls the Word the image

---

[77] C. Marc. 1.4.13 (20,4–7 Kl/H).

[78] C. Marc. 1.4.13 (20,8–10 Kl/H).

[79] C. Marc. 1.4.14 (20,13 Kl/H), referring to C. Marc. 1.4.4 (18,18–20 Kl/H). See also C. Marc. 2.2.34 (41,6–10 Kl/H) and Eccl. Theol. 2.19.2 (125,12–17 Kl/H), where Marcellus sarcastically comments that Asterius claims "to follow the scriptures simply and scrupulously," before suggesting that he is ignorant of a certain biblical passage.

[80] C. Marc. 1.4.14 (20,15–16 Kl/H) referring to C. Marc. 1.4.10 (19,16–18 Kl/H). More precisely, Asterius maintained that ascribing the generation of the Son to the will of the Father and denying that this birth involved suffering on the part of God was the very teaching declared by the wisest fathers in their own treatises. But Marcellus seems to have taken this passage as a general statement of the sources of his thought.

[81] C. Marc. 1.4.15–16 (20,16–24 Kl/H).

[82] C. Marc. 1.4.16–17 (20,24–29 Kl/H).

[83] C. Marc. 1.4.33–34 (24,35–25,17 Kl/H). The same fragment is preserved by Acacius of Caesarea *apud* Epiphanius, *Panarion* 72.6.2–3.

of the invisible God (Col 1:15).[84] Marcellus critiques Asterius' doctrine of the image of God in several ways. First, he claims that Asterius uses it "to teach that God is as different from the Word as a man seems to differ from his image," that is, that there is an ontological gulf between God and his Word.[85] Second, by definition, according to Marcellus, an image manifests what is absent, makes visible what is invisible. Thus, Marcellus identifies the image of God as Christ the incarnate Word, who is visible.[86] Accordingly, Marcellus accuses Asterius of faulty logic when he teaches that the pre-incarnate Word is an invisible image of the invisible God. It simply makes no sense given his belief in the essential visibility of images.[87] A third critique also suggests that Asterius' logic is flawed. Since Asterius identifies the Word as God, how can he also be the image of God? "For an image of God," writes Marcellus, "is one thing and God is another. Hence if he is an image, he is neither Lord nor God, but rather the image of the Lord and God. But if he really is Lord and God, the Lord and God can no longer be the image of the Lord and God."[88]

In response to these critiques, Eusebius rejects his opponent's understanding of the image of God and defends Asterius' doctrine.[89] For Eusebius, as for Asterius, the Word's status as the image of God denotes his likeness to God the Father. According to Eusebius, "the Son can be called the living image of his own Father at any time since he is as similar to the Father as possible (ὁμοιότατος)."[90] In support of this claim Eusebius cites Genesis 5:3, which speaks of Seth's being begotten according to the likeness and image of Adam. Thus, scripture shows that sons are so like their fathers that they can be called their images. Then Eusebius cites a number of scripture passages to show that the Word is the image of God: Philippians 2:6 ("form of God"), Hebrews 1:3 ("radiance of the glory and the character of the *hypostasis* of God"), and Wisdom 7:26 ("reflection of eternal light, a spotless mirror of the activity of God, and an image of his goodness").[91] Finally, Eusebius cites Colossians 3:9–10 to disprove Marcellus' belief that the incarnate Word is the image of God.[92]

---

[84] C. Marc. 1.4.30 (24,11–16 Kl/H); 1.4.31–32 (24,23–29 Kl/H); 2.3.24 (48,33–49,5 Kl/H).
[85] C. Marc. 1.4.30 (24,13–16 Kl/H).
[86] C. Marc. 1.4.31 (24,18–21 Kl/H).
[87] C. Marc. 1.4.31–32 (24,24–29 Kl/H); 2.3.24 (48,34–49,5 Kl/H).
[88] C. Marc. 1.4.33–34 (25,8–14 Kl/H).
[89] C. Marc. 1.4.35–37 (25,15–29 Kl/H).
[90] C. Marc. 1.4.35 (25,15–17 Kl/H).
[91] C. Marc. 1.4.36 (25,21–26 Kl/H). These were among the favorite passages of Eusebius when reflecting on the Word as the image of God; see also Eccl. Theol. 1.20.67–71 and 1.20.94. Incidentally, in Eccl. Theol. 1.20.71 Eusebius comments that Marcellus' interpretation of such titles as those in Heb 1:3 and Col 1:15–17 as referring to the flesh "is silly and incomprehensible in addition to being an incoherent interpretation" (93,3–4 Kl/H).
[92] C. Marc. 1.4.37 (25,26–29 Kl/H).

It is in *De ecclesiastica theologia*, however, that Eusebius develops his theology of the image of God in detail. According to Eusebius, the various "image" titles given to the Son (in Col 1:15; Phil 2:6; Heb 1:3) reveal his "relationship (σχέσις) to the Father's divinity, a relationship which is proper to him alone, as if to an only-begotten Son."[93] Furthermore, though being the image of God means that the Son has independent existence,[94] this does not result in there being two gods, because the Son's existence as the image of God insures the unity of God.[95] According to John 1:1, the Word is not *the* God (which to Eusebius would indicate a Sabellian identity of the Father and the Son), but rather the Word is with the God who is over all, being himself God "as an image of God, and an image not as in lifeless matter but as in a living son, who has also, with the greatest degree of exactness possible (ἀκριβέστατα), been constituted like (ἀφωμοιωμένῳ) the archetypal Godhead of the Father."[96] The Father is the only true God, but the Son is also true God, in the sense that he "possesses this as in an image."[97] While the Father is properly the *only* true God because he is the archetype of the image, the Son is true God because he is the image of God. And so, the Son's existence as the image of God secures both his independent existence and the unity of God. Furthermore, the one God is "made known through the Son as through an image. For that reason, the Son is also God, because, in him, as in an image, there is an expression (μόρφωσιν) of the Father."[98] Thus, the Son as image mediates knowledge of the Father. Eusebius explains how this invisible, interior mediation of the knowledge of God through the image of God operates (in contrast to Marcellus' notion of the visible incarnate Word's mediation as image of God):

> So then he who has seen him has seen the Father [John 14:9], because he and no one else is the image of the invisible God [Col 1:15] and the radiance of the glory of God and the character of his subsistence [Heb 1:3], and exists in the form of God [Phil 2:6] according to the apostolic teachings. For just as the one who has seen the king's image which is constituted exactly like him (τὴν ἐπ' ἀκριβὲς ἀφωμοιωμένην), receiving impressions from the lines of the form through the drawing, imagines the king, in the same way, or rather in a way surpassing all reason and

---

93 Eccl. Theol. 1.9.3 (67,23–25 Kl/H). Examples of this are found elsewhere when Eusebius states that, because the Son is the image of God, he possesses immortality (Eccl. Theol. 1.20.33) and the first-person passages in the Old Testament, such as Ex 3:14, "I am who am," are valid of him as well as the Father (Eccl. Theol. 2.20.15).

94 Eccl. Theol. 3.3.57 and 3.6.5.

95 Eccl. Theol. 1.20.72–74.

96 Eccl. Theol. 2.17.3 (120,30–33 Kl/H).

97 Eccl. Theol. 2.23.2 (133,28 Kl/H).

98 Eccl. Theol. 1.20.73–74 (93,16–18 Kl/H).

beyond any example, the one who with a clear mind and the eyes of the soul purified and illuminated by the Holy Spirit, and having gazed intently upon the greatness of the power of the only-begotten Son and Lord, and having reflected on how in him dwells the whole fullness of the Father's divinity [Col 2:9] and how all things were made through him [John 1:3] and how in him all things were created, those in heaven and those on earth, those visible and invisible [Col 1:16], and having considered how the Father begot him alone as only-begotten Son, who is constituted like him in all respects (κατὰ πάντα ἀφωμοιωμένον), by that power he shall also see the Father himself through the Son, seen as he is by those purified in their mind, concerning whom it was said, Blessed are the pure in heart, for they shall see God [Mt 5:8].[99]

Surely it is not by accident this is the final paragraph of *De ecclesiastica theologia*, save Eusebius' concluding admonition to his readers, and it serves as a fitting summary of Eusebius' theology of the image of God.

While Eusebius agrees with Asterius that the pre-incarnate Son is the image of God and sees this doctrine as central to a viable Trinitarian theology, Eusebius diverges from Asterius in his theological account of the image. Elsewhere I have argued that Asterius has a "participative" understanding of the Son as the image of God, whereas Eusebius' understanding is "constitutive."[100] In a "participative" understanding, the Son participates in the divine attributes of the Father by grace, but in a "constitutive" understanding, the Son's being itself was constituted to be as like the Father as possible without participating in the divine attributes. Furthermore, Eusebius nowhere defends or uses the key Asterian term "indistinguishable" (ἀπαράλλακτος) when describing the image of God.[101] It is not clear why Eusebius avoided this term, as it seems that it would have been conducive to his theology of the image of God, which is often said to be as similar to the Father as possible. At the same time, Eusebius places an emphasis on the fact that the Son is the *living* image of God that is not found in Asterius. Therefore, Eusebius takes his theology of the image of God in a different direction despite his basic agreement with Asterius.

A number of fragments of Marcellus refer to Asterius' doctrine that the Father and Son (or God and his Word) are two distinct *hypostases*.[102] Marcellus utterly rejects this idea, repeatedly affirming that God and his Word are inseparable

---

[99] Eccl. Theol. 3.21.1 (181,13–30 Kl/H).
[100] DelCogliano 2006:463–465 and 471–476.
[101] On the significance of this adjective, see DelCogliano 2006:465–471.
[102] Eccl. Theol. 2.19.1 (123,7–12 Kl/H); Eccl. Theol. 2.19.15–21 (126,1–127,6 Kl/H); Eccl. Theol. 2.21.5 (130,30–31 Kl/H); Eccl. Theol. 3.4.5 (158,33–34 Kl/H).

and undivided, stressing that the divine unity is a matter of a unity of personal subject.[103] Eusebius sees Marcellus' theology as blending the Father and Son into a single *hypostasis* and thus tantamount to denying the separate *hypostasis*—that is, the independent existence—of the Son (or Word).[104] Therefore, he repeatedly affirms the distinct *hypostasis* of the Son.[105] In addition, Eusebius explicitly refers to the Father and Son as two *hypostases*.[106] Nowhere, however, does Eusebius present his two-*hypostases* doctrine as a defense of Asterius'. Rather, this is a point of agreement between them.

Asterius' belief in two *hypostases* required him to account for the unity of God, for this belief was susceptible to a ditheistic interpretation, which Marcellus exploited.[107] A number of fragments of Marcellus preserve Asterius' view of divine unity in the Cappadocian's interpretation of John 10:30, "I and the Father are one."[108] The unity of the Father and Son is, according to Asterius, because of their exact agreement in everything, both words and deeds. Eusebius never explicitly defends Asterius' interpretation of John 10:30, but his own interpretation of the same verse is in harmony with his ally's. Eusebius denies that the unity of the Father and Son is a matter of their being one *hypostasis* and instead suggests, since he interprets John 10:30 in connection with John 17:21–23, that they are one by virtue of their "community of glory."[109] Like Asterius, and in contrast to Marcellus, Eusebius does not view the divine unity as a question of a unity of personal subject or a single divine *hypostasis*. Unlike Asterius, however, Eusebius does not locate their unity in their activities but in their shared glory. Elsewhere, Eusebius also stresses that the Father and Son are one because the Father is the unbegotten source and cause of the only-begotten Son—what is called derivational unity.[110] Therefore, while both Asterius and Eusebius think that the Father and Son are *hypostases* in a unity, they conceptualize this unity in different ways.

On two occasions, Marcellus quotes two snippets from Asterius on the incarnation ("that which came down in the last days" and "that which was born from the Virgin") in the context of affirming that it is only the Word who takes

---

[103] See Lienhard 1999:53–54.

[104] E.g. Eccl. Theol. 1.1.2 (62,34–63,4 Kl/H); 1.17.2 (77,22–24 Kl/H).

[105] E.g. Eccl. Theol. 1.20.77 (94,16–18 Kl/H).

[106] Eccl. Theol. 1.10.4 (69,6 Kl/H); 1.20.40–41 (87,25–29 Kl/H); 2.7.1–3 (104,3–14 Kl/H). Eccl. Theol. 2.7 is Eusebius' most detailed account of the two *hypostases*.

[107] Eccl. Theol. 2.19.15–21 (126,1–127,6 Kl/H).

[108] C. Marc. 1.4.55 (29,7–12 Kl/H); C. Marc. 2.2.15–19 (37,29–38 Kl/H); C. Marc. 2.2.20–22 (38,25–39,10 Kl/H); Eccl. Theol. 2.4.2 (102,27–30 Kl/H).

[109] Eccl. Theol. 3.19 (180 Kl/H). Marcellus records that Asterius called the authority given to the Word "glory" and "pre-cosmic glory" (C. Marc. 2.2.28 (40,5–7 Kl/H); Eccl. Theol. 2.1.5 (100,11–14 Kl/H)).

[110] Eccl. Theol. 2.6.

on flesh.[111] Unfortunately, he does not record who Asterius said was incarnated or his precise teaching on the matter. But, as we have seen, Asterius did not limit the title of the pre-incarnate Word to only "Word" as Marcellus did, but used titles such as "Son," "Only-Begotten," "image," and so forth. So it is most likely that Asterius spoke of the Son or even Jesus Christ as being incarnated.[112] This interpretation is corroborated when it is realized that the first phrase alludes to Hebrews 1:2: "but in these last days he has spoken to us by a Son . . ."[113] The fact that Asterius is citing Hebrews 1:2 may suggest that he said it was the Son who was incarnated. Eusebius' own doctrine of the incarnation in this regard agrees with Asterius. In fact, the second half of the second book of *De ecclesiastica theologia* is devoted to discussing the countless names by which scripture refers to the pre-incarnate Word. After running through the Johannine evidence, Eusebius quotes three Marcellan fragments on the topic, in one of which Marcellus quotes both Asterian snippets.[114] After this, Eusebius ransacks the Pauline epistles and other parts of scripture in his continuing quest to demonstrate the myriad names that scripture used for pre-incarnate Word.[115] Though he never alludes to Asterius himself or his expressions, Eusebius does affirm that scripture calls the pre-incarnate Word both "Son" and "Jesus Christ."[116] And

---

[111] The first fragment of Marcellus is found at C. Marc. 2.2.1 (35,1–5 Kl/H); Eccl. Theol. 1.18.2 (79,16–20 Kl/H); Eccl. Theol. 1.20.50 (89,13–17 Kl/H); Eccl. Theol. 2.10.3 (111,11–15 Kl/H); the second at C. Marc. 2.2.4 (35,21–25 Kl/H); Eccl. Theol. 2.1.1 (99,17–21 Kl/H). For Marcellus' teaching on the incarnation of the Word, see Lienhard 1999:59–61.

[112] Lienhard 1999:97 writes: "In Asterius' letter [i.e. the *Apologia*], as in the writings of many of his allies, the distinction between the preincarnate Son and the incarnate Christ is not crucial." In the next sentence Lienhard claims that Asterius said that the Son was "Spirit" before he came down. But this is a misinterpretation of the fragment of Marcellus on which this claim is based (C. Marc. 2.2.4 [35,21–25 Kl/H]; Eccl. Theol. 2.1.1 [99,17–21 Kl/H]): "So, what was 'that which came down' before the incarnation? Surely he [i.e. Asterius] would say, 'Spirit.' For if he should wish to say anything contrary to this, the angel who said to the Virgin, 'The Holy Spirit will come upon you,' [Luke 1:35] would not agree with him. But if he says that he is Spirit, listen to the Savior who says 'God is Spirit' [John 4:24]." In Greek the relevant portion is: τί τοίνυν ἦν τὸ κατελθὸν πρὸ τοῦ ἐνανθρωπῆσαι; πάντως πού φησιν· πνευμα. εἰ γάρ τι παρὰ τοῦτο λέγειν ἐθέλοι, οὐ συγχωρήσει αὐτῷ ὁ πρὸς τὴν παρθένον εἰρηκὼς ἄγγελος . . . Here Marcellus is trying to back Asterius into his own position. If he can get Asterius to admit, based on Luke 1:35, that it was the Spirit who came down in the incarnation, then based on John 4:24 he can convince Asterius that it was God, who is one with and the same as the Word, who was incarnated. So it seems unlikely that Asterius ever considered that it was the Spirit who came down in the last days and was born of the Virgin.

[113] The verse is of course followed by Heb 1:3, which had been central in explaining the doctrine of the image of God since Origen. In the Marcellan fragments, however, Asterius does not cite or appeal to this verse.

[114] Eccl. Theol. 1.20.50.

[115] Eccl. Theol. 1.20.51–87.

[116] E.g. Eccl. Theol. 1.20.58 (90,21–22 Kl/H); 1.20.60 (90,34–91,3 Kl/H).

so, while Eusebius does not explicitly defend Asterius in this matter, he agrees with his theology.

There are a number of other (mainly non-controversial) teachings of Asterius preserved by Marcellus which Eusebius never explicitly comments on or defends, but his own theology is in agreement with them. According to Marcellus, Asterius maintained that "God is the maker of all things."[117] Marcellus of course agrees with this, as does Eusebius.[118] Marcellus wrote that "the Father seems to be in the Word, even if it does not seem so to Asterius and to those who think the same things as he does."[119] Eusebius characterizes Marcellus' teaching here as nothing more than Sabellianism.[120] Thus he again agrees with Asterius, in that the Father and Son are distinct in number. When explaining his understanding of how the divine monad expands into a triad, Marcellus incorporates Asterius' own language in support of his theology, namely, "the Holy Spirit proceeds from the Father," which is a citation of John 15:26.[121] Asterius seems to have seen this verse as evidence for the Spirit's separate *hypostasis*, an interpretation Marcellus rejected.[122] Eusebius interprets the same verse in a way that agrees with Asterius', that the Father and Spirit are distinct, not conflated as Marcellus thinks.[123]

So far, we have only seen very little, if any, critique of Asterius on the part of Eusebius. All of it has been mild and implicit, in that Eusebius sometimes agrees with Asterius on basic doctrines, but articulates the detailed theology behind these doctrines in different ways. Yet, as mentioned above, Markus Vinzent claimed that in his anti-Marcellan writings Eusebius rejected Asterius' belief that the Son was a creature.[124] First of all, there is no text in which Eusebius explicitly faults Asterius for considering the Son a creature. Vinzent's claim of rejection must be based on his belief that this was Asterius' teaching and the fact that Eusebius in his anti-Marcellan writings is clear that the Son is not a creature.[125] But as far as I can tell, in the fragments of the *Apologia*, Asterius never claims that the Son is a creature.

---

[117] C. Marc. 2.2.26 (39,30–34 Kl/H); Eccl. Theol. 2.3.1 (101,28–32 Kl/H).

[118] E.g. Eccl. Theol. 2.14.16 (117,11–12 Kl/H).

[119] Eccl. Theol. 2.1.3 (99,30–31 Kl/H); Eccl. Theol. 2.19.14 (125,27–28 Kl/H).

[120] Eccl. Theol. 2.1.2–3 (99,21–29 Kl/H). It seems that Marcellus appealed to John 10:38 for this teaching; see Eccl. Theol. 2.11.4–5 (113,11–18 Kl/H).

[121] Eccl. Theol. 3.4.2–4 (158,2–26 Kl/H).

[122] Marcellus reports that Asterius said that there was three *hypostases* (of Father, Son, and Spirit) not once, but twice; see Eccl. Theol. 3.4.5 (158,33–34 Kl/H).

[123] Eccl. Theol. 3.5.6–8 (160,31–161,11 Kl/H).

[124] Vinzent 1993:26.

[125] See note 55 above.

Joseph Lienhard said that he did make such a claim based on a report of Marcellus preserved by Eusebius: "So then, how do those men full of deceit and villainy [see Acts 13:10], to speak as the Apostle does, transfer the passage [i.e. Ps 109:3] to what they think is his first creation, even though David clearly said this about his fleshly generation?"[126] It is true, as we saw, that Asterius interpreted Psalm 109:3 as a reference to the Father's eternal begetting of the Son, not the incarnation. But in this fragment, Marcellus speaks of unspecified Eusebian opponents in the plural. He could be including Asterius in the number of those who held this opinion, but this is not necessarily the correct interpretation. It seems more likely that this is a position that Marcellus believed to be held also by the other Eusebians whom he attacked, perhaps Eusebius of Nicomedia and Narcissus. Finally, the phrase "his first creation" may not even be the words used by the Eusebians. When Marcellus says that the Eusebians apply the verse to "what they think is his first creation" (τὴν πρώτην αὐτοῦ, ὡς οἴονται, κτίσιν), he seems to be giving his own polemical interpretation of their views, not their exact language.[127] For all these reasons, this fragment of Marcellus should not be considered to report a viewpoint of Asterius. Indeed, it is not considered as such in the two editions of Asterius fragments by Gustave Bardy and Markus Vinzent.[128]

Accordingly, Vinzent bases his claim of Eusebius "rejecting" Asterius on the issue of the Son's creatureliness mainly on Asterian fragments of the *Syntagmation* preserved by Athanasius. It is undeniable that some of these fragments speak of the Son as a creature.[129] But these are not texts that were attacked by Marcellus and thus were not subject either to the defense or the rejection of Eusebius in his anti-Marcellan writings. Yet Vinzent does see one Marcellan text preserved by Eusebius supporting the claim that Asterius held that the Son was a creature: "Where in the divine sayings will they be able to show us that there is 'one unbegotten and one begotten' in the way that they themselves believe he was begotten, when neither prophets nor evangelists, nor apostles have said this?"[130] The authenticity of the Asterian text purportedly quoted here by Marcellus is questionable for the same reason as for the rejected Asterian fragment discussed in the previous paragraph. Marcellus similarly attributes the idea to unspecified Eusebians in the plural, not specifically Asterius. Thus, there

---

[126] C. Marc. 1.4.32 (24,31–34 Kl/H). See Lienhard 1999:97.

[127] See the comments above on ancient citation techniques at p. 268. When quoting what are most likely the exact words of Asterius, Marcellus uses phrases such as "he wrote" (γέγραφεν) or "he said" (ἔφη, εἰρηκότος).

[128] Bardy 1936:351 does include it as text to be compared with C. Marc. 1.2.21, in which Marcellus faults Asterius for misquoting Ps 109:3. But it is not considered as a fragment.

[129] See particularly fragments 27 and 34 in Vinzent's collection (the latter is 9 in Bardy's).

[130] C. Marc. 1.4.52–53 (28,27–29 Kl/H). This is fragment 12 in Vinzent's collection.

is nothing in the fragment itself to suggest that it reports of the view of Asterius. In fact, Bardy did not include this fragment in his collection.[131] Yet, even if one should accept the Marcellan fragment as reporting a view of Asterius, calling the Son the "one begotten" is not the same as calling the Son a "creature."[132]

Therefore, if there is no evidence for the Asterius of the *Apologia* holding that the Son was a creature, then there is no basis for claiming that Eusebius rejected the teaching of Asterius on this point. Then how do we reconcile the teaching of the *Syntagmation* with the *Apologia*? The former was written in the early 320s, before the Council of Nicaea, whereas the latter appeared afterward. One possibility, I suggest, is that in this period Asterius, like Eusebius, came to realize the inadequacy of applying the term "creature" to the Son.[133] Or it may simply be the case that the fragmentary remains of the *Apologia* do not preserve the passages that spoke of the Son as a creature. However, since Marcellus was vehemently opposed to such a theology, it seems unlikely that he would have neglected to cite such passages. Even if this second possibility is closer to the truth of the matter, it still cannot be said that Eusebius has rejected Asterius' doctrine on the creatureliness of the Son, since there is no text of the extant fragments of the *Apologia* that teaches this.

## Conclusion

Of the three instances of mutual defense within the Eusebian alliance examined in this study, Eusebius' defense of Asterius is not only the most extensive but also the most genuinely a defense. Asterius' defense of the Nicomedian Eusebius engaged in a good deal of updating and revision, even as he defended him. The Caesarean Eusebius essentially rejected the theology of Paulinus and Narcissus while still claiming to defend them. In contrast, the same Eusebius defended or at least agreed with everything Asterius taught (at least as reported by Marcellus). In no case can we detect an explicit or even an implicit critique. It is true that at times Eusebius developed his theology in different directions than Asterius, but this fact should not obscure their fundamental agreement in doctrinal matters. And so, it may be concluded that, even if the main purpose of

---

[131] Vinzent's arguments for authenticity are based on parallels with genuine Asterian texts; see Vinzent 1993:175–176. I do not contest that the thought here is Asterian. But since it is not exclusive to Asterius and there are no indications that Marcellus intended to report a view of Asterius here, it seems best to agree with Bardy and not consider it a fragment of Asterius.

[132] On Asterius' use of begetting language, see p. 270 above.

[133] See note 55 above. Note that Eusebian conciliar documents of the 340s still affirmed that the Son was a creature, though in highly qualified language. The fact that such language is found in the Second Dedication Creed of 341, which otherwise strongly reflected Asterian theology, problematizes the suggestion that Asterius distanced himself from belief in the creatureliness of the Son.

Eusebius in his anti-Marcellan writings was to refute the theology of Marcellus, they can also be construed as writings in favor of Asterius. If *Contra Marcellum* were the title of both works, then the subtitle could certainly be *Pro Asterio.*

The anti-Marcellan writings of Eusebius played a key role in the development and transmission of Eusebian theology. He is first of all responsible for preserving precious fragments of the writings of Paulinus, Narcissus, and Asterius, much as he saved many texts, Christian, Jewish, and Greco-Roman alike, in his *Historia Ecclesiastica*, *Praeparatio Evangelica*, and *Demonstratio Evangelica*. But, just as in those works, so in the anti-Marcellan treatises, he is not merely a conserver. He engages with the theology of his fellow Eusebians, sometimes jettisoning it (as with Paulinus and Narcissus), sometimes developing it in new directions (as with Asterius), but in every case drawing upon his previous theological work and updating it to respond to contemporary concerns and challenges. And thus he achieved a classic expression of Eusebian theology that incorporated and expanded upon the views of Asterius, a theology that was enormously influential in the following decades.

# Works Cited

Anatolios, K. 2011. *Retrieving Nicaea: The Development and Meaning of Trinitarian Doctrine.* Grand Rapids.

Ayres, L. 2004. *Nicaea and its Legacy. An Approach to Fourth-Century Trinitarian Theology.* Oxford.

Bardy, G. 1936. *Recherches sur saint Lucien d'Antioche et son école.* Paris.

DelCogliano, M. 2006. "Eusebian Theologies of the Son as Image of God before 341." *Journal of Early Christian Studies* 14:459–484.

———. 2008. "The Eusebian Alliance: The Case of Theodotus of Laodicea." *Zeitschrift für Antikes Christentum* 12:250–266.

———. 2010. *Basil of Caesarea's Anti-Eunomian Theory of Names: Christian Theology and Late-Antique Philosophy in the Fourth-Century Trinitarian Controversy.* Vigiliae Christianae Supplements 103. Leiden.

———. 2011a. "Basil of Caesarea on the Primacy of the Name 'Son.'" *Revue des Études Augustiniennes et Patristiques* 57:45–69.

———. 2011b. "George of Laodicea: A Historical Reassessment." *Journal of Ecclesiastical History* 62:667–692.

Gwynn, D. 2007. *The Eusebians. The Polemic of Athanasius of Alexandria and the Construction of the 'Arian Controversy.'* Oxford.

Hanson, R. P. C. 1988. *The Search for the Christian Doctrine of God: The Arian Controversy 318-381 AD.* Edinburgh.

Inowlocki, S. 2006. *Eusebius and the Jewish Authors: His Citation Technique in an Apologetic Context.* Leiden.

Kidd, I. G. 1997. "What is a Posidonian Fragment?" In *Collecting Fragments. Fragmente sammeln,* ed. G. W. Most, 225–236. Göttingen.

Kinzig, W. 1990. *In Search of Asterius: Studies on the Authorship of the Homilies on the Psalms.* Göttingen.

Klostermann, E. and Günther Christian Hansen, eds. 1991. *Eusebius Werke IV: Gegen Marcell. Über die kirchliche Theologie. Die Fragmente Marcells.* 3. Aufl. GCS 14. Berlin.

Kopecek, T. 1979. *A History of Neo-Arianism.* Cambridge.

Lienhard, J. T. 1999. *Contra Marcellum. Marcellus of Ancyra and Fourth-Century Theology.* Washington, DC.

Luibhéid, C. 1976. "The Arianism of Eusebius of Nicomedia." *Irish Theological Quarterly* 43:3–23.

Most, G. W., ed. 1997. *Collecting Fragments. Fragmente sammeln.* Göttingen.

Opitz, H.-G. 1934–1935. *Athanasius Werke III/1. Urkunden zur Geschichte des arianischen Streites 318-328,* 1–2. Lieferung. Berlin/Leipzig.

Parvis, S. 2006. *Marcellus of Ancyra and the Lost Years of the Arian Controversy 325–345.* Oxford.

Schott, J. 2011. "Eusebius' Panegyric on the Building of Churches (HE 10.4.2–72): Aesthetics and the Politics of Christian Architecture." In *Reconsidering Eusebius: Collected Papers on Literary, Historical, and Theological Issues,* ed. Sabrina Inowlocki and Claudio Zamagni, 177–197. Vigiliae Christianae Supplements 107. Leiden.

Schwartz, E. 1911. "Zur Geschichte des Athanasius VIII." *Nachrichten der Akademie der Wissenschaften in Göttingen: Philologisch-historische Klasse,* 369–426. Göttingen. (= 1959. *Zur Geschichte des Athanasius, Gesammelte Schriften 3.* Berlin.)

Stead, G. C. 1973. "'Eusebius' and the Council of Nicaea." *Journal of Theological Studies* n.s. 24:85–100.

Strutwolf, H. 1999. *Die Trinitätstheologie und Christologie des Euseb von Caesarea.* Göttingen.

Vinzent, M. 1993. *Asterius von Kappadokien: Die theologischen Fragmente.* Vigiliae Christianae Supplements 20. Leiden.

———. 1997. *Markell von Ankyra: Die Fragmente [und] Der Brief an Julius von Rom.* Vigiliae Christianae Supplements 29. Leiden.

Wallace-Hadrill, D. S. 1960. *Eusebius of Caesarea.* London.

Williams, R. 2001. *Arius: Heresy and Tradition,* Rev. ed. Grand Rapids, MI.

# 14

# How Binitarian/Trinitarian was Eusebius?

## Volker Henning Drecoll

THE TRINITARIAN THEOLOGY of Eusebius is one of the crucial problems of the history of theology of the fourth century. It is often assumed that Eusebius' theology is a kind of standard theology, which was shared by many Eastern bishops in the fourth century. The Creeds of Antioch (especially the so-called second Formula of Antioch) seem to be a kind of summary of Eusebian theology that is remarkably different from Athanasius.[1] Furthermore, the antipathy of many Eastern bishops toward Marcellus and Photinus[2] and the appearance of the Pneumatomachians seem to have been caused by the specific profile of Eusebius's theology.[3] One important aspect of this profile is thought to be the neglect of the Holy Spirit in the Trinitarian debate, so Eusebius is known as a "Binitarian."

At the same time, Eusebius is known as an Origenistic thinker. Origen, however, has a Trinitarian theology.[4] Additionally, Eusebius did write a couple of chapters about pneumatology in book 3 of his *De ecclesiastica theologia* (hereafter Eccl. Theol.) and mentions the Holy Spirit in his *Praeparatio Evangelica* (hereafter PE). I would like to raise the question of how Binitarian/Trinitarian Eusebius in fact was. I will proceed in two steps:

1. The Binitarian structure of Eusebius' theology was asserted by some German scholars, especially by Kretschmar and Hauschild. The new approach of Holger Strutwolf aims to reconsider this "standard view," but needs further consideration itself.

---

[1] Cf. Hanson 1988; reprinted 1997:290–291; Simonetti 1975:151–154; Gwynn 2007:220–226. I doubt that there was any intention of the council of Antioch to replace the Creed of Nicaea, as Ayres 2004:120 suggests.

[2] Cf. Ayres 2004:101–103, 134–135.

[3] Cf. Drecoll 1996:140.

[4] Cf. the instructive analysis of Origenes, *De principiis* 1:3, 5–8 by Ziebritzki 1994:203–225.

2.  The pneumatology of Eusebius in his fight against Marcellus, especially in his Eccl. Theol. must be analyzed once again. My aim is to show that Marcellus was the first theologian of the fourth century who seriously raised the Trinitarian question. Thus, the impact of Marcellus (or the fight against him) produces the specific Trinitarian accent of the debate.

## The German Discussion about Eusebius' "Binitarism"

In his *Habilitationsschrift*, Georg Kretschmar[5] distinguishes three types of theology in the fourth century:

1.  An economical approach: the Trinity can only be understood in its close connection with the history of salvation;

2.  The large Origenistic group for whom it was familiar to speak of three hypostases;

3.  Binitarians.[6]

There is nearly no witness for the last group—except Eusebius. More precisely, we should say: the early Eusebius (who quoted Mt 28:19 without mentioning the Spirit), because Kretschmar observes that after the council of Nicaea in 325 Eusebius was well aware of the fact that he had to mention the Holy Spirit. He did so, e.g. in quoting Mt 28:19 in full, but his pneumatology is defective nonetheless.[7] In this respect his theology shifted away from Origen. Kretschmar suggests that this shift was caused by a modification of theological principles: While to Origen, cosmology and soteriology were deeply connected to each other, to Eusebius theology became mainly cosmology or a kind of metaphysical thinking.[8] To Origen salvation was accessible through the Son and the Holy Spirit. The Son had a double function for cosmology and soteriology, but the Spirit was mainly thought of as the way to salvation, i.e. pneumatology was just a part of soteriology. The shift from Origen to Eusebius, from cosmology and soteriology to cosmology alone, left no place for the Holy Spirit, while the cosmological significance of the Son was maintained and developed (especially in the apologetic discourse of the PE). This focus had a twofold effect: first, theology concentrated on the relation between Father and Son—with emphasis on the μονογενής the Holy Spirit having no place; second, the Holy Spirit was understood as the

---

5   Georg Kretschmar 1956.
6   Cf. Kretschmar 1956:2.
7   Cf. Kretschmar 1956:3–4.
8   Cf. Kretschmar 1956:7–8.

gift of God, not as God himself. Thus, Pneumatomachian theology was caused by Eusebius' theology, but cannot be traced back to an earlier stage of theology (e.g. an old Binitarian tradition from former centuries).[9]

Kretschmar's pupil (and, I have to add, my teacher) Wolf-Dieter Hauschild pursued this strategy, modifying Kretschmar's view considerably.[10] Above all, he was not convinced that Origen had a really Trinitarian theology. From his point of view, Origen's theology was always Binitarian. He concedes that Origen mentioned the Holy Spirit in various passages, but insisted on the fact that these passages were either not really concerned with Trinitarian theology or mentioned the Holy Spirit only because tradition forced him to do so.[11] The main argument of Hauschild is the double function of Christology: Christ is not only the creator whose wisdom and power can be recognized in the world, but he is the savior, too. He is the image of God, thus leading the believers to communion with God.[12] Even if he was able to describe this communion by pneumatological sentences, these sentences were merely traditional ones. In fact, he had no interest in and no place for an integration of the Holy Spirit into the Holy Trinity.[13] In this respect, Eusebius is directly dependent on Origen. Eusebius stressed the Father-Son relation, so the Holy Spirit was "after the Son," i.e. one of the created beings that cannot be distinguished from the angels in principle. Thus, Origenism is Binitarism, especially in the reception of Eusebius.[14] That is why the Pneumatomachians are not merely a short episode in the history of theology of the fourth century, as Kretschmar thought, but show the older tradition of the third century.

The perspective of Kretschmar and Hauschild is one of the points Holger Strutwolf aimed to reconsider in his *Habilitationsschrift*.[15] He wanted to demonstrate the theological significance of Eusebius, especially in his apologetic work PE. He opposes a view of Eusebius that reckoned him as a superficial theologian and opportunistic supporter of imperial power.[16] For his purpose, Strutwolf analyzes PE 11. According to Strutwolf, the structure of this book is Trinitarian: Eusebius starts with the Father; then he concentrates on the Son as second cause of the universe; and then only briefly adds the Holy Spirit. After that, however, he restarts with the Father who is the idea of the Good, the Son who is the realm of the ideas (*Ideenwelt*), and the Holy Spirit who is present in the passage about

---

[9]  Cf. Kretschmar 1956:12–14.
[10] Cf. Hauschild 1967.
[11] Cf. Hauschild 1967:131–136.
[12] Cf. Hauschild 1967:133–134.
[13] Cf. Hauschild 1967:135–140.
[14] Cf. Hauschild 1967:151–152.
[15] Holger Strutwolf 1999.
[16] Cf. Strutwolf 1999:16.

the demons.[17] Eusebius integrates the Platonic views about the Mind and the World-Soul into his description of the Son. For the relation between Father and Son, the Platonic structure of archetype and image is used predominantly.[18] That Eusebius mentions the pneumatology only briefly, shows according to Strutwolf that the Holy Spirit is only worthy of further consideration within the context of Trinitarian theology.[19] The parallelization with the World-Soul is intentional; the functions of the World-Soul, however, are already integrated in the functions of the second cause, the Son. That is why Eusebius purportedly considers the Holy Spirit mainly as a counterpart of the demons. This explains, according to Strutwolf, the structure of PE 11:

1. Chapters 9–13: God as being and unique (Father)

2. Chapters 14–19: The second cause (Son)

3. Chapter 20: About the Three principal Hypostases (Holy Spirit as part of Trinitarian Theology)

4. Chapters 21–22: The idea of the Good (≈ Father)

5. Chapters 23–25: The ideas (≈ Son)

6. Chapter 26: The demons (=> Holy Spirit)

In chapter 26, the Platonic idea of two "World-Souls" appears. To the good World-Soul (apparently identified with the Holy Spirit) is opposed the bad World-Soul, that is, the demons. Thus, Eusebius was able to describe the Holy Spirit as God (exactly because of his role as counterpart to the demons) and to integrate the Holy Spirit into his apologetic Trinitarian thought.[20] Compared with this, the pneumatological passage of the third book of Eccl. Theol. where Eusebius denies the divinity of the Holy Spirit is an exception for Strutwolf and can be explained by the polemical target of the book. Against Marcellus, he felt obliged to stress the Father-Son relation, thus denying the divinity of the Holy Spirit, but in all other contexts he distinguishes the Holy Spirit from the creatures, especially the angels.[21]

[17] Cf. Strutwolf 1999:103–104.
[18] Cf. Strutwolf 1999:161–165.
[19] Cf. Strutwolf 1999:194–197, 208–212.
[20] Cf. Strutwolf 1999:198–201, 213–217 with the result (Strutwolf 1999:223): "Es kann also festgehalten werden, daß Euseb in seinem apologetischen Doppelwerk nicht nur deutlich bemüht ist, den Heiligen Geist in die göttliche Trias einzubeziehen und von den Geschöpfen abzugrenzen, sondern auch in der Lage war, den Heiligen Geist in seinem Eingebundensein in die Trias als Gott zu bezeichnen. Diese Beobachtung steht allerdings in deutlichem Gegensatz zum in der Forschung verbreiteten Bild des Euseb als eines 'binitarischen Subordinatianers.'"
[21] Cf. Strutwolf 1999:224–230.

The result of Strutwolf's reading is twofold: Yes, Eusebius has a pneumatology; pneumatology is important to him, especially in the apologetic context. But in spite of this, his pneumatology is defective. In the apologetic context, it appears only within the Trinitarian discussion, not as an independent field of theological thinking. In the fight against Marcellus, it disappears behind the Father-Son relation.[22]

I have not found any traces of this German discussion about the pneumatology of Eusebius in Anglo-American literature. The questions raised by this are, for example, not present in Lewis Ayres' *Nicea and its Legacy*, though he knows Hauschild and Strutwolf.[23] The significance of these questions is considerable nonetheless. Not only does the emergence of Pneumatomachian theology deserve an explanation, but also the description of the Origenistic profile of Eastern theology as a whole cannot be done without the question of how Binitarian or Trinitarian it was. Therefore, I would like to reconsider a couple of texts mentioned in the contributions of Kretschmar, Hauschild, and Strutwolf, especially PE 11 and 7 and Eccl. Theol. 3.5–6.

## The Impact of Marcellus for the Trinitarian Theology of Eusebius

The structure of PE 11[24] is important for Strutwolf's argument as noted above. I doubt, however, that his analysis of the Trinitarian structure of Book 11, chapters 9–26 can be maintained. Not even the explicit divinity of the Holy Spirit as a part of Eusebius's theology can be proven by book 11. There are three arguments against Strutwolf's interpretation of that book:

1. The aim of Book 11 is to show how Plato's φυσιολογία fits the theology of the Old Testament, i.e. the philosophy of the Hebrews and especially Moses.[25] Thus, the structure of the following chapters is dominated by what we would expect from a handbook of Platonic philosophy. Accordingly, Eusebius starts with the Divine, then explains

---

[22] Cf. Strutwolf 1999:237: In Eusebius' theology, there are "zwei Perspektiven der eusebianischen Pneumatologie ... Wenn Euseb die Eigenständigkeit und damit das Proprium der drei Hypostasen betonen will, entfaltet er die Unterscheidung von väterlicher Hypostase und der des Sohnes in der Unterscheidung von urbildlicher und abbildlicher Gottheit und sieht dabei offenbar keine andere Möglichkeit, die innertrinitarische Eigenständigkeit des Geistes zu wahren, als dem Heiligen Geist den Titel θεός abzusprechen. Wenn er dagegen von der ursprünglichen Trias auf die Geschöpfe blickt, so kann er den Heiligen Geist als Gegenüber zu aller Kreatur mit dem Gottestitel bezeichnen und in die eine Vater und Sohn gemeinsame Gottheit miteinbeziehen."

[23] Cf. Ayres 2004:211–213, 451, 460. Cf. Haykin 1994.

[24] Cf. for the problem of dating the PE (and the DE) now Morlet 2009:80–93.

[25] For the concept of "Hebrews," cf. Ulrich 1999:59–68, 121–125; Johnson 2006:100–125.

the second cause, the ideas, the demons, and the immortal souls. Finally, he arrives at the cosmology, the stars, the change of the world and its end (which for Eusebius is the resurrection and the last judgment). Thus, the structure of Book 11 is not the sequence of Trinitarian thought and anthropology, but an ontological hierarchy of beings. Of course, Eusebius compares the Platonic thoughts with the theology of the Hebrews, thus stating that according to the Hebrews only God is the truly Good and that the Hebrews refer wisdom, justice, etc., directly to the Logos instead of to the ideas. But this does not lead to a Trinitarian structure of the argument. The next chapter simply proceeds on to the next level of the Platonic hierarchy. Therefore, I doubt that the demonology in chapter 26 is caused by the intention to integrate the Holy Spirit into divinity.

2.  The Holy Spirit is only briefly mentioned in the context of Trinitarian theology. Eusebius, however, does not assert the divinity of the Holy Spirit in this short text. He explains that according to the Hebrews after Father and Son there is the Holy Spirit, the third in order that belongs to the Trinity.[26] That the Holy Spirit belongs to the Trinity is shown by the fact that the Holy Spirit is superior to all beings and creatures, established before all noetic beings by the Son, being the third one in comparison with the first cause, the Father.[27] Eusebius does not explain how divine or not divine this third component is. It belongs to the Trinity, but also to the noetic beings, it is superior, but at the same time, "the third."

Eusebius quotes the famous passage of the Pseudo-Platonic letter 2 (*ep.* 2.312de)[28] which Clement used already in order to show that even Plato knew about the Trinity.[29] Then he adds that in addition to the first God there is the second cause and that the World-Soul is third, since the Platonists define the World-Soul as a third God.[30] He does not comment on this, but simply concludes his passage by saying that

---

[26] Eusebius, PE 11.20.1 (GCS Eusebius 8/2, 46,5–6 Mras).

[27] Eusebius, PE 11.20.1 (GCS Eusebius 8/2, 46,6–9 Mras).

[28] Eusebius, PE 11.20.1–2 (GCS Eusebius 8/2, 46,9–15 Mras).

[29] Clemens Alexandrinus, *Stromateis* 5,103,1 (GCS Clemens 2, 395,12–17 Stählin), cf. Eusebius, PE 13.13.29 (GCS Eusebius 8/2, 207,16–208,4 Mras).

[30] Eusebius, PE 11.20.3 (GCS Eusebius 8/2, 46,16–18 Mras). That the world soul is the third God according to the Platonists, is not precisely correct, e.g. Numenius seems to identify the third God with the cosmos in general, cf. Numenius, *Fragmenta* 11 (Collection des Universités de France, 53,11–16 des Places = Eusebius, PE 11.18.3 [GCS Eusebius 8/2, 40,19–41,2 Mras]) and 21 (Collection des Universités de France, 60,1–10 des Places = Proclus, *In Timaeum commentarius* 1 [303,27–304,7 Diehl]).

the divine scriptures describe the Trinity as a principle (ἐν ἀρχῆς λόγῳ). Then he gives a short note leading to the following section, in which the substance of the Good will be explained.[31]

Eusebius is very prudent in his statement about the Holy Spirit. He neither identifies it with the World-Soul nor does he reckon it as divine. He shows that what Plato described as a World-Soul and a third God can be compared with the Holy Spirit of Hebrew theology.

3. The subject of chapter 26 is not the Holy Spirit, but demonology. The Holy Spirit is not at all present in this section. Eusebius starts with the statement that there are not only good powers but also bad ones, too. Exactly on this point, Plato follows the words of the Hebrews. Then he quotes a section of *Nomoi* (896de) where two World-Souls are mentioned, a good one and a bad one. There is no identification of the World-Soul with the Holy Spirit in this text, but the quotation is given in order to show that Plato knew about bad spirits. That is why Eusebius quotes Job 1:6–7: Even Scripture speaks about the devil and the angels. In his description of the angels, the Holy Spirit is not present. Thus, I doubt that we can take this passage as a pneumatological one. It is just a passage about angels and demons.

From my point of view, PE 11 is of little or nearly no help for the pneumatology of Eusebius. This passage, however, is not the unique pneumatological one in the whole work. More important is perhaps PE 7.15.

This passage belongs to a context that is similar to the structure of book 11, because it wants to demonstrate that the Hebrews had a theology that is quite close to that of the Christians.[32] That is why, in PE 7.9, Eusebius starts with the δογματικὰ θεωρήματα, then he deals with the πρόνοια and the δημιουργία of the universe (7.10). The creating activity is explained by a description of the first (7.11) and the second cause (7.12–14). Two further passages describe ἡ τῶν λογικῶν σύστασις (7.15) and αἱ ἀντικειμέναι δυνάμεις (7.16); then follows the nature of human beings (7.17) and matter (7.18–22). This structure corroborates the analysis of book 11 given above. In both cases, Eusebius goes through the hierarchy of being, beginning with the highest nature, God-Father, and then proceeding step by step to matter. It becomes clear that pneumatology has no distinct and independent place in this structure, but is integrated into the

---

[31] Eusebius, PE 11.20.3 (GCS Eusebius 8/2, 46,18–21 Mras).

[32] This aim seems to be neglected in the analysis of Strutwolf 1999:201–208, cf. Inowlocki 2006:113–114, and Kofsky 2000:105: "Eusebius actually expounds his own Christian theology as if it were the theology of the ancient Hebrews." What he reports about the theology of the Hebrews, should, however, carefully be distinguished from his own expressions and his own terminology.

passage about the heavenly powers. That is why at the beginning of PE 7.15, Eusebius asserts that after the substance of the ἄναρχος καὶ ἀγένητος θεός, there is the Logos who is also μεγάλης βουλῆς ἄγγελος (Isa 9:5).[33] The heavenly spirits after the Logos cannot be numbered by human beings—they are too many and too different: we may compare them to the sun, the moon, and all other stars (cf. 1 Cor 15:41).[34] Describing this heavenly world (ὁ ἐν ἀσωμάτοις καὶ νοεραῖς οὐσίαις κόσμος), Eusebius says that after the Father there is the second power of the creating Logos (the sun of justice, cf. Mal 1:6)—while the third being in the place of the moon is the Holy Spirit. He has, according to the Hebrews, on the one side the same πρώτη καὶ βασιλικὴ τῆς τῶν ὅλων ἀρχῆς ἀξία καὶ τιμή, while on the other side he is εἰς ἀρχὴν τῶν μετὰ ταῦτα γενητῶν.[35] The term ἀρχή has a twofold meaning here: on the one side it means the creating principle, on the other side it means simply the beginning.[36] In this last respect the Holy Spirit passes what he receives to the beings below (especially the verb ἐπιχορηγέω carries this sense). The Holy Spirit receives his power from the second cause, the Logos, who receives everything from the highest nature, the πηγὴ θεότητος.[37] The difference between the Logos and the Holy Spirit becomes clear from the following explanation: the Logos receives everything that belongs to the highest nature; the individual and specific holy things, however, are transmitted to the Holy Spirit who passes these specific holy gifts to the beings below.[38] That is why the Hebrews, Eusebius continues, call the third and holy power ἅγιον πνεῦμα and ἀποθειάζουσιν, ὑφ'οὗ καὶ ἐφωτίζοντο θεοφορούμενοι.[39] The divine character of the Holy Spirit is directly linked to its sanctifying and illuminating power. After that, Eusebius pursues his overall strategy and explains (after the sun and the moon) the stars (that is, the angels).

---

[33] Eusebius, PE 7.15.1–2 (GCS Eusebius 8/1, 391,7–13 Mras).

[34] Eusebius, PE 7.15.3–4 (GCS Eusebius 8/1, 391,13–19 Mras). The interpretation of 1 Cor 15:41 is caused by the aim of the passage to elucidate the Hebrew's understanding of the heavenly world. While Logos and Holy Spirit are subordinated, they belong to the immense heavenly world that can be compared with the stars according to 1 Corr 15:41. I doubt that a specific Neoplatonic approach to consider the world soul as moon (cf. Strutwolf 1999:206–207) is present in the background of this passage. The functions of the world soul in Plotinus (and also in Plutarch) are very different from the function of the Holy Spirit described here by Eusebius.

[35] Eusebius, PE 7.15.5–6 (GCS Eusebius 8/1, 391,19–392,7 Mras).

[36] I doubt that the Holy Spirit is considered as ἀρχή in the same sense as the Father is ἡ ἀρχή (cf. Strutwolf 1999:202): He is not ἀρχή, but he has the same dignity (because of his sanctifying function). The Holy Spirit is called neither ἀρχή nor αἴτιον by Eusebius in this passage.

[37] Eusebius, PE 7.15.7 (GCS Eusebius 8/1, 392,7–16 Mras).

[38] Eusebius, PE 7.15.8–9 (GCS Eusebius 8/1, 392,16–27 Mras). Strutwolf is right in his observation of the relation between τὰ μὲν πάντα ... τὰ δ' ἐν μέρει (392,20–23). I agree with his description of the Holy Spirit as "das Prinzip der Verteilung der Tugenden unter die Vernunftwesen" (Strutwolf 1999:203), though I would prefer not to introduce the term "Tugenden" here.

[39] Eusebius, PE 7.15.10 (GCS Eusebius 8/1, 392,27–393,2 Mras).

In this concept, the Holy Spirit is integrated into the description of the heavenly world. His place is exactly in a kind of gray area between the θεοῦ λόγος and the angels. He is the τρίτη δύναμις and stands at the first place in the row of the spiritual beings. He leads the spiritual and sanctifying gifts to all angels and saints (ἐπιχορηγέω), but doing so, he passes on what he receives. His main function is the distributing function. Thus, he is considered to be divine by the Hebrews, but Eusebius himself is very prudent in his own expressions. While the Father is called ὁ μετὰ πάντων θεός and the Logos is called ὁ θεὸς λόγος, the Holy Spirit is "reckoned divine" (ἀποθειάζουσι) and placed on the highest ἀξία καὶ τιμή by the Hebrews. Eusebius does not express his own opinion in this respect. For Eusebius' Trinitarian theology, the passage is certainly a key one, but the context makes clear that, first, Eusebius' thinking concentrates upon the first and the second cause (Father and Logos); and that, second, he integrates the Holy Spirit into the heavenly hierarchy. There the Holy Spirit is certainly more than an angel: he has a special dignity and a special, distributing and sanctifying function; he can be called divine because of his close relation to the Logos. But he is not called θεός, nor is there an ontological explanation; the existence of the Holy Spirit is just explained by his function in the economy of salvation. It will become clear from the analysis of Eccl. Theol. 3.5–6 that it is exactly this concept Eusebius pursues and develops against Marcellus.

The most important passage for Eusebius' pneumatology is certainly Eccl. Theol. 3.5–6. Strutwolf is right in asserting that Eccl. Theol. 3.5–6 is caused by the fight against Marcellus.[40] This, however, does not mean that the passage is of less significance. From my point of view, it was particularly the struggle with Marcellus that caused Eusebius to incorporate pneumatology into his Trinitarian thought—very early in the fourth century and with important effects on the history of theology in the later fourth century. He could do so because he had developed some pneumatological ideas in PE 7. He picked up this passage and extended it in the Trinitarian controversy. Thus, Marcellus seems to be the reason for a really Trinitarian passage in Eusebius that became important for the history of theological thinking during the fourth century.

Before we analyze the text of Eusebius, we should consider the argument of Marcellus (consisting of four fragments) that Eusebius wants to refute.[41] Marcellus' argument is nearly a kind of syllogism, based on biblical quotations:

1. Hypothesis A: The Logos went out from the Father and came to us (Jn 16:28—this biblical reference is missing in the apparatus of Klostermann and Hansen).

---

[40] Cf. Strutwolf 1999:224.
[41] Cf. the commentary on the fragments (numbered as fragments 47–50) by Seibt 1994:323–333.

2.  Hypothesis B: The Holy Spirit went out from the Father (Jn 15:26) and he just preaches what he hears from the Logos (Jn 16:13–14).

3.  Conclusion: What proceeds (ἐκπορευόμενον) from the Father is sometimes called the Logos, at other times it is called the Holy Spirit. Therefore, the Son and the Holy Spirit belong to the μονάς both in the same sense. This proves the mystery, i.e. that the μονάς was extended (πλατύνεσθαι) to a Triad, remaining identical to itself. Thus, God (as a Monad extended to a Triad) is indivisible.[42]

Marcellus adds two further arguments: first, if the Son says "Take the Holy Spirit" (Jn 20:22) and the Holy Spirit receives everything from the Son (Jn 16:13–14), it is clear that what the disciples have is this Monad-Triad (the Holy Spirit being the Logos);[43] second, if the Son and the Holy Spirit are two different persons (as Asterius said), either the Holy Spirit went out from the Father, thus having no need of any help from the Son, or he receives everything from the Son, thus having no need of any direct relationship to the Father.[44] Conclusion: Asterius mentions the three hypostases several times, but this is apparently wrong (i.e. against the biblical witness).[45]

Since Marcellus' theology is based on the identification of the Triad with the Monad (by the verb πλατύνεσθαι), he takes into consideration not only the Son, but also the Holy Spirit. Thus, Marcellus is a truly Trinitarian theologian due to his understanding of God.

Marcellus develops his argument by using biblical quotations; it is an exegetical argument.[46] Therefore, Eusebius deals with exegesis in his refutation, too. He proceeds in five steps:[47]

---

[42]  Eusebius, Eccl. Theol. 3.4 (GCS Eusebius 4, 158,2–15 Klostermann and Hansen, hereafter Kl/H).

[43]  Eusebius, Eccl. Theol. 3.4 (GCS Eusebius 4, 158,14–18 Kl/H).

[44]  Eusebius, Eccl. Theol. 3.4 (GCS Eusebius 4, 158,19–26 Kl/H), cf. Eusebius, Eccl. Theol. 3.4 (GCS Eusebius 4, 158,28–31 Kl/H).

[45]  Eusebius, Eccl. Theol. 3.4 (GCS Eusebius 4, 158,33f. Kl/H).The hypothetical argument of Markell, fragment 47, in Eusebius, Eccl. Theol. 3.4 (GCS Eusebius 4; 157,32–36 Kl/H) may be skipped here, cf. on that Seibt 1994:326.

[46]  His argument relies on an exegetical method, a kind of "trial of replacement" ("Austauschprobe"): If the same thing is said about two things, it is plausible that they are synonymous—at least if the things said about them are specific enough. This is the case with the Son and the Spirit. Therefore from my perspective it is not the unity of perfection that is the backbone of the fragment (this is the opinion, however, of Seibt 1994:328).

[47]  The five steps are introduced by a short passage (Eusebius, Eccl. Theol. 3.5 [GCS Eusebius 4, 159,1–8 Kl/H]) and summed up in a conclusion (Eusebius, Eccl. Theol. 3.6 [GCS Eusebius 4, 156,22–36 Kl/H]). Cf. on this passage Strutwolf 1999:224–230.

1. First, he concentrates on the verb ἐξεληλυθέναι:[48] Of course, going out does not show identity. The Son was eternally with the Father, then he was sent into the world; for this purpose he went out from the Father. The Holy Spirit was always standing around God's throne (as the angels did), then he went out from the Father. Also others went out from God, e.g. the devil or an evil spirit. Thus, going out can be said about the Son and the Holy Spirit in a similar manner, but this does not mean identity.

2. The difference between the Holy Spirit and the Son is shown by the Spirit's operations:[49] various quotations, especially from the Gospel according to John, show that Christ spoke about the Holy Spirit as a different person. In particular, the announcement of the operation of the Holy Spirit as the "other paraclete" shows this difference. Jn 20:22 is not already the fulfillment of this announcement, but only the preparation, a kind of purification.[50]

3. Both the Father and the Son sent the Holy Spirit;[51] this is not contradictory, but shows only that Father and Son agree in their will, i.e. the Son does the will of the Father. The Holy Spirit is sent in order to teach the Christians more than was possible in the lifetime of Jesus (because of the audience that followed "the Jewish lifestyle"). Even regarding the forgiveness of sins, the disciples received higher and "fuller" charisms after the Ascension of Christ. Just this surpassing of the Holy Spirit, announced by Christ, shows that the Holy Spirit is different from the Son. In all the announcements, the Son speaks of the Holy Spirit as of a different person.

   It is in this context that Eusebius adds the famous sentence according to which the Holy Spirit is better and "higher" than all other noetic and rational substance, surpassing them in honor and glory (and that is why he is "bunched together" [συμπαρείληπται] with the Triad), but that at the same time he is less (ὑποβεβηκός) than the Son. This last sentence is not proven by the arguments given before, but leads to the following section:

4. The Holy Spirit receives everything that he reveals from the Father and the Son.[52] He is dependent on both. Both, the Father and the Son,

---

48  Eusebius, Eccl. Theol. 3.5 (GCS Eusebius 4, 159,8–29 Kl/H).
49  Eusebius, Eccl. Theol. 3.5 (GCS Eusebius 4, 159,29–161,20 Kl/H).
50  Cf. Strutwolf 1999:226.
51  Eusebius, Eccl. Theol. 3.5 (GCS Eusebius 4, 161,20–162,31 Kl/H).
52  Eusebius, Eccl. Theol. 3.5 (GCS Eusebius 4, 162,31–163,29 Kl/H).

are a) spirit and b) holy, but this is no proof of their identity with the Holy Spirit, e.g. the angels are called "spirits," too, but of course they are not equal to the Holy Spirit. The Holy Spirit has, however, a specific character, because he is the Paraclete. So we should preserve Mt 28:19 where all three (Father, Son, and Holy Spirit) are mentioned. Eusebius explains this by using 1 Cor 12:6–9. The Father is the origin and the donor of grace, the Son procures this by leading the Holy Spirit who distributes the charisms. This interpretation of 1 Cor 12:6–9 is directly dependent on Origen's explanation of Jn 1:3 in the *Commentary on John*.[53] There Origen explains how the Spirit is a) caused by the Son, and b) is distributing the charisms to the saints. In order to explain how these two points fit each other, Origen developed the idea that Christ is characterized by many aspects of his divinity (ἐπίνοια) and that the Holy Spirit is exactly these aspects. In establishing (Origen uses ὑφίστημι here) the Holy Spirit, Christ gives just these aspects to him, so the latter is as it were the hypostasis of these aspects. Thus, the Holy Spirit is caused by Christ's procuring his aspects as charisms for the saints. This puts both aspects (dependence and superiority) into one sentence. If we accept this Origenistic background of Eusebius's interpretation of Mt 28:19 by 1 Cor 12:6–9, it is absolutely not surprising that Eusebius in the last step deals especially with Jn 1:3 and the subordination of the Holy Spirit.

5. The Holy Spirit is not only led by the Son, but also caused by him according to Jn 1:3.[54] The Father decides who will receive grace, the Son leads the Holy Spirit, and the Holy Spirit distributes the charisms. The Son is not only the creator of the universe, but he also causes to subsist the Holy Spirit (of course in the sense of Origen's explanation of Jn 1:3). So there is a clear order: above all, there is God the Father who is over all and through all and in all (Eph 4:6); the Son is the only begotten God (cf. Jn 1:18). The Holy Spirit, however, is neither God nor Son, but has his origin from the Father in a manner comparable to the Son, while being at the same time one of those things that is brought into subsistence by the Son (Jn 1:3). The real problem of this sentence is the word "God" that is used in it. It means either God the Father or it means God in general (as a category). Thus, either the Holy Spirit is

---

[53] Origen, *Commentary on John* 2.10 (GCS Origenes 4, 64,11–65,35 Preuschen). Cf. Strutwolf 1999:229. Cf. the new translation with commentary by Thümmel 2011: especially 126–131, 248–251; cf. on this passage Drecoll 2003:479–487.

[54] Eusebius, Eccl. Theol. 3.5 (GCS Eusebius 4, 163,30–164,21 Kl/H).

not identical with the Father or he is not God or divine at all. Because of the juxtaposition of "nor Son" it seems more probable to me (*pace* Strutwolf[55]) that this refers to God the Father (the article is missing only because so-called "predicate nouns" regularly have no article, cf. Jn 1:1). From my perspective it is far from being certain that Eusebius here denies the divinity of the Spirit. He is just stressing the dependence and the specific operation of the Holy Spirit in order to refute Marcellus who is accused of the heresy of Paul of Samosata and others in the following sentence (the conclusion mentioned above).

The result of this analysis is that Eusebius is forced by Marcellus to explain why and in what respect the Holy Spirit is different from the Son. This leads Eusebius to a seven-page pneumatological passage. In his pneumatology, he clearly follows Origen. Thus, exactly the same problem that Origen was dealing with reappears in Eusebius: the Holy Spirit is dependent on the Son, but in his operation he is dealing with a higher degree than just creation or rational beings (that is the area of the Son's operation). Since the effect (in our case, the Holy Spirit) should not be higher than the cause (in our case, the Son), the higher value of the Spirit's operation seems to be contradictory to his being caused by the Son. But just like Origen, Eusebius refers to the fact that exactly the soteriological function of the Holy Spirit is closely linked to his being brought into subsistence by the Son. The Holy Spirit is what Christ gives to the saints; he establishes the body of Christ by the charisms that are the aspects of Christ's divinity.

Both Marcellus and Eusebius agree that the soteriological functions (as told by Scripture) allow statements about the ontological relationships between Son and Spirit. While to Marcellus these soteriological functions show the hidden and mysterious identity of Son and Holy Spirit (so we cannot speak of two different persons—against Asterius), to Eusebius the soteriological functions of the Holy Spirit and the Son show the ontological difference between them (so we should speak of different hypostases). But exactly this difference causes a problem: while the soteriological level leads to the assumption that the Holy Spirit is higher than the Son, it should be just the other way around regarding the ontological level. Nonetheless, Eusebius tried to follow Origen's interpretation of Jn 1:3, a strategy that tends to stress the identity of the Holy Spirit with Christ. Of course, this is not a valid argument against Marcellus, and so this tendency is "reduced." Therefore, the internal identity of the Holy Spirit with the Son is not stressed in Eccl. Theol. 3.5–6.

---

[55] Cf. Strutwolf 1999:229–230.

The polemical target of this pneumatology became important in the struggle of the Origenist theology against Marcellus and Photinus (in the forties and fifties—visible in the various Creeds of this time). Thus, the degree of divinity of the Holy Spirit became unclear. This was neither caused by "too much cosmology" in Eusebius (Kretschmar), nor by a continuity to a kind of proto-Pneumatomachian theology of Origen (Hauschild), nor by the defective attempt to consider the Holy Spirit as World-Soul and to integrate this thought into his apologetic work (Strutwolf). It was, however, caused by the controversy with Marcellus that revealed an internal problem of the Origenistic tradition. The attempt to bring together dependence and superiority of operation was based upon the close link between soteriological functions and ontological relations (as Origen preferred them). It was exactly this close link that seemed to be problematic in the struggle against Marcellus. Thus, stressing the difference between Son and Holy Spirit led to an overestimation of the dependence of the Holy Spirit on the Son. This raised the question whether the Holy Spirit was God at all. The Pneumatomachians drew their conclusions from this, clearly stating that the Holy Spirit was a creature (though different from all other creatures). The majority of the bishops, however, avoided being clear about this point. Thus, they preferred to speak about the Spirit's soteriological functions (that were considerably high and seemed to be "divine") and to say nothing about the divinity of the Spirit. The result of this we can see in Basil of Caesarea who struggled for more than fifteen years with this tradition.[56] Even the distinction between οὐσία and ὑπόστασις and the specific pneumatological profile of Basil can be understood in a better way, if we keep in mind the internal problems of the Origenistic pneumatology. Basil's strategy consisted of two steps:

I.   While he could use the ὁμοούσιος for the Son, he did not use it for the Spirit. For the Trinity as a whole, however, he could speak of μία οὐσία.

II.  Regarding pneumatology he applied Eusebius's mention of the Spirit's sanctifying function (of the angels, etc.) to the argument that exactly this high level guarantees that the Spirit is not a creature (though he did not use the word God in this respect).[57]

In this strategy, a certain measure of prudence is as present as the attempt to express definitely the divinity of the Holy Spirit. Exactly this strategy was widely accepted in 381.[58]

---

[56]   This is one of the results of Drecoll 1996:130–182.
[57]   Cf. Drecoll 1996:244–253.
[58]   Cf. Hauschild 1982:13–48.

So, how Binitarian/Trinitarian was Eusebius? To my mind, pneumatology as a part of Trinitarian thought in general was not extremely important to Eusebius; we have only a couple of pages about it in his work. So we may say: no, he was not really a Trinitarian theologian, but integrated the Holy Spirit in hierarchies between God, the Logos, and the angels. In the controversy with Marcellus, however, he felt obliged to say something about pneumatology. In so doing, he developed a considerably important pneumatology that was dependent on Origen. Regarding the impact of this pneumatology on the development of Trinitarian thought in the fourth century, we may say: yes, he became a Trinitarian theologian due to Marcellus. So, he was in fact a theologian whose position shaped the properly Trinitarian aspect of the theological discussion for approximately fifty years. The Trinitarian debate cannot be understood without the Trinitarian theology of Eusebius. I suppose there are not very many pneumatological passages for which we could claim a similar significance.

# Works Cited

Ayres, L. 2004. *Nicaea and its Legacy. An Approach to Fourth-Century Trinitarian Theology.* Oxford.

Drecoll, V. H. 1996. *Die Entwicklung der Trinitätslehre des Basilius von Cäsarea. Sein Weg vom Homöusianer zum Neonizäner.* Forschungen zur Kirchen und Dogmengeschichte 66. Göttingen.

———. 2003. "Der Begriff Hypostasis bei Origenes. Bemerkungen zum Johanneskommentar II,10." In *Origeniana Octava. Origen and the Alexandrian Tradition/Origene e la tradizione alessandrina.* Papers of the 8th International Origen Congress, Pisa, 27–31 August 2001, vol. II, ed. Lorenzo Perrone, 479–487. Bibliotheca Ephemeridum Theologicarum Lovaniensium 164B. Leuven.

Gwynn, D. M. 2007. *The Eusebians. The Polemic of Athanasius of Alexandria and the Construction of the 'Arian Controversy.'* Oxford.

Hanson, R. P. C. 1988. *The Search for the Christian Doctrine of God: The Arian Controversy 318-381.* Edinburgh.

Hauschild, W.-D. 1967. *Die Pneumatomachen. Eine Untersuchung zur Dogmengeschichte des vierten Jahrhunderts.* PhD diss. Hamburg University.

———. 1982. "Das trinitarische Dogma von 381 als Ergebnis verbindlicher Konsensusbildung." In *Glaubensbekenntnis und Kirchengemeinschaft. Das Modell des Konzils von Konstantinopel (381),* ed. Karl Lehmann and Wolfhart Pannenberg, 13–48. Dialog der Kirchen 1. Freiburg/Göttingen.

Haykin, M. 1994. *The Spirit of God: The Exegesis of 1 and 2 Corinthians in the Pneumatomachian Controversy of the Fourth Century.* Supplements to Vigiliae Christianae 27. Leiden.

Inowlocki, S. 2006. *Eusebius and the Jewish Authors. His Citation Technique in an Apologetic Context.* Ancient Judaism and Early Christianity 64. Leiden/ Boston.

Johnson, A. P. 2006. *Ethnicity and Argument in Eusebius' Praeparatio Evangelica.* Oxford Early Christian Studies. Oxford.

Klostermann, E. and Günther Christian Hansen, eds. 1991. *Eusebius Werke IV: Gegen Marcell. Über die kirchliche Theologie. Die Fragmente Marcells.* 3. Aufl. GCS 14. Berlin.

Kofsky, A. 2000. *Eusebius of Caesarea against Paganism.* Jewish and Christian Perspectives Series 3. Leiden.

Kretschmar, G. 1956. *Studien zur frühchristlichen Trinitätstheologie.* Beiträge zur Historischen Theologie 21. Tübingen.

Morlet, S. 2009. *La Démonstration évangélique d'Eusèbe de Césarée. Étude sur l'apologétique chrétienne à l'époque de Constantin.* Collection des Études Augustiniennes. Série Antiquité 187. Paris.

Seibt, K. 1994. *Die Theologie des Markell von Ankyra.* Arbeiten zur Kirchengeschichte 59. Berlin/New York.

Simonetti, M. 1975. *La crisi ariana nel IV secolo.* Studia Ephemeridis Augustinianum 11. Rome.

Strutwolf, H. 1999. *Die Trinitätstheologie und Christologie des Euseb von Caesarea. Eine dogmengeschichtliche Untersuchung seiner Platonismusrezeption und Wirkungsgeschichte.* Forschungen zur Kirchen- und Dogmengeschichte 72. Göttingen.

Thümmel, H. G. 2011. *Origenes' Johanneskommentar. Buch I–V.* Herausgegeben, übersetzt und kommentiert. Studien und Texte zu Antike und Christentum. Tübingen.

Ulrich, J. 1999. *Euseb von Caesarea und die Juden. Studien zur Rolle der Juden in der Theologie des Eusebius von Caesarea.* Patristische Texte und Studien 49. Berlin/New York.

Ziebritzki, H. 1994. *Heiliger Geist und Weltseele. das Problem der dritten Hypostase bei Origenes, Plotin und ihren Vorläufern.* Beiträge zur Historischen Theologie 84. Tübingen.

# 15

# Origen, Eusebius, the Doctrine of *Apokatastasis*, and Its Relation to Christology

ILARIA RAMELLI

IN ORIGEN'S THOUGHT, the doctrine of *apokatastasis* is interwoven with his anthropology, eschatology, theology, philosophy of history, theodicy, and exegesis; for anyone who takes Origen's thought seriously and with a deep grasp of it, it is impossible to separate the *apokatastasis* theory from all the rest, so as to reject it but accept the rest. Eusebius was an admirer of Origen and a follower of his thought;[1] this is also why he, significantly, chose to present himself as "Eusebius of Pamphilus"—that is, as the spiritual child of the strenuous defender of Origen, marking his adherence to the Origenian tradition. This, too, is probably why Eusebius always endeavored to avoid dealing with eschatology, and in particular with the doctrine of *apokatastasis*. His seems to have been a cautious move. However, upon close scrutiny, Eusebius does reveal his penchant for the doctrine of *apokatastasis*—a tendency not generally recognized by scholars[2]—in a few passages, especially those where he is commenting on 1 Cor 15:24–28. Here, Origen's influence is palpable, just as it is on Didymus, Gregory of Nyssa, and Evagrius, all of them supporters of the *apokatastasis* doctrine, and on Gregory Nazianzen.[3] It is natural that it is so, in that 1 Cor 15:28 announces the final submission of all creatures to Christ and Christ's submission to God, who will be "all in all." This was indeed one of the strongest New Testament *testimonia* in support of the doctrine of *apokatastasis*.

Indeed, Eusebius depends on Origen's interpretation of 1 Cor 15:28 and inclines to his conception of *apokatastasis*, also using this very term. My

---

[1]  On Eusebius's adherence to Origen, see Kannengiesser 1992:435–466; Ramelli 2011:21–49.

[2]  His reticence on eschatology was ascribed to scarce interest or to the idea that perfection was realized under Constantine. See respectively, e.g. Trisoglio 1978:173–182; Sirinelli 1961:480–481.

[3]  See further the discussion in I. Ramelli, *The Christian Doctrine of Apokatastasis: A Critical Assessment from the New Testament to Eriugena*. Leiden: Brill, 2013.

systematic investigation into Eusebius' use of ἀποκατάστασις and ἀποκαθίστημι (respectively "restoration" and "to restore") reveals, in addition to more trivial meanings (such as returning a possession to someone, or the well-known astronomical meaning of the return of a heavenly body to its initial position after a cycle), a frequent use of the terminology and notion of *apokatastasis*, strongly influenced by Origen's conception. For instance, commenting on the title of Psalm 5, "For the end, on her who inherits" (εἰς τὸ τέλος, ὑπὲρ τῆς κληρονομούσης), in *Commentary on Psalms* PG 23.581.25–30, Eusebius clearly joins eschatology and *apokatastasis*, by referring the latter to the *telos* and the inheritance of God. He also cites Psalm 15: "In Psalm 15 the inheritance [κληρονομία] itself was indicated, according to the words, 'The Lord is the portion of my inheritance' [. . .] you are the one who restores my inheritance to me" (ὁ ἀποκαθιστῶν τὴν κληρονομίαν μου ἐμοί: these very same words are repeated in *Commentary on Psalms* PG 23.157.38). Indeed, Eusebius sees important references to the notion of *apokatastasis* in the Psalms. In *Commentary on Psalms* PG 23.68.30, he reads Psalm 14 in reference to the "restoration [ἀποκατάστασις] of the perfect according to God." Likewise, in *Commentary on Psalms* PG 23.72.26, he deems Psalm 124 entirely devoted to the idea of *apokatastasis*, as is clear from its title itself: "*Apokatastasis*." And, given the *akolouthia* that both Eusebius and Gregory Nyssen read in the Psalms, the eschatological context is shown very well by the "titles" of the immediately following Psalms, all eschatological themes: "125: Expectation of the things to come; 126: Edification of the Church; 127: The call of the Gentiles; 128: The victory of the army of Christ; 129: The prayer of the martyrs."

An allusion to the notion of the eventual *apokatastasis* is even found in the *Oratio ad sanctorum coetum*, or *Constantine's Speech to the Gathering of the Saints*, written for Constantine (probably, rather than *by* Constantine),[4] at 11.16, in the context of a discussion of the relationship between free will and divine grace, which Origen also found compatible.[5] Above all, Eusebius insists on the notion of *anastasis* as *apokatastasis*, "resurrection" as "restoration," as did Origen and then Gregory of Nyssa. In *Commentary on Psalms,* Eusebius speaks of the eventual resurrection in terms of "renovation of humanity" and of *apokatastasis*, giving the very same definition of resurrection as restoration that will be offered by Gregory of Nyssa shortly after:

---

[4]   Or at least it was drafted by Constantine and written by Eusebius, as is indicated by the latter in VC 4.52. I do not intend to tackle this question here; the second solution is defended by Edwards 2007, to which I refer readers also for the relevant bibliography.

[5]   Cf. 12.1.

Eusebius: ἡ γὰρ ἀνάστασις εἰς τὸ ἀρχαῖόν ἐστιν ἀποκατάστασις.

*Commentary on Psalms* PG 23.1285.56

Gregory of Nyssa: ἀνάστασίς ἐστιν ἡ εἰς τὸ ἀρχαῖον τῆς φύσεως ἡμῶν ἀποκατάστασις

*On the Soul and the Resurrection* 156C

The resurrection is the restoration of humanity to its original condition, before the fall. The same expression, in its verbal form, is used again by Eusebius in *Commentary on Isaiah* 1.83.120: αὖθις ἀποκατασταθήσῃ εἰς τὸ ἀρχαῖον ("you will be restored again to your original condition"). Resurrection is described as a restoration to life, brought about by Christ, in *Oratio ad sanctorum coetum* 11.12: ἀντὶ δὲ θανάτου πάλιν εἰς τὸ ζῆν ἀποκατάστασις ("instead of death, being restored to life again").

Also, Eusebius, precisely like Origen (see especially in *Homilies on Jeremiah* 14.18 and *Commentary on Matthew* 17.19), read Peter's words in Acts 3:21—which he repeatedly cites—as a reference to the eventual universal restoration. In *Against Marcellus,* he explains Peter's expression, "the times of universal restoration," as the world to come, in which all beings will receive their perfect restoration:

> What else does the expression 'until the times of *apokatastasis*' [ἄχρι χρόνων ἀποκαταστάσεως] indicate to us, if not the aeon to come, in which all beings *must receive their perfect restoration* [δεῖ πάντα τῆς τελείας τυχεῖν ἀποκαταστάσεως]? [. . .] On the occasion of the restoration of absolutely all beings [τῆς ἀποκαταστάσεως ἁπάντων], as Paul says, the creation itself will pass on from slavery to freedom. For he says: 'Creation itself will be liberated from the slavery of corruption to the freedom of the glory of the children of God,' (etc).

*Against Marcellus* 2.4.11

The universality of the eventual *apokatastasis* is corroborated by Paul's words regarding the creation that will be liberated from enslavement to corruption. In *Eccl. Theol.* 3.9.1, Eusebius again cites Acts 3:21, once more connecting it to Paul's statement concerning the final liberation of all creation from corruption, in practically the same terms.[6] The similarity of the exegesis arises not

---

[6] "On the occasion of the 'restoration of all beings [τῆς ἀποκαταστάσεως ἁπάντων],' as Paul says, the creation itself will pass on from slavery to freedom. For he says: 'Creation itself will be liberated from the slavery of corruption to the freedom of the glory of the children of God.'"

only from the dependence on Origen's exegesis in both cases, but also from the common criticism of Marcellus of Ancyra's thought developed by Eusebius in both passages. The same interpretation of Acts 3:21 and the same criticism of Marcellus are found again at *Eccl. Theol.* 3.13.1–3.[7] And at *Eccl. Theol.* 3.14.2, Eusebius compares the "times of universal restoration" mentioned in Acts 3:21 to the second coming of Christ, assembling several Pauline statements on it.[8]

The final *apokatastasis* is described by Eusebius as a work of divine Providence, which brings about a rectification (διόρθωσις) of sin and the restoration of human nature to its original condition:

> What most fits piety is [. . .] to rectify [ἐπιδιορθοῦσθαι] the first sin by means of subsequent good deeds and the speedy return and restoration to what is proper and familiar [ἐπὶ τὴν τῶν οἰκείων. . .ἀποκατάστασιν]. For the end [τέλος] of humanity is not here on earth, nor the return to corruption and destruction, but above there, from where the first human being fell.
>
> *Preparation for the Gospel* 7.18.9

This is a thoroughly Origenian description of *apokatastasis*, identified with the very *telos* of humanity, in line with a notion that was already suggested by Clement of Alexandria.[9] Even the detail that *apokatastasis* is toward τὰ οἰκεῖα exactly reflects Origen's declaration that ἀποκατάστασίς ἐστιν εἰς τὰ οἰκεῖα, which in turn will be picked up by Gregory of Nyssa.[10] The idea that the *apokatastasis* is a work of divine Providence, and specifically dependent on Christ, is another important trait that Eusebius shares with Origen. Eusebius expresses it

---

7  "In the Acts of the Apostles Peter says, concerning our Savior, that heaven must keep him until the times of *apokatastasis* [ἄχρι χρόνων ἀποκαταστάσεως]. But Marcellus does not grasp the meaning of what is said and on the basis of this passage endeavors to circumscribe the duration of the reign of Christ, claiming that, by saying 'until the times of *apokatastasis*,' Scripture indicates a limit in the duration of his reign. He states that the same results also from the Psalm that says, 'Sit to my right, until I put your enemies as a stool for your feet'; and for this reason the apostle Paul said: 'For it is necessary for him to reign until he has put his enemies under his feet.' Indeed, Marcellus understood that 'until' in these passages indicates a limitation of time."

8  "Also the words, 'Sit to my right, until I have put your enemies as a stool for your feet,' and 'heaven must keep him until the times of *apokatastasis*,' have not been said in the sense that he will be no longer afterwards, but in the sense that, at the end of all, he will rise up from the throne of the Father and descend from heaven for the second time. The apostle teaches about this second descent by saying: 'The Lord himself, at an order, at the voice of an archangel, at the trumpet of God will descend from heaven, and first the dead will rise in Christ.'" For the translation of the last sentence, from 1 Thess 4:16, see Ramelli and Konstan 2007:579–593.

9  According to Clement, Paul teaches that "the *telos* is the hoped-for *apokatastasis*." See Ramelli 2013, section on Clement.

10  See Ramelli 2010. On Origen's Christian adaptation of the doctrine of *oikeiōsis* see eadem forthcoming b.

in *Commentary on Isaiah* 2.9, in which he explains, with Origen, that Christ-Logos, being the Way to the Father, purifies all those who run that way, leaving nobody contaminated by sin, and can thereby restore all to the Father: "Therefore, the Logos who is salvific [ὁ σωτήριος] and leads to the Father those who run his way and restores [ἀποκαθιστάς] them to the Kingdom of Heaven [. . .] there is nobody who travels this way and remains unpurified [ἀκάθαρτος]."

On another plane, Eusebius uses the notion of *apokatastasis* to express the action of restoration to life or health that was performed by Christ in his miracles; what is remarkable is that he too, like Origen, interprets this action on both the physical and the spiritual level, so that healing and resurrection also mean restoration.[11] The most interesting passage is *Fragments on Luke* PG 24.580.21–24, in which the double level of physical and spiritual healing and restoration is manifest: "first he will *restore* [ἀποκατασήσει] *them to salvation and health*, having opened the eyes of the blind and *healed every illness of their souls*; then he will prepare for them the spiritual banquet" (emphasis mine). Also, the notion of therapeutic and purifying punishments followed by the eventual *apokatastasis* is typical of Origen and reflected in Eusebius' *Demonstration of the Gospel* 10.6.3: "First they will be punished for their education [παιδευθέντες] for a short time; then they will be restored again [αὖθις ἀποκατασταθήσονται]." The basic concept of *apokatastasis* as a return to one's original condition (expressed by Eusebius, just as by Origen and Nyssen, with τὸ ἀρχαῖον) after an alteration has taken place, is expounded in *Eccl. Theol.* 2.9.4: "At first she was one thing; then she became something else, and then she is restored again to her original state [πάλιν εἰς τὸ ἀρχαῖον ἀποκαθισταμένην]." Eusebius, in *Preparation for the Gospel* 15.19.1–2, also reports the Stoic concept of *apokatastasis*, with which Origen had dealt a great deal, painstakingly underlying the differences between his own, Christian notion of *apokatastasis* and the Stoic one, characterized by necessity and by an infinite repetition of aeons.[12]

Eusebius was well acquainted with Origen's *Homilies on Jeremiah*, in which the reflection on the eventual *apokatastasis* is prominent because of the insistence on the theme of the restoration/return of Israel, which Origen saw as an allusion to the final *apokatastasis*. Eusebius too cites Jeremiah, expressly naming him, in reference to the *apokatastasis* in *Commentary on Psalms* PG 23.92.7: "after their fall" (διαπεσόντας), God "restores them again to their original condition" (πάλιν εἰς τὸ ἀρχαῖον ἀποκαταστῆσαι). The eventual *apokatastasis* is characterized

[11] For this duality of levels in Origen's notion of the resurrection, see Ramelli 2008; in Origen's conception of Christ's miracles, see Ramelli 2012. On Eusebius, see *Demonstration of the Gospel* 9.13.4; *Constantine's Speech to the Gathering of Saints* 11.15; cf. *Ecclesiastical History* (hereafter HE) 5.7.4.
[12] See on this Ramelli 2013, introduction and section on Origen.

in *Commentary on Psalms* 23.1049.22 as the return of all believers to unity: "the gathering of all the believers—those made worthy of the holy City of God—and their restoration to one and the same choir" (τὴν εἰς ἕνα χορὸν ἀποκατάστασιν).

Eusebius even refers the notion of *apokatastasis* to Christ's return to the Father after his incarnation, death, and resurrection, in many passages: "his divine restoration [ἀποκατάστασιν] to heaven" (HE 1.2.24); "the divine Scripture predicts, literally, the restoration [ἀποκατάστασιν] of Christ" (*Demonstration of the Gospel*[13] 4.16.42); "his restoration to God after his sojourn with humans" (DE 5.1.28); "the restoration [ἀποκατάστασιν] to the glory of God, which he has done with the help of the angelic and divine powers (DE 6.1.2); "because of his divine restoration [ἀποκατάστασιν] from the depth or because of his divine preexistence pertaining to theology" (DE 7.1.39); "for his glorious restoration/ return [ἀποκατάστασιν] to heaven" (*Commentary on Psalms* PG 23.720.6).[14] In this connection, the very transfiguration of Jesus on the mountain is presented as a figure of Jesus' restoration to his preexistent divinity in *Eccl. Theol.* 1.20.79: "he himself was seen as he was being restored [ἀποκαθιστάμενος] to a high mountain; the mountain signifies the preexistence of his divinity."

Further proofs that Eusebius adhered to Origen's doctrine of *apokatastasis* come from his polemic with Marcellus of Ancyra, whom Eusebius extensively quotes or paraphrases and whose exegesis of 1 Cor 15:28 may have influenced Gregory of Nyssa.[15] In *Against Marcellus* 2.4,[16] both he and Marcellus are taking Origen as an authority, especially with regard to the interpretation of 1 Cor 15:24–28. In Eusebius' passage, indeed, the submission of all beings to Christ and the eventual destruction of evil are announced. God, who took up humanity, will reign and, thanks to this the human being, who was deceived by the devil at the beginning, now will be constituted king by the Logos, and "will destroy all the authority and power of the devil." For "he must reign until he has put all enemies under his feet" (*C. Marc.* 2.4.1). Paul, as Eusebius reports, "says that the aim/end [τέλος] of the reign of Christ is that all be submitted to his feet [. . .] and when all are finally subjected to Christ [. . .] he himself will submit to him who has subjected all to him" (*C. Marc.* 2.4.1). Eusebius goes on to quote Marcellus, who quotes Paul in turn. Commenting on Psalm 109:1, quoted in 1 Cor 15:25, Eusebius observes that the distinction of two Lords therein ("the Lord said to my Lord ...") is due to the flesh assumed by the Son; thus it seems that the Son will sit to the Father's right only "at a certain time," when all enemies submit,

---

[13] Hereafter DE.

[14] See also *Commentary on Psalms* PG 23.312.8, where the implied reference is to Christ: "restore my soul from their bad deeds; protect my only-begotten daughter from the lions."

[15] See Hübner 1971:199–229; Hübner 1974:29–66; 283–290. See, however, the remarks in Ramelli 2011a.

[16] See Lienhard 1983:340–359.

during Christ's reign, and that the human form assumed by the Logos for the salvific economy (*C. Marc.* 2.4.7–8) will be abandoned at the end of his reign. For, after all enemies have submitted, another step begins. Indeed, Eusebius, like Origen, who in turn followed Paul's description of the *telos*, sees a further step at the end of all aeons and of Christ's reign, when all enemies have been reconciled and Christ's dominion is universal: precisely at this final stage comes the eventual *apokatastasis*. It is not only Marcellus, but Eusebius who supports this conception, since in *C. Marc.* 2.4.9–10 he continues saying that after Christ has submitted all beings (in what Origen considered to be a *salvific* submission[17]), "he will no more need this partial reign, because he will be king of *all, in a universal sense* [πάντων καθόλου]," together with God the Father (emphasis mine). In this way, Eusebius can maintain that Christ's reign will have no end, since, after reigning alone and achieving the submission of all enemies, he will hand the kingdom to the Father and will continue to reign along with the Father.

Then, Eusebius declares: "the human being, who once was deceived by the devil, thanks to the power of the Logos will be king and [. . .] will finally defeat the devil." It is notable that Eusebius explicitly describes this very fact as "the *apokatastasis.*" Indeed, it is at this point in his discussion that Eusebius inserts the reference to Acts 3:20–21, stating that the restoration of humanity and the complete triumph over evil will occur in "the times of universal *apokatastasis*" proclaimed by Acts 3:20–21. Eusebius clearly refers to this passage, presenting the times of "consolation" or "comfort" as the "times of universal restoration" (χρόνοι ἀποκαταστάσεως πάντων). As I have mentioned, Origen had already referred Acts 3:20–21 to the eventual *apokatastasis.*

Like Origen, Eusebius characterizes the final *apokatastasis* as unity.[18] He writes that "the times of universal restoration" will be when humanity attains unity (ἡνῶσθαι) with the Logos and in the future aeon all will receive complete restoration. It is significant that Eusebius uses ἀποκατάστασις again here, and *thrice* at that, to claim that "the *apokatastasis* of all" will be when all are finally liberated from captivity and can enjoy "the freedom of the glory of the children of God" (with the aforementioned quotation of Rom 8:21):

> The expression "until the times of restoration" [. . .] indicates to us the world to come, in which all beings [πάντα] must receive the perfect restoration [τῆς τελείας ἀποκαταστάσεως] [. . .] on the occasion of the *restoration of all beings* [τῆς ἀποκαταστάσεως ἀπάντων] creation itself will be transformed [. . .] from the slavery of corruption to the freedom of the glory of the children of God.
>
> *C. Marc.* 2.4.11 (emphasis mine)

---

[17] See Ramelli 2007.
[18] See the volume on John 13–17 in Novum Testamentum Patristicum, forthcoming.

Rom 8:21 was already used by Origen to describe the *apokatastasis*, especially in *Exhortation to Martyrdom* 13, in which he explains that God will reveal his treasures "when the whole creation is delivered from the bondage of the enemy into the glorious liberty of God's children." Origen evidently inspired Eusebius in this case too.

Both Eusebius and Marcellus speak Origen's language. After all aeons, they maintain, there will come the restoration, the *telos*, as in Origen's view.[19] The *telos* (1 Cor 15:24) will be after the sequence of all aeons, the submission of all enemies, and the elimination of evil, when Christ hands his kingdom to the Father (*C. Marc.* 2.4.12). This *telos*, after the Judgment, will conform to God's Providence (τῇ αὐτοῦ προνοίᾳ. . .τέλους τεύξεται). Again, the idea expressed here by Eusebius, that the eventual *apokatastasis* in the *telos* is the triumph of God's Providence, is a characteristic of Origen's *apokatastasis* doctrine.[20] From Origen, Diodore of Tarsus inherited it as well.[21]

Some of Marcellus' ideas are criticized by Eusebius in *C. Marc.* 2.4.13–14; in particular, Eusebius attacks his notion that the Logos will lose human flesh after the Judgment, the universal rectification (διόρθωσις), and the disappearance of all opposing powers. What is most remarkable in relation to my present argument is that Eusebius does not criticize the concept of the eventual vanishing of evil and universal rectification, which coincides with *apokatastasis*; rather, he takes on other issues concerning Christ and his keeping or discarding his humanity in the *telos*. Moreover, Marcellus only spoke of Christ as the Logos. Eusebius is concerned with criticizing Marcellus' Christology and, more generally, his Trinitarian "monoprosopic" theology,[22] rather than his eschatological notion of *apokatastasis* (*C. Marc.* 2.4.18–22). This is evident from the subsequent section, in which Eusebius' refutation develops exclusively on the Christological plane. But when Marcellus speaks of universal rectification and restoration, Eusebius has no objection whatsoever; indeed, he explicitly describes the scenario depicted by Paul in 1 Cor 15:24–28 as the eventual *apokatastasis*, the universal restoration that will take place in the *telos*. This is also why in *C. Marc.* 2.4.28 Eusebius defines Christ "the common savior of absolutely all."

Another work in which Eusebius criticizes ideas of Marcellus of Ancyra other than the doctrine of *apokatastasis* (which he endorses) is *Ecclesiastical Theology*. Here, at 2.8, Eusebius challenges Marcellus for, in his view, rejecting

---

[19]  Tzamalikos 2006:272–309; Ramelli 2010a.
[20]  See Ramelli 2011b.
[21]  See Ramelli 2013, section on Diodore.
[22]  See on this Ramelli 2011.

the begetting of the Son. However, Eusebius does not object to the doctrine of the final universal restoration. After the judgment, the following progression is delineated:

- First, the "rectification of all" or "setting right of all things" (τὴν τῶν ἀπάντων διόρθωσιν);

- next, "the disappearance of any opposing power";

- and then the submission of the Son to the Father, "so that the Logos will be in God, as it was before the world existed."

- After the end of this action, the Logos will be one with God, that God may be "all in all" (1 Cor 15:28 is quoted here).

This is Origen's conception of the *apokatastasis* as unity, which Eusebius does not attack; he only criticizes Marcellus' view that for a time the Logos was not with God. Eusebius returns to 1 Cor 15:28 in *Eccl. Theol.* 3.14–16, 18–20. In 3.14, he opposes Marcellus's conception of the Son and his interpretation of two crucial passages: Ps 109:1 (= 1 Cor 15:25) and Acts 3:21. Again, he explicitly refers "the times of universal restoration" of the latter passage to the submission of all to Christ. He refers 1 Thess 4:16 to the second coming of Christ: the Lord will descend from heaven, the dead will rise, and "we shall be always with the Lord." For "the Lord must remain in heaven until the end / accomplishment [ἕως τῆς συντελείας]. Then, at the end of all he will make his second and glorious coming, and will take his saints with him, so that they will be always with him, without end." Eusebius quotes 1 Cor 15:25–28 in full and insists that Marcellus in his exegesis was mistaken, but only on Christological and theological matters, and not on the universal *apokatastasis* itself. 1 Cor 15:28, Eusebius argues, does not predict a "universal confusion" of substances, but the spontaneous submission of all. This is in line with Origen's interpretation of these verses: the eventual submission of all to Christ and thence to God will be spontaneous and will coincide with the salvation of all. Eusebius too stresses that 1 Cor 15:26–28 predicts a universal submission that will be spontaneous and will coincide with universal salvation. Therefore, Christ is given glory as "the savior of *all in a universal sense*," because he will render all worthy of God:

When the apostle says that all beings [τὰ πάντα] will submit to the Son, he did not indicate a substantial union, but the voluntary obedience and glory [. . .] which *all beings* [τὰ πάντα] will render to him qua Savior and King *of all in a universal sense* [τῶν ὅλων]. In the same way, also the fact that he will submit to the Father means nothing else but [. . .] the voluntary obedience that he too will render to God the Father, *once he has prepared all* [τοὺς πάντας], that they may *become worthy* [ἀξίους] of the divinity of the Father.

*Eccl. Theol.* 3.15.3–6 (emphasis mine)

Soon after, Eusebius emphasizes that Christ is "the savior of *all in a universal sense*," and his reign will be rectifying and healing, according to a notion that was dear to Clement and Origen:[23]

Whenever they are unworthy [οὐκ ἄξιοι] of it, he himself, qua common Savior of absolutely all [κοινὸς ἁπάντων σωτήρ], assumes his reign, which *rectifies those creatures that are still imperfect and heals those which need healing* [διορθωτικὴν τῶν ἀτελῶν καὶ θεραπευτικὴν τῶν θεραπείας δεομένων] and thus he reigns, by putting the enemies of his kingdom under his feet.

*Eccl. Theol.* 3.15.6 (emphasis mine)

Christ's reign is thus the eschatological period during which Christ will exercise his power as Physician and during which the universal rectification will take place. In this way he will make all worthy of the encounter with the Father and of the enjoyment of eternal life. Eternal life will belong to those "worthy of the Kingdom," but Eusebius has just stated that Christ will make all worthy of it. All will then submit in a "salvific submission" (σωτήριον ὑποταγήν). This will coincide with the *apokatastasis*, which is described as θέωσις. As Origen did, Eusebius links the eschatological picture in 1 Cor 15 to Phil 3:20–21,[24] both passages that proclaim the eschatological submission of all to Christ. In *Eccl. Theol.* 3.15–16, Eusebius insists on the salvific character (again σωτήριον ὑποταγήν) of the eventual universal (τὰ πάντα) submission. In this perspective, if submission is universal, salvation too will involve all. In this way, Christ will be the source of "all goods," for all: Eusebius interprets the statement that "God will be all in all" (1 Cor 15:28) exactly as Origen has done. This will be the "perfect accomplishment" of the teaching of Paul concerning the *telos*: that God may be "all in all."

This eventuality was foretold in the Old Testament: God will inhabit not only a few who are worthy (βραχεῖς τοὺς ἀξίους), as is the case now, but "all" (ἅπασιν), who "will then have become worthy of the Kingdom." Origen likewise claimed that in the *telos* "not only in few or in many, but in *all* God will be all" (*On First Principles* 3.6.3). Eusebius adds that the Godhead will be "all in all" by offering itself to all (πᾶσιν) according to each one's capacity, which is also

---

[23] See Ramelli 2011b.
[24] See Ramelli 2005:139–158.

drawn from Origen; Gregory of Nyssa, too, an active reader of both Origen and Eusebius, elaborates on this idea.

*Apokatastasis* is described by Eusebius as "the culmination of the most blessed hope" (τῆς τρισμακαρίας ἐλπίδος . . . τῷ τέλει)[25] and identified with the very *telos*, when God will be "all *in all*" and will fill *all* (ἐμπιπλῶν τοὺς πάντας) and when the Son will rejoice in God's salvific action, here called κατόρθωμα or morally perfect action, and will continue in his never-ending reign. He will hand, safe, to the Father "all [πάντας] those who are ruled by him," or "his kingdom." Christ will return "all" to the Father once he has made all of them (τοὺς πάντας) perfect (τελειωθέντας), saved and completely healed (σώαν καὶ κατὰ πάντα ἐρρωμένην τὴν παραθήκην), after having sanctified them all as high priest. Even this last detail echoes Origen's exegesis of Hebrews.[26] "All" will be able to enjoy the Father's ineffable goods. Soon after, Eusebius expands on this: "God will then be 'in all [ἐν πᾶσιν],' namely those who have been made perfect by the Son [τοῖς ὑπὸ τῷ υἱῷ τελειωθεῖσιν][. . .] the Son will hand the Kingdom to God, showing him safe those with whom he was entrusted [σώαν τὴν παραθήκην] and prepared to adore God and to be saints; and God will be 'all in all,' becoming all to them."

Two other times Eusebius describes the final *apokatastasis* as the "the culmination of the most blessed hope," both at the end of the above-quoted passage, where it concerns the Son and "all the others" (λοιποῖς ἅπασιν), and in 3.18: "the most blessed *telos*" will be when the divinity, the supreme Good, will give itself as a gift to those who constitute the kingdom of Christ and have been saved and perfected by Christ during his reign, so that God will be all in all. Soon afterward, this final blessedness is again described as unity, according to Jesus's great prayer in John 17,[27] that all be "perfected into unity." Indeed, Eusebius, like Origen, strongly insists on unity, with quotations from John, especially John 17. In his view, as in Origen's,[28] all humanity's unity with God in the *apokatastasis* will be not a confusion of substance (συναλοιφὴν μιᾶς οὐσίας), but supreme perfection in virtue (τελείωσιν τῆς εἰς ἄκρον ἀρετῆς), to which "all" (οἱ ἄντες) will be led, once "made perfect" (τέλειοι κατεργασθέντες). All (οἱ πάντες) will achieve unity with God. As the Son is one with the Father, so will "all" imitate this oneness (πάντας). This is all Origenian material. Eusebius interprets other Old and New Testament passages as referring to the eventual *apokatastasis*, and

---

[25] Gregory of Nyssa *In Illud: Tunc et Ipse Filius* 13 analogously describes it as τὸ πέρας τῶν ἐλπιζομένων.

[26] See Ramelli 2008a:210–221.

[27] See the volume on John 13–17 in *Novum Testamentum Patristicum*, in preparation.

[28] See the item "Deification / Theosis" forthcoming in EBR: *Encyclopedia of the Bible and Its Reception*, vol. 6, Berlin 2013.

concludes with an anti-heretical statement: unity does not mean mixing up Father and Son in their hypostases,[29] nor humanity and divinity in their οὐσίαι. It is therefore clear that, exactly like Origen and Gregory of Nyssa,[30] Eusebius supports the doctrine of *apokatastasis* in a context of defense of orthodoxy.

In his exegesis of Luke[31] as well, Eusebius shows his close, albeit creative, adherence to Origen's eschatological conceptions. Here, Eusebius manifests the same choice as Origen, who had composed both *Homilies on Luke*—thirty-nine of which survive in Jerome's translation and in fragments—and a commentary on Luke, which is lost apart from some uncertain catenary fragments.[32] Indeed, the only patristic exegetical works on Luke that survive are Origen's homilies, 156 homilies by Cyril of Alexandria, handed down in Syriac, and ten books of Ambrose's *Expositions on the Gospel of Luke*, the first two of which depend closely on Origen, plus fragments from the homilies of Titus of Bostra.

What is more, in PG 24.549.6-36 Eusebius presents a description of the *telos* that is immersed in universalism, like that of Origen, and precisely follows Origen's very scheme, that in the end not only a *few* will be in communion with God, but *all* ("and not only in a few or in many, but *in all* God will be all, when there will be no more death, nor death's sting, nor evil, absolutely; then God will truly be 'all in all,'" *On First Principles* 3.6.3). It is notable that Origen expressed the very same idea precisely in his exegesis of Luke, by which Eusebius was clearly inspired for his own interpretation of that gospel: "John [*sc.* the Baptist] converts many; the Lord converts, not only many, but all. For this is the work of the Lord: to convert *all* to God the Father" (*Homilies on Luke* 4).

Eusebius even reiterates this scheme—*not only a few*, as in the present, *but all*, in the *telos*—thrice in just a few lines. At lines 8–13, he observes that, at the Transfiguration, only Moses and Elijah and three disciples were with Christ, but "at the end of the world, when the Lord comes with the glory of his Father, *not only* [οὐκέτι μόνον] Moses and Elijah will escort him, and *not only* three [οὐδὲ τρεῖς μόνοι] disciples will be with him, *but all* [ἀλλὰ πάντες] the prophets, the patriarchs, and the just will be." Again, at lines 19–25, Eusebius remarks that the

---

[29] See Ramelli 2012a.

[30] Origen supported it against Gnosticism and Gregory of Nyssa against Arianism. See Ramelli 2011ab.

[31] On which, see Johnson 2010.

[32] A problem with these fragments is that it is not always certain whether they come from the commentary on Matthew or that on Luke. Some scholars think that in the commentary on Matthew, which survives partially, Origen also commented on the parallels in Luke, so that in the commentary on Luke he only had to concentrate on the passages that are exclusive to Luke. See Lienhard 2009:xxxvi–xxxviii. Other colleagues, such as Tzamalikos 2012, 2012a, and 2012b, hypothesize that confusions in the attribution to the works on Luke or that on Matthew are due to the catenists.

divinity was only partially manifested, and only to Moses, but in the *telos* it will be manifested to all the saints, so that all will be able (δύνασθαι πάντας) to say that they have seen the glory of the Lord with an unveiled face.

The most important passage, and the most explicitly universalistic, is at the end of the short section I am considering, but its structure is the very same as that of the other two. Eusebius remarks that at the Transfiguration only three disciples fell down upon their faces, but in the *telos* "*no longer only* three disciples like at that time" (οὐκέτι ὥσπερ τότε οἱ τρεῖς μαθηταὶ μόνοι), but every knee will bend before the Lord, definitely "*all* knees" (πᾶν γόνυ) of all creatures in heaven, on earth, and in the underworld (with reference to Phil 2:10–11). Moreover, the conflation of Phil 2:10–11 and 1 Cor 15:24–28 for the description of the *telos* is typical of Origen,[33] and Eusebius continues it here.

Eusebius describes the eventual *apokatastasis* in *Commentary on Isaiah* 1.85 as well, calling it "the culmination of the goods" foreseen by the prophets, again with a reference to Acts 3:20–21, the importance of which for Eusebius' and Origen's view of the final *apokatastasis* I have already illustrated. Eusebius adds, in this connection, that the eventual restoration is in fact the ἀρχαία βουλή or "original intention" or "will" established by God "before the creation of the world and fulfilled at the end of the aeons" and described in Paul's terms as the submission of all enemies and destruction of evil and death,[34] when God will be "all in all" at the end of all aeons. The annihilation of evil is, in Eusebius as in Origen and Gregory, a *conditio sine qua non* for the eventual *apokatastasis*, and at the same time a robust argument in defense of it. The very notion that universal restoration will come at the end of all aeons is in perfect line with Origen's philosophy of history and eschatology.[35]

Following Isaiah's text, Eusebius foretells punishment for sinners, expressed in the form of the destruction of their cities in Isa 25:2. At the same time, however, he also predicts that the inhabitants will be saved and will escape from ruin (διασωθέντες). He praises Jesus as helper and defender, who will even save the pagans, although idolaters. The latter, in fact, would be "hopeless," and this is why Isa 25:8 says that "death swallowed" them, but Christ, whom Eusebius has just named the "Savior of all," frees them from error and spiritual death and prevents so many souls from perishing: "The Savior of all, who loves humanity, having liberated the souls of human beings from death [. . .] removed *every* tear from *every* face, [. . .] thus sparing the perdition of so many souls, out of his love for humanity." Within the same framework, Eusebius interprets Isa 25:8 as announcing the eventual eviction and disappearance of death, which had ruled

---

[33] See Ramelli 2010b.

[34] Πάσης κακίας ἐκποδὼν ἀρθείσης καὶ τοῦ ἐσχάτου ἐχθροῦ τοῦ θανάτου καταργηθέντος.

[35] See Tzamalikos 2007 and Ramelli 2010a.

over all; this eviction is indeed foretold in 1 Cor 15:26. Death, the destroyer of all humans, will be destroyed: "the Lord will destroy it so that it will not appear any more in any place [. . .] thus the last enemy, death, will be annihilated [. . .] the one who once destroyed all [τοὺς πάντας] will be destroyed." Eusebius, like Origen,[36] conceives of death as both physical and spiritual, and says that it will be eliminated thanks to Christ's salvific action for all, who will achieve eternal life, once liberated from evil (προτέρων ἠλευθερωμένοι κακῶν) and made by Christ worthy of God's promises (τῶν δ' ἐπαγγελιῶν τοῦ θεοῦ καταξιωθησόμενοι). According to Origen's and Eusebius' twofold conception of death, what Eusebius has described is liberation (not only from physical death, but from evil) and justification.

The punishment of Moab, as mentioned in Isa 16 and Jer 31, is contrasted by Eusebius with blessedness, but it is significant that Moab does not represent any part of humanity. It rather represents the powers of evil; what applies to Moab in the prophets is seen by Eusebius as referring to the opposing powers. Eusebius stresses the final destruction of death and adverse powers, in contrast with the humans' salvation; he does not speak of destruction or eternal damnation of human beings. When he mentions human creatures worthy of the promises (τῶν ἐπαγγελιῶν ἄξιοι), he indicates those who will have been rendered worthy by Christ. They will dwell in Jerusalem, that is, Christ himself, who will be "all" (πάντα) for all of them, with further reference to 1 Cor 15:28 and God's eventually being "all in all."

Eusebius clearly depends on Origen's doctrine of *apokatastasis* in several respects, and in particular in his exegesis of 1 Cor 15:28, a biblical pillar for Origen's doctrine of *apokatastasis*.[37] Origen's exegesis in turn proves extremely influential on Gregory of Nyssa, in *De Anima et Resurrectione* and *In Illud: Tunc et Ipse Filius*. As Origen in *Princ.* 3.5.7 opposes a subordinationistic interpretation of 1 Cor 15:28, Gregory opposes its "Arian" subordinationistic interpretation. He explains that Paul's statement indicates, not the Son's inferiority to the Father, but rather all humanity's salvific submission.[38] The background provided by Origen for Gregory's *In Illud* is evident in every passage of this work. The fact that Eusebius interprets 1 Cor 15:28 in the same way as Origen and, later, Gregory of Nyssa depends on his adherence to Origen's doctrine of ὁμοουσία between the Father and the Son and an anti-subordinationistic conception of their relationship. This may sound surprising in the light of the accusations of "Arianism" or "semi-Arianism" leveled against Eusebius, but in fact it is a natural consequence of his profound adherence to Origen's thought. Origen's

---

[36]  See Ramelli 2008.
[37]  See Ramelli 2007:313–356.
[38]  See Ramelli 2011a.

anti-subordinationism and his concept of ὁμοουσία between the Father and the Son have been demonstrated and it can even be asked whether it was through Eusebius that Constantine supported the inclusion of ὁμοούσιος in the Nicene creed.[39] Indeed, Christoph Markschies recently remarked that Eusebius is, not only an Origenian in general, but an Origenian *theologian*.[40] Nonetheless, this aspect in particular has scarcely been acknowledged or studied. It is hoped that the preceding examination will contribute to such an appreciation.

[39] Ramelli 2011:21–49. Beeley 2008:433–452, on Eusebius' Christology in his *Against Marcellus, Ecclesiastical Theology*, and *Theophany*, also rightly countered the interpretation of Eusebius' theology as subordinationistic and "semi-Arian."

[40] Markschies 2007:223–238.

# Works Cited

Beeley, C. A. 2008. "Eusebius's *Contra Marcellum*. Anti-Modalist Doctrine and Orthodox Christology." *Zeitschrift für Antikes Christentum* 12:433–452.

Edwards, M. J. 2007. "Notes on the Date and Venue of the Oration to the Saints (CPG 3497)." *Byzantion* 77:149–169.

Hübner, R. 1971. "Gregor von Nyssa und Markell von Ankyra." In *Écriture et culture philosophique dans la pensée de Grégoire de Nysse*, ed. M. Harl, 199–229. Leiden.

Hübner, R. 1974. *Die Einheit des Leibes Christi bei Gregor von Nyssa*. Leiden.

Johnson, A. 2010. "The Tenth Book of Eusebius' *General Elementary Introduction*: A Critique of the Wallace-Hadrill Thesis." *Journal of Theological Studies* 62:144–160.

Kannengiesser, C. 1992. "Eusebius of Caesarea, Origenist." In *Eusebius, Christianity, and Judaism*, ed. Attridge, H. and G. Hata, 435–466. Leiden.

Lienhard, J. 1983. "The Exegesis of 1 Corr. 15:28 from Marcellus of Ancyra to Theodoret of Cyrus." *Vigiliae Christianae* 37:340–359.

Lienhard, J. 2009, second ed. (original ed. 1996). *Origen: Homilies on Luke.* Washington, DC.

Markschies, C. 2007. "Eusebius als Schriftsteller. Beobachtungen zum sechsten Buch der Kirchengeschichte." In *Origenes und sein Erbe: Gesammelte Studien.* Berlin.

Ramelli, I. 2005. "'Nostra autem conversatio in caelis est' (Phil. 3.20)." *Sileno* 31:139–158.

———. 2007. "Christian Soteriology and Christian Platonism." *Vigiliae Christianae* 61:313–356.

———. 2008. "Origen's Exegesis of Jeremiah: Resurrection Announced throughout the Bible and its Twofold Conception." *Augustinianum* 48:59–78.

———. 2008a. "The Universal and Eternal Validity of Jesus's Priestly Sacrifice: The Epistle to the Hebrews in Support of Origen's Theory of Apokatastasis." In *A Cloud of Witnesses: The Theology of Hebrews in Its Ancient Contexts*, ed. R.J. Bauckham, D.R. Driver, T.A. Hart, and N. MacDonald, 210–221. London.

———. 2010. "The Doctrine of Oikeiōsis in Gregory of Nyssa's Theological Thought: Reconstructing Gregory's Creative Reception of Stoicism," Lecture delivered at the Twelfth International Colloquium on Gregory of Nyssa, Leuven, 14–17 September. Forthcoming in the proceedings. Leiden.

———. 2010a. "Αἰώνιος and Αἰών in Origen and Gregory of Nyssa." *Studia Patristica* 47:57–62.

————. 2010b. "*In Illud: Tunc et Ipse Filius*. . . (1 Corr 15,27–28): Gregory of Nyssa's Exegesis, Its Derivations from Origen, and Early Patristic Interpretations Related to Origen's." *Studia Patristica* 44:259–274.

————. 2011. "Origen's Anti-Subordinationism and Its Heritage in the Nicene and Cappadocian Line." *Vigiliae Christianae* 65:21–49.

————. 2011a. "The Trinitarian Theology of Gregory of Nyssa in his *In Illud: Tunc et ipse Filius*: His Polemic against 'Arian' Subordinationism and the Apokatastasis." In *Gregory of Nyssa: The Minor Treatises on Trinitarian Theology and Apollinarism. Proceedings of the 11th International Colloquium on Gregory of Nyssa (Tübingen, 17-20 September 2008)*, ed. V.H. Drecoll and M. Berghaus, 445–478. Leiden.

————. 2011b. "Origen and Apokatastasis: A Reassessment." In *Origeniana Decima*, ed. Kaczmarek, S. and H. Pietras, 649–670. Leuven.

————. 2012. "Disability in Bardaisan and Origen. Between the Stoic *Adiaphora* and the Lord's Grace." In *Gestörte Lektüre*, ed. M. Schiefer, 141–159. Stuttgart.

————. 2012a. "Origen, Greek Philosophy, and the Birth of the Trinitarian Meaning of Hypostasis." *Harvard Theological Review* 105:302–350.

————. Forthcoming. *The Christian Doctrine of Apokatastasis: A Critical Assessment From the New Testament to Eriugena.*

————. Forthcoming a. "*Strom.* 7 and Clement's Hints to the Theory of Apokatastasis." Proceedings of the International Colloquium Clementinum, Olomouc, 21–23 October 2010. Leiden.

————. Forthcoming b. "The Stoic Doctrine of *Oikeiōsis* and its Transformation by the Christian Platonist Origen."

Ramelli, I. and D. Konstan. 2007. "The Syntax of ἐν χριστῷ in 1 Thess 4:16." *Journal of Biblical Literature* 126:579–593.

————. 2011. *Terms for Eternity. Aionios and Aidios in Classical and Christian Authors.* New edition. Piscataway, NJ.

Sirinelli, J. 1961. *Les vues historiques d'Eusèbe de Césarée.* Dakar.

Trisoglio, F. 1978. "Eusebio di Cesarea e l'escatologia." *Augustinianum* 18:173–182.

Tzamalikos, P. 2006. *Origen: Cosmology and Ontology of Time.* Leiden.

————. 2007. *Origen: Philosophy of History and Eschatology.* Leiden.

————. 2012. *The Real Cassian Revisited: Monastic Life, Greek Paideia, and Origenism in the Sixth Century.* Leiden.

————. 2012a. *An Ancient Commentary on the Book of Revelation: A Critical Edition of the Scholia in Apocalypsin.* Leiden.

————. 2012b. *A Newly Discovered Greek Father: Cassian the Sabaite Eclipsed by John Cassian of Marseilles.* Leiden.

# 16

# Eusebius and Lactantius
## Rhetoric, Philosophy, and Christian Theology[1]

### Kristina A. Meinking

PHILOSOPHERS AND THEOLOGIANS of antiquity had long held that the supreme god was impassible and thus not subject to emotions. In his *De ira Dei*, however, Lactantius argues that the Christian God does have emotions and that anger, in particular, is critical to the divine nature. My aim in this essay is to outline the basic contours of Lactantius' argument and to suggest its significance, not only on its own, but also as a counter to Eusebius. Indeed, by examining Lactantius, we can better understand Eusebius. Both apologists lived through and wrote about the same historical events, both were steeped in the classical rhetorical tradition, and both manipulated that tradition in order to represent Christianity in very specific ways. Yet in corpus and in theological persuasion, these two Christian intellectuals maintained decidedly different opinions. In what follows, I argue that, in *De ira Dei*, we see the hallmarks and effects—strategic and unnoticed, intentional and conditioned—of an intellectual tradition that stands in marked contrast to that of Eusebius. These distinctions are especially apparent in two facets of the treatise: Lactantius' treatment of philosophers and his mode of argument. In both cases, where we would expect to see a privileging of philosophical hermeneutics and argumentation, we find instead the employment and elevation of Latin rhetorical discourse.

Scholars have long noted that Eusebius drew upon his rhetorical training across the constituent genres of his corpus and have likewise carefully studied his theological arguments in light of the rhetorical moves that he makes

---

[1] My thanks are owed to Aaron Johnson and Jeremy Schott for their invitation to be a part of the 2011 panel and to contribute to this volume. I have appreciated their advice and keen editorial eyes along the way, as well as the comments and suggestions of those present at the session.

therein.[2] In this way, Eusebius the theologian is markedly representative of the broader state of fourth-century Christian studies. Rhetorical influences in the works of John Chrysostom and Origen have also been examined for both their technical and their theological argument.[3] In all of these cases, rhetoric has been conceptualized as the handmaiden to theology and as an underpinning of a theologian's reading and reception of, especially, biblical texts. At the same time, the long tradition of Greek (and mostly Platonic) philosophy has been seen as the mechanism by which these theologians interpreted their sacred texts. Similarly, the arguments maintained by such philosophers were those with which Greek-writing Christian intellectuals are thought to have aligned their own theological claims. Despite a handful of author-based studies, for example, of Tertullian, Arnobius, and even Lactantius, little attention has been paid to the ways in which Christian intellectuals of the Latin tradition crafted their contributions to Christian theology.[4] That is to say that, although a general awareness of the importance of the rhetorical tradition has shaped the relevant scholarship about these individuals, our focus should now be on the consequences of different traditions of rhetorical training and techniques on Christian theology.

Lactantius' display of his rhetorical education and the tradition of which it is representative in *De ira Dei* also brings the effects of Eusebius' rhetorical training into clearer view. Two facets of *De ira Dei* will prove useful in determining the extent to which each apologist relied on similar or divergent traditions: first, the allusions to biblical texts; and, second, the rhetorical argumentation of the text. Lactantius' use of these methods is both pedestrian and at the same time unique. On the one hand, Lactantius reflexively and unconsciously draws upon his educational (and vocational) training, as do others like Origen and Eusebius. Yet, despite their shared description as "rhetorical," the educations and traditions of these two Greek-writing intellectuals remain distinct from that of Lactantius. On the other hand, however, the very nature of his Latin rhetorical training caused Lactantius to shape a different argument and, more crucially, to approach the theological problems at hand in a significantly different way.

One of the most obvious places that we would expect to find mention of divine wrath is in Lactantius' chronicle of the persecutions in his *De Mortibus Persecutorum*, a text which has parallels in Book 8 of Eusebius' *Historia Ecclesiastica*. Yet it is here that the idea of God's anger is surprisingly absent. Lactantius'

---

[2]  The bibliography here is vast, but Barnes 1981 and Drake 1976 have been particular influences on the present study.
[3]  Cameron 1994, Mitchell 2002 and 2005, Young 1997a and 1997b.
[4]  Barnes 1985, Simmons 1995, Digeser 2000.

prefatory comments indicate both relief at the end of persecution and conviction that those who offend God will eventually be punished:

> They who insulted the divinity lie low, they who cast down the holy
> temple are fallen with more tremendous ruin, and the tormentors of
> just men have poured out their guilty souls amidst plagues inflicted by
> heaven, and amidst deserved tortures. For God delayed to punish them
> that, by great and marvelous examples, he might teach posterity that
> he alone is God, and that with fit vengeance he executes judgment on
> the proud, the impious, and the persecutors.

Lactantius, *De Mortibus Persecutorum* 1.5–7[5]

The list begins with Nero and continues through Galerius and the eventual
triumph of Constantine (and Licinius), increasing in detail with each successive
emperor. Given Lactantius' expressed plan to show how the punishment of God
was meted out, some consideration of the anger that led to punishment seems
warranted. Yet there is no exploration of divine wrath, and only one mention
of it, wherein Aurelian is described as having "provoked the anger of God."[6] The
emphasis instead is on God as punisher (*vindex*) and on his judgment, and not on
the necessity of anger to these roles.

We see Eusebius taking a similar approach in his discussion of the persecutions, with one important exception: while Lactantius is focused on the description of God's punishment against the persecutors, Eusebius initially envisions
the persecutions as punishment for lax Christian attitudes and behaviors.[7]
Conflict and dissent among Christian leaders and congregations are here seen
as reasons for divine judgment (8.1.7), with a biblical quotation (Lamentations
2:1–2) about God's wrath provided as justification. Later in the book, divine
judgment is linked not to Christian suffering, but rather to God's punishment

---

[5] "Qui insultaverant deo, iacent, qui templum sanctum everterant, ruina maiore ceciderunt, qui
iustos excarnificaverunt, caelestibus plagis et cruciatibus meritis nocentes animas profuderunt.
Sero id quidem, sed graviter ac digne. Distulerat enim poenas eorum deus, ut ederet in eos
magna et mirabilia exempla, quibus posteri discerent et deum esse unum et eundem iudicem
digna vid<elicet> supplicia impiis ac persecutoribus inrogare."

[6] Lactantius, *De Mortibus Persecutorum* 1.6.1: "Aurelianus, qui esset natura vesanus et praeceps,
quamvis captivitatem Valeriani meminisset, tamen oblitus sceleris eius et poenae iram dei
crudelibus factis lacessivit." '*Ira*' appears three times in this text, as compared to sixty-two times
in *De ira Dei*.

[7] Eusebius, *Historia Ecclesiastica* 8.1.7. In taking this hard line against Christians themselves,
Eusebius' claims closely resemble those of Cyprian, d.258, whose work Lactantius, at least, knew
and admired (*Divinae Institutiones* 5.1.24–25).

of Galerius (8.16.3); this is also, interestingly, the only point in the book where God's anger is directly mentioned (8.16.2).[8]

Both *De Mortibus Persecutorum* and *Historia Ecclesiastica* were designed to serve specific apologetic purposes, yet even these purportedly historical accounts betray the theological opinions of their authors. Lactantius and Eusebius invoke the rhetoric of God's punishment as evidence of his judgment and his wrath in what they deem to be an appropriate context; elsewhere each writer makes a significantly different claim about the existence and function of divine emotions. In *Divine Institutes* 2.17.3–5, Lactantius tell us that God:

> suffers men to stray and to fail in duty even to himself while he remains just, gentle, and patient. In him is perfect virtue: perfect patience is necessarily in him also. Hence the view of some people that God does not even get angry, because he is not subject to emotions, which are disturbances of the mind: all creatures liable to emotional affect are frail. That belief destroys truth and religion utterly. Let us set aside for the moment, however, this topic of the wrath of God, because the material for it is quite large and needs to be treated more broadly in its own right.[9]

This programmatic statement comes immediately before Lactantius gives his readers a recapitulation of the book's material. The philosophers' refusal to attribute anger to God is presented as a significant factor in their greater misconception of the divine. It is also shaped as a topic worth its own separate treatment. Lactantius' awareness of his projects in both texts and of their relationship to one another is further evidenced in the second chapter of *De ira Dei*, where he refers to this passage and its broader context as ample proof of philosophical error.[10]

---

[8]   Eusebius, *Historia Ecclesiastica* 8.16.2–3: οὐκ ἀνθρώπινον δέ τι τούτου κατέστη αἴτιον οὐδ᾽ οἶκτος, ὡς ἂν φαίη τις, ἢ φιλανθρωπία τῶν ἀρχόντων· πολλοῦ δεῖ· πλείω γὰρ ὁσημέραι καὶ χαλεπώτερα ἀρχῆθεν καὶ εἰς ἐκεῖνο τοῦ καιροῦ τὰ καθ᾽ ἡμῶν αὐτοῖς ἐπενοεῖτο, ποικιλωτέραις μηχαναῖς ἄλλοτε ἄλλως τὰς καθ᾽ ἡμῶν αἰκίας ἐπικαινουργούντων· ἀλλ᾽ αὐτῆς γε τῆς θείας προνοίας ἐμφανὴς ἐπίσκεψις, τῷ μὲν αὐτῆς καταλλαττομένης λαῷ, τῷ δ᾽ αὐθέντῃ τῶν κακῶν ἐπεξιούσης καὶ πρωτοστάτῃ τῆς τοῦ παντὸς διωγμοῦ κακίας ἐπιχολουμένης. καὶ γὰρ εἴ τι ταῦτ᾽ ἐχρῆν κατὰ θείαν γενέσθαι κρίσιν, ἀλλά 'οὐαί,' φησὶν ὁ λόγος, 'δι᾽ οὗ δ᾽ ἂν τὸ σκάνδαλον ἔρχηται.'

[9]   Lactantius, *Divine Institutes* 2.17.3–5: "Nunc autem patitur homines errare, et adversum se quoque impios esse, ipse iustus, et mitis, et patiens. Nec enim fieri potest, ut non is, in quo perfecta sit virtus, sit etiam perfecta patientia. Unde quidam putant, ne irasci quidem Deum omnino, quod affectibus, qui sunt perturbationes animi, subjectus non sit; quia fragile est omne animal quod afficitur et commovetur. Quae persuasio veritatem, atque religionem funditus tollit. Sed seponatur interim locus hic nobis de ira Dei disserendi, quod et uberior est materia, et opere proprio latius exequenda."

[10]  Lactantius, *De ira Dei* 2.4: "Sed horum inperitiam iam coarguimus in secundo Divinarum Institutionum libro."

In *Divine Institutes*, Lactantius establishes a divide between philosophy and theology *qua* religion that carries into, and is equally evident in, *De ira Dei*. Indeed, the problem at the heart of *De ira Dei* is very much a theological one: is the supreme deity capable of anger? The question of the supreme god's impassibility, as well as his immateriality and immutability, had long been a subject of philosophical and theological debate. In response to their inheritance of a series of texts, most notably the Homeric epics, Greek philosophers adopted varied ways of negotiating the (philosophically) problematic depictions of deities as fickle, anthropomorphic, and subject to emotions. An example from the *Republic* is illustrative of the basic problem in its early formation. In the second book, during a conversation about the education necessary and appropriate for the youth in the ideal state, Socrates attacks the Homeric divinities. Having divided education into two parts, music and gymnastics, Socrates first addresses music, including literature. He defines bad literature as belonging to the realm of the poets, namely Homer and Hesiod, and, more precisely, as anything that carries the fault of "telling a bad lie." This kind of lie is one that consists of an "erroneous representation made of the nature of gods and heroes," like a painter who paints a portrait that lacks even the shadow of a likeness to the original.[11] It does not matter, Socrates says, whether or not these stories are meant to be read allegorically; what matters is that the youth, especially, will not know how to differentiate between the literal and the allegorical, and that this is too grave a risk to take.[12]

Heraclitus "the Allegorist," writing some five hundred years later, would agree with such critiques: "if he [Homer] meant nothing allegorically, he was impious through and through, and sacrilegious fables, loaded with blasphemous folly, run riot through both epics."[13] Heraclitus seeks to redeem Homer, however, and argues that in order to understand the poet, one needs to "recognize Homeric allegory" and to discern "what is said in a philosophical sense."[14] For Philo of Alexandria (20 BC–AD 50), allegory served a pedagogical function. In his *Quod Deus Sit Immutabilis*, Philo attributes the need to endow God with human characteristics to the human failure to comprehend anything other than the fact of God's existence.[15] Christians faced opposition similar to that

---

[11] Plato, *Republic* 2.377d–e.

[12] Plato, *Republic* 2.378d–e. On allegorical and figural reading in the Greco-Roman world, see Struck 2004, Dawson 1992, and Dawson 2002.

[13] Heraclitus, *Homeric Problems* 1.2. Despite some difficulties in dating (see Konstan and Russell 2005, xi–xii for discussion) the text was likely written around AD 100. Although references are made to other such treatises, the next earliest such work was that of Porphyry. For a discussion of the varieties of Homeric exegesis, see Lamberton 1989.

[14] Heraclitus, *Homeric Problems* 3.2.

[15] Philo, *Quod Deus Sit Immutabilis* 62.

against which Philo was writing in his treatise, for they too had inherited a series of texts in which the supreme deity was described in anthropomorphic and anthropopathic language.[16] As Karen Jo Torjesen succinctly states: "among Christians, the crisis was generated by the confrontation of a philosophical conception of divine incorporeality with biblical anthropomorphism."[17] Just as Heraclitus, Philo, and others did, Christians developed allegorical strategies for explaining such representations and moreover for offering an interpretation of them that would be consonant with their own cultural and intellectual traditions and inheritances.[18]

Despite the popularity and long-standing tradition of allegorical and figural reading among Greek theologians, however, there remained a persistent strand of literal interpretation among Christian intellectuals writing in Latin. In *De ira Dei*, Lactantius gives us a clear example of this: here, God's wrath is correct and essential. Against the Stoic and Epicurean straw men of the treatise, the apologist maintains that God has certain appropriate and necessary emotions, among which he counts anger. In choosing to affirm divine anger, Lactantius intentionally adopts a stance contrary to those of his predecessors and contemporaries. This choice could be attributed to his avowed, blatant dislike of philosophy and to his desire to appeal to a decidedly pagan audience. To take Lactantius' claims in *De ira Dei* at face value, however, and to accept that he abandoned one of the foremost intellectual traditions of his time out of mere dislike of it, is far too simplistic. Part of the challenge in finding an alternative is that Lactantius himself does not provide one; rather he informs us that he intends to meet the philosophers on their own terms. Both ancient and modern readers would correctly expect a treatment of the problem that is more obviously philosophical or theological. Yet this is precisely what he does not do. The arguments of the treatise are not so much philosophical as rhetorical, as Lactantius both confronts and conceptualizes the theological problem in terms of Latin rhetorical discourse and principles.

---

[16]  With the significant exception of the theological issues raised by the suffering and death of Jesus, the criticism leveled at Christians was directed at the representations of God found in the texts of the Old Testament, texts (and thus problems) that Christians thus inherited, or more properly appropriated, from Judaism. For discussions about the adoption of the Hebrew scriptures by Christians and what the content of those scriptures would have included, see, for example, Stern 2003; on the level of social interaction and literary representation, see Juel 2003; for a history of the scholarship on the question of Jewish-Christian relations and a call for a postcolonial critic's approach to the material, see Jacobs 2007.

[17]  Torjesen 2005:76. See also Stroumsa 1983, despite a now-outdated discussion of the Gnostics. That such anthropomorphic language continued to present problems in different contexts, on the medieval Jewish thinkers Saadia Gaon and Bahya Ibn Paquda, see Lobel 2008.

[18]  Dawson 1992 and 2002.

What Lactantius offers is a reasoned and organized defense of God's wrath, presented step-by-step and built upon the refutation of his opponents' claims. One of the ways he does this is by presenting a point in the opposition's argument and rebutting it with one of his own. Given the purportedly Christian bent of the treatise, one would expect to find a series of such rebuttals explicitly couched in scriptural examples and proofs. This expectation too is in vain: early on, Lactantius informs us that he will refrain from referencing biblical texts because they are viewed with such hostility by the philosophers.[19] Insofar as he intended his audience to understand him to mean direct and obvious references (e.g. quotation and exegesis), Lactantius fulfills this promise. The same cannot be said for more allusive and indirect references. In fact, he relies on scriptural themes and parallels, particularly those culled from the books of the Old Testament, at precise moments in the treatise. Three moments in *De ira Dei* are illustrative of this approach: his discussion of the master and slave (5.12–5.14); his argument for the necessity of evil (13.13; 13.17); and his definition of anger itself (17.7; 17.11–12; 17.17; 17.20–21). We shall briefly consider each of these.

In the fifth chapter of the treatise, Lactantius introduces the relationship between the master and the slave as a useful model for understanding the relationship between God and humans. He begins by attacking the Stoic idea of a supreme god who is free from vicious emotions, who is envisioned to be incapable of inflicting injury on anyone.[20] Where the Stoics see definitive difference between, e.g. anger and kindness, Lactantius sees the all-encompassing nature of the divine. A verse from Deuteronomy lies at the heart of this idea: "See now that I, even I, am he; there is no god besides me. I kill and I make alive; I wound and I heal; and no one can deliver from my hand."[21] The Deuteronomic expression of God's power to embrace such contradictions is thus brought to bear on the Stoics' inability to fathom that such apparent opposites could coexist. It is

---

[19]  Lactantius, *De ira Dei* 22.3–4.

[20]  Lactantius, *De ira Dei* 5.5–6. The idea of the calm and benevolent father against which Lactantius argues here is a marked contrast to his own idea of the justifiably emotional *dominus*. For discussions of how Lactantius fashions the claims of the philosophical schools whose opinions he attacks in the treatise, see Colish 1990, Harvey 2003, Micka 1943, Bufano 1951, Ingremeau 1998, Kendeffy 2000, and Althoff 1999.

[21]  Lactantius, *De ira Dei* 5.7. The precise parallel is in the verbs *vivificare* and *salvare* (see Ingremeau 1982:241–242, who notes that the prior verb pairing [*prodesse . . . nocere*] is classical, as in e.g. Cicero, *De Officiis* 3.25, which Lactantius cites elsewhere). The verse quoted above is Deuteronomy 32:39. All English translations of the Old Testament and the New are from the New Revised Standard Version. Lactantius' citation of Deuteronomy here also points to his privileging of the scriptural text, particularly this legalistic book of the Old Testament, over and against the ethical teachings of the Stoics (as he represents them). On the structure of Deuteronomy and in particular its exhortative strategies, see Penner and Stichele 2009.

never the case that God can be or have only one thing or another, or that he can have nothing, but rather that he has both elements of a pair.

Lactantius again invokes the analogy, this time more fully, to highlight the close dependence of these seemingly opposite emotions. In Lactantius' mind, the intertwined nature of love and hatred, and of anger and kindness, are exemplified by this social relationship:

> If any master has a good and a bad slave in his household, clearly he does not hate both or confer honor and favors on both. For if he does this he is both unjust and foolish. But he addresses the good one in a friendly manner, he honors him and appoints him to the command of his house and family and all of his own things, but he punishes the bad one with reproaches, with whippings, with nakedness, hunger, thirst, with fetters, so that by these things the latter may be an example to others to keep them from sinning, and the former to gain favor, so that fear may restrain some, and honor excite others ... And just as he who loves confers good things on those whom he loves, so he who hates inflicts evils upon those whom he hates. Because this proof is true it can be dissolved by no means.
>
> Lactantius, De ira Dei 5.12–5.14[22]

A parable that appears in both the Gospel of Matthew (24:45–51) and that of Luke (12:24–48, but especially 35–48) lies at the core of this idea.[23] In each version of the parable, Jesus tells the story of a master who has unexpectedly come home. If this master discovers that his slaves have behaved well and are alert upon his arrival, he rewards them; if however he finds that the slave believed him to have been delayed, has beaten other slaves and has otherwise abused the master's property, the master will "cut him into pieces."[24]

---

[22] With the following lines omitted from the quotation above: "Si quis dominus habens in familia servos bonum ac malum: utique non aut ambos odit aut ambos beneficiis et honore prosequitur—quod si faciat, et iniquus et stultus est—sed bonum adloquitur amice et ornat et domui ac familiae suisque rebus omnibus praeficit, malum vero maledictis verberibus nuditate fame siti conpedibus punit, ut et his exemplo ceteris sit ad non peccandum et ille ad promerendum, ut alios metus coerceat, alios honor provocet. Qui ergo diligit, et odit, qui odit, et diligit; sunt enim qui diligi debeant, sunt qui odio haberi. Et sicut is qui diligit confert bona in eos quos diligit, ita qui odit inrogat mala his quos odio habet; quod argumentum quia verum est, dissolvi nullo pacto potest."

[23] On the parable in its Matthean form and as part of a more contextual study of slaves and slavery in the New Testament, see Glancy 2000.

[24] Matthew 24:51 ("He will cut him in pieces and put him with the hypocrites, where there will be weeping and gnashing of teeth") and Luke 12:46 ("the master of that slave will come on a day when he does not expect him and at an hour that he does not know, and will cut him in pieces, and put him with the unfaithful"). The notes to each version of the parable mark it as

In its scriptural context, the passage is meant to be an allegory for what will happen upon the return of Jesus; the eschatological point of the story is that he can return at any moment and that those who worship him should be prepared for that arrival and the judgment that will come with it.[25] Lactantius' paraphrase omits the eschatological elements and construes the story as a simple example: the master's reaction to the state of affairs he discovers upon his return is illustrative of the natural balance between love and hate. While the language that Lactantius adopts to express this idea is ultimately scriptural, he also draws upon a classical parallel in the figure of Archytas of Tarentum.[26] Later in the treatise, Lactantius mocks those who tout Archytas as an example of restrained rage; Archytas is praised for having stopped himself from beating a slave who ruined his estate and for telling the slave that he would have beaten him had he not been angry.[27] In the first place, Lactantius takes issue with Archytas' forbearance with the slave: "it is a fault," he writes, "not to check the faults of slaves and children; for through their escaping without punishment they will proceed to greater evil."[28] The only situation in which Archytas' self-restraint would have been appropriate is if he had been angry at "any citizen or equal who injured him"—proper anger is reserved for those who are inferior to the individual holding authority, but anger is inappropriate when directed towards those who are equal to or above an individual in power or stature.[29]

---

intended to be read allegorically. Luke's version has an additional verse in which the severity of the punishments are meted out according to the degree to which a slave knew or did not know what was required of him. The slave who knew what was expected receives a severe beating, but the one who did not know, although he sinned, will receive a lesser beating.

[25]  In Matthew, the parable comes before three parables about the return of Jesus and the final judgment; in Luke, it is followed by a proclamation about the "time of judgment" (12:49–59). Glancy 2000:68 mentions the metaphorical meaning of this, and related parables with bibliography.

[26]  On Archytas' moral character as represented in the literary sources, see Huffman 2005, who fleshes out the *testimonia* he gives (283–288) by noting that the "basic point of this anecdote about Archytas and the similar ones about Plato is that one should never punish in anger (Diogenes Laertius *Lives* 8.20 has Pythagoras himself make the point) . . . Applied to the specific circumstances of punishing when controlled by anger, the point would be that, if we punish in anger, we will punish unjustly. This in turn could be judged morally problematic for two different reasons: (1) the person punished will suffer unjustly, (2) the person punishing will act unjustly and hence harm his own soul . . . The startling fact that the slaves escape all punishment is precisely what makes this version so memorable." (288). Cf. Ingremeau 1982:341.

[27]  Lactantius discusses the correct set of behaviors necessary for the punishment of slaves, with criticisms of Archytas' handling of his own slaves at 18.4–18.9 and 18.12.

[28]  Lactantius, *De ira Dei* 18.12: "servorum autem filiorumque peccata non coercere peccatum est; evadent enim ad maius malum per impunitatem."

[29]  Lactantius, *De ira Dei* 18.12: "esset igitur laudandus Archytas si, cum alicui civi et pari facienti sibi iniuriam fuisset iratus, repressisset se tamen et patientia furoris impetum mitigasset." Lactantius is not alone in thinking that anger has a specific and just use in specific contexts. Aristotle's definition of anger in his *Rhetoric*, for example, stresses the social aspect and utility of

The models of the power dynamic and that of reward and punishment provided by the analogy are indicative of the way in which Lactantius alludes to scriptural sources and associates them with examples drawn from stories familiar to those who were versed in the moral and ethical literature of the classical tradition. By refraining from a direct quotation or nominal reference to the parable, Lactantius allows the story to remain at a comfortable distance from the explicit scriptural accounts that his opponents so detest while simultaneously leaving open the possibility for a well-versed (Christian) reader to connect the abbreviated account given in *De ira Dei* with the Christian parable.[30] His criticism of the classical example of Archytas is not only a direct attack on the Stoics (and Plato, whom he also names), but also an echoing endorsement of the scriptural parable to which he had earlier alluded. Again we find a shift in meaning: the model presented is not so much eschatological as it is moral; the slave ought to obey and always expect the master lest he (rightfully) react in anger, and not necessarily because the final judgment could come at any moment. This is not to say that the eschatological element was completely absent from Lactantius' mind, but rather that his immediate concern in the treatise lies within the parameter of human behavior and its consequences.

Lactantius carries the discussion of anger's utility and appropriateness in God as he continues to argue against the Stoics. Particular attention is devoted to this idea in the thirteenth chapter, where the correlativity of opposites is expressed in terms of the mutual dependence of good and evil. The larger claim in this chapter is that both the Stoics and the Academics misunderstood the problem of evil: the Academics have used it to argue that the world was not made (by God) for humankind, and the Stoics have given the ridiculous reply that there is some benefit even in something that appears bad.[31] Lactantius proposes a solution:

> They could have answered more concisely and truly in this way: when God had formed man as if in his own image . . . he set before him both

---

the emotion as one properly directed towards those whom we regard as below us in power and status. For an overview of the moral dimensions of anger in antiquity, see Harris 2001.

30  Lactantius, *De ira Dei* 17.11. For the ways in which such stories would have circulated in the ancient Mediterranean see for example Lane Fox 1994.

31  Lactantius, *De ira Dei* 13.10: "Quod Stoici veritatem non perspicientes ineptissime reppulerunt. Aiunt enim multa esse in gignentibus et in numero animalium quorum adhuc lateat utilitatis sed eam processu temporum inveniri, sicut iam multa prioribus saeculis incognita necessitas et usus invenerit." Lactantius' presentation of the Stoic position on evil has resonances in Stoic theory about the emotions, in short, that it is human judgment of an initial impression that leads one to deem something as good or bad and to have a corresponding emotional reaction. For studies of the emotions in Stoic thought with consideration of the Christian opinion, see e.g. Sorabji 2000 and Graver 2007.

good and evil things, since he gave him wisdom, the whole system of which depends on the discernment of things evil and good . . . Truly, if only good things are put in sight, what need is there for deliberation, intellect, skill, or reason . . .?

Lactantius, *De ira Dei* 13.13 and 13.17[32]

The idea that humankind was formed in God's own image has clear scriptural parallels, but the more important resonance here is that God placed (*proposuit*) both good and evil before humans. According to Lactantius, it is because God endowed humans alone with wisdom (*sapientia*), itself the one trait that most links humans to their creator, that they are capable of distinguishing between good and evil; the entire reason (*ratio*) for which that wisdom exists is to recognize what is good and what is evil and to respond appropriately.[33]

Lactantius' articulation of this idea is phrased in scriptural terms; the lines above are modeled on a passage from Deuteronomy in which the covenant between God and the Israelites is renewed. *De ira Dei* 13.13 and 13.17 directly echo only two verses from the Deuteronomic passage; the intermediary verses are concerned with threats following upon disobedience of God's commandments.[34] The verses in question are 30:15 and 30:19:

See, I have set before you today life and prosperity, death and adversity. . . . . [19] I call heaven and earth to witness against you today that I have set before you life and death, blessings and curses. Choose life so that you and your descendants may live.[35]

---

[32] "Brevis igitur ac verius respondere potuerunt in hunc modum: deus cum formaret hominem veluti simulacrum suum, quod erat divini opificii summum, inspiravit ei sapientiam soli, ut omnia imperio ac dicioni suae subiugaret omnibusque mundi commodis uteretur. Proposuit tamen ei et bona et mala, quia sapientiam dedit cuius omnis ratio in discernendis bonis ac malis sita est . . . Positis enim tantummodo in conspectu bonis quid opus est cogitatione intellectu scientia ratione, cum, quocumque porrecerit manum, id naturae aptum et adcommodatum sit?"

[33] It is in this (their possession of *sapientia*) that humans are also differentiated from beasts, an important idea for Lactantius, not only for establishing the superiority of humankind in creation, but also for distinguishing just human emotions from the irrational and uncontrolled emotions of animals. See e.g. Lactantius, *De ira Dei* 7 (*passim*) and 17.14. We shall return to the significance of *ratio* below.

[34] On the interpretative statements and assumptions involved in adducing such "echoes," see the comments of Juel 2003:297–300.

[35] See Ingremeau 1982:306–307 for a discussion of *proposuit . . . bona et mala* and Ingremeau 309 for *positis in conspectu* in relation to the verses from Deuteronomy. The immediate context of the ideas that Lactantius incorporates have to do with the privileged status of the one true God above all other gods and an injunction to worship only him. The consequences for not doing so are here made very clear.

The direct scriptural references are those concerned with God's creation of both good and evil. The connection between the creation of good and evil—and humankind's ability to choose one or the other—would have been apparent to Lactantius as he sought to explain the existence of evil. This use of scripture presents us with a second example in which a biblical source is brought in to refute a Stoic claim.[36] It also gives us some insight to Lactantius' exegetical practice. Much as in his consideration of divine anger, Lactantius chooses not to engage in an allegorical or figural interpretation of an idea or concept that traditionally has been given a negative association. While the Stoics, Lactantius argues, interpret an apparent evil as an actual good, what they should do is admit that it is actually an evil and that, because it came from God, exists for a specific purpose.[37] Here Lactantius subtly deploys a scriptural model as a challenge to the philosophical argument of his opponents. The way in which he does so is illustrative of his methodology: since he knows that these opponents would not accept proof that is explicitly scriptural (such as would be announced by a direct quotation), he incorporates just enough of the Deuteronomic verse to allow for its recognition by those familiar with it, but not so much as to cast suspicion on his claims.[38]

The Deuteronomic excerpt also points to a particular framing of the obedience to the law and the legitimacy of God's wrath when the law is not obeyed. This is a theme that permeates the treatise. Lactantius often pairs it with presentations of his disagreement with the Stoics on specific points, and it forms a crucial element in his definition of anger. After dismissing the definitions of

---

[36] Lactantius had actually agreed with the Stoics until this point. His first concern is to dismiss the Academics who, he writes, challenge the Stoics by asking why, if God made everything for humans' benefit, there exist things that are contrary to human well-being (3.12). While the Stoics are correct to believe that God made the world for the benefit of humans, they were incorrect in their explanation of why evils (*mala*) exist; it is here that Lactantius draws on the scriptural text to refute a Stoic claim.

[37] As in his thinking through anger, Lactantius appears to prefer an attempt to work with apparent reality (anger is anger, evil is evil, etc.) rather than to try to find a way to make that reality fit with an ideal or to argue that it really means something other than what it initially appears to mean. The task that he set for himself, if we can extract it from this treatise, was to discover why things were the way they were—that is, why God created evil (in his view) and not how we might interpret evil.

[38] By doing so, Lactantius is asserting the following idea posited by Penner and Stichele 2009:249: "In fact, an analysis of early Christian oratorical discourse from the vantage point of the Greek and Roman rhetorical handbooks would suggest that, with respect to the deployment of the Hebrew Bible, it is difficult to draw a firm line between *exemplum* and *auctoritas* in so far as both scriptural citations and broader narrative references provide 'proof-texts' for the argument being developed. Such argumentation presumes the weight of the scriptural texts thus used and secures, in turn, the authority of the material that is cited."

the Greek and Roman philosophers, Lactantius provides his own.[39] According to the apologist, anger is "a movement of the mind, arising for the restraining of faults."[40] Lactantius seeks to claim that anger is the only appropriate reaction to an infraction of the divine law. Scriptural references and models are interspersed with his criticisms of the Stoic and Epicurean theories about anger, and biblical motifs are scattered throughout the chapter. In 17.7, for example, Lactantius endorses the view that both the just law and the good, unbiased judge will uphold a verdict that delivers retribution upon an offender. The belief that each individual will get his due grounds this claim and can be located in Isaiah 35:4, where the emphasis is just as much on the fact of divine vengeance as it is on the idea that one must await it.[41] Lactantius molds this idea to argue that God's anger and retribution come not from a desire to repay injury, but rather from the proper and fitting justice due to both those who obey and those who transgress the law.[42]

That God's anger is not a response to injury and is not intended injuriously are crucial components of Lactantius' idea and definition of divine wrath. The belief that humans are best understood as the slaves of God (already hinted at in chapter five, above) is equally relevant to Lactantius' position on the matter. Lactantius links the two ideas as follows:

> For the world is just as the house of God, and men just as his slaves; and if his name is a subject of derision to them, what kind or amount of forbearance is this, that he should cede his own honors to see wicked and unjust things done, and that he should not be indignant, which is peculiar and natural to him to whom sins are displeasing?

> Lactantius, *De ira Dei* 17.11[43]

Lactantius begins with a classical analogy and quickly shifts to a biblical idea: Cicero would agree that the world is the house of God (*mundus . . . dei domus*),

---

[39] The list comes at 17.13 and includes the definitions of the philosophers as presented by Seneca, Posidonius, and Aristotle; Cicero's definition comes later, at 17.20.

[40] Lactantius, *De ira Dei* 17.20: "Ergo ita definire debuerunt: ira est motus animi ad coercenda peccata insurgentis."

[41] Isaiah 35:4: "Say to those who are of a fearful heart, 'Be strong, do not fear! Here is your God. He will come with vengeance, with terrible recompense. He will come and save you.'" Cf. Psalm 27:4.

[42] Here Lactantius reformulates his discussion of the moral and ethical components of anger by closely linking them to the obedience or transgression of the law; the divine law becomes the arbiter of morality.

[43] "Nam mundus tamquam dei domus est et homines tamquam servi; quibus si ludibrio sit nomen eius, qualis aut quanta patientia est? Ut honoribus suis cedat, ut prava et iniqua fieri videat ut non indignetur, quod proprium et naturale est ei cui peccata non placent?" Cf. Ingremeau 1982:329–330.

but perhaps not that humans are the slaves of God (*homines . . . servi*).[44] In this instance, Lactantius' combination of the classical and biblical themes serves as a rebuttal of the Stoic claim for the unsuitability of anger, the attack of which he turns to in the next line.[45] Lactantius' complaint here is that the Stoics cannot see the difference between right and wrong or between just and unjust anger. The criticism itself is made on moral grounds, but at the same time it echoes his critique of the Stoics in chapter five. There the problem was that the Stoics interpret bad things as good things in disguise; here it is that they cannot discern any difference whatsoever. The scriptural model of humans as the slaves of their master (God) provides Lactantius with the basis for his argument and a framework for understanding the relationship between mortals and the divine. It also allows him to articulate why anger is fitting for God. With an appropriate object, and when it is employed for the sake of justice, anger has a fitting place, unlike the mere desire for revenge on account of which the Stoics (argues Lactantius) view anger as a negative attribute.[46]

Lactantius favors the models of God and of the divine-human relationship as expressed in some of the exhortative and disciplinary verses of the Old Testament scriptures. The Christian God for Lactantius, then, exists at some remove from the supreme deity envisioned by Plato and Heraclitus, as too from that of the Stoics and the Epicureans. Here Lactantius' deployment of allusions to passages from the Old Testament worked to rebut and undermine philosophical, and primarily Stoic, thought. Lactantius' claim towards the end of the text—that he cannot bring to bear the testimony of the prophets since it will not be accepted by his opponents—is not entirely honest.[47] He did in fact use biblical proofs and exempla in his argument, just not in so obvious a way as to attract attention and leave himself open to criticism. The subtle ways in which Lactantius formulated and supported his claims in *De ira Dei* are indicative of

---

[44] Ciceronian parallels: Cicero, *De Natura Deorum* 2.154; 3.26; *De Re Publica* 1.19; 3.14; Cicero, *De Legibus* 2.26; see also Seneca, *De Beneficiis* 7.1.7. Biblical parallels for *dominus . . . servi* and *servi Dei*: Genesis 50:17; 1 Ezra 5:11; Daniel 3:93; Acts 16:17; I Peter 2:16; Revelation 7:3.

[45] Lactantius, *De ira Dei* 17.12, cf. Lactantius, *Divinae Institutiones* 6.15.2; 6.16.1–11; and 6.19.1–11, to which Lactantius himself points his reader, another indication that *De ira Dei* came after the major work.

[46] The judicial and disciplinary aspects of Lactantius' understanding of divine wrath have scriptural parallels as expressed, for example, in 2 Maccabees. See the comments of Ingremeau 1982:337, who identifies the reference and argues that it indicates that Lactantius had in mind biblical ideas of God's wrath and divine punishment—although she does not think that he was necessarily aware of the depth of the parallel. A consideration of the excerpt above within its scriptural context, however, suggests that this was an intentional and precise use of the text. For a concise overview of 2 Maccabees with attention paid to its claims about both Judaism and Hellenism, see Himmelfarb 1998.

[47] Lactantius, *De ira Dei* 22.3–4.

his training in Latin rhetoric, for rhetoric provided Lactantius with a mode of argument, and moreover with principles of argumentation, that allowed him to achieve these ends. In addition, it equipped him with a mode of discourse suitable to, yet distinctly different from, the philosophical arguments of his opponents.

Often described as the "Christian Cicero," Lactantius has long received notice for the ways in which he emulates and imitates the famous classical rhetor's style.[48] Such studies, however, have neglected to question whether the apologist's allegiance to the genre is discernible in any other areas of the treatise. In the pages that remain, I quickly sketch the contours of the sort of education that Lactantius would have received in mid-third-century North Africa and the basic components of rhetorical works to which *De ira Dei* conforms. I then suggest that Lactantius adopted such rhetorical techniques not just out of habit, but also because he believed rhetoric to provide the soundest *ratio* for his material. Lactantius' disillusionment with philosophy, together with his training, educational and vocational, made rhetoric the most accessible and the most natural way for him to express his beliefs about the "true religion." Equally importantly, rhetoric gave him a way of articulating theological arguments that allowed him to be most persuasive to a specific audience.

To get a sense of what education might have been like in North Africa in the middle of the third century AD, we must look both backward to the texts, treatises, and techniques advanced by Cicero and Quintilian and also forward to the information passed on to us by Ausonius, Augustine, and others.[49] Generally, little is thought to have changed between the first century BC and the fourth century AD.[50] If what Ausonius writes about fourth-century education in Bordeaux can be taken as largely representative of the state of education in the empire at that time, at six or seven a child would pursue elementary studies in the *schola grammatici*, remaining there for about nine years.[51] Classroom numbers would decrease as the material and the cost of education became more difficult for families to manage.[52] One schoolroom exercise in particular

---

[48] The term seems to have originated with Pico de la Mirandola, in his *De studio divinae atque humanae philosophiae* (7).

[49] On Augustine, see Brown 2000:23–28. For the argument that we can use what Ausonius writes about education in his own day as representative of larger trends, see Booth 1979. Also useful to an extent (given our focus) is Kaster 1988.

[50] This is not to say that rhetoric remained static throughout the centuries separating Cicero and Lactantius (or Augustine, for that matter), but rather that there were elements of consistency to the basic progression of a young man through the Roman educational system and the values and knowledge imparted by that system.

[51] Booth 1979:7.

[52] See Augustine's oft-quoted statements about the cost of education at *Confessions* 2.5–6; see also Watts 2006:24–47 for a sense of education's cost—and cultural prestige—in late antique Athens.

has drawn attention for its value to teach students not only about the principles of speech and delivery but also about the social roles and responsibilities that young men would assume as adults: declamation.[53] It was in this exercise that students' skills were honed and sharpened with increasing precision until they could display mastery in the art of fashioning and delivering a convincing argument.

Declamation involved both skill and talent, both theory and practice.[54] Students would have to defend one or the other position while deploying both tactical and technical principles as they crafted an emotionally moving speech.[55] Pseudo-Quintilian's *Minor Declamations* offer some insight not only into the sorts of topics on which students would have to speak, but also into the pedagogical lessons they were meant to learn from them.[56] Many of these declamations required that the student adopt a persona, for example of a woman or soldier or someone of a social status other than their own.[57] To do so well necessitated the ability to think both within and across such categories, as well as to approach the speech with clear organization and thought; the student also would have relied on principles of distinction and definition.[58]

These exercises in delineation and differentiation were critical to success in oratorical pursuits beyond the classroom; in this respect the declamations practiced by students had as their goal the translation of the rules and methods of rhetorical theory into actual practice. The precise nature of those declamations and of the rules that governed them during the time in which Lactantius would have encountered and, later, taught them are beyond our reach. Certain principles, however, likely remained fairly stable, including the system of rhetoric proposed by Cicero and Quintilian as well as those outlined in the *Rhetorica ad Herennium*.[59] Thus, while the division of the *partes orationis* into five or six parts

---

[53] Bloomer 1997, who also spends time on the *hermeneumata* (see 72–78).

[54] As evidenced not least by Quintilian's division of his *Institutio Oratoria* into two parts (theory and education or teaching). Winterbottom 1982 has argued that Cicero's *Pro Milone* was designed with the specific purpose of retaining for educational purposes the theory as put into practice by the orator.

[55] The idea that a speech (as well as the orator delivering it) should have an emotional impression on the audience is important not only to Cicero but also to Aristotle, among others. Although this aspect of a text is more difficult to access in the case of *De ira Dei*, we should not discard its import and emphasis altogether.

[56] See Winterbottom 1982, with Fantham 1978 and Bloomer 1997.

[57] Bloomer 1997:58 and especially note 21.

[58] Bloomer 1997:57 and, with reference to a specific declamation, "The declaimer's first task is to redefine poisoning to include drugging. Again the declamation works by definition and it works out a conflict—the brave man accused of desertion—but shifts the blame to the stepmother" (67).

[59] Although such a statement elides the differences that originally existed between each of these individuals, as well as between various schools and traditions of rhetoric, my point here is that,

might have been a matter of opinion or preference (as it was even in Cicero's day), the fact that a speech could be divided into recognizable and purposeful sections was not.[60] Nor did the *officia oratoris* shift: *inventio, dispositio, elocutio, memoria,* and *actio* retained their importance.

Both Cicero and the anonymous author of the *Rhetorica ad Herennium* identify six structural components of a speech: the *exordium, narratio, divisio* (or *partitio*), *confirmatio, confutatio,* and *conclusio*.[61] Lactantius' treatise corresponds to this structure on a grand scale, although it admits of some modifications. The first three organizational elements listed by Cicero come in quick succession at the beginning of Lactantius' treatise: *exordium* (1); *narratio* (2.1–8); and *divisio* (2.9–10). Despite an unequal distribution of material, the remainder of the treatise (up to chapter twenty-two) consists of the *confirmatio*, which in this case often contains elements of refutation, or *confutatio*. Narrative elements are interwoven throughout these chapters of the treatise, but their primary function is to give Lactantius a platform for the articulation and exposition of his argument. Three programmatic statements, variously distributed, and their explication, form the bulk of the treatise (identifiable at 3; 6.2; 12.5; 15.12; 16; and 17.20). A *conclusio*, which Lactantius himself terms a "peroration in the manner of Cicero," shapes the final three chapters of the treatise (22–24).

Lactantius devotes the largest part of the treatise to the advancement of his own arguments about God's wrath and frequently merges these with a refutation of his opponents' claims, as we have seen above. This area, primarily of *confirmatio*, was considered the most important in rhetorical theory, since it was here that the orator could give an exposition of his arguments. It was here too that the rhetorician could showcase the most talent in deploying and displaying the very qualities that were necessary for him to be considered competent (at least) and innovative (at best) in his field. According to Cicero and the *Rhetorica ad Herennium*, those traits that made an orator an orator (or the duties, *officia oratoris*, as above) included: the degree to which he was able to find and develop his argument (*inventio*); the arrangement of that argument into its constituent parts (*dispositio*, consisting of the elements just discussed); his style (*elocutio* or *pronuntiatio*); his ability to memorize the speech to be delivered (*memoria*); and the delivery itself, with its attendant invocation of gesture and emotion (*actio*).[62] Our focus here will be on Lactantius' work in the area of *inventio*.

---

in the case of Lactantius especially, we are best able to detect the basic influences of Ciceronian rhetorical theory, which is unlikely to have undergone significant alteration since its formation.

60  On the different divisions of the *partes orationis*, see e.g. Clarke 1996:24–25. Cicero gives a six-fold division in *De Inventione* as does the *Rhetorica ad Herennium*; Quintilian has five, and others are said to have had four.

61  The speech could be divided into fewer of these as well, see Quintilian at 4.2–6.

62  Clarke 1996:23.

In Cicero's *De Oratore*, the interlocutor Antonius states that the process of *inventio* is the first to which the orator must attend when preparing his case.[63] Once the rhetorician has discovered the nature of the case, the next step is to identify "the point that cannot be removed without eliminating the dispute."[64] After this, he may advance to the third, namely to identify "the issue to be decided." The rhetorician's talent comes to the fore in the discovery of "the arguments bearing on the issue to be decided."[65] To find these, the orator must consider the arguments of both the defense and the prosecution, and he must realize that the specific circumstances of the case are in reality related to much more general categories. The question is not about the individual parties involved in the dispute, but rather the fundamental issue that is raised by the dispute.[66]

Lactantius applies this method to his framing of the question of divine anger. In its purest form, Lactantius' argument is concerned with whether or not God has anger.[67] This perspective is evident in the opening lines of the treatise, where Lactantius chastises the philosophers for their denial of this possibility and identifies his purpose in writing as being to dispel this error.[68] Shortly thereafter, Lactantius provides a clear statement of his argument: because some say that God has no emotions and other that he has only kindness, he too will follow this division. He refutes the other possibilities—that God has neither anger nor kindness, that God has only anger and not kindness, that God has only kindness and not anger—as he sets up his defense of the claim that God has both anger and kindness.[69]

Here Lactantius links God's anger to religion: God has anger because without it, no one would fear or worship him, and religion would be destroyed

---

[63] Cicero, *De Oratore* 2.104a. All translations from the text are by Wisse and May 2001.

[64] Cicero, *De Oratore* 2.132b; cf 2.104, where this is presented as the need to "establish the point of reference for the whole portion of the speech that specifically concerns the judgment of the issue itself."

[65] Cicero, *De Oratore* 2.132d: "Perspicua sunt haec quidem et in vulgari prudentia sita; sed illa quaerenda, quae et ab accusatore et a defensore argumenta ad id, quod in iudicium venit, spectantia debent adferri." The statement is followed by a sharp criticism of contemporary teachers who train their students only to seek two categories of cases.

[66] Cicero, *De Oratore* 2.132–2.127.

[67] Wisse and May 2001:151n75; the text of the note: "Antonius here summarizes (a particular version of) status theory, which was very important in contemporary standard rhetoric. He mentions, respectively, the conjectural status (*status coniecturalis*; developed in 2.105 below), the status of quality (*status qualitatis*; see 2.106), and the status of definition (*status definitionis*; see 2.107–109). His view differs from the standard view in two essential respects: (1) 'immediately' and (2) insistence that doctrine applicable to other than juridical cases."

[68] Lactantius, *De ira Dei* 1.1: "Animadverti saepe, Donate, plurimos id aestimare, quod etiam nonnulli philosophorum putaverunt, non irasci deum . . ."

[69] Lactantius, *De ira Dei* 6.1.

as a consequence.[70] The point that determines the case for Lactantius—the point that, if removed, would result in the destruction of his case—is that God's anger is born of the necessity to preserve religion, which is itself required for the existence of wisdom and justice, which are in turn necessary for the preservation of humankind, its civility and its institutions.[71] Although Lactantius adds a number of further arguments to this initial claim, it remains the most important to his criticism of his opponents. Lactantius' statements about the dependence of religion on God's anger, on the one hand, and humans' fear of God, on the other hand, here also help to explain the material that he discusses in the chapters that follow it.[72] For Lactantius to support this idea, he must convince his audience that religion is uniquely important to humans, he must explain what religion is, whom it is that they should worship, and why.

In both its structure and its argumentation, *De ira Dei* reflects the classical rhetorical training in which its author was most experienced; Lactantius' emulation of Cicero is not only stylistic but also formative. That Lactantius relied on the principles that he learned as a student and later taught as a rhetor should not surprise; that these strategies informed his theological perspective is a characteristic of his work that has parallels in the works and writings of his peers among the Greek-writing Christian intellectuals.[73] Lactantius' largely rhetorical argument, however, represents a distinct choice on the part of the author: *De ira Dei* fits neatly into no category—it is not clearly apologetic and certainly not the kind of homiletic or exegetical text the sort of which a Philo or Origen would write. Like his *Divinae Institutiones*, the text has judicial undertones, but it does not offer the kinds of precepts that are found in the longer

---

[70]  Lactantius, *De ira Dei* 6.2: "Haec tuenda nobis et adserenda sententia est: in eo enim summa omnis et cardo religionis pietatisque versatur. Nam neque honor ullus deberi potest deo, si nihil praestat colenti, nec ullus metus, si non irascitur non colenti." This should be read closely with 12.5: "Timor igitur dei solus est qui custodit hominum inter se societatem, per quem vita ipsa sustinetur munitur gubernatur. Is autem timor aufertur si fuerit homini persuasum quod irae sit expers deus, quem moveri et indignari, cum iniusta fiunt, non modo communis utilitas sed etiam ratio ipsa nobis et veritas persuadet."

[71]  Lactantius, *De ira Dei* 6 and 12.2.

[72]  Ingremeau 1982:37–44.

[73]  Although Jerome, for instance, fretted over whether or not he was more Ciceronian than Christian, at *Apology* 2.6 (and *Letter* 22), Jerome recounts a dream wherein, upon meeting heaven's judge and identifying himself as a Christian, the judge replies: "You lie: you are a Ciceronian. Where your treasure is, there is your heart." As a consequence, Jerome vows never again to read the classics. In this respect, Jerome's comments support the assertion of Leadbetter 1998:245 that "Christian intellectuals, in particular, had to struggle with classical learning. They could not ignore it because it formed the core of their own education and they used its forms—the letter, the speech, the treatise—to communicate their own position. That involved them in necessary compromise with something that they formally rejected." Lactantius would seem to be an exception to this statement.

work, nor is it necessarily prescriptive.[74] What the treatise does do, however, is to formulate a theological claim in rhetorical terms. It is not just that Lactantius looked toward his training in rhetoric or to the principles of reading and articulation that he could extract from it, but rather that he presented a doctrinal matter in a rhetorical framework.

Two considerations help to elucidate the reasons behind this choice. The first brings us back to Cicero, but this time our interest is with his idea of the relationship between rhetoric and philosophy. Points of dissent between rhetoricians and philosophers were many in antiquity, as each believed their own discipline to be best suited to the consideration of weighty matters. In its most basic form, the matter at stake was one that questioned training and preparation: could a rhetorician adequately expound upon a philosophical matter or was a philosopher appropriately equipped to criticize the art of the rhetorician? Cicero, in *De Oratore*, suggests that an individual could do both. In an oft-quoted excerpt, Cicero argues that the rhetorician can apply his art to any subject:

> But if we want to assign to the orator, besides his normal tasks, that other wide-ranging, unrestricted, and extensive group of questions, that is, if we think it is his duty to speak about good and evil, the things to be pursued and avoided, honorable or base, expedient or inexpedient, about virtue, justice, self-control, prudence, greatness of spirit, generosity, dutifulness, friendship, moral duty, loyalty, and all the other virtues and their corresponding vices, about the State, the exercise of power, military affairs, the political system, and human behavior—let us then take this group of questions upon ourselves also, provided that it be confined within moderate limits.
>
> Cicero, *De Oratore* 2.67[75]

---

[74] Digeser 2006 notes the legal language of the *Divinae Institutiones*.

[75] "Sed si illam quoque partem quaestionum oratori volumus adiungere vagam et liberam et late patentem, ut de rebus bonis aut malis, expetendis aut fugiendis, honestis aut turpibus, utilibus aut inutilibus, de virtute, de iustitia, de continentia, de prudentia, de magnitudine animi, de liberalitate, de pietate, de amicitia, de officio, de fide, de ceteris virtutibus contrariisque vitiis dicendum oratori putemus; itemque de re publica, de imperio, de re militari, de disciplina civitatis, de hominum moribus, adsumamus eam quoque partem, sed ita, ut sit circumscripta modicis regionibus." Cf. Cicero, *De Inventione* 1.1–3 and Cicero, *De Oratore* 2.34. See also the comments of Clarke 1996:61: "To appreciate his [Cicero's] contribution justly one must see it against the background of contemporary rhetorical teaching. One will then recognize the pertinence of the main theme of *De Oratore*. In emphasizing the importance of having something to say as well as knowing how to say it, and the desirability of combining the two main disciplines of the ancient world, rhetoric and philosophy, he was putting his finger on one of the weaknesses of ancient education."

That matters of a philosophical nature could and should fall under the juris-diction of the orator is thus an idea with which Lactantius would have been familiar; we see application of this principle in *De ira Dei*. It is not merely that Lactantius chose a medium of argumentation with which he was most comfort-able, but rather that he saw in that medium a justifiable and appropriate way to express a matter of Christian theology.

Nor is the relevance of rhetoric's principles to philosophical (or in Lactantius' case, theological) matters the only way to understand the argu-mentation of the treatise. The deeper motivation behind Lactantius' strategy was that he, like Cicero, saw in the proper exercise of rhetoric the pursuit of a reasoned and logical argument. Unlike philosophers, orators (in their own esti-mation) were required to stick to a specific plan and procedure by the adher-ence to which they approached the truth of the matter.[76] A good orator has been trained in and employs a good method (*ratio*); later in the text Cicero will argue that this method (*ratio*, again) depends on three means of persuasion.[77] Lactantius too frequently returns to the idea that it is because of the *ratio* of a matter (whether that matter be the speech, or treatise, itself, the argument, the emotions, or something else) that the answer to the question becomes apparent. He uses the term to mean not only "reason" but also "method" and "system." Thus, for example, some people do not understand the *ratio* of the "great and heavenly secret," *ratio* (and *ordo*) can "lead to the hiding place of truth," there is no *ratio* for men to hope if God is only the author of evils, and there is one *ratio* to which the emotions belong.[78]

Lactantius' use of *ratio* to mean "method" or "system" can take two forms. On the one hand, he invokes the term when he wants to mark a transition in the text or when he comments on his purpose; so that the matter may progress as it should it must be led by *ratio*.[79] On the other hand, his criticisms of his opponents are phrased as sarcastic comments on and assaults against their philosophical *ratio*. It is by virtue of the Stoics' "accurate method of reasoning" that they attri-bute only kindness to God and not anger, and thus "fall into the greatest error."[80]

---

[76] Cicero, *De Oratore* 2.32, where Cicero disparages orators who declaim "haphazardly" in the forum.

[77] Cicero, *De Oratore* 2.115: "Ita omnis ratio dicendi tribus ad persuadendum rebus est nixa: ut probemus vera esse, quae defendimus; ut conciliemus eos nobis, qui audiunt; ut animos eorum, ad quemcumque causa postulabit motum, vocemus."

[78] Lactantius, *De ira Dei* 1.9; 2.10; 3.2; 3.4; 4.12; 5.15; 7.1; 7.2; 7.5; 7.10; 7.15; 8.3; 9.1; 9.4; 9.8; 10.2; 10.11; 10.22; 10.25; 10.32; 10.34; 10.36; 10.38; 10.41; 10.51; 10.52; 11.10; 12.3; 12.5; 13.8; 13.13; 13.17; 13.20; 13.22; 13.24; 14.2; 15.5; 15.9; 17.2; 17.12; 17.13; 18.10; 22.3; 23.9; 24.6.

[79] See e.g. his use of *ratio* at 2.10: "Consideremus singula, ut nos ad latebras veritatis et ratio et ordo deducat."

[80] Lactantius, *De ira Dei* 5.15: "Ii vero, quos ratio et veritatis argumenti huius inducit, falso omnino sententia suscepta, in maximum errorem cadunt."

Lactantius is clearly mocking the Stoics and setting their false, philosophical reasoning against his own rhetorical methodology. This line of argument has parallels in the *Divinae Institutiones*, where *ratio* is also preferred as the means by which to come to the knowledge and worship of God.[81] Religion, for Lactantius, is a rational choice, thoughtful and reasoned out; it is not a system of beliefs to which one dedicates oneself based solely on revelation.[82] A decision reached by such a method requires a similar method of exposition and explication; philosophical terms and thought are inadequate to the task, but the principles of rhetorical argumentation provide the tools by which Lactantius can convince and persuade his audience. The rhetorical system and principles that Lactantius adopted for the purpose of persuasion indicate a conscious and intentional decision on the part of the apologist.

This was in many ways a natural choice, and one that reflects Lactantius' educational training and background as well as his vocation. I have argued that in it he found a method for the explication and presentation of theological arguments that he believed to contain greater reason and reasoning than methods of philosophical discourse. We come to see that he is the "Christian Cicero" in ways that outstrip mere stylistic parallels; the similarities between the two include a greater cultural project.[83] For Cicero, this involved the translation of Greek philosophical terms and ideas into Latin and the introduction thereof into Roman culture. For Lactantius, this involved the pairing of biblical ideas with familiar notions and the introduction thereof into an educated pagan culture of the Roman tradition. Rhetoric, although an ever-present and important facet of all intellectual production of the period, is the centerpiece of Lactantius' intellectual project.

It is primarily in this thorough dependence upon rhetoric—from the conceptualization of the problem to its articulation in the structure of the treatise—that Lactantius is ultimately distinct from Eusebius and others in the Greek Christian theological tradition. Lactantius' disavowal of philosophy belies a more complex factor at work, namely the epistemological basis that he took for granted. For Greek philosophers and theologians of the Platonic tradition (broadly construed), the tenets of that philosophical tradition were the benchmarks of validity; any attempt to square Christian doctrine with the beliefs held by their contemporaries had to account for the difficult discrepancies between

---

[81] Perrin 2001 provides an insightful analysis of this trend in the *Divinae Institutiones*; he references *De ira Dei* from time to time but focuses on the longer treatise.

[82] Perrin 2001:155.

[83] Evidence of this can also be found in the intertexual relationship between *De ira Dei* and Cicero's *De natura Deorum*, an exploration of which indicates the extent to which Lactantius saw himself as operating in a Ciceronian philosophical, theological fashion just as much as in a rhetorical one.

the two. Rhetoric for such intellectuals informed their defenses and exegeses largely insofar as it provided them with the tools to express ideas in clear and cogent terms. Rhetoric was for Lactantius, however, the epistemological basis of his understanding of Christianity and his articulation of Christian doctrine. It also suggests that he found it a useful tool with which to explicate ideas to his audience, including Constantine.

Nor was Lactantius alone in adopting this strategy. Other Christian intellectuals who wrote in Latin—Arnobius, Tertullian, Novatian, Cyprian, and Minucius Felix among them—also situated their theological claims in principles that we most readily identify as rhetorical. If Lactantius can be taken as representative of a dominant approach among Latin-writing Christian intellectuals, and if Eusebius can be taken as representative of the same among Greek authors, we have in these two key figures a poignant example of the variety of Christian intellectual thought of the third and fourth centuries, as well as the indication that these differences both began earlier and varied more greatly than has been previously suggested. It is not that Eusebius was not equally influenced by his rhetorical training and philosophical background, but merely that there were important distinctions between the intellectual world of Eusebius and that of Lactantius. This point has been heretofore overlooked in discussions of Lactantius and has bearing on how we ourselves approach the apologist's work. The debates and disagreements of the early fourth century might be more fully understood if the education, training, language, and origin of their authors are taken into account. Those rifts that have commonly been construed as theological have, perhaps, not as much to do with orthodox or heterodox belief as with the particular intellectual traditions upon which individuals drew, and the cultural, linguistic, and historical pasts that informed their understanding of an ever-shifting present.

# Works Cited

Althoff, J. 1999. *Zur Epikurrezeption bei Laktanz. Zur Rezeption der Hellenistischen Philosophie in der Spatantike*. Stuttgart.

Barnes, T. 1971. *Tertullian: A Historical and Literary Study*. Oxford.

———. 1973. "Lactantius and Constantine." *Journal of Roman Studies* 63:29–46.

———. 1981. *Constantine and Eusebius*. Cambridge, MA.

Becker, A. and A. Reed, eds. 2007. *The Ways That Never Parted: Jews and Christians in Late Antiquity and the Early Middle Ages*. Minneapolis.

Bloomer, W.M. 1997. "Schooling in Persona: Imagination and Subordination in Roman Education." *Classical Antiquity* 16.1: 57–78.

Booth, A. 1979. "Elementary and Secondary Education in the Roman Empire." *Florilegium* 1:1–14.

Brown, P. 2000. *Augustine of Hippo: A Biography*. Berkeley.

Bryce, J. 1990. *The Library of Lactantius*. New York.

Bufano, A. 1951. "Lucrezio in Lattanzio." *Giornale Italiano di Filologia* 4:335–349.

Cameron, A. 1994. *Christianity and the Rhetoric of Empire: The Development of Christian Discourse*. Sather Classical Lectures. Berkeley.

Casey, S. 1971–1980. "Lactantius' Reaction to Pagan Philosophy." *Classica et Medievalia* 32:203–219.

Clarke, M. 1996. *Rhetoric at Rome: A Historical* Survey. Routledge.

Colish, M. 1990. *The Stoic Tradition from Antiquity to the Early Middle Ages, volume 2: Stoicism in Christian Latin Thought through the Sixth Century*. Leiden.

Digeser, E. 2000. *The Making of a Christian Empire: Lactantius and Rome*. Ithaca.

———. 2006. "Religion, Law and the Roman Polity: The Era of the Great Persecution." In *Religion and Law in Classical and Christian Rome*, ed. C. Ando and J. Rupke, 68–84. Stuttgart.

Drake, H. 1976. *In Praise of Constantine, A Historical Study and New Translation of Eusebius' Tricennial Orations*. Berkeley.

Fantham, E. 1978. "Imitation and Decline: Rhetorical Theory and Practice in the First Century after Christ." *Classical Philology* 73.2:102–116.

Fox, R. L. 1994. "Literacy and Power in Early Christianity." In *Literacy and Power in the Ancient World*, ed. A. K. Bowman and G. Woolf, 126–148. Cambridge.

Garnsey, P. and A. Bowen, eds. 2003. *Lactantius: Divine Institutes.* Translated Texts for Historians 40. Liverpool.

Glancy, J. 2000. "Slaves and Slavery in the Matthean Parables." *Journal of Biblical Literature* 119.1:67–90.

Graver, M. 2007. *Stoicism and Emotion*. Chicago.

Harris, W.V. 2001. *Restraining Rage: The Ideology of Anger Control in Classical Antiquity*. Cambridge, MA.

Himmelfarb, M. 1998. "Judaism and Hellenism in 2 Maccabees." *Poetics Today. Hellenism and Hebraism Reconsidered: The Poetics of Cultural Influence and Exchange I.* 19.1:19–40.

Huffman, C. 2005. *Archytas of Tarentum: Pythagorean, Philosopher, and Mathematician King.* Cambridge.

Ingremeau, C. 1982. *Lactance: La Colère de Dieu. Introduction, Texte Critique, Traduction, Commentaire et Index.* Paris.

———. 1998. "Lactance et la philosophie des passions." In *Les Apologistes chrétiens et la Culture Grecque,* ed. B. Pouderon and J. Doré, 283–296. Paris.

Jacobs, A. 2007. "The Lion and the Lamb: Reconsidering Jewish-Christian Relations in Antiquity." In Becker and Reed 2007:95–118.

Juel, D. 2003. "Interpreting Israel's Scriptures in the New Testament." In *A History of Biblical Interpretation,* ed. P. Hauser and D. Watson, 283–303. Grand Rapids, MI.

Kaster, R. 1988. *Guardians of Language: The Grammarian and Society in Late Antiquity.* Berkeley.

Kendeffy, G. 2000. "Lactantius on the Passions." *Acta Classica Universitatis Scientarum Debreceniensis.* 36:113–129.

Konstan, D. and D. Russell, eds. 2005. *Heraclitus: Homeric Problems.* Atlanta.

Lamberton, R. 1989. *Homer the Theologian.* Berkeley.

Leadbetter, W. 1998. "Lactantius and Paideia in the Latin West." In *Ancient History in a Modern University,* ed. T. Hillard, et al., 245–252. Grand Rapids, MI.

Lobel, D. 2008. "Speaking about God: Bahya as Biblical Exegete." In *Philosophers and the Jewish Bible,* ed. C. Manekin and R. Eisen, 11–40. Baltimore.

Micka, E.F. 1943. *The Problem of Divine Anger in Arnobius and Lactantius.* Washington DC.

Mitchell, M. 2002. *Heavenly Trumpet: John Chrysostom and the Art of Pauline Interpretation.* Louisville.

———. 2005. "Patristic Rhetoric on Allegory: Origen and Eustathius Put I Samuel 28 on Trial." *The Journal of Religion* 85.3:414–445.

Ogilvie, R. 1978. *The Library of Lactantius.* Oxford.

Penner, T. and C. Vander Stichele. 2009. "Rhetorical Practice and Performance in Early Christianity." In *Cambridge Companion to Ancient Rhetoric,* ed. E. Gunderson, 245–260. Cambridge.

Perrin, M. 2001. "Lactance et la 'ratio' romaine et chrétienne." In *En deçà et au delà de la "ratio,"* ed. V. Naas, 153–160. Lille.

Pichon, R. 1901. *Lactance: étude sur le mouvement philosophique et religieux sous le règne de Constantin.* Paris.

Pohlenz, M. 1909. *Vom Zorne Gottes. Eine Studie über den Einfluss der griechischen Philosophie auf das alte Christentum.* Göttingen.

Schott, J. 2008. *Christianity, Empire, and the Making of Religion in Late Antiquity.* Philadelphia.

Simmons, M. 1995. *Arnobius of Sicca: Religious Conflict and Competition in the Age of Diocletian.* Oxford.

Stern, D. 2003. "On Canonization in Rabbinic Judaism." In *Homer, the Bible, and Beyond,* ed. M. Finkelberg and G. Stroumsa, 227–252. Leiden.

Sorabji, R. 2000. *Emotion and Peace of Mind: From Stoic Agitation to Christian Temptation.* Oxford.

Stroumsa, G. 1983. "The Incorporeality of God. Context and Implications of Origen's Position." *Religion* 13:345–358.

Struck, P. 2004. *The Birth of the Symbol: Ancient Readers at the Limits of their Texts.* Princeton.

Torjesen, K. 2005. "The Enscripturation of Philosophy: The Incorporeality of God in Origen's Exegesis." In *The Hermeneutics of Orthodoxy,* ed. C. Helmer, 72–83. Berlin.

Winterbottom, M. 1982. "Schoolroom and Courtoom." In *Rhetoric Revalued,* ed. B. Vickers, 59–70. New York.

Wisse, J. and J. May. 2001. *Cicero: The Ideal Orator.* Oxford.

Young, F. M. 1989. "The Rhetorical Schools and Their Influence on Patristic Exegesis." In *The Making of Orthodoxy,* ed. R. Williams, 182–199. Cambridge.

———. 1997a. "The Fourth Century Reaction Against Allegory." *Studia Patristica* 30:120–125.

———. 1997b. *Biblical Exegesis and the Formation of Christian Culture.* Cambridge.

# Afterword

## Receptions

JEREMY M. SCHOTT

## Late-ancient and Byzantine Receptions

IN MOST RESPECTS, Eusebius' biography is lost to historians. His successor, Acacius, penned a hagiographical *Life* that has not survived.[1] Eusebius, for his part, authored a *Life* of his mentor, Pamphilus, in which we might guess that he provided some autobiographical material, but this text has also been lost.[2] We can, however, trace the reception of Eusebius' writings in late antiquity. This short afterword to the foregoing collection of essays cannot pretend to be anything approaching a comprehensive account of ancient and modern receptions of Eusebius. Rather, in the spirit of the title "Tradition and Innovations," it aims to sketch some of the trajectories of Eusebius' *nachleben* and hopes to prompt further research on various historical and contemporary receptions of this major figure.

Eusebius' *Ecclesiastical History* served as the launching point for fourth- and fifth-century writers of ecclesiastical history. Later historians' assessments of Eusebius are mixed. Philostorgius "praises Eusebius, including what pertains to his history, [but] he says that he erred in orthodoxy."[3] Socrates includes a lengthy

---

[1] Socrates, *Historia Ecclesiastica* 2.4.

[2] Jerome (*Apology* 1.9, trans. NPNF) preserves a short fragment in Latin translation: "What lover of books was there who did not find a friend in Pamphilus? If he knew of any of them being in want of the necessaries of life, he helped them to the full extent of his power. He would not only lend them copies of the Holy Scriptures to read, but would give them most readily, and that not only to men, but to women also if he saw that they were given to reading. He therefore kept a store of manuscripts, so that he might be able to give them to those who wished for them whenever occasion demanded. He himself, however, wrote nothing whatever of his own, except private letters which he sent to his friends, so humble was his estimate of himself. But the treatises of the old writers he studied with the greatest diligence, and was constantly occupied in meditation upon them."

[3] Philostrogius, *Historia Ecclesiastica* 1.2, trans. Amidon 2007.

passage praising Eusebius "in order to refute those who have misrepresented him," perhaps having Philostorgius' critiques in view.[4] Evagrius Scholasticus praised Eusebius' style, but disparaged his orthodoxy, remarking that he "was particularly erudite . . . especially in the ability to persuade his readers to practice our faith, even if he was not capable of making them absolutely correct."[5] Eusebius' "continuators," however, did not necessarily adopt every dimension of Eusebius' historical methodology and aesthetic. Notably, they did not opt for extensive block quotations of literary and documentary texts as a compositional and narrative device.[6] When Socrates and Sozomen quote documents, for example, they take them from Eusebius' *Life of Constantine* and Athanasius' apologetic treatises. And although Eusebius describes it as a key feature of his work, subsequent writers of ecclesiastical history did not follow his interest in the history of Christian literature;[7] rather, in Gelasius, Rufinus, Philostorgius, Theodoret, Socrates, and Sozomen, the heresiological and conciliar threads of church history dominate. The literary-historical ingredient in Eusebius' oeuvre was distilled by Jerome, and became an important source for his own Christian literary history in *On Illustrious Men*.

As a testament to the influence of his quotational/documentary habits, Eusebius was also received as a source for later writers' histories and counter-histories. Athanasius, for instance, would mimic Eusebius' verbatim quotation of dossiers of letters. It is to Athanasius, for instance, that we owe the preservation of Eusebius' letter to Caesarea penned in the immediate aftermath of Nicaea; Athanasius quotes it verbatim in his polemic against Eusebius' successor, Acacius.[8] Much later, at the iconoclastic Council of Constantinople in 754, Eusebius' *Letter to Constantia* would be quoted as a major patristic *testimonium* against icons. The Seventh Ecumenical Council of 787 quoted Eusebius again, though this time to reject his authority. In the early ninth century, patriarch Nicephorus I quoted the letter again in a treatise aimed specifically at refuting it as an iconoclastic authority, setting it alongside other of Eusebius' letters in

---

[4] Socrates, *Historia Ecclesiastica* 2.21, trans. NPNF.

[5] Trans. Whitby 2000.

[6] Rufinus remarks on this explicitly in the preface to his translation of the HE: "Now it should be noted that since the tenth book of this work (i.e. the HE) has very little history in it, all the rest of it being taken up with bishops' panegyrics (e.g. Eusebius' own *Panegyric on the Building of Churches*, which comprises much of the tenth book) which added nothing to our knowledge of the facts, we have omitted what seemed superfluous and joined what history there was in it to the ninth book" (trans. Amidon 1997).

[7] Eusebius describes this as a key feature of his work in HE 1.1; 5.

[8] Athanasius, *De Decretis* 3.

order to impugn him as an Arian heretic, and therefore unworthy as a patristic authority in matters of doctrine.[9]

The extant literary-critical and heresiological receptions of Eusebius in late antiquity and the Byzantine world were mixed; he was most often regarded as a learned writer with a suspect personal and doctrinal history. In this short conclusion, I will outline briefly several illustrative receptions of Eusebius: by Rufinus and Jerome, in the late-fourth/early-fifth centuries, and by the patriarch and bibliophile Photius in the ninth century.

Eusebius figured prominently in the transmission of earlier Greek patristic literature, especially Origen, among Latin readers. Jerome included Eusebius in *On Illustrious Men*, his catalog of major Christian authors:

> Eusebius bishop of Cæsarea in Palestine was diligent in the study of Divine Scriptures and with Pamphilus the martyr a most diligent investigator of the Holy Bible. He published a great number of volumes among which are the following: *Demonstration of the Gospel* twenty books, *Preparation for the Gospel* fifteen books, *Theophany* five books, *Church history* ten books, *Chronicle of Universal history* and an *Epitome* of this last. Also *On discrepancies between the Gospels*, *On Isaiah*, ten books, also *Against Porphyry*, who was writing at that same time in Sicily as some think, twenty-five books, also one book of *Topics*, six books of *Apology for Origen*, three books *On the life of Pamphilus*, other brief works *On the martyrs*, exceedingly learned *Commentaries on one hundred and fifty Psalms*, and many others. He flourished chiefly in the reigns of Constantine the Great and Constantius. His surname Pamphilus arose from his friendship for Pamphilus the martyr.[10]

Jerome had visited the library at Caesarea, and in *On Illustrious Men* touches briefly on the history of the collection under Eusebius' successors.[11]

---

[9] On the use/rejection of Eusebius' *Letter to Constantia* as a patristic authority on icons see the pertinent portions of the Acts of the Seventh Ecumenical Council: Eusebius quoted by iconoclasts as authority (253A), quotation and refutation of *Letter to Constantia* (313A–317D) (trans. Sahas 1986). The Greek text of Nicephorus' polemic is in Pitra 1852:383–386. Annette von Stockhausen has published a new edition of the fragments of the *Letter to Constantia* (von Stockhausen 2002:92–105). The fragments of the letter are available in English translation in Mango 1972:16–18.

[10] Jerome, *De viris inlustribus* 81, trans. NPNF.

[11] Jerome reports that Acacius and Euzoius, Eusebius' immediate successors, "with great pains attempted to restore on parchments [i.e. in parchment codex form] the library, collected by Origen and Pamphilus, which had already suffered injury (*plurimo labore corruptam iam bibliothecam Origenis et Pamphili in membranis instaurare conatus est*)" (*De viris inlustribus* 113, trans. NPNF, slightly modified). In *De viris inlustribus*, Jerome mentions only Euzoius as renewing the library, but in a nearly identical sentence in *Letter* 34.1, he mentions both Acacius and Euzoius (*quam ex*

Interestingly, Jerome does not seem to know Eusebius' earlier works, such as the *General Elementary Introduction* and *Against Hierocles*. It was probably from the library at Caesarea that Jerome obtained his copy of Origen's *Commentary on the Twelve Prophets*, copied by Pamphilus: "I hug and guard [them] with such joy, that I deem myself to have the wealth of Croesus. And if it is such joy to have one epistle of a martyr how much more to have so many thousand lines which seem to me to be traced in his blood."[12] Jerome's brief catalog, of course, belies the depth of his reception of Eusebius. He translated (and updated) the *Chronici Canones* and *Onomasticon*, and drew heavily from Eusebius' *Commentary on Isaiah* in his own commentary on that text.

But, while Jerome values Eusebius' biblical scholarship in *On Illustrious Men*, written in the early 390's before the outbreak of the Origenist controversies, his assessment shifts in his later polemical exchanges with Rufinus. Jerome, for example, contended that the whole of the *Apology* had been authored not by Pamphilus, a true martyr, but by Eusebius, a known Arian.[13] Rufinus, moreover, had argued, in a short work *On the Falsification of the Books of Origen* appended to his translation of Eusebius' and Pamphilus' *Apology for Origen*, that doctrinally suspect material in Origen's corpus was due to interpolation by heretics. Jerome in turn contended that if there were an interpolator (a theory he found suspect), it may have been none other than Eusebius:

> Eusebius, who was a very learned man (observe I say 'learned' not 'catholic'; you must not as is your habit make this a ground for calumniating me) takes up six volumes with nothing else but the attempt to show that Origen is of his way of believing, that is, of the Arian perfidy. He brings out many test-passages, and effectually proves his point. In what dream in an Alexandrian prison was the revelation given to you on the strength of which you make out these passages to be falsified

---

*parte corruptam Acacius, dehinc Euzoius, eiusdem ecclesiae sacerdotes, in membranis instaurare conati sunt).* On these passages, see the discussion in Carriker 2003:23–27.

[12] Jerome, *De viris inlustribus* 75, trans. NPNF. The phrase *manu eius exarata repperi* need not imply that Jerome obtained a copy written in Pamphilus' own hand; rather, Jerome likely means that he has obtained a copy of the work made from an exemplar held in the library of Caesarea. The book Jerome describes was likely an exemplar in the library at Caesarea with a colophon similar to that transmitted, for example, at the conclusion of Esther in Codex Sinaiticus: "Collated and corrected against the Hexapla of Origen, as corrected by him. Antoninus the Confessor collated. Pamphilus corrected the volume in prison"; see also Carriker 2003:14–15. It is unlikely, in fact, that Pamphilus would literally have inked the page in his own hand (such work would have been done by professional scribes, or Pamphilus' *amanuensis*).

[13] "Eusebius, bishop of Caesarea, as I have already said before, who was in his day the standard bearer of the Arian faction, wrote a large and elaborate work in six books in defense of Origen, showing by many testimonies that Origen was in his sense a catholic, that is, in our sense, an Arian" (Jerome, *Apology* 1.8, trans. NPNF).

which he (Eusebius) accepts as true? But possibly he, being an Arian, took in these additions of the heretics to support his own error, so that he should not be thought to be the only one who had held false opinions contrary to the Church.[14]

Scholarship on the "Origenist controversy" has shown how Jerome, like Rufinus, had constructed his own literary persona on the back of Origen's works.[15] Insofar as "Origen" had come to the late-fourth century in large part via Caesarea, Eusebius and his works were also implicated in Jerome's presentation of himself as an orthodox man of letters. Thus, in his later career he would "spin" his earlier reception of Eusebius much as he tempered his earlier self-presentation as a scholar of Origen; in a letter of ca. 400, he would describe Eusebius as "the most open champion of the Arian impiety."[16]

The ninth-century patriarch of Constantinople, Photius, includes entries on several of Eusebius' works in his critical bibliography of late-ancient and Byzantine literature, the *Bibliotheca*. Besides cataloguing the library of this ninth-century bibliophile, the *Bibliotheca* includes descriptions of each work, often along with literary-critical assessments. Of Eusebius' works, Photius read: *Gospel Preparation, Gospel Demonstration, Ecclesiastical Preparation, Ecclesiastical Demonstration, Refutation and Apology, Ecclesiastical History, Against Hierocles, Apology for Origen,* and *Life of Constantine*.[17] Of the extant works he does not mention Eusebius' biblical commentaries, the *Chronicle, Onomasticon, Theophany,* or *Against Marcellus* and *Ecclesiastical Theology*. This need not necessarily imply that these texts were unknown or unavailable to Photius. The *Bibliotheca* is a record of Photius' reading over a specific period, and works tend to be recorded in "blocks" of similar texts or works of a particular author read in succession. Thus, the *Ecclesiastical History* is mentioned in a run of works of ecclesiastical history, while the *Gospel Preparation* and *Demonstration, Ecclesiastical Preparation* and *Demonstration,* and *Refutation and Apology* are mentioned in succession, likely because the reading of one of these apologetic works prompted the reading (or at least the cataloguing) of the others.

Photius also remarked on Eusebius' style. He found his phrasing/mode of expression (*phrasis*) "in no way pleasant, nor does it embrace brilliance."[18] He admired Eusebius as a "polymath" whose way of life was "smart and constant, even if he was wanting in respect of accuracy in his doctrines."[19] He is especially

---

[14] Jerome, *Apology* 2.16, trans. NPNF.
[15] Vessey 1993:135–145.
[16] Jerome, *Letter* 84.2, trans. NPNF.
[17] *Bibliotheca* 9, 10, 11, 12, 13, 27, 39, 118, and 127, respectively.
[18] *Bibliotheca* 13.
[19] *Bibliotheca* 13.

critical of Eusebius' account of the Council of Nicaea and the Arian controversy in the *Life of Constantine*. Eusebius would have it, for example, that the Arian "heresy" was merely a "dispute between Alexander and Arius" that was ameliorated successfully by the Council. Photius also chastises Eusebius for failing to record the judgments against Arius, Eusebius of Nicomedia, Theognis of Nicaea, and Maris of Chalcedon. Finally, Photius accuses Eusebius of dissimulation in his account of the depositions of Eustathius of Antioch and Athanasius.[20] Eusebius never mentions Eustathius by name, and portrays the events surrounding his deposition merely as "revolt and tumult," despite the fact that Eusebius was instrumental in the opposition against Eustathius.[21] As for Athanasius, Eusebius reports only that Alexandria was "filled with revolt and tumult" and describes the bishops sent by the Council of Tyre to investigate charges of murder against Athanasius as an intervention of bishops to restore peace. Photius was thus a close reader of the *Life of Constantine* and had compared Eusebius' narrative with parallel accounts in other ecclesiastical histories. Modern scholarship on the *Life* echoes many of Photius' observations.[22]

## Modern Receptions and Future Directions

The basic trajectories of modern scholarship on Eusebius are familiar to most. Among classicists, Eusebius' works have been important for their preservation of numerous quotations of otherwise lost works.[23] The *Gospel Preparation* is the main source of fragments of the so-called "Hellenistic Jewish historians," and contains a valuable cache of several key Middle Platonic texts. The *Ecclesiastical History* quotes many second- and third-century writers, such as Dionysius of Alexandria, Melito of Sardis, and Papias, whose works would otherwise remain unknown. In addition, several of the most important sources on second-century Montanism come from a dossier of polemical treatises quoted in the *Ecclesiastical History*.[24]

Jacob Burkhardt's *The Age of Constantine the Great* (1853) and Timothy Barnes' *Constantine and Eusebius* (1981) bracket over a century and a quarter's reception of Eusebius as a source for the histories of early Christianity and the "Age of Constantine." Consequently, that reception has centered on the *Ecclesiastical*

---

[20] The passages Photius has in mind are *Life of Constantine* 3.59.1–63.1 (Eustathius) and 4.41.1–48.1 (Council of Tyre/Dedication of Church of the Holy Sepulchre/investigation of Athanasius).

[21] Eusebius and Eustathius published polemics against one another as part of the dispute (Socrates, *Historia Ecclesiastica* 1.23, where Socrates likewise notes that Eusebius was accused of dissimulation in his account of Eustathius' deposition).

[22] See for example the commentary in Cameron and Hall 1999:305–306; 328–330.

[23] See Carriker 2003 for a reconstruction of Eusebius' library.

[24] HE 5.16–19.

*History* and *Life of Constantine* as works of "history" and the question of the reliability of those histories. Burkhardt's and Barnes' assessments of Eusebius also, in effect, mark the poles of the spectrum of modern appraisals—from utter liar, on the one hand, to fairly transparent source for the positivist reconstruction of events, on the other. Among historical theologians, Eusebius' works have figured, again, primarily as a source for narratives of the theological controversies in the decades surrounding the Council of Nicaea. For its part, the relatively younger field of Early Christian Studies, has, in a sense, emerged in the gaps and omissions of the Eusebian narrative. The emphasis of contemporary pedagogy on the history of various "Christianities," rather than the linear development of orthodox Christianity, for instance, can be read in part as a counter-narrative to Eusebius' teleological account of "the holy successions of the apostles."[25]

Along with Origen and Augustine, Eusebius is also one of the late-ancient Christian writers who appear regularly in comprehensive, globalizing histories of the sort that might be read in introductory courses on the history of Christianity, Western Civilization, or World History. In surveys of the history of Christianity, Eusebius appears as the primary source for the "Constantinian revolution" or "turn." In "decline" narratives of late antiquity/the later Roman Empire, Eusebius' panegyrical works are emblematic of the "orientalization" of the principate, Caesaropapism, and the "Christianization" of the empire. Selections from the final two books of the *Ecclesiastical History* or the *Life of Constantine* often appear in anthologies of primary sources, as epitomizing Christianity's dramatic transformation from persecuted minority to imperial religion, and, hence, affirm triumphalist narratives of Christianity over a dying paganism.

Current trends in the study of Eusebius, as represented by the contributions in this volume, follow, as one would expect, broader paradigm shifts across the humanities. Where scholarship of the twentieth century (the "long" twentieth century, bookended by Burkhardt and Barnes) was concerned in large part on Eusebius' historical and "Constantinian" works and their place in several classical "tropics" of late-ancient history, contemporary work on Eusebius has turned attention to works that have often stood on the periphery of the Eusebian corpus and situates the man and his works within a number of emerging perspectives.

Consequently, as several of the essays in this volume witness, new scholarship on Eusebius has been facilitated by (and is in turn prompting) the production of new critical editions and translations. The *Gospel Questions and Solutions*, for example, which reveals Eusebius in his role as bishop-scholar

---

[25] HE 1.1.1.

and bishop-educator, is now available in a true critical edition, as well as in French and English translations.[26] Work is afoot on an English translation of the *Ecclesiastical Theology* and *Against Marcellus*.[27] The *Commentary on Isaiah*, the earliest extant Christian commentary on Isaiah, is slated to appear in English.[28] The *Apology for Origen*, an important source for understanding the intellectual life of Pamphilus' circle and the reception of Origen at the turn of the fourth century, is now accessible in two excellent editions, as well as in French, German, and English translations.[29] The first extensive multi-volume commentary on the *Ecclesiastical History* is being published;[30] the equally complex and magisterial *Gospel Preparation* would benefit from similar treatment.[31] Modern critical editions of the *Prophetic Eclogues* and *Commentary on the Psalms* are in preparation.

The results of major archaeological excavations over three decades conducted by the Joint Expeditions to Caesarea Maritima are continuing to appear.[32] Although no digs have uncovered sites associated with Eusebius specifically, much more is now known about continuity and change in the urban landscape of Caesarea in late antiquity. The evidence suggests a city that maintained its character as Roman provincial capital and intermodal trading hub long into late antiquity. The inscriptions of Caesarea corroborate literary sources in evidencing a diverse population of Samaritans, Jews, Christians, Romans, and Greeks.[33] Knowing more of the material realities of the cityscape has facilitated more nuanced understandings of the setting of a work like the *Martyrs of Palestine*, which can now be appreciated as both a globalizing encomium of Christian martyrdom and a text embedded in the geographic and political specifics of

---

[26] Zamagni 2009; Miller et al. 2010 is based on Zamagni's edition and includes Syriac, Arabic, Latin, and Coptic fragments.

[27] Translations of both texts are being prepared by Kelley Spoerl. An Italian translation of *De Ecclesiastica Theologia* is available (Migliore 1998).

[28] As of this writing, an English translation by Jonathan Armstrong is scheduled to appear in Intervarsity Press's Ancient Christian Texts series (http://www.ivpress.com/cgi-ivpress/book. pl/toc/code=2920, accessed June 5, 2012).

[29] Edition, commentary, and French translation in Junod and Amacker 2002. Edition, commentary , and German translation in Röwekamp 2005. English translation and introduction in Scheck 2010.

[30] Morlet and Perrone 2012.

[31] On the *Gospel Demonstration* see the extensive new monograph by Sébastien Morlet (Morlet 2009).

[32] For an excellent summary of the significance of recent archaeological research on Caesarea see Patrich 2011:1–24.

[33] Holum and Lehman 2000. Though somewhat dated, the most comprehensive study of religious and ethnic diversity in Caesarea remains Levine 1975; Levine does an excellent job of collecting many anecdotes concerning Caesarea from a wide range of literary, archaeological, and documentary sources. On the Jewish population of Caesarea, including helpful summaries of Talmudic material pertaining to Caesarea, see: Levine, 1975:56–76 and Levine 1992:268–273. On the question of mulitlinguism in Caesarea, see Geiger 2001:27–36 and Geiger 1996:39–57.

Caesarea.[34] Promising work remains to be done on the reception of Caesarea as a pilgrimage site in the centuries following Eusebius and Pamphilus.[35]

A key feature of emerging research on Eusebius is a focus on heretofore ignored or marginalized works. While he is still known best as the "Father of Church History,"[36] history was, in fact, but a part of Eusebius' scholarship. As several of the papers in this volume make clear, Eusebius was a philologue,[37] and much of his corpus, including historical works like the *Chronici Canones*, were designed as tools for biblical study. Aaron Johnson and Elizabeth Penland have recently drawn attention to Eusebius' role as a student within Pamphilus' intellectual circle, and later, as an educator in his own right.[38] His successor, Acacius, and Eusebius of Emesa were among his mentees.[39] Indeed, current scholarship suggests that Eusebius' work might be contextualized better as a development of the philological activities of Pamphilus' circle than as propaganda for Constantinian politics. New work on the dating of Eusebius' works reinforces this: about two-thirds of the Eusebian corpus (including the *Ecclesiastical History*, *Gospel Preparation* and *Gospel Demonstration*, and *Chronological Canons*) was begun (and much completed) before Constantine wrested control of the eastern empire from Licinius in 324.[40]

This would situate Eusebius' theology not as "Nicene" or "Post-Nicene," but as an important witness of theological speculation and controversy in the two decades preceding Alexander of Alexandria's conflict with Arius and the ensuing "Arian" debacle. His theology of the Father and Son does not fit neatly into traditional mappings of "Arian" and "Nicene" theology. Instead, the theology of his later anti-Marcellan works is recognized as a development of ideas expressed in

---

[34] Patrich 2002:321–346.

[35] See, for example, Antoninus of Placentia, *Itinerarium* 45 (CCSL 175:174), on the martyrium of Pamphilus.

[36] As witnessed, for example, by the title of the "Eusebius" chapter in the recent *Cambridge History of Early Christian Literature* (Louth 2004:266–274, though the essay does contextualize Eusebius as a scholar trained in exegesis).

[37] As recognized by Lorenzo Perrone (Perrone 2005:413–429, an introductory essay that does justice to the range of Eusebius' literary corpus).

[38] Johnson 2011:99–118; Penland 2011:87–98.

[39] Socrates, *Historia Ecclesiastica* 2.9 (according to Socrates he was also taught by Eusebius' ally Patrophilus of Scythopolis).

[40] The dating of many of Eusebius' best-known works hinges on making sense of the publication history of the *Chronicle* and *Ecclesiastical History*. The trajectory of scholarship on dating these works can be traced in the following articles: Barnes 1980:191–201 (where Barnes' makes his well-know argument for an early date of the first edition of the HE), Louth 1990:111–123, and Burgess 1997:471–504 (where Burgess makes a convincing argument for a first edition of the HE in 313 and a second edition upon the accession of Constantine in 325). The *Gospel Preparation* and *Gospel Demonstration* were begun in the aftermath of Licinius' victory over Maximinus Daia in 313 (e.g. PE 4.2.11, where Eusebius mentions the execution of the *curator* of Antioch, Theotecnus, for his role in the persecution under Maximinus).

the earlier *Gospel Preparation/Demonstration* (even if with an avoidance of the label "second God" for the Son—a label occurring, in any case, only rarely in those earlier works). As several recent reconsiderations make clear, including Ilaria Ramelli's essay within the present volume, Eusebius might be better described as a third-century theologian working to make sense of a changing theological landscape. Eusebius, for instance, could conceptualize the Son as a second cause at the same time that he could accept the term ὁμοουσίος. Eusebius, moreover, was involved in theological disputes decades before he had ever heard of Arius. The chronological range of his theological writing—from the *Apology for Origen* (ca. 309), through the *Gospel Preparation* and *Gospel Demonstration* (ca. 313–325), to his anti-Marcellan writings (ca. 330s)—represents a particularly important perspective for rethinking the development of fourth-century theologies.[41]

Other recent scholarship has shown that Eusebius' theology, moreover, does not necessarily correspond point for point to his intellectual and political alliances. Eusebius was a "Eusebian," that is, part of the network of Eastern bishops that worked in varying degrees of concert against the political and theological interests of Alexander of Alexandria and his successor, Athanasius. He was not a "Eusebian," however, if the term is taken as Athansius would have it—as a loyal follower of Eusebius of Nicomedia. Recent scholarship paints a much more nuanced portrait of Eusebius' role in fourth-century ecclesiastical politics.[42] Rather than someone who followed in lockstep with the bishop of Nicomedia, Eusebius is now recognized as a theological and episcopal power-player in his own right. Within this volume, Mark DelCogliano's essay illuminates Eusebius' important role in ecclesiastical alliances. Eusebius was about a half-generation older than Eusebius of Nicomedia and several other "Eusebians," and as the dedications of his works and extant letters reveal, he anchored an alliance of bishops in Palestine and Phoenicia (e.g. Theodotus of Laodicea, Paulinus of Tyre, Patrophilus of Scythopolis). He played key roles in the Councils that deposed Athanasius and his allies Eustathius of Antioch and Marcellus of Ancyra.[43]

Eusebius was also genuinely engaged with developments in contemporary philosophy. Scholars have long recognized the prominence of Porphyry of Tyre in Eusebius' polemics—both as a potent critic of Christian literature and theology and as a useful bogey-man for polemical display—though as Sébastien Morlet

---

[41]  A comprehensive reconsideration of Eusebius' theology throughout his extant works remains to be written. Luibhéid 1981 remains an excellent study, though it evaluates Eusebius primarily in the terms of Nicene and post-Nicene theology.

[42]  Irshai 2011:25–38; Parvis 2006; Gwynn 2006; DelCogliano 2008:250–266; Bardy 1922:35–45.

[43]  He presided at the Synod of Antioch (ca. AD 328), where he declined election to the See of Antioch, and at the Synod of Tyre (AD 335) that deposed Athanasius (Eusebius' presidency is clearly implied by Epiphanius, *Panarion* 68.8.2); for a recent detailed reconstruction of the complex chain of events surrounding these depositions, see Parvis 2006.

and Aaron Johnson have pointed out, one must be careful not to overemphasize Porphyry's importance in Eusebius' works.[44] Eusebius clearly possessed a not-insignificant library of Middle- and Neo-Platonic literature. His theology can be read productively as a negotiation of issues of central concern in the Middle and Neoplatonic traditions at the turn of the fourth century.[45] The polemical literature surrounding the Great Persecution and Constantine's rise to power was also a *philosophical* literature that engaged issues of philosophical ortho-doxy, political philosophy, and ethics.[46] Even if his readings of Plato might seem farfetched to modern sensibilities (e.g. his apologetic claims for Plato's depen-dence on the Torah) he was indeed a *reader*, not a mere quoter, of Plato. The latter books of the *Gospel Preparation* represent a thoughtful, even if polemical, engagement with the Platonic corpus.[47] In Book 15, for example, Eusebius quotes and comments on a number of Middle- and Neo-Platonic texts that engage Stoic and Peripatetic doctrines concerning the soul, providence, and teleology. Eusebius pays particular attention to several second- and third-century philo-sophical writers who were likewise standard reading among Plotinus, Porphyry, and their circle, including Numenius, Atticus, Severus, Plutarch, and Alexander of Aphrodisias.[48] Much later, in the early 360s, "that wretched Eusebius" drew the ire of Julian, who had read the latter books of the *Preparation*.[49] These were "live" philosophical issues in the early fourth century, and Eusebius must be understood not merely as a polemical "quoter" but (like Origen before him) as participating alongside late third- and early fourth-century Platonists in heated debates over the reception of the Peripatetic and Stoic traditions.

Thanks to the (somewhat belated) arrival of the linguistic turn to late-ancient studies, Eusebius' works are no longer viewed as transparent "evidence" for the reconstruction of late-ancient history, but as complex literary texts that demand discursive and rhetorical analyses. Thus, the new reception of Eusebius is, like Photius' in the ninth century, literary-critical. Unlike Photius, however, modern scholarship has come to appreciate the importance of Eusebius' writing in the history of late-ancient literature, specifically, and the history and theory of western literature, more broadly.

Like other learned bishops, Eusebius was a prominent public orator. The "major works" of the Eusebian corpus (e.g. the *Life of Constantine, Ecclesiastical*

---

[44]  Morlet 2011:119–150; Johnson 2010: 53–58.
[45]  Strutwolf 1999.
[46]  Recognized increasingly in studies of philosophy, literature, and politics under the Tetrarchs and Constantine, see, for example, Drake 2000; Digeser 2000 and Digeser 2012; Schott 2008.
[47]  Des Places 1982; Schott 2003:501–531.
[48]  Compare, for example, Porphyry's list of authors commonly read in Plotinus' circle (*Life of Plotinus* 14) with the works quoted by Eusebius in the *Gospel Preparation*.
[49]  Julian, *Against the Galilaeans* in Cyril of Alexandria, *Against Julian* 221E–224E.

*History*, and *Gospel Preparation*) suggest a bookish scholar whose work centered on his library. But recent scholarship has given more attention to Eusebius' performance pieces. The two orations preserved as the *Tricennial Oration* (for which a new critical edition is in preparation)[50] and the *Panegyric on the Building of Churches* (delivered publicly at Tyre ca. AD 315)[51] represent the tip of an iceberg of sermonizing and other public oratory. As several of the chapters in this volume make clear, the writing of history was not aimed only (or even primarily) at providing an indelible record of the Christian past. "History" was a tool of suasive rhetoric. Reading works like the *Ecclesiastical History* and *Life of Constantine* as "rhetoric," on the one hand, brings into relief the immediacy and contingency of historical texts, and, on the other hand, as Finn Damgaard's essay does so effectively, troubles overly simplistic, linear readings of these texts as "propaganda." Where "propaganda" suggests a clear, hegemonic, unidirectional communication of *a specific* ideology, "rhetoric" intimates the complex inter-play of interests and counter-interests at work in Constantinian panegyric and polemic. In addition, as Kristina Meinking's essay demonstrates, Eusebius must be contextualized in terms of traditions of political rhetoric flourishing in Greek *and* Latin at the turn of the fourth century. If, as recent scholarship stresses, the fourth century witnessed a renewed flowering of classicizing rhetoric, a "Third Sophistic,"[52] then Eusebius, along with Lactantius, Constantine (e.g. the *Oratio ad Sanctos*), Methodius, and others, represent an important, and as yet unstudied, bridge between the second and third Sophistics. Eusebian scholarship seems poised to offer an account of Eusebius the rhetorician.

The Eusebian corpus also offers an excellent case study in various modes of intertextuality. In this volume, the contributions of Corke-Webster, DeVore, Olson, Damgaard, and Schott consider the warp and woof of the many texts within which and out of which Eusebius' own writing emerged. Theories of intertextuality are decidedly historical, for they emphasize the contingency of all texts within networks of previous and contemporary texts. Thus, Eusebius' writing becomes more completely legible when located within all of its myriad relationships with the classical texts, other patristic texts, contemporary polem-ical texts, Jewish texts, and so forth, to which it responds or reacts, upon which

---

[50]  By Harold Drake, to appear in the series Die Griechischen Christlichen Schriftsteller as Eusebius 1. 2: Rede an die Heilige Versammlung. Tricennatsrede, updating the previous edition by I.A. Heikel in the same series (http://www.bbaw.de/bbaw/Forschung/Forschungsprojekte/gcs/de/blanko.2005-06-28.6349238324, accessed 5 June, 2012).

[51]  On the Tyrian oration, see Smith 1989:226–247 and Schott 2011:177–198. For an earlier dating of the Oration at Tyre, see Amerise 2008:229–234.

[52]  On the "Third Sophistic" as a renewed (or, in other estimations, ongoing) classicizing aesthetic and cultural phenomenon in fourth-century rhetoric see, for example: Quiroga 2007:31–42; Van Hoof 2010:211–224.

it comments, or which it imitates. Studying Eusebius' writing in terms of "intertextuality," moreover, presses scholarship beyond traditional heuristics such as "dependence" and "influence." Theories of intertextuality, unlike models of literary influence or dependence, are non-linear. That is, although the relationships among intertexts are historically contingent, they are not bound to flow in one direction, whether from original to imitation, lemma to commentary, Mishnah to Gemara, and so forth. Thus, as Corke-Webster's essay demonstrates, Eusebius' deployment of the "model of the Maccabees" in his constructions of Christian martyrdom in the *Ecclesiastical History* is not merely a commentary on or a new interpretation of a Maccabean model, but a node at which the texts of 2 and 4 Maccabees, Origen's *Exhortation to Martyrdom*, and discourses around the Roman *familia* converge and diverge.

Eusebius' *oeuvre* is bluntly intertextual; even first readers of a work like the *Ecclesiastical History* are struck by his habit of arguing through extensive block quotation. As Aaron Johnson suggests in the "Introduction" to this volume, intertextual practice functioned for Eusebius as part of a broader "cumulative aesthetic" in late antiquity. Sabrina Inowlocki's recent monograph, *Eusebius and the Jewish Authors*, moreover, offers the first sustained interrogation of Eusebius' quotational habits.[53] While Eusebius is often disparaged for his penchant for extended quotation, Inowlocki demonstrates that this mode of composition had its own poetics; Eusebius develops new historical constructs, such as his famous distinction between "Jews" and "Hebrews," as well as arguments concerning the history of Jews and Judaism, through the skillful orchestration of quotations of Jewish authors. Each of Eusebius' works represents a new arranging of the books in the library. In publishing his works, Eusebius was thus also disseminating a particular model of "the Christian library," as well as specific modes of reading specific texts within that collection.[54] One could write an illuminating history of fourth- and fifth-century Christianity in terms of the various construals of the Caesarean library.

Methodologies informed by theories of intertextuality serve to trouble conceptions of texts as stable, fixed, and bounded, breaking open the text and revealing it as a web of consonances and dissonances. Other contemporary scholarship on Eusebius stresses the materiality of his literary projects. As Anthony Grafton and Megan Williams have shown, Eusebius is a major figure in the broader history of the book in western culture.[55] Eusebius' brand of biblical and historical scholarship prompted him to develop innovative modes of material presentation—from the visual representation of time in the *Chronici Canones* to

[53]  Inowlocki 2006.
[54]  Inowlocki 2011:199–224.
[55]  Grafton and Williams 2006.

the *Gospel Canons and Tables*, which included a marginal cross-referencing apparatus in colored inks in Gospel manuscripts. Consequently, the various intertextual relations that constitute the Eusebian corpus subsisted through specific kinds of books used in specific ways. Eusebius' genius lay not only in mediating biblical, patristic, Jewish, and "pagan" texts through his compositions, but in developing and disseminating particular materialities of reading. Indeed, the most widely copied of Eusebius' texts in late antiquity and the Byzantine and Western middle ages were his *Gospel Canons* and their attendant marginal notations in gospel manuscripts.

Current interdisciplinary research on the history of the book and genetic criticism emphasizes the material contingencies of textual production and transmission in any study of literature.[56] Thus, another area ripe for future study is the Byzantine manuscripts to which we owe the preservation of Eusebius' works. The earliest complete manuscripts of Eusebius' works are Syriac translations of the *Ecclesiastical History*, *Martyrs of Palestine*, and the *Theophany*.[57] Critical editions of these texts of course take account of these Syriac versions (indeed, the *Theophany* is complete only in Syriac); however, scholars have only begun to consider the import of differences and deviations among the Greek, Syriac, and Latin versions of the *Ecclesiastical History* for a "genetic" history of this text.[58] What, for example, might be the significance of the Syriac version's redaction of "Arian" passages and the alteration of Eusebius' detailed citation formulae in favor of more vague formulae, or Rufinus' editing of "Arian" material in his Latin version?[59] Might such a study illuminate not only the ideological/heresiological concerns of translators, but something of late-ancient attitudes towards,

---

[56] Both book history and genetic criticism have their origins in French literary theory and criticism, but have come into their own in the Anglophone humanities in the past two decades. The literature on both of these scholarly trajectories is vast; good introductions to theory and methodology in book history include: Febvre and Martin 1976, Cavallo and Chartier 1999, Chartier 1994. For an excellent introduction to genetic criticism, see the "Introduction" and collected essays in Deppman et al. 2004.

[57] The earliest extant fragment of the HE is *PBerl. Inv. 17076*, a papyrus fragment dated paleographically to the fourth century and containing HE 6.43.7–8.11–12. The earliest extant complete manuscript of the HE is *Codex Syriac 1*, housed in the National Library of Russia, St. Petersburg, which contains a subscription dating it to AD 462. *British Lib. Add. 14639* contains books 1–5 of the HE and dates to the sixth century. The Syriac versions of the *Martyrs of Palestine* and *Theophany* are very early (AD 411) and are included in *British Lib. Add. 12150*, an important manuscript that also contains the Pseudo-Clementine *Recognitiones* and Titus of Bostra, *Against the Manichaeans*.

[58] See Cassin, Debié, and Perrin 2012:185–206 for an example of an essay that treats the problem of the textual history of the HE in all its text-critical and genetic-critical complexity.

[59] Humphries 2008:143–164; Christensen 1989. Redactional aspects of the Syriac version are noted by Wright and McLean 1898:ix–x, but a detailed analysis study of the redactional habits of the Syriac version is a desideratum.

and assumptions about, "texts," "language," and "authorship" in the early Byzantine/late Roman world?

Most of Eusebius' extant works, moreover, come to us through Middle Byzantine manuscripts. The *Gospel Preparation* and *Against Hierocles* are preserved in the famous "Arethas Codex," which was produced by the scribe Baanes in AD 914. This manuscript is one of several that can with certainty be identified as belonging to the library of Arethas, the archbishop of Cappadocian Caesarea, which also included important extant manuscripts of Plato (*Codex Oxoniensis Clarkianus* 39), Euclid, and Aristides.[60] The "Arethas Codex" itself is also the primary conduit for a number of early Christian apologetic texts, including Clement's *Protrepticus* and *Paedagogus* and Athenagoras' *Apology* and *On the Resurrection*. The scholia preserved in Arethas' books, many in his own hand, are as important as the volumes themselves. The remains of Arethas' library and his scholia, together with Photius' *Bibliotheca*, therefore, offer an opportunity to explore in detail the theory and material practice of reading in Byzantium. And a cursory look at Arethas' library suggests that Eusebius figured prominently in Arethas' reading practice—his copy of Plato is corrected in several places against quotations of Platonic texts in the *Gospel Preparation*, for example.[61]

Importantly, interdisciplinary scholarship on Eusebius that attends to intertextuality, genetic criticism, and the history of the book also prompts us to recognize the contingencies of our own scholarly projects. If Eusebius' works and the Caesarean library were so axial in mediating "Hellenistic Jewish litera-ture," "patristic literature," and so forth—that is, if we know these literatures through Eusebius and Caesarea—then we must attend to the ways in which our own writings of late-ancient Christianity, Hellenistic Judaism, the Constantinian Empire, and so forth, are enmeshed within trajectories of Eusebian writing.

---

[60] Reynolds and Wilson 1991:57.
[61] Des Places 1957.

# Works Cited

Amerise, M. 2008. "Note sulla datazione del panegirico per l'inaugurazione della basilica di Tiro." *Adamantius* 14: 229–234.

Amidon, Philip. 1997. *The Church History of Rufinus of Aquileia. Books 10 and 11.* New York and Oxford.

Bardy, Gustave. 1922. "Sur Paulin de Tyr." *Revue des sciences religieuses* 2:35–45.

Barnes, Timothy. 1980. "The Editions of Eusebius' *Ecclesiastical History.*" *Greek, Roman, and Byzantine Studies* 21:191–201.

Burgess, Richard. 1997. "The Dates and Editions of Eusebius' *Chronici Canones* and *Historia Ecclesiastica.*" Journal of Theological Studies 48:471–504.

Cameron, Averil and Stuart G. Hall. 1999. Eusebius. *Life of Constantine.* Clarendon Ancient History Series. Oxford.

Carriker, Andrew. 2003. *The Library of Eusebius of Caesarea.* Leiden.

Cassin, Matthieu, Muriel Debié, and Michel-Yves Perrin. 2012. "La question des editions de l'Histoire ecclésiastique et livre X." In *Eusèbe de Césarée. Histoire ecclésiastique. Commentaire. Tome I. Études d'introduction,* ed. Sébastien Morlet and Lorenzo Perone, 185-206. Paris.

Cavallo, Guglielmo and Roger Chartier. 1999. *A History of Reading in the West,* trans. Lydia G. Cochrane. Amherst, MA.

Chartier, Roger. 1994. *The Order of Books,* trans. Lydia G. Cochrane. Cambridge.

Christensen, Torben. 1989. *Rufinus of Aquileia and the Historia Ecclesiastica, Lib. VIII-IX, of Eusebius.* Historisk-filosofiske Meddelelser 58. Copenhagen.

DelCogliano, Mark. 2008. "The Eusebian Alliance: the Case of Theodotus of Laodicea." *Zeitschrift für Antikes Christentum / Journal of Ancient Christianity* 12:250–66.

Deppman, Jed, Daniel Ferrer, and Micheal Groden, eds. 2004. *Genetic Criticism: Texts and Avant-textes.* Philadelphia.

des Places, Edouard. 1957. "Deux témoins du texte des *Lois* de Platon: Eusèbe, évêque de Césarée de Palestine; Aréthas, archevéque de Césarée de Cappadoce" *Wiener Studien* 70:254–259.

———. 1982. *Eusèbe de Césarée commentateur: Platonisme et Écriture Sainte.* Paris.

Digeser, Elizabeth DePalma. 2000. *The Making of a Christian Empire: Lactantius and Rome.* Ithaca.

———. 2012. *A Threat to Public Piety: Christians, Platonists, and the Great Persecution.* Ithaca.

Drake, Harold. 2000. *Constantine and the Bishops: The Politics of Intolerance.* Baltimore.

Febvre, Lucien and Henri-Jean Martin. 1976. *The Coming of the Book,* trans. David Gerard. London, originally published 1958 as *L'Apparition du livre.* Paris.

Geiger, J. 2001. "'Voices Reciting the Shema in Greek': Jews, Gentiles and Greek Wisdom in Caesarea." *Cathedra* 99:27–36 (in Hebrew).

———. 1996. "How Much Latin in Roman Palestine?" In *Aspects of Latin: Papers from the Seventh International Colloquium on Latin Linguistics Jerusalem, April 1993*, ed. H. Rosén, 39–57. Innsbruck.

Grafton, Anthony and Megan Williams. 2006. *Christianity and the Transformation of the Book: Origen, Eusebius, and the Library of Caesarea*. Cambridge, MA.

Gwynn, David M. 2006. *The Eusebians: The Polemic of Athanasius of Alexandria and the Construction of the 'Arian Controversy.'* Oxford.

Holum, Kenneth G. and Clayton Miles Lehman. 2000. *The Greek and Latin Inscriptions of Caesarea Maritima*. Joint Expeditions to Caesarea Maritima Excavation Reports vol. 5. Boston.

Humphries, Mark. 2008. "Rufinus' Eusebius: Translation, Continuation, and Edition in the Latin Ecclesiastical History." *Journal of Early Christian Studies* 16:143–164.

Irshai, Oded. 2011. "Fourth Century Palestinian Politics: A Glimpse at Eusebius of Caesarea's Local Political Career and Its Nachleben in Christian Memory." In Inowlocki and Zamagni 2011:25–38.

Inowlocki, Sabrina. 2006. *Eusebius and the Jewish Authors: His Citation Technique in an Apologetic Context*. Ancient Judaism and Early Christianity 64. Leiden.

Inowlocki, Sabrina and Claudio Zamagni, eds. 2011. *Reconsidering Eusebius: Collected Papers in Literary, Historical, and Theological Issues*. Supplements to Vigiliae Christianae 107. Leiden.

Inowlocki, Sabrina. 2011. "Eusebius' Construction of a Christian Culture: the Praeparatio evangelica as a Library." In Inowlocki and Zamagni 2011:99–224.

Johnson, Aaron P. 2010. "Rethinking the Authenticity of Porphyry, c. Christ. Fr. 1." *Studia Patristica* 46:53–58.

———. 2011. "Eusebius the Educator: The Context of the General Elementary Introduction." In Inowlocki and Zamagni 2011:99–118.

Junod, Eric and René Amacker. 2002. *Apologie pour Origène. Sources chrétiennes* 464–465. Paris.

Levine, Lee I. 1975. "R. Abbahu of Caesarea." In *Christianity, Judaism, And Other Greco-Roman Cults: Studies for Morton Smith at Sixty*, ed. Jacob Neusner, 56–76. Leiden.

———. 1975. *Caesarea Under Roman Rule*. Leiden.

———. 1992. "The Jewish Community at Caesarea in Late Antiquity." In *Caesarea Papers: Straton's Tower, Herod's Harbour, and Roman and Byzantine Caesarea*. Journal of Roman Archaeology. Supplementary Series 5, ed. R.L. Vann, 268–273. Ann Arbor, MI.

Louth, Andrew. 1990. "The Date of Eusebius' *Historia Ecclesiastica.*" *Journal of Theological Studies* 41:111–123.

———. 2004. "Eusebius and the Birth of Church History." In *The Cambridge History of Early Christian Literature*, ed. Frances Young, Lewis Ayres, and Andrew Louth, 266–274. Cambridge.

Luibhéid, Colm. 1981. *Eusebius of Caesarea and the Arian Crisis.* Dublin.

Migliore, Franzo. 1998. *Teologia ecclesiastica.* Collana di testi patristici, 144. Rome.

Miller, David, Adam McCollum, and Carol Downer. 2010. *Eusebius of Caesarea. Gospel Problems and Solutions.* Ancient Texts in Translation 1. Ipswitch.

Morlet, Sébastien. 2009. *La Démonstration Évangelique d'Eusèbe de Césarée. Étude sur l'apologétique chrétienne à l'époque de Constantin.* Paris.

———. 2011. "Eusebius' Polemic Against Porphyry: A Reassessment." In Inowlocki and Zamagni 2011:119–150.

Morlet, Sébastien and Lorenzo Perrone. 2012. *Eusèbe de Césarée. Histoire ecclésiastique. Commentaire. Tome I. Études d'introduction.* Anagoge 6. Paris.

Patrich, Joseph. 2002. "The Martyrs of Caesarea: the urban context." *Liber annuus Studii biblici franciscani* 52:321–346.

———. 2011. "Caesarea in the Time of Eusebius." In Inowlocki and Zamagni 2011:1–24.

Parvis, Sara. 2006. *Marcellus of Ancyra and the Lost Years of the Arian Controversy 325–345.* Oxford.

Penland, Elizabeth C. 2011. "Eusebius Philosophus? School Activity at Caesarea Through the Lens of the Martyrs." In Inowlocki and Zamagni 2011:87–98.

Perrone, Lorenzo. 2005. "Eusebius of Caesarea: Philology, History, and Apologetics for a Triumphant Christianity." In *Early Christian Greek and Latin Literature. A Literary History, Vol. I: From Paul to the Age of Constantine*, ed. Claudio Moreschini and Enrico Norelli, trans. Matthew J. O'Connell, 413–429. Peabody, MA.

Pitra, J.B. 1852. "Nicephorus. 'Contra Eusebium.'" In *Spicilegium Solesmense.* Paris.

Quiroga, Alberto. 2007. "From Sophistopolis to Episcopolis: The Case for a Third Sophistic." *Journal of Late Antique Religion and Culture* 1:31–42.

Reynolds, L.D. and N.G. Wilson. 1991. *Scribes and Scholars: A Guide to the Transmission of Greek and Latin Literature*, 3rd ed. New York.

Röwekamp, Georg. 2005. *Apologia pro Origene/Apologie für Origenes.* Fontes christiani 80. Turnhout.

Sahas, Daniel J. 1986. *Icon and Logos: Sources in Eighth-Century Iconoclasm.* Toronto and Buffalo.

Scheck, Thomas P. 2010. *St. Pamphilus. Apology for Origen with the letter of Rufinus on the falisification of the books of Origen.* Fathers of the Church 120. Washington, DC.

Schott, Jeremy M. 2003. "Founding Platonopolis: The Platonic Politeia in Eusebius, Porphyry, and Iamblichus," *Journal of Early Christian Studies* 11:501–531.

———. 2008. *Christianity, Empire, and the Making of Religion in Late Antiquity.* Divinations: Rereading Late Ancient Religions. Philadelphia.

———. 2011. "Eusebius' Panegyric On the Building of Churches (HE 10.4.2–72): Aesthetics and the Politics of Christian Architecture." In Inowlocki and Zamagni 2011:177–198.

Smith, Christine. 1989. "Christian Rhetoric in Eusebius' Panegyric at Tyre." *Vigiliae Christianae* 43:226–247.

Strutwolf, Holger. 1999. *Die Trinitätstheologie und Christologie des Euseb von Caesarea. Eine dogmengeschichtliche Untersuchung Seiner Platonismusrezeption und Wirkungsgeschichte.* Forschungen zur Kirchen- und Dogmengeschichte 72. Göttingen.

Van Hoof, Lieve. 2010. "Greek Rhetoric and the Later Roman Empire: The Bubble of the 'Third Sophistic.'" *Antiquité Tardive* 18:211–224.

Vessey, Mark. 1993. "Jerome's Origen: The Making of a Christian Literary Persona." *Studia Patristica* 28:135–145.

von Stockhausen, Annette. 2002. "Einige Anmerkungen zur Epistula ad Constantiam desEuseb von Cäsarea." In *Die ikonoklastische Synode von Hiereia 754: Einleitung, Text, Übersetzung und Kommentar ihres Horos,* ed. Torsten Krannich, Christoph Schubert, and Claudia Sode, 92–105. Tübingen.

Whitby, Michael. 2000. *The Ecclesiastical History of Evagrius Scholasticus.* Translated Texts for Historians. Liverpool.

Zamagni, Claudio. 2009. *Eusèbe de Césarée: Questions évangéliques.* Sources chrétiennes 523. Paris.

# Index Locorum

Eusebius

Against Marcellus (Contra Marcellum, C. Marc.): 1.1, 9; 1.2.20–22, 274; 1.4.9–10, 268; 1.4.12, 275; 1.4.14, 276; 1.4.27–29, 275; 1.4.30–34, 276–77; 1.4.32, 283; 1.4.35–37, 277; 1.4.52–53, 283; 1.4.63, 272; 2.4, 9; 2.4.1, 312; 2.4.9–10, 313; 2.4.11, 309, 313; 2.4.13–14, 314; 2.4.18–22, 314; 2.4.28, 314

Commentary on Isaiah (Commentarius in Isaiam, CI): 1.85, 319; 2.9, 310; 3.20–23, 173; 107.26–28, 180; 108.3–5, 180; 108.4, 180; 108.6–7, 181; 108.14–16, 180; 108.33–36, 180; 110.6–9, 182; 112.30–33, 182; 120.34–121.6, 183; 121.11–28, 184; 149.5–11, 176; 150.9–23, 177; 151.14–15, 177; 151.30–152.19, 178–179; 152.30–34, 178; 153.24–29, 179

Commentary on Luke: 24.549, 318–319; 24.580, 311; 540CD, 199; 549, 195

Commentary on the Psalms (Commentaria in Psalmos, CPs): 23.684C, 110; 23.720.6, 312; 23.92.7, 311; 23.1049.22, 311; 53.2, 160; 58.16–18, 157; 67.7, 159; 71.7, 158; 86.3, 159; 86.5–7, 161–162; 87.11, 154; 87.5, 157; 88.6, 157

Ecclesiastical History/Church History (Historia Ecclesiastica, HE): 1.1.1–2, 35; 1.2.23, 1031.2.24, 312; 1.3.19, 110; ; 1.13.1, 106; 3.6, 73; 5.pref.2–4, 36–37; 6.1.1, 646.2.11, 67; 6.2.12, 64; 6.2.3, 65; 6.2.4, 65; 6.2.6, 66; 6.3, 87; 6.19, 86; 6.27, 86, 89; 6.30, 86; 6.31, 28, 43; 6.32, 89; 6.32.3, 89; 6.4, 87; 6.8.1, 66; 7.18.4, 107; 7.22, 74; 7.32, 88; 7.32.25, 88; 8.1.7, 327; 8.12.3–4, 63; 8.16.2–3, 328; 9.9, 120

# Index of Subjects

CPSIA information can be obtained
at www.ICGtesting.com
Printed in the USA
JSHW020348120221
11808JS00002B/5